THE CAMBRIDGE HISTORY OF
CAPITALISM

The first volume of *The Cambridge History of Capitalism* provides a comprehensive account of the evolution of capitalism from its earliest beginnings. Starting with its distant origins in ancient Babylon, successive chapters trace progression up to the "Promised Land" of capitalism in America. Adopting a wide geographical coverage and comparative perspective, the international team of authors discuss the contributions of Greek, Roman, and Asian civilizations to the development of capitalism, as well as the Chinese, Indian, and Arab empires. They determine what features of modern capitalism were present at each time and place, and why the various precursors of capitalism did not survive. Looking at the eventual success of medieval Europe and the examples of city-states in northern Italy and the Low Countries, the authors address how British mercantilism led to European imitations and American successes, and ultimately, how capitalism became global.

LARRY NEAL is Emeritus Professor of Economics at the University of Illinois, Urbana-Champaign, Research Associate of the National Bureau of Economic Research, and Visiting Professor at the London School of Economics and Political Science. Specializing in financial history and European economies, he is author of *The Rise of Financial Capitalism: International Capital Markets in the Age of Reason* (Cambridge University Press, 1990), *The Economics of Europe and the European Union* (Cambridge University Press, 2007), and *'I Am Not Master of Events': The Speculations of John Law and Lord Londonderry in the Mississippi and South Sea Bubbles* (2012). He is co-editor of *The Origins and Development of Financial Markets and Institutions: From the Seventeenth Century to the Present* (Cambridge University Press, 2009).

JEFFREY G. WILLIAMSON is Emeritus Laird Bell Professor of Economics, Harvard University, and Honorary Fellow in the Department of Economics, University of Wisconsin-Madison. He is also Research Associate of the National Bureau of Economic Research, Research Fellow at the Centre for Economic Policy Research, and has been a visiting professor at seventeen universities around the world. Professor Williamson specializes in development, inequality, globalization, and history, and he is the author of around 230 scholarly articles and 30 books, his most recent being *Trade and Poverty: When the Third World Fell Behind* (2011), *Globalization and the Poor Periphery before 1950* (2006), *Global Migration and the World Economy* (2005, with T. Hatton), and *Globalization in Historical Perspective* (2003, edited with M. Bordo and A. M. Taylor).

Fundación **BBVA**

Cambridge University Press gratefully acknowledges the support of the BBVA Foundation in hosting and funding two workshops attended by contributors to the volume.

The BBVA Foundation expresses the BBVA Group's commitment to the improvement and welfare of the numerous societies in which it operates through the promotion of scientific research, innovation, and cultural creation, and their transmission to society using diverse channels and formats. Its work programs scrupulously respect the academic organization of knowledge and artistic creation and the principle of peer review, while facilitating the development of projects arising from the interaction of various fields and, particularly, emerging projects which move forward the frontiers of knowledge and thought. Among its multiple activities are the funding and co-organization of research projects, advanced training, lectures aimed at the general public, workshops, the endowment of special chairs, awards for researchers and creators (notably, the *Frontiers of Knowledge Awards* family, spanning eight categories and directed at the international community), publications under its own imprint and in partnership with academic publishers of excellence, and the recording and diffusion of classical and contemporary music.

Its areas of focus are Basic Sciences, Biomedicine, Environmental Sciences, Economics and Social Sciences, the Humanities and the Arts (particularly music and painting).

THE CAMBRIDGE
HISTORY OF
CAPITALISM

*

VOLUME I

The Rise of Capitalism:
From Ancient Origins to 1848

*

Edited by

LARRY NEAL

and

JEFFREY G. WILLIAMSON

Fundación **BBVA**

CAMBRIDGE
UNIVERSITY PRESS

University Printing House, Cambridge CB2 8BS, United Kingdom

Cambridge University Press is part of the University of Cambridge.

It furthers the University's mission by disseminating knowledge in the pursuit of education, learning and research at the highest international levels of excellence.

www.cambridge.org
Information on this title: www.cambridge.org/9781107583283

© Cambridge University Press 2014

First published 2014
3rd printing 2015
First paperback edition 2015

A catalogue record for this publication is available from the British Library

ISBN 978-1-107-58328-3 Paperback
ISBN 978-1-107-58459-4 Paperback set

Contents

Contents

Figures

Maps

Tables

Contributors

JEREMY ATACK, Professor Emeritus of Economics and History, Vanderbilt University

ALAIN BRESSON, Professor in the Department of Classics, University of Chicago

JOSÉ LUÍS CARDOSO, Research Professor at the Institute of Social Science of the University of Lisbon

ANN M. CARLOS, Professor of Economics and History, University of Colorado

OSCAR GELDERBLOM, Associate Professor, Department of History, Utrecht University

KARL GUNNAR PERSSON, Professor Emeritus of Economics, University of Copenhagen

C. KNICK HARLEY, Professor of Economic History, University of Oxford

MORTEN JERVEN, Associate Professor, School for International Studies, Simon Fraser University

WILLEM M. JONGMAN, Reader in the Department of History, University of Groningen

JOOST JONKER, Associate Professor of Economic and Social History, Utrecht University

ÉTIENNE DE LA VAISSIÈRE, Professor at the École Pratique des Hautes Études, Paris

MICHAEL JURSA, Professor of Assyriology, University of Vienna

FRANK D. LEWIS, Professor of Economics, Queen's University, Kingston, Ontario, Canada

LARRY NEAL, Professor Emeritus of Economics, University of Illnois, Urbana-Champaign and London School of Economics

PATRICK KARL O'BRIEN, Professor of Global Economic History, London School of Economics

ŞEVKET PAMUK, Chair of Contemporary Turkish Studies at the European Institute, London School of Economics

LUCIANO PEZZOLO, Associate Professor, Department of Humanities, University of Venice

TIRTHANKAR ROY, Professor of Economic History, London School of Economics

RICHARD SALVUCCI, Professor, Department of Economics, Trinity University, San Antonio, Texas

JEFFREY G. WILLIAMSON, Emeritus Laird Bell Professor of Economics, Harvard University

R. B. WONG, Professor of History and Director of the UCLA Asia Institute

Introduction

LARRY NEAL

Modern economic growth, defined as a sustained rise in per capita income with population growth (Kuznets 1966), has created higher levels of prosperity for many more people on earth than was ever thought possible before it began. Moreover, it began not so very long ago, perhaps as late as the middle of the nineteenth century and certainly not before the end of the seventeenth century. As modern economic growth emerged within a favored few nations and modern capitalism began to take on its distinguishing features, the wealth of nations began to diverge at the same time. Capitalism both shaped and responded to the structural changes required to sustain modern economic growth up to the present. The higher standards of living that came with modern economic growth stimulated efforts to imitate the successes of the first British and American examples. But the visible hardships that early capitalism inflicted on existing societies repelled others. Further, the connection between capitalism and modern economic growth was difficult to see in its early stages. Consequently, the spread of both modern economic growth and capitalism after the middle of the nineteenth century was fitful and uneven.

Even as the beneficial effects of modern economic growth became increasingly evident in the leading industrial nations, the spread of capitalism was restrained by local social, political, and cultural conditions in other countries, as demonstrated by the essays in Volume II, *The Spread of Capitalism*.

Collectively, however, those essays provide evidence that the capitalist system of coordinating economic activity through market signals to all the participants concerned was the root cause of the material advances so evident across the world at the beginning of the twenty-first century. Identifying capitalism as an economic system that generates modern economic growth, however, raises the question of whether continued growth in per capita income can be sustained and therefore whether capitalism as an economic system can be sustained. Those are questions dealt with throughout the essays in Volume II.

The question that the essays in Volume II do not raise, however, is: "Why did capitalism and modern economic growth take so long to get started in the first place?" The essays in Volume I, *The Rise of Capitalism*, try to answer that question. Their answer, essentially, is that it was hard – very hard – to coordinate the various factors needed to build and sustain permanent settlements in the first place, although such efforts usually raised per capita incomes (what economists term "economic growth on the intensive margin"). Then, it was even more difficult to sustain coordination over the long run in the face of successive shocks that arose naturally, either from external events or internal conflicts. Whether setbacks occurred from natural disasters, epidemic diseases, military defeats, or failures of leadership, they had the common feature of undoing whatever advances had been achieved earlier without laying a foundation for subsequent recovery. A consistent theme throughout the essays in Volume I therefore is to determine what features of modern capitalism were present at each time and place and, further, why the various precursors of capitalism did not survive setbacks and then subsequently continue the growth of both population and per capita incomes from their earlier levels.

Concepts of capitalism

What are the salient features of modern capitalism and how were these features manifested in earlier times? The scholarly literature refers variously to agrarian capitalism, industrial capitalism, financial capitalism, monopoly capitalism, state capitalism, crony capitalism, and even creative capitalism. Whatever the specific variety of capitalism denoted by these phrases, however, the connotation is nearly always negative. This is because the word "capitalism" was invented and then deployed by the critics of capitalists during the first global economy that clearly arose after 1848 and the spread of capitalism worldwide up to 1914. In the resurgence of a global economy at the beginning of the twenty-first century, however, scholars accept that there can be many varieties of capitalism and that there are comparative advantages to each variety (Hall and Soskice 2001).

Four elements, however, are common in each variant of capitalism, whatever the specific emphasis:

1 private property rights;
2 contracts enforceable by third parties;
3 markets with responsive prices; and
4 supportive governments.

Each of these elements must deal specifically with *capital*, a factor of production that is somehow physically embodied, whether in buildings and equipment, or in improvements to land, or in people with special knowledge. Regardless of the form it takes, however, the capital has to be long lived and not ephemeral to have meaningful economic effects. That means that each of the four features listed above has to have a long time horizon, spanning at least several years and preferably several human generations. Capital should also be productive and therefore in use throughout its economic lifespan, which may be shorter than its physical life due to obsolescence. Ownership of productive capital in whatever form it takes may be separated from its management, which leads one to consider explicitly the organizations and procedures created to operate, maintain, and expand or modify the capital stock.

Beyond these technical terms used by modern economists to define "capital" objectively for purposes of academic research, however, "capitalism" must also be considered as a system within which markets operate effectively to create price signals that can be observed and responded to effectively by everyone concerned – consumers, producers, and regulators. The effectiveness of the market-driven capitalist system depends upon the incentives its institutions create for all concerned, as well as the openness it provides to enable participants in the system to respond to incentives. Douglass C. North defines institutions as:

> the rules of the game of a society and in consequence [they] provide the framework of incentives that shape economic, political, and social organizations. Institutions are composed of formal rules (laws, constitutions, rules), informal constraints (conventions, codes of conduct, norms of behavior), and the effectiveness of their enforcement. Enforcement is carried out by third parties (law enforcement, social ostracism), by second parties (retaliation), or by the first party (self-imposed codes of conduct). Institutions affect economic performance by determining, together with the technology employed, the transaction and transformation (production) costs that make up the total costs of production. (North 1997: 6)

Beyond the basic elements of economic activity that are physically observable, therefore, the history of capitalism must also pay attention to the organizations such as guilds, corporations, governments, and legal systems that operate within and enforce the "rules of the game." Further, less observable elements such as informal institutions and mental models that govern individual responses to external conditions may determine the effectiveness of markets in creating and then sustaining economic growth (North 2005). Continued reallocation of resources within an economy is essential for

3

economic growth to be sustained, or regained after any setback, whether caused by external factors such as war, famine, natural disaster, disease, or internal factors such as a financial crisis or failures of leadership. Market signals are necessary to guide the reallocation of resources and to direct the effort required to continue or resume growth. The source of finance for the transition to the new state of the economy, however, may or may not be driven by market signals, depending on the existence of capital markets and the exigencies of command economies. Much attention has to be paid, therefore, to sources of financing and its effective deployment in the past, especially for the financing of long-distance trade and of long-lived projects that would be essential for sustaining economic growth, given the technology of the time.

Moreover, while a thoroughgoing market system with markets for labor, land, and capital as well as final consumption goods and services has its internal logic, it is necessarily embedded within broader political, cultural, and social systems. So the price signals generated within the capitalist market system have to be observed and responded to by political, cultural, and social groups as well as by consumers and producers within the economy (Ogilvie 2007). Capitalism, therefore, can be defined usefully as a complex and adaptive economic system operating within broader social, political, and cultural systems that are essentially supportive.

This operational definition of capitalism leads us to search for characteristics that may have been present in different historical settings when economic growth was achieved for a significant period (at least a couple of centuries, as with modern capitalism). Archaeological evidence of settled agriculture combined with urban complexes sets the earliest limit for useful historical inquiry into complex economic systems that may, or may not, evince signs of incipient capitalist institutions. Modern archaeology, for example, can identify the composition of food sources for ancient sites to determine the variety of cultivars and domesticated animals. Evidence of olive oil, wine, and preserved fruits might demonstrate that economic agents operated with time horizons of at least the several years required to bring olive trees, grape vines, or date palms to maturity for repeated harvesting. Aerial surveys that show up remains of irrigation works and canals, as well as ancient raised or terraced fields next to concentrations of housing, also provide tantalizing evidence of capital formation with long time horizons and increased productivity. With appropriate attention to documentation that may have been preserved for whatever reason, sources of finance and issues of contract enforcement may be adduced as well. Clay tablets found throughout the Middle East with arithmetic exercises and comparisons of different alphabets indicate the possibility of training specialists in record-keeping and disseminating market information, a very special kind of human capital and one found only within urban settings.

Whether these early efforts to maintain the flow of economic activity through reliable payments systems could be the basis for longer-lived economic projects remains open to question, basically because the evidence needed to demonstrate the connections of finance capital to real capital remains elusive. European scholars have the benefit of merchant accounts, correspondence, and even newspapers after the invention of the printing press, combined with repositories of legal disputes and decisions. Scholars in the rest of the world, however, have increasingly been able to uncover comparable evidence of their merchant entrepreneurs, especially after European contact. While the Italian development of the foreign bill of exchange has long been seen as an essential element in facilitating the rise of European capitalism, it is clear that the Arab empires that arose with Islam beginning in the seventh century used similar financial instruments. Both *hawala* (transfers of credits from one place in one currency to another place in another currency) and *saftaja* (transfer of credit from one place in one currency to another place in the same currency) financed the extensive trade of Arab and other merchants throughout the Mediterranean and into central Asia and northern India (Pamuk, Chapter 8). *Hundi* were the same technique used in southern India long before European contact when cotton textiles were doubtless exported to the rest of Eurasia (Roy, Chapter 7). Chinese merchants used *fei-ch'ien* (flying money) or *pien-huan* (credit exchange) as analogous financial instruments in their trade (Thompson 2011: 98; Wong, Chapter 6).

In the European case, these techniques of financing long-distance trade eventually interacted with the techniques of war finance to become the financial basis for European domination of global trade in the early modern period (Neal 1990). By contrast, the earlier emergence of comparable empires seemed to finance military efforts by the equivalent of capital levies, which not only disrupted the existing payments systems but also despoiled previous accumulations of merchant capital. While long-distance trade sustained and was sustained by both capitalism and economic growth, repeated wars, rebellions, and raids disrupted both capitalism and economic growth, making the eventual success of British mercantilist policy exceptional, as argued by Patrick O'Brien in Chapter 12.

It has long been accepted that the start of modern economic growth was due to industrialization as practiced first in Great Britain, although precursors of industrialization were evident in much of Europe, the Middle Eastern civilizations, and especially China and India well before the eighteenth century. Most books catalogued under the subject heading of "Capitalism, history" therefore deal with developments in western Europe from, at earliest, 1500 (Appleby 2010; Beaud 2001), but usually from 1700 on (e.g. Broadberry and O'Rourke 2010). They then expand their coverage to include mainly the United States, Canada, Australia, and perhaps Japan and Russia for the nineteenth century and later. More recently, however, scholars have attempted to take a much longer time perspective (Graeber 2011, Jones 1988; Morris 2010), and a much broader geographical range (Parthasarathi 2011; Pomeranz 2000; Rosenthal and Wong 2011).

In keeping with these initiatives, we take the view that the current world economy has been a long time in the making, so we look for the beginnings of the "rise of capitalism" as far back as archaeologists have been able to detect tangible evidence of some human activity that was consistent, if not fully congruent, with the practices of modern capitalism. Organized market activity that took place over long distances, and consequently with long time horizons and long-lived structures, has left archaeological remains as well as an occasional historical record. Most useful are signs of rising population density along with increasing consumption per capita, what Jones (1988) has called economic growth on the intensive margin, which coincided with economic growth on the extensive margin. These apparent contradictions to classical Malthusian theory that population growth before the advent of modern economic growth would dissipate temporary gains in per capita income from whatever source, can be called "Malthusian singularities."[1]

A variety of evidence acquired by using the tools of modern science has convinced archaeologists and many historians of the ancient world that high levels of per capita income did emerge episodically well before modern economic growth began in capitalist economies. Even more interesting, these episodes typically were accompanied by extended periods of population growth as well as technical improvements that seemingly presaged aspects of modern, high-income societies. Why they failed eventually to realize what might have been much earlier achievements of modern economic growth and rapid technical progress, however, remains a mystery, but a mystery that has stimulated all sorts of conjectural histories.

[1] James Hutton (1795) coined the term "singularity" for modern geology when he observed two quite separate strata of rock juxtaposed off the coast of Scotland. Exploring the possible incidents of such singularities worldwide then launched geology as a modern, truly global science.

It appears that the earliest evidence of Malthusian singularities is from the ancient civilizations of what is now known as the Middle East, mainly Babylon and Egypt. Most tantalizing in light of later developments in the Mediterranean world are the economic activities of the Phoenicians (Aubet 2001; Moscati 2001). The Phoenicians clearly developed cities and a market structure to support the inhabitants with provisions in return for specialized artifacts and protection over very long periods of time, periods certainly longer by orders of magnitude than the era of modern capitalism, and their trade routes covered the entire Mediterranean and the Atlantic coasts of Africa. It is an article of faith of Phoenician archaeologists that the first circumnavigation of Africa was by the Phoenician admiral Hanno, in the years around 425 BCE, for example. But they can only conjecture the economic significance of the artifacts they have uncovered and the quotidian functions of the sites they have identified, extensive as they are around the Mediterranean.

Unlike the contemporary civilizations in Mesopotamia and Egypt and later in Greece and Rome, there is very little textual evidence from the Phoenicians that can enlighten us about their economic organization. Aubet (2001), for example, infers that the extensive Phoenician settlements in Spain were mainly enclaves designed in the first case to gain access to the silver mines accessed upriver from Cadiz, but how the extensive trade was organized and financed first from Tyre and then from Carthage remains a matter of conjecture. Archaeological evidence of luxury goods obviously imported into Spain by the Phoenicians may indicate that these were gifts to local tribal elites to initiate profitable export trade for Phoenicians, much as Hudson's Bay agents did in the beaver trade of eighteenth-century North America (Carlos and Lewis, Chapter 15). But how Phoenicians organized, controlled, and sustained their long-distance trade remains unknown.

For later civilizations, modern archaeology has the benefit of classical texts that provide rich contexts for assessing the economic consequences of the material evidence that archaeologists have uncovered in overwhelming quantities. The huge archives of clay tablets and bullae uncovered from the excavations of ancient Babylon since the late nineteenth century, and now stored in museums around the world, have gradually been decoded. The mind-numbing details of their economic records, both from temples and private merchants, have been pieced together by teams of archaeologists to give us a compelling picture of a vibrant economy lasting for centuries starting 1200 BCE at the outset of the Iron Age and extending to the conquest of Mesopotamia by Alexander the Great in 332 BCE.

The case studies for the rise of capitalism

Michael Jursa (Chapter 2) introduces the archaeology-based reinterpretations of the economic experiences of ancient economies, based on his extensive analysis of the Babylon evidence. In his earlier work (Jursa 2010), he concluded that Babylonia in the sixth century BCE had reached higher levels of prosperity than in earlier periods of its history. "[T]he economy was growing, the productivity of (frequently market-oriented) agriculture was increasing, a substantial part of the urban population worked in non-agrarian occupations, there was a high degree of labour specialization, and the economy was largely monetized" (Jursa 2010: 815). In a word, basic elements of what became Western capitalism as described in later chapters made their documented appearance well before the rise of Greek city-states or of the Roman empire. Nevertheless, the life of individuals was uncertain and many remained ill and hungry while even members of the elite were on occasion arbitrarily put to death and had their property confiscated, and laborers were forced to work without food or clothing being provided. Moreover, the extensive building projects carried out by royal authorities seem to have been financed mainly from the spoils collected by continued raids into surrounding territories, especially that of the Phoenicians. This was hardly the basis for sustained economic growth, much less for embedding capitalist mental models in society.

Babylon's economic efflorescence lasted through Persian domination. Then it was interrupted by Alexander the Great's conquest in 331 BCE and the subsequent division of the previous empire into separate satrapies. Nevertheless, right up to the rise of Islam the basic elements of Babylon's economic success – irrigated fields of grain and groves of date palms combined with herds of sheep and cattle to produce high agricultural productivity – sustained higher standards of living in the cities created between and alongside the two rivers of Mesopotamia (Pamuk, Chapter 8).

Meanwhile, the Greek city-states began to proliferate, dominating the eastern Mediterranean from 1000 BCE until the rise of the Roman empire. In the process of establishing the concept of republican government and laying the intellectual basis for Western philosophy they also managed to combine rising population densities with rising per capita incomes. Recent discoveries by modern archaeologists demonstrate that a considerable amount of intensive economic growth took place in ancient Greece, growth that was based on technical innovation, division of labor, extensive trade, and radical improvements in financial and contracting practices, all within a favorable global institutional framework, as demonstrated by Alain Bresson, Chapter 3. Roman legions, however, effected another military revolution by establishing a standing professional army in place of mercenary hoplite troops favored by the dispersed Greek city-states, combining the legions with naval support on lines well established by Athens at the peak of its classical glory (Hale 2009). Extending the Grecian principles of finance, law, and contract enforcement to the furthest reaches of an expanding empire, the Romans took the Grecian precedents to yet another level of population growth and higher standards of living. It took the Antonine plague of the second century to bring down both population and per capita income in the western empire and the Justinian plague of the seventh century to halt progress in the eastern empire according to Willem Jongman, Chapter 4.

Demonstrating that even populations confined to the interior of the Eurasian land mass could engage in long-distance trade and generate independent technical innovations, the fabled Silk Road was traversed for centuries by profit-seeking merchants. The best known were the Sogdian traders, long before Marco Polo made Europeans aware of the existence of the Silk Road and the incredible wealth of Kublai Khan in the thirteenth century. Again, modern archaeologists have uncovered astonishing evidence of the prosperity centered on the trading emporia of Samarkand and Bukhara, which not only connected the various Chinese states over time with the Black Sea and the eastern Mediterranean but also extended trade routes south into India and north as far as the Baltic. All this trade, however, was conducted under the oversight of competing warlords upon whose favor depended the fortunes of the various merchants, not a favorable setting for the rise of capitalism according to Étienne de la Vaissière, Chapter 5.

All of these early experiments with combining intensive economic growth with extensive trading relations within the confines of the Eurasian land mass and extending into northern Africa came to a sudden stop at various times, but most generally and pervasively in the middle of the fourteenth century with the Black Death. At the time, all of Eurasia and much of northern Africa were actively engaged in long-distance trade, the reason why the bubonic plague spread so quickly and so completely across the continent (Abu-Lughod 1989). Chapters 6 through 8 take up the great civilizations that participated in the pre-Black Death trade across Eurasia and then responded to the disruption of trade and the devastation of population in distinct ways up to the modern period.

Imperial China takes precedence as the most advanced and most populous economy anywhere in the world at this time. Ray Bin Wong, Chapter 6, traces the complexity of China's political and economic arrangements through successive plagues, famines, and barbarian invasions cumulating with the challenge of the sea barbarians from their initial contact until the Taiping Rebellion lasting from 1850 to 1864. Rather than seeing the long course of Chinese history as unrelieved oriental despotism based on control and maintenance of large-scale irrigation works, he finds that the central government's capacity to command was limited by the scale of its empire, so that it needed to negotiate with its subjects, especially the regional elites, to create conditions desirable for them. This meant sustaining markets, both in land and labor as well as consumer necessities and luxuries, and the institutional arrangements that developed over time proved quite viable through successive changes of dynasties. Managing the resource constraints faced by a densely populated, by European standards, society was challenging but accomplished with light taxation, no central government long-term debt, or private corporations, in contrast to the European style of capitalism.

Tirthankar Roy, Chapter 7, examines the subcontinent of India where a variety of military states sought and established authority in the interior valleys while sundry trading ports tried to profit from trading relations either with the rest of Asia or with the competing empires to the west until the dynamism of the English East India Company subsumed both the competing warlords and the sea merchants. The commercial centers turned increasingly to meet the demands of the European markets, but at the expense of traditional industry, especially cotton goods. India's cotton textiles became the first victim of the deindustrialization that was to prove so general in the nineteenth century. Warlords in the interior retreated to their original territories where they could retain their rent-seeking privileges. The disastrous economic consequences of political rule by a profit-seeking corporation, which Adam Smith had derided in the case of the Dutch East India Company's rule over the Spice Islands and the Indonesian archipelago in the eighteenth century, became even more evident with the rule of the English East India Company in nineteenth-century India.

Şevket Pamuk, Chapter 8, extends his magisterial history of the Ottoman empire, which arose after the Black Death, back to its origins in the rise of Islam from the seventh century on and the economic practices that accompanied it. While the Middle East experienced much institutional change over the centuries preceding the Black Death, and indeed afterwards, independent city-merchant elites did not play the key roles that they did in western Europe (and earlier in the Phoenician and Grecian city-states). Cities were often under the rule of the central state and the economic responses of local artisans and merchants were directed by the priorities of the central authorities. Rather than geography, which was actually quite favorable for commercial interactions, or religion, which proved quite adaptable to economic pressures, it was the controlling interest of central authority in maintaining stable hierarchies that limited the Ottoman response to the challenges posed by the rise of western European capitalist economies in the nineteenth century.

Karl Gunnar Persson, Chapter 9, analyzes how the competing substates dotting the remains of the western Roman empire sought to sustain both independence from marauding invaders, whatever their origin, and some degree of economic self-sufficiency in light of the breakdown of traditional trade patterns. The trilemma posed by Evsey Domar (1970) that free labor, free land, and rent-seeking landlords could not coexist for long proves to be the case in medieval Europe. But all the possible solutions to the trilemma, whether enslaving labor, restricting access to land, or finding protection other than from rent-taking landlords, were tried out across medieval Europe. The new patterns of trade among the hundreds of sovereign states that arose set the stage for the eventual rise of capitalism in western Europe. Domar's explanation for serfdom in Russia turns out to apply only to Russia, as only there were landlords able to call upon higher authority to enforce serfdom. Elsewhere throughout Europe, free and mobile labor proliferated, especially in the cities that arose along traditional trade routes.

Within Europe, a variety of experiments led to the rise of capitalism as it finally emerged in the following centuries. Luciano Pezzolo, Chapter 10, compares the city-states of Genoa, Venice, and Florence, each with a distinctive political system, as they recovered from the devastation of the Black Death. All three relied heavily on family networks, a feature of later capitalist imitators after 1850, but in distinctive ways. The capture of the Genoese state by the permanent corporation of the Casa di San Giorgio proved most successful, perhaps because the powerful families of Genoa acknowledged the importance of turnover among themselves in governance of the corporation. Venetian families closed off political access to new families and by controlling the convoy system also prevented new competitors from arising. Florentine families split in violent opposition to one another, calling upon outsiders to support one side or the other, until the city's fortunes were squandered. The economic fortunes of all three cities yielded ultimately to the new mercantile states forming on the Atlantic coast of Europe.

The Dutch, who had emerged relatively unscathed from the Thirty Years War, indulged in a brief speculative fling on the prospects of exotic varieties of tulips, but mainly they concentrated on funneling the products of the East Indies through their ports united in the Dutch East India Company (VOC hereafter, for Vereenigde Oost-indische Compagnie). Oscar Gelderblom and Joost Jonker, Chapter 11, analyze why the world's largest joint-stock company at the time of its creation in 1607 could generate so much wealth and prosperity domestically for the Dutch economy during its golden age, but still fail to withstand the competition from the interlopers in their lucrative trade. Attempts at sharing the markets with the English East India Company and stifling the competition that arose occasionally from other European powers, including the French, Danish, Swedes, and even Austrians (after the Vienna Habsburgs gained control of the southern Netherlands in 1715) ultimately failed due to the political constraints imposed on the corporation, which could never expand its original capital stock after 1620. Previous trade routes along the ancient Silk Road and through the Indian Ocean also recovered, as noted in the preceding chapters on China, India, and the Arab caliphate.

Nevertheless, during its heyday as an independent, sovereign republic, the United Provinces provided an enviable example of the possibilities unleashed by merchant capitalism, even without creating industrial capitalism. The pacific competition among the port cities within the Low Countries and then, later, among the Dutch provinces in the north, led to product specialization. The ease of transport of goods and people along the extensive waterways provided extensive markets for the speciality of each city or province, resulting in higher productivity throughout the Low Countries. The successful revolt of the northern provinces, finally recognized by the Treaty of Westphalia in 1648, created a situation in which the merchant elites governing cities within the United Provinces could impose higher taxes and borrow at lower yields on their debt than could their counterparts in the southern provinces. The cities remaining in the Spanish (later Austrian) Netherlands were still subject to the impositions of a distant monarch, whether in Madrid or Vienna.

European mercantilism was a competition among the Atlantic port cities to see which could combine its resources most effectively to reap the profits anticipated from the new trades created by the European discoveries. The new markets included the regions discovered by the Europeans across the Atlantic and the all-sea route to the fabled Indies and the Spice Islands. Patrick O'Brien, Chapter 12, argues persuasively that only Britain managed to mobilize its naval and trading organizations to accomplish precedence over the competing powers of Spain, France, and the Netherlands. The Thirty Years War (1618–1648) wreaked havoc on the central European populations comparable to that suffered during the Black Death. Thirty years of unrelenting warfare generated new military technology and new means of public finance designed essentially to wage war, and set the stage for a century and half of state building across western Europe. When Oliver Cromwell emerged victorious in the English Civil War by keeping his New Model Army constantly in the field and using cheap cast-iron cannon to knock down the curtain walls of medieval castles throughout Ireland, Wales, and Scotland, he also created the fiscal basis for maintaining a standing navy in the future. The essential features of British capitalism were set, according to O'Brien, from that time forward, as succeeding monarchs kept intact the new tax system, which generated increasing revenues proportionately as the trade funneled through British ports expanded on the heels of naval victories.

While mercantile states competed, trying out their different approaches to capitalism in order to exploit the possibilities of settlement and trade with Asia and the Americas, the various European powers encountered previously isolated populations in sub-Saharan Africa, the interior of North America, and, most famously, in Latin America. The European contacts with these previously unknown societies had lasting consequences, both for the contact populations and the future of capitalism. The devastation of native populations and their virtual enslavement by the *conquistadores* of Spain led by Cortez in Mexico and Pizarro in Peru have cast a pall over the history of capitalism ever since. But, as Richard Salvucci, Chapter 13, demonstrates, the Spanish, and later the Portuguese, enterprises were hardly proto-capitalist initially. Only when later generations of colonial rulers had come to terms with the radically altered ratios of labor to land caused by the depopulation of native Americans, were they able to exploit the region economically, which led to colonial expansion throughout Latin America. The role of silver, mined and exported in large and rising quantities both to Europe and to the Indies, but ending up mainly in China, while it served the Spanish monarchs well for nearly two centuries in financing their military ventures, actually had little to do with the fiscal support of the viceroyalties of Mexico and Peru. Tobacco and sugar monopolies were far more important fiscally, and state exploitation was very much along pre-capitalist lines, extending even so far as the *obrajes* or textile mills that mimicked the workshops emerging in eighteenth-century England.

As the European markets for the goods continued to expand, these monopolies, based on plantation cultivation, relied on large numbers of slaves, leading to the slave trade. Again, this is identified with the rise of capitalism, even to the extent that capitalist advances in British industry have been identified with the profits that British slavers acquired from exporting slaves from the west coast of Africa to British, Spanish, and Portuguese America.

Morten Jerven, Chapter 14, reprises the complicated system of trading relations that developed on Africa's west coast to facilitate the trans-Atlantic slave trade. African chiefs readily provided the slaves demanded by British slave traders arriving from Bristol or Liverpool, but only after they set the prices for the slaves in terms of the European and Asian goods provided by the European merchants. Over time, slave prices rose as a consequence while Africans extended the sources for slaves further inland. Supplementary trade arose before the demise of the slave trade in many other goods, such as pepper, palm oil, and redwood, which proved to be the main trading activity between Old Calabar and Bristol after 1807 and the end of the British slave trade. Maintaining long-distance communications and finance so that the proper textiles from India could be shipped from England and the most profitable mix of slaves in turn shipped from Africa to the Caribbean sugar islands turned out to require personal relations for repeat transactions between African chiefs, such as Antera Duke in the Niger delta, and British ship captains, such as Thomas Jones out of Bristol.

Ann Carlos and Frank Lewis, Chapter 15, show that similar responses to European traders occurred among the North American Indians who, already actively engaged in long-distance and local trade, quickly turned European contact into expanded trading activity throughout the North American continent. While gift-giving corresponding to existing Indian practices, as long observed by anthropologists, became part of the Hudson's Bay Company's regular dealing with native Americans, it was just a courtesy to initiate the serious trading of goods that followed at each post's annual markets. The extent and variety of goods demanded by Indian tribes from the European traders kept increasing, especially when higher prices for beaver pelts were offered. Initial contacts of European capitalist agents with native populations, therefore, whether in Latin America, Africa, or the wildernesses of North America could be met with opportunistic responses leading to mutually beneficial exchanges and often were.

Knick Harley, Chapter 16, takes up the continuing puzzle of how European mercantilism eventually developed as European industrialization. While his work has shown that there was a British industrial revolution, its development into modern economic growth was more gradual and less driven by simply introducing factory systems into the textile trades, as striking as those symbols of early capitalism were and continue to be. Ultimately, British industrial practices could be easily imitated in much of nearby Europe, but typically were not. Lack of imitation was due to uneconomic factor prices in Europe for adopting British techniques that were energy intensive, capital using, and labor saving. The driving force for the differences came, most likely, from agriculture where English labor productivity had become markedly higher than in the European continent, excluding the Netherlands.

Both the Dutch and English had managed to create economically efficient organizations of agriculture, creating incentive-compatible contracts between operators and owners to maintain and attempt to increase high levels of productivity in terms of marketable produce. As British industrialization and expanded overseas trade kept rising, especially during the extended wars with France that culminated in 1815, Europeans sought different ways to imitate the British success, often as not by protecting domestic producers from British products. Only after 1850 did major policy changes in most European countries allow successful competition, starting with increased agricultural productivity. Adopting variants of British institutional arrangements, especially in representative government that promoted capitalistic enterprises in transportation, agriculture, and industry, proved to be the eventual key to success, but it was not realized in most cases even in Europe until after the mid nineteenth century (Cardoso and Lains 2010).

Jeremy Atack, Chapter 17, takes up the iconic case of rampant capitalism – the United States of America – by noting the importance of the English corporate form of shareholding and governance from the beginning of the colonization efforts by the British monarchs. Faced with virtually limitless stretches of land and motivated to make a profit from exporting whatever could be raised or gathered, the colonists in that *tabula rasa* pushed hard to extract that profit to the fullest extent possible. The expansion of a rapidly growing, but ever high-wage population, whether into arable land or commercial centers, remains one of the marvels of economic expansion that has continued into the twenty-first century. Atack places the corporation, with its profit orientation (even for the city and state governments that evolved), as the defining capitalist institution for creating the American economic success and posing continued challenges to the hegemony of the state.

The American South, with its increasingly peculiar institution of plantation slavery, created a dynamic tension with the northern states where agriculture was arguably, but perhaps less visibly, commercial as well, and based on family-owned and operated farms. These mounting tensions were managed for decades by political compromises combined with westward expansion – until the west coast was reached. With the United States already the largest capitalist economy in the world at the start of the Civil War, the Union armies emerged as the largest, most potent military force in the world at the end. The large-scale industrial corporation, long preceded by tens of thousands of small-scale businesses, especially in the north, then came into its own, driving American economic growth and political conflicts up to the present day.

The rise of capitalism and the challenges it posed to existing structures of economics, commerce, politics, and even religion, were especially evident to European observers at the time, starting with the observation of the increasing quantities of silver coming into the European markets in the second half of the sixteenth century and the impact this had on the trade patterns and military capacities of competing states. José Luís Cardoso, Chapter 18, argues that the contemporaries analyzing the causes and consequences of the rise of capitalism created a new science of political economy that was to have important policy consequences. Adam Smith's magnum opus built on a long tradition of preceding thought about the benefits of multilateral trade, but explicitly attempted to prescribe intelligent economic policy to state authorities (see Book v of the *Wealth of Nations*). His optimism about the possibilities of mutually beneficial trade leading to accumulating wealth and happiness among increasingly civilized societies did not have immediate policy consequences but was surely influential in the move to free trade by Britain after 1848.

That was also the year that Karl Marx and Friedrich Engels published their *Communist Manifesto* predicting the collapse of capitalism due to its internal contradictions, needing expanded markets but also needing increased exploitation of workers. But that was also the year in which John Stuart Mill published his *Principles of Political Economy*, the pinnacle of classical economics, which extolled the civilizing possibilities of the coming stationary state, which he anticipated would come soon. Both of these contradictory visions of the future of capitalism were ultimately discredited by the spread of capitalism that spun across the world for the next century and a half, which makes it odder still that both visions continue to resonate in the twenty-first century.

Conclusion

By accepting the inevitability of flux in the economic performance of the various economies in the past, the contributors to this history of the rise of capitalism have created a new meta-narrative that contrasts with the existing treatments of the history of capitalism. The first narratives created during the early twentieth century exuded a sense of triumphalism before the disasters of World War I. Following the trauma of the Great Depression, the next round of histories were searches for alternative forms of economic organization. The division of the world after World War II into Western capitalism in various forms competing with centrally planned economies led to another set of meta-narratives, often to justify alternative experiments in the so-called Third World economies. With the renewed experience of globalization since roughly 1980, the current generation of historical scholarship has searched for a compelling new meta-narrative that seems appropriate for bringing the experience of the past to bear on the challenges of the present.

The variety of policy responses to the collapse of the centrally planned economies in the 1990s made clear the difficulties of getting things right in order to achieve modern economic growth. If some versions of modern capitalism seemed more attractive than others to transition economies at the end of the twentieth century, the institutions required for successful imitation were difficult to create and then sustain (see Chapter 16 by Neal and Williamson that concludes Volume II). The problems of changing traditional political structures in order to accommodate effectively the possibilities of material improvement that became increasingly evident at different times were not easily overcome in the past, but on occasion they were. Just what were the essential features of the successful changes in political arrangements that complemented dynamic changes in the economies that prospered remains a matter of conjecture, but economists, political scientists, and historians are making great efforts to dissect what were the critical elements in the few cases of success that are amenable to investigation.

The British case is the most intensively studied, with the political arrangements that coalesced with the celebrated Glorious Revolution of 1688/1689 usually given pride of place. Acemoglu and Robinson (2012) argue that the Parliament that deposed James II was open to a broad range of economic interests, from hereditary landowners to overseas merchants with varying religious and geographical orientations. North and Weingast (1989) argue that Parliament constrained the predatory inclinations of the monarch, forcing him to accept the terms set by Parliament for extending new taxes, creating new debts, or establishing new enterprises. The "credible commitment" mechanisms so created were the essential aspect of the British constitution (still unwritten, however) that enabled entrepreneurs to prosper thereafter, eventually leading to the industrial revolution. Most historians of this episode, however, find events much more complex, and that a wide variety of commitment mechanisms were required, some of which predated the 1689 change of regime, while others took much longer to establish firmly (Coffman, Leonard, and Neal 2012). Regardless, all other cases of incipient capitalism have to be compared with the British example along several dimensions beyond the merely economic, but especially in terms of the political and legal institutions.

The obstacles to imitation were overcome in different ways by nation-states from the nineteenth century into the present. We know now that the innovations in follower countries went beyond merely mobilizing capital on an ever-larger scale in order to apply the latest technology. Political, social, cultural, and perhaps psychological adjustments were required as well if imitation was to succeed. Coordination of the various processes that make up any economy is the fundamental problem that has to be worked out for capitalism or its alternatives to operate at all. Coordination starts with combining several factors of production to create desirable goods and services; then becomes more complicated in distributing output among consumers scattered in space and varying in demand; and culminates by resolving the vexing issue of compensating the owners of the various factors of production.

While coordination problems are manifold and complex, perhaps they can be analyzed usefully as attempts to overcome various dilemmas, trilemmas, and other problems that arise within economies regardless of the degree to which they are capitalist, or industrialized, or market oriented. For example, modern macroeconomics at the end of the twentieth century has identified the theoretical basis for a specific trilemma confronted by nation-states participating in the global economy. Access to global capital markets requires free movement of capital to and from abroad, access to global commodity markets is increased with fixed exchange rates, while maintaining domestic tranquility requires an independent monetary policy. Unfortunately, not all three desirable economic policy regimes can be sustained at the same time. Eventually, one of the three desiderata has to be put aside (Obstfeld and Taylor 2004).

Sorting out this particular trilemma provides a useful analytical framework for assessing the development of global capitalism since the middle of the nineteenth century. Prior to that, the rise of mercantile capitalist economies in western Europe provided an interesting set of experiments with the leading powers – the Netherlands, the United Kingdom, and France – variously focussing on fixed exchange rates (Netherlands), capital mobility (the United Kingdom), and independent monetary policy (France) over the period roughly bounded by the Treaty of Westphalia in 1648 and the Treaty of Vienna in 1815 (Neal 2000). It bears repeating that the lesson from that long-run competition, essentially driven by the need to finance the increasing expenses of the military revolution in the successive wars from 1648 to 1815, was that maintaining capital mobility was most useful, as the British found (see O'Brien, Chapter 12).

Evsey Domar (1970) identified another, more fundamental trilemma in a classic paper where he put forth the hypothesis that the three elements of a pre-modern agricultural structure – free land, free peasants, and non-working landlords – could never exist simultaneously. At least one of the elements would have to be eliminated for a sustainable agricultural economy. Settled agriculture was repeatedly threatened by intermittent raiders, and farmers required military protection, which was typically provided by non-working landlords. In that case, either free land (western Europe) or free peasants (eastern Europe) had to be given up. Domar illustrated his hypothesis with a few examples drawn from his extensive reading in Russian history and the emerging literature on the profitability of slavery in the American South. The failure of serfdom to reappear in Britain or Europe west of the Elbe after the Black Death changed the land/labor ratio in favor of bondage remained an issue, however, an issue that Domar willingly handed to historians and political scientists. The contributions by Persson (Chapter 9) and Salvucci (Chapter 13) that follow in this volume explore other implications of the Domar trilemma.

For the very earliest periods, dominated by the rise and ultimate fall of empires, an interesting question is whether land-based empires had to become command driven at the expense of developing market capacities while sea-based empires could diversify their responses to exogenous shocks more readily by accessing new markets. Examples might include access to new sources of food supply for purchase, hiring military support in the form of mercenaries, or avoiding epidemics by restricting access to ports. If land-based empires were inherently unstable for the long run, how did the Egyptian empires manage to endure so long (Allen 1997) or the Chinese empires once they were established (Wong 1997)? What were the long-run implications for agricultural improvement and the rise of capitalism from Roman attempts to settle professional soldiers along the increasingly distant borders of the empire, an effort more successfully imitated later by the Austro-Hungarian empire, and even the Swedish empire, in comparison with the typical recourse to mercenaries by Athens, then the Italian city-states, and ultimately Great Britain?

Sir John Hicks, in *A Theory of Economic History* (1969), grappled with this problem by posing a provocative dilemma. Starting with the premise that human societies tend to be organized either from the top down (command economies) or from the bottom up (customary economies), Hicks hypothesized that while market-oriented economies could arise from time to time to provide an efficient allocation of resources or goods they had not prevailed through most of history. Societies confronted with shocks, whether from natural disasters, military invasions, or plagues, would naturally tend to respond with a command economy in order to mobilize resources as quickly as possible to confront the new challenge. Societies insulated from shocks, however, would tend to maintain their customary use of resources indefinitely whether their allocations were optimal for society as a whole or not. Because societies either did or did not experience shocks, they would become either command economies or customary economies. The market economy would always be in peril as a consequence. Either it would be thrust aside by the forces taking command or it would be allowed to wither away by popular indifference. The "command case" was the primary cause for the failures of early examples of market-oriented capitalism to survive shocks. The analyses of Karl Marx (usefully summarized in Marx [c. 1932]) variously argued two command cases that would lead to the collapse of capitalism: either internal contradictions among the economic rulers, or a revolution leading to a dictatorship of the proletariat. Later variants of this line of argument might be Rajan and Zingales (2003), who argue that entrenched capitalists can stifle creative responses to the challenges of shocks, or Rajan (2010), who argues that entrenched political rulers can maintain faulty policies in response to shocks. The "customary case" could explain the general failures of primitive populations to prosper, but could also be a cause for advanced economies to fail, whether because the capitalists failed to innovate (Schumpeter 1950) or the workers failed to respond to new opportunities for consumption (Bell 1976).

Hicks suggested that the rise of market-oriented economies depended upon independent city-states ruled by authorities committed to maintaining long-distance trade. The geography of the Mediterranean proved to be especially favorable for sustaining such economies, with Venice and Genoa as leading examples. Why Carthage, the flourishing center of Phoenician mercantile expertise before the creation of the Roman empire, could not prevail against Rome, however, was not considered by Hicks, save to make the point that market-oriented societies were vulnerable to either command or customary societies in conflicts. The contribution on China by Roy Bin Wong (Chapter 6 in this volume), however, shows that Hicks's dilemma can be overcome by bureaucratic elites in land-based empires as well, provided they can synthesize effectively the equivalent of an island economy that is self-sufficient and defensible.

An alternative resolution of Hicks's dilemma is to focus on the importance of developing a financial market for government debt. Hicks relied on the arguments of his friend, T. S. Ashton, to explain how Britain had managed to avoid either custom or command in responding to the challenges of the

Spanish, French, and Dutch in the eighteenth century. According to Ashton (1948), British interest rates, taken as the cost of capital, steadily fell over the eighteenth century, led by a fall in the yields on government debt. The problem with that argument is that interest rates on government debt were even lower elsewhere in Europe and much earlier than the eighteenth century (Chapter 10 in this volume). Nevertheless, a number of examples can be found where a financial revolution preceded a sustained economic expansion for a country (Rousseau 2003). If a government has the possibility of raising cash quickly by selling its bonds to a potentially large, diverse, and wealthy group of investors, it can then use its command of cash to purchase the resources needed to confront an external shock. The relevant markets for the needed labor, capital, goods, or services will then be enhanced and increasingly capable of responding effectively to subsequent shocks. In this way, a tendency for command economies to emerge can be diverted into a tendency for market economies to expand and deepen. This argument provides an example of how important is the focus of the individual contributions in this volume on the adaptability of the institutions in place in response to exogenous shocks. Did elements of command economies emerge? Did they then endure at the expense of markets for resources or specific commodities? If market responses did occur, how were they financed? By forced loans, forced circulation of currency, or drawing on external sources of supply through offering payment in sovereign bonds? Perhaps Marx was correct when he identified the British creation of a truly national debt funded explicitly by parliamentary commitment to servicing it with specific taxes after 1688 as the key element in the rise of modern capitalism!

References

Abu-Lughod, J. (1989). *Before European Hegemony: The World System A.D. 1250–1350*. New York: Oxford University Press.

Acemoglu, D. and J. Robinson (2012). *Why Nations Fail: The Origins of Power, Prosperity, and Poverty*. New York: Crown Publishers.

Allen, R. C. (1997). "Agriculture and the Origins of the State in Ancient Egypt," *Explorations in Economic History* 34: 135–154.

Appleby, J. (2010). *The Relentless Revolution: A History of Capitalism*. New York: W. W. Norton.

Ashton, T. S. (1948). *The Industrial Revolution, 1760–1830*. Oxford University Press.

Aubet, M. E. (2001). *The Phoenicians and the West: Politics, Colonies and Trade*. Cambridge and New York: Cambridge University Press.

Beaud, M. (2001). *A History of Capitalism, 1500–2000*. New York: Monthly Review Press.

Bell, D. (1976). *The Cultural Contradictions of Capitalism*. New York: Basic Books.

Broadberry, S. and K. O'Rourke, eds. (2010). *The Cambridge Economic History of Modern Europe*, 2 vols. Cambridge University Press.

Cardoso, J. L. and P. Lains, eds. (2010). *Paying for the Liberal State: The Rise of Public Finance in Nineteenth-century Europe*. Cambridge University Press.

Coffman, D., A. Leonard, and L. Neal, eds. (2013). *Questioning Credible Commitment: Perspectives on the Rise of Financial Capitalism*. Cambridge University Press.

Domar, E. (1970). "The Causes of Slavery or Serfdom: A Hypothesis," *Journal of Economic History*, 30(1): 18–32.

Drobak, J. N. and J. V. C. Nye, eds. (1997). *The Frontiers of the New Institutional Economics*. San Diego: Academic Press.

Findlay, R. and K. H. O'Rourke (2007). *Power and Plenty: Trade, War and the World Economy in the Second Millennium*. Princeton University Press.

Floud, R. and D. N. McCloskey (1981). *The Economic History of Britain*. Vol. 1: *1700–1870*. Cambridge University Press.

Graeber, D. (2011). *Debt: The First 5,000 Years*. Brooklyn, NY: Melville House Publishing.

Hale, J. R. (2009). *Lords of the Sea: The Epic Story of the Athenian Navy and the Birth of Democracy*. New York: Viking Press.

Hall, P. A. and D. Soskice, eds. (2001). *Varieties of Capitalism: The Institutional Foundations of Comparative Advantage*. Oxford University Press.

Harris, R. (2009). "The Institutional Dynamics of Early Modern Eurasian Trade: The Corporation and the Commenda," *Journal of Economic Behavior and Organization*, 71(3): 606–622.

Hatton, T. J. and J. G. Williamson (2008). *Global Migration and the World Economy: Two Centuries of Policy and Performance*. Cambridge, MA: The MIT Press.

Hicks, J. R. (1969). *A Theory of Economic History*. London: Oxford University Press.

Hutton, J. (1795). *Theory of the Earth, with Proofs and Illustrations*, 2 vols. Edinburgh: William Creech.

Jones, E. L. (1988). *Growth Recurring: Economic Change in World History*. Oxford: Clarendon Press.

Jursa, M. (2010). *Aspects of the Economic History of Babylonia in the First Millennium BC: Economic Geography, Economic Mentalities, Agriculture, the Use of Money and the Problem of Economic Growth*. Münster: Ugarit-Verlag.

Kuznets, S. (1966). *Modern Economic Growth: Rate, Structure, and Spread*. New Haven: Yale University Press.

Marx, K. (c. 1932). *Capital, the Communist Manifesto and Other Writings*, ed. Max Wastman. New York: The Mordern Library.

Morris, I. (2010). *Why the West Rules – for Now: The Patterns of History and What They Reveal About the Future*. New York: Farrar, Straus and Giroux.

Moscati, S. (2001). *The Phoenicians*. London and New York: I. B. Tauris.

Neal, L. (1990). *The Rise of Financial Capitalism: International Capital Markets in the Age of Reason*. New York: Cambridge University Press.

(2000). "How it All Began: The Monetary and Financial Architecture of Europe from 1648 to 1815," *Financial History Review*, 7(2): 117–140.

North, D. C. (1990). *Institutions, Institutional Change and Economic Performance*. Cambridge and New York: Cambridge University Press.

(1997). "Theoretical Foundations," in Drobak and Nye (eds.), p. 6.

(2005). *Understanding the Process of Economic Change*. Princeton University Press.

North, D. C. and B. Weingast (1989). "Constitutions and Commitment: The Evolution of Institutional Governing Public Choice in Seventeenth-Century England," *Journal of Economic History*, 49(4): 803–832.

North, D. C., J. Wallis, and B. Weingast (2010). *Violence and Social Orders: A Conceptual Framework for Interpreting Recorded Human History*. Cambridge and New York: Cambridge University Press.

O'Brien, P. (1988). "The Political Economy of British Taxation, 1660–1815," *Economic History Review* 41: 1–32.

Obstfeld, M. and A. Taylor (2004). *Global Capital Markets: Integration, Crisis, and Growth*. New York: Cambridge University Press.

Ogilvie, S. (2007). "'Whatever Is, Is Right'? Economic Institutions in Pre-industrial Europe," *Economic History Review*, 60(4): 649–684.

O'Rourke, K. H. and J. G. Williamson (1999). *Globalization and History: The Evolution of a Nineteenth-century Atlantic Economy*. Cambridge, MA: The MIT Press.

Parthasarathi, P. (2011). *Why Europe Grew Rich and Asia Did Not: Global Economic Divergences, 1600–1850*. Cambridge and New York: Cambridge University Press.

Pomeranz, K. (2000). *Great Divergence: China, Europe, and the Making of the Modern World Economy*. Princeton University Press.

Rajan, R. (2010). *Fault Lines: How Hidden Fractures Still Threaten the World Economy*. Princeton University Press.

Rajan, R. and L. Zingales (2003). *Saving Capitalism from the Capitalists: Unleashing the Power of Financial Markets to Create Wealth and Spread Opportunity*. Princeton University Press.

Rosenthal, J.-L. and R. B. Wong (2011). *Before and Beyond Divergence: The Politics of Economic Change in China and Europe*. Cambridge, MA: Harvard University Press.

Rousseau, P. (2003). "Historical Perspectives on Financial Development and Growth," *Federal Reserve Bank of St. Louis Review*, 85(4): 81–105.

Schumpeter, J. A. (1950). *Capitalism, Socialism, and Democracy*, 3rd edn. London: George Allen and Unwin.

Thompson, E. A. (2011). *Trust is the Coin of the Realm: Lessons from the Money Men in Afghanistan*. Karachi, New York and Oxford: Oxford University Press.

Williamson, J. G. (2006). *Globalization and the Poor Periphery before 1950: The 2004 Ohlin Lectures*. Cambridge, MA: The MIT Press.

Wong, R. B. (1997). *China Transformed: Historical Change and the Limits of European Experience*. Ithaca, NY: Cornell University Press.

2

Babylonia in the first millennium
BCE – economic growth in times of empire

MICHAEL JURSA

Introduction

Beginning in the nineteenth century, excavations in Iraq, Syria, and Iran have brought to light the remains of the civilizations that flourished in the ancient Near East in the third, second, and first millennia BCE. Among these finds, the written records, over 250,000 clay tablets inscribed with the cuneiform script, stand out. In the ancient world, this corpus is superseded quantitatively only by the source material in Greek; more text survives from antiquity in the ancient Near Eastern languages Sumerian, Assyrian, and Babylonian than in Latin (Streck 2011). Some 80 percent of the ancient Near Eastern text corpus are of socio-economic content – a mine of information on economic history that reaches back to a period very close to the first appearance of stratified urban societies.

The overabundance of qualitative and quantitative textual information notwithstanding, there are few extended treatments of the economic history of the ancient Near East that are informed by theoretical concerns and models as well as by an adequate understanding of the primary sources, and that also address economic development over time and changes in economic performance.[1] Research is hampered by the sheer mass of philological detail that has to be harnessed for the purpose of generalization, by the unequal distribution of the data (van de Mieroop 1997), and by the lack of archaeological research on

---

[1] Most of the data come from southern Mesopotamia, i.e. the region of modern Iraq. We will deal primarily with this region, leaving aside the less well-known economic development of ancient Iran, Syria, and the Levant. Of all general treatments of ancient Near Eastern history, Postgate (1994) and Liverani (2011) are the most thorough in their description of economic structures and development. See Van de Mieroop (1999) and Radner and Robson (2011) for the methodology of cuneiform studies.

the issue of overall demographic development, economic performance, and standards of living.[2]

The environment and the "traditional" paradigm of the ancient Mesopotamian economy

Ancient Mesopotamian societies were "complex peasant societies": strongly stratified, state-building societies characterized by a comparatively high degree of urbanization (Bang 2006: 55). The environmental conditions determined to a large extent the economic activities (e.g. Postgate 1994; Potts 1997; Wilkinson 2003; and Wirth 1962). Four principal ecological zones can be distinguished in southern Mesopotamia: the central alluvial plain, crisscrossed by rivers and irrigation canals; the swampy river deltas and other water-logged areas; the steppe bordering on the alluvium (the realm of the shepherds); and the cities. The principal economic activities associated with these zones were irrigation agriculture, hunting, and fishing, sheep-breeding and artisanal and other city-based non-agricultural activities. In northern Mesopotamia, the more hilly countryside permitted a mixture of irrigation and rainfall agriculture. The principal cereal crop, barley, was complemented in the south by dates: southern Mesopotamian agriculture was based on two leading crops, rather than one. Sesame was the main source of vegetable fat, barley beer and later a "beer" made of fermented dates were the principal beverages. Importantly, in southern Mesopotamia, where urbanism first arose, many essential natural resources, especially metal, stones, and good wood, were lacking and always had to be obtained from neighboring Iran, from the Levant and from Anatolia and, via the Persian Gulf, from India and Arabia.

The various forms of socio-economic organization that were adopted by the societies that flourished in this environment are often seen as variants of one basic model.[3] Following the terminology of Liverani (2011: 41–44), this model is founded on a dichotomy between a "domestic" and a "palatial" mode of production. The former is village based and involves agriculture at or near a mere subsistence level; producers and landowners are identical,

---

2 The principal exception is Adams (1981), a seminal study on the development of settlement patterns in southern Mesopotamia. See Matthews 2003 and Wilkinson 2003 for surveys of Near Eastern archaeology.

3 See Graslin-Thomé (2009: 91–131) and Jursa (2010a: 13–33) for a discussion of this and similar models, with further references, as well for other theory-based approaches to the economic history of the ancient Near East, including the reflexes of the "primitivist"–"modernist" and "substantivist"–"formalist" debates in this branch of ancient studies.

auto-consumption dominates, and exchange is limited, local, and predominantly reciprocal; full-time economic specialization is mostly absent. This
sector of the economy is subordinate to the "palatial" (or institutional) sector
that is dominated by large temple and palace households. Here producers
are in a servile status *vis-à-vis* the owners of the means of production (especially land); there is labor specialization and redistribution of goods within
the institutional household. This sector of the economy is city based, i.e. it is
closely linked with the process of urbanization. The institutional sector
depends for its survival on the (seasonal) labor and the surplus produced in
the "domestic" sector of the economy. Especially from the second millennium
onwards, this surplus is centrally collected by means of a "tributary system"
(see Liverani 2011: 52–53; Renger 2002, 2003, 2004; and e.g. Van de Mieroop
1999: 113–14; [for his approach, see Graslin-Thomé 2009: 116–118]).

The existence of other modes of production is conceded by the proponents
of this model. There is general agreement that in all periods of Mesopotamian
history, from the end of the fourth millennium BCE onwards (Powell 1994),
private land ownership (if not necessarily ownership of arable land) was
recognized and protected by law. However, there is considerable diachronic
variation – and equally considerable disagreement among scholars – regarding
the weight that has to be allotted to this and other economic subsistence
strategies compared with the two sectors of the economy, the institutional and
the (village-based) domestic (and communal), on whose interplay the dominant model of the Mesopotamian economy is founded. Complex systems of
bureaucratically administered redistribution within the framework of large
institutional households were certainly of major importance in the third
millennium. According to some scholars, essentially the entire population of
southern Mesopotamia was integrated into such households, while in later
periods, subsistence production on small plots dominated the life of the vast
majority of the population.[4] Others hesitate to subscribe to such sweeping
generalizations (e.g. Liverani 2011: 43; Van de Mieroop 1999: 115) or emphasize
the coexistence of the "private" sector of the economy next to the "institutional sector" also in the third millennium BCE (e.g. Garfinkle 2012: 27), but

---

4 E.g. Renger (2005; 2007: 193). See also Dahl (2010), who makes a case for late third-
millennium specialized craftsmen being permanently in state service without any scope
for working for the market. Following the lead of the influential classicist Moses Finley,
this view of the Mesopotamian economy has been taken as sufficient grounds for
excluding Mesopotamia – as "fundamentally different" – from consideration within the
wider context of the ancient (i.e. Greco-Roman) economy (see Jursa [2010a: 19] for
references).

agree that throughout the three millennia of documented ancient Near Eastern history the dominance of subsistence production and the "palatial" sector of the economy left at best limited scope for economic phenomena that can be classified as "capitalist" in that they depend – as defined in the introduction to this volume – on the government-backed interplay of private property rights, contractual relationships, and markets governed by supply and demand.

This "two-sector" paradigm of the Mesopotamian economy has been developed predominantly on the basis of evidence from the third millennium BCE, and it fits these data best. The model's significance for later periods is questionable – and has been questioned. While the continued existence and relevance of the "domestic" and the "institutional" (or "palatial," following Liverani) modes of production is beyond doubt, changes in their cumulative economic weight argue for a nuanced application of the two-sector model to later periods of Mesopotamian history. Its most sustained challenges come from the documentation for long-distance (and domestic) trade that proves the existence of market-based and profit-oriented commerce supported by complex social and legal institutions,[5] and from evidence dating to the first millennium BCE that shows a period of economic growth driven, *inter alia*, by increasing monetization and the market orientation of economic exchange. These phenomena will be treated in the remainder of this chapter.

Markets, long-distance trade and commerce in the ancient Near East: aspects of capitalism

Mesopotamian societies could procure important resources such as metals from neighboring regions by violence, through military raids, the imposition of tribute, or through institutionalized gift exchange with foreign rulers (e.g. Veenhof 2010: 40–41). Most often, however, such goods were obtained through trade. The best evidence comes from the first half of the second millennium. Especially northern Mesopotamian, i.e. Assyrian, data from around 1850 BCE document profit-oriented commerce in textiles and in base and precious metals that can be classified as "capitalist" according to the definitions set out in the introduction. The Old Assyrian caravan trade is

---

5 The best evidence for this dates to the first half of the second millennium BCE, but already in the third millennium BCE private entrepreneurial activity is well attested, in particular on the margins of the institutional economy (e.g. Jursa 2002; Garfinkle 2012).

documented by a corpus of 25,000 cuneiform tablets (e.g. Dercksen 2004; Veenhof 2008, 2010). Its basic structure will be summarized here. The hub of Assyrian trade was the city of Assur on the Tigris. Assyrian and foreign merchants imported to Assur textiles and copper (from the south), and tin and lapis lazuli from Iran; nomads from the city's wider hinterland brought wool which was woven into textiles in Assur in home-based workshops often run by women (typically, the wives of merchants). Assyrian traders paid for these goods with silver. This silver (and gold) was earned through the export of these goods to Anatolia.

The king of Assur's rights with respect to this crucial aspect of his city's economy were limited. The main administrative powers rested with the city assembly, a collective body which consisted of representatives of the city's elite (merchant) families and ran also the "city hall," the town's economic center. While the city, represented by the city hall, held the monopoly on some trade goods (meteoric iron and lapis lazuli), its main function in the economy was that of guaranteeing contracts, of defining the legal framework for all trading, which included guaranteeing the stability of the system of measures and weights and the purity of the precious metals traded, and of establishing the diplomatic relations with other regional powers on which the Assyrian caravan trade depended. The city also acted to limit competition to its merchants from traders originating in other cities (Veenhof 2010: 51–52). Bilateral treaties guaranteed Assyrian merchants the right of residence in foreign cities, including the right to establish trading colonies, extraterritorial rights, guarantees of safe conduct, and protection against brigandage (Eidem 1991: 189). The city hall also collected taxes on trade goods. The city delegated some of its power to the administration of several "colonies" established by Assyrian merchants in the commercial quarters of Anatolian cities; in their dealings with Anatolians, the Assyrian traders could count on the backing of the local representatives of their city.

The institutions of actual trading are abundantly documented. Trading firms were normally family based, but caravan ventures frequently were funded by "joint-stock funds" (*naruqqum*, "money bag," in Assyrian [Veenhof 2010: 55]). Up to around a dozen investors – family and business partners of the trader, but also simply rich citizens of Assur – pooled resources reckoned in a gold standard to finance a trader's business trip. Such investments were usually made for a decade, and were expected to yield to the investor double the amount invested, plus additional profits. Credit was frequently given and taken; debts bore interest, and sometimes also compound interest. Debt notes could be transferred; they were negotiable instruments similar to medieval bills of exchange.

Merchants were aware of the fluctuation of prices and market mechanisms and tried to benefit from them whenever they could. They were motivated by desire for prestige, as reflected in their large houses that have been excavated, and for profit, as expressed by a warning addressed to an overzealous merchant: "you love money, but you hate your life."

These Assyrian merchants are but the best-known case of Mesopotamian long-distance traders who worked in a setting that for all the involvement of the state – often export goods were surpluses originating from royal or temple estates, and in the first millennium long-distance traders were often royal merchants – bore all the imprints of market-based and profit-oriented trading.[6] Even when they acted for the state, merchants bore personally the risk of their activities and adopted various strategies to minimize it (Graslin-Thomé 2009: 381–428; Jursa 2002). Thus, market-based exchange dominated the realm of trade, especially long-distance trade, throughout ancient Near Eastern history. This sector of the economy was a realm of entrepreneurial activity that can be usefully analyzed with – for instance – the concepts of neoclassical theory. Nevertheless, it may be argued, in line with the "two-sector" model, that the Old Assyrian case, and the sphere of (long-distance) trade in general, are not characteristic of the dominant economic structures of most of ancient Near East history and of the lives lived by the vast majority of its population. As one of the most outspoken defenders of the role of private entrepreneurship in third millennium BCE Mesopotamia observes, it seems clear that "individuals in the ancient world often derived their impetus from a profit motive and . . . economizing choices were made in antiquity," but while "a large segment of the urban population . . . was free to engage in entrepreneurial activity," "the largest portion of the population . . . was absolutely dependent on the insti-tutions that controlled their labor" (Garfinkle 2012: 153). Only for the first millennium BCE, and in particular for southern Mesopotamia in the late seventh, the sixth, and the early fifth centuries BCE (the "long sixth century"), can one make a case for a general shift of the economy toward market-based transactions. This shift led to economic growth on the intensive margin which coincided with economic growth on the extensive margin – a possible case of a "Malthusian singularity."[7] The remainder of the chapter focusses on this evidence.

---

6 See van Driel (2002) and Garfinkle (2012) for the late third millennium BCE, Stol (2004: 868–99) for southern Mesopotamia (Babylonia) in the second millennium BCE, and Graslin-Thomé (2009) for the first millennium BCE.

7 See Goldstone (2002) and the introduction, p. 6.

Economic growth in first-millennium BCE Babylonia

The environmental and technological matrix of economic life in Babylonia in the first millennium BCE, including the long sixth century on which these pages will concentrate, did not differ significantly from that of earlier periods: Babylonia was still a predominantly agrarian society depending on irrigation agriculture with a double focus on barley and the more labor-intensive, but also more productive, cultivation of dates. Sheep-breeding was the third principal agrarian activity.

Within this framework, a certain set of interdependent ecological, demographic, and political factors cumulatively caused structural economic change. By the eighth century BCE, the climatic anomaly that had significantly contributed to the crisis of the Near Eastern world around the turn of the millennium had passed: the climate grew wetter, the river system in the alluvial flood plain of Mesopotamia stabilized, and conditions for agriculture production in southern Mesopotamia improved markedly. Population levels rose, and there began a phase of increasing urbanization (Adams 1981). Politically, the rise of the neo-Babylonian empire at the end of the seventh century brought to an end an extended period of unrest and war. As the center of an empire that stretched from the Levant to the foothills of the Iranian plateau, Babylonia could reap the benefits both of peace and of imperial domination.

Jointly, these factors triggered an expansion of the economy, and far-reaching change.[8] This development can be followed in great detail through a mass of qualitative and less abundant, but still substantial, quantifiable data. We focus here on the "long sixth century," which began with the rise of Babylonia at the end of the seventh century and came to an end in 484 BCE, when Babylonian rebellions against Xerxes and Persian reprisals caused major disruptions in the socio-economic fabric of the country. Over 20,000 cuneiform tablets document this period (Jursa 2005); many more remain unpublished. The result of the economic transformation in the 130 years (the long sixth century) following the fall of Assyria (612 BCE) and the rise of Babylon can be sketched as follows. Agricultural production increased overall and was strongly market oriented. A large (if unquantifiable) part of the urban population worked in non-agrarian occupations; there was a high degree of labor specialization. The majority of the urban and rural workforce consisted, for

---

8 The following argument is based on Jursa (2010a), where full documentation can be found. References here are selective.

the first time in Mesopotamian history, not of compelled laborers, but of free hirelings who were paid market wages in silver money. The economy was monetized to a greater degree than ever before – silver served not only for high-value transactions, but also as low-range money. Few among the urban population can have remained entirely untouched by the monetary economy. Consumption patterns suggest a significantly higher level of prosperity than in earlier periods of Babylonian history.

The interconnection of these phenomena, which will be described in more detail below, can be established through a "commercialization model" of Smithian inspiration (e.g. Hatcher and Bailey 2001: 121–173 and Millett 2001; Jursa 2010a: 783–800 for the application of the model to the present period). Demographic change is one important stimulus for agricultural and commercial development and technological progress, the agency of the state is another. Profiting from state-controlled investment in the agrarian infrastructure and generally lavish state spending,[9] population growth and a concomitant process of urbanization set in motion (and was in turn sustained by) a positive feedback cycle in the economy. This led to an increase in demand and to an increase in aggregate as well as per capita production. Urbanization allowed an increasing division of labor and economic specialization, and thus led to higher productivity. As administrative, religious, and economic centers, cities were foci of high consumption and depended on an increasing pool of non-agricultural labor. They stimulated the production of a growing agricultural surplus through offering market opportunities. The resulting modicum of economic growth not only offset (for a while) the Malthusian threat accompanying demographic growth but also allowed a noticeably (and quantifiably) higher general standard of living than in earlier (and later) periods. Some of the evidence that supports this model will now be discussed in brief.[10]

The demographic expansion in Babylonia from the seventh century onwards is best visible in the results of archaeological surveying. According to Adams (1981: 178), long-term demographic growth that began in this period led to a fivefold (or more) increase of the population in the region during a span of five to seven hundred years. Other estimates are more conservative

---

9 Labor for hire was widely available, as was incoming capital, in the form of booty and tribute acquired from the periphery of the Babylonian empire.

10 Note that structurally the forces that determined the economic development of the long sixth century and allowed southern Mesopotamian to enjoy a phase of exceptional prosperity are very similar to those that caused another episode of intensive growth and economic efflorescence in the same region in the early Islamic period (Pamuk and Shatzmiller 2014; Pamuk (Chapter 8 in this volume).

(Brinkman 1984), but it is certain that in the period under consideration many more people lived in Babylonia than in the preceding centuries. They also lived in larger settlements: urban settlements increased overproportionally, a result of "fairly abrupt, probably state-directed, policies of settlement formation" (Adams 1981: 178).

The agrarian basis of the economy underwent a deep structural transformation (Jursa 2010a: 316–468). Canal-building projects and state-sponsored land-reclamation schemes extended the cultivated area. Agricultural production also intensified qualitatively. In arable farming, seeding rates were higher, and the space between the furrows was reduced, in comparison to the second and third millennia BCE. Owing to the resulting greater investment of labor and resources, Babylonian cereal farming in the sixth century BCE produced on average about 25 percent higher returns than in earlier periods. Furthermore, very many landowners in this period favored date-gardening over arable farming, and turned fields into palm gardens. Peace and state-sponsored improvements of the irrigation system favored this society-wide trend towards long-term agricultural investment. The process is amply documented in the textual record. To cite just one example, the agricultural transformation of the region around the city of Nippur in central Babylonia can be traced through written records over a period of four centuries (Jursa 2010a: 405–418). An exclusively grain-farming area in the eighth century, Nippur saw some development in the sixth century[11] and had changed to the more intensive two-crop regime typical for the period by the fifth century. Importantly, date-gardening not only achieved higher surface yields than arable farming, but was also more productive in terms of the labor invested (by a margin of 10 to 100 percent (Jursa 2010a: 51–52). The preponderance of horticulture in the agricultural system of the period is a key factor for the entire economic structure: it caused a society-wide increase of the available agricultural surplus and led to an increase in the productivity per capita of agricultural labor, and thus of the largest sector of the economy.

Agricultural production diversified under the influence of (especially urban) markets. In the cities' hinterland, cash-crop production proliferated. Two examples illustrate the documentation that is available. One tablet archive furnishes evidence for cash-crop production of onions, which was directly stimulated by the markets in Babylon and by entrepreneurs

---

11 Which was comparatively slow and delayed in comparison to the development in northern and western Babylonia, especially around the city of Sippar and the region around the capital, Babylon.

specializing in the marketing of this niche product: the farmers grew large quantities of onions under contractual obligation to the middlemen who marketed their produce (Jursa 2010a: 216–18; Wunsch 1993, 2010). A temple archive demonstrates that the large institutional household in question, which, according to the traditional view of the "palatial economy," should have been essentially autarkic, in fact could not have survived economically without the market – the temple sold up to half of its agricultural income on the market against silver – money which was spent mostly to pay for hired labor and for the purchase of animals, especially sheep (Jursa 2010a: 572–576). Phenomena such as these cannot be accommodated by the traditional view of the Mesopotamian economy described above.

In earlier periods of Mesopotamian history, uncoined silver had served as a money of account and a standard of value as well as a high-value money that physically changed hands only in exchange for expensive goods (see Graslin-Thomé 2009: 238–254 and Jursa 2010a: 469–474). This role of silver changed in the course of the first centuries of the first millennium BCE. The eighth century still saw a comparatively "traditional" pattern of money usage – silver was mostly used for high-value transactions among professional traders and wealthy clients. By the sixth century, this had changed, and silver money was not the impractical high-value money it was previously. Many types of transaction were virtually always conducted with money, while there was none for which money was irrelevant. In an urban context, virtually all goods and services were available against the payment of silver, from the hiring of specialized and unspecialized labor to the buying of foodstuffs. The rural population earned money mostly as hired laborers in the city and on large building sites in the country and by selling cash crops on urban markets.

The importance of silver is reflected also by the terminology, which for the first time distinguishes silver qualities and degrees of purity, for which eventually, from about 545 BCE onwards, the state started to assume responsibility. Coins must have been in circulation at least in the Achaemenid period, if not earlier, but the Babylonian terminology was conservative and continued to ignore their existence. All forms of silver, coined or otherwise, were weighed, down to the Hellenistic period, so their worth depended on their intrinsic value. The expansion of the monetary economy caused the development of new contract forms, including innovative types of business partnership ventures. There were bilateral (or multilateral) partnerships in addition to commenda-type partnerships between one (or more) investor(s) and one (or more) agent(s). Babylonian law reached a considerable degree of abstraction here. The business company had a legal identity of its own; its assets were seen as distinct from the assets of the investors (Jursa 2010b). The legal and institutional requirements for a widespread use of productive credit were in place, although deposit banking in Babylonia only evolved in the late fifth and early fourth centuries. Such arrangements served a variety of purposes: tavern-keeping and beer-brewing, craft production, small-scale agricultural enterprises, regional and long-distance trade. However, the business partnership was primarily a means of financing small undertakings. The investors numbered usually two or three, and the silver sums invested remained comparatively modest. In most cases they represented the value of one or more donkeys, or one or more slaves, rarely as much as the value of a house. The financial capabilities of individual business companies did not surpass those of rich private households and did not even come close to those of institutional households.

Silver circulated on the market. For Babylonia in our period, the working of the commodity markets can be observed from the late seventh century onwards on the basis of qualitative and quite rich quantitative data; for the later centuries of the first millennium, there is an extremely rich collection of data in the "Astronomical Diaries" – texts which collect series of astronomical observations as well as price data and other "terrestrial" phenomena (e.g. Pirngruber 2012). Prices were demonstrably subject to seasonal fluctuations and to the laws of supply and demand. The statistical proof is conclusive: prices fluctuated unpredictably and could not be foreseen by consumers, and they were strongly interrelated through substitution and complementarity (e.g. Pirngruber 2012; Temin 2002; van Leeuwen and Pirngruber 2011). Transport costs, and hence transaction costs in general, were low in comparison to other ancient civilizations, owing to the ubiquitous presence of waterways.

Nevertheless, the case for market efficiency in Babylonia should probably not be overstated. Just as in the case of Egypt in late antiquity, for which a similar argument has been made (Rathbone 1997), these were "comparatively" well-performing, "comparatively" integrated markets: market failures were a common occurrence.[12] It may be conceivable to apply to these Babylonian markets Bang's concept of the "Bazaar economy" that he developed for the Greco-Roman world on the basis of comparative evidence (Bang 2006; 2008): "a stable and complex business environment characterised by uncertainty,

12 Several of the most explicit references to (physical) markets in fact point out that there was nothing to buy or sell (Jursa [2010a: 642] – note that these statements come from letters which report the exceptional, not the ordinary). The performance of Babylonian commodity markets is discussed, inter alia, in Pirngruber (2012) and Jursa (in press b).

unpredictability and local segmentation of markets" (Bang 2006: 79). The juxtaposition of a stable institutional background for commerce and instability resulting from contingent external factors is certainly useful and applicable to the Babylonian evidence, but it is less clear that we can see here a fundamental qualitative distinction, rather than gradual differences, that distinguished ancient markets from, for instance, homologous institutions of early modern Europe.

Social structures shaped the development of factor markets (Jursa in press a). The socio-economic environment was particularly favorable to the development of a labor market. The period experienced demographic growth, so manpower was available. Nevertheless, the "palatial" sector of the economy, the temple households and the royal establishment, did not have at its disposal a reservoir of dependent laborers that was sufficient for the state's huge investments in the agrarian infrastructure and ambitious public building projects. A substantial segment of the population had no institutional ties and could seek work freely; and even institutional depend- ants enjoyed a certain degree of freedom in taking up independent employ- ment, as did qualified slaves in private ownership (Dandamaev 1984). Much labor was contractual, based on agreements between two parties that in principle entered into the contract by their own free will. Wages were negotiated between the parties and depended on supply and demand: at harvest time, for instance, building workers could profit from the general labor shortage and demand extortionate wages. The development of wages over time followed that of commodity prices (Jursa 2010a: 673–681).

Hired mass labor is well attested in temple archives (Beaulieu 2005; Jursa 2010a: 661–681). For public building projects hired labor was as important as, or even more important than, compelled labor. Craft production in the city was dependent on monetized exchange, and on the availability of labor for hire; this led also to artisanal specialization and to the appearance of new trades. The best evidence here concerns smithing (Payne in Jursa 2010a: 688– 694), the baker's trade (Hackl in Jursa 2010: 708) and the freelance laundry business, a branch of the economy where also women entered the market place (Waerzeggers 2006). Much, if not most, of privately owned land was farmed out to free tenants or on analogous terms to slaves. Otherwise slaves appear within the area of private farming in a supervising, managerial capacity; they were found among the ordinary workforce only occasionally (Dandamaev 1984: 252–278; Jursa 2010a: 234–235). Finally, the system of com- pelled labor and military service for the state relied on the availability of substitute workers and soldiers whom the holders of land encumbered with

tax and service obligations could hire for service in their stead; these substitutes were paid high cash wages (Jursa 2011; van Driel 2002).

Three principal types of landholding can be distinguished: institutional
(royal and temple) estates; land held by individuals; and estates granted
to collectives by the state in return for military service and taxes (Jursa
2010a: 171–205, 316–468; van Driel 2002). The large, but frequently understaffed
and underexploited institutional estates were cultivated by compelled and
hired labor and by free (or, more rarely, slave) tenants; they were frequently
managed for the king, or for the temples, by private contractors who introduced an entrepreneurial element into the administration of state land. Royal
land grants were cultivated by the recipients of the grants, or by free tenants.
Much is known about land in private hands, the most innovative sector of
Babylonian landholding in this period. Private small-scale date-gardening on
private estates was the most intensive and most productive form of agriculture
in the sixth century and a forerunner of agrarian change (Jursa 2010a: 760).
Access to land for rent was in part regulated by interpersonal relationships of
sometimes long standing that were similar to a patron–client relationship, but
there is enough evidence for short-term leases and a rapid turnover of lessees
to suggest that both tenants, usually free men, and landowners were fairly
flexible. There was a wide possible range of economic relationships between
tenants and lessors reflecting the interplay of economic and social forces on the
"rental market." In general, contractual law and custom created a stable and
predictable institutional framework and outside the institutional sphere and its
partial reliance on the labor of dependants there is little in the sources about the
use of constraint and the exercise of power on the part of landowners.

Property rights were usually well defined and well protected; institutional
rights (or rights of the state) on land intersected with private property rights
only in a few clear cases. Areas that had been reclaimed by state intervention
were subject to certain types of taxation and labor service, and temples could
lay a vestigial claim to certain estates and demand a tithe. In neither case,
however, were there restrictions on the alienation of the land by the private
owners. In fact, only royal land grants to soldiers could not be sold (but they
could be pledged, rented, and inherited); otherwise there was no absolute
legal restriction on the buying and selling of land whatsoever. In practice royal
and temple land was alienated very rarely and only in extraordinary conditions; but the change of ownership of privately owned agricultural land is
extraordinarily well documented. It is justified to speak of a land market:
property rights were guaranteed by law, and the nature and the quality of
the land were decisive factors for the price. Nevertheless, the social

embeddedness of this market determined the framework within which it functioned; there was a mentality of avoiding the sale of land whenever possible, so that a majority of sales occurred under duress; and even then, land was preferably sold to social peers. These social constraints rendered the access to productive land through purchase difficult for outsiders. Where it occurred, it usually must be seen to imply a significant imbalance between the social power and the economic resources of the "outside" buyer and the seller.

Concentrating on data bearing on production, as the foregoing pages have done, the excellent performance of the Babylonian economy in the long sixth century (by the standards of the region in antiquity) is evident; it was growing on the extensive as well as on the intensive margin. The increase in labor productivity per capita follows most clearly from the general shift of agriculture from cereal farming to horticulture. This characteristic of the economy can be put into even sharper relief by focussing on consumption and the standard of living (Jursa 2010a: 804–816). For methodological issues, see, e.g. Morris (2004, 2005) and Scheidel (2010). In the absence of reliable and detailed archaeological studies on proxy data for living standards (stature, nutrition, mortality and life expectancy, disease patterns, and housing), textual data have to be used. Wheat wages, i.e. the quantity of wheat the average daily wage of an unskilled free worker could buy, are a crude but effective indicator of real income. In most ancient and medieval societies, daily wages of 3.5–6.5 liters of wheat predominate (Scheidel 2010), but Babylonians of the long sixth century earned wheat wages of 9.6–14.4 liters, significantly more than their Mesopotamian predecessors of the late third and early second millennia BCE (4.8–8 liters). This is a strong indication for unusually high prosperity levels during much of the long sixth century. A comparison of Old Babylonian (c. 2000–1600 BCE) and Neo-Babylonian dowry and inheritance documents, with their detailed list of household goods and material possessions in general, points into the same direction: urban households of the sixth century BCE owned a much wider range of household goods than their social homologues of the sixteenth or seventeenth centuries, and dowries and patrimonies were much richer (Jursa 2010: 806–811). These data support the production-oriented analysis summarized above; they give us a coherent image of a comparatively prosperous period which benefitted from internal economic growth owing to increasing agricultural productivity, the stimuli of a growing urban population, and a culture of comparatively free economic exchange with low transaction costs. Throughout much of the long sixth century, the economy also benefitted from incoming wealth owing to Babylonia's imperial domination over much of the Near East.

The state's contribution was arguably crucial for creating and sustaining this dynamic economy. The Neo-Babylonian empire, and later the Persian empire, mostly managed to maintain peace in the land, the decisive precondition for the economic development of the long sixth century. Second, large-scale state-sponsored building projects aiming at land reclamation and amelioration transformed parts of the rural landscape. Royal land allotment schemes of the seventh and early sixth centuries gave the initial impetus for the reclamation of the barren or underused land around the cities after decades of war and unrest. The Crown shaped the institutional, administrative, and technical foundations of Neo-Babylonian agriculture. It promoted commercial development by furthering entrepreneurial activities at the interface between the institutional and the private economy. It also interfered with the monetary system, by introducing various means for safeguarding the quality of silver (and by attempting to set fixed interest rates). Next to their investments in the agrarian infrastructure, the most important contribution of the Neo-Babylonian kings to the economic expansion during their reign consisted in their extravagant building activities. The huge new temples, palaces, city walls, and cross-country defense structures were financed to a large degree with tribute and booty from Assyria, Syria, and the Levant. These building undertakings brought large amounts of bullion into circulation and temporarily allowed many urban unskilled laborers to subsist largely on money wages because they could find employment for much of the year. Imperial domination is thus at the root of the inflationary process that caused the value of silver to fall to about a third of what it had been in the second millennium BCE, allowing silver to function as an all-purpose money for the first time in Mesopotamian history. Furthermore, royal demands for (cash) taxes and for labor and military service contributed to the increasing monetization of economic exchange; willingly or unwillingly, taxpayers were forced into the monetary economy.

In conclusion, the narrative that results from the reading of the evidence that is proposed here is that of a limited Smithian success story, as occasionally occurs also in other pre-modern economies. The interest of this case lies in its early date and in its particularities, in the combination of *longue-durée* factors of demography and climate with certain much more transient elements of *l'histoire conjoncturelle* and *événementielle*, to use the Braudelian terms. In particular, it was imperial domination that furthered agrarian development and the monetization of exchange that led to economic growth and increased prosperity. Correspondingly, it was also through political change, as an indirect consequence of the conquest of Babylonia by the Persians (539 BCE), that the particularly prosperous long sixth century came to an end; the country's prosperity was harnessed by a new ruling class in a way that eventually undermined its foundations.

In the later fifth century and thereafter, after an unsuccessful rebellion against Persian rule, the fortunes of the traditional Babylonian urban elites who had been the principal agents of the economic expansion of the preceding period declined. Their economic interests were no longer served by state politics as they had been under the Neo-Babylonian empire and, by institutional inertia, in the first decades of Persian rule. The expansion of large-scale land ownership of Persian nobles and Babylonian supporters of Persian rule introduced into the Babylonian socio-economic system a class of agents who depended for their prosperity on their use of political power rather than on commerce and agricultural business founded on a stable legal system and generally recognized property rights. The new elites had more power to compel labor than the Babylonian urban upper classes in the sixth century, and there may have been a tendency to extract from the province as much of the available resources as possible. Wage levels fell, and, if the sketchy data that are available have been read correctly, prosperity levels seem to have stagnated, if not declined. In the *longue durée*, the process of agrarian change and expansion that was initiated in the long sixth century continued in later centuries and laid the basis for the exceptional prosperity of Iraq in the early Islamic period. The development was not linear, however. The exceptional economic expansion of the sixth century had been created by a fortuitous combination of long-term economic and climatic background conditions and much more short-lived political factors. With the disappearance of the latter this short-lived Malthusian singularity came to an end.

References

Adams, R. McC. (1981). *Heartland of Cities: Surveys of Ancient Settlement and Land Use on the Central Floodplain on the Euphrates*. University of Chicago Press.

Andreau, J. et al., eds. (1997). *Économie antique. Prix et formation des prix dans les économies antiques*. Entretiens d'archéologie et d'histoire 3. Saint-Bertrand-de-Comminges: Musée Archéologique Départemental.

Attinger, P., W. Sallaberger, and M. Wäfler (2004). *Annäherungen 4, Mesopotamien. Die altbabylonische Zeit*. Orbis Biblicus et Orientalis 160/4. Fribourg and Göttingen: Academic Press/Vandenhoeck and Ruprecht.

Baker, H. D. and M. Jursa, eds. (2005). *Approaching the Babylonian Economy: Proceedings of the START Project Symposium Held in Vienna, 1–3 July 2004*. AOAT 330. Münster: Ugarit-Verlag.

Bang, P. F. (2006). "Imperial Bazaar: Towards a Comparative Understanding of Markets in the Roman Empire," in Bang et al. (eds.), pp. 51–88.

(2008). The Roman Bazaar: A Comparative Study of Trade and Markets in a Tributary Empire. Cambridge University Press.

Bang P. F. et al., eds. (2006). Ancient Economies, Modern Methodologies: Archaeology, Comparative History, Models and Institutions. Bari: Edipuglia.

Beaulieu, P.-A. (2005). "Eanna's Contribution to the Construction of the North Palace at Babylon," in Baker and Jursa (eds.), pp. 45–73.

Brinkman, J. A. (1984). "Settlement Surveys and Documentary Evidence: Regional Variation and Secular Trend in Mesopotamian Demography," Journal of Near Eastern Studies 43: 169–180.

Charpin, D. and F. Joannès, eds. (1991). Marchands, diplomates et empereurs. Études sur la civilization mésopotamienne offertes à Paul Garelli. Paris: ERC.

Clancier, Ph. et al., eds. (2005). Autour de Polanyi. Vocabulaires, théories et modalités des échanges. Paris: De Boccard.

Dahl, J. (2010). "A Babylonian Gang of Potters: Reconstructing the Social Organization of Crafts Production in the Late Third Millennium BC Southern Mesopotamia," in Kogan et al. (eds.), pp. 275–306.

Dandamaev, M. A. (1984). Slavery in Babylonia from Nabopolassar to Alexander the Great (626–331 BC). DeKalb, IL: Northern Illinois University Press.

Dercksen, J. G. (2004). Old Assyrian Institutions. Leiden: Nerderlands Instituut voor net Nabije Oasten (NINO).

Diakonoff, I. M., ed. (1982). Societies and Languages of the Ancient Near East: Studies in Honour of I. M. Diakonoff. Warminster: Aris and Phillips.

Driel, G. van (2002). Elusive Silver: In Search of a Role for a Market in an Agrarian Environment. Aspects of Mesopotamia's Society. Leiden: NINO.

Eidem, J. (1991). "An Old Assyrian Treaty from Tell Leilan," in Charpin and Joannès (eds.), pp. 185–207.

Garfinkle, S. J. (2012). Entrepreneurs and Enterprise in Early Mesopotamia: A Study of Three Archives from the Third Dynasty of Ur (2112–2004 BCE). Bethesda, MA: CDL Press.

Goldstone, J. (2002). "Efflorescences and Economic Growth in World History: Rethinking the 'Rise of the West' and the Industrial Revolution," Journal of World History, 13: 323–389.

Graslin-Thomé, L. (2009). Les échanges à longue distance en Mésopotamie au Ier millénaire. Une approche économique. Paris: De Boccard.

Hatcher, J. and M. Bailey (2001). Modelling the Middle Ages: The History and Theory of England's Economic Development. Oxford University Press.

Hausleiter, A. et al., eds. (2002). Material Culture and Mental Spheres. Rezeption archäologischer Denkrichtungen in der Vorderasiatischen Altertumskunde. Internationales Symposium für Hans J. Nissen, Berlin, 23.–24. Juni 2000. AOAT 293. Münster: Ugarit-Verlag.

Hilgert, M., ed. (2011). Altorientalistik im 21. Jahrhundert: Selbstverständnis, Herausforderungen, Ziele. Mitteilungen der Deutschen Orient-Gesellschaft 142 (2010). Deutsche Orient-Gesellschaft zu Berlin.

Jursa, M. (2002). Prywatyzacja i zysk? Przedsiębiorcy a gospodarka instytucjonalna w Mezopotamii od 3 do 1 tysiąclecia przed Chr [Polish: Privatization and Profit? Entrepreneurs and Institutional Households in Mesopotamia from the Third to the First Millennium BC]. Poznan: Poznańskie Towarzystwo Przyjaciół Nauk.

(2005). *Neo-Babylonian Legal and Administrative Documents: Typology, Contents and Archives.* Guides to the Mesopotamian Textual Record 1. Münster: Ugarit-Verlag.

(2010a). *Aspects of the Economic History of Babylonia in the First Millennium BC: Economic Geography, Economic Mentalities, Agriculture, the Use of Money and the Problem of Economic Growth.* With contributions by J. Hackl, B. Janković, K. Kleber, E. E. Payne, C. Waerzeggers, and M. Weszeli. AOAT 377. Münster: Ugarit-Verlag.

(2010b). "Business Companies in Babylonia in the First Millennium BC: Structure, Economic Strategies, Social Setting," in Wissa (ed.), pp. 53–68.

(2011). "Steuer. D. Spätbabylonisch," *Reallexikon der Assyriologie* 13(1/2): 168–175.

(in press a). "Factor Markets in Babylonia from the Late Seventh to Fourth Century BC," *Journal of the Economic and Social History of the Orient.*

(in press b). "Market Performance and Market Integration in Babylonia in the 'Long Sixth Century' BC," in van der Spek *et al.* (eds.).

Kogan, L. *et al.*, eds. (2010). *City Administration in the Ancient Near East: Proceedings of the 53rd Rencontre Assyriologique Internationale,* vol. 11. Winona Lake, IN: Eisenbrauns.

Landes, D. S., J. Mokyr, and W. J. Baumol, eds. (2010). *The Invention of Enterprise: Entrepreneurship from Ancient Mesopotamia to Modern Times.* Princeton University Press.

Larsen, M. T. (1982). "Your Money or Your Life! A Portrait of an Assyrian Businessman," in Diakonoff (ed.), pp. 214–245.

Leeuwen, B. van and R. Pirngruber (2011). "Markets in Pre-Industrial Societies: Storage in Hellenistic Babylonia in the Medieval English Mirror," *Journal of Global History* 6: 169–193.

Leick, G., ed. (2007). *The Babylonian World.* London and New York: Routledge.

Liverani, M. (1998). *Uruk la prima città.* Rome and Bari: Laterza.

(2011). *Antico Oriente. Storia società economia.* Rome and Bari: Laterza.

Manning, J. G. and I. Morris, eds. (2005). *The Ancient Economy: Evidence and Models.* Stanford University Press.

Matthews, R. (2003). *The Archaeology of Mesopotamia: Theories and Approaches.* London and New York: Routledge.

Morris, I. (2004). "Economic Growth in Ancient Greece," *Journal of Institutional and Theoretical Economics* 160: 709–742.

(2005). "Archaeology, Standards of Living, and Greek Economic History," in Manning and Morris, pp. 91–126.

Pamuk, Ş., and M. Shatzmiller (2014). "Plagues, Wages and Economic Change in the Islamic Middle East, 700–1500," *Journal of Economic History*, 74: forthcoming.

Pirngruber, R. (2012). "The Impact of Empire on Market Prices in Babylon in the Late Achaemenid and Seleucid periods, ca. 400–140 B.C." Ph.D. Thesis Vrije Universiteit Amsterdam.

Postgate, J. N. (1994). *Early Mesopotamia: Society and Economy at the Dawn of History*, 2nd edn. London and New York: Routledge.

Potts, D. T. (1997). *Mesopotamian Civilization: The Material Foundations.* London: Athlone Press.

Powell, M. (1994). "Elusive Eden: Private Property at the Dawn of History," *Journal of Cuneiform Studies* 46: 99–104.

Radner, K. and E. Robson, eds. (2011). *The Oxford Handbook of Cuneiform Culture.* Oxford University Press.

Rathbone, D. (1997). "Prices and Price Formation in Roman Egypt," in Andreau *et al.* (eds.), pp. 183–244.

Renger, J. (2002). "Wirtschaftsgeschichte des alten Mesopotamien. Versuch einer Standortbestimmung," in Hausleiter *et al.* (eds.), pp. 239–265.

(2003). "Oikos, Oikoswirtschaft," *Reallexikon der Assyriologie*, 10(1/2): 43–45.

(2004). "Palastwirtschaft," *Reallexikon der Assyriologie*, 10(3/4): 276–280.

(2005). "K. Polanyi and the Economy of Ancient Mesopotamia," in Clancier *et al.* (eds.), pp. 45–65.

(2007). "Economy of Ancient Mesopotamia: A General Outline," in Leick (ed.), pp. 187–197.

Scheidel, W. (2010). "Real Wages in Early Economies: Evidence for Living Standards from 1800 BCE to 1300 CE," *Journal of the Social and Economic History of the Orient* 53: 425–562.

Spek, R. J.van der, B. van Leeuwen, and J. L. van Zanden, eds. (in press). *A History of Market Performance from Ancient Babylonia to the Modern World*. London and New York: Routledge.

Stol, M. (2004). "Wirtschaft und Gesellschaft in altbabylonischer Zeit," in Attinger, Sallaberger, and Wäfler (eds.), pp. 643–975.

Streck, M. P. (2010). "Großes Fach Altorientalistik. Der Umfang des keilschriftlichen Textkorpus," in Hilgert (ed.), pp. 35–58.

Temin, P. (2002). "Price Behaviour in Ancient Babylon," *Explorations in Economic History* 39: 49–60.

Van de Mieroop, M. (1997). "Why Did They Write on Clay?" *Klio* 79: 1–18.

(1999). *Cuneiform Texts and the Writing of History*. London and New York: Routledge.

Veenhof, K. R. (2008). "The Old Assyrian Period," in Wäfler (ed.), pp. 13–263.

(2010). "Ancient Assur: The City, its Traders, and its Commercial Network," *Journal of the Social and Economic History of the Orient* 53: 39–82.

Waerzeggers, C. (2006). "Neo-Babylonian Laundry," *Revue d'Assyriologie* 100: 83–96.

Wäfler, M., ed. (2008). *Annäherungen 5, Mesopotamia. The Old Assyrian Period, part I*. Orbis Biblicus et Orientalis 160/5. Fribourg and Göttingen: Academic Press/Vandenhoeck and Ruprecht.

Wilkinson, T. J. (2003). *Archaeological Landscapes of the Near East*. Tucson: University of Arizona Press.

Wirth, E. (1962). *Agrargeographie des Irak*. Hamburger Geographische Studien 13. Hamburg: Institut für Geographie und Wirtschaftsgeographie.

Wissa, M. ed. (2010), *The Knowledge Economy and Technological Capabilities: Egypt, the Near East and the Mediterranean Second Millennium B.C. – First Millennium A.D. Proceedings of a Conference Held at the Maison de la Chimie Paris, France 9–10 December 2005*. Aula Orientalis Supplementa 26. Barcelona: Aula Orientalis.

Wunsch, C. (1993). *Die Urkunden des babylonischen Geschäftsmannes Iddin-Marduk. Zum Handel mit Naturalien im 6. Jahrhundert v. Chr.* Groningen: Styx.

(2010). "Neo-Babylonian Entrepreneurs," in Landes *et al.* (eds.), pp. 40–61.

Zawadzki, S. (2005). "The Building Project North of Sippar in the Time of Nabonidus," in Baker and Jursa (eds.), pp. 381–392

3

Capitalism and the ancient
Greek economy

ALAIN BRESSON

Can we speak of capitalism for the ancient Greek world, between *c.* 800 BCE and the Common Era? Or is the question totally irrelevant? Does the historical evolution of the ancient classical world, first Greece then Rome, justify a parallel with that of the "capitalist revolution" of early modern and modern Europe? Should we use a broader definition of "capitalism" to make sense of the "capitalist aspects" of societies of the past like those of the classical Mediterranean world? These are legitimate questions. But to begin with it is necessary to stress that reintegrating the economies of the past, those of Babylon or those of classical antiquity, into the debate on "capitalism" presents a series of most welcome advantages. First, this allows us to reopen a dialogue on economic development on the *longue durée* that had been interrupted for decades. Second, and no less interestingly, the possible similarities but also contrasting forms of organization between these sophisticated economies of the past and the modern "capitalist" societies lead to mutual interrogation on their forms of economic developments. The unrelenting question of the "failure" of ancient classical economies to accomplish the "big leap" toward modern capitalism and modernity can also be addressed with a new agenda.

Antiquity and capitalism

The possible "capitalist" character of the ancient economy was a heavily discussed topic among German academics at the end of the nineteenth and beginning of the twentieth centuries. This was a time of industrialization, accompanied by a radical transformation not only of the organization of production but of the whole social organization. In the space of three generations between *c.* 1830 and 1900, a still predominantly rural society, where agriculture and craftsmanship provided the bulk of production, was wiped out and replaced by a predominantly urban world, where heavy industry and mass production for a market were dominant. Banks and factories structured the new economic and social landscape. Capitalism, or so it seemed, could be analyzed as the association on the one hand of a new financial system that was able to mobilize huge financial means and on the other hand of new techniques of production and organization oriented towards mass production, scientific progress being at the heart of the matter. This combination allowed a huge increase in the quantity of energy and production available per capita. It also challenged the traditional values and forms of social life of the old regime that had prevailed for centuries. In Europe, it was certainly in Germany that the transition to the new social system was the quickest. The breakthrough was so massive and impressive that it could not help but impact the debates among social thinkers, economists, and historians of the new and brilliantly active German universities. This was also a world where the prestige of the classical world was still at its summit and where the members of the elite were commonly steeped in Latin and Greek. Thus it is no surprise that the question was raised of whether those prestigious civilizations of the past, Greece and Rome, with their prodigious achievements in art, literature, and philosophy, might have experienced a similar transformation. This was the starting point for a debate on the nature of the ancient economy that has continued ever since.

In fact from the start the controversy about the nature of the ancient economy developed in the framework of the debate on the policy that the German Reich was to adopt. Free trade was soon repudiated as a British trick to conquer foreign markets. The German state supported a policy of state intervention and closed economic development, with heavy customs duties on imported goods and low prices at export to conquer foreign markets. This policy of "national economy" was accepted and theorized by the various components of the German academic milieu. The German historical school of economics posited a holistic approach and vigorously opposed the British advocates of economic liberalism and their concepts based on the preferences of individuals on an open market.

This was the historical background to the debate that developed on the nature of the ancient economy. The basic question asked was whether the ancient economy shared features of the new "capitalist society." The answers were fiercely contradictory. But most of the protagonists shared the evolutionist perspective that impregnated European thought of the time, with the idea that each "stage" of human history was characterized by a specific form of economic and social organization. Among the leading figures of the historical school Karl Bücher was the one who took the strongest interest in the ancient economy. For him not only had the ancient world ignored capitalism, it was the anti-model of a capitalist society, as he advocated in his book on "the rise of the national economy," *Die Entstehung der Volkswirtschaft* (Bücher 1968 [1893]). For him, a capitalist economy was to be defined by the existence on the one hand of fixed capital in the form of machines, raw material, and appropriate buildings, and by the existence on the other hand of abstract capital in the form of loans, bonds, stock shares, and other financial tools. Finance provided the link between the several parts of the economy. For Bücher, far from having any "capitalist feature," the ancient world was at a stage of home production and consumption. Each household aimed to satisfy its own needs. Self-sufficiency was also the motto for the state. Trade and money played only a marginal role. It was only much later, after the stage of "city economy" (the middle ages), that a national economy corresponding to the era of capitalism could develop. We can easily understand why Bücher appeared to be the leader of what was soon to be styled as the "primitivist" school of ancient economics.

The most famous opponents of this theory were the historians Eduard Meyer and Karl Julius Beloch, who, on the contrary, saw a fabulously "modern" economic development in the ancient world (Finley 1979 and Schneider 1990). They insisted on the huge and unprecedented development of towns and of urban population, the introduction of coinage and general usage of money in transactions, the large development of trade. According to Meyer, one could also observe the existence of fabrics and of a competition between cities to make sure that their products would compare favorably on foreign markets. Besides, Meyer considered that "big money" (*das Großkapital*) was responsible for the disappearance of small farms. This would have made of the ancient Greek world an economy for a large part similar to that of our own times. This is the reason why, in contrast to Bücher, Meyer and Beloch can be defined as "modernists." The evolutionist imprint was present in the description of the various phases of development of the ancient Greek economy, which would have been similar to the phases of development of the middle ages, the early modern, and modern periods for western Europe.

In fact, it should have been clear from the start that large-scale factories and competition between cities to impose the products of their home industries on foreign markets did not characterize the ancient economy. This does not mean that there could not exist some large handicraft workshops. Such large workshops, with possibly a few dozen workers (sometimes up to 120 as in the case of the metic Kephalos in Athens in the fourth century, as mentioned by Lysias 12.19 [Todd 2000]) could indeed exist, but they were rare. Even if they could be organized on the basis of a technical division of labor (with specializations of tasks in the workshop), they did not require a considerable amount of capital, as the technology justifying considerable investment in machinery (as was the case at the time of the industrial revolution) was simply absent. Also, rivalries between ancient merchant cities were the norm. But these cities aimed normally to obtain trade privileges from other states rather than to compete in selling their industrial products at lower prices on an open market.

Thus if the question of the existence of capitalism is set in terms of the existence or not of big industry in the ancient world (whether Greece or Rome), the answer is without any doubt in the negative. But already at the time of the origins of the debate between "primitivists" and "modernists," one can observe an interesting shift in the debate on the "capitalist" nature of the ancient economy. The interrogation went beyond the existence or not of factories. For if Meyer was radically wrong in believing in the existence in the ancient world of factories comparable to those of his time, so was Bücher in defining the ancient world as an economic system based on self-consumption, ignoring market and finance. Thus Robert Pöhlmann already conceived the ancient economy as dominated by capital through the large development of trade, interest loans, rents, and slavery (Pöhlmann 1925). Its "capitalist spirit" was revealed by the existence of characters uniquely devoted to the research of profit. These were the men practicing chrematistics, the commerce of money, condemned by Aristotle. The famous *salve lucrum* ("Hail Profit") inscribed at the entrance to a Pompeii house might have been their motto.

Pöhlmann's themes were in tune with Werner Sombart's *Der moderne Kapitalismus* (1902). Indeed, strongly influenced as he was at that stage of his career by the Marxist perspective, Sombart insisted on the existence of two classes of population, the capital holders and the workers, who were deprived of any right of ownership of the means of production. He also stressed that capitalism needed a certain disposition of mind, which was characterized by an absence of a link with any specific national interest and by a uniquely rational approach to social or economic phenomena. In accordance with the prejudices of his time, Sombart linked capitalism with Judaism (Sombart 1913). For him, one of the key characteristics of the new capitalist firm was the double-entry bookkeeping system. It was invented in the world of the Italian merchant cities of the middle ages, but found its full accomplishment only with the full development of capitalism. Sombart considered that rational management of a capitalist firm was not possible without this system.

In many ways, Max Weber, who justifiably remains the giant of the theorists of the period, introduced themes that were similar to Sombart's.

For Weber, it was the Protestant faith that was at the origin of capitalism (Weber 1930 [1904–1905]). Besides, he insisted on the role in the development of capitalism of a general rational attitude towards life and labor. In this a crucial factor (more than the double-entry bookkeeping system advocated by Sombart) was the separation of the capital of the capitalist firm from individual property (Swedberg 1998: 7–21; Weber 1968 [1921–1922]). Of course these elements were totally lacking in antiquity, to which interestingly Weber devoted a special attention (Weber 1976 [1909]). Weber himself did not refrain from using the word "capitalism" for the ancient economy, provided it was limited to denoting the existence of a developed maritime trade, banking activity, a plantation economy, and of course of slavery (Love 1991: 9–55). But for him the absence of the specific features of capitalist development had also a negative side. The systematic neglect of agricultural improvements and the lack of technical progress in manufacture condemned that world to economic stagnation. Limited growth could take place as long as independent cities or states were able to exploit the possibilities offered by a fragmented Mediterranean. Stagnation was from the beginning to the end the defining characteristic of the ancient economy. In Weberian definition, this was the "ideal-type" of the ancient economy (Swedberg 1998: 193–196). The unification of the Mediterranean and the establishment of Roman rule, with its huge increase in the weight of the state, initiated a process of decline that could not be stopped and was fatal for the economy of the ancient world.

This was the state of the scholarly debate in the 1920s. Ever since and until the late 1980s, curiously, the debate has remained fossilized. It focussed even only on the most primitivist side of Weber, as was the case with the famous *Ancient Economy* of Moses I. Finley (Finley 1999 [1973]). Until one generation ago, ancient Greece was still assumed to have been a society dominated by an elite of wealthy landowners, living in towns and exploiting a poor rural countryside where people lived in crass poverty. The prevailing orthodoxy admitted the existence of trade, but considered that it was limited in extent, as it was supposed to supply almost exclusively luxury goods for the elites. Financial operations would have remained primitive and have consisted mainly of the usurious practices of private lenders. There might have been an expansion of population, or even of the quantities produced. But that (limited) expansion would have been purely extensive, i.e. it would have been the mechanical result of population growth. But no intensive growth, corresponding to a growth in per capita income, would have taken place. The lack of productivity growth was conceived to originate from the lack of technical progress, itself rooted in the lack of interest of the elites in any kind of investment in research.

The conclusion was clear: a stagnating economy and society based on the collection of land rents from poor and exploited peasants can hardly be described as capitalist. And this is why also the possible "capitalist" aspect of the ancient classical economy was now totally out of the picture. If this analysis was correct, ancient Greece should not have a place in a world history of capitalism.

This seemingly so well-established orthodoxy is now totally exploded. A new and much more dynamic picture of the ancient economy as a whole has emerged from recent research (Bowman and Wilson 2009; Scheidel 2012; Scheidel, Morris, and Saller 2007). This does not make the ancient Greek economy a "modern capitalist economy." But among the leading societies of the period corresponding to the period of c. 1000 BCE to 1700 CE, where the bulk of the aggregate product was also agricultural production, ancient Greece (and after it the early Roman empire) presents the characteristics of an exceptionally dynamic society and economy. A remarkable intensive growth took place, based on a highly favorable global institutional framework, division of labor, extensive trade, radical improvements in financial and contracting practices, and also technical innovation.

This does not make ancient Greece an authentic capitalist society, if we limit the definition to societies where human-produced capital (instead of land) is the major factor of production and where accumulation of capital in the framework of competitive markets is crucial to determine economic institutions. But it is quite sufficient to justify the place of ancient Greece in a world history of capitalism, both for the comparative evidence it provides for later and more elaborate economic developments, and simply also because in the *longue durée* it brought about a fundamental and lasting contribution in terms of technology, science, and economic institutions.

Growth, population and consumption

Measuring growth for societies of the past is always a difficult task. We can use only proxies that provide an evaluation for growth. Although figures or evaluation will be constantly an object of debate, the reality of growth is beyond doubt, and this totally changes the picture of a stagnant society of the old paradigm. It is in this sense that "Wealthy Hellas" is a perfect character-ization for the ancient Greek economy (Ober 2010). The economic expansion of the Greek world was not isolated to the Mediterranean area. It triggered and also was part of a larger expansion in which the West took a distinct leadership after 200 BCE. The statistics of shipwrecks in the period 700 BCE to

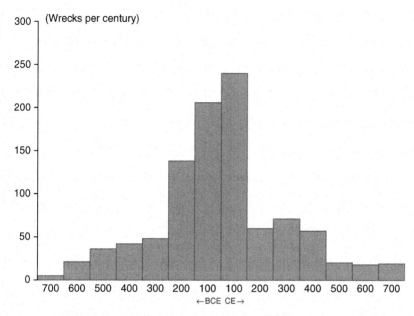

Figure 3.1 Mediterranean shipwrecks datable within hundred-year ranges, graphed according to an equal probability of sinking in any year during the date range for each wreck.
Source: Wilson 2011a: 35, Figure 2.4.

the Common Era (Figure 3.1) irrefutably translate this exceptional expansion of trade and thus of global prosperity in the period. After *c.* 50 CE barrels replaced amphoras. Insofar as amphoras are the best marker of shipwrecks, and barrels made of wood rot away, this means also that after the first century CE shipwrecks are no longer the reliable proxy for economic activity that they are until that date.

For ancient Greece, archaeological data (the number of occupied sites and the size of these sites) also provide inescapable evidence of a major demographic growth between the beginning of the first millennium BCE and the end of the fourth century BCE, although with various regional profiles (Scheidel 2007: 44–47). More specifically, between *c.* 750 and 300 BCE, the population may have multiplied by a factor of four (some scholars say even much more), while immigration out of Greece proper made it possible to create many new implantations of Greek population in southern Italy, Sicily, and also in northern Africa and around the Black Sea (Morris 2006b).

Without any doubt mainland Greece and the Kyklades carried more population *c.* 300 BCE than at the end of the nineteenth century. After

300 BCE, however, at least in mainland Greece and in the islands, a slow decline began, which became more pronounced at the end of the Hellenistic period. By contrast, in Asia Minor and in the neighboring islands, demographic growth continued until the end of the Hellenistic period, which means that the existence of regional profiles and contrasting evolutions also needs to be explained as well as the initial Greek population boom. How could Greece feed this growing population? The question needs all the more to be answered as archaeological evidence points not only to population growth but also to growth of per capita production and consumption.

This new prosperity can be observed in collective and individual consumption. Public goods such as sewers, fountains, stadiums, baths, and also public gardens, public festivals, and sometimes public libraries, now provided services that were basically unknown in other civilizations. The quality of these services sharply increased at the end of the classical and above all during the Hellenistic period. As for private consumption, it is also widely attested by the number of goods that were accessible to a far larger part of the population in the classical and above all Hellenistic period than five hundred years before. Larger houses were commonly equipped with tiled roofs and a cistern; clothes, basic household items (like cutlery or pots and pans, in ceramic or metal ware), generally adequate quantities of reasonably varied food, and also bath tubs, metal door locks, toys for children, sophisticated tombstones for the deceased (even slaves could sometimes expect to have the benefit of a small funerary monument) were now common consumer objects, attested both by vase paintings and by numerous archaeological discoveries (Morris 2004, 2005; Ober 2010).

This did not make of Greece a consumer society in the modern sense of the word, for scarcity, not affluence, was still prevalent. But at least it was a society where large sectors of the population had access to a wide range of basic or even semi-luxury goods. This finds no precedent until the beginning of the early modern period in countries like the Netherlands or England (where indeed consumption levels were even higher). The same could be said of the yearly per capita growth in capital income, even if it was only in the range of 0.07–0.14 percent (Ober 2010: 251). The aggregate growth rate for a very long period was much higher than that of any other society of the time. The same observation would hold true for any other society before the Dutch then British breakthrough of the early modern period. This means that the ancient Greek economy also managed to avoid the usual Malthusian trap, where per capita growth is quickly offset by demographic growth.

The specific framework of the city-state

To make sense of this growth of the Greek world in the archaic and classical period, an expansion that also held true for the new Hellenized regions of the Hellenistic world, we should observe that it is clearly linked to an original institution: a new and specific form of city-state. Until the big collapse at the end of the Bronze Age the political and economic institutions of the Greek world were no different from those of the empires of the Near East, especially the powerful Mesopotamian kingdoms. It was a world based on tribute in kind paid to a king by local peasant communities, with a sophisticated palace administration (Shelmerdine, Bennet, and Preston 2008). A little after 1200 BCE, just like the Near Eastern kingdoms, Mycenaean Greece entered a process of collapse (Deger-Jalkotzy 2008). After this general crisis at the end of the Bronze Age, oriental states reconstituted on similar bases with a tribute in kind and rations supplied by the king to his servants, officers, and soldiers. However, we can also observe in the first millennium BCE the growing role of precious metals, mainly raw silver, in transfers of value. Chunks of silver, duly weighed, could be used in transactions by the state, the temples, and even individuals. Silver still was not a unique and universal form of payment or store of value. Payments in grain or other goods, for instance for wages, were still common. But silver increasingly played the role of money in seventh- and sixth-century Babylon (and the same remark could be made for Mesopotamia and the most advanced parts of the Near East in the Achaemenid period). This created a new although specific form of a market economy (Jursa 2010: 469–753).

We should not forget that the alternative institution to the Greek city-state in the archaic and classical world was the tribute empire. At the end of the archaic period, after 525 BCE, all the empires in the East were unified into one only, the Persian empire, which enjoyed a remarkable period of expansion and success (Bedford 2007). The challenge and attraction of this system should not be minimized. In the Mediterranean-Middle Eastern world of the time, if there was an "institutional choice," it was between the hierarchic and bureaucratic empire dominated by one nation, the Persians, and the Greek model of organization.

The Greek world followed quite a different track. After the big collapse of the end of the Bronze Age, it reorganized from new bases (Morris 2006a). The new world of the Iron Age was based on a myriad of small-sized states, each developing a specific identity and frequently at war with its neighbors (Hall 2007). In the early Iron Age, an aristocracy of landlords and chieftains dominated peasants and concentrated in its hands both corvées and taxes in kind and the luxury goods brought from the Near East by long-distance trade (Morgan 2009; Osborne 2009: 35–65). But rather than transforming themselves into larger tributary states that would also progressively destroy and absorb their neighbors, these states took a different path.

The depth of the destruction of the previous Bronze Age palatial system was certainly an indispensable precondition of this specific track of the Greek world. The introduction of iron and other new technologies and a new start of long-distance trade brought about a new prosperity. Conceivably these aristocracies should easily have been able to capture the benefits of this new prosperity. But the permanent infighting between the city-states led to a different equilibrium. The ruling classes needed the help of peasant warriors to maintain the independence of the city-state. For this reason they had to yield unparalleled political privileges to the common people. The peasant soldiers owned their own military equipment and thus they could not be transformed into a mass of impoverished and politically voiceless rural dependants. Even though the explanation needs to be nuanced (Krentz 2007), it still resists criticism. For a long period, most city-states were unable to destroy and enslave their neighbors (Osborne 2009: 161–189). Besides, before the short Persian invasion at the beginning of the fifth century, mainland Greece was never threatened by an external enemy. (If this had been the case the microstates would have been replaced by a few or even one single powerful state, or the invader would have easily prevailed.) The result was an original situation of equilibrium both among the city-states and between the aristocracies and the people (Morris 2009).

Instead of a world dominated by a unique sovereign or that of a limited wealthy aristocracy facing a people both extremely poor and deprived of any political rights, we have a self-conscious people with a well-off middle class of peasant farmers that was able to check the will of the aristocracies to monopolize political power. This was not democracy. Democracy was a specific development at the very end of the archaic and beginning of the classical periods. But the combination of military and economic capability of the peasant farmers provided the basis for a specific form of political contract within the city-state. The characteristic of the archaic and classical Greek world is the emergence of a set of political agreements that ruled the life of the community.

As this was endlessly repeated in the laws and decrees as early as the second part of the seventh century BCE, the law had been discussed and voted on by the community and applied to everyone. Specific regulations made sure that, within the city, political power would not be monopolized by a small group of people or by a single individual. This does not mean that this never happened, but a striking characteristic of ancient Greek political life is that extreme oligarchic or tyrannical regimes (we would say today: dictatorships) were never stable and finally collapsed, and that sooner or later new more egalitarian systems regularly regained power. It is not by chance that at the end of the archaic period the Ephesian philosopher Heraclitus could proclaim that: "The people must fight in defense of the law as they would for their city wall" (Heraclitus tr. Waterfield [2000]: 45 fragment 53 = Diels-Kranz [1951–1952] fragment 22B44 = Diogenes Laertius *Lives of Eminent Philosophers* 9.2.2–3 Long [1964]).

In other words, the ancient Greek world was ruled by law. The law provided the fundamental institutional basis for the development of private property and safe contracting. In classical or Hellenistic Greece, if a contract was breached, the parties could come before the court. This was especially important for long-distance trade, as the cities offered the legal framework that was required for the security of transactions (Cohen 1973; Lanni 2006: 149–174 for the case of Athens). This in turn provided the institutional stability that was the best incentive for private individual initiative and economic progress. While in the archaic world only the wealthier had their say in the city, democracy corresponded to a phase of extension of actual civil rights to all the members of the community. This was to become the standard regime at the end of the classical period and during the Hellenistic period. This contract was decisively broken at the end of the Hellenistic period, the dominion imposed on Greece by the Romans corresponding also to a regime where the elites monopolized political power.

Market, finance, and business organization

Trade, both internal within the city and external trade with the outer world, Greek or non-Greek, played a crucial role in the ancient Greek economy. A specific characteristic of the Greek city was the existence of two institutions, the *agora*, or internal market, and the *emporion*, or market dedicated to international trade (Bresson 2000: 263–307). At the *agora*, everyone could bring their products and sell them freely under the protection of the law. In the ancient Greek cities, taxes were comparatively very low, around 10 percent for taxes on agricultural products. This means that peasants or other producers had incentives to bring much more produce to the market than in the Near East, where the level of taxes was much higher. Greek markets provided more than convenient vents for occasional surpluses; they also provided incentives for producers to concentrate on supplying specific products for specific markets. This meant that in the course of time, while for security reasons in an uncertain world subsistence farming was never abandoned, there was a reorganization of production in order to sell it to the market. The once prevailing idea of a Greek agriculture plagued by routine and inefficiency, and oriented only toward self-sufficiency, must be totally abandoned. Greek farmers knew perfectly well how to profit from the opportunities of the market.

What was true within the borders of the city-state was all the more true for international trade. International trade was extremely active and played a vital role in the life of the cities. It was also instrumental in the establishment of an international division of labor. As early as the end of the archaic period (800 BCE–480 BCE), and more and more so in the classical period, the expanding Greek population of Greece proper could not be fed with local production. The core of the Greek world (mainland and Aegean Greece) massively imported grain from the "new worlds" that had been created by Greek colonists in the previous centuries. The case of Athens is famous, with a population depending on between two-thirds and three-quarters of imported grain in the second half of the fourth century (Whitby 1998). But most other city-states of southern mainland Greece or the Aegean also massively imported grain from southern Italy, Sicily, Cyrene (Bresson 2011), Egypt, and from the Black Sea regions. To pay for these imports, Greek cities sold highly valuable commodities such as oil, wine, handicraft artifacts, luxury goods, or paid in silver, which they produced in large quantities.

The demographic expansion of the Greek world would not have been possible without this network of trade partners who sold their grain, as well as their raw metals or textiles. Access to imported "cheap" grain (as it could never have produced such large quantities of grain or other imported commodities) also made it possible for Greece to specialize in high-quality production. Far from being a closed society purely devoted to satisfying the most immediate needs of its own population, the ancient Greek world experienced the first "world economy" based on long-distance trade. Long-distance trade had existed before and in many contexts. This was the case, for instance, in the early second millennium BCE with the Assyrian colony of Kanesh in Anatolia, where tin and precious woolen cloths were imported from Assyria to Anatolia and gold and silver exported in the opposite direction (Veenhof 1997: 338–339 and Veenhof and Eidem 2008: 82–90). High-value goods were still privileged for long-distance trade in first-millennium BCE Mesopotamia (Graslin-Thomé 2009).

The specific case of the Greek world was that thanks to transport by sea and a sophisticated trading network, it was not only high-value items but also bulk consumption goods that were traded at a long distance. The initiative to produce the grain (except for Egypt, which was a different world even when the Greeks took control of the country in 332 BCE), the choice of production was always in the hands of farmers, whatever their social status. Further, the initiative of trade voyages was always taken by private individuals, although sometimes cities could substitute themselves as individual buyers to try to obtain a better share of the available goods on the international market. Even in this case, however, the actual transport of goods always remained in the hands of private actors. But traders needed both capital and a protective legal framework. In this field again the Greek world was strikingly innovative.

The role of the market in the ancient Greek (or Roman) economy remains one of the most hotly debated among scholars. The question of market is itself linked to, although not identical with, that of long-distance trade. Obviously, long-distance trade is seemingly one of the most visible forms of success of the ancient economy. Indeed, everyone now seems to agree that starting in the sixth century long-distance trade exchange in the ancient Greek world (and as a consequence of the Greek breakthrough, in the whole Mediterranean area) saw a regular and significant process of growth. Even if the proxy has its imperfections, this can be proved once and for all by the statistics of shipwrecks in the Mediterranean area from the archaic to the end of the Hellenistic period (see above Figure 3.1). Everything could be traded, from basic food items such as grain, wine, or oil, to more elaborate goods like ceramics, furniture, weapons, clothes, perfumes, and books, as well as raw or half-processed materials like iron, copper or lead ingots, wool, wood, and marble. The evidence for this long-distance trade, both that of the wrecks or of the archaeological finds on land and of the written sources, is now overwhelming and its significance cannot be denied any longer.

This did not make the ancient Mediterranean world a perfect or unified market that one might compare to the modern market. Indeed, despite the undeniable existence of long-distance trade, regional patterns are also clearly visible (Reger 2011 for the Hellenistic period). On the Roman side, the debate on the integration of the market seems to develop mainly in terms of the quantities involved or of the level of prosperity of the actors in trade (Wilson *et al.* 2012). It is also worth stressing that beyond costs linked to the technological level of the time, a major difference between the ancient Mediterranean and the modern world is that a large part of the goods came to the market as a result of political constraint: this was true for instance for the Persian satraps or for the Hellenistic kings when they sold or sometimes gave (which was even worse for market equilibrium) on the international market the grain they had collected as a tribute. This of course heavily impacted the activity of the producers who were operating in the market system of the city-state. This was also the case with the massive enslavement of foreign, usually "barbarian" populations. This had a major disruptive effect on a possible "market of labor."

A fundamental innovation of the ancient Greek world was the creation of a new monetary tool: coined precious metal (Howgego 1990, 1995: 1–18; Kroll 2012; Meadows 2008; and Schaps 2004). Beyond the technicalities and the basic requirement necessary to the implementation of the system (the presence of abundant sources of precious metal in the Aegean area), the transformation of raw silver money (as used in the Near East and in Greece before the introduction of coined money) into coins meant a radical transformation of the role of money in social relations. In the Mesopotamian or eastern Mediterranean tradition in general, money was kept totally private. It was a commodity selected by transaction partners and its precise composition was determined by the dominant parties in the transaction. In this regard, the state itself did not behave differently from any temple, banker, or landlord. In the Greek world, coined money meant that the city was present in all transactions, that all transactions involved the city and potentially all its members. Transacting in a city meant using only the currency to which the city gave the status of legal tender. Thus the space of valuable transactions was under the control of the city. These transactions were now socialized: instead of being the object of a pure balance of power between individuals, they became part of the reciprocity network that defined the Greek city (Bresson 2005a for late classical and Hellenistic periods). This is exactly what Plato had in mind when in the *Republic* (2 369c–371e) he defined the Greek city as a community whose members constantly transacted with one another to their mutual benefit (Bloom 1991: 46–48).

Thus, according to the region, from the end of the archaic or the classical period onward coinage became the basic form of money in the Greek city. It began with the minting of electrum, an artificial alloy of gold and silver, in western Asia Minor in the second half of the seventh century BCE. This integrated monetary system was a unique and radical innovation in the world of the time (Bresson 2009). Later, in the first half of the sixth century BCE, began the first strikes of pure gold and pure silver. These two precious metals dominated the most important transactions (involving heavy silver or even gold coins). Smaller-weight silver coins, and then bronze coins with fiduciary value first introduced in the second half of the fifth century) were used for even the smallest transcations. This flexible instrument made it possible to invest for instance in trade or other commercial business (a highly profitable operation if the voyage was successful).

More generally the fluidity of capital circulation made it possible to finance any business operation. This was true within the boundaries of the city as well as beyond it, for coins with internationally recognized value (what the Greeks called "the Greek money") allowed speedy and convenient transfers of value. Without any doubt also, money in the form of coinage was an instrument of state-building and a new mode of tax collecting (von Reden 2007: 58–83; 2010: 18–47).

Besides, credit, operated directly by individuals, by groups of "friends," by banks or by sanctuaries efficiently contributed to economic activity (Chankowski 2011; Cohen 1992: 111–189; Gabrielsen 2005; Millett 1991: 109–217). Greek city-states commonly borrowed funds, both within and beyond their borders (Migeotte 1984). It should be stressed, however, that there existed no trading of debt instruments, either for private or public debt (Andreau 2006). This is of course a striking difference with early modern Europe (Brewer 1989).

Analysts of business partnerships in the world of the Greek cities formerly lamented the primitiveness of the business partnership. The absence of the capitalist firm, with its evolved form of incorporated firm, with limited liability partnership and the legal personality of the enterprise, would have been sufficient proof of the backwardness of the ancient economy. The same remark was commonly made for the absence of double-entry bookkeeping, the only system by which it is possible to gauge the profitability of capital.

Indeed, the modern type of capitalist firm did not exist in antiquity, in Greece or later also in Rome. We should even observe that far from trying to organize permanent organizations, private operators did their best to atomize their business operations. For instance, instead of creating large-scale commercial firms, partners agreed to cooperate only on the basis of a single-shot business operation. There could be many investors and one or several active partners (traders and ship-owners). But they cooperated for a single voyage and a single operation. When the profits were shared, the obligations created by the contract were extinguished. There can be many reasons for this type of structure.

According to Coase's famous definition, a capitalist firm is first defined as an alternative to coordinating production and distribution through external markets (Coase 1937). But as a matter of paradox and by contrast to the medieval world, resorting to market in antiquity was so easy that it did not seem necessary to build permanent firms *proprio sensu*. Investors could contract in a series of different business operations, thus both minimizing risks and maximizing their profits by making for themselves the best choices of investment. Insofar as these business operations were segmented into a series of different business operations, calculating profit on invested capital was easy. It did not necessitate the complex bookkeeping operations that were *de rigueur* in the medieval trade firms, first of all because only precise accounting made it possible to share the profits among the partners of the firm. But interestingly also they do not present the concentrated forms of organization that can be observed as early as the beginning of the second millennium BCE in the Assyrian colony of Kanesh (Veenhof 1997; Veenhof and Eidem 2008: 90–93). As it operated in a very different institutional framework, geographically more diverse but with comparatively good legal guarantees, Greek business organization was less concentrated, more fragmented, but thus also more flexible.

If we want to find the "firms" of antiquity (although commonly with one single owner only) this is easily done. They are to be identified mainly (but not exclusively) in the rural world, where large farms were operated by slave workers. Within the farm, the market ceased to exist and slaves had to obey the orders as soldiers would do in the army. Indeed, the market created the conditions of existence of the farm, as on the one hand the land, the farm building, the tools, and the workers could be bought on the market, and as on the other hand the farm would produce for the market. The investment capital could itself be borrowed, which made the farm a perfectly "capitalist" business. But on a daily basis, and this is a crucial difference with the modern capitalist world, the farmer did not resort to the market. Far from it, he did his best to avoid resorting to it. While credit is central for the operations of the modern capitalist firm (to buy the raw material or make the investments necessitated by a given contract), it played no role in the productive operations of the ancient farm, where the farmer or his agent did his best to produce everything he could on the farm (for example seeds, tools, food supplies, draft animals, etc.) and maximize his money revenue when he sold his crops (Bresson and Bresson 2004). This is why accounting did not develop the way it did in the late medieval or early modern periods. The Greek world created, however, a sophisticated system of single-entry bookkeeping, as can be observed in the large estates of Ptolemaic Egypt or at Delos to manage the both large-scale and complex financial operations of the sanctuary of Apollo (Bresson and Aubert in press).

Slavery and other forms of forced labor

Slavery also perfectly illustrates the specific form of constraint brought about by the ancient state on the market. The image of slavery has long been associated with forms of backward and sluggish economies. Nothing could be further from the truth. In reality, the form of slavery conventionally styled "chattel-slavery" practiced in the ancient Greek world not only was compatible with a market-oriented economy and intensive growth, but made sense only in connection with it.

Admittedly, in mainland Greece various forms of forced labor coexisted for a while. A first type (chronologically the first to have been in force) was that of the peasant communities who had to work the land of a master (Garlan 1988: 85–106). This was a form of collective serfdom, as famously was the case with the Spartan helots (Hodkinson 2008). These peasants could not be sold on the market. But their dependence was hereditary. This was the system that had long prevailed in southern Greece, in the traditional cities of Sparta and Crete. These cities were characterized by their poor connection to the market, among other things by their desire (to various degrees) to separate themselves from international trade. But this traditional model was challenged by cities on the model of Athens, which each unified their territory, pooled their resources, and created pockets of domestic markets. In these cities, the constraint of labor was based on "chattel slavery," on a workforce that was bought and sold on the international market, any form of enslavement of the local population being prohibited. Most of the time, slaves came from non-Greek, "barbarian" regions around the Aegean or further away (Garlan 1988: 45–55). It was clearly the constraint of force – based on the efficient military organization of the free population the core of which was the citizen body – that allowed the system to persist.

The proportion of slaves in the global population has always been a matter of debate. But one thing is certain: in most developed cities of classical or Hellenistic Greece, slavery was a massive phenomenon. Slaves were employed in every possible kind of activity, as it is possible to show for Athens (Fisher 2003: 34–78). This was the case for agricultural production in family farms or (in larger numbers) in estates specializing in mass production for the market (especially for oil and wine production, which required a large workforce). This was also the case in mining (where human losses were heavy in the production conditions of the time) just as in masonry or all forms of craftsmanship, from ceramics to textile or weapon production. Slaves could also be used as secretaries, teachers, and managers, and slave women were commonly forced into prostitution. Free laborers were also present in many sectors, working side by side with slaves, as can be observed in the public construction sites (Feyel 2006). However, there should be no doubt that after the archaic period – at least in the most advanced Greek cities, those that were rich in capital and trade networks – the major part of the aggregate production in both agriculture and crafts was produced by slaves.

The economic impact of slavery on production was massive. Resorting to slavery was not "uneconomic," in the sense that it would have negatively impacted production. The economic analysis of the Roman slave system in terms of individual cost of the slave, profitability, and constraints of management (Scheidel 2012) is also fully valid for the Greek one. The basic reason for resorting to chattel slavery was the market, not only because the slave workforce was provided through the market, but because it gave the possibility of increasing the return on investment (ROI), although with no increase of labor productivity. Free workers would never have accepted the appalling conditions of the slaves working in the mines (for instance) or more generally the endless days imposed on them (Scheidel 2007: 62–63). But the slaves had no other choice but to accept them if they wanted to avoid the horrible penalties that masters could inflict. That the slaves were directly a means to increase the return on investment and bypass the bottleneck of automation is famously put forward by Aristotle (*Politics* 1.4.3 1253b 34–39, tr. Barker [1948: 14]: if objects could move from their own movement, "a shuttle would then weave of itself and a plectrum would do its own harp-playing. In this situation managers would not need subordinates and masters would not need slaves." This does not mean, however, that slavery would have prevented innovation (on this question see below).

The basic reasons for resorting to slavery were (1) a relative shortage of labor (compared to exploitable resources), meaning by this a high demand for goods or services that could be produced by slaves and high wages for the free labor force; (2) an accumulation of capital and physical access in people who could be enslaved (Scheidel 2008). Along these lines, it can easily be explained why classical Athens saw such a massive development of slavery. The rich silver ores of Laurion (in southern Attica) exploited by slaves (Rihll 2010) provided a huge profit. In turn, this profit allowed both a comparatively high income for the free population (Loomis 1998) and a large amount of capital to buy slaves on the international market. At that time the vast "barbarian" periphery could provide as many slaves as were needed. In that sense the slaves of the Laurion silver mines were at the core of the system, as the silver they extracted enabled the Athenians to purchase or seize a massive input of foreign slaves.

By massively increasing the aggregate input of labor, slavery was one of the basic factors of accelerated economic growth in the classical and Hellenistic world. Insofar as they were overexploited as a workforce and were not compensated for the work they performed, slaves were not commonly supposed to reproduce themselves (even though some reproduction took place, it was not sufficient to maintain the number of slaves at a constant level). The slave system thus relied upon a permanent input of a fresh workforce from the more or less barbarian periphery, of men, women, and children who were enslaved after war or were the victims of piratical raids, or simply were sold by their families. If not constantly at the same level, the aggregate demand for slaves was thus permanent and can be considered to be a fundamental characteristic of the ancient Greek economy (the same observation could be made for the Roman economy, where the demand for slaves became vertiginous in the last centuries of the republic and at the beginning of the empire).

The cost of raising this workforce was almost nil for the world of the Greek cities. Beyond the cost of fetching and transporting them to the markets where they would be sold, this was a completely beneficial operation. In aggregate terms for the whole of the ancient world, the global balance of slavery, in terms of production, was even largely positive, as the slaves were transferred by constraint from zones of low technical productivity to zones of high technical productivity, where they would be used to perform a quantity of work vastly superior to that they would have performed in their home environment. But of course it was the Greek side that benefitted from that extra return on investment and output. Growth in the world of the Greek cities would never have been so intensive without slavery. In that sense, it is undisputable that the old question of whether or not "Greek civilization was based on slave labor" (Finley 1983: 97–115) should be answered positively.

As in most sectors the productivity of an overexploited slave was inevitably superior to that of a free worker, slavery was thus a growth accelerator, above all in the conditions of the ancient world where the chattel-slave workforce was given enough incentives to maintain a minimal level of natural reproduction. This maximized the return on investment of slave buyers. It thus becomes clear that slavery was a crucial factor in the process of growth of the ancient Greek world. It allowed massive and quick increases of the production put into the market. In the short run, it also boosted the profits of the capital holders and the process of capital concentration.

Initially, in a world where only limited pockets of highly productive slave economy existed, the cities that had made the choice to make use of chattel slavery benefitted from a huge comparative advantage. Those that kept traditional forms of labor exploitation were marginalized or collapsed. This remained true as long as a comparative advantage existed with zones that had not yet adopted the chattel slavery system; in other words as long as the products of the slave farms or workshops could find a market with a comfortable margin for the producers. The association of slavery and trade, especially long-distance trade by sea in the Mediterranean, is the secret behind the "Golden Age" of the end of the archaic period and the classical period. The cities of the Aegean area were able to sell *en masse* the labor-intensive goods produced in the slave farms or the high-quality craft products to a whole series of customers, especially the states of the eastern Mediterranean – Egypt and Persia.

In their own way, these states were rich and developed, but they did not base the exploitation of their workforce on slavery. They might want to import a specific series of Greek products for the needs of the state in the case of Egypt, or both of the state and the elite aristocracies in the case of the Persian empire. This was the case also with the chieftains of the "barbarian periphery," who were attracted by Greek weapons, luxury products, or wines. This was the case finally in many Greek cities more or less recently planted in newly colonized Mediterranean zones, or in various non-Greek city-states of the eastern and western Mediterranean, where the slave system may have existed but not on the massive scale of the Aegean Greek cities. In the Hellenistic period, part of this comparative advantage could be maintained. The conquest of the Persian empire and the creation of Greek kingdoms in the East even opened new markets. At the same time, however, the ever-growing transfer to the western Mediterranean of the technologies and institutions (massive slavery) that had been key to the achievements of the previous period began to impact at various degrees growth in the Aegean area. The process was of course directly linked with the political expansion of Rome, which became a huge and autonomous pole of growth.

When Rome conquered the whole of the Mediterranean world and transformed it into one single empire and potential market, the comparative advantage of the Greek trading cities began to disappear. Chattel slavery could be introduced everywhere, although in various proportions – in Roman Egypt, it was probably of the order of only 7–15 percent (Scheidel

2008:106). But what was now more and more lacking were the non-chattel slavery zones that could absorb the production of the core of the slave economy. In other words, the very existence of the slave system inevitably began to impact growth. A striking characteristic of growth in the ancient world considered as a whole is that although a high level of prosperity was maintained for a while, the Roman world began to experience a phase of negative growth that accelerated over time. The drawback, or contradiction, of growth based on slavery was that it also prevented the creation of a large class of wage-earners, who might also have represented a potential large-scale market.

Energy and technological innovation

Given that throughout antiquity agriculture remained by far the main sector of production and that the rural world was supposedly always dominated by routine, it has long been supposed that technological innovation, as a whole, was very limited in the ancient world. But this analysis can no longer be accepted. What remains true, however, is that the *systematic* application of science to technological innovation, which is one of the main characteristics of the modern capitalist economy, remained unknown in the ancient world, even though there were some remarkable technological applications of science that proved to be of fundamental importance.

Even the view of unchanging agricultural techniques should be challenged. Ancient Greek agriculture was not purely based on an inefficient routine and on household production and self-sufficiency. Indeed, a certain routine was inevitable. Experience of the past led to an attitude of risk avoidance in the face of strong climatic, war, or market uncertainties. Home consumption, in a world where land transport was very costly, made also perfect sense; this meant that the family and the slaves produced the majority of their own food. But nevertheless, and quite remarkably, ancient Greek agriculture was not doomed to low productivity and inefficiency. If not in its basic technologies of production (despite innovations in the detail and despite some significant improvements like the introduction of the watermill or the oil press, but which concerned only limited phases of the production process), it experienced major transformations in its structures and orientations. For instance switching from grain to wine or oil production allowed a spectacular increase in the production of calories per hectare (see Jongman, Chapter 4 in this volume). Agriculture was thus also increasingly market oriented, always aimed at improving seeds and even did not ignore the selective breeding of livestock or crop rotation.

That said, ancient Greek agriculture was strongly handicapped by a lack of cheap and good metal tools, of fertilizers (particularly acute as the Mediterranean climate limited herding) and of non-human or animal energy input. In this it faced the limitations experienced by nearly all traditional systems of farming before the industrial revolution. The yield increase in ancient Greek agriculture was certainly much more limited than the spectacular leap forward of British agriculture in the eighteenth century. It was, however, quite remarkable for the time.

The list of technological innovations of the ancient Greek world is long and impressive. It reflects an entrepreneurial spirit that was willing to innovate and take risks (Greene 2000, 2007, and 2008; Wilson 2002 and 2008). For some sectors like energy (with water power), the technological base of the ancient world remained in place until the "industrial revolution" (a term that seems to be back in favor) of the eighteenth and nineteenth centuries. Among this long list of innovations we should mention objects that are now so familiar to us that we might forget that they have a history, for instance the bound book in the form it has today (Roberts and Skeat 1983), the glass bottle (Stern 2008), or the already mentioned coined money. The analysis of technical innovation in two sectors will serve to illustrate its forms and consequences.

The first sector is the technology of ship-building, which underwent radical transformations at the end of the archaic period (McGrail 2008; Wilson 2011a and b). Instead of the sewn-planked shells of the Greek ships of the archaic age, the adoption of the technology of tenon and mortise joints (which was known in the east as early as the second millennium BCE) made it possible to build ships that were both much larger and much sturdier. While for the late archaic period the ships for long-distance trade seem seldom to have had a cargo capacity over c. 30 metric tons, in the late classical and early Hellenistic period that capacity seem to have reached commonly 60 to 100 tons, with some larger ships already up to 120 tons (and possibly above). After 100 BCE, the capacity of the ships kept on increasing, with many ships over 100 tons and some in the range of 300–500 (Wilson 2011b: 214–215). Improvements in the rigging and in the technology of anchors (originally in stone, later in iron and lead, allowing a better hooking into the seabed), usage of sounding weights, of more sophisticated sounding helms or bilge pumps brought also vital contributions to the technology of navigation. The construction of better-protected ports and of lighthouses on the model of the famous pharos of Alexandria – prefiguring the even more spectacular developments of the imperial period – began in the

Hellenistic period (Blackman 2008). This was also the case of the use of cranes to load and unload the ships.

Without these innovations it would have been impossible to build a sustainable network to transport the thousands of amphoras (commonly already 3,000 in each ship in the late classical period), thousands of tons of grain, and more generally the various goods that were transported by way of direct navigation on the high sea to various very distant ports of the Mediterranean (Arnaud 2011; Wilson 2011a). Indeed, this was vital in the process of international division of labor and growth of the world of the Greek cities and Hellenistic kingdoms.

The second sector in which innovation was spectactular was energy, with the introduction of the watermill (Wikander 2008). This invention of the third century BCE had a much wider development in antiquity than previously envisaged (Wilson 2002). For the first time, it was possible, thanks to a complex arrangement of wheels and gears, to transform the energy of flowing water and to use it for a specific purpose, first to grind grain with a circular movement. It is now certain that this new technology was quickly adopted. A further step was made under the Roman empire, when combining a connecting rod with a crank allowed the rotary movement of the waterwheel to be transformed into a reciprocating movement. This was the principle of the Hierapolis sawmill (first half of the third century CE), an innovation later attested in various parts of the Roman empire, especially for stone sawing (Ritti, Grewe, and Kessener 2007). The modern capitalist system is legitimately linked to its capacity to master the technologies for exploiting diverse sources of energy, which are key for sustained growth. It is striking that the first operational system of transformation of energy was invented, and extensively used, by the ancient Greeks.

Admittedly, however, despite its interest, the watermill was not an "all-purpose" source of energy. This meant that despite its huge interest it impacted only limited segments of the production process. For instance for grain production, waterpower was crucial in the process of grain grinding, but of course had strictly no impact on the production of grain proper (Zelener 2006). Only the "all-purpose" sources of energy of modern times ended in a revolution of every single segment of the production process. This invites us to revisit the successes but also the limits of ancient innovation.

The traditional paradigm was that slavery had been a major factor in limiting technological innovation (Michell 1940: 167–168). The availability of a low-cost slave workforce (so it was argued) would have been a disincentive for technological innovation. This view was expressed at a time when the

ancient world was supposed to have experienced neither growth nor technological innovation, two views that are now totally exploded. What has now to
be explained is how a comparatively significant process of innovation could go
hand in hand with slavery (Rihll 2008).

As observed above, competition between farmers or craftsmen was the
rule, and the cost of buying and managing slaves had to be carefully monitored. The fundamental reason why slavery did not seriously hinder technological innovation was the basic cost of the slave, i.e. the investment in capital
represented, and then the cost of it maintenance in a chaotic market (which
justified resorting to conditional manumission, the new freedman having
to work for his next master when he needed him, while for the rest he had
to earn his own living). As soon as a new technology was available at a
reasonable cost, it was widely adopted, as is proved by the diffusion of the
watermill, a technology which massively saved animal (but also sometimes
slave) workforce. In a competitive market, it was always comparatively
attractive to use a new technology *and* slaves, rather than slaves only. If
indeed some innovation potential was, however, probably lost, it was only
insofar as the slaves (at least those working in the hardest conditions of the
mines or the large latifundiary farms) had no direct interest in innovation. But
even this would not be true of slaves working independently in a shop or
workshop and paying a fixed rent to their master, for innovation could allow
them a quicker accumulation of the sum of money that would allow them to
buy their own freedom.

Technological progress had two origins. First of all and overwhelmingly it
originated in the capacity of innovation of independent farmers or craftsmen
who were competing with one another and who tried to innovate to capture a
larger share of profit, if only to survive in the market. Introducing an
innovation meant saving time and money. Innovating could correspond to
transfers of technologies that besides were already known. This was the case
for the transfer of a technology from one branch of production to another, like
the molding for the production of ceramic products, which became common
in the Hellenistic period (Rotroff 1997 and 2006). This was also the case with
the adoption of a technology already developed in another geographical area,
such as for ship-building that of the above-mentioned tenon–mortise joint,
developed in Greece at the end of the archaic period but originating in the east
Mediterranean; or that of the rotary mill originating in the western
Mediterranean but adopted and improved by the Greeks in the Hellenistic
period. It could correspond also to a genuine creation of a new technology,
like that of glass blowing in Phoenicia and Judaea in the early first century BCE

(Stern 2008), or of a new machine like in the case of the watermill or later of the water sawmill.

The second source of innovation was, however, sometimes scientific research. This was the case with the mathematicians and scientists of the Museum of Alexandria, whom the third century Ptolemaic kings had invited from all over the Greek world, or of members of other schools like Archimedes from Syracuse (third century BCE also). The gear, the screw, the connecting rod, and the piston were the "byproducts" of this abstract (and certainly not directly profit oriented) research that were to prove decisive for the creation of machines like the watermill, the screw-press (used in antiquity to crush olives or grapes) or the Archimedean screw (used as a pump in ships or in the mines).

This raises the famous case of the existence (or not) of a "rational mind" in these developments. "Enlightenment" and a new culture systematically oriented toward progress have been advocated as the decisive factor of modern capitalism and the industrial revolution (Mokyr 2009). This new culture itself would have been based on the new dignity obtained by the bourgeoisie in the eighteenth and nineteenth centuries and from then on its liberty to innovate in economic affairs (McCloskey 2010). This is what has been labeled an "idealist" approach (Clark 2012). Indeed, the systematic research for profit and the "new dignity" of the bourgeoisie are part of the equation of the industrial revolution. But it is hard to conceive how this new attitude would have been possible if it had not been based on a pre-existing economic transformation of which the "historical materialist" analysis so fundamentally allows us to make sense. But this brief detour through modernity invites us to consider the question of a possible "ancient Enlightenment."

Did there exist in the ancient world attitudes toward rational forms of behavior, and thus potentially toward rational forms of economic behavior, that can be identified during the industrial revolution? It is very easy to prove the existence of "rational attitudes" in the behavior of ancient Greek free citizens, as they systematically aimed at basing their decisions on their chance of success or failure, rather than on religious or other forms of traditional belief. The most advanced scientists of the Hellenistic period were able to conceive the earth's rotundity and to measure fairly accurately its circumference. In the second century CE, Ptolemy's *Geography* proposed a description of the world of his time where every location was defined by coordinates of latitude and longitude. As for the application of science to technological innovation, it can even be proved that even for the modern industrial revolution empirical discoveries, trials, and errors and, more generally, non-scientific rather than scientific processes were crucial in the first stage

(Allen 2009). Interestingly, the abstract principles of thermodynamics were developed by Carnot in the 1820s only, that is one century after the implantation of Newcomen's steam engine (Mokyr 2009: 124–144).

Growth, limits to growth and ancient Greek "capitalism"

The ancient Greek world enjoyed for a long period unprecedented economic growth. This growth originated fundamentally in an original institution, that of the city-state. The rule of the law established equality in contract as it established equality between citizens at the assembly. But this in turn also triggered the implementation of a comparatively efficient domestic and international market, which exploited the resources of the Mediterranean milieu with an energy of no cost, viz. wind (Bresson 2005b). It also contributed to an active division of labor and to a comparatively unprecedented process of innovation.

If coined money made it easier to accumulate capital and to make vast fortunes, a striking feature of the Greek cities remains the existence of a large class of well-off people, who fully benefitted from the existence of the model of the city-state. As for the lower class, it benefitted from the systems of protection implemented by the city, which maintained a minimal food supply at a reasonable price or even the service of public physicians at affordable cost. There were periods of severe food shortages in Greek antiquity, but except in time of war large-scale famines typical of the Near Eastern Mediterranean world or even of the European medieval world were unknown. Income inequality within the average ancient Greek city was certainly lower than that of most more recent societies and, of course, much lower than that of its contemporary oriental counterparts. This contributed in a large measure to the global economic success of the world of the ancient city-states.

These achievements were challenged by the Roman conquest, which implemented a much less egalitarian regime. The paradox is that it was the unification of the Mediterranean and the exploitation of the possibilities offered by a seemingly "unified" market, along with the corresponding undermining of the old model of the city-states, that prepared the collapse of the whole system. The previous huge commercial profits based on a core–periphery model (where the core profited from a continuous arrival of slaves) were now out of the question. Besides, the widening of the social gap between the elites and the people now became inevitable, as the former were no longer under pressure to yield any social or political concessions. This in turn undermined the power of innovation linked to the existence of the market by decreasing the incentive for the majority of people to improve their own conditions of existence. Finally, by suppressing freedom of speech and freedom of political debate, it also irremediably damaged the capacity of scientific innovation. After a regular increase until the end of the Hellenistic period, the number of mathematicians and scientists regularly decreases during the Roman empire, until finally in the fifth century it becomes negligible (Keyser 2010). The contrast with the booming atmosphere of scientific innovation of the world of the ancient city-states from the archaic to the Hellenistic period is striking.

There remains to envisage the question of the steam engine, as despite nuances in the immediate impact of this new technology (Mokyr 2009: 123–126) it still symbolizes the new capitalist industrial revolution and became actually its driving force, if not immediately, at least in the nineteenth century. The cost of energy in the form of fuel (wood only) remained extremely high in antiquity in general (except in Roman Britain where interestingly coal seams began to be exploited on a grand scale). But the core of the Mediterranean world was deprived of coal, which might have provided this alternative source of energy. While with Heron the school of Alexandria had conceived the principle of a steam engine (Keyser 1992), there remained fundamental engineering difficulties to be solved, in terms of quality of metals and of metal fabrication, before an actual steam engine might have been developed. But fundamentally, the absence of coal in the core of the Mediterranean world meant that for basic reasons of cost the development of a steam engine was absolutely out of the question (Bresson 2006).

For these reasons, insofar as the "engines of growth" of the previous centuries were now at a standstill, the Roman empire found itself vulnerable to exogenous shocks. It is in this sense, and in this sense only, that the history of the ancient Greek world followed by that of the Roman empire was an interrupted story. What was lacking for development was not a specific ideology, supposedly because rentier landowners would have constantly neglected their role of entrepreneurs. What took place was the collapse of a core–periphery model of profit, the collapse of the legally egalitarian model of the Greek city-state, and with these the collapse of a form of rational research for profit and positive attitude toward free debate and scientific research. In lieu of the static "ideal type" paradigm of the Weberian model, a dynamic new-institutional analysis allows us to make better sense of the complex history of the ancient classical world, of its unprecedented growth of specific "capitalist" type, but also of its limitations and of is final failure.

References

Allen, R. C. (2009). *The British Industrial Revolution in Global Perspective*. Cambridge University Press.

Andreau, J. (2006). "Existait-il une dette publique dans l'Antiquité romaine?," in Andreau *et al.* (eds.), pp. 101–114.

Andreau, J., C. Béaur, and J. -Y. Grenier, eds. (2006). *La dette publique dans l'histoire*. Paris: Comité pour l'Histoire économique et financière de la France.

Archibald, Z. H., J. K. Davies, and V. Gabrielsen, eds. (2005). *Making, Moving and Managing: The New World of Ancient Economies, 323–31 BC*. Oxford Books.

(2011). *The Economies of Hellenistic Societies, Third to First Centuries BC*. Oxford University Press.

Arnaud, P. (2011). "Ancient Maritime Trade and Sailing Routes in their Administrative, Legal and Economic Contexts," in Wilson and Robinson (eds.), pp. 59–78.

Barchiesi, A. and W. Scheidel, eds. (2010). *The Oxford Handbook of Roman Studies*. Oxford University Press.

Barker, E. (1948). *The Politics of Aristotle*, trs. E. Barker. Oxford: Clarendon Press.

Bedford, P. R. (2007). "The Persian Near East," in Scheidel *et al.* (eds.), pp. 302–329.

Blackman, D. J. (2008). "Sea Transport, Part 2: Harbors," in Oleson (ed.), pp. 638–670.

Bloom, A. (1991). *The Republic of Plato*, trs. A. Bloom, 2nd edn. New York: Basic Books.

Bowman, A. and A. I. Wilson (2009). *Quantifying the Roman Economy: Methods and Problems*. Oxford University Press.

Bresson, A. (2000). *La cité marchande*, Bordeaux: Ausonius.

(2005a). "Coinage and Money Supply in the Hellenistic Age," in Archibald *et al.* (eds.), pp. 44–72.

(2005b). "Ecology and Beyond," in Harris (ed.), pp. 94–114.

(2006). "La machine d'Héron et le coût de l'énergie dans le monde antique," in Lo Cascio (ed.), pp. 55–80.

(2009). "Electrum Coins, Currency Exchange and Transaction Costs in Archaic and Classical Greece," *Revue Belge de Numismatique et de Sigillographie* 140: 71–80.

(2011). "Grain from Cyrene," in Archibald *et al.* (eds.), pp. 66–95.

Bresson, A. and J.-J. Aubert (in press). "Accounting in Greece and Rome," in Bresson *et al.* (eds.).

Bresson, A. and F. Bresson (2004). "Max Weber, la comptabilité rationnelle et l'économie du monde gréco-romain," *Cahiers du Centre de Recherches Historiques (EHESS)* 34: 91–114.

Bresson, A., E. Lo Cascio, and F. R. Velde, eds. (in press). *The Oxford Handbook of Ancient Economics*. Oxford University Press.

Brewer, J. (1989). *The Sinews of Power: War, Money, and the English State, 1688–1783*. New York: Knopf.

Bücher, K. (1968 [1893]). *Industrial Evolution*. Trs. from the third German edn. New York: A. M. Kelley.

Calder, W. M. III and A. Demandt (1990). *Eduard Meyer. Leben und Leistung eines Universalhistorikers*. Leiden and New York: Brill.

Chankowski, V. (2011). "Divine Financiers: Cults as Consumers and Generators of Value," in Archibald *et al.* (eds.), pp. 142–165.

Clark, G. (2012). Review of Mokyr 2009, *Journal of Economic Literature* 50(1): 85–95.

Coase, R. H. (1937). "The Nature of the Firm," *Economica* 4(16): 386–405.

Cohen, E. E. (1973). *Ancient Athenian Maritime Courts*. Princeton University Press.

  (1992). *Athenian Economy and Society: A Banking Perspective*. Princeton University Press.

Dal Lago, E. and C. Katsari, eds. (2008). *Slave Systems: Ancient and Modern*. Cambridge University Press.

Deger-Jalkotzy, S. (2008). "Decline, Destruction, Aftermath," in Shelmerdine (ed.), pp. 387–416.

Diels, H. and W. Kranz (1951–1952). *Die Fragmente der Vorsokratiker*. Griechisch und Deutsch von Hermann Diels. Herausgegeben von Walther Kranz, sixth edn. Hildesheim: Weidmann.

Feyel, C. (2006). *Les artisans dans les sanctuaires grecs à travers la documentation financière en Grèce*. Paris: De Boccard.

Finley, M. I. (1983 [1981]). *Economy and Society in Ancient Greece*, ed. with introduction by B. D. Shaw and R. P. Saller. London: Penguin Books.

  (1999 [1973 and 1985]). *The Ancient Economy*. Berkeley: University of California Press.

Finley, M. I., ed. (1979). *The Bücher-Meyer-Controversy*. New York: Arno Press.

Fisher, N. R. E. (1993). *Slavery in Classical Greece*. Bristol Classical Press.

Gabrielsen, V. (2005). "Banking and Credit Operations in Hellenistic Times," in Archibald *et al.* (eds.), pp. 136–164.

Garlan, Y. (1988). *Slavery in Ancient Greece*. Ithaca and London: Cornell University Press.

Graslin-Thomé, L. (2009). *Les échanges à longue distance en Mésopotamie au Ier millénaire. Une approche économique*. Paris: De Boccard.

Greene, K. (2000). "Technological Innovation and Economic Progress in the Ancient World: M. I. Finley Re-Considered," *Economic History Review* 53: 29–59.

  (2007). "Late Hellenistic and Early Roman Invention and Innovation: The Case of Lead-Glazed Pottery," *American Journal of Archaeology* 111: 653–671.

  2008. "Historiography and Theoretical Approaches," in Oleson (ed.), pp. 62–90.

Hall, J. M. (2007). "Polis, Community and Ethnic Identity," in Shapiro (ed.), pp. 40–61.

Harris, William V., ed. (2005). *Rethinking the Mediterranean*. Oxford University Press.

Harris, W. V. and K. Iara, eds. (2011). *Maritime Technology in the Ancient Economy: Ship Design and Navigation*. JRA Supplementary Series 84. Portsmouth, RI: Journal of Roman Archaeology.

Heinen, H., ed. (2010). *Antike Sklaverei. Ruckblick und Ausblick*. Stuttgart: Steiner.

Hodkinson, S. (2008). "Spartiates, Helots and the Direction of the Agrarian Economy: Toward an Understanding of Helotage in Comparative Perspective," in Dal Lago and Katsari (eds.), pp. 285–320.

Howgego, C. J. (1990). "Why did Ancient States Strike Coins?" *Numismatic Chronicle* 150: 1–25.

  (1995). *Ancient History from Coins*. London and New York: Routledge.

Jursa, M. (2010). *Aspects of the Economic History of Babylonia in the First Millennium BC: Economic Geography, Economic Mentalities, Agriculture, the Use of Money and the Problem of Economic Growth*. Münster: Ugarit-Verlag.

Keyser, P. T. (1992). "A New Look at Heron's 'Steam Engine'," *Archive for History of Exact Sciences* 44: 107–124.

  (2010). "Science," in Barchiesi and Scheidel (eds.), pp. 859–881.

Krentz, P. (2007). "Warfare and Hoplites," in Shapiro (ed.), pp. 61–84.

Kroll, J. H. (2012). "The Monetary Background of Early Coinage," in Metcalf (ed.), pp. 33–42.

Lanni, A. (2006). *Law and Justice in the Courts of Classical Athens*. Cambridge University Press.

Lo Cascio, E., ed. (2006). *Innovazione tecnica e progresso economico nel mondo romano*. Bari: Edipuglia.

Long, H. S. ed. (1964). *Diogenes Laertius. Vitae philosophorum*. Oxford: Clarendon Press.

Loomis, W. T. (1998). *Wages, Welfare Costs and Inflation in Classical Athens*. Ann Arbor: University of Michigan Press.

Love, J. R. (1991). *Antiquity and Capitalism: Max Weber and the Sociological Foundations of Roman Civilization*. London and New York: Routledge.

Manning, J. G. and I. Morris (2005). *The Ancient Economy: Evidence and Models*. Stanford University Press.

McCloskey, D. (2010). *Bourgeois Dignity: Why Economics can't Explain the Modern World*. University of Chicago Press.

McGrail, S. (2008). "Sea Transport, Part 1: Ships and Navigation," in Oleson (ed.), pp. 606–637.

Meadows, A. (2008). "Coinage," in Oleson (ed.), pp. 769–777.

Metcalf, W. E., ed. (2012). *The Oxford Handbook of Greek and Roman Coinage*. Oxford University Press.

Michell, H. (1940). *The Economics of Ancient Greece*. Cambridge University Press.

Migeotte, L. (1984). *L'emprunt public dans les cités grecques*. Paris: Les Belles Lettres.

Millett, P. (1991). *Lending and Borrowing in Ancient Athens*. Cambridge University Press.

Mokyr, J. (2009). *The Enlightened Economy: An Economic History of Britain 1700–1850*. New Haven: Yale University Press.

Morgan, C. (2009). "The Early Iron Age," in Raaflaub and van Wees (eds.), pp. 41–63.

Morris, I. (2004). "Economic Growth in Ancient Greece," *Journal of Institutional and Theoretical Economics* 160: 709–742.

(2005). "Archaeology, Standards of Living, and Greek Economic History," in Manning and Morris (eds.), pp. 91–126.

(2006a). "The Collapse and Regeneration of Complex Society in Greece, 1500–500 BC," in Schwartz and Nichols (eds.), pp. 72–85.

(2006b). "The Growth of Greek Cities in the First Millennium BC," in Storey (ed.), pp. 27–51.

(2009). "The Eighth-Century Revolution," in Raaflaub and van Wees (eds.), pp. 64–80.

Ober, J. (2010). "Wealthy Hellas." *Transactions of the American Philological Association* 140: 241–286.

Oleson, J. P., ed. (2008). *The Oxford Handbook of Engineering and Technology in the Classical World*. Oxford University Press.

Osborne, R. (2009). *Greece in the Making, 1200–479 BC*. London and New York: Routledge.

Parkins, H. and C. Smith (1998). *Trade, Traders and the Ancient City*. London and New York: Routledge.

Pöhlmann, Robert von (1925). *Geschichte der sozialen Frage und des Sozialismus in der antiken Welt*, 2 vols. Munich: C. H. Beck.

Raaflaub, K. A. and H. van Wees (2009). *A Companion to Archaic Greece*. Chichester and Malden, MA: Wiley-Blackwell.

Reden, Sitta von (2007). *Money in Ptolemaic Egypt: From the Macedonian Conquest to the End of the Third Century BC*. Cambridge University Press.

(2010). *Money in Classical Antiquity*. Cambridge University Press.

Reger, G. (2011). "Inter-Regional Economies in the Aegean Basin," in Archibald *et al.* (eds.), pp. 368–389.

Rihll, T. (2008). "Slavery and Technology in Pre-Industrial Contexts," in Dal Lago and Katsari (eds.), pp. 127–147.

(2010). "Skilled Slaves and the Economy: The Silver Mines of the Laurion," in Heinen (ed.), pp. 203–220.

Ritti, T., K. Grewe, and P. Kessener (2007). "A Relief of a Water-Powered Stone Saw Mill on a Sarcophagus at Hierapolis and its Implications," *Journal of Roman Archaeology* 20: 138–163.

Roberts, C. H. and T. C. Skeat (1983). *The Birth of the Codex*. Oxford University Press.

Rotroff, S. I. (1997). *Hellenistic Pottery: Athenian and Imported Wheelmade Table Ware and Related Material*, 2 vols. Princeton, NJ: American School of Classical Studies at Athens.

(2006). "The Introduction of the Moldmade Bowl Revisited: Tracking a Hellenistic Innovation," *Hesperia* 75: 357–378.

Schaps, David M. (2004). *The Invention of Coinage and the Monetization of Ancient Greece*. Ann Arbor: University of Michigan Press.

Scheidel, W. (2007). "Demography," in Scheidel, Morris and Saller (eds.), pp. 38–86.

(2008). "The Comparative Economics of Slavery in the Greco-Roman World," in Dal Lago and Katsari (eds.), pp. 105–126.

Scheidel, W., ed. 2012. *The Cambridge Companion to the Roman Economy*. Cambridge University Press.

Scheidel, W., I. Morris, and R. P. Saller, eds. (2007). *The Cambridge Economic History of the Greco-Roman World*. Cambridge University Press.

Schneider, H. (1990). "Die Bücher – Meyer Kontroverse," in Calder and Demandt (eds.), pp. 417–445.

Schwartz, G. M. and J. J. Nichols (2006). *After Collapse: The Regeneration of Complex Societies*. Tucson: University of Arizona Press.

Shapiro, H. A. (2007). *The Cambridge Companion to Archaic Greece*. Cambridge University Press.

Shelmerdine, C. W., ed. (2008). *The Cambridge Companion to the Aegean Bronze Age*. Cambridge University Press.

Shelmerdine, C. W., J. Bennet, and L. Preston (2008). "Mycenaean States: Economy and Administration," in Shelmerdine (ed.), pp. 289–309.

Sombart, W. (1902). *Der moderne Kapitalismus*. Vol 1: *Die Genesis des Kapitalismus*. Leipzig: Duncker and Humblot.

(1913). *The Jews and Modern Capitalism*. Trs. from the German edn 1911. London: Unwin.

Stern, E. M. (2008). "Glass Production," in Oleson (ed.), pp. 520–547.

Storey, G. R. (2006). *The Archaeology of Preindustrial Cities*. Tuscaloosa: The University of Alabama Press.

Swedberg, R. (1998). *Max Weber and the Idea of Economic Sociology*. Princeton University Press.

Todd, S. C., trans. (2000). *Lysias (The Oratory of Classical Greece)*. Austin, TX: University of Texas Press.

Veenhof, Klaas R. (1997). "Modern Features of Old Assyrian Trade," *Journal of the Economic and Social History of the Orient* 40: 336–366.

Veenhof, K. R. and J. Eidem (2008). *Mesopotamia: The Old Assyrian Period*. Göttingen: Vandenhoeck and Ruprecht.

Waterfield, R. (2000). *The First Philosophers: The Presocratics and Sophists*. Trs. with commentary R. Waterfield. Oxford University Press.

Weber, M. (1930 [1904–1905]). *The Protestant Ethic and the Spirit of Capitalism*. English trs. T. Parsons and A. Giddens. London and Boston: Unwin Hyman.

(1968 [1921–1922]). *Economy and Society: An Outline of Interpretative Sociology*, ed. G. Roth and C. Wittich. New York: Bedminster Press.

(1976 [1909]). *The Agrarian Sociology of Ancient Civilizations*. London and Atlantic Highlands, NJ: Humanities Press.

Whitby, M. (1998). "The Grain Trade of Athens in the Fourth Century BC," in Parkins and Smith (eds.), pp. 102–128.

Wikander, Ö. (2008). "Sources of Energy and Exploitation of Water Power," in Oleson (ed.), pp. 136–157.

Wilson, A. I. (2002). "Machines, Power and the Ancient Economy," *Journal of Roman Studies* 92: 1–32.

(2008). "Machines in Greek and Roman Technology," in Oleson (ed.), pp. 337–366.

(2011a). "Developments in Mediterranean Shipping and Maritime Trade from the Hellenistic Period to AD 1000," in Robinson and Wilson (eds.), pp. 33–59.

(2011b). "The Economic Influence of Developments in Maritime Technology in Antiquity," in Harris and Iara (eds.), pp. 211–233.

Wilson, A. I. and Robinson, D., eds. (2011). *Maritime Archaeology and Ancient Trade in the Mediterranean*. Oxford University Press.

Wilson, A. I., P. F. Bang, P. Erkamp, and N. Morley (2012). "A Debate on the Market," in Scheidel (ed.), pp. 287–317.

Zelener, Y. (2006). "Between Technology and Productivity," in Lo Cascio (ed.), pp. 303–318.

4

Re-constructing the Roman economy

WILLEM M. JONGMAN

The modern orthodoxy

For the last few decades, the modern orthodoxy on the Roman economy has been a simple one: the vast majority of the population lived at or near subsistence, and that changed little over the lifetime of Roman civilization (Finley 1985; Jongman 1988: 15–62). The wealth that existed was only that of a tiny landowning elite, and the splendor of, for example, Roman public architecture was the splendor of imperialism. The Roman economy was an underdeveloped and stagnant economy without economic growth. This was the ultimate world of the *longue durée* where nothing ever changed, and the explanation for the stagnation was a cultural one: the dominant value-system prevented elite involvement in trade and manufacturing. As a result, these sectors of the economy remained small, and the market remained unimportant. The elite were acquisitive for sure, but failed to develop an innovative economic rationality aimed at profit maximization. Interest in technological innovation was non-existent outside the world of the military. Elite mentality was a landowner mentality, averse to risk, and often more concerned with self-sufficiency than maximizing profit. The market was not the only institution that remained underdeveloped as a result; the same applied to the banking sector or the monetary system. The state failed to develop an economic policy beyond the fiscal one of ensuring revenue, as it could neither conceive of the economy as a concept, nor see a role for itself within it. As a result of all this, the economy did not grow. Analytically, and following in the footsteps of substantivist economic anthropology (and their precursors in the historical school in German economics), modern economic theory was deemed irrelevant for this cultural explanation of Greek and Roman economic stagnation. Thus, ancient economic historians of the last few decades took an altogether different theoretical turn from their colleagues in more modern periods.

From their side of the great divide, historians of more recent periods happily concurred with histories of their own that most often began only around the year CE 1000: before that, "nothing happened." Change only came with the growth of medieval and early modern commercial cities and a commercial bourgeoisie (or even only with the industrial revolution). Between them, ancient and more modern economic historians thus used a simple model of historical development where movement was in only one direction. Discussion of the ancient economy was mostly limited to what it was not, and why not.

The virtue of this pessimistic model was that it underscored the difference between our modern prosperous capitalist world and the world of a more distant past without modern economic growth. It was the product of the realization that the preindustrial past is indeed a foreign country, and a world we have lost. No one could any longer write what Michail Rostovtzeff once wrote:

> I have no doubt that some, or most, modern Italian cities differ very little from their Roman ancestors. . . . We may say that as regards comfort, beauty and hygiene the cities of the Roman Empire, worthy successors of their Hellenistic parents, were not inferior to many a modern European and American town. (Rostovtzeff 1957: 142–143)

The weakness of that contrast between the modern world and the preindustrial past is that it all too easily ignores the possibility of changes within preindustrial society, and the differences between some preindustrial societies and others. Not all preindustrial societies lived close to bare subsistence. Some clearly were far more prosperous and successful than that, even if they did not experience an industrial revolution or modern economic growth (Allen 2009).

Our Renaissance ancestors, for example, were clearly aware of such differences, and viewed classical antiquity (and more particularly ancient Rome) as superior to their own age. In fact, living with, for example, perhaps 35,000 people in the ruins of a city of Rome that had once had a million inhabitants, their admiration and awe were quite understandable. Rome was and for centuries remained a source of inspiration and admiration, culturally, administratively, and economically. This was an admiration that only began to fade when modern Europe for the first time began to surpass ancient Rome during the early phases of the industrial revolution. Roman engineers had set a high standard, and Rome had used more iron and other metals than any previous society (and many subsequent ones), but it had not built an Iron Bridge, or harnessed steam power. The appreciation for Rome's achievement was thus squeezed out by liberal optimism about the modern age, and a new Romantic medievalism that denied that the middle ages had been a dark age at all, and instead claimed them as the cradle of the modern world.

Of course modern economies are far more successful than preindustrial ones. On average we live at least twice as long, there are far more of us, and yet our standard of living is much higher than at any time in the preindustrial past. Finally, that standard of living improves virtually every year, by quite a lot, and for more and more of the world population. The past has indeed become a foreign country. And yet that does not necessarily reduce all of the preindustrial past to an unchanging world where life was forever brutish and short. One popular model for preindustrial economic change is the Malthusian: with population growth, marginal labor productivity declines, and thus labor incomes. This was only reversed by positive checks such as famines and epidemics, when reduced populations once again allowed a higher labor productivity. Thus, the long-term trends in population and popular prosperity moved in opposite directions. The historical question is whether this is all there was to it: was there no escape from Malthus?

Actual performance: population and other trends

Interestingly, there was hardly any empirical testing of the pessimistic modern orthodoxy. There was criticism of the thesis that the Roman elite were not involved in trade and manufacturing, but hardly anyone tried to measure actual economic performance: we all thought we knew that the Roman economy did not perform particularly well, and none of us ever imagined how we could actually measure such economic performance empirically. All most of us did was discuss possible explanations for stagnation. Data are indeed an issue, since apart from a few exceptions we have no archival or other documentary records to give us statistics. The biggest exception is Roman Egypt, where the dry desert conditions have preserved some sets of administrative documents written on papyrus. Even those, however, are only a tiny proportion of what an early modern historian would have, although they are indeed enough to demonstrate that in Roman times both public and private written administrations did exist in abundance.

Beyond Egypt, almost the entire modern history of ancient Rome was written on the basis of ancient literary accounts by mostly elite authors. These anecdotal accounts mostly lack any reliable quantitative information, and at the very least require serious deconstruction of their authors' biases. Thus, data on wages and prices are exceptionally thin on the ground. Modern historians with an interest in ancient Greece and Rome may not realize that, for example, the ingenious reconstructions of Roman GDP are often based on little more than a handful of data points (Goldsmith 1984; Hopkins 1980; Lo Cascio and Malanima 2009; Maddison 2007; Scheidel and Friesen 2009; Temin 2013). It is like reconstructing changes in twentieth-century US GDP on the basis of little more than the price of a hamburger in Kentucky in the 1930s, a car in Virginia in the 1960s, an electrician's wage in San Francisco in the 1990s, and the tax revenue of a village in Louisiana in the 1940s (see Scheidel 2010 for wages and prices). In short, these reconstructions are composites from vastly different regions and periods, and offer little possibility of differentiating through space and time. Growth, as a process of precisely change over time, remains invisible in these reconstructions. Yet there are quite simply too few observations for anything better. Thus, much quantification may look like the real thing, but that is deceptive.

The last few years have shown the potential of an altogether different research methodology, however. Although we do not have the written records of Roman economic activities, we do have their material remains. Modern Roman archaeologists have moved away significantly from the Indiana Jones stereotype, and are concerned with the wholesale reconstruction of past economic and social life (apart from much else). Their methodologies are sophisticated, and the results can bring us closer to the reality of ancient life. These new methodologies can be grouped into three. The first is that of the increased resolution of modern detailed excavation, including archaeological science. The second is that of settlement archaeology, and field surveys in particular, where surface data from larger areas are collected to reconstruct patterns of habitation and land use. The third is that of the aggregate analysis of classes of finds such as fine table wares, amphoras, or shipwrecks. If one shipwreck is moderately interesting, an analysis of the chronology and geographic distribution of all known shipwrecks is many times more informative. By professional tradition, archaeologists often still focus on the unique and the particular, but influential studies of aggregate data sets are beginning to change that. In particular, many of these data allow the construction of time series, and thus the analysis of economic change over time. With the shift from cultural explanations to actual performance the use of archaeological proxies for classic variables like population or production and consumption is more relevant than ever.

These new categories of evidence and new methods also invited new types of explanation beyond the cultural. Modern economic theory hesitatingly acquired a more prominent role in the debate than before, if only to identify the relevant variables (Jongman 1988, although substantively more pessimistic; Jongman 2012b). Finally, and again unlike nearly all research of the last few decades, this involved some serious quantification.

The new time series data do indeed contradict the modern orthodoxy that Roman society was one of extreme poverty and stagnation, where nothing ever changed. First and foremost, I will show that many parts of the Roman world witnessed dramatic population growth during the last few centuries BCE, not only in its core areas, but also in many of the newly conquered territories, followed by an equally dramatic decline from mostly the late second century CE (and a temporary late antique recovery in the eastern empire, but not in the western). The chronology of this process is best visible in Roman Italy, where decades of archaeological field surveys have produced a detailed mosaic of changes in settlement patterns and habitation densities from the Iron Age to the early medieval period (Ikeguchi 2007; Launaro 2011). Archaeologists have often emphasized the unique nature of the region they have worked in themselves, but it is now abundantly clear that nearly all regions of Italy followed an underlying pattern of population growth from perhaps the late fourth or early third centuries BC until roughly sometime in the second century CE (Jongman 2009; Lo Cascio and Malanima 2005). After that, demographic decline set in, sometimes dramatically. Clearly, during the Roman period the landscape filled up to an unprecedented extent, to become dramatically depopulated again in late antiquity and the early middle ages. Figure 4.1 juxtaposes recent demographic reconstructions from two regions, Nettuno and the Albenga valley, to demonstrate the remarkable similarities.

Italy, moreover, was by no means unique: other regions also show high population densities in the Roman period. In the Rhineland, for example, detailed archaeological research in some exceptionally well-studied regions has provided what are probably the best estimates for very long-term population trends in Europe. Here, densities in Roman times were massively higher than in the periods before and after (Figure 4.2).

Population densities in many parts of the empire were only surpassed in modern times, and the total population of the empire grew to at least some 60 million people, if not significantly more (according to some scholars up to 90–100 million) (Scheidel 2007a). With the growth of population, cities grew even more in size and number (see below p. 92). The Roman empire became more deeply urbanized than any later society in preindustrial European history, with more and bigger cities, and a critically more urban lifestyle.

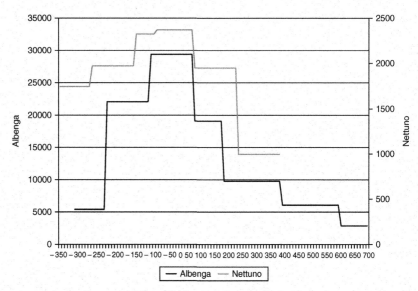

Figure 4.1 Population trends from field survey data, totals per region (De Haas, Tol, and Attema 2010; Fentress 2009)

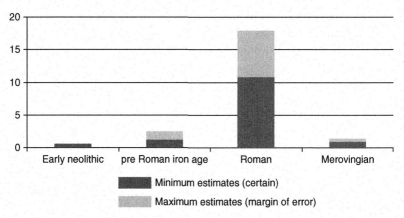

Figure 4.2 Population densities in the Rhineland (per km²) (Zimmermann *et al.* 2009: 377)

The million dollar question is, of course, whether all of this was a good thing. Did high population density depress labor productivity and thus popular standard of living (as I once argued and as some still do), or was it in fact the product of economic success and prosperity (as I have argued more recently) (Jongman 1988, 2007b; Scheidel and Friesen 2009). Did population densities get perilously close to a Malthusian ceiling, and is this indeed the explanation for the subsequent decline, first in the later second century CE and second from the mid sixth century when epidemics ravaged the empire's population? Or did standard of living not suffer under population growth, and was there a non-Malthusian explanation for that subsequent decline? Similarly, did cities grow so large because they drew masses of desperate and destitute peasants driven off their land, as has indeed been argued, or did they grow because of increased and beneficial division of labor between town and country, and an increased demand for urban goods and services, and thus for urban labor (Hopkins 1978; Jongman 2003a)? Did cities grow because of increased prosperity and become engines of further economic growth? Did trends in population and prosperity move in viciously Malthusian opposite directions, or not? Were they perhaps both part of the same economic success story?

I want to argue that crucial performance indicators show dramatic aggregate and per capita increases in production and consumption from the third century BCE, or sometimes a bit later, until the Roman economy reached a spectacular peak during the first century BCE and the first century CE, lasting until perhaps the middle of the second century CE (de Callataÿ 2005; Hong et al. 1994). As I argued earlier, we do not have serious data on Roman wages, let alone over any length of time. With some ingenuity there is one good exception, however. We have a good series of implied slave prices from the Delphi manumission inscriptions (Hopkins 1978: 161). These show that precisely during the period of a massively increasing slave supply in the second and first centuries BCE, the price of manumission, and by implication the price of slaves, was increasing. Since the price of slaves represents the net present value of future labor income above subsistence, this suggests that labor incomes were indeed rising during these centuries (Domar 1970; Jongman 2007b: 601–602).

There is good archaeological evidence that standard of living was indeed rising. An example is afforded by an analysis of field survey data on population and consumption of goods with high income elasticity. Again, we turn to the Nettuno survey, but this time we compare the time series of reconstructed population numbers with the time series of amphoras sherds and fine table ware. Both of these are high-income elasticity goods, and thus good markers of increased prosperity. Simple series of amphoras and fine ware consumption are only moderately interesting, however, because we know population also increased: we want to see changes in per capita consumption. Therefore, Figure 4.3 uses the demographic data for Nettuno in Figure 4.2 as a denominator for the reconstruction of a trend in per capita consumption of amphoras and fine wares.

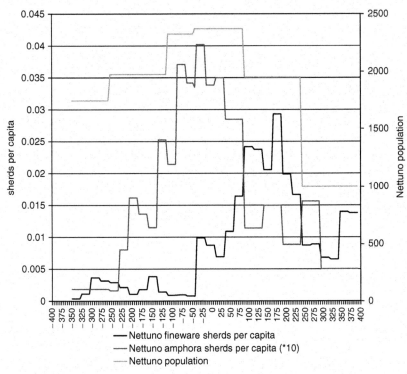

Figure 4.3 Population and per capita consumption in Nettuno. Data from De Haas, Tol and Attema 2010

Similar trends can be found in data on diet. Finds of animal bones on Roman sites used as a proxy for meat consumption show a rapid increase from the later fourth century BCE in Italy, and also in the provinces after they had been conquered by Rome. Figure 4.4 charts these data for the Roman empire as a whole, though some regions are inevitably better represented than others.

The same trend can be seen in the growth of the installed capacity of fish farms and fish-salting installations along the coast (Wilson 2006). There was now a clear demand for expensive traded proteins. Recent data from the main sewer of Herculaneum reveal an exceptionally rich and varied diet in CE 79, and not just for elite households (Rowan forthcoming). Similarly, data on food plants show a fabulous improvement in the range of fruits and vegetables that were consumed in northwestern Europe after the Roman conquest (Bakels and Jacomet 2003). Interestingly, much of this variety did not survive the demise of the Roman empire.

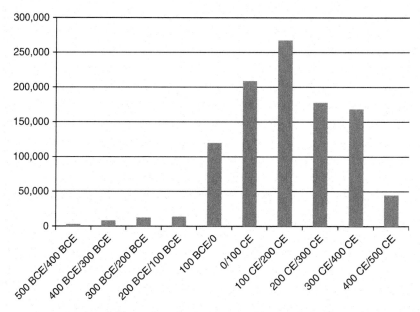

Figure 4.4 Dated animal bones from the Roman empire (Jongman 2007b 613–614, based on King 1999)

Production of raw materials and manufactured goods shows similar trends. Greenland ice core data show significant peaks from the first century BC to the second century CE in metal pollution as a product of Roman mining activity, and the trend in coal exploitation in Roman Britain (Figure 4.5) also shows a rise in the early Roman period, a decline during the third century crisis, recovery in the fourth century, and ultimate collapse with the end of Roman rule (de Callataÿ 2005; Hong et al. 1994; Malanima 2013).

Wood finds from Germany show that building activity had exploded during the Roman period, to decline steeply thereafter. The beauty of wood data is that they are dated by tree rings, and the chronological resolution is, therefore, only one year. Figure 4.6 thus charts the number of wood finds per year.

A recent reconstruction of the chronology of public building construction in Roman Italy (Figure 4.7) shows a steady increase in the volume of theatres, amphitheatres, porticoes, public baths, and the like until about CE 170, a substantial dip thereafter, and major decline from the early third centry CE (Heinrich 2010). This, of course, is not just a measure of public purchasing power, but also of elite commitment to civic culture and public life. I write

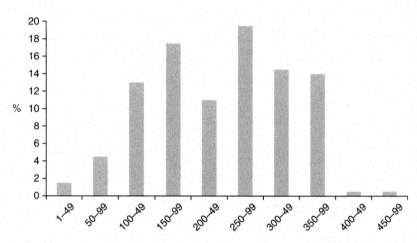

Figure 4.5 Chronology of coal exploitation in Roman Britain (Malanima 2013; Smith 1997: 322–324)

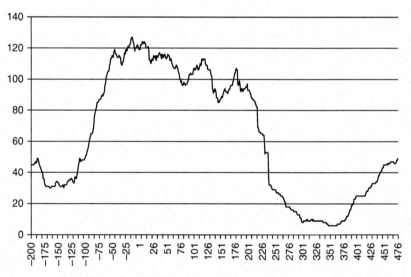

Figure 4.6 Chronology of wood consumption in western Germany (number of dated wood finds per annum) (Holstein 1980). The author is very grateful to Dr. Thomas Frank of the laboratory for dendro-archaeology of the University of Cologne for retrieving a digital copy of these data

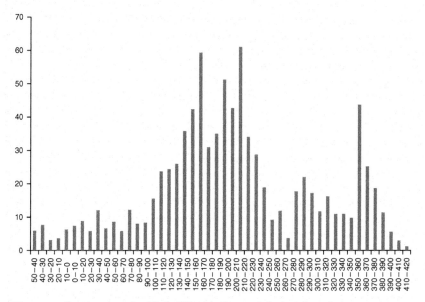

Figure 4.7 Construction of public buildings in Roman Italy (number of buildings) (Heinrich 2010)

elite, because it was the local elite who funded large parts of these building projects.

The Roman economy thus not only witnessed substantial and continued increases in population as well as in aggregate production, but for a while the Roman people also enjoyed higher per capita incomes as demonstrated by improved diets and material culture. I think there are now good reasons to believe that it reached levels of economic performance not achieved again for a very long time to come, and perhaps only in Britain and the Netherlands in the early modern period.

Finally, it is important to emphasize that the prosperity did not remain confined to a small elite of imperial magnates. Roman material reached even modest households in faraway provinces. Terra Sigillata tableware was produced in huge quantities and was exported and subsequently imitated on an imperial scale, to be recovered from urban sites and smaller farms alike. Urban society shows the presence of a large and prosperous sub-elite. Pompeii, for example, may have had a political elite of probably a hundred families, but the city counted at least some five hundred grand and elaborately decorated town houses that could only be inhabited by a well-to-do family with half a dozen or a dozen domestic slaves (Wallace-Hadrill 1994). Outside the city's freeborn elite of a hundred, many if not most of the other four hundred owners of these grand houses were freed slaves who after manumission had continued the careers they had in fact started when as slaves of their masters they had been secretaries, bookkeepers, business agents, and the like (Jongman 1988; 2007a; Aubert 1994). For these people there were many opportunities for upward mobility. As a result, and perhaps surprisingly, Roman social inequality was perhaps less than in some other preindustrial societies (Milanovic, Lindert, and Willamson 2011). For a while, Roman society was not only quite prosperous, but also relatively inclusive (cf. Acemoglu and Robinson 2012).

What contributed to the success?

If the Roman economy was indeed as successful as I think, there is something to be explained. The most skeptical explanation would be to argue that all this was the product of Roman imperialism, and only lasted for as long as the income from this imperialism had worked its way through the (Italian) economy (Scheidel 2007b). This explanation has three points in its favor. The first is that it draws proper attention to the magnitude of Roman rapacity and cruelty in the formative stages of the empire. Rome's war effort was gigantic, but so was the initial capital transfer (including enslaved human capital) and the subsequent stream of income from extortion and taxation (not always easy to distinguish from each other). The second is that it draws attention to the importance of Rome as a large political and economic unit. Previous research has often only treated the empire as a multitude of cities with their territories, and little more. Size does indeed matter. The third point is that it has an explanation for the subsequent economic decline of the empire.

There is little doubt that huge sums were transferred from the provinces to the imperial center, but the consequences are not so clear. Keith Hopkins came up with an alternative optimistic model many years ago: Roman taxation in rich interior provinces such as Asia Minor and the expenditure of that money in the Italian center and in the frontier provinces stimulated those interior provinces to develop an export industry to earn back the money they paid in taxes (Hopkins 1980, 2002). This then kindled the kind of long-distance economic integration of the empire that benefitted everyone.

To test these models against reality, Italian examples are quite irrelevant as both a growth scenario and an exploitation scenario would show Italian prosperity. The real test is what happened in the provinces: did they prosper or suffer under Roman rule? In my view, they prospered, and I do think we have enough data to support this. Demographically, there is little doubt that after the initial conquest, population went up in many if not all conquered provinces. It is equally obvious that these provinces became increasingly connected to the imperial economy. They began to produce for distant markets, and they began to consume food and manufactures from other distant lands.

A recent study of Roman Baetica (modern day Andalusia) shows in great detail how that region became connected to Roman markets, and how it benefitted, in part by exporting olive oil to the city of Rome (Haley 2003). In Rome itself, Monte Testaccio, an artificial mound of mostly discarded oil amphoras from Baetica, testifies to the size of this export. It has a volume of 580,000 cubic metres, implying an estimated import of 7.5 million liters of olive oil per annum from this source alone. The Rhine region and Roman Britain are other obvious and well-studied examples of provincial regions that benefitted: as mentioned above, diet in that part of Europe improved enormously with the advent of Rome, and so did housing conditions, or material culture inside the house. As every field archaeologist knows, Roman levels are incomparably richer than what is below or above them. There is more and nicer pottery, there is more and better kitchen equipment, and there is vastly more iron and bronze in tools, locks, hinges, stoves, and many other applications. And there are clear signs of many technological advances in the wake of the Roman conquest. It was good to live in the Roman empire, and it was good to have been conquered by Rome. Why else did barbarians try to enter the empire, but to benefit from it?

If Roman imperialism cannot be the explanation for a prosperity that extended well beyond the imperial center, we need other explanations for that success, and also for the subsequent decline. We shall thus look into classic candidates such as institutions, division of labor, and technology, and we need to distinguish between factors that explain the initial growth and factors that explain the ultimate decline (they can be the same, but they need not be).

If there is one lasting legacy of Roman achievement, it must be Roman law, and more specifically Roman civil law. To this day it remains the foundation of many modern legal systems, and it dealt successfully with many pressing issues that could have harmed the economy. It guaranteed private property, it discouraged dishonesty in business, and it made it relatively easy to enforce contracts, even over longer periods of time. We now know against earlier skepticism that the law was in fact used extensively and knowledgeably, in both large and small contracts, in litigation, and in administrative documents (Terpstra 2013). These legal documents have survived as wooden writing tablets from the Vesuvian area, from the wet soil along Hadrian's wall in Britain, and in even smaller numbers from a few other regions. They have also survived in larger numbers as papyri from Roman Egypt. The law was used, and made transactions easier.

Thus, Roman law is certainly part of the story of Roman economic success. On the other hand, it is hard to see how it can explain the beginning of that story. It developed relatively late, it would seem, and mostly in response to demand from an increasingly sophisticated society. Finally, its most impressive articulations only occurred in the later empire, precisely when the economy was facing real difficulties. So Roman law cannot explain the original growth, or the final decline.

We can also see that both the state and private enterprises used extensive administrations to keep track of their affairs. For each assessed person a tax collector in Roman Egypt kept records of previous years together with those of the present, in order to check for consistency, and army units kept extensive records of pay and other financial affairs: soldiers received much of their pay as entries in a savings account with their unit's administration. We have the administration of one large estate in Roman Egypt, and again we see extensive record-keeping (Hopkins 1991; Rathbone 1991). The grain distributions (about 400 kg in twelve monthly rations of 33 kg each) to some 200,000 adult male citizens in the city of Rome were only practical because the recipients had to present a personalized token on a specified day and at one specified counter out of the forty-five at the Porticus Minucia, and where lists were kept of the 150 or so recipients of that day and at that counter (Jongman 1997). Precise land registers were also kept, for taxation purposes, but also to record ownership and mortgages. Similarly, Rome's central administration kept records of all individual soldiers (300,000 or even more at any one time), and their entitlements. From its early days, Rome had held a census of people and property every five years. After all, before the introduction of a professional army from 107 BCE it needed to record who could serve in the army, and it needed to record citizens' worth, because political status and voting rights largely depended on wealth (Nicolet 1976). Thus, the empire critically depended on written records, and on a sufficiently wide-ranging literacy to exploit them to the full (Hopkins 1991). However, there is no indication that, apart from the census, written records were used in the earlier stages of Rome's economic expansion. Of course, writing existed in Egypt before Roman times, but in Italy itself writing and most written administrations seem to have followed rather than initiated the economic boom.

This brings me to the wider issue of government and bureaucracy. Roman emperors of the first and second centuries CE repeatedly insisted on the importance of good government. We may cynically dismiss the pretension, but Roman rule was by the law. Roman emperors were advised by lawyers to insure that their decisions followed legal precedents. Under Augustus, the earlier privatized system of provincial tax collection was brought under central control, if only to avoid the excesses of the previous period. From the time of Augustus again, a system of imperial bureaucratic administration evolved, with separate departments such as the treasury, and staffed by imperial slaves and freedmen (Millar 1977; Weaver 1972). Nothing like it had existed before, even though Augustus in typical style used the preceding model of Roman senior magistrates who used their private servants for state business. The difference was one of scale, and it was a big difference.

This central government provided infrastructure such as roads for the empire, harbors, and enormous warehousing complexes such as those in Ostia and Portus, or frightfully expensive aqueducts that would often remain the main urban water supply until modern times, or benefits for the city of Rome and elsewhere (Hodge 1992; Keay *et al.* 2005; Laurence 2002; Rickman 1971; Robinson and Wilson 2011). Romans of the republican and early imperial period were citizens rather than subjects, and were entitled to the benefits of that citizenship. Thus, citizens in Rome were sometimes given large cash handouts. Each month they were given generous rations of grain to cover about half a family's calorific requirements. Each day some seven thousand Roman men could be seen carrying home their monthly 33 kg of wheat, a graphic reminder of the benefits of imperial rule. In the second century CE inhabitants of the cities of Italy received a similarly valuable benefit in coin (*alimenta*) (Jongman 2002). Gladiatorial games provided magnificent entertainment in Rome and many other cities of the empire (Hopkins 1983). In Rome these were staged by the emperor so no one could upstage him, but elsewhere they were mostly paid for by local magistrates.

One benefit of Roman rule was internal and external security. From the age of Augustus the *pax Romana* provided more security than a typical preindustrial state could afford, and certainly during the peak of its economic success in the early imperial period piracy and brigandage were much reduced. In those days, Roman cities did not need or have defensive walls. The same applied to external security during these years. Rome's professional armies not only rarely lost a battle, but often the mere presence of their overwhelming fighting power was intimidating enough for potential enemies to not even contemplate a fight (Campbell 1984). Roman legions were better trained, better paid, better led, and better equipped than any opposition. Until the later second century CE they undoubtedly paid for themselves economically by the peace that they maintained.

Money is another important institution for an advanced economy, and again there is no doubt that Rome's achievements were impressive. In the early empire Rome had essentially (though with some exceptions) created one integrated monetary system that covered most of its territory with a stable monetary system and supplied denominations to cover the entire range of transactions, from fiduciary small change in bronze, to silver *denarii* and all the way to high-value gold coins (*aurei*) worth almost a year's subsistence food for one person (Burnett 1987). Recent research has shown that this coinage was widely used. Per capita monetary stock was exceptionally large by the standards of a preindustrial economy, and there is now ample evidence for extensive monetization of small transactions in even remote districts (Duncan-Jones 1994; Harl 1996; Harris 2006; Howgego 2009; Jongman 2003b). The system also worked well in the sense that there was little or no inflation until the late second century CE, and rampant inflation only raised its head much later. The successful creation and maintenance of this monetary system during the most successful four centuries of Rome's economic history is thus testimony to Rome's achievement, but again, it is hard to imagine how it can be used to explain either Rome's early growth, or Rome's ultimate decline.

Compared with other powers in the region Rome was relatively late in producing its own coinage, and even then it did originally only in southern Italy where at the beginning of the third century BCE it had to compete with the southern Italian Greek coinage. In 211 BCE, during the Second Punic War, Rome finally introduced the system with a lighter silver *denarius* that was to remain the foundation of its monetary system until the middle of the third century CE. The (silver) money stock increased during the second and first centuries BCE, with the increase in population, the size of the empire, and production and consumption per capita (Hopkins 1980:109). The growth of the silver coinage tailed off in the later first century BCE, when Rome began to mint golden *aurei* as well. From that moment onwards, to estimate the total money stock, these gold coins have to be added. As mentioned above, the per capita gold, silver, and bronze money stock was probably larger per head than in even the most advanced early modern European economies (Jongman 2003b).

The system began to disintegrate in the later second century CE. In earlier centuries Rome had debased its coinage only rarely and not by much, and mostly in response it would seem to years of bad harvests and thus disappointing tax incomes (in the absence of public debt this is all the state could do). This did indeed begin to change in the 160s, but only slowly at first. The cause seems to have been a combination of disappointing tax returns in the wake of the Antonine plague, increased military spending to cope with military unrest at the frontiers, and problems in mining districts such as Spain that made it much harder to strike new coins to pay for public expenditure. For the first time prices also began to rise during this period. In Egypt, the only region where we have some half decent data, many prices seem to have roughly doubled in the wake of the Antonine plague (Scheidel 2002; but see Bagnall 2002). After the death of so many, the per capita money stock had increased dramatically. Since the aggregate stock of money (M) had remained roughly the same, and also the velocity of circulation (V), the reduction in the number of transactions (T) from a lower population must have pushed up prices (P) in the classic equation $MV = PT$. This rather than any still quite minor debasement must have caused the late second-century inflation. The monetary system responded to the crisis, and did not cause it.

Apart from coinage, Rome also had a banking sector. Traditionally, Roman banking is seen as relatively crude: it could not create money, and bankers were insufficiently rich to cope with the demands at the top of the social and economic scale (Andreau 1999; Finley 1985). For that, private deals between members of the landowning elite remained necessary. For lack of good evidence it is hard to see what Roman bankers could and could not provide. Importantly for such a large empire, money could be and was transferred on paper from one part of the empire to another. Large public projects were completed, and complex business ventures like sailings of big ships to India were financed, even if we do not quite know how. The Roman economy was not constrained by a lack of capital.

Monetary integration is but one aspect of the larger story of economic integration over the empire's huge territory. People, goods, and services could and did travel over enormous distances, connecting markets into one large system. The Mediterranean was the hub, of course, facilitating cheap sea transport in the core, and helped by a high-quality infrastructure of good harbors and warehousing (Robinson and Wilson 2011). Maritime shipping increased enormously in the second century BCE, when Rome became the dominant power in the Mediterranean, first in the west, but soon also in the east, with commercial nodes such as Rhodes and Delos. The most visible sign of the booming shipping business is the massive increase in the number of dated shipwrecks (see this volume, p. 49). But it was not just the Mediterranean that showed an increase in long-distance trade. The Red Sea and its harbors witnessed a booming trade with India (Nappo 2007).

Harbors were connected by river and land transport to inland markets. The Rhine and other rivers in France and elsewhere connected the Mediterranean economy with northwestern Europe and England. The empire's expensive network of well-built roads, with bridges and tunnels where necessary, would remain unsurpassed until modern times. Of course, the original impetus was military, but from the very beginning the roads were also used for private travel and transport.

The benefits were such that a new and much larger and more integrated "global" economy emerged where more advanced technologies could spread rapidly, and where goods could now be traded over much longer distances, adding greatly to the quality of life for even quite ordinary Romans. The empire became increasingly integrated by a network of long-distance communication and transportation. In its most mature form, when the market had become large enough, this was then sometimes followed with increased local production of imitation wares.

At the very local level, Roman villas were often located precisely along roads, to facilitate the transport of their produce to urban markets, and to make personal travel more comfortable. A good example is the Via Appia from Rome to Capua, built in the later fourth century BCE. It followed Rome's conquest of that city, but it was also part of a larger scheme to drain the fertile Pontine marshes. It stimulated the construction of new villas and more commercial agriculture along its route, and both responded to and further stimulated the urban growth that took off in precisely this period. If we look at the chronology it is thus apparent that the globalization of the Roman economy and the growth of long-distance trade followed upon an earlier urban growth and a growth of market agriculture. That seems to be where the story actually begins.

At the peak of its economic success the Roman empire was indeed an exceptionally urbanized society (Hanson 2011). There were perhaps 2,500 cities in the Roman empire, of which more than 400 were in Italy alone. Roman society at its height was an urban society. Cities played a pivotal role in the economy. Unlike in the medieval world, there was no economic, social, or legal divide between town and country. The landowning elite lived primarily in cities, drawing rents from their agricultural estates. Thus, and unlike in the feudal world, the urban economy was founded on the largest sector of the economy rather than living at its margin. Cities were the connecting nodes in the network of local rural–urban exchange and in the system of long-distance transport and communication. Thus, the empire was administered from cities, and Roman culture was urban culture. Even small Roman towns had some public buildings such as temples, a forum, porticoes, or a public bath. These were all recognizably Roman, whether in Britain or in the Syrian desert.

Roman cities were not only more numerous than for a long time afterwards, but many were also much larger. There were numerous cities with a few tens of thousands of inhabitants, and at least half a dozen in the range 100,000–200,000. On top of that there were really large cities such as the world had never seen, and would not see again for a long time. Roman Carthage, Alexandria, and Antioch each had 200,000–500,000 inhabitants for a combined population of a million or so. Finally, there was the city of Rome itself. During the last two or three centuries BCE its population had grown to perhaps one million inhabitants by the time of Augustus, a size that would not be equaled again until the Chinese cities of the Sung dynasty, or until London around 1800, during the early stages of the industrial revolution (Jongman 2003a). In the early imperial period perhaps 5 percent of the empire's population lived in cities with more than a hundred thousand inhabitants.

The importance of these larger cities is that even though the vast majority of cities were indeed, as many have said, small, the majority of urban inhabitants lived in large or even very large cities, and much more so than in medieval or early modern Europe. Economically, socially, and culturally, theirs was a true big city life. This is not often recognized, but it has important consequences. The Roman urban experience was truly urban, with a complex and sophisticated market for specialized urban goods and services, and advanced division of highly skilled labor. This applied to the manufacturing or building industry as much as to the food trade or financial services. Elite purchasing power was huge, and so was demand for goods that had to come from far afield. Romans in the provinces could expect to be supplied with ceramics or food produced in distant parts of the empire, and could communicate with relatives at the other side of their known world.

In a preindustrial economy there is always one condition that has to be met for such urbanism to be successful: agrarian productivity growth. Supporting a large nonagricultural sector is only possible if agriculture is productive enough. This is all the more important under conditions of high population density. After all, the problem of such agricultural systems is that of declining labor productivity in agriculture under population pressure. In the Roman empire, and in its core regions in particular, population densities were indeed comparatively high. Thus the Malthusian specter of declining labor productivity and low labor incomes was looming. It would have pushed the economy into the Jan de Vries peasant model of adaptation to population pressure: peasants avoid the market and try to produce all their needs for themselves (de Vries 1974: 4–17; Boserup 1965). What were the possibilities for Roman farmers to avoid this grim scenario, and avoid declining labor productivity?

As we saw, the early urban growth in late fourth and early third centuries BCE Italy went hand in hand with the rise of a new agriculture of wine and olive oil production on rather larger farms (Hellenistic villas is what they are often called, but the term is rather grand for a larger farm) (Terrenato 2001). The output of these farms was quite evidently too large for their own consumption, and not surprisingly they were often located near good transport opportunities. Their market was in the newly founded or expanded towns. This invites scrutiny of their business logic: how did they escape from the dismal prospect of declining labor productivity? The crop choice is revealing: with wine and oil it was possible to produce about five times more calories per hectare than with cereals (Jongman 2007b). Thus, if Romans drank enough wine and consumed enough olives and olive oil, the often quoted demographic ceiling was lifted in one stroke. These market crops permitted much larger populations, in both towns and in the country. It was also economically attractive to produce these crops, because these were expensive calories. The few prices that we have from early imperial Italy suggest that wine was perhaps five times more expensive per calorie than wheat, and oil at least twice as expensive. So with these crops revenue per hectare could be ten to twenty-five times higher. Of course, these were also labor-intensive crops, so costs were also higher, but not nearly as much. The partial switch to wine and oil averted the nightmare of declining agricultural labor productivity, made good use of the growing population, and was highly profitable (Jongman forthcoming).

Since these were more expensive calories, the switch was dependent on a preceding increase in prosperity, of course. This in turn could then provide the positive feedback for further growth. In principle we have two candidates for this. The first is the prosperity brought about by Roman imperialism. The late fourth and early third centuries BCE were the time when Rome conquered Italy. The puzzle is that the switch not only occurred in Roman territories, but also elsewhere in Italy, and before Roman conquest (Terrenato 2001). Rising prosperity was not just a Roman phenomenon. The second candidate is to look at climate. This was, after all, roughly the beginning of the so-called

Roman warm period (McCormick *et al.* 2012). Analytically a more beneficial climate can be seen as technical progress: the production function itself shifts because the same quantities of land, capital, and labor now produce more than before. It is an attractive explanation, even though the data are not yet as good as one would like.

What were the limits to growth?

The imperial economy was thus a high-level equilibrium, where total factor productivity could be high because prosperity was high, and because a system of state institutions and public services was maintained that could only be afforded because the empire was successful. The system seems to have declined from the later second century CE when the so-called Antonine plague ravaged the empire's population, inaugurating a period of increased oppression and military turmoil (Jongman 2012a; Lo Cascio 2012). In the west that was the end of the story, but in the east there was a big recovery, until at least the Justinian plague of the sixth century.

Everything else being equal, a dramatic epidemic such as the Antonine plague should have increased labor productivity, and labor incomes. That was what happened after the Black Death of the fourteenth century. However, this does not seem to have occurred in the second or early third century. There are a few contested indications from Egypt that real wages in the immediate aftermath of the Antonine plague improved, but the overwhelming bulk of the evidence points to not only economic contraction, but also to a decline in prosperity for ordinary people (Bagnall 2002; Scheidel 2002). Cities were hit hard, and urban elites in many cases retreated to their estates in the countryside. Thus, in the cities the fabric of civic culture began to disintegrate. Fewer gladiatorial games were given, public building came to a stop (Figure 4.7), and prominent citizens no longer acted as civic benefactors (Figure 4.8) as they had done before. Part of their role would begin to be taken over by Christianity, with its ideal of charity for the poor and the indigent.

Long-distance trade was interrupted in many regions, and so was manufacture of traded goods (Erickson-Gini 2010). The sea trade to India that suffered a similar economic crisis was virtually abandoned (Nappo 2007). In the countryside we not only witness the signs of dramatic demographic contraction, but also of a concentration of properties (Duncan-Jones 2004). The smaller farms seem to almost disappear, and so do even the smaller estates. In many regions this is the period when the landscape began to be

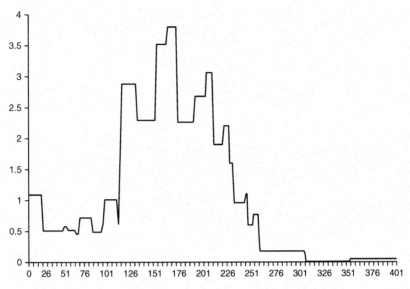

Figure 4.8 Benefactions in (part of) Asia Minor (Zuiderhoek 2009: 18).

dominated by truly large and increasingly fortified estates. In the legal system this increased inequality is expressed in the erosion of the value of citizenship, and the rise of the new social and legal distinction between *honestiores* with status and property and *humiliores* within citizenship who could be beaten tortured or crucified as punishment (Garnsey 1970). So altogether it would seem that the Roman world took a different turn from that of Europe in the fourteenth century, and a turn that looked more like eastern Europe's second serfdom. Rome had changed from an inclusive society to a more extractive one (Acemoglu and Robinson 2012).The high-level equilibrium was destroyed.

One explanation for this turn of events could be that the period of favorable weather had indeed come to an end (McCormick *et al.* 2012; Jongman 2012b). As in the years preceding the Black Death, the years before the Antonine plague had witnessed some of the worst weather for a long time, and those were only the beginning of a centuries-long period of much less favorable climatic conditions (Campbell 2010).

The demographic and economic collapse of the late second century took a while to translate into other fields, and the achievements of the Severan emperors of the late second and early third centuries are truly impressive in this respect; but the inevitable had to happen with the military and political troubles of the half-century between 235 and 284. After that, the story took a different turn, with the great divergence between the eastern and western Roman empires: the west steadily declined, but the east showed miraculous recoveries, with substantial population growth, an explosion of commercial agriculture in for example Judaea, a resumption of the trade with India, and a reinvigorated urban life in many areas. One reason may have been that this was indeed a colder and wetter period, harming the northwest, but benefitting precisely the Levantine regions. In the east, this new prosperity lasted until the reign of Justinian, when a new epidemic, this time of the real plague, killed off huge numbers. Interestingly, it is now apparent that this epidemic too was preceded by a major climatic event. The eastern economy never really recovered.

References

Acemoglu, D. and J. A. Robinson (2012). *Why Nations Fail: The Origins of Power, Prosperity, and Poverty.* New York: Random House.

Allen, R. (2009). "How Prosperous Were the Romans? Evidence from Diocletian's Price Edict (AD 301)," in Bowman and Wilson (eds.), pp. 327–345.

Andreau, J. (1999). *Banking and Business in the Roman World.* Cambridge University Press.

Aubert, J.-J. (1994). *Business Managers in Ancient Rome: A Social and Economic Study of Institores, 200 B.C.–A.D. 250.* Leiden: E. J. Brill.

Bagnall, R. (2002). "Effects of Plague: Model and Evidence," *Journal of Roman Archaeology* 15: 114–120.

Bakels, C. C. and S. Jacomet (2003). "Access to Luxury Foods in Central Europe during the Roman Period," *World Archaeology* 34: 542–557.

Boserup, E. (1965). *The Conditions of Agricultural Growth.* London: Allen & Unwin.

Bowman, A. and A. Wilson, eds. (2009). *Quantifying the Roman Economy: Methods and Problems.* Oxford Studies in the Roman Economy I. Oxford University Press.

Burnett, A. (1987). *Coinage in the Roman World.* London: Seaby.

Campbell, B. M. S. (2010). "Nature as Historical Protagonist: Environment and Society in Preindustrial England: The 2008 Tawney Memorial Lecture," *Economic History Review* 63: 281–314.

Campbell, J. B. (1984). *The Emperor and the Roman Army 31 B.C.–A.D. 235.* Oxford University Press.

de Callataÿ, F. (2005). "The Greco-Roman Economy in the Super Long-run: Lead, Copper and Shipwrecks," *Journal of Roman Archaeology* 18: 361–372.

De Haas, T., G. Tol, and P. Attema (2010). "Investing in the Colonia and Ager of Antium," *Facta* 4: 225–256.

de Vries, J. (1974). *The Dutch Rural Economy in the Golden Age 1500–1700.* New Haven: Yale University Press.

Domar, E. (1970). "The Causes of Slavery or Serfdom: A Hypothesis," *Economic History Review* 30: 18–32.

Duncan-Jones, R. P. (1994). *Money and Government in the Roman Empire.* Cambridge University Press.

(2004). "Economic Change and the Transition to Late Antiquity," in S. Swain and M. Edwards (eds.), *Approaching Late Antiquity: The Transformation from Early to Late Empire*. Oxford University Press, pp. 20–52.

Erickson-Gini, T. (2010). *Crisis and Renewal: Nabataean Settlement in the Central Negev during the Late Roman and Early Byzantine Periods*. Oxford: Archaeopress.

Fentress, E. (2009). "Peopling the Countryside: Roman Demography in the Albenga Valley and Jerba," in Bowman and Wilson (eds.), pp. 127–161.

Finley, M. I. (1985). *The Ancient Economy*, 2nd edn. London: Chatto and Windus.

Garnsey, P. D. A. (1970). *Social Status and Legal Privilege in the Roman Empire*. Oxford University Press.

Goldsmith, R. W. (1984). "An Estimate of the Size and Structure of the National Product of the Early Roman Empire," *Review of Income and Wealth* 30: 263–288.

Haley, E. W. (2003). *Baetica Felix: People and Prosperity in Southern Spain from Caesar to Septimius Severus*. Austin: University of Texas Press.

Hanson, J. W. (2011). "The Urban System of Roman Asia Minor and Wider Urban Connectivity," in Bowman and Wilson (eds.), *Settlement, Urbanization, and Population*. Oxford Studies on the Roman Economy. Oxford University Press, pp. 229–275.

Harl, K. W. (1996). *Coinage in the Roman Economy, 300 B.C. to A.D. 700*. Baltimore, MD: Johns Hopkins University Press.

Harris, W. V. (2006). "A Revisionist View of Roman Money," *Journal of Roman Studies* 96: 1–24.

Heinrich, F. B. J. (2010). "Publieke constructies in Romeins Italië (225 v.Chr.–425 n.Chr.): een conjuncturele benadering," in P. Attema and W. Jongman (eds.), *Archeologie en Romeinse economie*. Special issue of *Tijdschrift voor Mediterrane Archeologie*, 44: 14–21.

Hodge, A. T. (1992). *Roman Aqueducts and Water Supply*. London: Duckworth.

Holstein, E. (1980). *Mitteleuropäische Eichenchronologie*. Mainz: von Zabern.

Hong, S., J. P. Candelone, C. C. Patterson, and C. F. Boutron (1994). "Greenland Ice Evidence of Hemispheric Lead Pollution Two Millennia ago by Greek and Roman Civilizations," *Science* 265: 1841–1843.

Hopkins, K. (1978). *Conquerors and Slaves*. Cambridge University Press.

(1980). "Taxes and Trade in the Roman Empire (200 B.C.–A.D. 400)," *Journal of Roman Studies* 70: 101–125.

(1983). *Death and Renewal*. Cambridge University Press.

(1991). "Conquest by Book," in M. Beard *et al.*, *Literacy in the Roman world*. Ann Arbor: Journal of Roman Archaeology Supplement 3, pp. 133–158.

(2002). "Rome, Taxes, Rents and Trade," in W. Scheidel and S. von Reden (eds.), *The Ancient Economy*. Edinburgh University Press, pp. 190–230.

Howgego, C. (2009). "Some Numismatic Approaches to Quantifying the Roman economy," in Bowman and Wilson (eds.), pp. 287–295.

Ikeguchi, M. (2007). "A Method for Interpreting and Comparing Field Survey Data," in P. Bang, M. Ikeguchi, and H. Ziche (eds.), *Ancient Economies and Modern Methodologies*. Bari: Edipuglia, pp. 137–158.

Jongman, W. M. (1988). *The Economy and Society of Pompeii*. Amsterdam: J. C. Gieben and ACLS Humanities Ebook.

(1997) "Lemma 'cura annonae'," in H. Cancik and H. Schneider (eds.), *Der Neue Pauly. Enzyklopädie der Antike*, vol. III. Stuttgart/Weimar, pp. 234–236.

(2002). "Beneficial Symbols: *Alimenta* and the Infantilization of the Roman Citizen," in W. Jongman and M. Kleijwegt (eds.), *After the Past: Essays in Ancient History in Honour of H. W. Pleket.* Leiden: E. J. Brill, pp. 47–80.

(2003a). "Slavery and the Growth of Rome: The Transformation of Italy in the First and Second Century BCE," in C. Edwards and G. Woolf (eds.), *Rome the Cosmopolis.* Cambridge University Press, pp. 100–122.

(2003b) "A Golden Age: Death, Money Supply and Social Succession in the Roman Empire," in E. Lo Cascio (ed.), *Credito e moneta nel mondo romano.* Bari: Edipiglia, pp. 181–196.

(2007a). "The Loss of Innocence: Pompeian Economy and Society between Past and Present," in J. J. Dobbins and P. W. Foss (eds.), *The World of Pompeii.* London: Routledge, pp. 499–517.

(2007b). "The Early Roman Empire: Consumption," in W. Scheidel, I. Morris, and R. P. Saller (eds.), *The Cambridge Economic History of the Greco-Roman World.* Cambridge University Press, pp. 592–618.

(2009). "Archaeology, Demography and Roman Economic Growth," in Bowman and Wilson (eds.), pp. 115–126.

(2012a). "Roman Economic Change and the Antonine Plague: Endogenous, Exogenous, or What?," in E. Lo Cascio (ed.), pp. 253–263.

(2012b). "Lemma 'Formalism–substantivism debate'," in *The Encyclopedia of Ancient History.* New York / Oxford: Wiley-Blackwell.

(forthcoming). "The New Economic History of the Roman Empire."

Keay, S., M. Millett, L. Paroli, and K. Strutt (2005). *Portus: An Archaeological Survey of the Port of Imperial Rome.* Archaeological Monographs of the British School at Rome 15. London: British School at Rome.

King, A. (1999). "Diet in the Roman World: A Regional Inter-site Comparison of the Mammal Bones," *Journal of Roman Archaeology* 12: 168–202.

Launaro, A. (2011). *Peasants and Slaves: The Rural Population of Italy (200 B.C. to A.D. 100).* Cambridge University Press.

Laurence, R. (2002). *The Roads of Roman Italy: Mobility and Cultural Change.* London: Taylor and Francis.

Lo Cascio, E., ed. (2012). *L'impatto della peste Antonina.* Bari: Edipuglia.

Lo Cascio, E. and P. Malanima (2005). "Cycles and Stability: Italian Population before the Demographic Transition (225 B.C.–A.D. 1900)," *Rivista di Storia Economica,* 21(3): 197–232.

(2009). "GDP in Pre-Modern Agrarian Economies (1–1820 AD): A Revision of the Estimates," *Rivista di Storia Economica* n.s. 25(3): 391–419.

Maddison, A. (2007). *Contours of the World Economy, 1–2030: Essays in Macroeconomic History.* Oxford University Press.

Malanima, P. (2013). "Energy Consumption and Energy Crisis in the Roman World," in W. Ham (ed.), *The Ancient Mediterranean Environment between Science and History.* Leiden: E. J. Brill, pp. 13–36.

McCormick, M., U. Büntgen, M. A. Cane, E. R. Cook, K. Harper, P. Huybers, T. Litt, S. W. Manning, P. A. Mayewski, A. F. M. More, K. Nicolussi, and W. Tegel (2012). "Climate Change during and after the Roman Empire: Reconstructing the Past from Scientific and Historical Evidence," *Journal of Interdisciplinary History* 43(2): 169–220.

Milanovic, B., P. H. Lindert, and J. G. Williamson (2011). "Pre-industrial Inequality," *The Economic Journal* 121(551): 255–272.

Millar, F. (1977). *The Emperor in the Roman World (31 B.C.–A.D. 337)*. London: Duckworth.

Nappo, D. (2007). "The Impact of the Third Century Crisis on the International Trade with the East," in O. Hekster, G. de Kleijn, and D. Slootjes (eds.), *Crises and the Roman Empire: Proceedings of the Seventh Workshop of the International Network Impact of Empire (Nijmegen, June 20–24, 2006)*. Leiden: E. Brill, pp. 183–199.

Nicolet, C. (1976). *Le métier de citoyen dans la Rome républicaine*. Paris: Gallimard.

Rathbone, D. (1991). *Economic Rationalism and Rural Society in Third-Century AD Egypt: The Heroninos Archive and the Appianus Estate*. Cambridge University Press.

Rickman, G. E. (1971). *Roman Granaries and Store Buildings*. Cambridge University Press.

Robinson, D. and A. Wilson (2011). *Maritime Archaeology and Ancient Trade in the Mediterranean*. Monograph 6. Oxford Centre for Maritime Archaeology.

Rostovtzeff, M. (1957). *The Social and Economic History of the Roman Empire*, 2 vols., 2nd edn. Oxford University Press.

Rowan, E. (forthcoming). "Sewers, Archaeobotany and Diet at Pompeii and Herculaneum," in M. Flohr and A. Wilson (eds.), *The Economy of Pompeii*. Oxford Studies on the Roman Economy. Oxford University Press.

Scheidel, W. (2002). "A Model of Demographic and Economic Change in Roman Egypt after the Antonine Plague," *Journal of Roman Archaeology* 15: 97–114.

(2007a). "Demography," in W. Scheidel, I. Morris, and R. Saller (eds.), *The Cambridge Economic History of the Greco-Roman World*. Cambridge University Press, pp. 38–86.

(2007b). "A Model of Real Income Growth in Italy," *Historia* 56(3): 22–46.

(2010). *Prices and other Monetary Valuations in Roman History: Ancient Literary Evidence*. http://www.stanford.edu/~scheidel/NumIntro.htm, accessed may 15.

Scheidel, W. and S. Friesen (2009). "The Size of the Economy and the Distribution of Income in the Roman Empire," *Journal of Roman Studies* 99: 61–91.

Smith, A. H. V. (1997). "Provenance of Coals from Roman Sites in England and Wales," *Brittannia* 28: 297–324.

Temin, P. (2013). *The Roman Market Economy*. Princeton University Press.

Terpstra, T. T. (2013). *Trading Communities in the Roman World: A Micro-economic and Institutional Perspective*. Leiden: E. J. Brill.

Terrenato, N. (2001). "The Auditorium Site and the Origins of the Roman Villa," *Journal of Roman Archaeology* 14: 5–32.

Wallace-Hadrill, A. (1994). *Houses and Society in Pompeii and Herculaneum*. Princeton University Press.

Weaver, P. R. C. (1972). *Famila Caesaris: A Social Study of the Emperor's Freedmen and Slaves*. Cambridge University Press.

Wilson, A. (2006). "Fishy Business: Roman Exploitation of Marine Resources," *Journal of Roman Archaeology* 19: 525–537.

Zimmermann, A., J. Hilpert, and K. P. Wendt (2009). "Estimates of Population Density for Selected Periods between the Neolithic and A.D. 1800," *Human Biology* 81(2–3): 357–380.

Zuiderhoek, A. (2009). *The Politics of Munificence in the Roman Empire: Citizens, Elites and Benefactors in Asia Minor*. Cambridge University Press.

5

Trans-Asian trade, or the Silk Road deconstructed (antiquity, middle ages)

ÉTIENNE DE LA VAISSIÈRE

Economic history at a Eurasian scale is a challenge, especially in the long run and with sources written in a whole array of languages and scripts – Chinese, Gandhari, Pali, Latin, Arabic, Persian, Armenian, Sogdian, Tamil, Aramaic, Greek, and Italian dialects are only some of the languages used by traders on the various Asian roads in antiquity and the middle ages. It is therefore quite natural that studies on the economic history of the trans-Asian trade have suffered from a Europe-centered bias from the outset. These studies were primarily concerned to find a way to think about the history and power of the West, and taking the west as their focus was easier than grappling with non-Western languages. The question of the origin of European capitalism was in this regard central, whether it was ascribed to the Italian trading cities of the thirteenth century or to the maritime powers of sixteenth- and seventeenth-century Europe. I will obviously integrate this European perspective into this chapter, and especially the remarkable results gathered by the specialists of the Roman papyri and Italian archives on the Asian part of the trade of Rome, Venice, or Genoa. But I will try nevertheless to provide first and foremost an Asian, and more precisely a central Asian, perspective on the trans-Asian trade, central Asia being, with the Indian Ocean, one of the two main arteries of trade during this period. The trade of Samarkand totally lacks any Western documentation and has no obvious link with Western growth, and so, has been passed over in this European-centered search for the origins of capitalism. I will focus on the silk trade, certainly the longest-distance trade, although comparisons will be provided with the more "regional" the trades, by which I mean long-distance trades linking only parts of the ancient world, such as the trade in pepper in the Indian Ocean from the Malabar coast to Egypt. I will try to draw comparisons to evaluate the economic importance of these various trades.

A short chronological overview

It is certainly useful to ascertain first the chronology. If important during some periods, usually quite short and limited, the trans-Asian trade was certainly not continuous up to the eleventh century. The so-called Silk Road – a quite recent image (1877) rather than an actual scientific concept – was poorly trodden during centuries and was not a permanent east–west link, as is too often believed.

A trickle of Chinese silk might have crossed Eurasia before the second century BCE: silk has been found in various cemeteries of Europe and Asia in antiquity, from the Celtic ones in Hallstadt to the Kerameikos cemetery in Athens or in Pazyryk. There was a prehistory of the Silk Road through the Scythian world, about which we know almost nothing except that some silk circulated. However, silk was not important enough to have been noticed in any textual source – and Greek sources cannot be regarded as uninterested in Asia. Traveling for unknown reasons in unknown hands, silk cannot have played anything but a small role in the economy of these societies, perhaps as a most infrequent and exotic marker, among several more important ones (see the discoveries of Pazyryk), of some social status. Some other goods in early antiquity are much more adequate for analysis of distance trade in Asia, as lapis lazuli for instance, which was traded as early as the fourth millennium BCE from the unique mine in the Kokcha valley, near the Pamirs, to Mesopotamia and Egypt and later to India, but not to the north or to China (Herrmann 1968).

The actual starting point of the Silk Road is well described in the Chinese dynastic histories. With the Han attempts to establish an alliance with the nomadic tribes of central Asia at the end of the second century BCE, the Chinese embassies were loaded with presents among which silk rolls played a major part. This created in central and western Asia a market in want of more regular contact with China, independent of political events. The first merchants who reacted to these political embassies by organizing expeditions up to China were in the first century BCE from the Indo-Iranian borderlands, from Gandhāra (nowadays northern Pakistan) and then Bactria (northern Afghanistan), soon to be united during the first century CE in the Kushan empire. These merchants were accustomed to long-distance trade – in the fifth century BCE traders of Balkh were already selling precious stones (lapis, carnelian?) along the Indus. The second-century BCE report of Zhang Qian, the first Chinese envoy to western central Asia wrote on Bactria that "some of the inhabitants are merchants who travel by carts or boats to neighbouring countries, sometimes journeying several thousand li" (*Shiji*, 123.3162; a li is roughly half a kilometer). These traders in a few generations managed to establish trading colonies in northern China. In a way, the creation of the Silk Road can be regarded as the combination of the old Middle Eastern trade with the Han expansionist policy. The systems coalesced.

The starting point of long-distance maritime trade was quite different. Direct trade between the Red Sea and the western coast of India with the monsoon winds was undoubtedly of growing importance since their 'discovery' by Hippalus *c.* 100 BCE. Berenike, the major port of trade of Roman Egypt on the Red Sea, reached its apogee in the first century CE, when Pliny the Elder (XII.41) wrote that "by the lowest reckoning, India, China, and the Arabian peninsula take from our empire 100 million sesterces every year – that is the sum which our luxuries and our women cost us." Out of this 100 million, one half was for Arabian perfumes and we do not know the shares of Chinese silk imported to India by the Kushan traders and spices in the remaining half. In view of these amounts, it has been argued that the 25 percent tax on imported goods may have been an important source of income for the Roman state in the first and second centuries CE. This trade strongly declined after the middle of the second century and up to the middle of the fourth century, as demonstrated by the excavations in Berenike (Sidebotham 2011), only to then experience a major renaissance up to the end of the fifth century.

The inland trade might have crumbled in the third century, as China was shaken by internal troubles and secessions, while the Kushan empire was destroyed by the Sassanid invasion. Silk is seldom mentioned in third-century Latin authors. The two last testimonies to this bygone period were in the third century: a text mentioning the Kushan trading community in Gansu and a set of commercial letters, the so-called Sogdian Ancient Letters (La Vaissière 2005: Chapter 2), which describe in 313 the death of Indian traders in Luoyang. Both associate the traders of the Kushan empire with newcomers, the Sogdians. They were originally the pupils and apprentices of the Kushan merchants, coming from the by then poorer regions of central Asia more to the north (Samarkand, Bukhara, Tashkent). Part of the commercial Sogdian vocabulary is of Bactrian origin, while some of the earliest Sogdian traders are known in India. The Sogdian Ancient Letters show the presence of Sogdian merchant communities in the main cities of inner China and Gansu, organized within networks. We have evidence of the replacement of Bactrian merchants by Sogdians in the fourth century and of a renewal of the Silk Road in the fifth century after a decline and then a disruption of about two centuries.

From the fifth to the first half of the eighth centuries, the Silk Road may have been at its apex, with Sogdians as the main long-distance caravan merchants in central Asia. Until the mid-eighth century, and unlike the trade in antiquity, for which the sources are spotty at best, we do have ample proof, archaeological and textual, of continuous inland trade. The Sogdian diaspora was the main continental medium for export and import of luxury products in China and so controlled the principal trans-Asiatic trade route. Besides silk, the Sogdians traded musk, slaves, precious metals and stones, furs, silverware, amber, relics, paper, spices, brass, curcuma, sal ammoniac, medicinal plants, candy sugar, and perfumes, etc. (Schafer 1963; Skaff 1998b). Sogdian trade was greatly diminished by two events in the eighth century. The conquest of Sogdiana by Arab armies was slow and difficult, and it partially ruined the country, while China itself was ruined by the An Lushan rebellion in 755. We have very little information about the period from the mid eighth century to the late ninth century, given the lack of Chinese and Arabic sources on central Asia. Continuous wars all over central Asia certainly weakened Sogdian trade. Although some Sogdian merchants traveling to China are still mentioned in the first third of the tenth century, references to them disappear afterwards.

Meanwhile, maritime trade with China had grown to overtake continental caravan trade in the ninth century. At least since antiquity, maritime long-distance trade is known to have reached China. However, in antiquity its eastern branch, between India and China, seems to have been less developed than the western one between India and the Roman world. It is mainly in the Sassanian period (224 to 651 CE) that maritime trade between Iran, Ceylon, Indonesia, and China actually developed. In the west the Sassanian Persian Gulf superseded the Red Sea. Some archaeological remains of Sassanian warehouses have been discovered on the shores of the Persian Gulf and of the Indian Ocean and the Sassanian dynasty seems to have practiced an aggressive commercial policy (Kervran 1994, 1999; Whitehouse and Williamson 1973). Persian traders were familiar figures on the trade maritime roads up to southern China. But we have in the sixth-century text of the Nestorian, Cosmas Indicopleustes, a hierarchy of the trade routes of Asia, which pointed out that it was by caravan routes, rather than by sea, that Persia received most of its silk (Cosmas Indicopleustes, II: 45–46). In the ninth century, however, the decline of the land routes might have triggered a rise in the oceanic trade, starting from the Persian Gulf (Siraf, excavations of Whitehouse). Several Arabic and Persian books, among them especially the *Aḥbār aṣ-Ṣīn wa l-Hind*, testified to this trade. In Chinese sources, the major harbors of southern China sheltered Persian colonies, Zoroastrian, Muslim, and Christian. From an archaeological point of view, the excavations of the major trade port of Shiraf have shown thousands of sherds of Chinese stoneware, and later chinaware, as well as in all the other Muslim harbors in contact with the Indian Ocean. By comparison only a few sherds of chinaware have been discovered after decades of excavations in Samarkand (Sokolovskaia and Rougeulle 1992).

In central Asia, the major trade was no longer an east–west trade, but a south–north one. The trade of the Samanids in the tenth century resumed the old northwestern Sogdian road leading from Iran to southern Russia and the Urals and the northeastern one toward the nearby Turkic tribes. These were roads already familiar to the Sogdians, but within very different economic conditions. More than one million Samanid coins have been discovered in eastern Europe. By contrast, no Samanid coin has been found in China. We have no reasons from the extant archaeological or written sources to believe that an important caravan trade linked China with the West during this period.

With the tenth century long-distance trade seems to have changed in Asia. We should no longer speak of the "Silk Road" but rather simply of the multifaceted long-distance trade of Asia. With the transfer to the West of silk technology in the sixth century the Near and Middle East became gradually self-sufficient (Jacoby 2004), while in China itself, silk lost part of its role as a currency in favor of silver ingots. Most of the remaining trade must have been seaborne: in central Asia the former networks split into two halves, a Muslim network to the west, of which the Qarakhanid empire seems to have been the political expression – its territory fits neatly the zone of commercial expansion of the Samarkand traders as described in the geographical texts of the tenth century – and in the east a Uyghur one operating from Turfan to the Chinese states. In between, the actual relations seem to have been quite limited. The inland Silk Road was reduced to a very small path from *c*. 750 to *c*. 1100 and faded away after the Mongols in the face of the growing importance of the regional networks.

The creation of the Mongol empire in the thirteenth century was from a commercial point of view a gigantic reshuffle of these networks as the Mongols made use of both Muslim and Uyghur traders in a variety of roles. The unification of Eurasia allowed Chinese silk, which still benefitted from a comparative price advantage due to the abundance of production in China, to be present again on the markets of Europe (Jacoby 2010). But this revival of an actual land Silk Road was only possible if security and unity were maintained all over the road to the Near East, namely if protection costs could be lowered by Mongol official protection. Decline was swift to come in the fourteenth century with the wars between and within the various *uluses*, exacerbated by the Black Death. After that, the image is simply no longer relevant, if it ever was, given the complexity of the trades all over Asia.

Economics of silk

As a major home production of northern China, silk was omnipresent in economic life. It irrigated both the private, commercial networks and the official taxation system. The Tang dynasty tax system combined collection of grains, corvée, and a tax in kind, payable in textiles. In silk-producing areas, mainly northern China, this tax was 20 feet of silk and 3 ounces of silk floss per head. Up to the ninth century the standardized silk roll, 12 meters long by 0.56 meters wide in the middle of the Tang period, was a quasi-currency. Large amounts could be paid in silk rolls, and sometimes silk was required. The importance of its role, beginning with the Han and up to the middle period of the Tang (eighth century), has been explained as a proof of insufficient coin production. It declined afterward – from 780 taxes had to be paid in coins instead of goods – although from time to time in case of lack of coins payment in goods could be restored.

As the state in China had a large control over silk distribution through the taxation system, private commercial exportation, understood as the trade of small or major professional traders, was only one of the two major possibilities of despatch of silk to the West, the other one being the action of the state. Unfortunately, due to the nature of the sources, we know much more about the latter than about the former, although some comparison could be made.

Within the official sphere, there were two major reasons to despatch silk to the rest of Asia. Diplomatic or tributary relationships with the nomads were a first possibility, while the inclusion of part of Asia in the currency sphere of China is a second one.

But it is also clear that at the western receiving end were traders. If in the east the Chinese state was powerful in its control of the economy, from central Asia westward, private networks of central Asian traders despatched and sold the rolls. So we have to consider two interfaces: how silk trickled down from the hands of the nomadic elites – silk as tribute – or the Chinese officials – silk as money – to the hands of the traders themselves.

From tribute to trade: *ortaq* traders

The concept of *ortaq* is extremely important to link the tributary and commercial aspects of the Silk Road. More often than not, in the long run, China
had to buy peace from its northern nomadic neighbors by paying heavy
tributes to them, generally in silk rolls. These were easily transported over
the Gobi desert and were completely foreign to the productive knowledge and
capacities of the nomadic world. These rolls could be used for domestic
consumption, especially as a social tool for marking the hierarchies among
the nomadic elites. But domestic consumption was certainly insufficient to
absorb the thousands or hundreds of thousands of rolls sent on a yearly basis
by the Chinese power. Huge quantities of silk were ready to be despatched
further to the west from the centers of the nomadic power, usually Mongolia
itself, or the upper part of the bend of the Yellow River, or the northern side of
the Tian Shan. Several possibilities can be contemplated here. Certainly rolls
could be used as a currency within the nomadic empires: we do have texts
testifying to the payment of Türgesh warriors in silk rolls (Ṭabarī II, 1689). But
the major intermediaries were the traders.

In the Mongol period, Mongol princes and traders were linked by a special
relationship named *ortog*, from *ortaq* in Turkish. The *ortaq* trader in the Mongol
empire is a merchant whose capital has been supplied by a Mongolian prince or
official (Allsen 1989; Endicott-West 1989). A Yuan dynasty vocabulary defines it
as "the name for the practice whereby government funds used for trade were
distributed as capital to earn interest" (quoted in Endicott West 1989: 130).
Seventy percent of the benefits should have been for the government, and 30
percent for the *ortaq* (Sen 2006: 431, quoting the *Yuanshi* 94.2402). The *ortaq*
traders soon became major players in the empire, succeeding for instance in
farming the taxes of China or of Iran (Aigle 2005: 123f., 141f.) for their Mongol
masters. The system of the *ortaq* traders extended well beyond the frontiers of
the Mongol empire. For instance at the end of the thirteenth and beginning of
the fourteenth centuries the sea trade between the Malabar coast and Iran was
entirely controlled by the two brothers Tibi. One, Maliku-l Islam, controlled the
main entrepôt of the Persian Gulf, the island of Qays, and acted as *ortaq* for
the Mongols, farming on their request the taxes of Fars. The other brother
was the vizier of the lord of the Malabar coast. There,

> whatever commodities and goods were imported from the remotest parts of
> China and Hind into Malabar, his agents and factors should be allowed the
> first selection, until which no one else was allowed to purchase. When he had

selected his goods he despatched them on his own ships, or delivered them to merchants and ship owners to carry to the island of Qays. There also it was not permitted to any merchant to contract a bargain until the factors of Maliku-l Islam had selected what they required ... and the trade was so managed that the produce from the remotest China was consumed in the farthest west. (Vaṣṣāf 1871: 35)

Later in the text of the historian Vaṣṣāf, we see Fakhr-ud din, the son of Maliku-l Islam, acting as an ambassador and *ortaq* between the Ilkhans of Iran and the Yuan Mongol dynasty in China:

with presents of cloths, jewels, costly garments, and hunting leopards, worthy of his royal acceptance, and ten tumans (one hundred thousand pieces) of gold were given to him from the chief treasury, to be employed as capital in trade. Fakhr-ud din laid in supply of necessaries for his voyages by ships and junks, and laded them with his own merchandize and immense jewels and pearls, and other commodities suited to Timur Kha'an's country, belonging to his friends and relations, and to his father. (Vaṣṣāf 1871: 45)

As regards economic history, the main importance of the *ortaq* association between the Mongol state and the traders is that they allowed the transfer of tribute toward actual trade. This was a major economic tool by which taxes on China or Iran became capital for traders through the intermediary of tribute to the Mongols.

We naturally wonder whether the origins of the institution cannot be dated further back, to the special relationship between the Sogdians and the Turks. We can be sure that *ortaq* traders were known well before the Mongol period. They were known in the eleventh-century dictionary of Kashgari, and before that in the Uyghur documents of the ninth and tenth centuries (Hamilton 1986: 138). However, the earliest attestation, not of the name but of the institution, goes back to the very beginning of the involvement of the Sogdian traders in the economic life of the Turkish empire, *c.* 567:

Maniakh, the leader of the Sogdians, took this opportunity and advised Sizabul that it would be better for the Turks to cultivate the friendship of the Romans and send their raw silk for sale to them because they made more use of it than other people. Maniakh said that he himself was very willing to go along with envoys from the Turks, and in this way the Romans and Turks would become friends. Sizabul consented to this proposal and sent Maniakh and some others as envoys to the Roman Emperor carrying greetings, a valuable gift of raw silk and a letter. (Menander Protector 1985: 111–115)

Maniakh was the *ortaq* of the Turkisk prince Sizabul, proposing to increase the profit he earned by the Chinese tribute by selling it to the main markets of Asia, the Sassanians – in a previous attempt – and the Greeks. However, the institution at this early stage is not clearly differentiated from diplomacy; this evolution would take place during the six centuries separating Maniakh from his Mongol counterparts.

From currency to trade: silk in central Asia

Chinese empires expanded to central Asia mainly during the Han and the Tang periods, and a unification of China with central Asia took place during the Mongol period. The cost of maintaining armies and administrations in central Asia was important and has been studied quite precisely for the Tang period (Skaff 1998a: 81ff.).

To pay for it, the most convenient way was to transfer rolls of silk. The salary of a soldier or an administrator was calculated in grains, then in coins, and then converted into and actually paid in standardized rolls of silk. For instance, instead of sending 7,200 liters of millet from inner China, or 160 kg of bronze coins, the administration in 745 would pay a middle-level administrator in the army at Dunhuang with 83.5 bolts of silk every six months. We have precise documents showing the army sending convoys loaded with thousands of rolls of silk to the Chinese armies and colonies in central Asia, an image very different from the standard idea of the caravan trade. At the same date, two convoys for a total of 15,000 bolts of silk were sent from the army stationed in Dunhuang to the state warehouse 700 km to the east to bring back the salaries of the soldiers (Trombert 2000: 109–111). It was most certainly the same during earlier periods of Chinese colonization of central Asia, as we have documents from the late third century showing thousands of rolls of silk in stock in Chinese military warehouses in central Asia, while some of this silk was used to buy grain for the soldiers (Lin 1985: 235, 291).

The next step of the rolls toward the West is known from Chinese documents and Arabic texts on central Asia: the roll of silk was a local currency, which could be used on the markets to buy goods. An entire economic system was born out of the needs of the Chinese army: wholesale traders of grain for instance were paid in rolls of silk to provide flour to the Chinese soldiers. Similarly, when Samarkand surrendered to the Arabic armies in 712, the amounts to be delivered were labeled in silver dirhams in the treaty, with immediately following rates of conversion for various goods by which the ransom would be actually paid, among which were standard Chinese silk rolls

(La Vaissière 2005: 271). During the periods of important Chinese colonial presence in central Asia, the Silk Road can be better described as an administrative delivery of cash to cover bargains made in different monetary zones.

Private trade

The question arises whether the trade in administrative silk existed on top of a flow created by the traders themselves. At any time over the long run, private trade from China to the West could be totally disturbed and indeed ruined by the intervention of the state. The sending of silk to the West by the Chinese army or the Chinese diplomacy at a cost paid by the state could only destroy the trading networks between inner China and central Asia. Conversely, it created opportunities for traders operating further west, from Chinese-controlled central Asia to the Middle and Near East, as exemplified by the willingness of Maniakh to be the *ortaq* of the Turkish *qaghan* between central Asia, Iran, and Byzantium. If we do not have any detail on precise individual traders in China ruined by such practices, it is clear from a social point of view that during the heyday of Chinese control of central Asia and sending 5 millions bolts to Gansu and Xinjiang annually, the sons of the western trading families established in China quit the job of traders and caravaneers to be hired into the administration or the army. The army had hired former caravaneers to help transport the huge loads of silk to the West. We do have precise social data on that phenomenon, which seems to confirm the above analysis of a ruin of the private networks caused by Chinese conquest of the West (La Vaissière and Trombert 2004: 958).

It should, however, be said too that these periods of administrative involvement in the West are on the whole infrequent, taking place in not more than four centuries out of fourteen centuries of Chinese interest in the West before the Mongols. In any case they are rarer than periods of tribute paid to nomads. The tributes themselves were quite fluctuating and most of the time not as important as those paid to the Turks or the Uighurs in periods of general political distress in northern China.

The normal situation should have been private trade. Unfortunately, we have no data, no account book or statistics, to evaluate the private flow. For the Tang period, the only quantitative data we know is that a rich trader in Paykant, a small trading Sogdian town near Bukhara, had 5,000 silk rolls at hand to reclaim his life from the invading Arab general Qutayba b. Muslim in the early eighth century (Ṭabarī II: 1188–1189). For the Mongol period we know some assets of rich Italian traders and companies in Italy, and the amount of some commendas to Iran, India, or western central Asia (Bautier 1970: Lopez 1943), but none actually from China. A theoretical example in the medieval trader handbook of the Genoese agent Pegolotti (1866), the *Practica della Mercatura*, gives, however, a capital of 25,000 golden florins to a trade venture by land to China in the first decades of the fourteenth century. In Islamic sources we do have a few actual examples, proving the much more important quantities transported by sea trade: a Karimi merchant made the sea route to China five times, and the last time in 1304 he brought back to Egypt "300 buhârs of silk [nearly 40 t.] 450 ratl of musk [195 kg] an enormous quantity of Chinese pottery, and a splendid collection of vessels of jade, inlaid with gold, consisting of large plates" (al-Khazraji, quoted in Lane and Serjeant 1948: 114). We know that the dues paid on these goods came to 300,000 dirhams, that is an amount quite equivalent – but for the taxes only! – to the 25,000 florins of capital of Pegolotti's example.

The chronology summarized above shows the strict dependency of this trade on the absence of political disturbance. Trade sharply declined or ceased completely in times of wars, pillages, invasions: after the invasion of Gansu by the northern Wei in 439, the central Asian traders there were captured and sent, together with a great part of the population of the province, to north-eastern China, and it is only a generation later that long-range contacts resumed and that the king of Sogdiana could send an embassy to reclaim them (*Weishu* 102.2270). Travel in these difficult times was only possible in huge caravans of hundreds of traders, with private guards, and pack animals, raising sharply the cost of transport, by contrast with the much smaller groups traveling quite freely (once they received their official passport) in less dangerous periods. Problems of trust over a long distance seem to have been solved on a familial basis.

Quantitative data

It would be extremely interesting to be able to evaluate the quantities of goods traveling on the Silk Road according to these various possibilities. If this is impossible, we do have, however, some ideas about the quantities officially sent to the West by the Chinese state. In the first half of the eighth century more than 5 million pieces of fabric – mostly silk, but also high-quality hemp cloth – were sent each year by the Tang on the Silk Road to pay for their troops and administration in Gansu and central Asia.

This amount should be compared with the numbers of rolls paid as tribute to the nomadic powers to the north. These numbers are usually quite vague.

For instance during the climax of Turkish power, in the 560s and 570s, a text says that the Zhou and the Qi, the two dynasties vying to control northern China, each paid the Turks 100,000 pieces of silk per year to assure their neutrality or possibly their services against the rival dynasty (*Zhoushu* 50.911). The two dynasties thus emptied their treasuries in order to obtain the good graces and military services of the Turks. The silk that Maniakh and his Sogdians proposed to the *qaghan* to sell in the Persian empire was this tribute silk. But 100,000 means here "a lot" rather than anything precise. For the first decades of the ninth century, however, we are on a firmer ground: Chinese sources mention the number of 500,000 silk rolls paid yearly to the Uyghurs (Beckwith 1991). This number is confirmed by an independent source, a Muslim ambassador to the Uyghur empire (Tamīn b. Baḥr, 1948: 283).

The Mongol period is quite different as silver and paper notes replaced silk as the currency, and indeed a silver road might have developed during this period through central Asia. However it seems that if we base ourselves not on texts written by medieval historians or writers but on actual Uyghur documents the taxes theoretically in silver were paid quite often in kind, and especially in silk yarn. The revival of Chinese silk on the European markets may be linked not only with the dynamics of the Muslim traders in the empire, but also with a phenomenon strictly similar to that testified for the Tang period, silk as currency (Schurmann 1956).

With these numbers it is clear that the periods of both Chinese military control in central Asia, and silk as a currency, should have seen the maximum flow of administrative silk to the West, that is in the Han and the Tang period. There is a one-to-ten range between the known numbers of silk as tribute and silk as currency. Even though the texts are silent on that, it might be not by chance that the Arabs pursued a very aggressive policy of military conquest in central Asia during the very period of climax of Tang silk despatch to the West, during the first half of the eighth century

The Chinese army in central Asia, with its huge expenditures in silk rolls, created some economic flows of bulk goods. For instance a routine army document describes how 600 kg of steel were sent from the Tian Shan to the Chinese army some 2,500 km further east (Trombert 2000: 99), and similarly a Sogdian king proposed to deliver grain over long distance to a campaigning Chinese army some 1,000 km to the northeast.

However, as regards quantities, caravan trade could carry much less than maritime transport. Take for instance a text describing a sixth-century huge caravan of 600 camels with its 240 Sogdian traders. It carried among other goods 10,000 rolls of silk, that is *c.* 5 tons of silk out a total possible load of *c.* 120 tons.

A bigger caravan is mentioned for the early tenth century between central Asia and the upper Volga, of *c.* 3,000 beasts of burden, which, if camels, could carry *c.* 600 tons. But the boat described in the unfortunately unique Muziris papyrus arriving from the Malabar coast of India *c.* 150 CE might have carried as much as a whole big caravan, and the average boat of the Roman trade with India 300 tons (De Romanis 2012). One hundred twenty such boats were sent annually to India in the first century CE, for a total freight of *c.* 36,000 tons; 180,000 camels would have been needed to compete. It is very clear from the sources that huge caravans were not frequent, and in the low periods of trans-Asian trade there were only a few of them each year. While caravan trade could not evolve technologically, the Chinese junks of the fourteenth century could carry three times as much as the Muziris boat (Sen 2006: 425).

Prices and costs

It has been possible to calculate that in a period of tranquility, the first half of the eighth century, the cost of transport added to the benefit of the traders doubled the cost of a bolt of silk between Dunhuang, at the eastern end of central Asia, and Samarkand, from 14 to 28 silver coins (La Vaissière 2005: 271), with the bias that silver was much rarer in Dunhuang. With the same data in Samarkand 1g of gold had the purchasing power of 84 g of silk. At the western end of the road, we do have also the maximum price fixed by law for silk in the Byzantine empire under Justinian, 8 nomismata a pound, that is 36.4 g of pure gold for 324 g of raw silk, a 1 to 9 ratio, and for a later period of Justinian's reign a 1 to 5 ratio (Oikonomides 1986: 34), proving the high volatility of prices depending on the political context (the wars with the Turks and the Persians of the Byzantine emperors were wars with the silk providers).

During the short revival of the Silk Road as a result of the security on the inland roads created by the Mongol unification of the steppe, that is from the 1290s to the early 1340s, just before it fell into disuse, the price of plain silk from China to Italy tripled (Lopez 1952: 75). The *Practica della Mercatura* describes quite precisely the security of the roads in the first half of the fourteenth century and gives an idea of the actual costs of transport once distinguished from the costs of security:

> You may calculate that a merchant with a dragoman [translator] and with two men servants, and with goods to the value of twenty-five thousand golden florins, should spend on his way to Cathay from sixty to eighty sommi [ingots] of silver, and not more if he manage well; and for all the road back again from Cathay to Tana [on the Azov sea], including the expenses of living and the pay

of servants, and all other charges, the cost will be about five sommi per head of pack animals, or something less. And you may reckon the sommo to be worth five golden florins, You may reckon also that each ox-waggon will require one ox, and will carry ten cantars Genoese weight; and the camel-waggon will require three camels, and will carry thirty cantars Genoese weight; and the horse-waggon will require one horse, and will commonly carry six and half cantars of silk, at 150 Genoese pounds to the cantar. And a bale of silk may be reckoned at between 110 and 115 Genoese pounds.

(Pegolotti 1866: 153–154)

This would mean an extremely low total cost of transport of about 3–4 percent for the Mongol part of the road.

A few years later, when troubles began to interrupt the transfer of silk bolts in the Mongol empire, the price of silk immediately doubled on the Italian markets.

Consequences on the economy: the early middle ages

The Chinese expansion in central Asia was discussed at the imperial court and various opinions were given in favor of or against the conquest. From these discussions, whether of Han or Tang times, it is quite clear that China never regarded these conquests as economically profitable. Pointed comments were made on their very high costs, while in favor of conquest only military and diplomatic reasons are actually given (Skaff 1998a: 62ff.). As external trade toward central Asia was totally dominated by the central Asian diaspora, there was no internal social incentive from Chinese traders in favor of the conquest. But trade is sometimes mentioned in some more precise discussions of these topics in the sources. To allow the flow of central Asian traders into China is one of the recurrent arguments in the texts: a blockade and high taxes raised by the king of Turfan was the reason put forward by the emperor for the conquest of the oasis in 640, although this move was resisted by some courtiers who insisted on the high cost of maintaining armies so far away from the central plain. Moreover, the Tang dynasty was aware of the useful-ness of these foreign traders for lowering the costs of maintaining armies: on the northeastern frontier, in Manchuria, far away from central Asia, the Tang had implemented a systematic policy of settling communities of foreign merchants (La Vaissière 2005: 143). An active commercial presence could have reduced the exorbitant costs of the Tang military presence in those distant regions. More generally, it is possible that the government had the

Sogdians inscribed on the population registers, in the same way as they had the Chinese, in order to make it easier to keep track of them and their movements within Chinese territory. The government also authorized these foreign merchants to pay in silver coins at markets. The spread of Sogdian commerce in the Chinese provinces and Sogdian control of certain aspects of commerce in the capital were the fruits of a deliberate Tang policy to advance the role of foreign merchants in commerce. While it is usually considered that the very negative attitudes of well-read Chinese toward the commercial professions came to an end only from the second half of the eighth century – a development which led to the merchant civilization of the Song in the eleventh century – in practice the Tang had in fact had recourse to the efficient services of these foreign merchants since their assumption of power (La Vaissière and Trombert: 2004).

We naturally wonder whether this development of Sogdian trade within China itself, and its interest in silk, led to an evolution toward some forms of early capitalism. Indeed, a text, quite isolated, and coming from a literary source, is intriguing:

> He Yuanming, from Dingzhou, was a very wealthy man. He managed three post-stations. Near each of them he established inns where merchants could stop, dealing especially with arriving Sogdians. [His] assets were enormous and in his house he had five hundred damask weaving machines.
> (*Taiping guangji*, Chapter 243, trs. in Qi 2005: 118)

It is presumed that He Yuanming was himself of Sogdian origin because of his name. This example shows an integration of distant trade with production, and a separation of capital from work. We have similar examples from tenth-century central Asia, but for regional trade only (Sims-Williams and Hamilton: 1990).

To calculate the global imbalance of Chinese involvement in the Silk Road is impossible given the paucity of our documents, but it would necessitate taking into account not only the actual enormous cost of maintaining the Chinese presence there, and the private trade of the central Asians on the caravan tracks, but also the participation of these central Asian traders in the trade in China, the possible increase of production – provided that the example of He Yuanming might be generalized – and the lowering of costs to China. While the Tang experienced some very powerful Chinese commercial companies, it seems nevertheless that the foreigners had something to propose that the Chinese could not. The Silk Road was also a road of commercial skills, the nature of which is unknown for lack of any juridical text.

It is obvious that international trade was an important part of the central Asian oasis activities and it has been assumed that trade played an important role in the development of these oasis states. But in fact we do not have any quantitative data, and the textual data on antiquity are very limited. We do have one textual proof that the economy of the Kroraina oasis kingdom in the third-century Tarim basin was dependent on Chinese silk for upper-level economic transactions. For the Tang period a Chinese pilgrim through central Asia wrote about Sogdiana that "Both parents and child plan how to get wealth, and the more they get the more they esteem each other . . . The strong bodied cultivate the land, the rest [half] engage in money-getting [business]." And later, with regard to Samarkand: "the precious merchandise of many foreign countries is stored up here." Other Chinese sources add "They excel at commerce and love profit; as soon as a man reaches the age of twenty, he leaves for the neighboring kingdoms; to every place that one can earn, they have gone." These testimonies are corroborated by other contemporary observations on the Sogdians. Thus, an Armenian geographer writes "The Sogdians are wealthy and industrious merchants who live between the lands of Turkestan and Ariana" (texts in La Vaissière 2005: 160).

However, it is still to be demonstrated that the global growth that central Asia undoubtedly experienced from the fourth to the tenth centuries is directly linked to international trade rather than agricultural new developments. For instance the expansion of the Sogdian settlements to the north, to Semirech'e region, the northern foothills of the Tian Shan (northern Kirghizia), is usually described as a consequence of the Silk Road going this way. However, archaeological excavations demonstrate that, from the beginning, these were agricultural ventures on virgin lands by nobles which created these towns, and that it is only later that traders made use of them as stopovers. Moreover if we turn toward the global, Asian, picture, this importance of international trade in central Asia has to be balanced by the relatively meager population of these regions. If the Sogdians might have numbered a few hundreds of thousands, Turfan, one of the turning points of the Silk Road, never housed more than a mere 50,000 inhabitants (Skaff 1998: 365ff.). These numbers should be compared to the 70–80 million of Han Chinese under the Tang (Pulleyblank 1961) and similarly the millions of inhabitants of the other great powers of the time. Even in Turfan, it was recently pointed out that most of the population had no link whatsoever with international trade (Hansen 2005).

But the focus of the argument on the economic importance of the Silk Road in the economic history of antiquity and middle ages has actually been on the receiving societies, not on China or the countries of the go-betweens. It has been argued that, whatever the small volume of luxury trade, its importance for the receiving societies was nevertheless enormous. Wallerstein, in dismissing luxury trade in favor of the trade of bulk goods, in his analysis of the capitalist growth of Europe in the sixteenth century would have grossly underestimated the fact that each unit of luxury good traveling afar conveyed an enormous value, compensating for the limited number of units. Moreover, in anthropological terms, the luxury items would have been essential tools of social discrimination (Schneider 1977). Indeed, the early middle ages is a good period to demonstrate this: in the Byzantine empire, silk garments were major political tools of the imperial order, with strict rules governing their use. A special official organization was created for dealing with silk trade and controlling distribution in the Byzantine empire (Oikonomides 1986: 34f.). Later, the various Muslim empires and the Mongols made use of the bestowal of luxury garments by the sovereign or his representatives as a major tool for distinguishing eminent members of the elite (Allsen 1997: 79f.). But this shift toward anthropological reasons leaves open the crucial question of whether or not silk itself induced a greater economic activity than other goods produced internally which might equally have been used as social discriminatory tools. To resort to silk might have weakened the internal growth of the receiving countries, the upper position in the hierarchy of goods being imported and so not playing any role in the growth of production in the country. The creation of an industry is a different point, which supposes a technological transfer – the well-known story of the monks bringing silkworm eggs to Byzantium hidden in their sticks – or at least a constant flow of raw material, which in the conditions of transport of the time meant production in neighboring countries. Before that transfer, and speaking of a very long-distance and fragile trade originating from faraway China, there is no reason to argue in favor of any economic growth induced by this luxury trade.

The Mongol mirage

The Mongol empire is obviously a different question. The traditional importance of imported luxury textiles as a social marker in nomadic societies, combined with the conquest of most of Eurasia, gave to the active pro-trade policy of the Mongols an impact unseen in previous centuries. The *ortaq* traders of the Mongolian princes, present in the whole empire, had for sure access to resources of gigantic scale. The policies of the Mongols were not limited to trade, but included also the major transfer of populations, and especially of weavers, as with the weavers from Herat, transported to Besh Baliq in 1221, north of Turfan (Allsen 1997: 40), or the Samarkandi transported north of Beijing (Pelliot 1927).

However, the greatest part of historiography has been marred by a Europe-centered vision of this trade. Indeed, due to the lack of actual documents on the trade with China, Marco Polo and Pegolotti's *Practica della mercatura* are regarded as the best testimonies on Mongol trade. Consequently, the importance of the northern direct road from the Italian colonies of the Black Sea to China has been exaggerated. The specialists of the Italian archives demonstrated more than forty years ago that the Chinese silk which arrived by this road was of bad quality, was actually cheaper on Italian markets than Middle Eastern silk, and that it never represented more than a limited part of the amount of silk available in Europe. From the archives of the main silk town of medieval Europe, Lucca, Bautier demonstrated that six camel-carts of raw silk a year were enough to provide Lucca with all the Chinese silk it needed (Bautier 1970: 289). The actual hinterland of the Italian cities of the Black Sea never went beyond Tabriz in Iran and Urganch south of the Arak Sea. Further east, for all the celebrity of Marco Polo, the number of actual Western traders who took this road up to China was very limited, and the Western colonies of Almaligh and Khanbaliq were not very populous (Petech 1962). Moreover, it has recently been argued that even as regards the Venetian and Genoese involvement on the Black Sea, long-distance trade was not the main reason for it but rather the regional and Mediterranean trade in bulk goods such as grain. Long-distance trade was a valuable add-on, but it was left to private merchants with no direct involvement of the two rival cities (Di Cosmo 2010). As regards Europe, the actual important trade was, as ever, a trade in bulk goods on the maritime margins of the Muslim and Byzantine lands, from Tana in the north to Syria in the south. What the *pax Mongolica* opened mainly was access to Iran, either directly from the northern Syrian coast, or through the Golden Horde. Pegolotti has a few paragraphs on the road to China, and pages on the road to Tabriz. As regards Asia, and the global picture, the main trade was as ever the Muslim one, and in second position, the Uyghur one. The picture is similar as regards the sea trade: at the end of the thirteenth century, Marco Polo reminds us that for one load of pepper exported to Europe from the Malabar coast, a hundred were exported to China.

That said, we are limited by the present state of the historiography. Except for the studies of Allsen, which are more qualitative than quantitative (Allsen 1997, 2001), very little has been done on the actual main commercial relationship in the Mongol period, that of China with Iran. It is to be hoped that hundreds of Persian, Chagatay, Arabic, or Armenian documents might be waiting to be read in manuscript and used for reconstruction of this trade from the point of view of an actual economic history of Asia. For want of these studies, it is nevertheless still possible to assert the importance of the trans-Asian exchanges by studying the flow of silver from China to the west, that is, mainly the Muslim Middle East. The Mongols created a gigantic secured commercial zone mainly between Ilkhanid territories in Iran, Iraq, and Syria, the Golden Horde in the western steppe, and China in which the currency was the silver ingot, the *som*, the consequence of which is visible in all the Eurasian mints, inside and outside the Mongol empire. In this first silver age, new coins with a very white silver coming probably from Yunnan were minted from Cyprus or Trabzon to Bangladesh, all over Asia in contact with the Mongol empire. The actual consequence of the Mongol "silk road" was actually a first silver age (Kuroda 2009).

Most of this silver went through the usual intermediaries of the Middle East. The reason for that is clear from Allsen's studies of the extraordinary desire for luxury Islamic textiles among the Mongol hierarchy. On top of tribute and deportations, the Mongols paid for the precious *nasîj* (gold brocade) textile of the Muslim world with their *sommo*, as well as with silk by way of the networks of the *ortaq* traders all over their empire. While the Middle East was draining Chinese silver, and certainly silk too, although we are lacking here the statistics we have for Europe from the Italian archives, it was also draining European silver. This phenomenon is ubiquitous in all the sources of this period, tons of silver being transferred toward the Middle East. We are, however, unable to discriminate between what was linked with the usual Mediterranean trade and what was actually linked with the Mongol Silk Road.

But two remarks should, however, be made to qualify the actual economic importance of the Mongol period in the long run. The first one is that it was quite limited in time: as regards the northern road, from China to the Black Sea as described by Pegolotti, it was in actual regular use for at most half a century – *c.* 1290–1343 – a period of safe travel itself interrupted by succession struggles, as noted by Pegolotti himself. The southern roads, through the Muslim parts of the empire, lasted only slightly longer, from *c.* 1260 to 1335. Afterwards, engulfed in political battles, both roads declined sharply, especially after the 1360s. The trade returned to Egypt and Syria (Ashtor 1983: 64ff.). The second and main point is that this trade was totally embedded in politics. The Mongols did not hesitate to ruin the Italian trading ports of the Black Sea, from which they obviously greatly benefitted, for purely political reasons – a contestation of the Mongol power there. Similarly, if we see the rising power of the *ortaq* as a powerful group at the Mongol courts in the Chinese and Persian sources, it is because the main aim of this group seems to have been to control the farming of the Chinese and Iranian taxes, not to create a safe legal environment for trade, and they usually lost everything as soon as the political tables turned. This is true even for major traders external to the system. For instance the head of the above-mentioned Tibi dynasty in the island of Qays was eager to farm the taxes of Fars, but eventually lost a lot of money from the political intrigues at the Mongol court, and finally the rival dynasty of Hormuz took over power in the Persian Gulf (Aubin 1953: 89–100). The crumbling of the central Asian silk trade during the period of disintegration of the Mongol empire in the 1340s proved also that the Mongol empire did not modify in the long run the organization of trade in Asia and might indeed have weakened it. The China trade reverted to the sea, never controlled by the Mongols.

The Mongol period is a political experiment in what could have been the trade policy of the first actual world empire; but the Western historiography is marred by its fascination with the great opening it represented for its own traders. Actually, if we are to evaluate the Mongol period globally, the reshuffle of the trading networks was most probably an artificial and ultimately a destructive one. Many of the main trading towns of central Asia, such as Samarkand or Balkh, or in Iran and Iraq – Baghdad – were destroyed, and the successor state of Tamerlane did no better. We do not know how the trading networks might have been reconstituted in central Asia after the end of the Mongol empire, but a limited revival took place in the early fifteenth century in the east (Rossabi 1990), while in the long run the Muslim traders developed a trade quite similar to what took place half a millennium previously in the Samanid period, a trade between Muslim Central Asia, Russia, and Siberia (Burton 1993).

Far from giving support to the grandiose theories that have been built on its importance, trade from China to the Near East was a discontinuous and quite often highly political phenomenon, which never allowed itself more than limited growth, mainly among the go-betweens. As regards the silk trade in antiquity and the middle ages, it cannot be demonstrated with the sources we have that it stimulated in itself growth in Iran or Byzantium. Moreover, transport and protection costs over such distances simply forbade any international specialization. The three periods of politically much reduced transportation costs do not show any proof of a systemic economic change and were not only entirely vulnerable to external political shocks but were political shocks in themselves.

Webs of knowledge

What did stimulate growth, however, was knowledge, the well-known transfer of actual techniques. The arrival of silk or paper technologies in the West did create new industries, if the arrival of Western cotton in medieval China did not. But it would be naïve to reconstruct a too direct causative link. Quite often the knowledge arrived, but no consequences followed. For instance we now have archival proof that paper was known in pre-Islamic Iran, but that it took several centuries for a take-off of its use. Another point is that quite often these transfers were not directly linked with trade itself except for the knowledge of the road: refugees, migrations, religious networks were as much or even more important. Some refugees transmitted the secrets of glass-making to China, some monks transmitted silk technology to Byzantium, some pilgrims expanded the *qarez* irrigation techniques all along the Hajj networks.

In fact what have mattered more is something broader, the sheer knowledge of the existence of others, a basic geography of the world that diplomacy and trade created, especially among the Middle Eastern countries situated in between all the contacts. As early as late antiquity, an image of the world was created, with the idea of the four (or more) kings of the world (Chinese, Indian or Iranian, Nomad, Greek), probably originating from India, and pervading the whole Asian continent up to the tenth century: this is known from Umayyad palaces to Chinese Buddhist texts or Sogdian paintings (La Vaissière 2006). Among this division of the world it is remarkable that the Chinese were par excellence the gifted craftsmen, while the nomads provided professional warriors. Whatever quantities might have traveled on an irregular basis, an international division of labor was contemplated, even if not actually realized. The Muslim geographers inherited from this basic geography and developed their much broader vision of the world. They had an actual, if patchy, knowledge of the whole Eurasian and African landmass, from Japan to Madagascar and Senegal. Their central position allowed them to control the flow of data between the various great blocks during most of the middle ages. The Mongol invasion broke this monopoly on knowledge.

After the failure of the twelfth-century attempts of the Sicilian kings to integrate Muslim geographical knowledge into the Christian world, the novelty of the thirteenth century in Europe was the discovery of the possibility of trade, which proved to be more important in the long run than the actual trade. This is what led the Portuguese around Africa to the Indian Ocean, in search of spices and Christians. Two centuries after the failed attempt of the

Genoese Vivaldi brothers, but in direct intellectual continuity, Bartolomeu Dias and Vasco De Gama managed to pass into the Indian Ocean. Similarly the Spanish went to America with a Genoese navigator, Christopher Columbus, this stranded medieval traveler, who had learned his purely medieval geography of the world from the fourteenth-century *Ymago mundi* of Pierre d'Ailly. In a striking symmetrical attempt to break Muslim centrality, the early Ming supported the maritime expeditions of Zheng He (1405–1433), which made use of the Muslim knowledge of the maritime roads for the benefit of the Chinese empire.

In a way, and as the Ming eventually put an end to these attempts, it might be argued that the *mirabilia* of Marco Polo in the long run mattered more than the redirections of trade forcefully implemented by the Mongol nobility: not actually the goods that these marginal Genoese and Venetian traders brought back, but the knowledge of a world beyond the Muslim world, the depth of Asia totally forgotten since Theophylact Simocatta's depiction of the Turks and China during the second stage of the Silk Road. It seems to be a mistake to try to link with a single economic reasoning the actual inland trade of the Mongol period seen from an economic perspective and the economic expansion of sixteenth-century Europe. By the thirteenth century the important trade was already the maritime one, and its importance was only to grow, as the caravan trade had reached its technological limits half a millennium before Gengis Khan. But to understand the actual link between the inland Silk Road and the growth of Europe, we have to step outside economic history, and take into account the mobilizing power of the newly created *Ymago mundi*.

References

All the Chinese texts are quoted according to the standard Zhonghua Shuju edition.

Aigle, D. (2005). *Le Fārs sous la domination mongole. Politique et fiscalité (XIIIe-XIVe s.)*, Cahier de Studia Iranica 31. Paris: Association pour l'Avancement des Études Iraniennes.

Allsen, T. (1989). "Mongolian Princes and Their Merchant Partners, 1200–1260," *Asia Major* 2(2): 83–126.

   (1997). *Commodity and Exchange in the Mongol Empire: A Cultural History of Islamic Textiles.* Cambridge University Press.

   (2001). *Culture and Conquest in Mongol Eurasia.* Cambridge University Press.

Ashtor, E. (1983). *Levant Trade in the Later Middle Ages.* Princeton University Press.

Aubin, J. (1953). "Les princes d'Ormuz du XIIIe au XVe s.," *Journal Asiatique* 241: 177–238.

Bautier, R.-H. (1970). "Les relations économiques des Occidentaux avec les pays d'Orient, au Moyen Âge, points de vue et documents," in M. Mollat (ed.), *Sociétés et compagnies de commerce en Orient et dans l'Océan Indien. Actes du huitième colloque international d'histoire maritime.* Paris: SEVPEN, pp 263–331.

Beckwith, C. (1991). "The Impact of the Horse and Silk Trade on the Economies of T'ang China and the Uighur Empire," *Journal of the Economic and Social History of the Orient* 34: 183–198.

Burton, A. (1993). *Bukharan Trade, 1558–1718*. Bloomington, IN: Indiana University Press.

Cosmas Indicopleustes (1968–1973). Trs. W. Wolska-Conus, *Topographie chrétienne*, 3 vols. Sources Chrétiennes, 141, 159, 197. Paris: Éditions du Cerf.

De Romanis, F. (2012). "Playing Sudoku on the Verso of the 'Muziris papyrus': Pepper, Malabathron and Tortoise Shell in the Cargo of the Hermapollon," *Journal of Ancient Indian History* 27: 75–101.

Di Cosmo, N. (2010). "Black Sea Emporia and the Mongol Empire: A Reassessment of the Pax Mongolica," *Journal of the Economic and Social History of the Orient* 53: 83–108.

Endicott-West, E. (1989). "Merchant Associations in Yüan China: The Ortog," *Asia Major* 2(2): 127–154.

Hamilton, J. (1986). *Manuscrits ouïgours du IXe Xe siècle de Touen Houang*. Paris: Peeters.

Hansen, V. (2005). "The Impact of the Silk Road Trade on a Local Community: The Turfan Oasis, 500–800," in E. de la Vaissière and E. Trombert (eds.), *Les Sogdiens en Chine*. Paris: EFEO, pp. 283–310.

Herrmann, G. (1968). "Lapis-Lazuli: The Early Phases of its Trade," *Iraq* 30: 21–57.

Jacoby, D. (2004). "Silk Economics and Cross-Cultural Artistic Interaction: Byzantium, the Muslim World, and the Christian West," *Dumbarton Oaks Papers*, 58: 197–240.

   (2010). "Oriental Silks Go West: A Declining Trade in the Later Middle Ages," in C. Schmidt Arcangeli and G. Wolf (eds.), *Islamic Artefacts in the Mediterranean World: Trade, Gift, Exchange and Artistic Transfer*. Venice: Marsilio, pp. 71–88.

Kervran, M. (1994). "Forteresses, entrepôts et commerce. Une histoire à suivre depuis les rois sassanides jusqu'aux princes d'Ormuz," *Itinéraires d'Orient. Hommages à Claude Cahen*. Res Orientales vi. Bures-sur-Yvette: GECMO, pp. 325–351.

   (1999), "Caravansérails du delta de l'Indus. Réflexions sur l'origine du caravansérail islamique," *Archéologie islamique* 8–9: 143–176.

Kuroda, A. (2009). "The Eurasian Silver Century, 1276–1359: Commensurability and Multiplicity," *Journal of Global History* 4: 245–269.

La Vaissière, É. de (2005). *Sogdian Traders: A History*. Leiden: Brill.

   (2006). "Les Turcs, rois du monde à Samarcande," in M. Compareti and É. de la Vaissière (eds.), *Royal Nawruz in Samarkand: Proceedings of the conference held in Venice on the pre-Islamic painting at Afrasiab*. Supplemento 1, *Rivista degli Studi Orientali*, vol. 78. Pisa/Rome: 147–162.

La Vaissière, É. de and E. Trombert (2004). "Des Chinois et des Hu. Migrations et intégration des Iraniens orientaux en milieu chinois durant le Haut Moyen-Âge," *Annales. Histoire, Sciences Sociales*, 59(5–6): 931–969.

Lane, A. and R. B. Serjeant (1948). "Pottery and Glass Fragments from Littoral, with Historical Notes," *Journal of the Royal Asiatic Society of Great Britain and Ireland*, 2: 108–133.

Lin, M. (1985). *Loulan Niya chutu wenshu*. Beijing: Wenwu chubanshe.

Lopez, R. (1952). "China Silk in Europe in the Yuan Period," *Journal of the American Oriental Society* 72: 72–76.

Lopez, R. S. (1943). "European Merchants in the Medieval Indies: The Evidence of Commercial Documents," *Journal of Economic History* 3: 164–184.

Menander Protector (1985). In R. C. Blockley (trs.), *The History of Menander the Guardsman*. ARCA, 17. Liverpool: Francis Cairns.

Oikonomides, N. (1986). "Silk Trade and Production in Byzantium from the Sixth to the Ninth Century: The Seals of Kommerkiarioi," *Dumbarton Oaks Papers* 40: 33–53.

Pegolotti, F. B. (1866). *Cathay and the Way Thither*, trs. H. Yule, vol. III. London: Hakluyt Society, pp. 143–173.

Pelliot, P. (1927). "Une Ville musulmane dans la Chine du Nord sous les Mongols," *Journal asiatique* 21(1): 261–279.

Petech, L. (1962). "Les marchands italians dans l'empire mongol," *Journal asiatique* 250: 549–574.

Pliny (1945). *Natural History*, vol. IV, books 12–16, trans. H. Rackham. Loeb Classical Library 370. Cambridge, MA: Harvard University Press, p. 63.

Pulleyblank, E. (1961). "Registration of Population in China in the Sui and Tang Periods," *Journal of the Economic and Social History of the Orient* 4: 289–301.

Qi, D. (2005). "The Hejiacun Treasure and Sogdian Culture," in É. de la Vaissière and E. Trombert (eds.), *Les Sogdiens en Chine*. Paris: EFEO, pp. 107–121.

Rossabi, M. (1990). "The Decline of the Central Asian Caravan Trade," in J. Tracy (ed.), *The Rise of Merchant Empires: Long-Distance Trade in the Early Modern World*. Cambridge University Press, pp. 351–371.

Schafer, E. (1963). *The Golden Peaches of Samarkand: A Study of T'ang Exotics*. Berkeley: University of California Press.

Schneider, J. (1977). "Was There a Precapitalist World-System?," *Peasant Studies* 6(1): 20–29.

Schurmann, H. (1956). "Mongolian Tributary Practices of the Thirteenth Century," *Harvard Journal of Asiatic Studies* 19(3/4): 304–389.

Sen, T. (2006). "The Formation of Chinese Maritime Networks to Southern Asia, 1200–1450," *Journal of the Economic and Social History of the Orient* 49(4): 421–453.

Sidebotham, S. (2011). *Berenike and the Ancient Maritime Spice Route*. Berkeley: University of California Press.

Sims-Williams, N. and J. Hamilton (1990). *Documents turco-sogdiens du IXe–Xe siècle de Touen-houang*, Corpus Inscriptionum Iranicarum, II/III. London: SOAS.

Skaff, J. (1998a). "Straddling Steppe and Sown: Tang China's Relations with the Nomads of Inner Asia (640–756)." Unpublished dissertation, University of Michigan.

(1998b). "Sasanian and Arab Sasanian Silver Coins from Turfan: Their Relationship to International Trade and the Local Economy," *Asia Major* 9(2): 67–115.

Sokolovskaia, L. and A. Rougeulle (1992). "Stratified Finds of Chinese Porcelains from Pre-Mongol Samarkand (Afrasyab)," *Bulletin of the Asia Institute* 6: 87–98.

Ṭabarī (1879–1901). *Tārīkh al Rusul wa'l Mulūk*, ed. M. J. de Goejer *et al.*, 15 vols. Leiden: Brill.

Tamīn b. Baḥr (1948). In V. Minorsky (trs.), "Tamīn ibn Baḥr's Journey to the Uyghurs," *Bulletin of the School of Oriental and African Studies* 12(2): 275–305.

Trombert, É. (2000). "Textiles et tissus sur la Route de la Soie. Éléments pour une géographie de la production et des échanges," in M. Cohe, J. P. Drège, and J. Giès (eds.), *La Sérinde, terre d'échanges*. Paris: La documentation française, pp. 107–120.

Vaṣṣāf, Tajziyat al-amṣār wa-tazjiyat al-aʿṣār (1871), trs. H. M. Elliot, in *The History of India, as told by its Own Historians. The Muhammadan Period*. London: Trubner & Co.

Whitehouse, D. and A. Williamson (1973) "Sasanian Maritime Trade," *Iran* 11: 29–49.

6

China before capitalism

R. B. WONG

Introduction

Did capitalism cause industrialization? Was it either necessary or sufficient? Many of our responses to such questions depend upon how we account for technological change between the sixteenth and nineteenth centuries. If we think that capitalism as an economic system made possible the technological changes leading to industrialization, then Europe had capitalism and no other world region did. If capitalism as practiced in Europe did not produce the crucial technological changes, we can possibly use the term "capitalism" to describe economic practices in other world regions; at a minimum we can disentangle the issues of explaining industrialization from those of explaining capitalism. The advantages of separating capitalism from industrialization are even clearer when we move to the twentieth century and consider the Soviet and Chinese industrialization experiences. If we accept the premise that capitalism was neither necessary nor sufficient to create industrialization, we can frame our understanding of how they are connected to each other in nineteenth-century western Europe and North America by looking to earlier periods, both within and beyond Western settings.

Industrialization requires the mobilization and concentration of capital. Large private firms and well-developed financial markets of the second half of the nineteenth century confirm a good fit between the demands of industrialization and the institutions of capitalism. The repeated episodes of major technological change that enabled the creation of new industries, markets, and products depended on financing of multiple kinds best achieved with well-developed capital markets. Modern economic growth is impossible to imagine without sophisticated financial markets and large firms, some of which dominate their markets. This intimate connection between capitalism and modern economic growth has been read backward into earlier eras of history, leading economic historians of many world regions to search for institutions and practices similar to those found in Europe. Some of these scholarly practices implicitly move through respecifications of an empirical proposition: (1) early modern European capitalist practices created economic growth and dynamism to (2) only early modern European capitalist practices could create economic growth to (3) the absence of early modern European capitalist practices means the absence of economic growth.

Through an assessment of Chinese economic history before the late nineteenth-century development of capitalist firms and markets transforming China's economy, this chapter seeks to query this sequence of propositions. To do so I make a distinction between economic growth as a general category and industrialization as a more specific species of economic growth. I put forward that the Chinese economy had three of the four features that editor Larry Neal has suggested we find in capitalism. Their presence in an economy that is not capitalist, at least by the criterion of having large firms able to amass large amounts of capital and control major portions of their markets, means that one can find private property rights, enforceable contracts, and price-setting markets outside capitalist systems. Neal's fourth feature of "supportive governments" is more complicated to assess. It makes little sense, at least to me, to consider as "support" any government policies and activities that are not implemented with the purpose of affecting economic conditions and possibilities. By this criterion, the role of war-making by early modern European states, whatever its positive economic consequences, in large measure probably does not qualify as government support for a healthy economy able to grow – unless we look only at winners and discount the losses suffered by competing actors motivated to achieve the gains that went to others.

For evaluating the possibilities of economic growth before industrialization, the efficacy of the institutions of private property, contract enforcement, and price-setting markets all matter. The Chinese economy did in fact exhibit all these features without, however, also creating large concentrations of capital by firms able to dominate particular markets. How China mobilized and managed natural and financial resources in the absence of the kinds of capital markets and firms controlling large amounts of capital that we see in early modern Europe shows a government support for economic growth that we do not find in Europe. While these Chinese fiscal mechanisms are not in any simple sense substitutes, they help us to understand how the early modern Chinese economy was able to grow without the institutions of European commercial capitalism. In addition, the presence of commercial capitalism in Europe did not mean that those economies especially advanced in commercial capitalism also necessarily took the lead in creating industrial capitalism, as the Dutch case reminds us. Finally, the ideas and institutions animating Chinese political economy before the late nineteenth century continue to be key conceptual resources and material practices in China's twentieth-century economic transformation, even if less obviously so than the case of European movements from commercial to industrial capitalism. Without recognition of the relevance of late imperial Chinese political economy to subsequent economic change, it remains too easy to assume that early modern Chinese practices present problems and that modern foreign institutions introduce possibilities. Half-truths get us only half way.

Agriculture and rural craft production

One of the European images of imperial despots that recurs from the early modern era forward is of a ruler who owns all the land in his realm. There is no private property in the eastern empires of some European imaginations, nor really any distinction between the ruler's wealth and that of his government. Certainly for China, the image of a ruler controlling all the resources of his realm as he wishes, with the ability to appropriate people's land at whim, is ill conceived. Early imperial rulers pursued with some success the promotion of independent peasant farming households which they could tax to support their government. But these rulers were vulnerable to the power of the empire's land-rich families to shut the state and its bureaucratic rule out of their territories. In subsequent centuries, political ideology stressed a society of smallholders to support the government, while the agrarian reality included the persistence and in some places even growth of large estates. Some of the peasants working the land of these estates were subjected to a servile status that limited their mobility and their incomes (Wu Tingyu 1987). The structural persistence of large land holding would persist in multiple forms into China's late imperial period, in global terms the early modern era, but despite these challenges, agricultural taxes would supply at least half and often more than two-thirds of state revenues between the late fourteenth and early nineteenth centuries. The late imperial state was able to some degree to meet the early imperial aspiration of basing its fiscal support on peasant farming households. From the tenth through the thirteenth centuries, however, direct agricultural taxation proved less important than either early imperial aspirations would have led us to expect or late imperial practices would demonstrate.

Whatever the disparities in land ownership between the richest and poorest strata of rural society, the scale of agricultural cultivation was almost always small plots tended by individual farming households. The social organization of agricultural production was based on family farming across varied ecological conditions. Improved technologies of tilling, sowing, fertilizing, weeding, and harvesting spread across the empire after the third century, but always enabling improvements for family farming, not creating alternative forms of agriculture. By the tenth century a contrast began to emerge between the northern half of the empire, dominated by dry-field farming, and the spread in the south of irrigated paddy agriculture, a phenomenon that has led some scholars to argue for a Chinese agricultural revolution between the eighth and twelfth centuries (Elvin 1973: 113–130). This "revolution" involved improvements in soil preparation, the more extensive use of fertilizers, and the development of new seed strains offering higher, more consistent, or earlier-ripening harvests. In the south especially it meant the improvement of hydraulic technologies and more elaborate irrigation networks. Finally, the growth of commercial demand for cash crops beyond basic food grains encouraged the exploitation of lands previously uncultivated.

This set of Chinese agricultural changes, be they considered a revolution or not, came several centuries before the early modern European agricultural changes, also considered a revolution by some scholars. Both of these transformations saw improved technologies making possible higher agricultural outputs which in turn were connected to increased commercial circulation of grain and the abilities of agriculture in some parts of China and Europe to support larger urban populations not needing to grow their own food. In other ways, however, the Chinese agricultural changes were different. First, they required more technological change and financial investment because the requirements of extending irrigation technologies across larger and varied landscapes required capital to build and subsequently to maintain. Second, the Chinese agricultural revolution raised productivity and expanded production without changing the basic organization of production by the agricultural peasant household; it promoted the viability of an existing social order rather than promoting social change in the manner of the English enclosures. Third, and perhaps most surprisingly, three basic features of the eighteenth-century changes in European agricultural technology were previously used together in north China and they appear together nowhere else – the plow with a curved iron mold-board, the seed-drill, and the horse-hoe (Bray 1984: 566). What were other revolutionary developments for Chinese many centuries earlier, such as irrigation technologies, were by and large not technologies that Europeans employed, if at all, until well after their agricultural revolution.

The expansion of agriculture in Song dynasty (960–1279) China, together with improvements in transport, made possible the creation of new kinds of commercially oriented cities in which craft production reached new levels of output. These developments were jointly enabled by the efforts of common people to develop cash-cropping and craft production and government projects to improve the waterways for the transportation of goods over long distances. New institutions facilitated the growth of trade within the empire and from coastal areas to areas beyond the empire (Elvin 1973: 131–199). The development of paddy agriculture allowed the more intensive use of land for rice production. While specialists differ in their assessments of how widespread the growing of paddy rice became during the Song, they affirm that the scale of rice production grew enough to support long-distance trade in rice by merchants who purchased rice from both peasants and richer households and sold rice to brokers who in turn supplied retail shops in towns and cities. The expansion of agriculture also included the opening of new dry land fields and the growing of cash crops. Increased textile craft production was made possible by increased planting of cotton, hemp, and the raising of silkworms. Food crops beyond grains became commercial; sugarcane was planted in southern parts of the empire, while fruits and vegetables were grown in many areas. Chinese consumption of medicinal plants and herbs also expanded commercially in this period, as did commercial fisheries. Forest lands were planted commercially with trees and bamboo; these provided raw materials used in making paper, lacquer, and baskets (Qi Xia 1987: 139–181).

The expansion of the market in mid-imperial China certainly did not affect all parts of the empire to the same degree any more than commerce was widespread in medieval Europe. Evidence of commercial growth in many parts of the empire does, however, make clear that a familiar combination of agricultural growth, urbanization, and craft expansion were all taking place in mid-imperial China. Commercial growth depended to some extent upon the creation of credit instruments that allowed merchants to sell goods in one area and be paid in another. The use of credit compensated for the inability of the copper and iron coin supply to expand at a pace needed to support the growing commercial economy. The development of these credit policies was intimately connected to the Song state's growing appetite for resources as it faced military threats. The state paid for frontier military supplies with vouchers that could be redeemed elsewhere in the empire, often for other goods the state also controlled. A secondary market for buying and selling credit instruments developed. The state's continued efforts to expand its revenue ultimately included an excess of printing paper money which undermined the monetary and credit systems (Mou 2002). Before reaching that point, however, the state proved aggressively able for some two centuries to take advantage of the empire's expanding market economy.

Economic expansion depended crucially on the spread of intensive agricultural production. The impact of increased abilities to shape the natural environment through water control projects yielded both clear and positive economic gains and generated less visible and more troubling environmental problems. For example, the reclamation of land along the lower reaches of the Yangzi River began in the eighth century and was largely completed by the thirteenth century. Additional land reclamation occurred along the edges of the Hangzhou Bay to the river's south (Shiba 1998). The creation of polder lands resembled in many ways the Golden Age Dutch projects of land reclamation from the North Sea that took place some eight centuries after such projects began along the Yangzi (de Vries and Woude 1997: 27–32). The initial work of constructing sea walls, cutting channels, and enclosing land was undertaken by officials who mobilized the labor and capital to reclaim land. The purpose of this investment was not simply to create economic opportunities for peasants; it was to enable more peasants to pay taxes. For more than a century beginning in 1263 the Yuan and Ming governments depended heavily on the grain levied from irrigated lands in six prefectures along the Yangzi River. In Yuan times, of the nearly 40 percent of the empire's revenues that came from grain in this area, some 40 percent was from lands over which the state claimed direct ownership (Shiba 1998).

For subsequent centuries, evidence is available for how communities managed and paid for the use of the dyke systems that regulated the influx and outflow of water from paddy lands. Some did so by apportioning levies on households according to the amount of land they had benefitting from the system (Li 2012). Such systems could be sustained economically and environmentally for considerable periods. From one perspective we could think of such community arrangements as an example of the effectiveness of community institutions and hence a kind of customary activity, but we could equally consider this to be a basic benefits / cost-driven system that emulated the fee for service that a single-source provider might develop in a market setting. The state also played a role in water management, but the levels of effort it made ebbed and flowed. After an eighteenth-century era of official oversight, the state was largely conceding management control over water control projects during the nineteenth century to local elites (Morita Akira 2002). This kind of self-management paralleled in broad measure steps the government was also taking to remove some of its oversight on certain types of community-based granaries which stored grain for use during the lean spring season and to be called upon especially in years of bad harvest (Will and Wong 1991). For water control this political disengagement meant that elites could manage community resources for their own benefit without the presence of officials as arbiters of different interests. But it also meant that people, especially richer and more powerful individuals, could take advantage of the state's less visible presence to capture profits from creating paddy lands through draining swamps and building enclosures.

In the mid-Yangzi region, for example, there were two waves of expanding rice cultivation through the creating of paddy lands, one beginning in the late fourteenth century and ending in the early seventeenth century and a second beginning in the late seventeenth and eighteenth centuries with a decline by the late nineteenth century. This effort was part of a broader empire-wide initiative of the first Ming emperor (r. 1368–1398) to create a temporary bureaucracy of officials who organized the building and repair of 40,987 reservoirs and dams, 4,162 canals and 5,418 dykes and embankments in different parts of the empire. As the basic infrastructure for water control management was completed or repaired it fell upon local people to continue the maintenance and sometimes expansion of the water control projects. The power of elites to act in their own interest in ways that disadvantaged others meant that officials were in some cases inclined to use coercion in order to impose a different allocation of benefits. The state's use of command was intended to define a more general public interest threatened by private profit seekers upsetting an ecological balance by rendering an area more vulnerable to flooding (Perdue 1982; Will 1985).

The development of water control projects to increase the productivity of crop land and to improve transportation routes involved a mix of state command to marshal resources and labor to execute large projects and local community efforts to manage the costs and benefits of irrigation channels crucial to rice paddy agriculture. Both state and community efforts at water control were tied to market production and exchange. Top-down organizational efforts initiated by officials as well as the bottom-up organizational practices of local elites and common people served to maintain and expand a market economy in which many commodities, both crops and crafts, came from agrarian households that served as the primary units of commercial production and consumption. Beyond the state's varied roles in water control projects that became economically important by the mid-imperial period, officials of the early modern era promoted the spread of best practices to more backward areas. These efforts included seed selection and crop cultivation as well as handicraft technologies. Officials as well as literati compiled agricultural handbooks detailing information on crops and cultivation methods. The botanical encyclopedia published in 1708, *Guang Qunfangpu* [Enlarged Flora] included sections on grains, textile fiber plants, vegetables, and trees. The Qianlong emperor personally wrote the preface for a wide-ranging compilation on agriculture entitled *Shoushi tongkao* [Compendium of Work and Days] (Deng 1993).

The sparse data available to calculate or infer levels of land productivity suggest improvements in at least some areas between the tenth and eighteenth centuries. Some of the few scholars who have assembled scattered information disagree over the relative importance of technology improvements and productivity gains (Li Bozhong 2003; Liu 2013). Whatever the precise levels of productivity and their changes over time or variations among regions, the land could be more densely settled in paddy agriculture regions than in dry farm areas. The increasing development of household-based craft production in the early modern era created an agrarian economy in which markets proved basic institutions, supported in large measure by state policies recognizing the benefits of market exchange.

The early modern growth of an agrarian empire's commercial economy

Between the sixteenth and eighteenth centuries, the development of market towns through which cash crops and crafts moved to locales nearby and distant could be found in many parts of the empire. Some areas, like Jiangnan, the area around today's Shanghai, or the Pearl River delta region, in which is located today's Guangzhou, developed more markets and trade than areas of northwest or southwest China. But even the least commercialized parts of the empire were not innocent of trade developments. Other regions, like north China and the southeast coast, had active commercial economies and in both cases these were tied to trade across the empire's frontiers. In the north China province of Shandong, for instance, peasant households developed crafts and food processing activities to complement their crop cultivation. They engaged in cotton or silk cloth production, paper-making, tobacco or grain processing, and making incense or pottery production. Those near the sea included commercial fishermen as well as households that produced salt. Specialized markets for grain and cotton attest to the commercial circulation of daily use items; there were markets at which peasant households could buy soy beans for fertilizer cakes, raw materials like cotton for handicraft production, and implements used to crop the land (Xu Tan 1998). In central China an expansion of commerce was powered by the increased production of rice made possible through increased paddy rice cultivation beginning in the sixteenth and seventeenth centuries and becoming important nationally by the eighteenth century as a key source of food supply for the empire's major commercial region, downstream along the Yangzi River. In addition to this major long-distance trade based on the rice that peasant households grew to sell on the market, other households began planting and selling other cash crops, including cotton, tobacco, and tea. On the region's markets other crops and crafts produced in the region circulated, including hemp cloth, iron, coal, and paper, as well as commodities brought into the region, such as salt (Ren Fang 2003). Beyond the villages of peasants planting crops and producing crafts, there were households engaged in mining and fishing. The early Ming vision of a settled agrarian society was transformed into a related but different reality of commercialized agrarian society in which the movements of goods and resources was a basic feature of a settled society largely composed of peasant households.

China's most developed markets were in the lower Yangzi region, commonly called Jiangnan. Specialized markets for raw cotton, silk thread and mulberry leaves, grain, silk cloth, cotton cloth, tea, and other daily life commodities were formed in addition to more general markets where indigo, seed oils for cooking, and paper products also flourished. Jiangnan markets were connected to markets in other parts of the empire. Jiangnan merchants went to other parts of the empire and merchant groups from other parts of the empire came to Jiangnan. Jiangnan trade also went overseas (Fan Jinmin 1998; Zhang Haiying 2002). Some of the rural craft production in Jiangnan households was no doubt of a higher quality than found elsewhere in the empire. The connections between such textile-producing peasant households and urban firms that completed some production processes created a tighter and denser set of production relationships than was typical of other places. But even in these highly commercialized conditions, production and exchange supported the viability of an agrarian society composed of small peasant households. More generally across the empire peasant households were connected to market exchange. Many produced cash crops; still others engaged in craft production. Hill lands were brought under expanded cultivation for tea, tobacco, and indigo used to dye cotton blue. All peasant households had to buy at markets their iron implements for crop cultivation and their pottery for food consumption and storage. Peasant households were thus both market producers and market consumers.

The maritime trade of merchants in the southeastern coastal province of Fujian allows us to consider trade networks from the vantage point of one particular area that engaged both in trade within the empire and beyond. The growing eighteenth-century trade with Taiwan, administratively part of Fujian province in the eighteenth century, brought Taiwanese rice and sugar onto mainland markets. The commodities moving north along the coast included items from southeast Asia, such as sapanwood, sharks' fins, pepper, tin, and frankincense, but Fujian products were more abundant, including tea, tobacco, textiles, paper, earthenware, preserves and candies, medicinal herbs, and fruits, many of these products being particular local specialities. Some ships went to Tianjin and others went further north to Manchuria. The return voyages brought back craft and crop goods particular to northern and Yangzi region locales – various kinds of silk and satin, medicinal herbs, wheat, beans, salt, red dates, and dried mussels (Ng 1983:133–167).

Some sophisticated production took place in specialized sites separated from agriculture. State demand for elegant silks and refined pottery helped spur the production of quality products. We know from the continued and changing production of pottery and textiles that the Chinese must have had the capacity to impart knowledge about sophisticated production techniques. Clearly the levels of sophistication in ceramics production, especially porcelain at Jingdezhen, and in the range of silk fabrics produced in Jiangnan cities and towns, suggests the generation and transmission of considerable technological knowledge (Fan Shuzhi 1990: 188–231; Finlay 2010; Liang Miaotai 1991). But to date we lack the kind of empirical details for technical knowledge transmission that allow us to make comparably documented Chinese comparisons with European practices. It appears that Chinese craft guilds were not as serious or successful at protecting knowledge within the guild as were European guilds. The movement from urban to rural setting of technologies that could be pursued in rural households was a basic feature of early modern Chinese history, most visible in cotton textiles. We also see the development of multiple centers of pottery production, among which some sharing of techniques seems the only reasonable way to account for the similarities of patterns even if not the same level of technical sophistication. The influence of state production and consumption was not limited to textiles and pottery. The emperors also enjoyed receiving gifts of watches and automatons. Because these devices frequently broke down the court had to develop repair shops; from learning how to repair these mechanisms, Chinese craftsmen developed abilities to make these gadgets themselves. From the imperial household the technologies spread to craftsmen working in wealthy

Jiangnan and to the southern port of Guangzhou who met the taste for clocks among wealthy consumers that began in both Jiangnan and south China (Pagani 2001). During the eighteenth century, foreigners could even buy these "foreign" goods in China had their own presents brought from Europe not survived the journey.

At the same time as the Chinese court's attraction to foreign mechanical devices spread into society more generally, the silks and porcelains produced for the court by special workshops spawned broader craft industries that fashioned products in great demand in early modern Europe and colonial America. These silks and porcelains joined other craft goods produced both by highly skilled artisans as well as those made in peasant households, as commodities entering long-distance trade circuits. Within the empire, grain was also an extremely common good traded over long distances. Several regionally identified merchant groups pursued trade, either within their own provinces or in some cases on a broader spatial scale. The two largest groups were Shanxi merchants and Huizhou merchants (Zhang Haipeng and Wang Yanyuan 1995; Huang Jianhui 2002). The Shanxi merchants established themselves by transporting grain to the troops stationed in northwest China. For this service they received licenses to buy salt. In addition Shanxi merchants began to develop Chinese trade in tea and textiles with Mongolians and Russians. Huizhou merchants from Anhui province also became involved in the salt trade as well as many other trades in the southern half of the empire. Additional merchants from Fujian were major actors in the maritime trade between coastal China and southeast Asia. Contrary to the image of China being closed off to foreign trade after the government's halting of Zheng He's early fifteenth-century expeditions, private trade continued, at times expanding and at others contracting, influenced in part by the degree to which the state attempted to restrict private overseas trade.

The country's main commercial routes followed rivers. The most important was the Yangzi River and the tributaries that feed the river in its upper and mid reaches. The Huai and Yellow rivers in the north and Pearl River in the south all had commerce flow along them, as did several other rivers in the northeast and central parts of the empire. In addition to riverine commerce, there were major commercial routes that went from the southwest through central China to the capital in Beijing, routes from Urumuqi in the northwest to both Beijing and Shanghai, and routes across north China (Niu Guanjie 2008). To the west of Urumuqi lay the central Asian oases especially famous in earlier centuries for comprising the Silk Road. Beyond the ports of coastal China were sea routes to Korea, Japan, Taiwan, and the Ryūkyūs, as well as those to southeast Asia and from there further west.

To understand the institutions that promoted a flourishing commercial economy across and beyond the vast spaces of China's agrarian empire, the following section looks more closely at how production and exchange were organized.

Contracts, firms, and markets

Wu Chengming and his colleagues estimated the value of trade in the early nineteenth century to have been around 400 million liang of silver – at a time when the central government's revenues were roughly 10 to 15 percent of that amount. For the two most important commodities, grains and cotton cloth, he estimates more than 20 percent of grain and 15 percent of cotton cloth entered long-distance trade, the balance being in local and regional trade. Of course, "regional" trade in the Chinese empire was on a spatial scale similar to larger European countries (Xu and Wu 2000: 173–178). The size and value of Chinese trade means that the basic economic challenges of exchange were routinely solved. Early modern Chinese merchant groups working several land and water routes over long distances within the empire and to places beyond managed to solve basic issues of establishing trust, securing financing, and resolving disputes. But we have, certainly relative to some European cases, far less information about the kinds of formal and informal institutions used to achieve these circuits of exchange.

Kinship and native place provided important principles of linking people into networks that provided the bases for developing relationships of trust. South China cases of lineage kinship relations being important to the formation of business enterprises form one model of Chinese business behavior (Faure 1989; Ruskola 2000). Native place associations established for sojourning merchants in cities outside their home towns gave people access to larger and denser sets of relations than they would have had on their own. Yet despite the importance of kinship and native place in Chinese commerce, there were countless cases of traveling merchants agreeing to market transactions with people they may not have known well. They were counseled in merchant manuals to be careful with their goods and their money when on the roads or rivers and to present themselves honorably to others (Lufrano 1987). For some goods it is clear that trademarks or brand names affirmed a level of quality of goods, as is shown in the trade between Shanxi and Mongolia (Liu Jiansheng et al. 2005: 206).

Chinese firms beyond the family had several organizational forms in which kinship and native place may have contributed considerably to the pool from which people drew to form a firm. More generally, Chinese commercial practices included mechanisms to mobilize capital as well as dispute resolution mechanisms that used a mix of community institutions and government regulation and resolution powers. Though very different from the institutional mixes that emerged in early modern Europe for both financial markets and judicial means of commercial dispute resolution, we cannot easily infer from the organizational differences any basic difference in their relative effectiveness in their different contexts.

For certain kinds of trade we do have information about the organization of exchange. Merchants from the southeastern province of Fujian worked sea routes north to ports within the empire, east to the island of Taiwan, and south to ports in southeast Asian countries. Ship-owners in the eighteenth century were registered with the state; some traveled with their cargo; others hired a captain and crew to go without them. Yet others took on partners, especially for the larger ships sailing to southeast Asia which were larger and more expensive to operate. More than a thousand boats worked the coastal route north in the 1720s, while several tens of larger boats made their way to southeast Asia each year. Information on individual voyages suggests that the merchants whose goods were loaded on a ship often were relatives. In rare instances when there is evidence of the same ship making separate voyages some of the same merchants are found again but with some being different. The financing of maritime trade by Fujian merchants used systems of individuals having capital shares on specific voyages. The individuals involved typically had some kinship or at least native place relationship that supplied the basic network of relations within which people came forth to put shares of capital into a voyage (Chen Zhiping 2009: 91–93). When disputes emerged over the liability for risks in voyages that were failures or incompletely successful they were often resolved within existing networks of relations. But when the commercial disputes involved merchants from different counties, officials could become involved in adjudicating the competing claims (Chen Zhiping 2009: 260–276).

Shipping merchants who unloaded their goods in Fujian ports sold their goods to government-licensed brokers (*yahang*) who affirmed the quantities, quality, and prices of goods and recorded transaction details. This basic organization of trade was common to many regions of the empire. From the state's perspective, brokers were expected to manage the fair and efficient operation of exchange of goods that moved over the empire's various trade routes. Their importance was magnified for those based in Canton (known today by its Mandarin Chinese name Guangzhou) who dealt with European merchants. It was their responsibility to maintain social order and manage economic relations with foreigners. Officials considered the presence of foreign merchants a source of potential social discord as well as commercial dispute.

Paul Van Dyke's discovery and analysis of more than a hundred bilingual contracts between Chinese and either Dutch, Danish, or Swedish, demonstrates that contracts were essential to creating trust between foreign merchants and Chinese. But contracts were not drawn up necessarily to fit within Chinese law. Nor were there Chinese courts to which disputes could be easily taken. Instead, contracts were written agreements that explained the terms of a transaction. They could include Chinese merchants receiving goods on credit or borrowing funds from foreign merchants, a practice not permitted by Chinese law. But the state was not irrelevant to the resolution of disputes. Contracts were introduced into the process of dispute resolution; an investigation team of merchants, translators, and sometimes only, an official considered the merits of a particular dispute and recommended to the authorities how they thought the dispute would be best resolved. One of the two highest state officials, either the governor-general or the Hoppo (the Ministry of Revenue official managing tax collection on foreign trade) accepted the suggestions or asked the investigation team to come up with an alternative. Suggestions that struck officials as especially helpful and possibly relevant to future disputes could be put into law with an imperial edict. Many disputes involved the debts incurred by the Chinese brokers to foreign merchants. The issue was not that incurring such debts was prohibited by law, but rather how to resolve the issue in practical terms so that foreign merchants continued to engage in trade that officials could tax (Van Dyke 2011: 31–49).

From a contemporary point of view, it would seem that eighteenth-century Chinese law was not effective, but from an early modern European vantage point where multiple courts of law were on offer as venues for different kinds of contractual dispute, Chinese practices seem simply one more way for merchants to use government and law in order to settle disputes. It is difficult to create metrics for early modern era legal practices that are judged by economic effects, but the growth of the porcelain, tea, and silk trades to Europe and colonial America suggest that the Chinese institutional nexus for foreign trade did not stifle exchange in a consequential fashion. More challenging to this trade was increasing European mercantilist-inspired anxiety about the outflow of silver bullion to pay for these goods, which contributed to the development of opium as substitute. For present purposes, what is significant about the use of contracts in Chinese foreign trade with Europeans is the similarities they share with the ways in which contracts were used within the empire for the far more frequent and widespread transactions within China.

Contracts were used by merchants doing long-distance trade within the empire as they were by European merchants working across comparable expanses within Europe. While the Chinese did not develop the kinds of legal institutions early modern Europeans created, Chinese officials did participate in the resolution of commercial disputes. More generally, the numbers of cases coming before county magistrates increased in the eighteenth century. This rise meant the emergence of litigation experts, both to represent parties to a dispute and to advise magistrates seeking to negotiate settlements based on sets of precedents and regulations or laws that were sometimes collected at the provincial level (Macauley 1999). Many of the commercial cases address issues of debt similar to those present in the Canton trade with Europeans – the so-called traveling merchants (*keshang*) had problems with brokers who developed debts with them. At a general level, officials tried to strengthen the ability of traveling merchants to negotiate terms with brokers; in specific cases of dispute they sought to have the disagreeing parties agree mutually on a settlement. By the late nineteenth century the state was promoting the establishment of merchant organizations, translated into English as chambers of commerce (*shanghui*) to manage much of the dispute-resolution process under official oversight (Ch'iu Peng-Sheng 2008; Fan Jinmin 2007). The process of dispute resolution depends on the existence of contracts and settlement processes involving major and complementary roles for both officials and the merchants themselves.

Some of the difficulties encountered through market transactions between traveling merchants and resident brokers were avoided by some commercial firms that were composed of a head office in one city and branches in other cities or towns. Among Shanxi merchant firms, for example, the firm itself could be composed of two or more individuals putting in capital and sharing management or a structure in which the individual(s) supplying capital were different from those providing the management; for this second kind of firm both the capital provider and the person managing the firm were issued with shares which determined their portions of the firm's profits (Liu Jiansheng *et al.* 2005). One way in which investors spread their risks was to have shares in multiple firms; the investors formed a network of individuals who in any given locale were likely to be investing with others in more than a single operation. Shanxi firms were sometimes organized with a head office in one town and branches in two or more others. Very clear rules stipulated the balancing of accounts and reporting of transactions by each and between them (Liu Jiansheng *et al.* 2005: 172, 204). Chinese firms more generally were typically partnerships with capital contributed in varying amounts and the management functions often in the hands of only one partner. Chinese entrepreneurs with large amounts of capital often invested in multiple firms, sometimes with many of the same other individuals; thus, there was a network of investors who undertook different partnerships. Partners had stakes in firms according to the amounts of capital they invested; in the salt brine evaporation business in Sichuan, firms could bring in additional capital by adding shares to those already in the firm (Zelin 2005: 38–45).

Early modern Chinese firms seem rarely to have grown to become dominant actors on any particular market. They did not, in other words, become commercial capitalists in the particular sense of concentrating large amounts of capital and achieving market control over some kinds of commodity. The major exceptions to this generalization were the Chinese merchants chosen by the state to deal with European merchants in Canton and the merchants licensed by the state to buy and sell salt. In both cases, these entrepreneurs who amassed large amounts of capital in a single set of operations were only able to do so because of the institutional arrangements created by the state. Though the specifics for each of these cases differs from the range of specifics formulated in European countries for maritime trading companies operating overseas, a similar logic of the state allocating limited opportunities for wealth accumulation to create capitalist operations can be said to be at work. But in the Chinese case, to be sure, government-created and regulated business operations were a minor part of the empire's commercial economy. Firms were generally multiple in any market and required small amounts of capital that could be met through partnerships by individuals who, if they had additional capital, chose to invest in other partnerships rather than commit more capital to a single operation. The commercial economy had no particular need for capital markets able to mobilize large amounts of capital for a limited number of large firms.

The mix between informal and formal mechanisms in both financial markets and commercial-dispute resolution in China suggests a relationship between custom and law different from European experiences. European law involves crystallization and codification of custom into formal law. But Chinese law works with social mechanisms of dispute resolution in a more intimate and connected fashion. "Custom" (*fengsu*) in Chinese refers to local practices which sometimes government regulations and law can accommodate and at other times not accept; in either case law and custom are generally conceived to be quite distinct from each other. Capital mobilization clearly depended on trust among people who were close to each other through either kinship or native place, but more formal documents were drawn up to stipulate their shares of capital in a particular venture. At the same time, these documents were "legal" in the sense that officials used them in determining difficult disputes and they were social in a more general sense of being affirmed by the people themselves as a document stipulating their agreements.

When we turn to land and labor markets a similar set of challenges present themselves. There were active land markets in early modern China but the transactions were institutionally constructed differently from modern land contracts. Two aspects of Chinese land contracts seem to suggest constraints imposed by custom. First, contracts typically refer to land being first offered to kinsmen before being sold to others. Second, many contracts include clauses allowing for the redemption or repurchase of land at some future date according to some stipulated price; such contracts could even allow subsequent generations to seek return of land sold by ancestors (Yang Guozhen 2009). Similarly, when we look at labor markets we observe that where early modern European households sent family members out of the home to find wage-earning work as domestics or laborers, Chinese family members were far more likely to remain at home, sometimes doing similar kinds of work for which Europeans gained wages but not themselves passing through some more explicit and formal labor market. Custom then seems to be at work in place of markets in the Chinese case. For both land and labor markets we could reasonably argue that Chinese markets were restricted in their effective operation by customary practices and as a result opportunities to use resources most efficiently were not realized. But such an inference depends on assumptions about land and labor use that may not be extremely relevant to early modern Chinese conditions, as suggested below.

Irrespective of ownership, the use of agricultural land in China was almost always by small plots. Thus, the production functions into which land was entered did not vary in the ways they could have were there real economies of scale. Such economies of scale would have been achieved with certain mechanical technologies, assuming it was economically profitable to change capital/labor ratios in the ways that cultivating the land in larger units would make possible. But in the absence of either the economic incentive of relative factor prices making capital-using technologies more profitable or the availability of technologies to achieve such kinds of production, it is not exactly clear how much difference selling land to a wider selection of people than already available in most Chinese locales would have made. The significance of the customary constraint of selling first to kin seems therefore at most not very strong. The practice of allowing land repurchases or redemption in conditional sales would harm efficiency if the productivity of the land were consistently higher when operated by the buyer rather than the seller. But if that is not true it again is not clear what the economic losses of allowing repurchases would be.

What Chinese officials were concerned about were the possibilities that land sales were often made by families falling upon hard times, whose opportunities to recover the government wanted to enhance by making it possible for them to redeem land previously sold. They did not want in the early modern era any more than they wanted in the early imperial era to support the growth of land concentration in the hands of the rich and the creation of households having to rent land or leave the land altogether.

Surviving land contracts suggest that land did change hands with some significant frequency in early modern China (Yang Guozhen 2009). The results could increase concentration of ownership in some locales, but need not. Even when people became landlords by buying land from others, the basic unit of production remained the household, which worked plots of land as tenants when not owners. The scale and mix of capital, land, and labor did not vary dramatically as a result of there being a land market. The state did not want to see land ownership become more concentrated, even as officials wished to simplify the complicated conditions of land being reacquired by a seller who claimed to retain rights of redemption on a plot that he or his relative had alienated many years before. Improvements in agricultural productivity were achieved through technologies that were suitable for this scale of operation.

The importance of the early modern Chinese agrarian household as the basic unit of production across the empire included both its crop and its craft outputs. Thinking of this household as a small firm making production decisions, labor was typically allocated to multiple activities; some were part of crop cultivation, while others concerned craft activities. A typically gendered division of labor became enshrined in the expression "men plow, women weave" (nangeng nuzhi). The desire and ability of Chinese households to expand their production activities to provide income-producing opportunities that kept all members of the family at home contrasts with the preferences and mechanisms created by early modern European households to make wage labor an option, in particular for young women who left their homes to engage in service in other households as well as other kinds of employment. Labor markets developed more generally in early modern Europe for work in both rural and urban settings (Knotter 2001; Lucassen 2001; Schlumbohm 2001). In early modern China there were people who worked as wage laborers in the countryside but only those who were utterly landless, lacking the money to own or rent land, became wage labor. Because the individual household was the unit of production and it typically pursued a mix of crop and craft activities, labor market development was more limited than in early modern Europe. In economic terms, the difference can be conceived as a different dividing point between the firm and the market in these two world regions in the early modern era.

In brief, early modern China had less developed capital and labor markets than early modern Europe, but this does not mean that firms were less able to combine capital and labor in efficiently productive ways. As we have seen, officials certainly promoted the viability of the smallholder agrarian household as a unit of crop and craft production. More generally, as we see in more detail below, the early modern Chinese state was pro-market but also, in some basic ways anti-capitalist. The government did not favor the concentration of land, market control by a few large firms, or the creation of a large landless population dependent on wage labor. This does not mean, however, that the state did not actively pursue and enable economic growth.

State support for economic development

Defining state support for economic development is not straightforward. It may be tempting to read back anachronistically the kinds of policies useful in the twentieth century to earlier eras and equally tempting to look for what were supportive policies in one part of the world as a guide for what was needed in another. Nevertheless, the possibilities and appropriateness of state support for economic development clearly must vary according to the contexts within which governments find themselves – an agrarian society before industrialization clearly includes situations very different from those in which industrialization has occurred as well as those in which industrialization has become a consciously conceived aspiration. I understand state support for economic development to come from intentional efforts to improve economic conditions that actually succeed. Governments may have other motives as well as economic development, but the notion of state support should not, it seems to me, include cases of unintended consequences; rather, only those instances where deliberate intent is coupled with some measure of success count as examples of government support.

With this framing in mind, consider the basic orientation of Chinese officials adopted toward supporting the economy, a set of activities basic to Chinese ideas about good governance. Unlike the advice early modern European rulers were offered by texts such as Machiavelli's *The Prince*, much of the ancient Chinese advice written between the sixth and fourth centuries BCE, a period preceding the first imperial unification of 221 BCE, proposed to rulers how best to persuade people that they were proper rulers. Many suggestions included a focus on promoting the material security of people living with the uncertainties of harvests subject to nature's vagaries and the troubles that government extraction to pay for armies could cause. Material well-being was, not surprisingly in an agricultural society, associated with having land and being able to enjoy the fruits of one's labor without heavy taxes. The logical precedence of people satisfying their needs before they could contemplate more abstract issues of fairness and justice made government efforts at promoting material security a basic condition for achieving political legitimacy. From this connection came the corollary that people, and especially elites, had a right to rebel when rulers failed to meet expectations. The fiscal principles that flowed from ancient ideas about good governance continued to be influential in the early modern era (Wong 2012).

The Chinese government's efforts to tax lightly were intended to enable people to grow wealthier and hence to provide an ever larger economy from which the state could gather resources in the future. If society can become enriched, then even if the state is temporarily poor it can subsequently gain the resources it needs. If, however, society is impoverished, even if the state is at some moment rich, it will subsequently become poor because it will not be able to raise the revenue it later needs to meet its routine expenses. The logic at work here stresses the importance of limiting the amounts of resources sent from the people up to the government in order to enable the people to prosper and to be better able in the future to meet the government's need for resources. Chinese views place fundamental importance on the material successes of the people as the basis upon which to sustain a sensible government. A basic premise necessary for this logic to work was a society of peasant households that could pay taxes to the government. A society of large landlords collecting rents from their tenants would put a powerful elite between the government and common people. As a result, Chinese political thinking stressed the importance of land tenure and linked production and taxation to those institutional conditions.

Chinese governments also turned at several points in the long imperial era to indirect taxation. But surprisingly from the vantage point of European history, indirect taxation did not increasingly replace direct taxation between the sixteenth and nineteenth centuries. The issues of whether or not the state should directly control certain kinds of production and distribution and should tax commercial commodities came up several times, but arguably without any conclusive agreement on how to tax commerce until the late twentieth century. A major debate took place at the Han dynasty court during the reign of Emperor Wu (r. 187–141 BCE) regarding the advisability of the government directly controlling salt and iron production and distribution. Those opposed to official control claimed the state was interfering with the people's ability to enrich themselves through production and trade. Those advocating a government monopoly wanted to prevent rich merchants from grasping all the profits coming from control over important commodities and to assure for the state the revenues that came from controlling salt sales. They were opposed to a few rich people controlling crucial resources, what we might consider a kind of capitalist practice, claiming that the government was able and willing to see that resources circulated more widely according to supply and demand (Hsiao 1979: 457–462). Related debates about the government's role in the economy emerged again in the mid eleventh century in response to Finance Minister Wang Anshi's expanded use of state monopolies and commercial taxation, once again to fund pressing military expenditures (Li Huarui 2004; Liu 1959). For much of Chinese dynastic history, however, agricultural taxes rather than commercial taxes supplied the bulk of resources for Chinese imperial states. Whatever pressure military expenditures placed on the state, they were basically met by raising most revenues from the land. This reliance on peasant agriculture as the main source of fiscal and political support for the state led to repeated stress on taxing the people lightly and setting expenditure levels according to available revenues.

By the early modern era, state support for peasants opening up new lands to expand their bases of production created tensions between economic benefits and environmental costs. The choices made by Chinese officials and people about land use come out clearly in the case of forest land management. The clearing of forested land to allow crop cultivation is a seemingly one-directional movement toward ever-decreasing forest cover in China. Highland area clearance in the middle and lower Yangzi regions typically exhausted the newly cleared land quickly (Osborne 1998). In north China a gradual decline of forest land as peasants cleared land and searched for wood to use as fuel continued well past 1850 and was not reversed by the Republican era government promoting reforestation (Pomeranz 1993: 120–145). But beneath this picture of secular decline descending into crisis we know of some efforts at managing forest lands to promote if not always assure their survival. For example, lineages in south China held forest land as common property and set up rules to limit access and define acceptable use (Menzies 1994: 75–98). Nor was the trade-off simply between economic profit and environmental preservation. The Huizhou merchants who managed the timber trade supplying the porcelain kilns of Jingdezhen with fuel were mindful of maintaining the forests from which they cut down timber as renewable resources (Menzies 1994: 77). They understood the need for an economically sensible management plan for a commercially valuable resource to avoid rapid depletion.

Identifying Chinese awareness of the detrimental impact of some use of resources, such as forest lands, certainly does not negate the long-term large-scale process of deforestation and spreading problem of fuel scarcities. But the presence of multiple institutional arrangements to manage forest lands, both as collective goods and as private goods, for both social preservation and economic use, alerts us to China grappling with what become in other parts of the world the modern problems of making trade-offs between conservation and economic profits. The Qing state also clearly cared about certain lands as sacred and symbolic spaces and others as sites for imperial hunts. Officials and elites pursued multiple strategies of land use that reflect the competing demands of the market, sacred and symbolic spaces, and the dependence of poor communities on woodlands, another example of how resources could be variously governed by market, command, and custom.

When we turn to water-use management we discover that the Chinese also had a rich array of experiences in managing water flows for transportation, the irrigation of crop land, and flood control. Sometimes water control projects were concerned primarily with one purpose, but often there were competing interests and priorities that made decision-making at best complex and at worst ineffectual. Water was in some instances a public good or at least one requiring governmental investment in infrastructural support. But water was also a resource that could be regulated by local organizations that apportioned water for irrigation purposes and charged people for the maintenance and upkeep of water control projects according to the estimated benefits they each received from the irrigation works. Property rights to water were both less developed and more complex than those developed for land. As with forest land destruction, the Chinese began to face environmental challenges attending the regulation of water flows along their large rivers by the early modern era.

Certainly the state's support of water control efforts was in part self-serving – expanding the productive base increased the economic output that the state could tax. This could be seen as meeting the maxim of storing wealth with the people because it was creating the people's ability to create additional wealth that enabled the state to gather more taxes. Beyond the normative motivations, it is striking that the state was able to mobilize capital and labor for major water control projects in a command economy fashion at the same time as it allowed local community organizations to manage irrigation works according to benefit/cost calculations. It also attempted to balance the interests of producers and merchants for irrigation water and transportation routes, as it remained mindful that wealthy people seeking to create new polder lands undermined the viability of transportation routes and subjected their locales to increased dangers from flooding by reducing water surfaces. As with issues of land management, Chinese efforts to meet competing objectives meant of necessity an inability to meet the desires of all parties. But such situations, perhaps unusual for other early modern governments, have become far more typical of the modern era.

Regarding markets and trade, official attitudes varied. Salt production and trade were controlled by officials as a source of revenue. Some trade networks, like those for grain, were actively promoted by officials as a means to assure that annual imbalances within given regions could be mitigated through variable movements across them. Chinese officials generally permitted trade within the eighteenth-century empire to take place with minimal taxation and regulation. Excepting the government monopoly over the production and distribution of salt, trade was taxed at a few ports at low rates, accounting in some years for less than 5 percent and in other years as much as a little over 10 percent of total government revenues between the late seventeenth and early nineteenth centuries (Zhou Zhichu 2002). These light rates could even be lifted on grain in order to give merchants incentives to transport supplies along routes serving people suffering from grain shortages. Indeed, officials expressed great concern over grain supplies since these were considered the foundation of social security and accordingly political stability. Those officials serving in regions relying on commercial imports expressed strong support for market principles of supply and demand for people in their jurisdictions directly benefitting from grain imports. Officials in grain-exporting regions, however, worried about shipments leaving their jurisdictions in years of poor harvests. Throughout the empire officials expressed a mix of attitudes toward the holding of grain off markets. When they perceived hoarding to be market manipulation by a handful of rich and powerful people, they labeled such activities unacceptable ways to raise prices by holding goods off the market. However, officials also noted that keeping grain off local markets was necessary to transport it to other markets where prices were higher; such movements of grain from areas of low price to those with higher prices were understood as beneficial (Wong 1999).

Spatial differences in the economic policies pursued across the empire reflected the government's recognition of different challenges and opportunities present across its diverse natural and social environment. In the most developed commercial areas, officials basically promoted the smooth operation of markets. In economically less developed areas officials promoted production and certainly by no later than the mid eighteenth century expected increased production to create more trade. Coastal areas where people were eager and able to pursue maritime trade presented particular challenges and opportunities. In the late seventeenth century, the newly installed Qing dynasty was uncertain about the loyalty of populations living along the southeastern coast; disrupting trade was considered an acceptable economic price to pay for enhancing political security. At other times, officials recognized the importance of maritime trade to people living in coastal areas (Wong 2004). By 1500 the late imperial state possessed a complex tradition of policy options to shape economic activity, both to raise revenues and to achieve a stable social order. Official choices fluctuated. Two general approaches define the endpoints of possibilities. First, the state could choose activist and interventionist policies to control or direct economic activities; such efforts included the regulation of mining and the exchange of salt vouchers for grain shipments to troops in the northwest (Terada Takanobu 1972: 80–119). Second, the state could satisfy itself with monitoring private-sector efforts and even informally delegate responsibility or depend on others to help achieve its goals; examples include market surveillance and reliance on elites for famine relief (Mann 1987; Will 1990). In between the extremes of direct state control and indirect monitoring lay all sorts of efforts to redirect, channel, or limit private sector economic practices.

Amid considerable variation in techniques there was basic agreement through the eighteenth century about the type of economy officials sought to stabilize and expand in order to maintain a society in which most people stayed in villages where both cash crops and handicrafts were produced. Officials generally agreed to rely principally on agrarian taxes and to tax lightly. Because they were able and willing through much of the eighteenth century to move their resources across county and provincial borders, not only to the capital but also to other areas experiencing particular demands, be they caused by harvest failures or military needs, officials did not have much need to borrow money – they were able to move resources through space rather than take on loans to be repaid with future taxes. In at least some ways therefore the state intended some of its actions to complement and extend the natural reach of the market. In other ways it sought to balance the logics of customary circulation within a local area, at least for grain supplies, with the demands of market exchange taking food grains over long distances. Market, customary, and state circuits of circulation all proved durable and connected to each other in ways that complemented each other as they also constrained or qualified the kinds of actions taken within each.

Across all areas, the state invested in both water control operations and, especially during much of the eighteenth century, in maintaining large grain reserves to aid the poor and to protect people more generally against harvest shortfalls. The government understood that light taxation allowed more wealth to remain with people which in turn made them less likely to cause social conflict and more likely to be productive and pay the taxes levied upon them. To appreciate the elements of Chinese economic policies and practices that were parallel to those found in other parts of the world as well as those that were more distinctive to this particular world region, the final section of this chapter compares China's pre-1850 economy with those of other empires, Europe, and the China that would follow after 1850.

China in comparative contexts

Among empires

An earlier generation of scholarship contrasted empires from modern national states, considering empires a more ancient form of rule over larger territories than are typical of national states in recent times. This general approach stressed historical change throughout the world following an arc of empires collapsing, to be replaced by regimes governed by ideas and institutions first developed in western Europe. This approach made the world of national states a system of political regimes different from all that came before in world history. It allowed for the study of regimes of varying sizes and amounts of wealth and power, but it ignored the construction of European overseas empires in the same era as national states were being formed. To confront these difficulties, some scholars have consciously extended the rubric of "empire" to cover more diverse political forms across many historical eras. Jane Burbank and Frederick Cooper in their *Empires in World History*, for instance, focus "on the different ways empires turned conquest into governing and on how empires balanced incorporation of people into the polity with sustaining distinctions among them" (Burbank and Cooper 2010: 15): To achieve incorporation, rulers send out their agents – civilian administrators, military officers, judges, and tax collectors – and coopt local leaders to serve them, often with titles bestowed by the imperial regime. Burbank and Cooper suggest that:

> [e]mpire was a variable political form, and we accent the multiple ways in which incorporation and difference were conjugated. Empires' durability depended to a large extent on their ability to combine and shift strategies, from consolidating territory to planting enclaves, from loose supervision of intermediaries to tight, top-down control, from frank assertion of imperial authority to denial of acting like an empire. Unitary kingdoms, city-states, tribes, and nation-states were less able to respond as flexibly to a changing world. (Burbank and Cooper 2010: 16)

This definition of empire is capacious so that many different regimes qualify – empire as a category is durable over time even if specific empires are not. While empires have a repertoire of strategies and techniques to deploy, not many seem able to deploy their choices effectively for more than a few generations. The ability to use different techniques of direct and indirect rule and to co-opt local leaders as well as depute loyal followers from the center, points to the limits of both.

What empires in general lack is much in the way of rule-governed administrators forming a bureaucracy. Such conditions provide a basic contrast to Max Weber's famous formulation of modern bureaucratic rule. Weber saw this form of rule to be fundamentally different from whatever forms of personalistic use of administration were forged by pre-modern rulers, including those who commanded empires. Yet a rule-governed bureaucracy is precisely what the Chinese empire developed over the centuries from the time of the Han empire and its temporal counterpart of Rome, through its mid-imperial era when the Abbasid caliphate flourished and sent troops to help the Tang court quell a military rebellion, and especially in its late imperial era when the Ottoman, Mughal, and Russian empires achieved their heights of power and success but together ruled less land than the Qing empire.

The expansion of bureaucratic capacities of rule between the early, mid and late imperial eras included growth in the absolute size of the bureaucracy, the delineation of offices within a vertically structured hierarchy of offices, as well as the creation of functionally specific offices outside the template of routine administration. The principles and practices developed in the Chinese empire were shared to varying degrees by governments in

Korea and Vietnam and inspired less successful efforts at state building in the Ryūkyū kingdom. But the Chinese imperial experiences with developing bureaucratic rule were longer lasting and affected far larger populations than those attempted elsewhere. The substance of good governance and the goals of bureaucratic rule included many elements reviewed in this chapter as policies designed to influence the organization of economic activities across the empire. The plausibility of even imagining, let alone implementing, policies on subjects such as land ownership and management, food supply storage and circulation, and water control for production and transportation could not have existed without routine access to resources and the ability to mobilize manpower to pursue major projects. Such abilities could be considered part of the Chinese empire's command economy, except that such a characterization would fail to focus adequately on the intent and impact of such policies, which were at least as much to promote the material well-being of its subjects as they were to enrich the coffers of the state and depended upon active support of market institutions, the recognition of private property rights, and the use of contracts. None of this fits obviously within conventional definitions of empire.

Consider Sir John Hicks's *A Theory of Economic History*, which proposes a conceptually clear way to think about the economies of empires in contrast to those of other kinds of polities. Hicks suggested that the development and sustaining of markets is rare in world history. Markets are vulnerable to collapse when warfare and social disorder reduce people to reliance upon custom for principles of mutual support. They are equally vulnerable to the rapacious grasp of despotic states, such as empires, which impose command structures that undercut market principles. If Hicks's suggestions are entered into a broader and more recent discussion among historians of what makes empires different from other polities in world history, we can begin to see what made the Chinese empire so different from other empires. If other empires were individually fragile, and if command economies were part of the common repertoire of strategies to which they all appealed, perhaps China's political capacity for reproduction depended in part upon its nurturing of a commercial economy to complement and integrate with its more command-oriented policies. China does not fit Hicks's image of empires and therefore the relationship he posits between political forms and economic institutions becomes less clear. For China specifically, it is not easy to make a clear distinction between custom, market, and command in the manner conceived by Hicks or more generally in the manner often applied to European history, in which choices between the three logics are seen as mutually exclusive.

The durability and capacity for expansion exhibited by commercial institutions that developed in China after the tenth century makes clear the compatibility of the market in China with Chinese imperial institutions of rule. These institutions were by no means typical of empires generally. But this is only half of the contrast of China with other empires. For the state to develop its economic policies there had to be effective economic institution building from below to make market exchanges possible. The capacity of the Chinese to organize themselves efficiently and effectively for both production and exchange is attested by the visible growth of agricultural and craft production after the tenth century and by their continued development and the further elaboration of merchant organizations in subsequent centuries. In part the ability of production and exchange to expand across much so much of the Chinese empire after 1400 depended on the political stability imperial rule typically provided over the subsequent four and a half centuries. Other imperial spaces were usually conquered and defeated all within four and a half centuries so it was impossible for these imperial regimes to provide the peaceful conditions conducive to economic expansion possible in China. Yet peaceful conditions over vast territories were not in fact a necessary condition for commercial growth, as other empires had pockets of commercial production and exchange. So too in fact did conflict-ridden early modern Europe. As we turn to compare China and Europe, one of the first contrasts to consider is the possibility for commercial growth in a largely peaceful empire in China and in a typically war-torn continent in Europe during the early modern era.

China and Europe

From the vantage point of the most successful moments of the Han and Roman empires, China in the early modern era was, as it had been for many of the previous centuries, a large and relatively peaceful empire, while Europe was politically fragmented and vulnerable to war. In one basic sense, peace made possible the material security of *domestic* trade over long distances in China while in Europe the same trade was *foreign* and subject to disruptions and violence not present in China. We therefore should expect, *ceteris paribus*, that more long-distance commerce was possible in early modern China than in early modern Europe. The great variety of routes that entered multiple channels of exchange within the Chinese empire do in fact appear to carry a greater diversity of goods over a longer total distance than did commerce within Europe. Despite having different economic institutions, as well as different mixes of formal and informal mechanisms, it is not likely, let alone obvious, that Chinese institutions were less successful in promoting economic growth than European ones were. We are led to imagine such differences in Europe's favor from the association of early modern European practices with subsequent modern economic growth. Such exercises are part of a larger effort made to account for what Kenneth Pomeranz memorably labeled the "great divergence" between the Chinese and European economies that became starkly visible in the nineteenth century. Scholars have put forward many interpretations, the relative importance of which is difficult to evaluate because we lack models that can discern persuasively the ways in which different plausible causal mechanisms will necessarily interact, as well as the data to test them in commensurate ways.

For Pomeranz himself, the "great divergence" depended crucially on English access to New World cotton, a windfall gain made possible first by colonization and then the subsequent expansion of slavery (Pomeranz 2000). Empirically it is certainly the case that early modern Europeans went overseas and imposed regimes of exploitation and extraction, especially in the Americas. But this opportunity only mattered to economic growth in the manner Pomeranz explains because of the changes in cotton textile technology that created the massive increase in British demand for raw cotton in the early nineteenth century. Technological change was a necessary condition for the economic significance of American cotton. Secondly, and equally importantly to those wishing to stress the crucial significance of the European access to the New World, it is necessary to separate out the particular institutional features of colonialism and slavery from the more general issue of agricultural production in one area being exported to another according to the principles of market exchange. Slavery need not have been the basic labor relationship behind cotton production for the exchange to have taken place – cotton may have been cheaper under this regime and thus the demand for cotton would have declined without slavery, but how different would the basic comparative advantage of British textile mills over other producers have been with a different agricultural labor regime?

Questions separating out the political processes from the economic impacts of new areas of production entering into larger networks of exchange, and asking which features of those processes were necessary or not for other economic changes we subsequently observe, cannot be answered very easily through appeal to data because we are asking a counterfactual. This problem is related to a more general contrast of China and Europe that places the two world regions at extremes among those that do and do not have territorially large polities. The political fragmentation of Europe as a region is directly connected to the incentives of European rulers to carry their competition overseas. The economic impacts for winners of this competition were less obvious than a singular examination of the antecedents to the nineteenth-century British rise would lead us to expect. Spain was certainly the European winner in Latin America and it was thus able to exploit the silver mines of the New World. Its increased amounts of silver did not lead to major economic growth. Successful rent-seeking does not necessarily translate into positive economic change. Political competition of Europeans within and beyond Europe affected the distribution of spoils but it did not always contribute to changing an economy for the better.

Jean-Laurent Rosenthal and I have suggested some important economic impacts of the political differences of empire versus political competition among small polities in the early modern era (Rosenthal and Wong 2011). We suggest that in early modern times there were any number of important forms of craft manufacturing that, *ceteris paribus*, were more likely to locate in the countryside than in the city because labor costs were cheaper in the countryside and labor was the major factor of production in many processes. Labor was cheaper because food costs were lower in the countryside and public health risks in cities raised the costs of urban employment. Thus we need to be able to account for the greater likelihood of craft manufacturing locations in European cities than in the countryside. We argue a major reason was the threat of warfare. For the early modern era the threat of warfare was higher within Europe than it was within China. Additionally, when warfare fears were higher in China, as they were between the tenth and thirteenth centuries, crafts were more urban than they subsequently became. Also consistent with our proposition, those times and places in Europe where we see the efflorescence of rural crafts faced fewer threats of war. While in the early modern era generally, this contrast of more rural sites of craft production in China compared to urban ones in Europe favored China over Europe, there were long-run consequences of a very different order. At the same time as labor was cheaper in the countryside, capital was cheaper in cities because monitoring costs were lower and information about borrowers was cheaper to obtain. Because capital was cheaper in cities than the countryside and labor was more expensive, relative factor prices created a European bias in favor of capital over labor. Since the use of technologies typically involved additional capital expenditure, the likelihood of such changes being made was higher in Europe than in China. The demand for technological change in early modern Europe was thus higher than in China irrespective of the particular supply functions for science and technology present in the two world regions.

In a chapter that is part of a work on capitalism in world history we might ask how significant capitalism itself was to the emerging economic contrasts of China and Europe. The reasons Rosenthal and I suggest for the visible nineteenth-century differences begin far earlier in the political histories of the two world regions but depend neither on the institutions of private property, contracting, and market institutions nor on government support for economic development. If we follow the definition of capitalism as concentrating large amounts of capital among a limited number of firms that develop and control markets, then we do in fact have a plausible candidate to explain early modern era differences between China and Europe because the expansion of maritime European commerce and production did in fact involve a limited number of firms mobilizing considerable amounts of capital to develop and control new markets. The market economy that expanded in China was not motored by a similar set of actors.

An explanation for these differences in terms of the political economies of the Chinese and European world regions could be offered but is certainly beyond what is possible in this chapter. More relevant is the issue of whether or not early modern European commercial capitalism created industrial capitalism. It may seem intuitively obvious that industrial capitalism emerged out of commercial capitalism, and there are venerable approaches to understanding the emergence of modern economies that promote just such views. But if the "industrial" part of capitalism is what is key to modern economic growth, it is the development of those capacities and possibilities that deserve particular attention in accounts of nineteenth-century economic change. Once industrial possibilities are available in terms of technologies and skills, the question emerges of the range of institutional settings that can support and indeed promote industrialization and modern economic growth. To understand what capitalism means, the issue becomes some version of establishing varieties of capitalism or the limits of capitalism as a covering term for key economic activities in the contemporary world. China's more recent past becomes one venue to consider our explanatory challenges and choices.

China before 1850 and its influences on more recent times

Scholars working on the Chinese economy beginning in the late nineteenth century typically find little relevance in economic practices preceding the twentieth century for understanding either modern economic growth or the character of China's contemporary economy. Certainly, if our baseline is roughly 1850 we are encountering China as it is torn apart by major rebellions, and the reconsolidation of government abilities to sustain rule over the empire in the 1860s never includes the kind of effective government support for the agrarian economy that was seen in the previous century. If, however, we address earlier Chinese economic practices, their plausible relevance to subsequent economic growth cannot be dismissed so easily by reason of their non-conformity to European institutions. Whether we look from the vantage point of the state's approach to economic activities or from the perspective of economic agents organizing their production and exchange, the relevance of past practices may be no less significant than they are to understanding changes in the economies of other better-studied world regions, such as Europe or North America.

The imperial Chinese state had only two major episodes of significant state involvement in industrial production and distribution before the late nineteenth century. This is not perhaps all that surprising since the possibilities for industry were limited globally before the nineteenth century. As briefly mentioned earlier in this chapter, early imperial and mid-imperial era Chinese states implemented policies of control over both production and distribution, first of salt and iron, and in the later period over a larger variety of commodities. What became more typical in the late imperial period, or early modern era in world history terms, were close official relations with certain kinds of merchants who were given government licenses to engage in heavily regulated trades, like salt and exchanges with Europeans, and a kind of looser complementary relationship with a far larger number of merchants who organized commercial exchange and were expected to manage matters with minimal direct intervention by officials; in aggregate their activities dwarfed the more limited trade in salt and with foreigners that made a select few merchants very wealthy. The early modern Chinese state did not depend greatly on indirect taxes or government monopolies and thus lacked the incentive to forge the far closer relations between government officials and merchants found in both early modern European history and the histories of other world regions; Chinese officials and merchants fashioned more complementary roles based more on a division of labor than a fusion of their interests – merchants organized commercial exchange and officials by and large left them to manage their own affairs. Given this background it therefore is not surprising that the initial late nineteenth-century responses of the Chinese state to the opportunities and threats posed by Western industrial technologies led officials to fashion a partnership with entrepreneurs to establish shipyards, mining operations, and factories predicated on complementary interests but without clear rules for how to manage their relations (Chan 1980).

By the early twentieth century, the Chinese state had made a set of bureau-cratic reforms establishing a new ministry for industry, which was subse-quently changed to include agriculture and commerce. In conception and intent, at least, China's last imperial state was beginning to fashion the bureaucratic apparatus to promote a general vision of promoting agriculture, industry, and commerce together; such an overall vision represented the expansion and extension of an earlier set of concerns with promoting the expansion and stability of the agrarian economy that existed before Western-created industrial technologies became available (Wang Kui 2008). Though the state fell in 1911 and its new bureaucratic apparatus could not be effectively elaborated upon by Republican era governments, economic actors themselves achieved some of the results hoped for by early twentieth-century state efforts at creating linkages between agriculture, commerce, and industry.

The development of new industries in the quarter century following the founding of the Republic of China in 1912 included both industries built in cities, most especially Shanghai as well as factories formed in more modest towns, and the introduction of new technologies into rural household production. An important example of rural crafts being invigorated by new technologies can be seen in the north China county of Gaoyang, where an iron-gear loom imported from Japan allowed the expansion of craft production among households who formed a large number of small firms engaged in different kinds of textile production. The practices of these households largely followed those of rural Chinese households across much of the country in late imperial times, suggesting the abilities of such a system to take advantage of technologies suitable for labor-intensive production (Grove 2006). In Nantong, a county in Jiangsu province on the northern banks of the Yangzi River upstream from Shanghai, former Qing dynasty and republican government official Zhang Jian began a new cotton textile factory; benefitting from his official connections for some of his initial equipment and imbued with a vision of creating new economic possibilities in the town that served as the county seat, Zhang Jian's textile company became the cornerstone of a larger and diversified set of commercial operations that went into decline after his death (Köll 2003). In this case too we can see elements of past problems and possibilities for Chinese entrepreneurs made into a fundamentally new compound by the introduc-tion of new technologies, managed in a distinctive manner that drew upon both native and foreign approaches to management. These changes take place well beyond the most visible urban centers of industrial change, of which Shanghai is by far the most important. But the changes in Shanghai were by no means either separate from or replacements for production that took place in small towns and agrarian households. A basic complementarity between new production in Shanghai and production in the area around the city developed in the 1920s and 1930s (Rawski 1989: 344). Evidence of economic development involving rural, small-town, and city-based production began to emerge in at least parts of the country before the Japanese invasion of 1937. While easily dismissed as limited in scale and modest in spatial reach, compared to what happened in industrializing European countries in the nineteenth century, if we were to take an area of Europe as large as China, it would include many places as devoid of industrial transformation as 1930s China was. Thomas Rawski posed a quarter century ago the counterfactual of how the Chinese economy might have grown in the absence of the Japanese invasion (Rawski 1989). While it is difficult to imagine very precisely what would have occurred, it is not impossible that economic growth spanning some rural and urban areas that included the persistence and transformation of craft-based technologies in the countryside and construction of labor-intensive factory production in small towns would have taken place.

The disruption of war led the Nationalist government to uproot much of the capital stock in the Shanghai region and other places threatened by and subsequently taken over by the Japanese. They moved a large amount of physical plant to their wartime capital of Chongqing. During the war the government also took over a number of enterprises. The subsequent sequence of decisions by the People's Republic in the first half of the 1950s to develop state-owned industries and remove private enterprises was, thus, not as radical a rupture as it seems when viewed solely as the result of the importation of a Soviet model of a planned economy. Less typically remarked upon, but arguably at least as significant an economic change came from the efforts to deindustrialize the countryside – to transform agrarian China into agricultural China stripped of its craft industries and small-scale factories ill-suited to fit within a Soviet-style planned economy.

Largely successful, the destruction of craft industries left the countryside largely agricultural. State efforts to promote some rural-based producer goods industries in the late 1950s are remembered largely for the failures of so-called backyard steel furnaces. The notion of sophisticated technologies requiring both capital and management expertise being transmuted into forms plausible in rural settings seems at best risible; there were, however, better results with chemical fertilizer plants. More significantly, small-scale industries outside the state plan in the Shanghai area developed in the early 1970s to supply larger firms under the state plan with inputs that the larger firms were unable to secure in adequate quantities within the plan (White 1998: 112–151). Well before officials allowed the economy outside the planned sector to grow as the initial phase of economic reforms, enterprises operating under the plan began to move outside the constraints of the plan. The state's subsequent decisions to foster economic growth and industrialization outside the plan thus followed and extended practices begun at local levels.

Looking at the Chinese economy's remarkable growth since the late 1970s, it is easy to forget that a sophisticated commercial economy was developing over the several centuries preceding 1850. We can explain China's late twentieth-century growth in terms of conventional economic principles that see development as the product of adopting practices successful in creating economic growth elsewhere in the world. We can quickly identify the gross inefficiencies and irrationalities of the planned economy that had stripped China of its markets and subjected firms and people to administrative control and political manipulations. If we extend our perspective back to the mid and late nineteenth century we confront a weak state, a society threatened by domestic unrest, and an economy visibly backward compared to the industrializing economies of western Europe and North America; pockets of growth in China clearly involve access to foreign markets, capital, and entrepreneurship. What is added to our conventional view of China's recent economic transformation by extending our historical perspective to earlier centuries?

Much of the rapid growth of the 1980s in the gross value of industrial input came from the development of township and village enterprises (TVE). These enterprises were formed outside the planned economy and typically in rural and small-town settings. Lacking a formal institutional environment to guarantee contracts for sales, to set up bank loans, or to hire workers, Chinese enterprises proceeded with informal mechanisms that owed much to the history and repertoire of commercial practices that the Chinese had variously employed before 1949. Setting of industries in the countryside where they could absorb some of the agricultural surplus labor that would otherwise migrate to existing larger urban centers or continue to languish in agriculture meant that the countryside once again had industries. They were different to be sure from the smaller-scale craft industries of the past, but in contrast to the general equivalences of urban and industrial and of rural and agricultural that marked both earlier Western industrialization experiences and China under the planned economy, 1980s China was more similar to an earlier China (Wong 2002).

Moving through the 1990s and into the new millennium, it became increasingly clear that the Chinese state's exit from a planned economy and embrace of market exchange did not mean a retreat from government accepting a menu of responsibilities, challenges, and opportunities different from those on offer in many other developing and developed societies. The state became a major owner of several of the country's largest enterprises as several other governments were divesting themselves of state ownership stakes in major companies. The Chinese state does not have the same kind of philosophical commitment to a clean and complete separation of state and society as Western governments, whose economic policies tend to qualify an ideal anchored in earlier historical practices; Chinese practices too are tied to earlier problems and possibilities, even when not explicitly recognized. The gap, for example, between central and local officials allows room for flexibility and abuse – flexibility can mean multiple positive responses to central directives that accommodate local contexts, while abuse results from the ability of local leaders to flout rules and prohibitions because the center lacks the capacity to monitor local officials adequately and cannot consistently create effective incentives to encourage the behavior they seek. The Chinese economy exhibits two traits that from most Western perspectives are difficult to reconcile, and make more sense when seen to result from the efforts of bureaucratic control on a large-scale political setting coupled with the spaces for organizing activity from below. On the one hand, the government continues to play a very large role as manager of big enterprises and on the other, much entrepreneurial activity from the bottom up continues to proceed with inadequate government regulation and control. The resolution of disputes still depends on forms of negotiated settlement that accommodates poorly the expectations of foreign actors for the institutions they typically work under.

Historically, China's large territorial size and large population have created problems and positive possibilities particular to China and foreign to Europe. But as the European Union grapples to become a new kind of polity that builds a vertically integrated administration over a land mass more comparable to China's than at any point since the era of the Han and Roman empires, it is discovering many of the difficulties and challenges encountered repeatedly in Chinese history. It does so, of course, within a different tradition of political ideas and institutions and will not likely come to resemble China very closely. Symmetrically, we might adjust our expectations to recognize that China may not necessarily become more like a Western polity or economy.

China's economic advances into the world economy, an economy dominated by powerful capitalist economies, have led many observers to consider contemporary China a capitalist economy. At the same time both Chinese and international evaluations of China's economy stress differences between Chinese practices and those elsewhere. Some Chinese stress that theirs is a *socialist* market economy while others, including many World Trade Organization members, regard China as a "non-market economy." At stake is the role of the state in the economy, a role that includes many features that resonate with earlier expectations of what Chinese governments do in a commercial economy. Observers implicitly if not explicitly divide Chinese traits into those that have developed through emulation of foreign practices and those that remain elaborations upon earlier Chinese practices, and see one set as desirable and the other as negative. China's economic experiences before 1850 help us see what China has become thereafter, even if there remains room for debate over how to characterize the economy's traits and how it fits into the world of contemporary capitalism.

References

Bray, F. (1984). *Science and Civilization in China*. Vol. VI: *Biology and Biological Technology*. Cambridge University Press, Part 2.

Burbank, J. and F. Cooper (2010). *Empires in World History: Power and the Politics of Difference*. Princeton University Press.

Chan, W. (1980). "Government, Merchants and Industry to 1911," in John Fairbank and Kwang-ching Liu (eds.), *Cambridge History of China*. Vol. XI: *Late Ch'ing*, part 2, *1800–1911*. Cambridge University Press, pp. 416–462.

Chen Zhiping (2009). *Minjian wenshu yu Ming Qing Dongnan zushang yanjiu* [Non-official Documents and Research on Lineage Merchants in Southeast China during the Ming and Qing Dynasties]. Zhonghua shuju.

Ch'iu Peng-sheng (2008). *Dang falü yu jingji: Ming Qing Zhongguo de shangye falü* [When Law Meets the Economy: Ming Qing Chinese Commercial Law]. Wunan tushu chuban gongsi.

Deng, Gang (1993). *Development versus Stagnation: Technological Change and Agricultural Progress in Pre-modern China*. Greenwood Press.

Elvin, M. (1973). *The Pattern of the Chinese Past*. Stanford University Press.

Fan Jinmin (1998). *Ming Qing Jiangnan shangye de fazhan* [The Development of the Ming Qing Period Jiangnan Commercial Economy]. Nanjing daxue chubanshe.

　(2007). *Ming Qing shangshi jiufen yu shangye susong* [Ming Qing Commercial Dispute Resolution and Commercial Disputes]. Nanjing daxue chubanshe.

Fan Shuzhi (1990). *Ming Qing Jiangnan shizhen tanwei* [A Study of Ming Qing Era Jiangnan Market Towns]. Fudan daxue chubanshe.

Faure, D. (1989). "The Lineage as Business Company: Patronage versus Law in the Development of Chinese Business," in *Second Conference on Modern Chinese Economic History*. Academia Sinica, pp. 347–376.

Finlay, R. (2010). *The Pilgrim Art: Cultures of Porcelain in World History*. University of California Press.

Grove, L. (2006). *A Chinese Economic Revolution: Rural Entrepreneurship in the Twentieth Century*. Rowman & Littlefield.

Hicks, J. (1973). *A Theory of Economic History*. Oxford University Press.

Hsiao, K. (1979). *A History of Chinese Political Thought*, vol. I. Trs. F. W. Mote. Princeton University Press.

Knotter, A. (2001). "Problems of the 'Family Economy': Peasant Economy, Domestic Production and Labor Markets in Pre-industrial Europe," in M. Prak (ed.), *Early Modern Capitalism: Economic and Social Change in Europe, 1400–1800*. Routledge, pp. 135–160.

Huang Jianhui (2002). *Ming Qing Shanxi shangren yanjiu* [Studies of Ming Qing Era Shanxi Merchants]. Shanxi jingji chubanshe.

Köll, E. (2003). *From Cotton Mill to Business Empire: The Emergence of Regional Enterprises in Modern China*. Cambridge, MA: Harvard University Asia Center.

Li, B. (2003). "Was There a 'Fourteenth-Century Turning Point'?" in Paul Jakov Smith and Richard von Glahn (eds.), *The Song-Yuan-Ming Transition in Chinese History*. Cambridge, MA: Harvard University Asia Center.

Li, C. (2012). "Beneficiary Pays: Forging Reciprocal Connections Between Private Profit and Public Good in Hydraulic Reform in the Lower Yangzi Delta, 1520s-1640s," *T'oung Pao* 98: 385–438.

Li Huarui (2004). *Wang Anshi bianfa yanjiu shi* [A History of Research on Wang Anshi's New Policies]. Renmin chubanshe.

Liang Miaotai (1991). *Ming Qing Jingdezhen chengshi jingji yanjiu* [Studies of the Ming Qing Period Jingdezhen Urban Economy]. Jiangxi renmin chubanshe.

Liu, G. (2013). "Agricultural Productivity in Early Modern Jiangnan," in B. K. L. So (ed.), *Economic History of Lower Yangzi Delta in Late Imperial China*. Routledge.

Liu Jiansheng et al. (2005). *Ming Qing Jinshang zhidu bianqian yanjiu* [Studies of Institutional Change among Ming Qing Era Shanxi Merchants]. Shanxi renmin chubanshe.

Liu, T. C. (1959). *Reform in Sung China: Wang An-shih (1021–1086) and his New Policies*. Harvard University Press.

Lucassen, J. (2001). "Mobilization of Labour in Early Modern Europe," in Maarten Prak (ed.), *Early Modern Capitalism: Economic and Social Change in Europe, 1400–1800*. Routledge, pp. 161–174.

Lufrano, R. (1987). *Honorable Merchants: Commerce and Self-Cultivation in Late Imperial China*. University of Hawaii Press.

Macauley, M. (1999). *Social Power and Legal Culture: Litigation Masters in Late Imperial China*. Stanford University Press.

Mann, S. (1987). *Local Merchants and the Chinese Bureaucracy, 1750–1950*. Stanford University Press.

Menzies, N. (1994). *Forest and Land Management in Imperial China*. Macmillan Press.

Morita, Akira (2002). *Shindai no suiri to chi'ikki shakai* [Qing Dynasty Water Control and Local Society]. Chūgoku shoten.

Mou Kenhe (2002). *Songdai xinyong piaoju yanjiu* [Studies of Song Dynasty Credit]. Yunnan daxue chubanshe.

Ng, C.-K. (1983). *Trade and Society: The Amoy Network on the China Coast 1683–1735*. National University of Singapore Press.

Niu Guanjie (2008). *17–19 shiji Zhongguo de shichang yu jingji fazhan* [Chinese Markets and Economic Development, 17th–19th Centuries]. Huangshan shushe.

Osborne, A. (1998). "Highland and Lowlands: Economic and Ecological Interaction in the Lower Yangzi Region under the Qing," in M. Elvin and T. Liu (eds.), *Sediments of Time. Part I: Environment and Society in Chinese History*. Cambridge University Press, pp. 203–234.

Pagani, C. (2001). *Eastern Magnificence and European Ingenuity: Clocks in Late Imperial China*. University of Michigan Press.

Perdue, P. (1982). "Water Control in the Dongting Lake Region during the Ming and Qing Periods," *Journal of Asian Studies* 41(4): 747–765.

Pomeranz, K. (1993). *The Making of a Hinterland: State, Society, and Economy in Inland North China, 1853–1937*. University of California Press.

(2000). *The Great Divergence: Europe, China and the Making of the Modern World Economy*. Princeton University Press.

Qi Xia (1987). *Songdai jingji shi* [Song Dynasty Economic History], Vol. 1. Shanghai renmin chubanshe.

Rawski, T. (1989). *Economic Growth in Prewar China*. University of California Press.

Ren Fang (2003). *Ming Qing Changjiang zhongyou shizhen jingji yanjiu* [Studies of the Market Economy in the Middle Yangzi Region during the Ming Qing Period]. Wuhan daxue chubanshe.

Rosenthal, J. L. and R. B. Wong (2011). *Before and Beyond Divergence: The Politics of Economic Change in China and Europe*. Harvard University Press.

Ruskola, Teemu (2000). "Conceptualizing Corporations and Kinship: Comparative Law and Development Theory in a Chinese Perspective," *Stanford Law Review*, 52(6): 1599–1729.

Schlumbohm, J. (2001). "Labour in Proto-industrialization: Big Questions and Micro-answers," in M. Prak (ed.), *Early Modern Capitalism: Economic and Social Change in Europe, 1400–1800*. Routledge, pp. 125–134.

Shiba, Y. (1998). "Environment versus Water Control: The Case of the Southern Hangzhou Bay Area from the mid-Tang Through the Qing," in Mark Elvin and T. Liu (eds.), *Sediments of Time. Part 1: Environment and Society in Chinese History*. Cambridge University Press, pp. 135–164.

Terada Takanobu (1972). *Sansei shōnin no kenkyū* [Research on the Shanxi Merchants]. Dohosha.

Van Dyke, P. (2011). *Merchants of Canton and Macao: Politics and Strategies of Eighteenth-century Chinese Trade*. Hong Kong University Press.

Vries, J. and A. van der Woude. (1997). *The First Modern Economy: Success, Failure and Perseverance of the Dutch Economy, 1500–1815*. Cambridge University Press.

Wang Kui (2008). *Qingmo shangbu yanjiu* [A Study of the Late Qing Dynasty Ministry of Finance). Renmin chubanshe.

White, L. (1998). *Unstately Power*. Vol. 1: *Local Causes of China's Economic Reforms*. M. E. Sharpe.

Will, P. E. (1985). "State Intervention in the Administration of a Hydraulic Infrastructure: The Example of Hubei Province in Late Imperial Times," in S. R. Schram (ed.), *The Scope of State Power in China*. SOAS and Chinese University Press, pp. 295–348.

(1990). *Bureaucracy and Famine in Eighteenth-century China*. Stanford University Press.

Will, P.-E. and R. B. Wong (1991). *Nourish the People: The State Civilian Granary System in China, 1650–1850*. University of Michigan Center for Chinese Studies.

Wong, R. B. (1999). "The Political Economy of Agrarian China and its Modern Legacy," in T. Brook and G. Blue (eds.), *China and Capitalism: Genealogies of Sinological Knowledge*. Cambridge University Press, pp. 210–45.

(2002). "The Political Economy of Chinese Rural Industry and Commerce in Historical Perspective," *Études Rurales (Le retour du marchand dans la Chine rurale)* 161–162: 153–164.

(2004). "Relationships between the Political Economies of Maritime and Agrarian China, 1750–1850," in G. Wang and C.-K. Ng (eds.), *Maritime China and the Overseas Chinese Communities*. Harrassowitz Verlag, pp. 19–31.

(2012). "Taxation and Good Governance in China, 1500–1914," in B. Yun-Casalilla and P. K. O'Brien with F. Comín Comín (eds.), *The Rise of Fiscal States: A Global History, 1500–1914*. Cambridge University Press.

Wu Tingyu (1987). *Zhongguo lidai tudi zhidu shigang* [A History of Chinese Land Systems]. Jilin daxue chubanshe.

Xu, D. and C. Wu, eds. (2000). *Chinese Capitalism, 1522–1840*. Macmillan Press.

Xu Tan (1998). *Ming Qing shiqi Shandong shangpin jingji de fazhan* [The Development of Shandong's Commercial Economy in the Ming-Qing Period]. Zhongguo shehui kexue chubanshe.

Yang Guozhen (2009). *Ming Qing tudi qiyue wenshu yanjiu* [Studies of Land Contract Documents of the Ming Qing Era]. Zhongguo renmin daxue chubanse.

Zhang Haiying (2002). *Ming Qing Jiangnan shangpin liutong yu shicang tixi* [Commercial Circulation and Market Structures in Ming Qing Era Jiangnan]. Huadong shifan daxue chubanshe.

Zelin, M. (2005). *The Merchants of Zigong: Industrial Entrepreneurship in Early Modern China*. Columbia University Press.

Zhang Haipeng and Wang Yanyuan, eds. (1995). *Hui shang yanjiu* (Studies of Huizhou Merchants). Anhui renmin chubanshe.

Zhou Zhichu (2002). *Wan Qing caizheng jingji yanjiu* [Research on Late Qing Fiscal Administration]. Jilu shushe.

7

Capitalism in India in the very long run

TIRTHANKAR ROY

Any general account of capitalism in India needs to be mindful of two characteristics of the region. First, Indians have been doing business with the outside world for millennia. The Indian subcontinent has long enjoyed a central place within intersecting webs of commercial and cultural exchange, thanks to a coastline thousands of miles long, convenient access from Africa and southeast Asia, the presence of skilled artisans, and a robust seafaring tradition. Second, there was, and still is, an extraordinary degree of regional diversity within the Indian subcontinent. For example, if the coasts and the deltas engaged routinely in foreign trade, the uplands, the great flood plains, and the arid areas in the interior did so to a much smaller extent; and partly because of this difference, merchants and bankers located in the interior were of a different kind from their counterparts on the seaboard. These features, namely, a propensity to engage with the world and great diversity among business firms, characterized Indian history from very early on. And because they were so enduring, any general account of Indian capitalism should be a long-range one.

This chapter will present such an account. The plot that holds this narrative together is the interplay between diversity and difference on the one hand, and attempts by regional states to bridge diversity and difference on the other. By diversity is meant the presence of two distinct capitalisms, one based in the capital cities of powerful empires that formed in the landlocked interior, and the other based in the seaboard, ruled by weaker states. The former was dependent on grain trade and the fiscal system, the latter on foreign trade. The distance between them was bridged through the imperial ambition to join maritime trade. These attempts, it is shown, succeeded in a limited way in the seventeenth century, and intermittently before. The game took a dramatic turn in the wake of Indo-European trade when, for the first time in Indian history, a merchant-ruled seaboard state began to rule the interior. The ground was thus set for a process of convergence between the two worlds.

The meaning of the change cannot be fully grasped except in relation to the dialectical movement that had been characteristic of Indian capitalism.

The chapter needs to make frequent use of two concepts, capitalism and convergence. What do I mean by these terms? "Capitalism" tends to enter comparative economic history in three different ways: as a mode of production in orthodox Marxism; as international trade in the world systems analysis; and as institutions in current discourses on international development. I will ignore the orthodox definition for reasons explained in the next section, and deal with trade in the first half of the chapter and with institutions in the second half. In turn, "convergence" will mean either more exchange between different trading orders, or greater resemblance between them in institutional terms.

Two capitalisms

In the 1960s and the 1970s, Marxist historiography followed Karl Marx's *Capital* to define capitalism with reference to production relations, especially, extensive use of wage labor (Desai 1991). The definition cannot be easily employed in doing global and comparative history, production relations being a concept too tied to specific production sites to be quite portable. One alternative explored was to designate Europe capitalist and non-Europe as non-capitalist. "The capitalist penetration," Robert Brenner writes, "of the 'third world' through trade and capital investment not only has failed to carry with it capitalist economic development, but has erected positive barriers to such development," allowing "old modes of production" to dig in deeper inside India and China (Brenner 1977: 26; see also n. 2). Such an approach would not find favor today. For India, the scholarly enterprise saw its fullest flourish in an exchange known as the "mode of production" debate, which deliberated on the appropriate characterization of the Indian agrarian system as it had evolved from the colonial times (essays in Patnaik 1990). This debate died without heir. It proved unsure in dealing with business history, engaged in semantics more than real history, and found diversity within the Indian experience difficult to handle.

Interestingly, in his remarks on India, which had first appeared in journalistic writings before *Capital* was published, Marx followed a different way of understanding economic systems, one that emphasized the state rather more than capital–labor relations. Possibly, the emphasis arose from Marx's famous belief that private property did not exist in Asia (Thavaraj 1984). Be that as it may, it was this conception that led to the most influential attempt to read the history of capitalism in India.

In 1969 an article was published on the subject (Habib 1969). The article belonged in a line of interpretive scholarship that employed the concept of capitalism in order to draw broad distinctions between the economic trajectories of the West and the East. Earlier characterizations of Asian business had made use of notions such as peddling (J. C. Van Leur), pre-capitalist (J. H. Boeke), and non-materialistic (Max Weber). The Habib article followed a different tradition, that of James Mill and Karl Marx, to focus on the relationship between the Mughal imperial state and the big merchants and bankers of the imperial realm. The argument was that a centralized and revenue-hungry state had left the capitalists too dependent on a "parasitical" system of "direct agrarian exploitation by a small ruling class" (Habib 1969: 77). Apparently, the Indian capitalists were left with little outlet for their enterprise outside the cities of courtly power.

Despite the differences between models of capitalism, the shared assumption until the 1980s was that India represented an impure version of capitalism, the purest manifestation of which was to be found in the modern West. Interpretations of world history and Indian history implicitly retained the assumption. Frequent use was made of "class" in order to define the distinctiveness of the Indian experience, especially the distinct pattern of economic change experienced during British colonial rule, at a time when world economic inequality reached unprecedented levels (Bagchi 1982).

A major challenge to the assumption came in the 1980s and 1990s from research on maritime trade along the littoral. This scholarship revealed quite another order of enterprise in early modern India, one that did not fit the picture of a politically dependent world of business. In this realm, the states were smaller and weaker than those inland, the capital-owning merchants did different kinds of business from those located in the cities of the empire, and the relationship between the state and the merchant was different too. Research on Indian Ocean trade showed not only how deeply European commercial success in Gujarat, Coromandel, and Bengal depended on the agency, accommodation, and partnership of Indian merchants and bankers, but also how little direct influence the land-based empires exercised on coastal entrepreneurship.[1] Large swathes of the coast were ruled by states that

---

[1] On the history of the English and the Dutch companies, see Chaudhuri (1978), Furber (1951), and Prakash (1998, 1985). On Indian textiles, essays in two recent collections are state of the art: Riello and Parthasarathi (2010), and Riello and Roy (2010).

remained at a remove from those that had formed inland, a circumstance that enabled the English East India Company to acquire port sites where it could function unmolested as landlord. Trade in the Indian Ocean, and India's strategic role as a transit point, were shown to be of great antiquity. The scholarship also showed that the decline of the Mughal empire might have made the coastal entrepreneurs politically more ambitious than before, even drawing them closer to collaboration with the Europeans. In this way, the early modern commercialization was seen as preparatory to the start of a merchant-ruled empire in the eighteenth century.

On one point, the historiography of inland commerce and the historiography of coastal commerce were in agreement. Both considered that the "potentialities" of their preferred version of capitalism to lead to a full-blown industrial society had been limited.[2] In Habib's narrative, the promise was not fulfilled because the merchants were too dependent on the despotic state. Others have taken pains to replace the picture of dependent capitalists with one of free and institutionally advanced capitalists in the eighteenth century. Indian businesses in this reading were "sophisticated" (Perlin 1983: p. 69; Ray 1995: 455). But they lost their freedom to negotiate terms as European colonial rule consolidated in the region. Indian merchants became increasingly oriented to Europe and were coordinated by European capitalists.

In this way, these two stories, one about the business world of the Mughal empire ruling the Gangetic plains and another about the business world of the coasts, converged into one that we can call the story of capitalism interrupted. What lent this story relevance and purpose was the need that many Indianists felt to explain the failure of nineteenth-century India to become as capitalist as western Europe, leading to a historiography "dominated by forebodings of colonial conquest and decline" (Washbrook 2007).

Revisiting this grand narrative of decline and fall is not the aim of the present chapter. There are two reasons why that is not so. First, the decline and fall idea looks odd in the backdrop of a capitalistic resurgence that has occurred in south Asia in the more recent times. Surely the resurgence had owed something to colonial India's trading heritage? The decline and fall story would suggest, implausibly, that it did not. Second, whether or not the prospect of capitalism was obstructed by colonial rule is a rhetorical question.

---

2 Some of the mechanisms that frustrated the progression of Indian traders toward this nirvana were deindustrialization, decline of Indian shipping, and the transformation of Indian traders into comprador capitalists. See Perlin (1983) and Wallerstein (1986) for arguments about the end of the capitalistic efflorescence.

We should, instead, use these scholarships to do real business history, by which I mean pay more attention to the empirical propositions they advance.

So far in the historiography of early modern India, the maritime and the interior have remained discrete worlds. The two form subjects of different specialisms, partly because the relevant archives are different, until late in the eighteenth century when the East India Company records begin to display considerable interest in the Gangetic plains. The two specialisms have been even engaged in a fierce debate over who is more right as to the cause of economic decline in the eighteenth century (Marshall 2003).

It is the argument of the chapter that these two orders of commercial enterprise, one based on land and the other ocean bound, do not represent alternative interpretations of history, but should be combined to construct the picture of a dichotomous business world. The dualism between the land and the sea predated the early modern times by centuries because it was primarily geographical in origin. But it was also a field of political action, because land-based powers wanted to control the sea, albeit with insufficient means, until a limited success in the endeavor was achieved in the 1600s. Thereafter, Indo-European trade added a new dimension to this politics by steadily empowering the seaboard militarily and politically.

In order to see how the politics evolved through these stages, we should start our journey from much earlier times.[3]

Early trade to 1200

A quick glance at the map of the Indian subcontinent will show us that its topography would have presented any long-distance trader living before the age of steam with a great advantage and a great disadvantage at the same time. The immediately visible geographical advantage of the region was its long coastline, situated conveniently in the middle of the sea route between south-east Asia and west Asia. Both these regions belonged in ancient maritime commercial networks. The Arabian Sea, Persian Gulf, and the Red Sea supplied merchandise from India's Konkan and Malabar coasts with access to west Asian, Mediterranean, European, and north African markets, and the Bay of Bengal likewise supplied the produce of Bengal and Coromandel with access to markets in Burma, Cambodia, Sumatra, Java, and China.

On the other hand, the cost of bulk transportation over land was ordinarily very high. If data compiled in the eighteenth and nineteenth centuries are any

---

3 The next three sections draw on Roy (2012).

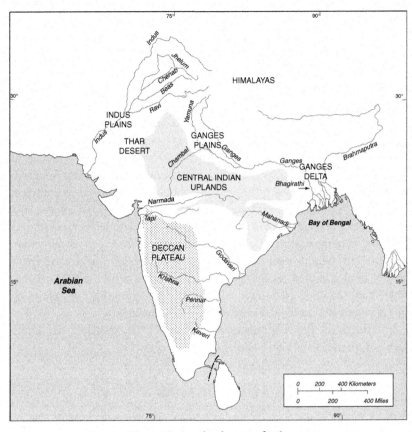

Map 7.1 Geographical zones of India

indication, the cost of moving cargo per ton/mile by carts was two to three times that of boats, and by bullock caravans two to three times that of carts. These differences were the result of the time taken to move goods as well as the varieties of risk and depreciation that applied to these modes of transportation. In major trade routes that traversed the Himalayan passes, caravan costs became astronomical given the limited capacity of the pack animals and the high risk of their death. Bullock carts were suitable for transporting goods over a few miles, and unsuitable for long-distance transportation. Even for limited transit, carts were rarely used in central and southern uplands (see Map 7.1). Boats could not move over long distances outside the Ganges and Indus basins, because few rivers other than the Himalayan snowmelt ones were navigable. In the Bengal delta, which had a dense network of navigable rivers, river morphology changed so much from one area to another that boat construction and navigational knowledge tended to be locally rooted. The situation was not conducive for mass transportation systems to develop. In deltaic Bengal and the lower reaches of the Ganges and the Indus, where relatively placid and deepwater channels could be found, inland navigation was limited by seasonal fluctuations in water level and by mud, eddies, sudden appearance of sandbanks, and pirate attacks (Roy 2011a).

A relatively easy access to the oceans from the seaboard, and a relatively difficult access from the interior to the seaboard, gave ancient commerce a distinctive character. Organized trading and banking developed along two axes – the seaboard and the imperial cities. Merchants and bankers on the seaboard lived on maritime trade; those in the interior depended directly or indirectly on the land revenue system and to a limited extent overland trade. Income from maritime trade provided much-needed revenue to the seaboard states, but was in itself not enough to sustain large armies and bureaucracies. Strong political hubs were usually located inland, inside states that made use of the revenues to be had from the riparian plains.

Exceptions to this picture were present. Perhaps the most important case of a large state that seemed to bridge the land and the sea was the south Indian Chola at the turn of the second millennium CE, who operated from one of the largest and geographically most accessible deltas in the peninsula, that of the River Kaveri. Similar examples would be hard to find elsewhere. The Ganges delta, by comparison, was larger in size but far less accessible from inland as well as from the sea. How well the Chola achieved the integration is also a debatable issue.

In respect of the direction and composition of commodity trade, the seaboard clusters looked mainly outward whereas the inland clusters looked mainly towards local consumption. The two worlds came into contact all the time. Major caravan routes crisscrossed the Deccan plateau, and moved along the river valleys of the peninsula. Still, the costs of carriage being as high as described above, caravan trade could not conceivably have had enough capacity to carry the produce of the interior agrarian societies on a large scale. Instead, the goods that it was profitable to carry were the relatively highly priced low-bulk commodities. The most important of such tradable goods were fine textiles, spices, silks, pearls, diamonds, fine ceramics, gold, and other precious stones such as lapis lazuli.

The seaboard commercial clusters accessed these high-value, low-bulk goods. But they also accessed a variety of goods from the immediate vicinity. Despite the vast length of the seafront, ports did not grow up randomly.

In fact, ancient Indian ports almost without exception situated themselves on estuaries that sheltered them from the violence of the monsoon on the one hand, and secured them an easy way to procure raw material, foods, and traded goods by rivers from within the delta on the other hand. The physical link between the sea and the land was achieved by means of rivers. Cambay/Khambat on the River Mahi, Surat on the Tapi, Broach/Bharuch/Bharukacchha/Barigaza on the Narmada, Arikamedu on the Ponnaiyar, Tamralipti/Tamluk on the Rupnarayan, Saptagram/Satgaon on the Saraswati, Masulipatnam in the Krishna delta, Hooghly on the Bhagirathi, Balasore/Baleshwar with easy access to Budibalang and Subarnarekha, Sonargaon on the Shitalakhya, Old Goa on the Mandovi, the Malabar ports Muziris (exact site still debated) and Kollam/Quilon on the inland waterways – all of these sites were within easy reach simultaneously of the sea and of the inland via the rivers on which they were situated. The fundamental distance between the landed and the maritime business worlds remained intact, because the rivers that these hubs were situated on were not ordinarily navigable beyond a few miles, even though the river valley often supplied an easy land route for caravan traffic. The long-term fortunes of these sites depended upon local geographical factors. They declined or were abandoned because the rivers that they lived on silted up or changed course. Commercial fortunes, in this way, depended on the unstable environment of the larger region.

Reflecting the same kind of dependence, the monsoon wind imposed pronounced seasonality upon trade, the functioning of the ports, and the rhythm of transportation. Even the most considerable ports had the character of a seasonal fairground, doing brisk business in the winter months followed by a long period of lull. Cesar Frederick saw this phenomenon in Betore, the most important point of Portuguese trade in lower Bengal about 1565, where "a village [was] constructed every year" and burnt down after the trading season.[4] The same thing happened to Chaul, another considerable port on the Konkan. Harbors had a makeshift character. Ship and boat construction came in a bewildering variety along the coast, for evidently the shipwrights had to solve local issues. For example, ship design needed to adapt to the monsoon winds rather than ocean currents. The preoccupation with adaptation to local constraints led Indian shipping to pay less attention to long-distance voyages and the challenges that such voyages entailed. Therefore, even as intra-Asian trade provided enough profitable opportunities to the traders located on the seaboard, the Indian trading system was technologically ill equipped to

4 See Kerr (1824: 178–181) on Cesar Frederick's account of trade in lower Bengal.

venture beyond the Arabian Sea or the Bay of Bengal. The knowledge of how to build large ships did exist, but it was not commercially employed. Voyages that might take months rather than weeks were not the priority for traders or shipwrights.

From long before the beginning of the Common Era, and almost 1500 years after, the most powerful states in India tended to form hundreds of miles away from the coast. Few maintained anything more than a very tenuous and indirect link with the littoral or the littoral kingdoms. In their turn, the Maurya and Satavahana empires (*c.* 320 BCE to *c.* 100 CE), the Gupta empire (*c.* 250–550), the Kusans (200–0 BCE), even the much later Delhi sultanate (1206–1526), Mughal (1526–*c.* 1750), and Vijayanagar empires (1336–1565) were in effect landlocked. Their capital cities were located months, or even a whole year's journey, away from the nearest seaport. It has been said above that the state that did manage to break this cleavage to some extent was that of the Chola (850–1280), who developed on the southeastern coast of India, where the deltas were wider, more easily accessible from inland, and had plentiful fertile land.

Even though inland states were far away from the littoral, as they enlarged they did try to take control of the coast or build more secure contacts with the coastal world of commerce. States that lived mainly on land taxes still had an interest in road building to open up military supply routes. From time to time, empires also secured large chunks of overland routes, and connected them to the sea. Before the Common Era, the Satavahana empire achieved this integration to feed the Indo-Roman trade from Coromandel. The Kusans at the turn of the Common Era secured overland traffic between the upper Indus plains and central Asia. The Gupta empire in west central India secured traffic between the political center in Ujjain and the Gujarat littoral. The Chola in the twelfth century achieved an unusual extent of land and sea integration.

This picture of two distinct trading clusters, one ocean going and another land based, with not enough contact or exchange between them, was thus susceptible to attempts by the interior world to create a militarily and politically stable access to the sea. Success in this respect began to take shape from the thirteenth century onward with the slow spread of Islam southward and eastward.

A deeper integration: 1200–1600

About 1206 a Turkic Mamluk general of the Afghan warlord and ruler Muhammad Ghori built a powerful state in north India, inaugurating the sultanate of Delhi. About the same time, other warlords were carving out estates in the eastern part of the Gangetic plane. During the next centuries, as Delhi grew stronger, military supply routes penetrated into Gujarat, Deccan, and Bengal from Delhi, settlements of northerners in these regions increased, and so did trade contact. The expansion of northern political power and pan-Asian courtly culture southward and eastward was of a different order of expansion from those in the past. For one thing it was supported by a massive expansion in mobile cavalry armies. Perhaps military technology explains best the possibility of holding on to distant outposts of the empire. For another, Islam supplied a cooperative principle among communities that colonized land frontiers, cleared forests, and sometimes supplied soldiers to the state.

Between 1300 and 1600, the authority of Delhi or its vassals increased sufficiently to open up east–west, north–south, and trans-Himalayan trading-cum-military routes. The conquest by Delhi's vassals of Malwa, Deccan, Gujarat, and Bengal was the foundation upon which a sustainable integration of roads, inland waterways, and the sea could build itself during the Mughal empire in the seventeenth century.

These developments had little effect on the long-term pattern of commercialization in the region. The imperial states still lived on land taxes in the main. The coastal states were still small, semi-autonomous, and only intermittently allies of the inland empires. The cost of moving cavalry into the hilly coasts of western India or into swampy Bengal was still too high. The sultanate, the Mughals, the Vijayanagar empire in the south were all interested in overseas trade, but an overwhelming percentage of their income came from land, and landed estates maintained the military aristocracy.

Despite these broad elements of continuity, the Indo-Islamic empires did strengthen trading contacts in the region. They did so in two principal ways. They integrated markets in the wider Islamic world of Asia, connecting India with the Silk Road for instance. And second, while connecting north India with south India, eastern with western Deccan, Bengal and the Ganges delta with the imperial core, thus stimulating trade along the Ganges itself, the empires managed to create a few ports on the sea that more firmly belonged to the land-based states. These ports, Surat in the Mughal province of Gujarat, Hooghly in Mughal Bengal, and Masulipatnam on Coromandel (a port sponsored by the Deccan state of Golkonda, see Map 7.2) represented, in political if not economic terms, a closer integration of inland states and maritime trade than before.

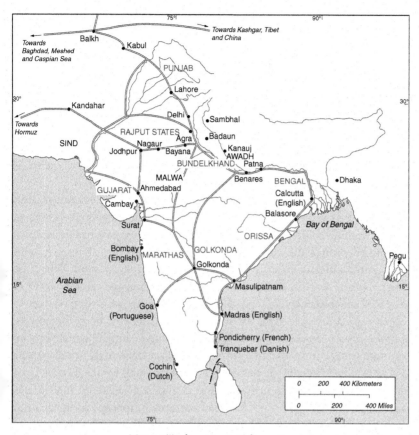

Map 7.2 Trade routes in India c. 1650

It would be difficult to explain the beginnings of European commercial enterprise on the Indian coasts without reference to this prior, deeper, integration.

Indo-European trade: 1600–1800

The European interest in Indian goods began on a serious scale after Vasco Da Gama discovered the sea route to India around the Cape of Good Hope (1498), thereby bypassing the Arab and Mediterranean merchants who controlled the Indo-European trade via west Asia. The interest was at first an indirect one. Cotton textiles were procured from India in order to pay for Indonesian spices. Textiles were also a handy medium of exchange in the African trades in slaves and ivory. In turn, warhorses from west Asia were a convenient means of payment for Indian textiles. Horses for textiles and textiles for spices were ancient forms of exchange in the Indian Ocean world. The Portuguese interest was to take a share of the maritime exchange so as to divert a part of the spice trade between Europe and Asia to the sea route from the overland or Mediterranean route. From the mid-seventeenth century, however, India became a more central piece in the operation. The demand for Indian cotton cloth in European markets increased, whereas silver procured from Spanish America replaced all other articles as the most important medium of exchange in India, thus delinking Indo-European trade from Asian trade.

In the sixteenth century, the Portuguese mariners could still conceive of an empire on the sea, in defiance of Arab merchants and indigenous merchants on the western coast of India, because the inland empire had little naval capacity to control the coast. In the seventeenth century, however, both Surat and Masulipatnam were seats of provincial administration. When the Dutch and the English East India Companies entered the trading world in search of Indian textiles (c. 1615), they were militarily not strong enough to contemplate a struggle with the inland states. Conquest being out of the question, they needed to establish footholds in the existing imperial ports by negotiating trade treaties with Agra or Golkonda, or one of the smaller states that were usually keen to invite foreign merchants both for the income from trade and for reasons of security against opportunistic neighbors. Indeed, this sanction from the inland states gave the northern Europeans an upper hand with respect to the Portuguese, and equally, served the inland states to create a deterrent against the Portuguese.

In the Indian Ocean world, the Europeans represented two organizational principles that were not indigenous to the region. The hardware and the knowledge to carry out intercontinental trading voyages was one of these. Ship sizes were on average smaller in the seventeenth and eighteenth century than in the era of peak Portuguese power (mid to late 1500s), but they were still larger than those operating in coast to coast trade in India, sufficiently large to carry many guns. More than the potential for causing violence, shipping technology brought the knowledge of markets beyond Asia into contact with Asian goods. It also had a deep impact upon technological change along the coast. It spread the knowledge of cast-iron founding, and led Indian ship construction and navigation technology toward European standards. A second distinctive feature of Indo-European trade, more relevant with the English and the Dutch traders, was the institution of the joint-stock company, which was unknown in this world. Thanks to joint-stock organization, these were firms much larger in scale and better able to weather risks than the family firms that ruled the Indian business world. They were also more specialized in specific goods, not necessarily luxuries. And being specialized, they needed to make use of long-period contractual transactions. The fair-ground style of trading on the Indian coasts, therefore, was not compatible with the European mode of doing transoceanic business.

While these were their strengths, the chartered companies suffered from weaknesses too. The English company had formed out of a Crown-delivered monopoly. But it had few effective means available to impose that monopoly. Indeed, it needed to share its monopoly trading rights with its own employees stationed abroad in order to supply them with enough incentive to work for the company and deal with the huge risks that trading overseas entailed in early modern times. But this factor created a fundamental conflict of interest between principals and agents. The agents could abuse the privilege, or be seen to do so. The agents in their turn felt that they needed to fend for themselves in a hostile world that the principals did not understand. Along an undefined fringe of the company's business, therefore, there existed a vast network of private traders and company employees doing private trade. Some were punished, but most survived with little effective check on them.

Historians of Indo-European trade remind us how deeply the Europeans depended on Indian partners and agents in carrying out their business. Building networks of collaboration was indeed an important feature of the trade. In the records of European business, we hear about several kinds of indigenous business firms. The wealthiest and politically the most powerful class were the bankers. Those who ruled Surat and Masulipatnam were the group Ashin Das Gupta called ship-owning merchants (Das Gupta 2001). People like Mullah Abdul Ghafoor, who owned a large number of ships plying the west Asia route, were, not unlike the owners of the chartered companies, stationary heads of trading firm who did not take a direct interest in the navigational and technological side of the business. They hired ship captains and gave away a part of the trading rights as an incentive in order to carry out their own business deals effectively. These groups the Europeans did not collaborate with much, but had to remain friendly with, for the former commanded much political power.

On the other hand, the Europeans had regular dealings with bankers. The Indian banking firms at this time had close links with the regional, and sometimes the imperial, courts, for many of them lent money to the rulers and supplied war finance. Considerable money circulated among the nobility or among the city merchants in Mughal India. Deposit bankers of Agra in the seventeenth century, for example, had as their main clients the military-political elite of the same cities (Habib 1964). Individual firm histories remain scarce. But we do know quite a lot about one entity, the Jagatseth of Bengal, thanks to the company's complex relationship with it. The firm of Jagatseths held the license to carry on a variety of monetary functions that should ordinarily be done by the state. They were as big and powerful as the Bengal Nawab's hold on the monetary system was precarious, and money was valuable in Bengal because of Indo-European trade. As Spanish silver entered India in larger quantities, the business of licensed money-changing grew in scale. For remittance, currency, and short-term loans, the Europeans relied mainly on reputable Indian family firms. The dependence increased during warfare and led to a ranking of these firms on a scale of loyalty and friendliness.

Indian textile merchants entered the companies' books as "brokers" or contractors who monitored the long-period advances of money. For local transportation of goods and materials, the companies relied entirely on Indian caravan operators and on the coast-to-coast shipping largely owned by Indians. Skilled artisans, such as weavers and textile processors, were again in close contact with the companies.

Two general features of these Indo-European partnerships deserve special notice. First, almost always the Europeans contracted with those individuals who they thought were leaders of their communities. Social leadership had to be harnessed for business purposes, for there was hardly any other way that contracts could be enforced. The Europeans did not have enough policing powers, nor could they take recourse in indigenous law for the purpose. Surat and Masulipatnam had strong governments, but they did not possess a well-defined framework of commercial law. No mercantile community was strong enough to impose its law upon others. Law, such as it was, had been endogenous to community norms and enforced by community leaders and elders. Indo-European business, therefore, created, utilized, and sometimes strengthened hierarchies. Second, the wide network of contracts weakened, if not ended, the pronounced seasonality of much littoral trade of an earlier era. The textile contracts were year-round contracts, and kept the business side of the trade busy throughout the year, even though the transportation side continued to be ruled by the monsoon wind pattern.

There was yet another distinctive tendency of Indo-European trade: its need to concentrate over space. Although the weavers were spread far and wide, it made sense to invite some of the commercial and processing services to settle near the warehouses, called factories. The sheer scale of the business, and the physical concentration of the final market in the seaport, made a concentrated settlement economical for all parties. The options in this regard were limited in Surat and Masulipatnam, as the risk that the facilities the English created would be poached upon by the Dutch was very great. This was one of the drivers behind the push for whole new settlements of trade on the part of the European traders.

The three port cities that the English Company set up in India (c. 1630–1690) were much more than new urban centers. Bombay, Madras, and Calcutta were not fairgrounds and emporia in the way the Indian ports still were. Instead, they represented occupationally specialized sites with an overwhelming interest in commissioning textile production, a precursor to a nineteenth-century model of urbanization. They were set apart from Mughal cities in the interior. These three ports redefined the relationship between geography and commerce. With the exception of Calcutta, and perhaps Portuguese Goa, the ports were located on sites that did not rely on river-borne trade in order to access the interior. They were not even located on rivers of any significance. Even Calcutta, which was situated on a river, did not rely on the river a great deal to conduct its main businesses. Instead, these ports looked towards the Indian Ocean, and being a set of three, could consider achieving coast-to-coast integration in trade and naval capability (see Map 7.3 on the regional and coastal trade networks). They were, therefore, secured by means of a superior naval force compared with the indigenous coastal states, and could serve as a haven for those indigenous capitalists who wished to leave the quarrelsome states in the interior.

In their origin, Bombay, Madras, and Calcutta were small port sites acquired partly by accident, exposed to attacks by enemies, and without a secure future. Still, as the Mughal empire began to crumble in the early eighteenth century, the well-defended company towns rose as safer destinations for Indian merchants and artisans. For the first time in Indian history, capital, artisanal skills, and enterprise fled from the inland to the seaboard. What was a trickle in the second half of the eighteenth century became a flood in the early nineteenth. Perhaps the best illustration of this trend comes from the rather rough data we have on town size. Between 1680 and 1800, the combined population of Delhi, Agra, and Lahore dropped from 1.2 million to 300,000, whereas that of Madras, Bombay, and Calcutta increased from about 100,000–200,000 to more than a million.

Trade historians see in the emergence and meteoric rise of Bombay, Madras, and Calcutta a diversion of trade from the established centers,

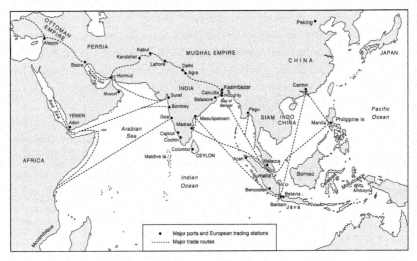

Map 7.3 Maritime routes and ports in India with European presence, *c.* 1700

Surat, Masulipatnam, or Hooghly. In fact, the new cities also gained by drawing capital away from the Gangetic plains, and represented a different business culture in coastal India. For one thing, Madras and Bombay broke the geographically conditioned dependence of port cities upon internal navigation and interior roads. These were, even more than Surat, ocean-bound ports. For another, Surat and Masulipatnam were cities that did not belong to merchants; in these cities the merchants did not make laws, in Bombay, Madras, and Calcutta, they did.

By 1800, then, the significance of Indo-European trade had changed. It now represented a shift in the balance of political power between the land and the sea. The seaborne trading world triumphed over overland trade. Until that moment of transition, there had been a clear disjuncture between foreign trade and political power. Strong states did not form on the coasts. The company's territories broke that pattern. The fortunes of businesses were still tied to the fortunes of the state. That factor did not change in the port cities. But then, in these cities, the state belonged to the merchants and this was a new element.

From the viewpoint of the costs of carrying out trade, the rise of the British colonial empire in the nineteenth century made little difference directly. It did, however, free up European private trade from the shackles, however ineffective, that they were subject to in the era when the company was still a monopoly. In the first half of the nineteenth century, a whole gamut of new businesses sprang up in the three port cities. All of these entailed a larger scale of and sustained transactions between the coastal merchants and resources or commodities that came from inland. All of these also entailed partnerships between European private merchants and Indian capitalists. Some of the businesses then begun failed to sustain themselves. Iron-smelting in charcoal furnaces was one example. On the other hand, some trades, such as indigo manufacture and export, made many fortunes before dying out. Opium trade brought Indian and European private traders and Chinese coastal traders into a relation of deep mutual dependence, giving rise to such hybrid Anglo-Sino-Indian towns as Hong Kong and Singapore. Parsi shipwrights of Bombay profited from Indo-China and Indo-Burma trades forged in the early nineteenth century. Cotton export and tea manufacture and export survived to become major fields of investment. Overall, this new era in Indo-European partnership created a foundation of capitalistic enterprise that was pan-Asian, straddling the land and the sea, and ready to take on bigger challenges in the industrial era. Without the cosmopolitan foundation of Bombay and Calcutta, the subsequent industrialization of the two cities, wholly exceptional in the poor tropics, cannot be explained.

Much of this entrepreneurial drive was confined to the port cities established by the company. How estranged that world had grown from the political economy of the Gangetic plains was starkly exposed during the great Indian mutiny of 1857. At one level, the mutiny was a revolt of a loose alliance of disgruntled Indian soldiers and the landed aristocrats, both hailing mainly from the upper Gangetic plains, against the rule by the company. These groups had quite different reasons for opposing the company, which was one reason why the rebellion eventually failed. But at another level, the mutiny demonstrated the support that the regime commanded from Indian capitalists. In none of the three ports was there a threat to the military effort. Indeed, the ports were the locus of the counter-resistance, thanks largely to the Indian bankers and merchants based there, who demonstrated their support to the company regime by making sure that the supply lines worked smoothly. There were not many examples of merchants allying with the ancient regime even in the interior. In line with my reading of Indian history, the mutiny represented the last stand taken by the regimes of the interior, and their eventual retreat demonstrated how decisively capitalist loyalties had shifted over to the cosmopolitan trading regime on the seaboard.

Having finished with the narrative, let me now move on to the qualitative dimensions of the change. Did the convergence of the two capitalist orders lead to an institutional convergence? Were institutions of capitalism different between the Indians and the Europeans, between the interior and the seaboard?

Institutions of capitalism

The modern definition of capitalism as a bundle of institutions is owed to Max Weber's discussion in *General Economic History* of the "rational-legal state" as one of the two preconditions of the emergence of a market economy, the other one being an "economic ethic" (Collins 1980). Weber's emphasis on the necessity of a formal legal code based on citizenship is of particular relevance to the economic history of the nineteenth century, which saw a formalization of economic laws not only in Europe, which Weber studied in detail, but also outside Europe and in regions ruled by the European colonial powers. In the 1980s, new institutional economic history absorbed the Weberian paradigm as its own, and gave it a distinctive twist by means of an emphasis on transaction costs and the importance of an enforceable secure title to private property as one of the conditions for mitigating transaction costs (North 1986).

In the 1990s, contributions on new institutional economic history emphasized the importance of social norms, and suggested that the formation of a bureaucratic state and social norms could lead to different, sometimes alternative, frameworks of regulation and in turn of capitalism. A non-Weberian strand within new economic sociology stressed that in a variety of preindustrial market exchanges, trust and stable contracts were attained without the agency of the state. In analytical economic history, norm-based associations and rule-based associations were contrasted in interpretations of pre-modern trade and the rise of the West (Greif 2006). That socially sanctioned mediation and state-enforced contract laws could be substitutes in mitigating transaction cost in a variety of exchanges was also an already familiar hypothesis in economic anthropology and African economic history (Landa 1994; Lonsdale 1981). The relationship between social norm and positive law took a prominent place in the literature on law and economics as well (McAdams 2001).

Weber was famously outlandish on India, partly because he did not extend the institutions paradigm to India and China, confining himself instead to the elusive "ethic" point in discussing non-Western societies. But has the new institutional economic history done any better? Unfortunately it has not. In current applied research it tends to be assumed that the rational-legal paradigm was an import from the West into the non-West (see discussion in Roy 2011b). This is true insofar as laws and legal procedures were coded better after colonial conquest. It is not true in respect of the contents of property law. Security of property right was not a serious point of difference between Europe and India in the eighteenth century or before. After all, Indians were trading as much as the Europeans in the preindustrial world. It would follow that private property was seen by the respective states to be useful and worthy of protection. That should not mean that the political context did not matter. It mattered not because states succeeded or failed to protect private property, but for a different reason. States earned their taxes, or borrowed, from different kinds of business, and therefore could choose allies among business groups selectively, giving rise to different profiles of firms according to the political set-up. Politics neither suppressed not actively promoted enterprise, but reinforced its dualist character in India.

What about social norms? Greif (2006: 26) suggests that "interest-based, self-governed, non-kin-based organizations" played a major role in the modernization of Europe, whereas kin-based ethnic cartels took their place in such Old World trading zones as those of India and China. The early efflorescence of global business in western Europe was a result of the nature of commercial associations in the region, reducing a variety of transaction costs and providing a basis for the formation of commercial law. By implication, in the non-European societies, laws of association and contract were late to form and were often borrowed from the West in the course of colonization, conquest, and other types of coercive contact. This discussion on norms leads us to frame a relevant question. Were Indian business combines kin based or associational?

Institutions before European trade

Economic historians of ancient India suggest that Indian merchant groups in the pre-Islamic periods formed collective bodies, and that these collectives included *both* kin-based and non-kin-based types. There is a great deal of material in the Hindu Dharmasastras and the Buddhist literature on urban guilds. These literatures do not suggest that the kin-based types were the only kind of guild. But they do suggest that the kin-based ones were prominent in public life. Kingly duties toward the merchants were framed in the Dharmasastras with reference to protection of caste rather than protection of professions (Roy 2010). Kin-based associations, therefore, commanded a particular moral-religious force in India, which derived from the equation between strict marriage rules and perceived purity of character. This feature was indeed distinctive of Indian capitalism. Intra-community marriage was practiced in many business communities of the world. But making purity of character a function of marriage was not as common elsewhere as in India. Needless to add moral character was a very important business asset in the pre-modern world.

Sponsorship of religious institutions also came mainly from merchants, and worked as a uniting factor among merchants stationed in distant locations. Jainism and Buddhism were both religions of merchants and religions carried afar by mobile merchants. In south India, mobile Hindu merchants set up temples along trade routes that served as rest stops, means to secure intracommunity connection, and possibly as fortified storage of grains and valuables as well.

These mobile merchant groups bridged the agrarian and maritime worlds of business to a limited extent. Indeed, the weak political link between land and sea seemingly pushed some of the mobile merchant groups into becoming organized military-political bodies. They functioned from within guilds. They were often strategic allies of the land-based states. They maintained multiple bases, and they represented far-flung merchant networks buttressed by powerful codes of conduct. So powerful could these codes be that community elders were known to punish code-breakers with death. While these features could be found in varying degrees among wealthy commercial groups in both northern and southern India, much evidence of a symbiotic coexistence of merchants and rulers, as well as of guilds that operated over long distances, comes from medieval south India.

Interestingly, the medieval south Indian guilds were non-kin based at the height of their power, as far as we can ascertain. This height was reached around the early centuries of the second millennium of the Common Era, or during the late Chola dynastic period. Historians suggest that with the emergence of the landlocked and agrarian Vijayanagar empire in the fourteenth century, these groups tended to become more sedentary, shed their military-political role, and possibly retreated into a kin- and caste-based model of association. Much of this is speculative, but it does caution against treating Indian commercial institutions as either static or of one kind.

We do not know enough about commercial institutions in the centuries immediately preceding Indo-European trade to make general statements. The safer position to hold is that diversity rather than uniformity ruled. In port towns, major business centers, and in negotiations with the state, some degree of non-kin cooperation was possibly quite common. Relics of these professional associations could be seen in Gujarat in the eighteenth century. In the late eighteenth century, similar associations could be found in Benares, as Bayly (1983) has noted. On the other hand, wherever members of a guild or association routinely dealt in scarce assets – knowledge, money, or land – the guild seemed to converge into a kin-based, caste-based unit. Business partners were rarely known to be recruited from groups not already connected by kinship, marriage, and bonds of caste and community. Any association that needed to secure trust because it traded in valuable capital, tended to make use of socially constructed relations to secure that trust.

Did the interior and the littoral worlds differ systematically on the point of business institutions? One can at best be speculative on this issue. It is possible that the merchants and bankers who coordinated the revenue system and grain trade were more important to the states than were the merchants who participated in maritime trade, for commercial revenue was only one of the income sources of the coastal states, but land tax was the principal revenue of all states. This situation could sometimes lead to an exploitative dependency of the merchant upon the states. But more often, it enabled the fiscal merchants to become officers of the court, and led them to demand and receive a variety of privileges in respect of banking and tax concessions. The political role of the merchants increased during warfare, and during periods of revenue scarcity. Comparatively, the merchants and bankers on the littoral were less politically connected, and to that extent were perhaps more reliant on their own community support systems. These were the very groups the Europeans did business with.

Institutions after European trade

In the seventeenth century, when the Europeans expanded trading operations on the Indian coast, the organizations that they wrote about invariably had families of powerful merchants and bankers at the center. These family firms appeared to the Europeans to be, socially speaking, extraordinarily insular. In most parts of the world, a business deal with outsiders was closed with a meal taken together. In India, inviting Europeans to the dining area of an Indian merchant home would be a sacrilege. Equally stringent barriers were maintained in respect of seclusion of women, a fact that the Europeans, many of them young males, bitterly complained about. The wealthier the business community, the stricter were the barriers. Debarred so firmly from entering the personal and social spheres of Indian merchants, the Europeans drew the conclusion that business ethics of the Indians were internal to their homes and understood only by their relations. There may have been some exaggeration and flatness to this picture. To some extent, the insularity that the Europeans observed may have been a reaction to the very presence of the Europeans in this milieu. Still, the picture could not be far from reality. The indigenous literature of the time confirms the predominance of endogamous business communities.

Indian businesses had adapted to the predominance of family firms and the moral-cultural character of commercial law well enough. Factor market transactions were mainly conducted within communities and were governed by codes that only the members understood. Commodity market transactions were largely conducted at auction sales, and did not need an elaborate and explicit system of formal law. The opportunistic and seasonal nature of all long-distance trade had made commercial relationships of a contingent and impermanent kind. Auctions and spot sales, rather than long-period bulk contracts, were far more common in the fairground pattern of trade.

This difference in the character of business firms – families in the Indian setting as opposed to companies among the Europeans – connects with an important debate about Indian business after European entry. A number of early readings of Indian Ocean trade tried to explain why the Indian coastal merchants declined and the Europeans succeeded in the Indian Ocean. Frederic Lane thought the answer was gunships; André Gunder Frank argued that the answer should be sought in access to Spanish American silver (Frank 1998; Lane 1979). J. C. Van Leur, William Moreland, and A. I. Chicherov were the prominent representatives of a school of thought attributing European success and Asian decline to differences in business organization (Das Gupta 2001). All of them acknowledged the existence of large volumes of trade in the Indian Ocean before European entry, but all considered the Indian merchants to be conservative, even backward, on the point of business organization. Family firms and a reliance on retail business, what Van Leur called "peddling," made them individually weak and inconsequential. Disputing this view, Ashin Das Gupta showed the large scale of some of the ship-owning merchant firms in the Arabian Sea trade, and the command over political and financial capital that they enjoyed (Das Gupta 2001). Das Gupta's own explanation for the decline of Indian capitalists was the contemporaneous decline of the large territorial empires in west and south Asia, which weakened the Asian capitalists who formerly traded between hubs protected by these regimes.

We now know that the question is a wrong one to ask. In all likelihood there was no decline in Indian shipping at all, nor was there much competition. Europeans were entrenched from the start in transoceanic routes, whereas the Indians traded in the Arabian Sea and the Bay of Bengal. On the coast, only some groups like the ship-owning merchants disappeared. But many new groups emerged, in trade as well as shipping, in the port cities where private European traders offered them capital and market access. The Parsis are one of the best-known examples. Overall, there were more cases of adaptation than decline. There was a creative destruction of the old Asian merchant, and the rise of a new class who operated on a pan-Asian scale. The bazaar, to use the term popularized in this context by Rajat Ray, proved extraordinarily adaptable (Ray 1995).

These stories of decline or survival beg the question of why the Indian coastal traders did not join transoceanic trade. The only credible answer to the question must look at how the firms were organized, and what kind of risk-bearing capacity their organization entailed. Indian Ocean trade offered economies of scale, and the Europeans could operate on a large scale. The English and the Dutch overseas trading enterprises were differently organized not only from Indian firms, but also from the Portuguese Crown monopoly (Steensgaard 1974). They functioned on the basis of joint stock, which allowed them to pool in large amounts of capital, spread and share risks, and build an elaborate infrastructure consisting of forts, factories, harbors, and ships. The monopoly charter that the English received from the Crown also reduced competition, allowed a larger scale of operations, and in turn enabled more investment in military capability and trading infrastructure. The Indians, being organized around communities and families, were too divided to form large professional combines. Being family firms, they needed to be risk averse to avoid exposing the family to danger (Das Gupta 2001).

Recent research by economists studying early modern trade suggests that the Europeans solved one problem – that of scale – only to give rise to another – contract failure. When they first entered the Indian Ocean, they purchased what it was possible to buy on the spot from the bazaars, usually with the mediation of contractors hired from local business communities. But as the volume of transactions expanded, spot-market purchases needed to be replaced with long-period contracts. Compared to contemporary Indian merchant firms, the English East India Company was a specialized firm. It dealt in few goods, but these it bought on a very large scale. Being specialized, the company contracted with a specific set of suppliers repeatedly year after year and paid out sums of money as advances. These sums were advanced over a whole year.

Contractual sale of goods was not unknown in India before, but contractual sale on such scale by a single firm had no historical precedents. Contractual transaction carried hazards. In Indo-European trade, the transacting parties were neither protected by state law, nor did they share the same customary law. Conflicts around the terms and enforcement of contracts, therefore, were extremely common. Not by accident then, the merchant-explorer Jean-Baptiste Tavernier devoted an entire chapter in his famous travelogue (c. 1660) to the subject of the "frauds" practiced in India (Tavernier 1889). These conflicts imparted to the Indo-European trade an air of instability. The subject of contract failure, long obscured by the historian's obsession with the "rise" and "decline" of ethnic groups, has now entered the historiography of Indo-European trade (see Kranton and Swamy 2008; Roy 2011c). With hindsight, the company dealt with the instability in their own ports by using sovereign authority. It would be far fetched to explain the colonial conquest as a political response to the challenge of contract enforcement, but the fact remains that no other response was as effective.

Territorial acquisition raises a question about the company's own organizational structure. Did its territorial acquisition happen by design or by accident? On this question, two radically different perspectives can exist, depending on interpretation of what kind of a firm the English East India Company really was. On the one hand, it is possible to see the company as a unitary command and control system, where the agents acted on the wishes of the principals, and the principals knew what the agents were doing. This reading would be consistent with the picture of the company drawn in the influential contributions of Ann M. Carlos and Stephen Nicholas, who argue that the chartered companies were analogous with modern multinationals, insofar as both shared strategies that enabled the managers to economize on transaction cost and reduce opportunism by agents (Carlos and Nicholas 1988). If indeed the principals were in control of the actions of the agents, it would follow that the decisive steps towards conquest and port-building in India were taken in full knowledge of the principals and under their command.

On the other hand, historians like Holden Furber suggested that the actual move to own ports did not follow a conscious decision from above, but was undertaken by the agents against the knowledge of and despite resistance from the owners of the company. In short, territorial expansion was the result of a split personality within the firm. Far from being like a modern hierarchical firm, the company was a pre-modern form of partnership between sedentary merchants and bankers on the one hand and peripatetic sailors and soldiers, with regulated privilege to conduct private trade, on the other. "The real antithesis," Furber wrote, is between those who stood to profit from the extension of empire in India and those who had been accustomed to profiting solely through trade, the former group being drawn from every class of English society and the latter consisting of the London merchants, ship-owners, and sea captains dominant in the company's courts of proprietors and directors.   (Furber 1940: 636)

The two classes of people – the City merchants and outstation factors, sailors, and soldiers – did share a common interest in the profits of Asian trade, but were not friends otherwise. The local agents, in their capacity as traders, tended to engage more with the Indian elite. A decisive change of balance in the partnership could see the sailors-cum-soldiers try to establish a sphere of political authority defying the wishes of their principals. Between 1690 and 1760, the cleavage was widening, just as the collapse of the Mughal empire and Anglo-French wars in India in the wake of the War of Austrian Succession and the Seven Years War supplied the means and the motivations to those who believed that an empire was more profitable than trade.

Such debates about how distinct the European organization was and what that distinctness meant for Indian history will not be easily settled, because the answer will depend on what we are trying to explain. A theory of political adventurism and a theory of business success are quite different pursuits. But there cannot be any dispute that territorial expansion succeeded in the end also because the company cities were, institutionally speaking, worlds apart from the Indian littoral zones. They were sovereign, legislating spaces where merchants made laws, an unheard of concept on the seaboard. This concept attracted not only European merchants but also a substantial section of the Indian merchants. The migration of capital empowered the ports and drained the interior of fighting power.

Institutionally speaking, colonization had an ambiguous effect upon the Indian business community. The cohesion of kin-based groups had earlier depended on the king as guarantor of the juridical autonomy of business communities. The company state unwittingly made this guarantee weaker than before by creating new law courts with the power to override community rules. From their early beginning in the port cities, these courts needed to settle disputes that arose within communities, and brought therein by disgruntled upstarts who considered a rule by community elders irksome. The port cities also offered opportunities for business partnerships that cut across communities, which would entail exchange of capital, information, and skill between socially unrelated groups, and therefore needed a framework of law that would be less cultural and more formal (Roy 2011b).

Do we then see dissolution of communities in the nineteenth century? We do not. The great paradox of colonial legislation in India was that it adopted a dualist principle to begin with – English common law for Europeans and, by default, communal-religious law for Indians. As a result, while these courts could test and challenge the juridical autonomy of the community, the courts also displayed a bias for settling cases in favor of the Indian tradition. For other reasons too, while disputes over tradition multiplied, tradition did not necessarily become weaker. Strengthening collective bonds was one of the strategies that individuals adopted when entering unknown forms of enterprise, or transacting with unknown people. The outcome, then, was the emergence of opposite tendencies, which explains why communities survived to the twentieth century while battling challenges from within and without, and why court cases over division of property among old business families drag on interminably even today.

Conclusion

This outline has consisted of two intersecting themes – convergence between the littoral and the interior trading worlds, and an uneasy but inevitable meeting of distinct business cultures. That the two processes interacted cannot be questioned, but many aspects of their interaction remain unknown.

The nineteenth-century globalization reshaped these processes in unprecedented ways. The railways and the steamships effected integration of the land and the sea to an unprecedented degree. The railways made a huge difference to the costs of overland trade. The British empire, formed of a diverse collection of world regions with a shared official language and mutually compatible legal regimes, brought down transaction costs in exchanges between parts of the empire. The empire, therefore, was crucial to expanding the axes of interaction from commodity to capital, labor, and technology. Economic laws, especially in the sphere of commercial exchanges, broadened the scope of contracts. The railways and new trading activities attracted capital from London. New currency regimes reduced the risks of overseas investment. The abolition of slavery encouraged the tropical plantations to import Asian labor.

But although these were introduced in the nineteenth century, the meaning of these developments cannot be understood outside the context of the convergence between the interior and the seaboard that had begun centuries before.

References

Bagchi, A. K. (1982). *The Political Economy of Underdevelopment*. Cambridge University Press.

Bayly, C. A. (1983). *Rulers, Townsmen and Bazaars: North Indian Society in the Age of British Expansion 1770–1870*. Cambridge University Press.

Brenner, R. (1977). "The Origins of Capitalist Development: A Critique of Neo-Smithian Marxism," *New Left Review* 104: 25–92.

Carlos, A. and S. Nicholas (1988). "'Giants of an Earlier Capitalism': The Chartered Trading Companies as Modern Multinationals," *Business History Review* 62: 398–419.

Chaudhuri, K. N. (1978). *The Trading World of Asia and the English East India Company, 1660–1760*. Cambridge University Press.

Collins, R. (1980). "Weber's Last Theory of Capitalism: A Systematization," *American Sociological Review* 45: 925–942.

Das Gupta, A. (2001). *The World of the Indian Ocean Merchant, 1500–1800*. Oxford University Press.

Desai, M. (1991). "Capitalism," in T. Bottomore (ed.), *A Dictionary of Marxist Thought*. Blackwell.

Frank, A. G. (1998). *ReOrient: Global Economy in the Asian Age*. University of California Press.

Furber, H. (1940). Review of A. Mervyn Davies, *Clive of Plassey: A Biography*, Charles Scribner's Sons, 1939, *American Historical Review* 45: 635–637.

(1951). *John Company at Work: A Study of European Expansion in India in the Late Eighteenth Century*. Harvard University Press.

Greif, A. (2006). *Institutions and the Path to the Modern Economy: Lessons from Medieval Trade*. Cambridge University Press.

Habib, I. (1964). "Usury in Medieval India," *Comparative Studies in Society and History* 6: 393–419.

(1969). "Potentialities of Capitalistic Development in the Economy of Mughal India," *Journal of Economic History* 29: 32–78.

Kerr, R., ed. (1824). *A General History and Collection of Voyages and Travels Arranged in Systematic Order*, vol. VII. London: Hakluyt Society, pp. 178–181.

Kranton, R. E. and A. V. Swamy (2008). "Contracts, Hold-up, and Exports: Textiles and Opium in Colonial India," *American Economic Review* 98: 967–989.

Landa, J. T. (1994). *Trust, Ethnicity, and Identity: Beyond the New Institutional Economics of Ethnic Trading Networks, Contract Law, and Gift-Exchange*. University of Michigan Press.

Lane, F. (1979). *Profits from Power: Readings in Protection Rent and Violence-controlling Enterprises*. Albany, NY: State University of New York Press.

Lonsdale, J. (1981). "States and Social Processes in Africa: A Historiographical Survey," *African Studies Review* 24: 139–225.

Marshall, P. J., ed. (2003). *The Eighteenth Century in Indian History*. Oxford University Press.

McAdams, R. H. (2001). "Signalling Discount Rates: Law, Norms, and Economic Methodology," *Yale Law Journal* 110: 625–689.

North, D. (1986). *Institutions and Economic Growth: An Historical Introduction*. Ithaca: Cornell University Press.

Patnaik, U., ed. (1990). *Agrarian Relations and Accumulation: The "Mode of Production" Debate in India*. Oxford University Press.

Perlin, F. (1983). "Proto-Industrialization and Pre-Colonial South Asia," *Past and Present* 98: 30–95.

Prakash, O. (1985). *The Dutch East India Company and the Economy of Bengal 1630–1720.* Princeton University Press.

(1998). *European Commercial Enterprise in Pre-colonial India.* Cambridge University Press.

Ray, R. K. (1995). "Asian Capital in the Age of European Domination: The Rise of the Bazaar, 1800–1914," *Modern Asian Studies* 29: 449–554.

Riello, G. and P. Parthasarathi, eds. (2010). *The Spinning World: A Global History of Cotton Textiles*, 1200–1850. Oxford University Press.

Riello, G. and T. Roy, eds. (2010). *How India Clothed the World: The World of South Asian Textiles 1500–1850.* Brill.

Roy, T. (2010). *Company of Kinsmen: Enterprise and Community in South Asian History 1600–1940.* Oxford University Press.

(2011a). "Where is Bengal? Situating an Indian Region in the Early Modern World Economy," *Past and Present* 213: 115–146.

(2011b), "Law and the Economy of Early Modern India," in D. Ma and J. L. van Zanden (eds.), *Law and Long-term Economic Change: A Eurasian Perspective.* Stanford University Press.

(2011c). "Indigo and Law in Colonial India," *Economic History Review* 64: 60–75.

(2012). *India in the World Economy from Antiquity to the Present.* Cambridge University Press.

Steensgaard, N. (1974). *The Asian Trade Revolution of the Seventeenth Century.* University of Chicago Press.

Tavernier, J. B. (1889). *Travels in India by Jean Baptiste Tavernier*, Vol. II. Macmillan.

Thavaraj, M. J. K. (1984). "The Concept of Asiatic Mode of Production: Its Relevance to Indian History," *Social Scientist* 12: 26–34.

Wallerstein, I. (1986). "Incorporation of Indian Subcontinent into Capitalist World-Economy," *Economic and Political Weekly* 21: PE28–PE39.

Washbrook, D. (2007). "India in the Early Modern World Economy: Modes of Production, Reproduction and Exchange," *Journal of Global History* 2: 87–111.

8

Institutional change and economic development in the Middle East, 700–1800

ŞEVKET PAMUK

Introduction

The Middle East region had one of the most vibrant economies in the world from the eighth until the end of the eleventh centuries. Economic prosperity during the so called Golden Age of Islam was based, above all, on rising productivity in agriculture. Located between the two major sea areas, the Indian Ocean and the Mediterranean, and at the center of major intercontinental routes, economies of the region also enjoyed a strong urban network and wide range of manufacturing activities. The deepening of the division of labor, the growth of new occupations and skills in manufacturing and services as well as agriculture, high rates of literacy and the long list of technical innovations, all point to an episode of intensive growth and economic efflorescence in Abbasid Iraq. Complex institutions for credit, commercial and other business partnerships, long-distance trade, and shipping were developed during this period. These institutions were imported into Italy in the eighth or ninth centuries and formed the basis of European commenda and contributed to the development of the European institutions of business, commerce, and finance in later centuries (Abu-Lughod 1989; Ashtor 1976; Lombard 1975; Udovitch 1970, 1975). After the eleventh century, however, the center of gravity began to shift away from the urban centers of the Middle East toward the mercantile states of Italy and the later to the Low Countries and England. (Abu-Lughod 1989; Ashtor 1976; Shatzmiller 2011).[1]

The author would like to thank Larry Neal, Jeffrey Williamson, the authors of the other chapters and Roger Owen for many helpful comments and suggestions on earlier versions of this essay.

1 The term Middle East was coined only recently, during the last century or two. Nonetheless, I prefer to use this term rather than the earlier Near East because of its convenience.

It has long been debated whether the cause of this divergence was a series of external shocks such as the Crusades, the Mongol invasion, the Black Death, and shifts in the intercontinental trade routes. Admittedly each of these external shocks had a significant and long-lasting impact on the economies of the region. However, the Black Death had a severe impact on other regions of the world as well, most notably on Europe. It is clear that northwestern Europe absorbed this shock and responded to it much more positively in the following centuries (Borsch 2005; Pamuk 2007). The shift of the intercontinental trade routes to the Atlantic Ocean undoubtedly had an impact on the region. By that time, however, the Middle East had already begun to lag behind southern and northwestern Europe.

In this chapter I will first examine the evolution of institutions in the region in three different areas, land regime, private finance, and public borrowing, to show there were many changes over the millennium from the rise of Islam until the modern era. While these were often in response to the changing circumstances, they also reflected the social structure and prevailing power balances in these societies. I will also argue that how towns and urban areas related to the state, how urban areas are included in state policies, and how they influenced the shaping of institutions are the keys to understanding long-term institutional and economic change in the region. Even though local urban councils led by the notables and local craftsmen, including the guilds in the Ottoman era, enjoyed a good deal of autonomy, political power in the region was concentrated in the hands of the ruler and the state elites around him. In contrast, the influence of various social groups, not only of landowners but also of merchants, manufacturers, and moneychangers over economic matters, including the policies of the central government, remained limited. This political configuration and the related institutions persisted into the modern era. As a result, societies in the Middle East did not develop institutions more independent of the state and the state elites and more in favor of the private sector.

Long-term trends in wages and incomes

I begin with some estimates of population in order to give an idea of the orders of magnitude. The population of the Islamic states of the Middle East including Iran and North Africa but excluding Anatolia is estimated to have varied between 20 to 35 million during the medieval era, from the seventh to the fifteenth centuries. These numbers indicate clearly that the population of the Middle East was much smaller than those of south Asia and China during the medieval era. It was roughly comparable to the population of southern and western Europe early in the medieval era, but the population of the latter began to outstrip the population of the Middle East approximately after the year 1100. Moreover, while the population of these three other areas increased significantly from the sixteenth through the eighteenth centuries, the population of the Middle East did not change very much until the nineteenth century (Issawi 1981; McEvedy and Jones, 1978).

A good amount of wage and price data for the medieval and early modern Middle East has made it possible in recent years to learn more about the long-term trends in wages and incomes in the region and compare them with the neighboring areas. In what follows I prefer to state these findings qualitatively since the margins of error associated with the existing estimates for both the Middle East and Europe do not allow a high degree of precision, especially for the earlier periods.

A recent study has concluded that because of the two long-lasting demographic cycles, the first known as the Justinian plague that began in the middle of the sixth century and lasted until the ninth century and a second one known as the Black Death that began in the middle of the fourteenth century, as well as an episode of intensive growth known as the Golden Age, the purchasing power of the daily wages of unskilled workers as well as average incomes in the Middle East not only exhibited significant medium- and long-term fluctuations but also remained well above the subsistence minimum for a large part of the medieval era. It has been estimated that the purchasing power of unskilled wages in the region remained mostly between 1.3 and 2.0 times the subsistence minimum, and that average incomes remained mostly within an interval that ranged from two to three times the subsistence minimum during the medieval era (Pamuk and Shatzmiller 2014).

Direct comparisons of wages and incomes between the Middle East and Europe for the period before the thirteenth or fourteenth centuries are not possible at the moment since we do not have reliable estimates for the levels of real wages or GDP per capita for most European regions or countries. Nonetheless, it appears that from the eighth through the tenth centuries, and possibly until a later date some time in the eleventh century, real wages and incomes in the more prosperous regions of the Middle East were higher than those in the more prosperous regions of Europe. After that date, however, a divergence between the Middle East and parts of Europe began to emerge. Parts of the Middle East, Iraq, Iran, and Syria but not Egypt were adversely affected by the Mongolian invasions during the thirteenth century, although the long-term implications of these invasions may not have been as significant as many have assumed. More importantly, southern and later northwestern

Europe began to experience sustained increases in wages and per capita incomes. Differences in incomes and standards of living between the more prosperous areas of the Middle East and those of southern Europe, if not northwestern Europe, had become apparent by the first half of the fourteenth century, before the arrival of the Black Death.

The initial impact of the Black Death in the Middle East was similar to that in most parts of Europe as real wages and per capita incomes rose sharply in both areas. With the recovery of population, however, real wages began to decline. Recent research points out that in many European countries real wages at the end of the eighteenth century were no higher than those in the fifteenth century. Similarly, recent GDP per capita estimates suggest that in many cases average incomes at the end of the eighteenth century were not higher than the peaks reached in the aftermath of the Black Death (Allen 2001; Alvarez-Nogal and Prados de la Escosura 2013; Broadberry et al. 2010; van Zanden 1999). Long-term trends in the Middle East were similar in this respect. Our estimates indicate that real wages in Cairo and Istanbul around the 1780s were no higher than the peak levels attained during the fifteenth century. The major exception to this pattern occurred in northwestern Europe, in the Low Countries and in Britain, where during the early modern era, well before the industrial revolution, it is estimated that per capita incomes but not wages began to exceed the levels attained during the era of the Black Death.

One also needs to be careful not to overstate the differences in real wages and average incomes between Europe and the Middle East in the era before the industrial revolution. Differences in urban wages between the more advanced regions of Europe, that is, England and the Low Countries and the eastern Mediterranean, rarely exceeded two to one before the nineteenth century. Differences between the rest of Europe and the eastern Mediterranean were even smaller until after the industrial revolution. The emerging gap was not due to a decline in the Middle East but due to the rise of wages and incomes first in southern and then in northwestern Europe. For this reason, it is more appropriate to talk about the rise of Europe than the decline of the Middle East during the late medieval and early modern eras (Özmucur and Pamuk 2002; Pamuk, 2007).

Institutions and institutional change

Institutions and institutional change have been identified in recent decades as key variables that help explain the widely disparate economic performance of different societies over time. Based on the successful experience of western Europe and European offshoots, Douglass North and others have argued that long-run economic change is attained because the underlying framework persistently reinforced incentives for organizations to engage in exchange and productive activity. Institutional economics and economic historians have come to recognize that institutional change is usually not in the direction of most efficient outcomes and a society rarely arrives at or creates institutions that are conducive to economic growth. In most cases, institutions have favored activities that restrict opportunities rather than expand them. Similarly, rather than reinforcing incentives toward productive activity, in most cases states have acted as instruments for transferring resources from one group to another or promoting their own survival at the expense of others. In short, the process of institutional change has not always been favorable to economic growth (Acemoglu and Robinson 2012; North 1990).

How economic institutions are determined and why they vary across countries is not sufficiently well understood. Institutional economics proposes a number of causes or determinants of institutions. Most important among them are (1) geography or resource endowments; (2) religion or more generally culture; and (3) social conflict or political economy. Economic institutions in the Middle East have certainly been influenced by geography or resource endowments. The most important example in this respect is Egypt, where the land regime, fiscal institutions, and the role of the central government have been shaped to a large degree by the needs of irrigated agriculture. With the exception of Egypt, however, the geography or resource endowments of the region were not very different from those of other temperate areas of the world. A favorable location can also be a substantial stimulus for economic development. In fact, the location of the Middle East between Europe and Asia provided significant opportunities for commercial development as it enabled the region to turn more towards the Indian Ocean in the Middle Ages while Europe was going through its Dark Ages. Similarly, it is difficult to deny that the shift of the intercontinental trade routes to the Atlantic Ocean had an impact on the region. By that time, however, the Middle East had already begun to lag behind southern and northwestern Europe. For these reasons, I do not consider geography or resource endowments as the leading determinant of institutions in the region or the primary cause of the long-term change in its relative economic standing.

Religion and/or culture have long been offered as a primary cause of the differences in economic outcomes between the Middle East and western Europe. Weber's analysis of Islamic societies emphasized the contrasts between them and those in western Europe in a number of areas including religion and law as well as the political system (Weber 1968). More recently, Timur Kuran (2010) has pointed to Middle Eastern institutions rooted in Islamic law, including inheritance law, commercial law and others, as past and in some cases continuing obstacles to economic development. As a result, he has argued, even though Middle Eastern institutions may not have caused a decline in economic activity, they have turned into handicaps by perpetuating themselves during the centuries when the West developed the institutions of the modern economy. Culture and religion certainly influenced institutions in the region. However, like Weber, Kuran has minimized the considerable differences that has existed within Europe and within the Middle East and has presented idealized versions of societies, institutions, and patterns of long-term economic change in each of these two regions. As a result, he has overlooked institutional changes in Islamic societies, changes in Islamic law, and the varieties of Islam that emerged in response to the many different conditions. He has also tended to minimize if not ignore the large body of evidence that Islamic societies often circumvented or adapted those religious rules that appeared to prevent change, including economic change. Moreover, Islamic law has not been an autonomous sphere isolated from these societies. Recent research in the Ottoman archives has shown, for example, that political authority was closely involved in the interpretation of law and the day-to-day administration of justice in the early modern Ottoman empire (Gerber 1994; Hallaq 2005; Udovitch 1970). Once it is allowed that so-called Islamic rules can and do change or be circumvented, it becomes necessary to understand why and how.

Those in the recent institutional economics literature adhering to a social conflict or political economy explanation of economic institutions argue that because different groups and individuals typically benefit from different economic institutions, there is generally a conflict over the choice of economic institution. Institutional change, even when socially beneficial, will be resisted by social groups who stand to lose economic rents or political power. Consequently, the process of institutional change involves significant conflict between different groups, ultimately resolved in favor of groups with greater economic and political power. The distribution of political power is, in turn, determined by political institutions and the distribution of economic power. For this reason, political economy and political institutions are considered as key determinants of economic institutions and the direction of institutional change (Acemoglu and Robinson 2012; Ogilvie 2007; Rodrik, Subramanian, and Trebbi 2004).

The same literature also argues that for long-term economic growth, institutions should not only offer incentives to a narrow elite but also open up opportunities to a broader section of society. Institutions that provide incentives to invest in land, physical and human capital, or technology are more likely to arise when political power is in the hands of a relatively broad group with significant investment opportunities. The state can be a major player in this context as it often decides on the rules and often maintains the coercive power necessary to enforce them.

In a related recent study, Acemoglu, Johnson, and Robinson (2005a) have offered an explanation for why strong private property rights emerged in western Europe, especially in Britain and the Netherlands, beginning in the sixteenth century. They argue that Atlantic trade – the opening of the sea routes to the New World, Africa, and Asia and the building of colonial empires – contributed to the process of west European growth between 1500 and 1850 not only through its direct economic effects, but also indirectly, by inducing fundamental institutional change. Atlantic trade in Britain and the Netherlands altered the balance of political power by enriching and strengthening commercial interests outside the royal circle, including various overseas merchants, slave traders, and colonial planters. Through this channel, it contributed to the emergence of political institutions protecting merchants against royal power. In short, they argue, the Atlantic trade played a key role in strengthening segments of the bourgeoisie and the development of capitalist institutions in these countries. In contrast, where the power of the Crown was relatively unchecked, as in Spain, Portugal, and France, they emphasize that trade was largely monopolized and regulated, the Crown and its allies became the main beneficiaries of the Atlantic expansion, and the same induced institutional changes did not take place. Areas lacking easy access to the Atlantic, such as Venice and Genoa, on the other hand, did not experience any direct or indirect benefits of Atlantic trade.

This argument also suggests that the causal relationship between institutions and economic development is not necessarily one directional, running from institutions to economic development. Economic development or its absence also influences the institutions and their evolution. In other words, just as the expansion of Atlantic trade helped the merchants shape the capitalistic institutions in northwestern Europe, the low levels of economic transformation in the economies of the Middle East may have limited the economic and political power enjoyed by merchants and manufacturers. These low levels of economic development helped maintain a different pattern of institutions, one that was not friendly to merchants or more generally to the private sector.

Institutional change in the Middle East

Contrary to many clichés and misconceptions, societies of the Middle East experienced a good deal of institutional change during the millennium from the rise of Islam to the modern era. By examining the evolution of institutions in three different areas, land regime, private finance, and public borrowing, this section will argue these changes were not caused by the requirements of Islam or geography but reflected power balances in society as well as responses to changing economic needs.

Land regime

The evolution of the land regime in the Middle East during the late medieval era exhibited a great deal of variation but it is safe to say Islamic law was not the primary determinant of the emerging patterns. Instead, these were closely associated with the changes in social structure and political power. In the early centuries of Islam, states distributed to their notables portions of their territory, and ownership or control of the land was subject to regular payments of the tithe. These transfers were irrevocable. In later centuries, however, along with the increase in military needs and the rise of the new military elite, a new arrangement emerged. When governments began to experience difficulties in payments to officers and the troops, they began to grant military officers the fiscal rights of lands under government control instead of payments in cash. The officers were expected to use the tax revenues from these lands as payments for themselves and the troops. These arrangements were not permanent, however; they ended with the term of office or military service.

The Seljukids extended this practice throughout their wider empire and began to confer whole provinces in Iran, Iraq, Syria, and Anatolia. These land grants similarly expanded in Egypt during the Fatimid and Mamluk eras. Their status was subject to long swings of the pendulum depending on invasions, conquests, and the strength of the central government. During periods of decentralization or weakening of the central government, the revocable nature of the grants faded and they became more hereditary. During periods of increasing power by the central government, on the other hand, the hold of former military officers and their descendants on these lands weakened and their control reverted back to central government which often chose to distribute the fiscal rights to new individuals (Ashtor 1976: 168–331; Borsch, 2005: 26–27; Cahen 1971; Lambton 1953; Tsugitaka 1997).

Conquest of new lands from non-Muslim populations, the periodic repetition of conquests, and invasions also weakened hereditary control over land by military elites. In the longer term, states remained strong enough to prevent the emergence and consolidation of private ownership on land. As a result, private property on land remained precarious and was never firmly established in most parts of the region. In Egypt, for example, where geography gave a stronger hand to the government, the individual *ikta* was unhereditary, short term and constantly subject to the winds of political and military fortune in the late medieval centuries. Mongol invasion in the thirteenth century tended to weaken the central governments in the region and strengthen control by local rulers. With the disintegration of the Ilkhanids, the Mongols of Persia, however, local control over land began to take root once more. On the other hand, the rise of Ottoman control over large areas of the region in the fifteenth and sixteenth centuries strengthened state control and the establishment of state ownership over land. While the extent of control over land by local elites varied over time and space, it is clear that a land-based, hereditary aristocracy did not emerge in the region during the millennium before the modern era.

The spread of the *ikta* did not benefit the peasantry, since it eroded their status as free cultivators even though the recipients of an *ikta* were not, strictly speaking, the possessors of an estate but merely the recipients of fiscal revenues. They usually resided in urban areas, many in distant towns, and had little contact with the actual cultivators. They dealt with the cultivators through intermediaries, representatives who would go down to the estate to collect the taxes. These fiscal rights did not take root for periods of time long enough to evolve into private property, however.

The evolution of the *ikta*, and more generally the land regime in the Middle East during the late medieval centuries, remains an understudied subject. It is not possible to do justice to its complexities here. Two things are clear, however. The *ikta* showed significant variations, across the region. Even more importantly, these variations and more generally the evolution of the land regime, was not due to Islam but was linked, above all, to the changing power balances between the central governments and state elites, on the one hand, and various other groups in the provinces. The same applies to the Ottoman land regime during the early modern era.

During the early stages of Ottoman territorial expansion, lands taken over from the neighboring states in the Balkans began to be registered as state lands. In contrast, private property on land continued in areas taken from the Islamic principalities in Anatolia. With the centralization drive in the second half of the fifteenth century, however, state ownership of agricultural lands was established as the basic form in most core regions of the empire, in the Balkans, Anatolia, and Syria. Hereditary usufruct of state lands was then given to peasant households, which typically cultivated with a pair of oxen and family labor. The peasant family farm thus emerged as the basic economic and fiscal unit in the countryside. Ottoman central administration refused to recognize private ownership in agricultural lands with the exception of orchards and vineyards in urban areas until the reforms of the nineteenth century (Inalcik 1994: 103–179).

In the state lands, taxes collected from the peasant cultivators were converted to a large provincial army under the *timar* system. In this prebendal system, *sipahis*, state employees, often chosen for their wartime valor, lived in the rural areas, collected mostly in-kind taxes from agricultural producers and spent the revenues locally on the training and equipment of a predetermined number of soldiers as well as their own maintenance. The Ottoman central administration did not attempt to impose the *timar* regime in all of the conquered territories, however. Eastern Anatolia, Iraq, Egypt, Yemen, Wallachia, Moldavia, and the Maghrib remained outside the *timar* system.

The power of the Ottoman central administration declined and the influence of the provincial notables (*ayan*) rose after the sixteenth century. Even though the *ayan* obtained greater control of the tax collection system in the provinces, they could not extend their power to establish private property of land. The central administration refused to recognize private ownership in agricultural lands, with the exception of orchards and vineyards in urban areas, until the reforms of the nineteenth century and the Land Code of 1858. Local courts, which had jurisdiction over matters of property, rarely approved sales of agricultural land during the seventeenth and eighteenth centuries. When records listing the assets of the provincial notables are examined, it is clear that land ownership was only a small part of their holdings. Their economic power was achieved and extended through the control of the tax collection process. In these state lands usufruct thus remained in the hands of peasant households. In other words, the *ayan* were unable to translate their power into a more lasting autonomy (Keyder and Tabak 1991).

State power was not the only obstacle in the way of private ownership of land, however. Commercialization of agriculture, including exports of agricultural commodities, remained limited until the nineteenth century. In addition, in a landscape dominated by small peasant holdings, it was not easy to find wage labor. Large farms or estates using year-round labor thus remained few in number. The exceptions were mostly in the Balkans, where expansion of long-distance trade and greater population density provided greater support for larger estates oriented toward commercial agriculture. In Egypt, on the other hand, institutions of land ownership and taxation, as well as the techniques and organization of cultivation, depended closely on the irrigation of fertile land. Large holdings and sales of agricultural land were more frequent there (Cuno 1992; Shaw 1962).

Another important category on land was the *vakif* or pious foundation. Islamic law allowed individuals who had private property, including land under private ownership, to convert some or all of these assets to *vakif* status and direct their future income for a predetermined purpose. At the time of the endowment, private ownership terminated. A board of trustees was then appointed to rent out or otherwise manage the property designated as *vakif* and direct the revenues towards the designated purpose. Control of the board of trustees over these lands usually weakened over time and tenants began to enjoy greater autonomy and pay less in rent. Despite occasional state expropriation, substantial amounts of agricultural land as well as urban real estate remained under *vakif* status throughout the Ottoman centuries, but the extent of both *vakif* lands and legally recognized private property on land was only a fraction of the land under state ownership until the nineteenth century.

Institutions of private finance

It has often been assumed that the prohibition of interest in Islam prevented the development of credit, or at best, imposed rigid obstacles in its way. Similarly, the apparent absence of deposit banking and lending by banks has led many observers to conclude that financial institutions and instruments were, by and large, absent in Islamic societies. It is true that a religiously inspired prohibition against usurious transactions was a powerful feature shared around the Mediterranean during the middle ages, both by the Islamic world and Christian West. While the practice of *riba*, the Arabic term for usury and interest, is sharply denounced in a number of passages in the Qur'an and in all subsequent Islamic religious writings, already in the medieval era, Islamic law had provided several means by which the anti-usury prohibition could be circumvented just as the same prohibitions were circumvented in Europe in the late medieval period. Various legal fictions, based primarily on the model of the "double sale" were, if not enthusiastically endorsed by jurists, at least not declared invalid. It is thus clear that neither the Islamic prohibitions against interest and usury nor the absence of formal banking institutions prevented the expansion of credit and trade in the medieval Middle East.

Similarly, neither the Islamic prohibitions against interest and usury nor the absence of formal banking institutions prevented the expansion of credit in Ottoman society. Utilizing the Islamic court records, the late Ronald Jennings has shown that dense networks of lenders and borrowers flourished in and around the Anatolian cities of Kayseri, Karaman, Amasya, and Trabzon during the sixteenth century. Over a twenty-year period which his study covered, he found literally thousands of court cases involving debts. Many members of each family and many women are registered in these records as borrowing and lending to other members of the family as well as to outsiders. These records leave no doubt that the use of credit was widespread among all segments of the urban and even rural society. Most lending and borrowing was on a small scale and interest was regularly charged on credit, in accordance with both Islamic and Ottoman law, with the consent and approval of the court and the *ulema*. In their dealings with the court the participants felt no need to conceal interest or resort to tricks in order to clear legal hurdles. Annual rates of interest ranged from 10 to 20 percent (Jennings 1973).

One important provider of loans in Istanbul, the Balkans, and the Anatolian urban centers were the cash *vakifs*, pious foundations established with the explicit purpose of lending their cash assets and using the interest income to fulfill their goals. These endowments began to be approved by the Ottoman courts in the early part of the fifteenth century and had become popular all over Anatolia and the Balkan provinces by the end of the sixteenth century. The endowments began to allocate their funds increasingly to their trustees during the eighteenth century. The trustees then used the borrowed funds to lend at higher rates of interest to large-scale moneylenders at Istanbul who pooled the funds to finance larger ventures, most importantly, long-distance trade and tax-farming (Çizakça 1996: 131–133).

Not surprisingly, a lively debate developed during the sixteenth century within the Ottoman *ulema* regarding whether the cash *vakif* should be considered illegitimate. The cash *vakifs* were opposed by those who believed that only goods with permanent value such as real estate should constitute the assets of a pious foundation and that the cash *vakifs* contravened the Islamic prohibition of interest. The majority of the *ulema*, however, remained eminently pragmatic and the view that anything useful for the community was useful for Islam ultimately prevailed. During the heated debate, Ebusuud Efendi, the prominent, state-appointed religious leader (*seyhulislam*) of the period, defended the practice from a purely practical point of view, arguing that abolition of interest taking would lead to the collapse of many pious foundations, a situation that would harm the Muslim community (Mandaville 1979).

Despite this pragmatism, however, the cash *vakif* faced serious shortcomings. The interest they charged was fixed by the original founders and could not respond to later changes in market conditions. More importantly, their capital was limited primarily to the original endowment and whatever could additionally be added by reinvesting the profits and other marginal means. Since the original capital was essentially composed of the savings of a single individual, no matter how wealthy, such funds were bound to remain small and the potential for growth remained limited over the long term. Moreover, the Ottoman cash *vakifs* rarely lent to entrepreneurs; they provided mostly consumption credit. It is interesting, however, that as the borrowing requirements of the central government rose sharply in the eighteenth century, the cash *vakifs* responded quickly to the new and growing demand. Financiers began pooling the funds of large numbers of small cash *vakifs* and lending these funds to the central government. In short, Ottoman institutions of credit exhibited a good deal of pragmatism but changed only to a limited extent during the early modern era. They also remained mostly uninfluenced by developments in Europe until the eighteenth century (Çizakça 1996). We will discuss alternative explanations for this pattern below.

Business partnerships

Even though there was no insurmountable barrier against the use of interest-bearing loans for commercial credit, this alternative was not pursued in the medieval Islamic world. Instead, numerous other commercial techniques were developed which played the same role as interest-bearing loans and thus made the use of loans unnecessary. These included a variety of business partnership forms such as *mudaraba* or *commenda*, credit arrangements, transfers of debt and letters of credit, all of which were sanctioned by religious theory. Long-distance trade was thus financed not by simple credit relations involving interest but by a variety of Islamic business partnerships the specifics of which depended on the nature of the risks and the resources provided by the different partners (Çizakça, 1996:10–32, 66–76; Udovitch 1970: 170–217).[2]

Ottoman merchants widely used the varieties of Islamic business partnerships practiced in the Islamic world since the classical era (Çizakça 1996:

---

2 In essence, the *mudaraba* was identical to the commenda of Europe; for discussions of the Islamic origins of commenda, see Ashtor (1972), Pryor (1977), and Udovitch (1962).

66–76; Udovitch 1970: 170–217). Evidence from Islamic court records on commercial disputes and their resolution indicate that Ottoman jurists were well informed about the teachings of medieval Muslim jurists and, in general, adhered closely to the classical Islamic principles in disputes arising from these partnerships. There were some innovations over the centuries; for example, some interesting combinations of *mudaraba* and putting-out activities were developed.

Ottoman institutions of private finance thus reflected a high degree of pragmatism and the willingness to circumvent the Islamic prohibition on interest. However, there was limited change in either the institutions or lending. Similarly, evidence from hundreds of business partnerships indicates that classical Islamic partnership forms underwent limited changes in the early modern era (Gedikli 1998). Ottoman business partnerships as well as the cash *vakifs* remained relatively small, of short duration, and with limited capital. Under these conditions it is not surprising that European business organizations began to dominate Ottoman overseas as well as domestic trade late in the early modern era.

It is important to explore the reasons why the cash *vakifs* did not turn into more formal lending institutions and why there was little change in the Islamic forms of private partnership during the Ottoman era. One explanation points to the rigidity of Islam and Islamic institutions, assuming that Islamic rules, prohibitions, and forms did not change over time even in the face of demands to change them (Kuran 2010). However, we have already pointed to the pragmatism and flexibility exhibited by various segments of Islamic society, economy, and states in the face of daily, practical demands. In contrast, Murat Çizakça has suggested that the continued dominance of small-scale firms or partnerships was probably the most important reason for the limited changes in this area. In other words, demand for change in these institutions was not sufficiently strong (Çizakça 1996). This line of reasoning suggests that the causal relationship between institutions and economic development was not one directional. Just as economic institutions influence the degree and direction of economic development, economic development or its absence also influences institutions and their evolution.

There is another important and related reason for the limited nature of institutional change in this area. The private sector, the merchants, and producers were never in a position to influence the state elites and push for institutional changes that would favor the growth of the private sector during these centuries. In other words, because the state elites were able to retain their leading position in Ottoman society and politics, the influence of various social groups, not only of landowners but also of merchants, manufacturers, and moneychangers, over economic matters, and more generally over the policies of the central government, remained limited.

Institutions of state borrowing

The evolution of Ottoman fiscal institutions during the seventeenth and eighteenth centuries provides a good example not only of the flexibility and pragmatism of the Ottoman state but also of its ability to contain the challenges it faced with the habit of negotiation to coopt and incorporate into a broad alliance the social groups that challenged its authority (Pamuk 2004).

While loans to kings, princes, and governments were part of the regular business of European banking houses in the late medieval and early modern periods, in the Islamic world advances of cash to the rulers and the public treasury were handled differently. In the face of the prohibition on interest, they took the form of tax-farming arrangements in which individuals possessing liquid capital assets advanced cash to the government in return for the right to farm the taxes of a given region or fiscal unit for a fixed period. From the very beginning the Ottomans relied on tax-farming for the collection of urban taxes. Until late in the sixteenth century, however, the agricultural taxes, which constituted the largest part of the tax revenues, were collected locally and mostly in kind within the prebendal *timar* system. State finances were relatively strong during this period thanks to the revenues obtained through the rapid territorial expansion of the empire, and the state did not feel the need to increase the revenues collected at the center (Inalcik 1994: 212–214).

With the changes in military technology during the sixteenth century and the need to maintain larger, permanent armies, however, pressures increased to collect a larger part of the rural surplus at the center. As a result, the *timar* system began to be abandoned in favor of tax-farming and the tax units began to be auctioned off at Istanbul (Darling 1996; Inalcik 1980). Deterioration of state finances during the seventeenth century increased the pressures on the central government to take greater advantage of the tax-farming system for the purposes of domestic borrowing. Especially during periods of war when the fiscal pressures were greatest, the central government began to increase the length of the tax-farming contracts from one to three years to three to five years and even longer. It also demanded an increasingly higher fraction of the auction price of the contract in advance. Tax-farming was thus converted to a form of domestic borrowing with the actual tax revenues being used as collateral by the central government.

Further steps were taken in the same direction with the introduction, in 1695, of the *malikane* system in which the revenue source began to be farmed out on a lifetime basis in return for a large initial payment to be followed by annual payments (Genç 1987; Özvar 2003). One rationale often offered for this system was that by extending the term of the contract, the state hoped that the tax contractor would take better care of the tax source, most importantly the peasant producers, and try to achieve long-term increases in production. In fact, the *malikane* allowed the state to use tax revenues as collateral and borrow on a longer-term basis. In comparison to the straightforward tax-farming system, it represented an important shift towards longer-term borrowing by the state.

With the extension of their term and the introduction of larger advance payments, the long-term financing of these contracts assumed an even greater importance. Private financiers thus began to play an increasingly important role in the tax collection process. Behind the individual, often a Muslim, who joined the bidding in the tax-farming auctions, there often existed a partnership that included financiers as well as the agents who intended to organize the tax collection process itself, often by dividing the large initial contract into smaller pieces and finding subcontractors. Non-Muslims were prohibited from holding most *malikane* contracts but Greeks, Armenians, and Jews were very much part of this elite as financiers, brokers, and accountants. These arrangements were mostly in the form of Islamic business partnerships involving both Muslims and non-Muslims (Çizakça 1996). Over the course of the eighteenth century, some one to two thousand Istanbul-based individuals, together with some five to ten thousand individuals in the provinces, as well as innumerable contractors, agents, financiers, accountants, and managers controlled an important share of the state's revenues. This grand coalition of Istanbul-based elites and the rising elites in the provinces constituted a semi-privatized but interdependent component of the regime (Salzman 1993). Many provincials were able to acquire and pass from one generation to the next small and medium-sized *malikane* shares on villages as long as they remained in favor with local administrators or their Istanbul sponsors. For both the well-connected individuals in the capital city and those in the provinces, getting a piece of government tax revenues became an activity more lucrative than investing in agriculture, trade, or manufacturing.

In the longer term, however, the *malikane* system actually led to a decline in state revenues because of the inability of the state to regain control of the revenue sources after the death of the individuals who had purchased them.

The central government thus began to experiment with other methods for tax collection and domestic borrowing from the 1770s onwards. Rising military expenditures and increasing fiscal pressures during wartime were once again responsible for the institutional changes. After the end of the war of 1768–1774, which had dramatically exposed the military as well as financial weaknesses of the Ottoman system, the financial bureaucracy started a new and related system of long-term domestic borrowing called *esham*. In this system, the annual net revenues of a tax source were specified in nominal terms. This amount was divided into a large number of shares which were then sold to the public for the lifetime of the buyers. The annual revenues of the source continued to be collected by the tax-farmers. As the linkage between the annual government payments to *esham* holders and the under-lying revenues of the tax source weakened, the *esham* increasingly resembled a life-term annuity quite popular in many European countries of the period. Eager to make sure that the Islamic law prohibition against interest rates and usury did not apply to the new instrument, the govern-ment declared that an *esham* share was not structured as and did not constitute a loan since the government had the option to redeem them whenever it wished (Genç 1995).

The remarkable evolution of Ottoman institutions of tax collection and state borrowing from short-term tax farming to lifetime tax farms to govern-ment borrowing with tax revenues as collateral and finally to government annuities and bonds illustrates, in the face of the apparent prohibition of interest by Islamic law, the state's pragmatism as well as its ability and will-ingness to reorganize in response to changing circumstances, albeit slowly and often with considerable time lags. The central government not only experi-mented with new fiscal and financial institutions but it was also willing to come to terms with the limits of its political and administrative power by entering into broad alliances with elites and financiers in the capital city as well as those in the provinces in order to finance its urgent needs, which escalated rapidly and dramatically during periods of war. The option of borrowing in the European financial markets was not available to the Ottomans until the middle of the nineteenth century.

The sharp contrast between the extensive changes in the institutions of public finance and the limited changes in the institutions of private finance during the early modern era is equally striking. This makes it all the more difficult to explain institutional changes or their absence in the Middle East in terms of the rigidities of Islamic law. Instead, such contrasts need to be explained either in terms of the different levels of demand for different kinds of institutional changes and/or in terms of political economy and the disparities between the powers of state elites who needed and favored changes in the institutions of public finance, unlike the economic elites of the private sector, merchants, artisans and financiers who favored changes in the institutions of private finance.

Urban political economy and institutions

The previous section has shown that societies of the Middle East exhibited a good deal of variation and experienced a good deal of institutional change during the millennium before the modern era. It has also argued that these changes were not caused by the requirements of Islam or changes in geography but reflected the changes in economic needs and social structure. This section will focus on how towns and urban areas related to the state, how urban areas were included in state policies, and how they influenced the shaping of institutions as these provide the keys to understanding long-term institutional change in the Middle East. Together with a good deal of regional and intertemporal variation, we can discern some common and persistent features in this respect. Even though the urban councils led by the notables and local producers organized around the guilds enjoyed varying degrees of autonomy, political institutions were often shaped by the sovereign and the state elites around him. Moreover, economic institutions and policies in these societies were shaped to a large degree by the priorities and interests of these state elites. In contrast, the influence of various social groups, not only of landowners but also of merchants, manufacturers, and moneychangers over economic matters, and more generally over the policies of the central government, remained limited. The state elites often exhibited a good deal of pragmatism, flexibility, willingness to negotiate, and ability to adapt their institutions to changing circumstances. Ultimately, however, pragmatism and flexibility were utilized for the defense of an order in which the sovereign and the state elites had the power to shape the political institutions.

In the early centuries of Islam the region had one of the most vibrant economies in the world. It enjoyed strong and expanding urban networks, growing consumer demand, an increasing range of manufacturing activities, and a highly commercialized and monetarized economy well linked to other areas of the ancient world. Economic prosperity was based, above all, on rising productivity in agriculture, thanks to political stability, greater security, expansion of irrigation, and the introduction of many new crops. Growing specialization and division of labor in the non-agricultural sector led to the expansion of manufacturing in food processing, textiles, ceramics, ivory, leather, metal, paper, wicker, wood, and other sectors. The available manuals and scientific works also document a long and impressive list of technical adaptations and innovations in agriculture and food production, ship-building and navigation, textiles, leather and paper, chemicals, soap-making, glass and ceramics, mining, metallurgy, and mechanical engineering, including the use of water power (Pamuk and Shatzmiller 2014). The deepening of the division of labor, the growth of new occupations and skills in manufacturing and services as well as agriculture, and the long list of technical innovations all point to an episode of intensive growth and economic efflorescence in Abbasid Iraq of the kind that has been observed rather infrequently in the preindustrial era (Goldstone 2002).

In addition to the trade across the Indian Ocean, the region developed strong commercial linkages with both central Asia and northern Europe during this period. The very large hoards of silver dirhams found in the Volga region and in Scandinavia points to the access of Islamic lands to large deposits of central Asian silver and the large output of silver coinage by the mints of the Islamic state at a time when the economies of Carolingian Europe and the Byzantine empire suffered from shortages of specie. The rise of long-distance trade and greater commercialization were accompanied by the rise in taxes collected in cash and the growth of the use of Islamic letters of credit (Shatzmiller 2011).

Political leadership in these early centuries had spanned many groups in society, including landowners, merchants, and producers as well as the religious elites. The merchants and more generally the economic elites were able to acquire political power and had a good deal of influence on domestic politics and the government in this period. They were also able to develop extensive trade links and develop long-distance trade from north Africa to central Asia and across the Indian Ocean. The cities of the Middle East became centers of manufactures, producing staple goods for local markets – textiles, metalwork, pottery, leather goods, processed foods, and luxury goods, especially fine textiles for a wider market. The accumulation of capital in the hands of these manufacturers and retail traders remained limited in comparison to those involved in long-distance trade, however. The merchants, and more generally the economic elites, had more autonomy from government intervention and they enjoyed more support during this early period. They also had a good deal of influence on domestic politics and the government (Ibrahim 1990).

Rise of new state elites

Islamic societies began to experience an important change in the middle of the ninth century, however, as soldiers and officers for the Islamic armies began to be recruited from the fringes of the empire rather than the towns and cities of Iraq and Syria or the Bedouin tribes of the Arabian desert. One important reason for this shift was the labor shortages that had their origins in the Justinian plague of the sixth century, which kept recurring at least until the ninth century and possibly later. Another motive was to ensure that soldiers would not be involved in party conflicts and would remain loyal to the central government. The new policy meant that the members of the military began to be recruited from a social group different from the rest of society. While these soldiers, and especially their descendants, gradually assimilated into society, it was virtually impossible for a member of the local indigenous population to become a part of the military ruling elite. This divorce of the military elite from the rest of the society, by origin, custom, and even language, became a distinctive feature of many medieval Islamic societies (Blaydes and Chaney 2013: 9–12; Crone 1980: 74–81; Kennedy 1986: 158–162). Later in the Ottoman era, the reliance on the *devshirme* system for recruiting soldiers and state officials from the sons of Christian peasantry reinforced this division between the state elites and the rest of society, even though the Ottomans abandoned that system after the sixteenth century. While imported slaves played a prominent role as soldiers and officers in the military and as state elites, their numbers and role in the economy remained limited, especially after the Zanj rebellion by black slaves working in plantations in Iraq during the ninth century. Aside from those in the military and government, most slaves in the medieval and early modern Middle East worked as household servants.

With the rise of the power of the new military and political elites, urban politics and social organization began to change. The new state elites, to some extent in collaboration with religious elites, began to dominate urban politics. This new urban political configuration soon began to shape political as well as economic institutions. The economic policies and practices of the government began to reflect the interests and priorities of the new military and political elites. The entrepreneurs or the private sector, consisting of merchants and craftsmen, continued to have a good deal of economic power. There were many rich merchants, and governments both central and local depended on them for various services. However, merchants and private-sector producers played a limited role in the shaping of the institutions (Lapidus 1984: 117–130). It has been observed that Islamic law did not recognize the town as a separate entity and some have argued this is one of the key shortcomings of Islamic law that help explain the long-term economic stagnation of the region (Kuran 2010; Weber 1968). In fact, it was the relative weakness of local participative institutions and absence of political autonomy for the town that explained both the absence of the town in Islamic law and also why merchants were unable to shape the institutions in the direction they preferred (Cahen 1970: 522).

The relationship between governments and the merchants was not a relationship between equals. Governments tolerated and even encouraged the activities of the latter. At the same time, however, the state elites opposed economic and institutional changes when they thought these changes would transform the existing order and make it more likely that they would lose political power. For their part, the merchants could not achieve the sufficiently powerful identity of interests with their rulers which would have enabled them to influence the government to use its material and military resources to further their own commercial interests. They certainly could not declare *l'état c'est moi* but they could plausibly claim, during the best of times, *l'état n'est pas contre moi* (Udovitch 1988).

The apparent and important exception to this picture were the Karimi ("great") merchants who enjoyed the support of the government early on and played an important role in the long-distance trade of Egypt with India and China, especially in the spice trade on the Indian Ocean during the twelfth and thirteenth centuries (Ashtor 1978; Labib 1976). It is clear, however, that the political power or input into government policy enjoyed by them was limited. Towns and cities in the Middle East were under the control of central authorities and the appointed governors during this period. The Karimi merchants took part in politics only indirectly, since the authorities set limits on their capital and their freedom to trade. Even though government policies tended to support the Karimis in the earlier period, they began to turn against them in the fourteenth and especially the fifteenth centuries. In addition to the deteriorating economic conditions in Egypt, the decline of the Karimi merchants was due to excessive government taxation and attempts by the Mamluk rulers to wrest control of the spice trade by setting up government monopolies.

Priorities and policies of the Ottoman state

Late medieval and early modern states all had to address a common range of economic problems. The most basic of these were related directly to the maintenance of the states themselves. The provisioning of the capital city, the armed forces, and to a lesser extent of other urban areas, taxation, support, and regulation of long-distance trade and maintaining a steady supply of money were among the leading concerns of economic policy.[3] In their economic policies, states did not pursue the public interest in some abstract sense of the term. Instead, both the goals and design of economic policies as well as institutions related to their implementation were shaped by the social structure and by the social and political influences acting on the state. In the Ottoman case, economic institutions and the policies of the government in Istanbul began to reflect much more strongly the priorities of the central administration after the successful centralization drive of Mehmed II in the second half of the fifteenth century. The influence of various social groups over these policies remained limited.

One important priority was the provisioning of the urban areas, which was seen as necessary for political stability (Genç 1989; Inalcik 1994: 44–54). The central government wanted to assure a steady supply of goods especially for the capital city and it was very much aware of the critical role played by merchants in this respect. With the territorial expansion of the empire and the incorporation of Syria and Egypt during the sixteenth century, long-distance trade and the control of the intercontinental trade routes became increasingly important and even critical for these needs.

The emphasis on provisioning also necessitated an important distinction between imports and exports. Imports were encouraged as they added to the availability of goods. As a result, the Ottomans never used protectionism as an economic policy. They did not attempt to protect domestic producers from the competition of Indian textiles during the seventeenth and eighteenth centuries, for example. In contrast, exports were tolerated only after the requirements of the domestic economy were met. As soon as the possibility of shortages emerged, the government did not hesitate to restrict the activities of the merchants and prohibit the exportation of basic necessities, especially foodstuffs and raw materials.

Another priority for the Ottoman central administration was to keep other social groups in check. Just as it tried to prevent the emergence of powerful landed elites in the rural areas, so the Ottoman central administration tried to prevent rapid accumulation in the hands of merchants, guild members,

---

3 One should add the qualification that for most societies in the late medieval and early modern periods, it is difficult to talk about an economic sphere separate from the political, administrative, and fiscal (Miller 1963).

former state employees, and tax-farmers. Local guilds enjoyed a good deal of autonomy throughout the Ottoman era. Urban notables whose roots lay in local councils acquired substantial power and began to control large parts of the tax-farming system during the seventeenth and eighteenth centuries. The central bureaucracy was reluctant to give these groups greater power. Nonetheless, it continued to negotiate with them and play one group off against the other. In part because of the opposition of the central administration, local notables were unable to coordinate collective action and change the formal political institutions in their favor even at the height of their power during the eighteenth century.[4]

The state and the private sector in the early modern era

The government's attitude toward merchants and more generally the private sector remained ambiguous. On the one hand, the private businesses were considered indispensable for the functioning of the urban economy. The state often encouraged the activities of merchants, large and small, domestic manufacturers more or less independent of the guilds, and moneychangers as long as they helped sustain the urban economy. When the merchants found opportunities to pursue their activities with less intervention from the government, they often flourished (Hanna 1998). Yet the activities of merchants occasionally led to higher prices of raw materials, bringing pressure on the guild system and more generally the urban economy. Thus the central administration often considered as its main task the control of merchants, not their protection. The control of merchants was much more difficult than the control of guilds, however. While the guilds were fixed in location, the merchants were mobile. Needless to say, the official attitude toward financiers, and moneychangers was similarly ambiguous (Inalcik 1969; Islamoğlu and Keyder 1977).

One of the most extreme examples of Ottoman state policies toward domestic merchants involved the meat supply of the capital city. By the second half of the sixteenth century, Istanbul had emerged, once again, as the largest city in Europe. The state strove to keep food prices at low levels in the capital city. For this purpose, it often tried to make use of the price

---

4 Acemoglu and Robinson (2006) have developed a model to examine the circumstances under which political elites, fearing political replacement, are likely to block technological and institutional change.

ceiling system. For its meat supply the capital depended on large numbers of live animals transported on foot or by sea. When the announced price ceilings for meat were established below market prices, however, merchants refused to bring livestock to the capital. In response, the Ottoman state began to identify wealthy merchants and assign to them the task of supplying meat to the capital city. Merchants who were given this assignment often ended up with large losses and faced sharp declines in their wealth. Not surprisingly, they tried to avoid this responsibility. The state soon began to assign for this task merchants who were engaged in illegal activities or who offended the government. This example suggests that while the state needed the merchants for the provisioning of the cities and especially the capital city, on important issues, it could follow practices rather unfriendly to the merchants. These harsh practices were softened after the sixteenth century and the capital city began to rely increasingly on markets for its meat supply (Greenwood 1988).

Such practices did not mean, however, that the Ottoman state regularly expropriated the property of merchants or guild members. In fact, the Ottoman state made a distinction between the property of private merchants and guild members and the property of employees of the state. Assets accumulated by public servants, especially high-ranking officials during their careers, were considered as the property of the state and they were often if not regularly confiscated after they died or left office. In contrast, the state usually did not intervene to expropriate the assets of private individuals. One important exception occurred during the power struggle between the central government and the urban notables in the provinces around the turn of the nineteenth century, when the central government began to expropriate the properties of prominent urban notables with the argument that many of these assets had been accumulated through tax-farming and other dealings with the state. It may be useful in this context to make a distinction between institutions that shape and enforce contracts and those that enforce property rights (Acemoglu and Robinson 2005). As was the case in many other pre-modern societies, institutions that tended to support markets and enforce contracts tended to function better in the early modern Ottoman empire than the institutions related to the protection of property rights.

In a recent study Nelly Hanna (2011) offers important insights into the activities and life trajectories of the artisan entrepreneurs of Egypt during the Ottoman era. The artisan entrepreneurs stood at the top of the artisan community but were more modest than the largest of the merchants. They were usually not constrained by the guilds and acted as small capitalists, engaging in textiles, sugar, oil, and leather manufacturing. They maintained strong links to the countryside, diversified their activities and their investments into local and long-distance trade and tax-farming. Hanna emphasizes the limits of the command economy and argues that the economic expansion in Egypt during the seventeenth and eighteenth centuries provided many opportunities for accumulation for artisan entrepreneurs as well as merchants. Nonetheless, neither the artisan entrepreneurs nor the merchants received much support from the state. On the contrary, even during the good times they had to watch for the intrusions and encroachments by the state and the state elites. The latter not only levied and collected taxes and tried to regulate the activities of merchants and artisans but they also engaged in entrepreneurial activities themselves, most importantly in tax-farming where they had privileged if not exclusive access. The economic expansion ended with the outbreak of a power struggle within the state elites during the 1760s. The Mamluks or imported state elites with slave origins eventually gained control of the Egyptian economy as well as politics, pushing out the merchants and artisan entrepreneurs and establishing their own networks not only in tax collection but also in production and trade.

Just like the merchants of the region during the medieval period, Ottoman merchants were able to develop trading networks and large presences in south Asia and north Africa. However, the inability of Ottoman and especially the Muslim merchants to control a significant share of the trade with Europe hurt them in the longer term. One important obstacle faced by the Muslim merchants was the restrictions against them created in Europe. From the twelfth century onwards, most European countries promulgated laws forbidding the lengthy sojourn, permanent settlement, or engagement in commerce by foreign nationals, including Muslims. Other factors contributed to the weak presence of Ottoman merchants in Europe. While the governments of European countries often encouraged, backed, and supported merchants who were their subjects or citizens, the rulers or governments in the Middle East did not view the protection of the merchants who were their subjects and who operated outside the boundaries of their countries a matter worthy of their attention. One major reason for this was that the governments felt that the activities of the merchants abroad did not yield any revenues or otherwise provide a fiscal advantage to the central treasury.

The basic message to local merchants operating abroad was that their state was indifferent to their activity and hence no backing or protection was granted to them when they needed it. As a result, those Muslim merchants who wished to operate in foreign lands directed their energies to areas where the population was mostly Muslim or in which large Muslim communities existed, in central Asia, south and southeast Asia and to some extent in north Africa. They had also been active in the trade with Europe but began to lag behind non-Muslim Ottoman merchants who were able to take advantage of their growing international networks and connections with European merchants (Gilbar 2003). By the eighteenth century, Muslim merchants were mostly excluded from the rapidly growing European trade. The fact that the wealthiest Ottoman merchants were non-Muslims, mostly Greeks and Armenians, made it even more difficult for their economic power to be converted to political influence during the eighteenth and nineteenth centuries.

The Ottoman central administration's success in keeping the merchants, urban notables, and other groups in check does not mean that the enduring cliché about the strong and despotic states in the Middle East is true. In fact, the Ottoman state had only limited power and capacity in many areas. For example, only a small fraction of the taxes collected from the peasant and urban producers in the large empire reached the central treasury. Most of the tax revenues were actually retained by the local elites who controlled the tax-farming system. A recent study found that per capita tax collections of the Ottoman central administration lagged significantly behind all European states during the seventeenth and eighteenth centuries, even after corrections are made for the differences in per capita income levels (Karaman and Pamuk 2010). Geography also played an important role in this respect. The large size and great geographical diversity of the empire made it much more difficult for the Ottoman state to collect taxes and more generally to pursue effective policies. The large scale also made it difficult for the local elites to coordinate their actions and challenge the central administration to change the political institutions and acquire greater power.

Privileges to European merchants

While the policies of governments in the region toward local merchants were characterized by a great deal of ambiguity, the same governments were willing and ready to offer legal, commercial, and other privileges to European merchants, beginning as early as the twelfth century. These privileges were granted not because the Islamic governments were coerced by the more powerful European states. Through these privileges, the rulers sought to increase the circulation of goods, especially luxury goods, in their local markets and to increase state revenues from trade. Another motive was to use the privileges as an instrument of foreign policy and gain influence and friendship in Europe. The privileges for the European merchants included lower tariffs or even exemptions from certain kinds of duty. It is clear that local merchants did not have much say in this process as the privileges often put them at a disadvantage against their European counterparts (Inalcik 1973).

These privileges played an important role in the transfer of large segments of the long-distance trade of the Middle East as well as coastal and long-distance shipping to Euroepan merchants in the following centuries. As local merchants became weaker, it became even more difficult for them to provide input into their government's trade policies or change the commercial or economic institutions in the region. With the rise of the Atlantic trade, the merchants of northwestern European countries increased their power substantially. They were then able not only to bring about major institutional changes in their countries but also to induce their governments to defend and develop their interests in the Middle East more forcefully. Merchants of the region thus found it even more difficult to compete against their European counterparts after the sixteenth century.

As European states and merchants increased their economic and political power, they also began to influence the direction of institutional change in the region. The privileges provided to the European merchants were expanded substantially during the eighteenth century. They ceased to be unilateral grants and began to be referred to as the "capitulations" due to the many headings they were grouped under in the original Latin texts in the medieval era (van den Boogert 2005). By the nineteenth century, these privileges made it increasingly difficult for the local merchants to compete on an equal footing with the Europeans, and they became a striking example of exclusionary institutions. The capitulations could be abolished only after World War I and the dissolution of the Ottoman empire.

Conclusion

Until the end of the eleventh century, the Middle East region had one of the most vibrant economies in the world. The Islamic states enjoyed a strong urban network, wide range of manufacturing activities, and a highly commercialized and monetarized economy well linked to other areas of the Old World. After the eleventh century, however, the center of gravity of the ancient world began to shift away from the urban centers of the Islamic states and toward the mercantile states of Italy, the Low Countries, and England. Nonetheless, the differences in the standards of living between the two regions remained limited until the industrial revolution. Urban wages in the Middle East did not exhibit a long-term downward trend during the early modern centuries. This and other evidence suggests that it is probably more appropriate to talk about the rise of Europe than the decline of the Middle East.

This chapter has argued that despite the growing divergence with western Europe, many institutional changes took place in the medieval and early modern Middle East. For an explanation of the direction of institutional change, it focussed on the internal organization of societies in the Middle East and how their social and political organization may have influenced political and economic institutions. In the late medieval and early modern Middle East, political institutions and economic policies and practices of the government often reflected the interests and priorities of the state elites. The private sector, landowners, merchants, manufacturers, and moneychangers enjoyed a good deal of local power and autonomy, but formal political institutions did not sufficiently allow the representation of their interests in central government and in central government policy. Moreover, these groups were never able to achieve the sufficiently powerful identity of interests with their rulers which would have enabled them to influence the government to further their own commercial interests. For their part, the state elites considered the merchants and the private sector indispensable for the functioning of the economy. The state tolerated and even encouraged their activities. When the merchants found opportunities to pursue their activities with less intervention from the government, they often flourished. At the same time, however, the state elites opposed economic and institutional changes when they thought that these changes would transform the existing order and make it more likely that they would lose political power. Institutional change thus remained selective and reflected, above all, the interests and priorities of the state and the state elites.

Differences in government policies and the institutional environment between western Europe and the Middle East remained limited during the medieval era. With the rise of the Atlantic trade, however, the merchants in northwestern European countries increased their economic and political power substantially. They were then able not only to bring about major institutional changes in their countries but also to induce their governments to defend and develop their commercial interests in the Middle East more forcefully. Merchants of the region thus found it even more difficult to compete against them after the sixteenth century. As they began to lag behind the European merchants even in their own region, it became even more difficult for them to provide input into their government's trade policies or change the commercial or economic institutions in the direction they preferred. Beginning early in the nineteenth century, economic policies and institutional changes in the Middle East also began to reflect the growing power of European states and companies.

The weaknesses of the merchants, and more generally of the private sector in the Middle East, persisted well into the twentieth century. When the Great Depression led to the collapse of an economic model based on agriculture and accelerated if not initiated the debates about industrialization, it was argued throughout the region that the private sector could not undertake this kind of resource mobilization. Reliance on private entrepreneurs and on the law of supply and demand would be wasteful, it was believed, and would not extricate the economy from its trap. As a result, it was the state elites and state enterprises that took the lead in industrialization in Turkey during the 1930s, a strategy called *étatisme*. This model was replicated after World War II in Egypt, Syria, Iraq, and across North Africa as import-substituting industrialization was led not by private enterprises but by the state sector (Richards and Waterbury 1996: 173–204).

As a leading political scientist of the region recently observed, one of the most important historical legacies in the Middle East today is the large discrepancy between the economic and political power of the merchants and more generally of economic elites. As was the case in the past, merchants in most parts of the modern Middle East can become wealthy but they cannot expect to attain political power or influence (Özbudun 1996: 135–137). This absence, on the part of the economic elites, of political power and capacity to influence economic institutions explains better than any other single factor, better than geography or resource endowments, Islam or culture, the growing economic divergence between western Europe and the Middle East during the late medieval and early modern eras.

References

Abu-Lughod, J. L. (1989). *Before European Hegemony: The World System A.D. 1250–1350*. Oxford University Press.

Acemoglu, D. and S. Johnson, (2005). "Unbundling Institutions," *Journal of Political Economy* 113: 949–995.

Acemoglu, D. and J. Robinson (2006). "Economic Backwardness in Political Perspective," *American Political Science Review* 100: 115–131.

(2012). *Why Nations Fail: The Origins of Power, Prosperity and Poverty*. London: Profile Books.

Acemoglu, D., S. Johnson, and J. Robinson (2005). "The Rise of Europe: Atlantic Trade, Institutional Change and Economic Growth," *American Economic Review* 95: 546–579.

Allen, R. C. (2001). "The Great Divergence in European Wages and Prices from the Middle Ages to the First World War," *Explorations in Economic History* 38: 411–447.

Alvarez-Nogal, C. and L. Prados de la Escosura (2013). "The Rise and Fall of Spain (1270–1850)," *Economic History Review* 66: 1–37.

Ashtor, E. (1972). "Banking Instruments between the Muslim East and the Christian West," *Journal of European Economic History* 1: 553–573.

(1976). *A Social and Economic History of the Near East in the Middle Ages*. University of California Press.

(1978). *Studies on the Levantine Trade in the Middle Ages*. London: Variorum.

Blaydes, L. and E. Chaney (2013). "The Feudal Revolution and Europe's Rise: Political Divergence of the Christian and Muslim Worlds before 1500 CE," *American Political Science Review* 107(1): 16–34.

Boogert, M. H. van den (2005). *The Capitulations and the Ottoman Legal System, Qadis, Consuls and Beratlis in the 18th Century*. Leiden and Boston: Brill.

Borsch, S. J. (2005). *The Black Death in Egypt and England*. Austin, TX: The University of Texas Press.

Broadberry, S., B. Campbell, A. Klein, M. Overton, and B. Van Leeuwen (2010). "British Economic Growth, Some Preliminary Estimates, 1300–1850." Unpublished manuscript.

Cahen, C. (1970). "Economy, Society and Institutions," in P. M. Holt, Ann K. Lambton, and B. Lewis (eds.), *Islamic Society and Civilization*. Cambridge University Press, pp. 511–538.

(1971). "Ikta," in *Encyclopedia of Islam*, 2nd edn. Leiden: Brill.

Cipolla, C. M. (1963). "The Economic Policies of Governments," and "The Italian and Iberian Peninsulas," in M. M. Postan, E. E. Rich and E. Miller (eds.), *The Cambridge Economic History of Europe*, Vol. III. Cambridge University Press, pp. 397–429.

Çizakça, M. (1996). *A Comparative Evolution of Business Partnerships: The Islamic World and Europe with Specific Reference to the Ottoman Archives*. Leiden: Brill.

Crone, P. (1980). *Slaves on Horses: The Evolution of the Islamic Polity*. Cambridge University Press, pp. 74–81.

Cuno, K. (1992). *The Pasha's Peasants. Land, Society and Economy in Lower Egypt, 1740–1858*. Cambridge University Press.

Darling, L. T. (1996). *Revenue-Raising and Legitimacy: Tax Collection and Finance Administration in the Ottoman Empire, 1560–1660*. Leiden: Brill.

Gedikli, F. (1998). *Osmanli Şirket Kültürü, XVI–XVII. Yüzyillarda Mudarebe Uygulamasi*. Istanbul: Iz Yayincilik.

Genç, M. (1987). "A Study of the Feasibility of Using Eighteenth Century Ottoman Financial Records as an Indicator of Economic Activity," in H. Islamoğlu-Inan (ed.), *The Ottoman Empire and the World Economy*. Cambridge University Press, pp. 345–373.

(1989). "Osmanlı Iktisadi Dünya Görüşünün Ilkeleri," *Istanbul Üniversitesi Edebiyat Fakültesi Sosyoloji Dergis* 3(1): 175–185.

(1995). "Esham," in *Islam Ansiklopedisi* Ankara: Türkiye Diyanet Vakfi.

Gilbar, G. (2003). "The Muslim Big Merchants-Entrepreneurs of the Middle East, 1860–1914," *Die Welt des Islams* 43: 1–36.

Goldstone, J. (2002). "Efflorescences and Economic Growth in World History: Rethinking the 'Rise of the West' and the Industrial Revolution," *Journal of World History*, 13: 323–389.

Greenwood, A. (1988). "Istanbul's Meat Provisioning: A Study of the Celepkesan System," Ph.D. dissertation, University of Chicago.

Hanna, N. (1998). *Making Big Money in 1600: The Life and Times of Ismail Abu Taqiyya, Egyptian Merchant*. The American University in Cairo Press.

(2011). *Artisan Entrepreneurs in Cairo and Early-Modern Capitalism (1600–1800)*. Syracuse University Press.

Ibrahim, M. (1990). *Merchant Capital and Islam*. Austin, TX: University of Texas Press.

Inalcik, H. (1969). "Capital Accumulation in the Ottoman Empire," *The Journal of Economic History* 29: 97–140.

(1973). "Imtiyazat," in *Encyclopedia of Islam*, 2nd edn.

(1980). "Military and Fiscal Transformation in the Ottoman Empire, 1600–1700," *Archivum Ottomanicum* 6: 283–337.

(1994). "The Ottoman State: Economy and Society, 1300–1600," in H. İnalcik and D. Quataert (eds.), *An Economic and Social History of the Ottoman Empire, 1300–1914*. Cambridge University Press, pp. 9–409.

Islamoğlu, H. and Ç. Keyder (1977). "Agenda for Ottoman History," *Review, Fernand Braudel Center* 1: 31–55.

Issawi, C. (1981). "The Area and Population of the Arab Empire: An Essay in Speculation," in A. L. Udovitch (ed.), *The Islamic Middle East 700–1900*. Princeton, NJ: Darwin Press, pp. 375–397.

Jennings, R. C. (1973). "Loans and Credit in Early 17th Century Ottoman Judicial Records," *Journal of the Economic and Social History of the Orient* 16: 168–216.

Karaman, K. and Ş. Pamuk (2010). "Ottoman State Finances in Comparative European Perspective, 1500–1914," *The Journal of Economic History* 70: 593–627.

Kennedy, H. (1986). *The Prophet and the Age of the Caliphates: The Islamic Near East from the Sixth to the Tenth Century*. Longman, pp. 158–162.

Keyder, C. and F. Tabak, eds. (1991). *Landholding and Commercial Agriculture in the Middle East*. Albany, NY: State University of New York Press.

Kuran, T. (2010). *The Long Divergence: How Islamic Law Held Back the Middle East*. Princeton University Press.

Labib, S. Y. (1976). "Karimi," in *Encyclopedia of Islam*, 2nd edn.

Lambton, A. K. S. (1953). *Landlord and Peasant in Persia: A Study of Land Tenure and Land Revenue Administration*. London: Oxford University Press.

Lapidus, I. (1984). *Muslim Cities in the Later Middle Ages*. New York: Cambridge University Press.

Lombard, M. (1975). *The Golden Age of Islam*, trs. J. Spencer. Amsterdam: North Holland.

McEvedy, C. and R. Jones (1978). *Atlas of World Population History*. Harmondsworth: Penguin Books.

Mandaville, J. E. (1979). "Usurious Piety: The Cash Waqf Controversy in the Ottoman Empire," *International Journal of Middle East Studies* 10: 289–308.

Miller, E. (1963). "France and England," in M. M. Postan, E. E. Rich and E. Miller (eds.), *The Cambridge Economic History of Europe*, Vol. III. Cambridge University Press, pp. 282–91.

North, D. C. (1990). *Institutions, Institutional Change and Economic Performance*. Cambridge University Press.

Ogilvie, S. (2007). "'Whatever Is, Is Right?'. Institutions in Pre-Industrial Europe," *Economic History Review* 60: 649–684.

Özbudun, E. (1996). "The Continuing Ottoman Legacy and State Tradition in the Middle East," in L. Carl Brown (ed.), *Imperial Legacy: The Ottoman Imprint on the Balkans and the Middle East*. Columbia University Press, pp. 133–157.

Özmucur, S. and Ş. Pamuk (2002). "Real Wages and Standards of Living in the Ottoman Empire, 1489–1914," *The Journal of Economic History* 62: 292–321.

Özvar, E. (2003). *Osmanlı Maliyesinde Malikâne Uygulaması*. Istanbul: Kitabevi.

Pamuk, Ş. (2004). "Institutional Change and the Longevity of the Ottoman Empire, 1500–1800," *Journal of Interdisciplinary History* 35: 225–247.

(2007). "The Black Death and the Origins of the Great Divergence inside Europe, 1300–1600," *European Review of Economic History* 11: 289–317.

Pamuk, Ş. and M. Shatzmiller (2014). "Plagues, Wages and Economic Change in the Islamic Middle East, 700–1500," *Journal of Economic History* 74 (forthcoming).

Pryor, J. H. (1977). "Origins of the Commenda Contract," *Speculum* 52: 5–37.

Richards, A. and J. Waterbury (1996). *A Political Economy of the Middle East*, 2nd edn. Boulder, Westview Press.

Rodrik, D., A. Subramanian, and F. Trebbi (2004). "Institutions Rule: The Primacy of Institutions over Geography and Integration in Economic Development," *The Journal of Economic Growth* 9: 131–165.

Salzman, A. (1993). "An Ancien Regime Revisited: Privatization and Political Economy in the Eighteenth Century Ottoman Empire," *Politics and Society* 21: 393–423.

Shan, S. J. (1962). *The Financial and Administrative Organization and Development of Ottoman Egypt, 1517–1798*. Princeton University Press.

Shatzmiller, M. (2011). "Economic Performance and Economic Growth in the Early Islamic World, 700–1000," *Journal of the Economic and Social History of the Orient* 54: 132–184.

Tsugitaka, S. (1997). *State and Rural Society in Medieval Islam: Sultans, Muqta's and Fallahun*, Leiden: Brill.

Udovitch, A. L. (1962). "At the Origins of the Western Commenda: Islam, Israel, Byzantium," *Speculum* 37: 198–207.

(1970). *Partnership and Profit in Medieval Islam*. Princeton University Press.

(1975). "Reflections on the Institutions of Credits and Banking in the Medieval Islamic Near East," *Studia Islamica* 56: 5–21.

(1988). "Merchants and *Amirs*: Government and Trade in Eleventh Century Egypt," *Asian and African Studies* 22: 53–72.

Weber, M. (1968). *Economy and Society*, ed. G. Roth and C. Wittich, 3 vols. New York: Bedminster Press.

Zanden, J. L. van (1999). "Wages and the Standard of Living in Europe, 1500–1800," *The European Review of Economic History* 3: 175–197.

9

Markets and coercion in medieval Europe

KARL GUNNAR PERSSON

Introduction

Medieval Europe was literally built on the ruins left by the disintegrated Roman empire (McCormick 2001; Wickham 2005, 2009). But during that long period of recovery up to the early modern period Europe was transformed from an economic backwater into the most advanced region in the world. By 1500 GDP per head in the leading areas of Europe, that is Spain, England, the Low Countries (divided into Belgium and Holland in the table) and Italy (comprising mainly northern and central Italy) was three to five times that of a subsistence income, estimated at some 400 dollars in constant 1990 prices (cf. Table 10.1). This accomplishment seems paradoxical in the light of the popular but prejudiced view of medieval Europe as culturally retarded, institutionally unsophisticated, and economically and technologically stagnant.

Medieval Europe started from a position where many of the gains from advanced specialization and vibrant trade had been lost. Cities had been deserted, roads and bridges had not been maintained, mints and workshops had been closed down, and the Mediterranean world was about to be split along religious lines with the advancement of the Arab civilization after the decline of the western Roman empire. But population started to grow again in a sustained way in the eighth century after centuries of ravaging epidemics, political fragmentation, and catastrophic population shocks. Not only did Europe manage to rebuild and repopulate its cities and re-establish long-haul transport, but it also managed to reach levels of technological, economic, cultural, and institutional sophistication never experienced before in world history. The recovery was linked to regional specialization

Thanks to Bas van Bavel and the editors for comments on a draft and to the Carlsberg Foundation for research funding.

stimulated by trade and "Smithian" forces of increasing division of labor that generated markets for goods, services, and factors of production. Population increase also permitted the higher level of aggregate demand that was a necessary condition for spending on more productive "high fixed cost and low variable cost" investments such as roads, bridges, ships, and water- and windmills.

The expansion of trade and markets in post-Roman medieval Europe has not passed unnoticed. Usually labeled the "commercial revolution" it has been at the center of research, and rightly so (Britnell 1993; Favier 1987; Lopez 1971). Together with the history of advances in technology (White 1962) these studies fostered a dynamic interpretation of the medieval economy. This view challenged the prevailing more pessimistic view relying more on the constraints of Malthusian conditions. Scholars like M. M. Postan and E. Le Roy Ladurie had turned their attention to the consequence of population growth in economies with limited land, which eventually became a binding constraint. In this interpretation the medieval economy could not escape stagnation in the long run because of alleged technological inertia. The postulate of insufficient response of technological progress to resource constraints is a cornerstone in the Malthusian interpretation of the pre-industrial economy, making periods of relative affluence, at best, transitory events. A positive technological shock would increase income per head only in the short run and would eventually lead to a permanently higher population level at long-run subsistence incomes. The assumption of insignificant technological progress, however, has been challenged by the idea that division of labor not only increases labor productivity but also enables "learning by doing" which continues to increase productivity.

The appeal of the Malthusian interpretation of pre-industrial economic history stems from its simplicity: income and population are endogenous and the outcome is deterministic with income per head remaining at subsistence level (cf. Clark [2008] for a recent restatement of the Malthusian story). However, the standard interpretation of the Malthusian model is but a special case of a wider model. Once *permanent* technological progress is admitted for the steady state, income can remain at above subsistence level, as it actually did in many regions of medieval Europe. The outcome will depend on the relative strength of diminishing returns as opposed to the rate of technological progress (Persson 1988). In a sense, the interpretation of the medieval period can be framed as a controversy between dynamic "Smithian" and stagnationist "Malthusian" forces (Persson 2010: 60–73). A combination of the two admits for the diversity of income levels in medieval Europe, which had largely escaped the bare-bones subsistence economy.

The essential question is not whether markets existed but how penetrating markets were in daily life. Recent research actually underpins the view that markets, although often imperfect, were or became more pervasive than previously believed. Markets remained thin for non-standardized commodities, and commodities were less standardized than today, and it is therefore difficult to assess whether alleged deviations of, say, land prices from equilibrium price originated in the hazards of a particular negotiating context or because there were constraints set by family or kinship or coercion by landowning elites. A wide variance in prices at a given point in time cannot conceal that movements in prices over time and space reflected demand and supply conditions fairly quickly. The ever-advancing division of labor and regional specialization built on a lively trade and its response to changes in relative prices. In what follows it will be demonstrated that land, credit, and commodity markets were certainly not restricted to the core parts of Europe but have been recorded in the more peripheral parts like Scandinavia as well (Franzén 2006: 44–58, 102–25). Property rights were usually well defined and the procedures for exchange fairly standardized. Local courts were set up early on to settle conflicts regarding credit and debt. The value of money was known also in the very periphery of Europe as told in Icelandic sagas: Halldor, a warrior, could easily see that King Harald Hårdråde was trying to pay him with debased coins after a campaign and refused to be enlisted for a new campaign. So much for king and country!

There is no denying that un-freedom was on the rise at the end of the first millennium. Markets were operating in a context where coercion, particularly over labor, was present. Although the volatility of prices posed problems especially for the poor, coercion was even worse. As noted by Christopher Dyer, "[a]ll of our evidence for peasant opinion suggests that they felt no gratitude for being protected from market forces" (Dyer 2005a: 427).

However, as we will see, un-freedom in the form of slavery and serfdom was neither as pervasive nor as permanent as commonly believed. Outright slavery was marginal and virtually extinct in most of Europe in the beginning of the second millennium, although trade in slaves continued from the west to the eastern Mediterranean. With a significant share of the population in serfdom not only labor markets but also markets for land were affected because serfs met barriers when buying land and contracting leases. The terms of the contracts with landowners were affected by the coercive power of the lords. Despite those constraints, markets for goods and factors of production were revitalized and lively, especially in areas close to urban centers and trading emporia. Commodity markets were the first to recover but were soon followed by lively land markets and, indeed, labor markets. Although informal credit existed alongside the development of land and commodity markets the decisive innovations in banking and finance came during the last centuries in the medieval era.

Understanding un-freedom in medieval Europe

Economic systems rely to a varying extent on command. That is true also for a capitalist system: workers voluntarily contract to work for a specified time period in a firm but the work is organized by command. In the medieval economy the element of command and coercion was, at times, extended to what in a capitalist economy is the sphere of contracting between independent buyers and sellers of commodities, factors of production, and (labor) services. The medieval economy witnessed first the rise and then the decline of un-freedom, which is essentially the denial of the right of free contracting in markets. However in the end un-freedom was giving way to a system that recognized an individual's right to contract in all markets.

Evsey Domar, best known as a pioneering growth economist, suggested a persuasive although, as he admitted, incomplete theory of serfdom and slavery.[1] Domar focused on the problem for a landowning elite of extracting rent if peasants were paid the marginal product. In a land-abundant economy the marginal product was approximately equal to the average product, meaning that landlords could not extract a land rent from a *free* peasant who was paid the marginal product. The heart of the matter was peasant liberties: the liberty to choose whom to work for and the liberty of geographical mobility. *Net leybeigen, dann sye haben freien zug*, as the contemporary German saying put it. Not being a serf gave you the right to move away, to negotiate a new and better contract. As a consequence the land rent would converge to zero as long as the liberty of laborers was not denied. To secure a land rent in a land-abundant economy landowners needed to restrict the bargaining power given by the right of *freien zug*. Serfdom was essentially a way for a landowner to deny or restrict labor mobility, that is, to dictate a "subsistence" income below

---

1 I have deliberately avoided the terms "feudal" and "feudalism" in this chapter because these concepts have become more of an obstacle than a guide to the understanding of the medieval period. The feudal connotation suggests an overwhelmingly agrarian and autarkic economy in which customary bonds of delegation and subordination dominate social and political relations. "Feudalism" also conveys a view of a particular "mode of production" in which manors were the prime site of agrarian production, which is an unacceptable simplification. As a contrast I will focus on the transitional nature of command in the medieval period and how command was eroded by market forces.

marginal product when market forces would have helped peasants to negotiate better economic conditions.

The rent extracted from unfree peasant households varied over time and location. In exchange for the right to use a piece of arable land and to have access to the common the peasant paid a rent in kind or in money and/or in labor services performed at the lord's estate. On top of that there were a number of dues or fines linked to marriage, *merchet*, and the generational shift of plot, *heriot*, and entry fines. There was an ongoing conflict between landowners and enserfed peasants, or villeins, where the latter resisted new or old dues laid upon them. The efficiency of policing the area determined the incidence of fugitives who would actually take the risk of moving to the free frontier land. The decline of serfdom in Domar's perspective would happen when *labor* shortage had been replaced by *land* shortage after centuries of uninterrupted population growth. When labor was chasing land and marginal output on free frontier land had declined sufficiently land rents could be expected to rise. Landlords could now rely on market forces to extract rents from labor rather than using the command of force and laying restrictions on individual rights. Although elegant and simple, Domar's theory cannot grasp the complexity of European experience.

To enforce a peasant income below the marginal product of labor, landlords had to agree not to outbid each other in their search for labor to occupy their vacant land. Essentially, landlords had to establish a monopsonistic cartel that determined the rent peasants had to pay. If there was a labor shortage all members of the cartel would face vacancies, that is unused land, and as a consequence a single landlord would be tempted to earn a lot more by just offering households a slightly smaller rent and thereby fill the vacancies. When all landlords followed this strategy, then land rents would be squeezed. There were formidable coordination costs and a high risk of coordination failures in reaching and monitoring a ban on employing fugitives and stopping peasants from moving into land where the aristocracy had not yet extended its property rights. It is reasonable to argue that the larger the vacancy rate, the more difficult it would be to impose the necessary discipline within the cartel. It is well known that cartels are inherently unstable. However, as labor becomes less scarce the cartel might become more stable. The policy of the Crown, the central authority, was essential for the possibility of maintaining an agreement among landlords not to compete for labor from other estates, what we can call the "employ no fugitive" rule. That rule was difficult to monitor without the assistance of the state, except in densely populated areas. If landlords could externalize the administration and monitoring costs of fugitives to the state, the probability of the sustainability of serfdom would increase. However, the cooperation of the state was far from given. The state might claim property rights over frontier land and would therefore typically raise revenue by taxing new occupants of such land. In non-frontier lands the state often competed with lords over rents. In that perspective the state had little interest in maintaining or helping to establish serfdom.

Local lords could claim jurisdiction over their own territory but would need the state and/or the cooperation of other lords to pursue fugitives outside the territory. Practices varied but lords were not always successful in claiming that there was a personal bond between lord and serf. If there was none a lord had little chance of fugitives being returned. This problem increased in importance with city growth. *Stadtluft macht frei*, as the contemporary saying had it. Health hazards in cities were probably more of a problem for a refugee than the risk of being returned to the estate.[2] While it is possible that landowners could sustain an agreement not to outbid each other in the search for labor, at least within a limited geographical area, it would be much harder to extend that agreement to employers in cities, especially when cities became increasingly independent from aristocratic jurisdiction. A high level of urbanization can therefore be seen as incompatible with serfdom.

Timing and incidence of serfdom

The evidence suggests that un-freedom re-emerged in western Europe with a considerable time lag *after* the demise of the Roman empire (e.g. Bonnassie 1990: 154–164; Wickham 2005: 570–579). The essential new element in medieval un-freedom, the fact that serfs were subjected to the private justice of their lords, emerges in the ninth and tenth centuries, a century or so earlier in much of France. The Roman decline seems to be associated with a weakening of both central and local power and an increase in peasants rights over their own labor and land. In areas untouched by Roman civilization the peasantry had a tradition of independence and self-ownership and the aristocracy was weak. Many parts of Europe had still not been Christianized and the Church was therefore absent as landlord. In the centuries after the Roman decline the weakened aristocracy was not potent enough to impose restrictions on labor

---

2 A widespread, although contested, custom gave escaping serfs the freedom from being forcefully returned after one year and a day within the city walls. Lords tried, but in the end failed, to stem the exodus to cities.

mobility or to establish the discipline of a monopsonistic cartel, with the peasantry as the major beneficiary.

As the coercive elements of serfdom were tightened in the closing centuries of the first millennium there was still land that could be reclaimed, and often aristocracies had to give in to market pressures by offering more generous contracts to attract or keep labor. Geographically separated areas such as Catalonia and the Low Countries illustrate this condition well. Although the timing of aristocratic revival differed across continental western Europe it seems to be a general trend (Feller 2007: 169). Peasant resistance, documented in various parts of Italy, could delay the process somewhat, and there were large differences in the coercive power of lords also within small areas, although these differences tended to melt down over time (Figueras 2005: 480–481). By and large, settler areas were built on the consensual agreement of peasants in the labor-scarce frontier regions, as shown most clearly by the medieval history of Spain under the "reconquest" (MacCay 1977).

Serfdom was, if not preceded by, clearly associated with a concentration of ownership of land in the hands of the lay and ecclesiastical elites. In fact, the imposition of aristocratic burdens and servitude was often the consequence of military annexation such as the Carolingian occupation and subjection of eastern Germany (Saxony) at the end of the eighth century, which met fierce resistance from the local peasantry in the mid ninth century. The process of aristocratic land-grabbing gained momentum in the eighth century, with free holding peasants as the major victims, leading to occasional but largely unsuccessful peasant uprisings. In other parts of Europe local landlords exploited any sign of weakness of the state by claiming the right to collect taxes and fees previously collected by the state.

The eleventh and twelfth centuries witness attempts to increase the fines paid by villeins. Although a free peasantry was not wiped out entirely it declined in importance. However, the coercive power of the landholding elites was never absolute. Customary rights of the peasantry retarded the onslaught of the landlords, but the latter had the advantage of running the courts and keeping the records. The jurisdictional power of the local aristocracy increased, however, which had adverse consequences for the peasantry. *Mals usos* or bad customs, that is, arbitrary exactions, were laid upon the tenants and freeholders alike. But in any given location you would typically see a wide variety of contractual forms, from heavily burdened serfs to free tenants with lighter burdens as well as freeholders. The only group of workers who experienced an improvement in social standing were slaves, who were elevated to serflike legal status. The misperception of the extent of European un-freedom is partly a consequence of a bias imposed by the availability of written sources. Estates, specifically ecclesiastical estates, kept records that have survived; freeholding peasants did not keep records.

The precise composition of the labor force is not known but at most serfs were, in Christopher Dyer's words, "a substantial minority." Although this generalization is articulated with reference to England it is probably roughly true for medieval western Europe, with the exception of Scandinavia with its large independent peasantry.

Peasant households remained the major locus of agricultural production even if the consolidated estate, the manor, gained in importance with the establishment of serfdom. Manors had land worked by serfs who owed labor services performed at the lord's manor. The extent and nature of labor services varied but was usually expressed as days per week, varying between one and three days a week or the equivalent expressed in weeks per year. The serfs also had their own plot to cultivate for their own consumption and the market. This form of management of production was, however, less wide-spread and less permanent than commonly believed. The manorial organiza-tional form, which continental scholars often call bipartite,[3] never employed a majority of agricultural producers even in these areas where it was most widely diffused. Besides, serfdom was not necessarily associated with labor services on an estate managed by the lay or ecclesiastical lord. It was quite common for the entire estate, or most of it, to be subdivided into peasant-managed plots paying rents to the landlord.

Why this drift toward a manorial organization gained momentum in the ninth century is not entirely clear and it is not a Europe-wide phenomenon. The core of the manorial organization was located in the area between the Loire and Rhine rivers, that is, in the former Carolingian empire. It later spread eastwards, but was virtually absent or weak in southern France, in Scandinavia, and eastern Europe. In Italy manors were less consolidated and seigniorial rights were weak in major regions, such as Tuscany (Wickham 1996). There is no direct link between plantations in antiquity worked by slaves and manorial production management. In fact manorial production does not appear until the late eighth century in France, perhaps a century earlier in part of the Low Countries, where there was no history of plantation

---

3 For southern France see Duby (1971: 173). The French term is *régime domaniale, sistema curtense* in Italian, and in the German literature *Villifikationswirtschaft* is the accepted terminology.

production in antiquity, unlike in Italy. English manors can be traced back to before the Norman Conquest, which invalidates the claim that manorialism was a Norman import. In fact the homeland of the Normans, Normandy in France, had barely any trace of manors. Moreover, if manorial production was a substantial part of total agricultural production it probably never was the dominant source of agricultural output. In England at the end of the thirteenth century the distribution of land according to production suggests that about a quarter of the arable land was under direct manorial management, an equal share was free land, and free and un-free tenants cultivated the rest (Campbell 2000: 55–58).

One interpretation of the rise of manorialism is that by the close of the first millennium commodity markets had started to thrive and that manorial organization permitted an intensification of a marketable surplus. This argument is also suggested as an explanation of eastern European serfdom in the early modern period (Kula 1976). However, there is reason to question the efficiency of manorial production. Serfs lacked motivation and the inherent tendency to shirk necessitated a costly monitoring of work effort. A more likely explanation looks at the manorial organization as a way of securing a rent in the form of labor services in a period when peasant households were difficult to discipline. It should be remembered that the submission of an independent peasantry had not taken place without open resistance. The extension of the manorial sector varied substantially across regions. In the Low Countries, an area covering present-day northern France, Belgium, and the Netherlands, the manorial organization was emerging in the densely populated regions suitable for cereal production, but was virtually absent in areas of land reclamation, such as Holland and the coastal regions of Flanders, which were much less densely populated. In that respect the northern part of the Low Countries resembled northern Germany, which was colonized, at least partly, by people from the Low Countries (van Bavel 2010). It is likely that the cartel agreement was easier to police in densely populated areas where local landlords actually could oversee and sanction each other and repatriate fugitives.

Un-freedom was not necessarily linked to the expansion of manorial organization of production. Tenants could be denied the right to move without having to perform labor services. Rents and other dues were then paid in money or in kind. In Catalonia, for example, manors were virtually absent but serfdom was not. The Catalonian case illustrates the complicated dynamics of a local aristocracy trying to extend its coercive power over peasants while sometimes constrained by central power, and the opportunities of peasants to reclaim land at the frontier over which the aristocracy had no property rights

(Freedman 1991). The strategy of the aristocracy oscillated between attempts to impose stricter control over peasants and concessions in regions bordering the areas where land could be reclaimed. Serfdom arrived much later in Catalonia than in the rest of continental Europe, not until the eleventh century.

Sweden and Norway were exceptional in being characterized by labor shortage relative to the land possible to reclaim. Their peasantry did not succumb to aristocratic authority as in the rest of Europe to the south. The Crown became a substantial owner of land before the Reformation, particularly in areas of recent settlement, for example northern Sweden, and had no interest in restricting the mobility of potential settlers. Serfdom was never introduced, although attempts to bind the leaseholders to the estate were made in both Sweden and Denmark when labor shortages became acute in the second half of the fourteenth and mid fifteenth centuries (Büchert Netterstøm 2005; Myrdal 2012). Slavery was phased out later in Sweden than on the continent but the former slaves did not become serfs but crofters. In Sweden freeholders remained the single most important occupational group and after the Black Death manorial production, as in Denmark, decreased and demesnes, which never became widespread, were increasingly leased out to peasant households (Henriksen 1995; Myrdal 1999, 2012). Peasants on Crown land paid taxes to the state while tenants on land held by the aristocracy were exempted from taxes but paid rents. In practice the difference between tax and rent became blurred. Denmark and the Danish parts of southern Sweden were different. Manorial production was more prominent but serfdom was not successfully introduced until the end of the medieval period with the exception of Jutland. The late arrival of serfdom in Denmark as well as its absence in Jutland, hard hit by the plagues, seems to be associated with landlords' inability to establish the discipline of a cartel as well as peasant resistance. Competition among lords for the scarce labor was too stiff and made their attempts to introduce serfdom in the late fourteenth century fail, despite the helping hand of the Crown.

The timing, incidence, and nature of serfdom varied substantially in medieval Europe. Although Domar was correct in pointing to the problem of extracting a rent in a land-abundant economy as a driving force for serfdom, we have seen that the ability of the landowners, lay and ecclesiastical, to introduce and uphold elements of un-freedom depended on a multitude of conditions. The landowners had to be able to extend ownership of land to settler areas, which was not easy if the state saw these areas as a potential source of revenue or as long as these areas were too vast for efficient authority to be exercised. This explains why the population decline after the collapse of the Roman empire was associated with a strengthening of the peasantry. Furthermore, landowners had to overcome the inherent instability of a cartel, which was difficult when landlords had a high fraction of their land vacant. But even when the aristocracy were able resist the temptation to poach labor from other estates, the burden of rent reflected to some extent the opportunity income of the runaway serfs. In areas with land that could be reclaimed at the frontier by peasant households landlords offered a lighter burden to keep their labor, *if* coercion was unsuccessful, as it often became.

The conditions for the emergence of serfdom seemed to be labor shortage, a small and declining independent peasantry, a high concentration of land in the hands of lay and ecclesiastical elites, a low level of urbanization, a tight network of lay and ecclesiastical landowners and, finally, a state which cooperated with the aristocracy.

The decline of serfdom

The decline of serfdom before and especially after the Black Death in western Europe is associated with a decline in manorial production. Manorial organization in the Low Countries did not survive the tensions created by growing opportunities for peasants to defect and migrate to cities, to other estates, and areas of land reclamation, including northwestern Germany. The independence from a lord's jurisdiction granted to cities also helped the swift transformation. The decline of manorialism was accompanied by the dissolution of or relaxation of labor services. The decline of manorial organization started early in the Low Countries, which had large areas of recent and ongoing land reclamation. Already by the twelfth century this was complete in many regions and the manumission of serfs was more or less completed before the Black Death, when it was only starting in other parts of Europe (van Bavel 2010: 86–93). A wave of manumissions is documented in France starting in the mid thirteenth century, and similar tendencies are seen elsewhere on the continent. However, it is by no means a coordinated and fast transition, but rather slow and gradual (Feller 2007: 169–70).

Old habits, however, did not always die silently. The fairly late enfranchisement, the fight against *mals usos*, arbitrary and contested fees, in Catalonia was, for example, accompanied by fierce social conflict during the fifteenth century. By the mid fourteenth century the process of enfranchisement was, if not completed, clearly underway in France, but at a very early stage in England. In northern and central Italy manumissions gained momentum in the twelfth and thirteenth centuries as peasant communes were formed as a counterforce to the local lords, often with the support of urban elites. Some of these communes were free of (heavy-handed) interference from landlords. A *borgo franco* could be established either by escaping submission or by the formation of new villages, as population growth continued. Individual freedom was gained by a contractual agreement: freedom could be bought at a price, but often simply as the result of a gradual erosion of lordly powers (Nobili 2006: 32–34; Panero 2006: 399–401). In Germany there had been a relaxation of the implementation of serfdom in that serfs were allowed greater freedom but these practices were reversed when labor shortages resurfaced after the Black Death (Scott 2005).

First of all, serfs were freed from arbitrary exactions and the regular fines paid at generational shifts. The humiliating intrusion into private life, into matters of love and marriage, typical of serf status was also disappearing. Serfs could be granted freedom as part of a pious act of the ecclesiastical lords but more often this was a commercial transaction. Villages or individual households bought their freedom and urban financiers were extending loans to peasants to complete the transaction. Given the continuous population increase freedom was also gained by peasants taking up reclaimed land, often on sharecropping contracts agreed with landlords. However, peasants who occupied or gained leases on newly reclaimed land were usually not forced to do labor services. Even if manumissions often were consensual they were probably also provoked by the perceived risk of social conflict or shirking in the execution of labor services. Market forces also worked in favor of landowners after centuries of population growth.

The gradual decline of serfdom before the Black Death is easy to explain in a Domar framework. As we have just noted, serfs were willing to pay for the right to become free tenants. The fact that the decline continued despite the labor shortage after the Black Death in western Europe is more of a puzzle in the Domar context. As population growth continued in the first centuries of the second millennium market forces permitted landowners to negotiate favorable rents without the element of command implied by the manorial organization, and increasingly labor services were transformed into money rents. In the end serfdom declined and land rents were determined by market forces rather than by command and coercion. By the fourteenth century landlords did not have to chase labor because labor chased vacant tenancies and was willing to pay market rates. The decline of serfdom was not a deliberate political reform, as were the reforms in Russia and Prussia in the late and early nineteenth century respectively or those in late eighteenth-century Denmark, but a slow erosion of customs which had become obsolete and redundant. When landlords could extract a rent from tenants without cumbersome and often inefficient forced labor at the manor, estate production declined. Besides, the ongoing differentiation of the peasantry, discussed in the next section, created a class of landless laborers and smallholders, which could be employed as wage labor on the estates. However, after the Black Death in the course of the fifteenth century the abolition of serfdom became more of a disorderly retreat from privileges and arbitrary exactions not possible to defend in face of a peasantry that had opportunities to move to vacant land or cities. Not that landlords did not try to suppress the peasantry; but they failed and met resistance, sometimes violent. However, the outcome differed across Europe. In many parts of Germany the resistance and peasant revolts in the early sixteenth century brought only temporary relief (Rössener 2005), but in England and most of western Europe serfdom was virtually abandoned by then. Attempts to introduce serfdom in Scandinavia in the aftermath of the Black Death failed partly because of inter-lord rivalry in securing labor.

The gradual erosion of serflike customs was accelerated by the changing nature of the intergenerational transfer of tenancies. Peasants had the conditional right to transfer a tenancy provided the transferee accepted the obligation to pay the entry fine, and other dues linked to the tenancy, as discussed in next section. Before the Black Death most of these transfers were within the family or involved close relatives. After the Black Death, however, it became quite common that there was no heir willing to take on the tenancy. Landlords with vacant land were unable to act as a collective, the familiar instability of a monopsonistic cartel, and therefore had to offer concessions to potential tenants. The hereditary nature of tenancies also changed when serfdom was phased out. Land leases became market-driven contracts with a specified time span.

Conversion of in-kind levies to money rents was an ongoing process in the medieval period, reflecting the increased monetization of the economy. As early as the ninth century economic transactions relied heavily on the use of money as a means of payment and account. Even if actual payments could rely both on money and commodities the actual accounting was usually expressed in the prevailing currency (Feller 1998: 376–378). Earlier scholarship (Duby 1962: 462–500) viewed this as an unbroken process but more recent scholars, while not denying the general direction of the process, point to periods of regress. The more profound changes in the organization of agrarian production, the dismantling of manorial production, stimulated the commutation of labor services to payments in money. It seems as if commutation occurred first in highly commercialized and monetized areas. When landlords were forced to transform their estates into parcels that were leased out to peasants the need for labor services declined. There were periods of windfall gains for rent-paying tenants if rents were fixed for longer periods in nominal terms and inflation persisted. We also witness, usually short-lived, attempts by landlords to reverse the tide and reintroduce labor services as a means to secure stable rents in real terms. Another way was to opt for shorter lease contracts, so that rents could be renegotiated more often.[4]

Can we summarize this bewildering historical set of information into a unified approach?

1 Serfdom was concentrated to a few centuries before and after the year 1000 but never affected more than a substantial minority of the peasant population.
2 Serfdom assumes a critical mass of concentration of land in the hands of lay and ecclesiastical elites, which had the tacit or active consent of the state, which helped to overcome inter-lord competition for labor.
3 The presence of much vacant land before, say, 700, in continental western Europe and in Scandinavia and eastern Europe before 1500 made monopsonistic cartel-building difficult or unstable.
4 The spontaneous dissolution of serfdom in most of western Europe in the century before the Black Death was consensual and driven by market forces. In a sense it could be said that coercion was no longer needed for landowners to extract a rent.
5 After the Black Death the monopsonistic cartel could not be rebuilt because of intense competition among lords, the reluctant support or resistance from central authorities, and the rise of the cities, which were outside the private jurisdiction of the aristocracy and became a safe haven for fugitive serfs and tenants.

The market for land

Documentation of land sales appears in the first written sources available for the medieval epoch. In Italy it is possible that there was an unbroken, although at times feeble, link back to the Roman period (van Bavel 2008). In Catalonia, which is one of the best-documented areas of Europe around the end of the

---

4 Laurent Feller (2009) has edited a volume representing the state of the art research on the issue.

first millennium, about 70 percent of the written records actually refer to land transactions. There are two major types of transaction that need to be separated. The first are sales of land properly speaking when the ownership title of land was at stake. The second, equally vigorous market deals with sales of tenancies, that is, of leases of land. In the second case, the ultimate ownership of land remained in the hands of lords, lay and ecclesiastical, but the right to occupy the land could be transferred from one household to another at a price. The lords and urban elites increased their share of total land by purchases from freeholders while ecclesiastical authorities not only bought land but also benefitted from donations. The market for both leases and free land therefore became increasingly important, especially after the decline of the manors, or estate-managed agriculture. New land was continuously added by means of land reclamation to the market either under sharecropping contracts or as freeholds.

Since tenancies were held in long-term contracts, say, ninety-nine years, a large proportion of land transactions were matters of intergenerational transfers *post mortem* from father or mother to son or daughter and were only indirectly linked to actual market forces. The incoming occupier had to pay an entry fine, although the right to inherit the tenancy was usually not in question. It was in fact in the interest of the lord to keep the tenancy active and the actual rent extracted from the tenant would vary with the strength of customary constraints relative to market forces and lords' authority. The intergenerational transfer of land was an important source of income for the aristocracy. Apart from the entry fee there was a death fee, *heriot*, and a marriage fee, *merchet*. There was also some diversity in the relative size of the entry fee relative to the yearly rent, the former being much larger. In periods of aristocratic pressure or increasing land hunger lords attempted to increase fees. Not all tenancies passed to relatives after the death of the occupier. Especially after the Black Death it became more common for a tenancy to be left idle, and with lords unable to exert their authority on relatives the terms of the lease contracts had to be softened.

Inter vivos transfers of tenant land bring us to a market for tenancies or leases, though some, but not the dominant part, of these transfers were also between close relatives. Landlords had an ambiguous attitude toward sales of leases, in which a villein sold the tenancy to a buyer. Lords rightly feared that the whole order on which their authority was built could be eroded by these practices. Therefore they were initially actively involved in these transactions. There is great uniformity across Europe in the way the landlords adjusted to the pressure for an active land market, although the timing of more active land markets differed across regions. There were restrictions on to whom these sales could be made. By and large the buyer had to be of the same status as the seller, a villein, and had to pay the entry fines and accept the labor services or charges that came with the tenancy. Lords were reserved the right of preferential treatment in that a delay of a month or so was permitted before the sale became effective, and furthermore the lord could repurchase the tenancy at the price offered by the highest bidder. However, the supervision of these transactions tended to be relaxed over time and especially so in regions that were more intensively commercialized, such as eastern England, the Paris basin, or the region around Barcelona (Figueras 2005: 488–489). It is clear that land prices reflected the quality of the land and/or the potential of improving it and for that matter proximity to urban markets (Brunel 2005: 102–106; Desportes 1979: 402–412).

When land was transferred from one tenant to another permanently it opened up the possibility of the former tenant gaining freedom from villein status, that is, manumission. The implication of an expanding land lease market then suggests that villein rights had improved from a state of strict servile status (Schofield 2005a: 241, 250). But it did not stop there. Villeins were also active in the market for free land. As Schofield notes:

> By engaging freely and openly in a market in free land the *villein* brought into question the very nature of his or her servility, and, through his or her dealings, established common law precedents of behavior that might serve to reduce any present or future claims of his or her lord.

The lords tried to extend their jurisdiction over the free land acquired by peasants to stop the erosion of their authority. But it worked both ways as free men leased "unfree" land. By the end of the thirteenth century the most entrepreneurial villeins had acquired free land in and outside the manor (Schofield 2005b: 282–283).

Tenancies were bought and then sublet in some regions, although there was initial resistance from landlords since they feared that rents escaped from them in this process. Typically, entrepreneurs of urban or rural descent saw the opportunities of intensive land use near expanding urban markets which substantially increased the profits from land, which were shared by the occupier and the owner of the lease.

While *post mortem* transfers were predominantly interfamily except in periods of severe demographic shocks, there was some resistance from lords toward partible inheritance. As population continued to grow holdings tended, however, to become smaller. There is some, but not undisputed, evidence that peasant households prepared for the generational shift by accumulating land which was then parceled out to the heirs, and there were cases when parents gave up their holdings in old age altogether against a promise of a future income, a sort of "pension." *Inter vivos* sales of holdings, on the other hand, tended to be outside the circle of close relatives and contributed to a differentiation of peasant society into classes of small and large tenants even though single transactions usually dealt with very small plots. However, a surprisingly large number of transactions took place in the villages. The reason for the differentiation of land ownership was an asymmetry in the timing and the conditions regarding sales and purchase. Tenants with smallholdings were more at risk in periods of harvest failures and borrowed with the holding as collateral or simply sold off small parcels of land. Typically, local credit markets saw a surge in activity in the months before the harvest when granaries were empty. Loans usually were short term, up to a year. If the peasant could not pay the creditor in due time the holding would end up in the hands of a creditor who could be an urban grain trader or a rich peasant in the village. Poor peasants usually sold land when there was much land on the market and prices were low, and often failed to buy back when supply had shrunk and prices had increased (Campbell 1984: 107–134; Dyer 2005b: 235). On average and with due consideration of regional differences between 1 and 2 percent of agricultural land changed ownership on a yearly basis.

From an early date medieval peasants, aristocrats, the clergy, and increasingly urban entrepreneurs were actively involved in land transactions, which had all the characteristics of a lively market economy. It is likely that the peasantry became more stratified as regards the size of landholdings. Some peasants of humble origin managed to increase their holdings of tenancies and/or free land and relied partly on hired labor supplied by tenants and peasants with smallholdings and the landless, who needed to supplement their income by salaried work. However, it also seems as if peasant communities gained a degree of autonomy by increasing the realm of market transactions that empowered them in bargaining with landlords and the state.

Alongside freeholders and tenants with fixed rents there was also a considerable presence of sharecropping tenants. This contractual heterogeneity might reflect differences in preferences with risk-averse tenants opting for sharecropping contracts since risk was shared with the landowner, unlike in a fixed-rent contract. It has also been suggested that the prevalence of sharecropping might reflect imperfections or the absence of capital markets with the implication that the landless had difficulties raising the working capital needed to enter a fixed-rent contract (Ackerberg and Botticini 2000).

Technology, indivisibilities and production organization: precursors of the capitalist firm

In a modern capitalist economy larger firms are vertically integrated units of planned resource allocation competing in input and produce markets. This element of planning and command seems at first sight to be a negation of the market economy and is in need of an explanation. By and large, production units in the medieval economy were smaller and less integrated; they performed a small number of tasks and bought intermediate goods on the market.

Ronald Coase (1937) suggested that the modern vertically integrated firm emerged because the transaction costs in using markets to coordinate the supply chain from intermediate to the final product became large relative to the costs of integrating separate production stages into a single firm under centralized non-market command. This is an important insight and it applies to the vertical integration of previously separate producers relying on market interaction. In this process independent producers tend to become hired labor under the guidance and command of an entrepreneur. However, large-scale firms also have their origin in purely technological conditions, namely the existence of indivisibilities in equipment, that is the economies of scale inherent in operations that rely on considerable fixed investment. Both the Coasean forces and economies of scale explain the changes of the production organization in medieval Europe. The major technological accomplishment of the medieval period is the development and diffusion of the first general purpose technology in history, namely the mill driven by water or wind. Watermills had been known and used since antiquity, while windmills arrived in Europe only in the twelfth century.

As we have demonstrated in the previous sections, the large-scale units in agriculture, the manors, never dominated production and reached their largest share of total output when they relied on forced or serf labor. When it became increasingly difficult to extract labor services by force from tenants the manors tended to disintegrate at the close of the medieval era. The reason was that there were neither strong economies of scale in agriculture nor Coasean gains from reducing transaction costs. That might explain the persistence of the household as the typical production unit in agriculture. In the non-agricultural sector the small-scale production units also dominated but there was nevertheless a trend toward larger units and the number of hired hands was generally larger and became increasingly so over time. There were also changes in the organization of non-agricultural production that "internalized" markets into entrepreneurial direction and management.

By and large the organization of work in cities is less well documented in written sources than agricultural production. The evidence there is suggests that workshops were small, often family based with few, if any, employees except apprentices as long as producers supplied the local market (Keene 1990). In the past a village craftsman or a farming household could supply the village with cloth but this small-scale production could not survive the forces of Smithian specialization. While some operations remained in rural areas, others moved into urban areas, in particular the direction and organization of production, that is, purchases of inputs and sales operations. The production of, say, woolen cloth was separated into a number of stages from washing the wool, combing, carding, spinning, weaving, fulling, and dyeing but these stages were, as a rule, not integrated vertically into a single workshop or factory. Master craftsmen were usually organized in separate guilds each representing a specific stage in the production process and they relied on intermediate goods markets for inputs into production. Production units remained small. A master craftsman employed family members and a limited number of apprentices and perhaps a few hired hands. With a growing market the nature of non-agricultural production changed. Economies of scale were exploited in the marketing of produce and transaction costs were reduced by the *Verlag*-system, known in the English literature as the "putting out" system. In the export-oriented manufacturing sector new and enlarged firm structures emerged. The putting out system relied on the merchant supplying working capital, the literal translation of the German word *Verlag*.

This system was firmly established in the leading woolen industry regions, such as Flanders, already by the twelfth century. A merchant capitalist, the clothier (*lanaiuolo*, *drapier*) introduced an element of centralized direction and management of production and sales. With the increase in the scale of production as well as the extended time between purchase of imported raw material and sales to export markets there was an increasing need for working capital. As the woolen industry developed production became geographically separated from the major raw material suppliers. High-quality wool was exported from England and dyestuffs from France to Flanders, which had a concentration of larger production units. When the artisans no longer were supplied locally by raw material and produced for a distant market the merchant entrepreneur stepped in as an intermediary but initially not as an owner of the tools and equipment. The capital was sunk in raw material, intermediate goods moving from one production stage to the next, and finally becoming inventories of commodities for final consumption. Some of the simple operations might be performed on the premises of the merchant entrepreneur, but the more complicated operations, of which dyeing was one, were usually performed by master craftsmen in their own workshops.

Means of production, that is, fixed capital as opposed to working capital, were generally owned by the artisans as a sign of their independence or non-proletarian status. In areas dominated by export-oriented production some producers were proletarians however. They worked for a piece-rate wage for a single entrepreneur rather than negotiating a price for the product with other buyers, and they often leased the equipment used in production. The transaction costs were due to the logistics of moving products at various stages of production from one production site to another. Other costs were related to potential fraud and negligence due to the problems of monitoring the quality and use of the raw material or the intermediate goods throughout the production process. Guild restrictions made it sometimes difficult for the merchant entrepreneur to take production in house but it became increasingly common for the entrepreneur to set up a workshop for some of the preliminary work to be done. In the woolen industry the washers and sometimes combers, carders, and spinners could be employed within the premises of a merchant entrepreneur. Other stages of production were outsourced to independent producers owning their own equipment such as weavers, fullers, and dyers. Many of these operations were performed by women in surrounding rural areas giving their household an additional source of income during the idle periods in the agricultural sector.

In a sense you see a hybrid of the modern firm and the traditional putting out system. It differs from a modern firm in that in-house production is a fairly small part of the total valued added, but the fraction of in-house production varies a lot also in modern firms. On the other hand production was not organized as a chain of sales and purchases from a large number of independent producers relying on specialized spot markets. There is an entrepreneurial direction of the flow of goods from the supply of raw material to the marketing of the final goods and the entrepreneur is the residual claimant, as in a capitalist enterprise. In many respects we are dealing with an integrated firm since subcontracting artisans were paid a piece-rate wage, which was determined in advance and not in spot markets. However, all the stages of production of a commodity were as a rule not physically placed in a single factory.

Since far from all apprentices actually became master craftsmen they found employment as journeymen and formed the core of a skilled working class, separated in status from day laborers in transport and unskilled workers in the building trades. In the export-oriented textile industries, such as the tapestries in the Low Countries, some entrepreneurs could coordinate the operations of up to a hundred master craftsmen and workers, but on average not more than around twenty five (Stabel 2004: 207). Most of these workers or subcontractors would work in their homes or workshops using their own tools or leasing them from the merchant capitalist, and only a limited number were under the roof of the merchant. Subcontractors were usually paid by piece and the raw materials or the intermediate goods were provided by the entrepreneur.

In a Coasean perspective the *Verlag* or putting out system seems to reduce the transaction costs in contracting a long supply chain from raw material to final product but the "requirement" that a firm should be a physical unit, not explicitly suggested by Coase, is not fulfilled. In a sense the central authority in the *Verlag* system is similar to the modern outsourcing firm. Some of the operations, the design, planning, and monitoring of the production and sales, remain in the "headquarters" with merchant entrepreneurs, while other operations are outsourced to independent producers or workers performing their duties in their homes or workshops. But it is (the owner of) capital, i.e. the entrepreneur financier who is the residual claimant, that is the one who hires labor, and not the subcontracted craftsman who hires capital. It is, of course, possible that this order of things is related to imperfections in the capital markets that made it difficult for workers to "hire" capital.

The impact of technological indivisibilities for production organization is evident in manufacturing using water and wind power. Water and wind-powered devices were applied to almost all production lines and most stages in production of a wide variety of commodities. Take the production of iron as a case. Waterwheels were used to pump water from pits, to drive hammers to crush the iron ore, to drive bellows in the furnaces and hammers to purify the iron from slag, to polish steel tools, etc. In continental Europe early use of waterwheels in metallurgy stems from the first part of the eleventh century and there is archaeological evidence from the periphery (Sweden) by the end of the twelfth century. The proliferation of the new technology was driven by one simple rationale: the technologies it replaced were typically low fixed-cost but high variable-cost techniques. At a low level of output the latter had lower unit costs. Grinding grain for flour can be done by hand-driven grinding stones, and bellows could be driven by foot or hand. A wind- or water-driven mill would be unfeasible at low levels of aggregate demand, which explains why the diffusion of the technology comes as population density and aggregate demand rose. The productivity advantages of high fixed-cost and low variable-cost technology require a threshold level of demand to materialize. At a high level of aggregate demand such a technology is a labor saving device very much like the pivotal innovation of the medieval period: movable type typesetting and printing, which is introduced when real wages are at a historical peak. But Gutenberg's typesetting technology has its obvious advantage in large print runs that pay off the fixed costs of typesetting.

Initially landlords were those who had the means to invest in mills, but during the first half of the second millennium an "independent" milling sector evolved, with tenants leasing and operating the mills. In cities the burghers invested in mills and leased the operations to millers or others with an appropriate skill or profession such as a grain merchant. Some leaseholders became entrepreneurs operating several mills with hired hands. Domesday Book records about six thousand mills by the end of the eleventh century in England and the number, now also including windmills, had doubled by 1300. Most of the expansion of mills took place outside the manorial sector, which also demonstrates the diversification of the uses of mills. Landlords and the gentry remained an important source of finance for the establishment of mills and a set of well-defined types of lease contracts developed, which demonstrated the underlying rational economic reasoning dominant at the time. Apart from the construction costs there were considerable maintenance costs and risk of major breakdown of the material. It is not surprising therefore to find carpenters among the leaseholders of mills. By and large leasing contracts made the leaseholder increasingly responsible for the maintenance costs the longer the contract period was (Langdon 2004: 193–197). Over time the contract length increased and some leases became hereditary, but shorter contracts were often linked to an advance payment to secure the owner against negligence. However, having assumed most or all maintenance costs the leaseholder was subject to unexpected and costly maintenance shocks. It is therefore not surprising to find leaseholders forming partnerships pooling the risks and sharing the proceeds of the milling operation.

However, not all partners were necessarily participating in production or advancing equal amounts of capital. Some were sleeping partners and there were also salaried workers. Germain Sicard's remarkably detailed treatise (1953) on the mills in Toulouse in southern France reveals the astonishing modernity of the corporate structure found in two mills along the Garonne river, but there is evidence of similar development elsewhere. These mills required building dams over the river to redirect water and leave passages for boats. The magnitude of these infrastructural works involved considerable funding needs. Following the governance system over three centuries it is possible to trace not only a separation of ownership from involvement in production but also between ownership and administration. Owners had originally some relationship to the actual activity but became mere equity- or shareholders with little say in the daily operations of the mills. Over time owners also gained limited liability. These partnerships differed from partner- ships in trade, which had limited duration. Shares in milling corporations were traded and the corporations existed for centuries.

In mining and metallurgy John Nef (1987) also discovered a "cleavage between capital and labor" in the more advanced sites of production on the European continent triggered by the scale of investment needed. Partnerships evolved all over Europe, for example in the copper mining of Stora Kopparberg in Sweden and the extraction of silver in Tuscan Montieri. In metallurgy the investment in waterwheels and their maintenance required larger workshops, typically a master craftsman with a number of apprentices and hired workers. However, these workshops were not large by modern standards: few of them employed more than ten workers. There are excep- tions, of which the silver producing workshops in Germany, the *Saigerhütten*, are the most impressive. They are described in great detail and with illustra- tions by Agricola in *De re metallica*. These workshops powered by water integrated the many steps in silver production into one "factory." Finance originated from territorial lords, the state, from the combined efforts by partnerships of producers, and increasingly from urban entrepreneurs and merchants. Mining also became more capital intensive when the deposits first exploited, often ores that had broken through the surface or were situated just below, were exhausted. Pits below the surface were more difficult to dig and maintain, in particular because of the need to pump water. In that process of increasing capital requirements the original partnerships of producers were indebted and eventually became victims of takeovers from the city merchants who had provided the credit. Many independent producers became wage- laborers. Ownership of the pits and the furnaces was not centralized but held by fairly large groups of investors who delegated the actual management to professionals.

We see here the contours of a modern enterprise. The increasing reliance on a salaried workforce replaced an organization built upon partnership or association of independent producers or the subcontracting of master crafts- men. Where mining was scattered in fairly small sites, as was the case in Sweden, the traditional organization persisted into the early modern period. Furnaces were built and used by a group of farmer-miners who used the furnace in succession usually during the low season in the agricultural cycle. Although the partners often had humble origins they gained in status, privileges, and wealth over generations, becoming a sort of aristocracy. The traditional landed aristocracy was gradually crowded out as owners by the state and the mining "aristocracy". The output of each furnace was of course limited but still Sweden became a major supplier of forgeable iron, so-called *osmundjärn*, to the European market in the late medieval period (Geijerstam and Nisser 2011: 38–53). In the mining areas in continental Europe, however, territorial lords maintained their grip over the mineral resources even though they leased out the actual mining and processing to enterprises run by partnerships with links to the marketing and shipping of the produce.

Although producing units became larger they remained small by modern standards. However, they introduced several new elements, the most important being an increasing reliance on salaried labor, capital as the residual claimant in the *Verlag* system, and a vertical integration of different stages of production replacing markets with high transaction costs.

Labor markets

Labor markets introduce the essential distinction between the residual claimant, the entrepreneur or capitalist, and the hired laborer. It is owners of capital who hire labor and not the other way round. The development, or re-emergence, of medieval labor markets was intimately tied to the increasing importance of non-agricultural trades and urban growth from the beginning of the second millennium. In rural areas the gradual decline of labor services opened up a market for wage labor at large estates and for freeholders and the demise of un-freedom permitted a freer flow of labor to cities. Cities became less dependent on fugitives. They were dominated by commodity production and trade and these activities outweighed public and private administrative activities by say three to one. Large cities developed a very sophisticated division of labor with several hundreds of specific occupations. For example, textile production, which perhaps employed 10 to 15 percent of the urban population, had not just fullers, weavers, dyers, and shearers but specialists like button-makers. There were specialists in music instrument production, metal and leather processing – leather was the plastic of the pre-industrial era – glass-making and then of course a full variety of food processing. It is by all accounts a Smithian world of gains from specialization.

Most of the activities were regulated by guilds but control was not always efficient. There was outsourcing of some lines of production to suburban and rural areas. In the most advanced areas of northwestern Europe, central Holland, the proto-industries employed up to about half the rural population (van Bavel 2007). In some cases the urban population chased the polluting industries out of the city centers. Other activities were moved to production sites that had access to water-powered mills, for example fulling (Barron 2004: 64–83).

The labor market had been growing continuously since the revival of the European economy and by the fourteenth century it was considerable. Estimates suggest that in the most advanced areas of Europe about half the adult population was involved with and accustomed to wage labor (Dyer 2005c: 211–214). However, because much of that wage labor was seasonal, especially in rural areas, the share of the adult population in permanent wage labor was smaller. Rural wage labor was concentrated at the peaks in the agricultural cycle, such as harvest work by cottagers and landless workers, who to some extent were migrant harvest workers. There was a flow in both directions between rural and urban areas witnessed by the fact that urban day wages increased in harvest time when day laborers deserted the cities. But rural households, particularly women, were also working for piece-rate wages for urban entrepreneurs in the woolen putting out industry as weavers and spinners. This work was typically performed when the demand for labor in agriculture was at its seasonal low point.

In cities the wage-laborers were a rather heterogeneous group. Unskilled workers were employed in the building trades and transport, often on short contracts, working along as helpers to master craftsmen. Unlike the textile industries, where piece-rate wages dominated, day or weekly wages were the norm in construction. Larger cities had spot markets for workers employed per day or week where employers and workers met by sunrise and agreed by trust or by written contract, the latter usually for longer-period contracts (Geremek 1968: 126–127). Contracts were often quite detailed, specifying length of duty, tasks, and wage. Workshops employed family members and apprentices, which normally lived in the master craftsman's house, as did servants. Larger workshops could employ a few journeymen who had finished their apprenticeship. They were skilled workers and lived in their own quarters like the adult unskilled workers. A journeyman would aspire to set up his own workshop, but an increasing number failed to do so and remained salaried workers for most of their lives. The skilled labor force also had an inflow of former independent master craftsmen who had failed to sustain their business. Quite a few master craftsmen, and in sectors like the export-oriented woolen industry an increasing share, became wage workers for merchants and *Verlag* entrepreneurs. These weavers, shearers, fullers, or dyers might work in their own workshop and remain members of their guilds, but under contract from a single employer paying a piece-rate wage.

The share of unskilled workers, apprentices, dropouts from apprenticeships and servants in the total urban labor force was substantial, perhaps a third of the adult population in cities (Schulz 1985: 37–38). In rural areas wage labor varied but on average it was about the same fraction of total labor force. Social conflicts erupted occasionally, with the subordinate classes opposing the established guilds of master craftsmen and merchants who dominated politics in the cities. Apprentices occasionally organized boycotts against particular master craftsmen and "walk-outs" to improve employment conditions. Apprentices had a vulnerable position, forced as they were to fulfill a lengthy training period with little pay while living in the master craftsman's house-hold. There are few signs of permanent organizational structures similar to modern trade unions, however. Guilds formed late in the middle ages were often organizing groups hitherto denied formal organization rights by the established guilds.

By and large, rural labor markets were more competitive than urban markets because the latter had barriers to entry for an increasing number of professions as we move into the fourteenth and fifteenth centuries. Wages were paid either as time wages, per day or for longer periods, or as piece-rates. The large swings in real wages were driven mainly by the strong volatility in the prices of subsistence goods. In many occupations wages were supple-mented by the provisioning of food or meals, which stabilized consumption. Large shocks to the labor supply, such as the Black Death, generated a sharp rise in both nominal and real wages. Authorities all over Europe tried to stem this increase by wage freeze regulation, statutes of labor, which, however, largely failed.

It is important to distinguish between time and piece-rate wages because it has bearing on the issue of wage discrimination. Women were generally paid lower time wages for a given task, say, a day of threshing, and this phenom-enon has often been interpreted as a sign of gender discrimination. However, it is likely the lower wage just reflected the lower productivity in tasks demanding great physical strength and endurance. Investigating piece-rate wages, say the threshing of a bushel, there is no sign of women being discriminated against (Hatcher 2001: 192). In urban professions the problem is different, simply because women were excluded from many skilled professions and the numbers of skills exclusive to women, such as silk weaving in some cities, were quite limited. Over time it also seems as if women were marginalized in some traditional female occupations such as wool weaving, not because of outright discrimination but because weaving became more physically demanding. It was quite common for women to acquire the same skills as men, for example, in brewing, without formal recognition, with lower pay as a consequence.

Apart from the growing salaried workforce of mainly unskilled workers on farms and in cities a substantial share of the workforce remained self-employed and owned or leased the means of production. But in non-agricultural production the distinction between self-employment and salaried work became vague when the self-employed worked for piece-wages contracted by merchant entrepreneurs. Many self-employed therefore were connected to the market economy mainly through the labor market.

From local to long-distance trade

The major source of productivity advances in the medieval economy was division of labor. However, sophisticated division of labor and regional specialization triggered by comparative advantages are built upon frequent exchange among people who know each other mainly by reputation, if at all. As long as division of labor is rudimentary, exchange is predominantly spot exchange among people who know or get to know each other easily at local markets. As division of labor gains momentum, as it does in the second millennium, a period usually referred to as the commercial revolution, trade becomes increasingly long distance, with a separation not only in space but also in time of contracting and contract fulfillment, between shipping goods and payment of goods. It eventually involves trade between strangers. This is the context for what has been called the "fundamental problem of exchange." The difficulties in establishing lasting long-distance trade relationships between strangers are embedded in imperfect and asymmetric information, uncertainty, and greater risks as compared to spot exchange. Contract enforcement problems were formidable because legal traditions and procedures differed between cities and nations. One major accomplishment in the first half of the second millennium was the establishment of an institutional framework needed for exchange to handle the "fundamental problem of exchange" (Greif 2000; Milgrom, North, and Weingast 1990). If a sedentary merchant trader, say, in Bruges, provided the financing and the goods in the transaction and used an agent in some other city to conclude the trade that agent could exploit the fact that full information was not immediately revealed to the principal. For example the agent might claim, rightly or wrongly, that the quality of goods in transit had deteriorated and fetched a price lower than expected. Trust relationships in a family firm certainly helped to avoid the problem of fraudulent behavior and the persistence of that type of firm indicates their value in maintaining trust between principals and agents. Greif (1989) has pointed out the importance of reputation and effective sanctions against breach of confidence within closely knit ethnic communities. However, there is an evolution from trade relying mainly on family and kin relationships in which peer pressure was a major mechanism to secure proper conduct to exchange relations built upon the use of formal institutions of contract enforcement and conflict resolution.

The first signs in what is known as the commercial revolution in the second millennium of medieval Europe is the establishment of periodic fairs such as the Champagne fairs in France, which attracted merchants and bankers from most of western Europe. The location of these fairs southeast of Paris made them a convenient crossing point for merchants and moneychangers from northwestern and southern Europe and Italy in particular. Although just semi-sedentary these fairs also provided legal services to facilitate the solution of contractual disputes. Officials at fairs could bar merchants with a reputation for fraudulent behavior. As trade continued to expand and increasing volumes of trade became seaborne, these fairs were replaced by permanent trading emporia with financial and more formalized contract-enforcing services in the major cities of Europe. This development saw the repopulation of a number of cities which had declined or been abandoned in the post-Roman period as well as the establishment of new cities (Verhulst 1999).

Merchants were typically organized along ethnic lines, such as the German Hanse, a confederation of traders from major German cities. Similar organizations grouped traders from other regions. These merchant guilds attempted to gain monopoly control over trade routes, but also contributed to conflict resolution among members and protected members from predatory actions of local rulers. To some extent these associations emerged when the public legal infrastructure was poorly developed. Where public institutions were strong merchant guilds were weak, and vice versa (Grafe and Gelderblom 2010; Gelderblom 2004).

As the scale of trade increased from the tenth and eleventh centuries new ways of reducing agency problems developed. Merchants' houses transcended the constraints of kin and the family firm and included external partners. Such firms were based on formalized profit sharing and increasingly relied on well-specified contracts between principal and agent, between merchant and employee, or between principal and agents or correspondents. Contract fulfillment was overseen by law enforcement institutions rather than by informal sanctions and peer pressure.

Local merchant houses that previously used to employ agents developed into vertically integrated "multinationals" with a branch structure run by agents who became partners with a claim on profits or a mix of salary and profit. This innovation evolved when international trade relied more on permanent market networks rather than the periodic fairs typical of the early phase of the "commercial revolution." The size of trading firms increased, which necessitated a larger and wider group of investors. All employed were not partners but employees were monitored and diligent behavior could be helpful in elevation to partnership status. The demise of the periodic international fairs did not mean that fairs devoted to domestic and regional exchange disappeared, however (Epstein 1994).

Transport costs differed widely with packhorses being the most expensive and in fact the only means available over some of the passes across the Alps. Transport by cart reduced costs considerably. Transport of goods like courier services were handled by specialists and on a regular basis. Commodities were reloaded at times, exploiting the opportunity of much cheaper water rates, approximately 15–25 percent of road transport charges. However, open seas maritime trade often added considerable mileage. For example, most of the gains from lower transport charges between say, Bruges and Venice, were lost by the long distance over sea relative to the land passage. The carrying capacity of ships in maritime trade increased approximately by a factor of five over the first half of the second millennium but manning did not increase proportionally, which reveals increasing labor productivity in shipping. Modern insurance with the merchant paying a fee develops in the fourteenth century with rates around 10–15 percent of value of cargo, compared to 1–2 percent in late nineteenth century trade. This dramatic fall over time reflects safer ships and the extinction of pirating at sea and robbery in transports on land.

We have only scattered quantitative data on the aggregate trade but all evidence suggests a significant increase in trade and in trade/income ratios, although the latter were probably closer to 5 than 10 percent of national income. Surprisingly the demographic shocks of the fourteenth and fifteenth centuries did not stop the ongoing process of specialization and trade (Findlay and O'Rourke 2007: 120–124).

The Baltic and northern export trade, which was controlled by the German Hanse, consisted of furs, wax, amber, timber, and salted herring from the Baltic area, copper and iron from Sweden, dried and salted cod from Norway, and live cattle and butter from Denmark. These commodities were exchanged for manufactured goods such as woolen cloth from the Low Countries, salt, spices, and wine. Grain was shipped from the southern Baltic ports to northwestern Europe. Italy specialized in exports of high-quality metal manufacturing (for example weapons) and textiles: wool, linen, silk, and cotton, and imported raw wool from England and Spain. Many of the spices and luxury goods from the Islamic world came through Italy.

Money and credit

With the political disorder following the decline of the Roman empire the monetary system also disintegrated. Long-distance trade fell and trading emporia were deserted. Minting of gold coins ceased. There was probably a revival of barter trade alongside the use of ingots of silver and gold in settlements because of the scarcity of money. When Europe was recovering minting started again but only silver was minted (Spufford 1988). In the Carolingian period a strict order of denominations is introduced. This long-lived monetary system consisting of 12 pennies (*deniers*) amounting to 1 shilling (*sou*) and the pound (*livre*, *lira*) consisting of 20 shillings was introduced and survived in Britain until February 15, 1971. Gold coins were not struck on a regular basis and extensive scale until the mid thirteenth century. Silver coins were used mainly for local trade and little remained of the Carolingian silver content regulation in coins by the beginning of the second millennium.

In fact a bewildering number and types of coins had developed, which reveals the fast expansion of mints and the political diversity of Europe at this time. In the Holy Roman empire alone some seventy different currencies were used and struck by up to five hundred mints. Virtually every market town of importance had or obtained a mint in the first centuries of the second millennium, and for rulers debasement of coins was a major source of revenue, which led to a long-term decline in silver content of coins. The inflationary impact of debasement was less than proportional, however, to the loss in silver content of monies (Munro 2012). Varying inflation rates and the multitude of monies were probably not a great impediment to trade as it was predominantly local. There was also a circulation of token coins struck in small denominations used for petty trade. Gold coins, in particular those struck in Florence and Venice (or imitations of them struck elsewhere), were mainly used in international trade and in payments between rulers in political settlements. Unlike silver coins, the florins and Venetian gold ducats were remarkably stable in gold content over the centuries. The use of money with an intrinsic value is of course very costly. The wear and tear alone reduced the metal by up to 0.5 percent per year. That fiat money did not develop on an extensive scale was mainly due to the risk of counterfeiting. Prevailing minting technology did not produce counterfeit proof coins. The usual way of identifying good money was to assess the content of precious metal, which deterred counterfeiters.

Money markets became increasingly well integrated over time. Boerner and Volckart (2010) measured the extent of money market integration by proposing that in an integrated money market the law of one price should prevail. In this context that means that the currencies in use should be exchanged so that the same silver/gold price ratio prevailed in all markets. There were deviations of the silver/gold price ratio across regions and nations but there was a significant decline in variance of the ratio before the early modern period. Another finding was that commodity market integration seems to precede money market uniformity. Where trade expanded there was also a drift toward monetary unions.

The expansion of long-distance trade stimulated other means of payment such as the promissory note and the bill of exchange. The bill of exchange developed in the thirteenth and fourteenth centuries and it is essentially a promise of payment to a payee and his principal at some future date. It was of great use in long-distance trade and exploited the fact that trading partners in different locations could offset debts and credits. By clearing debt and credit bills locally merchants and bankers could minimize the use of specie, which greatly reduced the risk of theft, apart from the cost of transporting heavy bullion between long-distance markets. Although initially developed by Mediterranean merchants the Italian merchant bankers were instrumental in introducing them to northwestern Europe. In the Baltic, Hanse cities like Lübeck and Danzig later followed these practices or used simpler substitutes like the "bill obligatory" (North 2013).

The diffusion of the bill of exchange as a short-term credit and payment instrument was also first linked to the migration and settlement of Italians in other busy areas of northwestern Europe. Given the diversity of currencies moneychangers were essential participants in the trading network. They gradually developed banking services when accepting deposits and developing a type of fractional reserve banking as well as services such as transfers between accounts. Thereby payments, both local and international, were made through simple bookkeeping transfers between demand accounts. The rationale of these innovations was of course to minimize the use of specie in transactions. The primitive forms of fractional reserve banking that developed were predictably associated with occasional failures that alerted the city authorities, who tried and sometimes succeeded in banning the practice for shorter or longer periods.

Credit and the charge of interest were also a concern of the Church, witness its ban on usury as a form of theft. Although usurious lending had been condemned since antiquity the scholastic discussion and the ambition of Church regulation was intensified as the scale of trade expanded in the thirteenth century. What constituted usury was not crystal clear because there were exceptions to the general rule that rent on a loan constituted usury, and an ongoing discussion in the Church. Furthermore, if payment of a loan was delayed the lender could ask for compensation. This constituted a loophole for borrowers and lenders who deliberately, but tacitly, delayed repayment so as to agree on a positive interest rate. More controversially some theologians, a contested minority, argued that a lender was entitled to charge interest since this could be interpreted as the opportunity income, that is the income forgone by the money not being invested, say, in trade. The usury ban was hence not a ban on profits on investment. Ownership of land and property as well as investment in trade ventures gave the owner the right to earn a profit, the residual income, if any, from that investment.

Quite a lot of borrowing and lending was private and informal in nature and poorly documented, partly because of the usury ban. This type of informal credit market was revealed when indebted people died and creditors made claims on the estate of the deceased, not always with much success. Casual credit markets of this type are not limited to the more advanced parts of Europe but are found in peripheral Sweden in the late medieval period as well (Franzén 2006). Bills of exchange concealed the interest rate on the credit by rigging the exchange rate between currencies used in the advance of funds in one city and later payment in another city and in another currency. This practice was difficult to discover by authorities because bills of exchange were private contracts. The most severe sanction against usury available to the Church was excommunication but this was reserved for serial and grave offenders. The Church also offered a "passport to heaven" for "sinners" who donated to the Church (Galassi 1992). The financial risk faced by lenders was twofold. They were occasionally fined, especially if the interest rate charged was above some, usually quite high, threshold level, which varied over time and location. More seriously, borrowers attempted to be released from their debt, and sometimes succeeded, by revealing usurious contracts to authorities.

Minorities, for example Lombards and Jews, were tolerated and often licensed as lenders and moneychangers but suffered from legal insecurity and public scorn, leading to occasional clampdowns on their activity. Pawnbrokers were licensed "usurers" in some cities but mostly provided short-term credit for consumption rather than trade or investment. By and large interest rates on short-term loans were higher than on long-term borrowing.

The impact of the usury ban is therefore difficult to assess. It certainly did not stop lending at an interest (see Table 10.3 for the evolution of interest rates). Usury laws made lending more difficult and more costly, and it is likely that the protection usury laws were supposed to offer borrowers was counter-productive, at least to the extent that the expected fines and costs involved in lending affected the interest charged. Some lenders regularly paid the fines and in some cities the definition of a usury rent amounted to very high annualized interest rates. However, more often than not the Church turned a blind eye to "usury" as long as interest rates charged were not too high (Heers 2012). So credit and debt were everywhere in late medieval society.

Bruges, a busy trading and manufacturing city, is a telling case. Its role in international trade of course made its financial infrastructure more sophisticated but ordinary people also typically lived in houses with a mortgage or rented from a landlord who had a mortgage. There were also other forms of credit such as unpaid bills long overdue. If there were debts, there was of course credit. As a rule real estate was held as collateral. Hostellers, pawnbrokers, and moneychangers formed the backbone of the financial network, and the latter were developing clearing and transfers between demand accounts apart from actual payments and exchange of coins. The payment services seem mostly to have been used by the export-oriented trades. The moneychangers serviced just a small fraction of the most active merchants and manufacturers in the city, including hostellers and a considerable part of foreign merchants. Some merchants deposited money with the hostellers, who in turn deposited money with the moneylenders, and thus functioned as a sort of intermediary as well by providing, directly or indirectly, some clearing and transfer services.

A primitive variety of paper money was established when bills of exchange could be endorsed and made negotiable (transferable) in the fifteenth century but this practice was not uniformly accepted until later in the early modern era. Financial sophistication was unevenly diffused over Europe and was most advanced in and around the major cities. By and large, trade in the Baltic was later in adopting promissory notes and bills of exchange, but here as elsewhere in northwestern Europe Italian merchant bankers were pioneers, although local merchants did adopt the financial innovations (North 2013).

Not only was private debt flourishing but public debt as well. City authorities especially in the Low Countries, northern France, and Italy were heavily dependent on so called *rentes*, a sort of annuity. The collateral of public debt was future tax income. The public was occasionally forced to purchase the *rentes* and in some cities secondary markets in this instrument developed (Munro 2003).

The Church was heavily dependent on the merchant bankers to transfer the tithes collected locally to Rome and Avignon. The Italian bankers had a near monopoly of this activity, which paid off handsomely with commissions ranging between 1 and 5 percent of the sums transferred. Correspondents in Bruges were particularly important in transfer operations involving Scandinavia and the Baltic. A merchant banker could advance a credit to the papacy to cover purchases in, say, Bruges, and the merchant was reimbursed by the income owed to the Holy See by, say, the Church in Poland. The Holy See occasionally borrowed money but only exceptionally is it admitted that the lender charged interest (Renouard 1941).

How competitive were medieval markets?

The prevailing view of medieval commodity and labor markets is that they were characterized by barriers to entry erected by guilds, which led to technological inertia and other welfare losses. Guilds were not new to the medieval epoch but had their roots in the Roman economy, and were reinvented and gained a foothold in the medieval epoch. It is a legitimate suspicion that they imposed deadweight losses on society, although that claim has been disputed (see Ogilvie 2008 vs. Epstein 1998, 2008). Strong views are articulated but there are no precise estimates of the magnitude of the alleged losses. Most arguments are based on a priori reasoning, that is arguments that refer to the expected effects of a cartel or monopoly with the counterfactual being a perfectly competitive economy. The assessment of the impact of guilds would lead to negative conclusions if compared to such a counterfactual. The problem is, of course, that the counterfactual is not factual: markets were often too thin to generate equilibrium outcomes.

Did guilds impede technological progress? The medieval period was a period of slow productivity growth, but there is no evidence that productivity growth in the guild-run urban sector was slower than in the agrarian sector. Direct estimates of changes is labor productivity reveal modest rates of growth by modern standards, say around 0.15 to 0.25 per year in agriculture (Persson 1991, 2010). However, productivity growth in urban trades seems to be higher. Clark (2008) suggested that labor productivity growth in nail production in England was higher or around 0.4 percent per year. It has also been noted than many non-agricultural products tended to record falling relative prices. Iron prices in Sweden, a major export product, were falling at a rate of about 0.5 percent relative to other prices between 1300 and 1500. Assuming a modest increase in labor costs, being the principal production cost, the approximate conclusion is that there is a significant growth of labor productivity in that sector similar to Clark's estimate of productivity in nail output. For Swedish shipping similar results are documented (Edvinsson and Söderberg 2011).

The power of guilds did not extend beyond city limits and the widespread adoption of the watermill as a source of energy in all sorts of industries in the first half of the second millennium largely took place where natural conditions were favorable, within or outside city limits. The simple dichotomy between producer guilds and consumers, the latter being allegedly exploited by guilds, is difficult to defend. Guild members were of course both producers and consumers. However, that does not exclude inefficient outcomes. Guilds were supposed to set quality standards on the produce, a practice which has some similarities to modern branding, which is a type of imperfect competition but is certainly not unknown in modern capitalist economies. Furthermore some guilds, for example in the dominant textile sector, increasingly developed trade union functions when members did not obtain master (employer) status.

Although guilds might exert local market power, regionally and internationally traded goods were integrated in the sense that price levels and movements were correlated. The extent of correlation fell with distance but was significant and large also between markets for wheat, which did not trade directly with each other, say London and Strasbourg (Söderberg 2007).

Shocks and resilience

A telling indicator of the robustness of an economic system is its resilience and capacity to absorb shocks. And shocks there were! With agriculture as the major sector harvest failures had strong short-term effects on prices, land rents, and real incomes. Serious output shocks, say in the order of a 10–15 percent decline in output, which occur once in a lifetime, at most, in a modern economy were much more frequent, say, once every seven to ten years.

These shocks caused excess mortality but did not destroy the fabric of society. Even more perplexing is the resilience of the medieval economy when faced with the Black Death, the plague which reduced the European population by about a third in the mid fourteenth century and with occasional minor outbreaks until the mid fifteenth century. Again, the Black Death destroyed people but not institutions. The economic effects revealed a market economy at work. The speed of diffusion of the disease from ports on the Black Sea to the Mediterranean and later to northwestern Europe and as far away as Iceland reveals the major trade links and the intensity of trade. As expected, wages increased, land rents fell, and age at marriage declined. The fifteenth century was known as a golden age for labor. It seems as if workers were at a backward-bending supply curve of labor because the days worked per year fell as real wages increased. Consumption patterns drifted toward more meat and less cereals.

There is no denying that the plague left deserted villages and reduced urban populations, but there does not seem to have been a permanent shock to the extent of specialization. The long-run trend visible in the medieval period of an increasing proportion of the labor force in non-agrarian professions was not reversed. In fact the more advanced areas witnessed a significant increase in the share of the non-agrarian labor force, as high as 50 percent in Holland at the end of the fifteenth century and around 35 per cent in England, and on average you can see a more muted increase in the relative share of non-agrarian professions. This change in the occupational pattern of the labor force reveals a change in production and consumption with an increasing share of income directed to non-food items. Ultimately this is related to an increase in income per head if we subscribe to Engel's law.[5]

There must of course have been initial disturbances in international trade but increases in ship size were not permanently halted. The rise in real wages may have stimulated a drift towards labor-saving technological inventions, with Gutenberg's typesetting and printing as one example.

Concluding remarks

Most of the economic institutions associated with a capitalist economy were present or emerged in the medieval era. It was, as Jacques Heers suggests by the title of his recent monograph (2012) *la naissance du capitalisme*, capitalism in

---

5 Engel's law, after the nineteenth-century Prussian statistician, suggests that the share of income spent on food declines with increasing income per household.

its infancy. The cleavage between capital and labor was becoming more articulated. Markets for land, labor, capital, and commodities were thin but penetrated every corner of Europe. Property rights might have been contested more often and legal protection was biased in favor of the elites, in particular the landowning class. Intellectual property rights, however, were largely absent or inefficient compared to modern patent right protection. Although insurance institutions were developing they were mainly focussed on commercial risk. It was not difficult to raise funds for trade and investment even if the sums involved were quite modest by modern standards. International payments supported fast growing trade in food, raw materials, and luxuries. Capital markets operated markets for public as well as private debt. The public courts settled those contractual disputes, which were not handled by civil society.

Economic man was no stranger to medieval society. Human behavior had that mix of self-interested pursuit and concern for others that modern man displays. Medieval man was, however, more at risk and faced more imperfect markets, and market outcomes might have been thwarted more by inherited power than in a modern capitalist economy where privileges and power come with wealth rather than titles and status. But in the end privileges, authority, and political power and decrees could not stop wages from increasing when labor supply dried up, or prices from rising when harvests failed. The property-owning classes were carefully calculating profitable ventures and skillfully adjusted to Church doctrine sometimes by deceit and sometimes by donations. Labor quitted employers and cities if there were better alternatives elsewhere. Farmers reacted predictably and swiftly to changes in prices.

Markets were more volatile and difficult to predict because medieval man did not master nature sufficiently to avoid frequent harvest shocks and therefore lived closer to frequent economic disasters. There was a thin line between success and failure and there was little institutional support for the poor. For the poor life was "nasty, brutish and short." And opulence was neighbor to poverty.

References

Ackerberg, D. A. and M. Botticini. (2000). "The Choice of Agrarian Contracts in Early Renaissance Tuscany: Risk Sharing, Moral Hazard, or Capital Market Imperfections?," *Explorations in Economic History* 37: 241–257.

Barron, C. M. (2004). *London in the Middle Ages: Government and People 1200–1500*. Oxford University Press.

Bautier, R. H. (1953). "Les foires de Champagne. Recherche sur une évolution historique," *Recueils de la Société Jean Bodin* 5: 97–145.

Bavel, B. J. P. van (2007). "The Transition in the Low Countries: Wage Labor as an Indicator of the Rise of Capitalism in the Countryside, 1300–1700," *Past and Present* 195, Suppl. 2: 286–303.

(2008). "The Organization and Rise of Land and Lease Markets in Northwestern Europe and Italy, c.1000–1800," *Continuity and Change* 23(1): 13–53.

(2010). *Manors and Markets: Economy and Society in the Low Countries, 500–1600*. Oxford University Press.

Bonnassie, P. (1975). *La Catalogne au milieu du Xe à la fin du XIe siècle. Croissance et mutations d'une societé*. Association des publications de l'Université de Toulouse-Le Mirail.

(1990). *La Catalogne au tournant de l'an mille*. Paris: Albin Michel.

Boerner, L. and O. Volckart (2010). *The Utility of a Common Coinage: Currency Unions and the Integration of Money Markets in Late Medieval Central Europe*. Working Paper No. 146/10, Department of Economic History, London School of Economics.

Bourin, M. and P. Freedman (2005). *Forms of Servitude in Northern and Central Europe*. Turnhout: Brepols Publishers.

Britnell, R. (1993). *The Commercialization of English Society, 1000–1500*. Cambridge University Press.

Brunel, G. (2005). "Le marché de la terre en France septentrionale et en Belgique," in Feller and Wickham (eds.), pp. 99–111.

Büchert Netterstrøm, J. (2005). "Protection and Serfdom in Late Medieval and Early Modern Denmark," in Bourin and Freedman (eds.), pp. 369–384.

Campbell, B. M. S. (1984). "Inheritance and the Land Market in a Peasant Community," in Smith (ed.), pp. 87–134.

(2000). *English Seigniorial Agriculture 1250–1450*. Cambridge University Press.

Carus-Wilson, E. M. (1941). "An Industrial Revolution in the 13th Century," *Economic History Review* 11: 39–60.

Clark, G. (2008). *A Farewell to Alms: A Brief Economic History of the World*. Princeton University Press.

Coase, R. (1937). "The Nature of the Firm," *Economica* 4(16): 386–405.

Desportes, P. (1979). *Reims et les Rémois aux XIIIe et XIVe siècle*. Paris: Service de reproduction des thèses.

Dilcher, C. and C. Violante, eds. (1996). *Strutture e trasformazioni della signoria rurale nei secoli X–XII*. Bologna: Il Mulino.

Domar, E. (1970). "The Causes of Slavery and Serfdom: A Hypothesis," *Journal of Economic History* 30(1): 18–32.

Duby, G. (1962). *L'économie rurale et la vie des campagnes dans l'occident médiéval*. Paris: Aubier.

(1971). *La société aux XIe et XIIe siècles dans la région mâconnaise*. Paris: Écoles des Hautes Études en Sciences Sociales.

Dyer, C. (2005a). "Villeins, Bondsmen, Neifs and Serfs: New Serfdom in England, c. 1200–1600," in Bourin and Freedman (eds.), pp. 419–435.

(2005b). "Seigniorial Profits on the Landmarket in Late Medieval England," in Feller and Wickham (eds.), pp. 219–236.

(2005c). *An Age of Transition? Economy and Society in England in the Late Middle Ages*. Oxford: Clarendon Press.

Edwards, J. and S. Ogilvie (2011). "Contract Enforcement, Institutions, and Social Capital: The Maghribi Traders Reappraised," *Economic History Review* 65(2): 1–24.

Edvinsson, R. and J. Söderberg (2011). "Prices and the Growth of the Knowledge Economy in Sweden and Western Europe before the Industrial Revolution," *Scandinavian Economic History Review* 59(3): 250–272.

Epstein, S. R. (1994). "Regional Fairs, Institutional Innovation, and Economic Growth in Late Medieval Europe," *Economic History Review* 47(3): 459–482.

(1998). "Craft Guilds, Apprenticeship, and Technological Change in Preindustrial Europe," *Journal of Economic History* 58: 684–713.

(2008). "Craft Guilds in the Pre-modern Economy: A Discussion," *Economic History Review* 61: 155–174.

Favier, J. (1987). *De l'or et des épices. Naissance de l'homme d'affaires au Moyen Âge.* Paris: Fayard.

Feller, L. (1998). *Les Abruzzes médiévales. Territoire, économies et société en Italie centrale du IXe au XIIe siècle.* Paris: École française de Rome.

(2007). *Paysans et seigneurs au Moyen Âge, VIIIe–XVe siècles.* Paris: A. Colin.

(2009). *Calculs et rationalités dans la seigneurie medieval. Les conversions de redevances entre IXe et XVe siècle.* Paris: Publications de la Sorbonne.

Feller, L. and C. Wickham (2005). *Le marché de la terre au moyen age.* Rome: École française de Rome.

Figueras, L. T. (2005). "Le marché de la terre et la seigneurie dans la Catalogne medieval," in Feller and Wickham (eds.), pp. 479–542.

Findlay, R. and K. H. O'Rourke (2007). *Power and Plenty: Trade, War and the World Economy in the Second Millennium.* Princeton University Press.

Fourquin, G. (1964). *Les campagnes de la région parisienne à la fin du Moyen Âge.* Paris: Presses universitaires de France.

Franzén, B. (2006). *Folkungatidens monetära system. Pennningen mellan pest och patriarkat.* Stockholm: Almqvist & Wiksell.

Freedman, P. (1991). *The Origin of Peasant Servitude in Medieval Catalonia.* Cambridge University Press.

Galassi, F. L. (1992). "Buying a Passport to Heaven: Usury, Restitution, and the Merchants of Medieval Genoa," *Religion* 22: 313–326.

Geijerstam, J. af and M. Nisser. (2011). *Bergsbruk – gruvor och metallframställning.* Stockholm: Norstedts.

Gelderblom, O. (2004). "The Decline of Fairs and Merchant Guilds in the Low Countries, 1250–1650," *Jaarboek voor Middeleeuwse Geschiedenis* 7: 199–238.

Geremek, B. (1968). *Le salariat dans l'artisanat Parisien aux XIIIe-XVe siècles.* Paris: Mouton.

Grafe, R. and O. Gelderblom (2010). "The Rise and Fall of the Merchant Guilds: Re-thinking the Comparative Study of Commercial Institutions in Premodern Europe," *Journal of Interdisciplinary History* 40(4): 477–511.

Greif, A. (1989). "Reputation and Coalitions in Medieval Trade: Evidence on the Maghribi Traders," *Journal of Economic History* 49(4): 857–882.

(2000). "The Fundamental Problem of Exchange: A Research Agenda in Historical Institutional Analysis," *European Review of Economic History* 4: 251–284.

Hammer, C. (2002). *A Large Scale Slave Society in Early Medieval Bavaria.* Abingdon: Ashgate Publishing Group.

Hatcher, J. (2001). "Women and Work Reconsidered: Gender and Wage Differences in Late Medieval England," *Past and Present* 173: 191–198.

Heers, J. (2012). *La naissance du capitalisme au Moyen Âge. Changeurs, usuriers et grands financiers*. Paris: Perrin.

Henriksen, I. (1995). "The Danish Second Serfdom Revisited," in A. M. Møller (ed.), *Folk og Erhverv, tilegnet Hans Chr. Johansen*. Odense Universitetsforlag, pp. 17–34

Holbach, R. (1994). *Frühformen von Verlag und Grossvertrieb in der Gewerblichen Produktion (13.–16. Jahrhundert)*. Stuttgart: Steiner.

Howell, M. C. (2010). *Commerce Capitalism in Europe, 1300–1600*. Cambridge University Press.

Keene, D. (1990). "Continuity and Development in Urban Trades: Problems of Concepts and the Evidence," in P. J. Corfield and D. Keene (eds.), *Work in Towns*. Leicester University Press, pp. 1–16.

Kula, W. (1976). *An Economic Theory of of the Feudal System: Towards a Model of the Polish Economy 1500–1800*. London: Schocken Books.

Langdon, J. (2004). *Mills in the Medieval Economy*. Oxford University Press.

Lopez, R. (1966). *The Birth of Europe*. New York: M. Evans.

(1971). *The Commercial Revolution of the Middle Ages, 950–1350*. Englewood Cliffs, NJ: Prentice Hall.

MacCay, A. (1977). *Spain in the Middle Ages: From Frontier to Empire, 1000–1500*. London: Macmillan.

McCormick, M. (2001). *Origins of the European Economy: Communications and Commerce* A.D. *300–900*. Cambridge University Press.

Milgrom, P. R., D. C. North, and R. Weingast (1990). "The Role of Institutions in the Revival of Trade: The Law Merchant, Private Judges, and the Champagne Fairs," *Economics and Politics* 2(1): 1–23.

Miskimin, H. (1975). *The Economy of Early Renaissance Europe, 1300–1460*. Cambridge University Press.

Munro, J. H. (2001). "The New Institutional Economics and the Changing Fortunes of Fairs in Medieval and Early Modern Europe: The Textile Trades, Warfare, and Transaction Costs," *Vierteljahrschrift für Sozial- und Wirtschaftsgeschichte* 88: 1–47.

(2003). "The Medieval Origins of the Financial Revolution: Usury, Rentes, and Negotiability," *The International History Review* 25(3): 505–562.

(2012). "The Technology and Economics of Coinage Debasements in Medieval and Early Modern Europe: With Special Reference to the Low Countries and England," in J. H. Munro (ed.), *Money in the Pre-Industrial World: Bullion, Debasements and Coin Substitutes*. London: Pickering & Chatto.

Murray, J. M. (2005). *Bruges, Cradle of Capitalism, 1280–1390*. Cambridge University Press.

Myrdal, J. (1999). *Jordbruket under feodalismen 1000–1700*. Stockholm: Natur och Kultur.

(2012). "Scandinavia," in H. Kisikopoulos (ed.), *Agrarian Change and Crisis in Europe, 1200–1500*. London: Routledge, pp. 204–249.

Myrdal, J. and M. Morell (2011). *The Agrarian History of Sweden: From 4000* BC *to* AD *2000*. Lund: Nordic Academic Press.

Nef, J. U. (1987). "Mining and Metallurgy in Medieval Civilization," in Postan, Rich, and Miller (eds.), pp. 693–761.

Nobili, M. (2006). "Schiavitù, 'servaggio' e 'dipendenza signorile'. Lo svolgimento delle relazioni di dipendenza del coltivatori delle campagne dell'Italia centro settentrionale nell'opera di Cinizio Violante (Secoli VIII–XIII)," in Violante and Spicciani (eds.), pp. 27–40.

North, M. (2013). "Merchants and Credit in the Hanseatic Area, 1300–1700," in Gerard Caprio (ed.), *Handbook of Key Global Financial Markets, Institutions, and Infrastructure*. London: Elsevier.

Ogilvie, S. C. (2004). "Guilds, Efficiency, and Social Capital: Evidence from German Proto-industry," *Economic History Review* 57(2): 286–333.

(2008). "Rehabilitating the Guilds: A Reply," *Economic History Review* 61(1): 175–182.

(2011). *Institutions and European Trade, Merchant Guilds 1000–1800*. Cambridge University Press.

Panero, F. (2006). "Manumissioni di 'servi' e affrancazioni di 'rustici' nell'Italia settentrionale, secoli X-XIII," in Violante and Spicciani (eds.), pp. 385–404.

Persson, K. G. (1988). *Pre-Industrial Economic Growth, Social Organization and Technological Progress in Europe*. Oxford: Basil Blackwell.

(1991). "Labor Productivity in the Medieval Economy: The Case of Tuscany and the Low Countries," in B. Campbell and M. Overton (eds.), *Land, Labor and Livestock*. Historical Studies in European Agricultural Productivity. Manchester University Press, pp. 124–143.

(2010). *An Economic History of Europe, Knowledge, Institutions and Growth: 600 to the Present*. Cambridge University Press.

Polanyi, K. (1957). *The Great Transformation: The Political and Economic Origin of Our Times*. Boston: Beacon Press.

Postan, M. M. (1966). "Medieval Agrarian Society in its Prime: England," in M. M. Postan (ed.), *The Cambridge Economic History of Europe*. Vol. I: *The Agrarian Life of the Middle Ages*. Cambridge University Press, pp. 548–632.

(1973). *Essays on Medieval Agriculture and General Problems in the Medieval Economy*. Cambridge University Press.

Postan, M. M., C. Postan, and E. Miller, eds. (1987). *The Cambridge Economic History of Europe*. Vol. II: *Trade and Industry in the Middle Ages*. Cambridge University Press.

Postan, M. M., E. E. Rich, and E. Miller, eds. (1965). *The Cambridge Economic History of Europe*. Vol. III: *Economic Policies and Organization in the Middle Ages*. Cambridge University Press.

Renouard, Y. (1941). *Les relations des Papes d'Avignon et des compagnies commerciales 1316–1378*. Paris: De Boccard.

Rössener, W. (2005). "Die Leibeigenschaft als Problem in den Bauernaufständen des Spätmittelalters im Südwestdeutschen Raum," in Bourin and Freedman (eds.), pp. 289–312.

Schofield, P. R. (2005a). "Manorial Court Rolls and Land Markets in Eastern England c.1250–1350," in Feller and Wickham (eds.), pp. 237–271.

(2005b). "The Market in Free Land on the Estates of Bury St Edmunds, c. 1086-c.1300," in Feller and Wickham (eds.), pp. 273–295.

Schulz, K. (1985). *Handwerksgesellen und Lohnarbeiter. Unterzuchungen zur oberrheinischen und oberdeutschen Stadtgeschichte des 14. bis 17. Jahrhunderts*. Sigmaringen: Jan Thorbecke Verlag.

Scott, T. (2005). "South-West German serfdom reconsidered," in Bourin and Freedman (eds.), pp. 1115–1128.

Sicard, G. (1953). *Aux origines des sociétés anonymes. Les moulins de Toulouse au Moyen Âge.* Paris: Armand Colin.

Smith, R., ed. (1984). *Land, Kinship and Life-Cycle.* Cambridge University Press.

Söderberg, J. (2007). "Grain Prices in Cairo and Europe in the Middle Ages," *Research in Economic History* 24: 189–216.

Spufford, P. (1988). *Money and its Use in Medieval Europe.* Cambridge University Press.

(2003). *Power and Profit: The Merchant in Medieval Europe.* London: Thames and Hudson.

Stabel, P. (2004). "Guilds in Late-medieval Flanders: Myth and Realities of Guild Life in an Export-oriented Environment," *Journal of Medieval History* 30: 187–212.

Verhulst, A. (1999). *The Rise of Cities in North-West Europe.* Cambridge University Press.

Violante, C. and A. Spicciani (2006). *La signoria rurale in Italia nel medioevo.* Pisa: ETS.

Volckart, O. and N. Wolf (2006). "Estimating Financial Integration in the Middle Ages: What can we Learn from a TAR model?," *Journal of Economic History* 66: 122–139.

White, L. T. (1962). *Medieval Technology and Social Change.* Oxford University Press.

Wickham, C. (1996). "La signoria rurale in Toscana," in Dilcher and Violante (eds.), pp. 343–409.

(2005). *Framing the Early Middle Ages: Europe and the Mediterranean 400–800.* Oxford University Press.

(2009). *The Inheritance of Rome: A History of Europe from 400 to 1000.* London: Allen Lane.

10

The *via italiana* to capitalism

LUCIANO PEZZOLO

The economic history of Italy is surprising in many ways. The great medieval cities have offered abundant material for scholars of modern capitalism. The merchants' leading role, the innovations in accounting and commercial practices, the legal rules and commercial institutions, and the emergence of a new mentality – all have been considered elements characteristic of early capitalism. Italy can rightly be regarded as the cradle of commercial and financial capitalism. On the other hand, contemporary Italy demonstrates the grave limits of European capitalism, a capitalism where personal and client relationships carry a special weight, and where corporate groups (parental, client, and organizational clans with specific interests) play a central role in both the organization and the distribution of resources beyond the marketplace (Sapelli 1997: 95–105). The Italian case presents a Mediterranean version of continental capitalism, where kinship and social groups form a base of reciprocity and relationships of trust. In contrast to the "northern" version, in Italian capitalism the presence of the state appears nearly irrelevant in the face of the pervasive force of familial logics. Nonetheless, the state and family create what is only an apparent contradiction, given that the latter has often been viewed as an obstacle to the development of a shared sense of state in southern Europe. The southern extended family is thought to have assumed functions that elsewhere, that is in northern states where the nuclear family prevails, would have been the prerogative of public institutions. Thus the growth of the welfare state in the north implies a reduction in the role of the family; by contrast, the strength of family ties in the Mediterranean has been seen as an alternative to certain responsibilities of the state. Despite this, Italian history shows that there is not a marked conflict between family and state: rather, these are elements that complete one another in a tight dialectic where the boundaries shift only marginally in response to external shocks. Italian territorial states in the Renaissance, for example, did not destroy the political strength of lineage, but rather in some ways reinforced its role (Herlihy 1969; Mineo 1995).

Before continuing, however, it is worth clarifying the fundamental concepts that form the base of this essay. The state of the *ancien régime* was a fairly flexible political and social institution that reflected the power relationships in that society. The state institutions mediated between the needs and goals of the ruling classes and the pressures that came from the classes that did not share political power. These dynamics came together in a context dominated by concepts of class, status, and honor. Individuals acted within a system characterized by class relations, i.e., social hierarchy was determined by birth, by status, and by one's lineage. The context was the jurisdictional state, a system where different jurisdictional spaces coexisted and sometimes vied for prominence. These consisted of local bodies, lordships, feuds, municipalities, corporations, and central organs, all of which characterize the state of the *ancien régime*.

The term "family" refers to two systems: on the one hand lineage, which represents the patrilineal structure, founded on the agnatic transmission of name and blood; on the other the *parentado*, made up of cognatic ties which stem mostly from women's marriages. These are two structures, one vertical and the other horizontal, which form a complex system and which heavily influence the choices and options of the members of the elites. The sense of "family" for lower classes was narrower, limited to close descendants. In addition to consanguinal and residential ties we must add what can be called, borrowing an anthropological term, "fictive kinship," characterized by relations of godparenthood, ritual brotherhood, and so on. The crucial importance of lineage is balanced by the equally important elements of friendship and the sense of honor within this social system.

The system was therefore composed of both formal and informal elements that determined, in the broader context of international economy and local interests, the political and economic paths of the Italian peninsula. In the late middle ages, some Italian political units managed to create organizations with scale economies that supported the interests of economically powerful groups, who in turn formed most of the political ruling class. The development of these organizations was enhanced by the heated political competition that characterized medieval and Renaissance Italy and that simplified the political geography of the peninsula as territorial states emerged over the fifteenth century. The system based on concepts of lineage, friendship, clientage, and neighborhood generated multiple internal relationships (Coleman 1989), which in turn supported the formation of social capital at the base of the medieval commercial revolution. The Italian case shows how close connections between huge informal networks and formal institutions promoted economic growth.

Table 10.1 *GDP per capita levels in 1990 international dollars, 1300–1800*

	Italy Central-north	Castile	France	Southern Flanders	Holland	England	India	Japan
1300	1,808					716		525
1400	1,788				1,195	1,070		525
1500	1,550	1,295	1,330	929	1,454	1,119		
1600	1,350	1,382	1,300	1,073	2,662	1,054	792	572
1700	1,440	1,230	1,440	1,264	2,105	1,561	728	627
1800	1,430	1,205	1,410	1,497	2,408	2,125	646	639

Sources: Broadberry *et al.* 2011: 61; Malanima 2003: 290, Malanima 2011: 189.

The medieval expansion and Italy

Between the tenth and the fourteenth centuries, Europe experienced extraordinary economic and institutional changes. Around the tenth century the European continent appeared underdeveloped compared to China and the Arab world, but three centuries later the gap had been bridged and evidence suggests that the level of the Western economy was even higher than that of the Near East and Asia. If we consider the rate of urbanization as a marker of economic dynamics, then the European growth is evident. The percentage of Europeans who lived in cities of over ten thousand inhabitants doubled between the ninth century and 1300, and Italy in that period tripled its urban population (van Zanden 2009: 40). It is likely that the central and northern part of the Italian peninsula was at the time one of the richest areas in the whole world, a level of wealth that was never again attained until the end of the pre-industrial age, as Table 10.1 shows.

The reasons for this growth are still under debate. Some stress technological innovations in the agrarian sector to explain the rise of population and trade. Others argue that the new institutional framework (legislation, politics, and guilds) promoted a significant expansion of trade by lowering transaction costs, which in turn sustained population growth. Although the period appears to have been stimulated by favorable market conditions rather than by population growth, it is likely that interplay between demographic and institutional factors was at work. The table also shows that during the early modern period Italy witnessed a slow and steady decline. Although in absolute terms the wealth of the peninsula did not drop dramatically, it lagged behind in comparison to other countries (namely England and Holland).

Although trade in the Mediterranean had never disappeared, it is clear that the early middle ages witnessed a decrease in the intensity of commercial activities on a large scale. However, as early as the ninth century there was a significant widening of exchange networks. Cities in southern Italy first led the recovery, due to their traditional relationship with the Muslim world and the Byzantine empire. This tradition permitted Italians to develop the know-how, the financial and juridical tools, and the accounting techniques common to Muslim merchants (Lieber 1968). At first Sicily and Amalfi were the main foci of trading connections; Genoa and Pisa were the protagonists of the next phase. In the early twelfth century the merchants of the two northern cities pushed their interests towards the eastern Mediterranean and a harsh struggle broke out between them, which was eventually won by Genoa. By this time Venice had expanded its influence over the Adriatic Sea, having by the eighth century already established commercial relations with the eastern Mediterranean (Abulafia 1977; Lopez 1976; Tangheroni 1996). In fact, by the early ninth century Venice was playing a central role in the commercial routes of the Mediterranean and the Po valley, although these routes had not yet achieved the level and scope of activity in Europe that was to come.

Why did the Italians become the protagonists of the commercial rise? No doubt the geographical position of Italy is critical. The peninsula was the natural link between the Byzantine and Muslim areas on the one hand, and the European continent on the other. Economic differences encouraged brokerage activity as the European demand for manufactured and luxury goods grew, albeit slowly. The Byzantine and Arab merchants were not particularly interested in European markets, for these were considered unattractive. Starting from the tenth century, moreover, Muslim fleets were unable to maintain their predominance over the Mediterranean waters. This prevented the Levantine merchants from seizing favorable opportunities as the European economy began to grow. The spaces left empty by the Muslim merchants, and the growing difficulties of the Byzantine empire, opened the way for the Italians. The initial phases of Italian maritime and commercial expansion are marked by intense pirate activity, so that there was no clear line dividing merchants from pirates. In the western Mediterranean, galleys from Pisa, Genoa, and Muslims from Andalusia battled for dominance; the Genoese engaged the Venetians in the eastern Mediterranean as well (Balard 1978: 587–598; Bruce 2006; Katele 1988).

Italians turned out to be very effective in raising the capital to invest in long-distance trade. They overcame the limits of traditional trade networks based on kinship and ethnicity, and were able to mobilize resources from a wide area of investors. Moreover, while the merchants belonging to traditional networks found themselves unable to organize the protection of their trips from pirates and competitors, the Italians instead proved particularly effective at this, either by organizing protected convoys or by strengthening the crews themselves with a significant armed presence. In 1259, for example, a contract in Genoa stipulated that a crew of fifty sailors consist of forty armored men and ten crossbowmen; in the middle of the fourteenth century a light galley was required to be equipped with 160 cuirasses, 160 gorgets, 170 helmets, at least 24 crossbows, 5000 quarrels, as well as lances and javelins. In 1302 the Venetian government ordered that thirty bowmen had to travel on every merchant galley (Dotson 1994: 330; Lane 1969: 164; Van Doosselaere 2009: 57–60, 182–183).

The fleets of the great Italian cities represented a massive military strength. By the late thirteenth century Venice was able to deploy around one hundred ships and Genoa as many as one hundred and sixty. A fleet of one hundred galleys embarked about 20,000 men and, despite the Black Death, the average size of the Venetian and Genoese fleets doubled between the thirteenth and the fourteenth centuries. It is worth noting that in the fourteenth century the Genoese fleet was mobilized every two years and that Venice was also engaged for as long in the eastern Mediterranean. The two great maritime powers chose two completely different models for managing naval warfare. Venice deployed rather early a permanent fleet, whose construction and management was controlled directly by the government, while Genoa had a tiny nucleus of state galleys which was integrated, when necessary, with private ships. This did not prevent the Genoese from adopting technological innovations ahead of their rivals, such as the extensive use of trireme galleys, which were larger, heavier, and better armed than the earlier biremes (Dotson 2003).

The roles of Genoa and Venice also developed by means of colonial expansion in the eastern Mediterranean and Black Sea. Venetians and Genoese had profited from the long process of disintegration of the Byzantine empire to enjoy privileges and to occupy territories that permitted them to control the routes between east and west. Critical to the success of Italian merchants was the effectiveness of warships in support of their motherland's commercial interests. The Chrysobull of 1082 sanctioned the military role played by Venice in defense of the Byzantine empire, which was under threat from the Normans. With this act the Venetians gained commercial privileges and fiscal exemptions, and reinforced their role as intermediaries even in territory under imperial sovereignty (Jacoby 2009). In 1111 the Pisans, and in 1155 the Genoese, obtained analogous privileges, which were consolidated in the decades that followed. The period of the crusades (1095–1391) offered further possibilities for expansion for Venice in particular, which culminated with the taking of Constantinople in 1204 and the creation of the Latin empire of the east (1204–1261). Toward the middle of the thirteenth century Italian merchants, supported by efficient fleets, had established a sort of hegemony over exchanges between Europe and the Levant. Violence and its shadow loomed over economic activities and represented a destabilizing factor, particularly in the area of long-distance trading. The damage was not so much caused directly by conflicts as by the general climate of insecurity they brought about. The anxiety created by war and insecurity due to piracy and banditry caused a surge in transaction costs and influenced choices accordingly. It is noteworthy that in the early fourteenth century the improvement of defense capabilities and the adoption of marine insurance in Genoa were a response to the resurgence of piracy in the Mediterranean. At the same time, some governments – *in primis* the Venetian one – themselves supported piracy activities. In these (and other) ways, the effective use of violence provided Genoa and Venice with competitive advantages in long-distance trading (Pezzolo 2007).

In addition to their efficient methods of coercion, Italian merchants developed organizational innovations designed to improve their efficiency and reduce transaction costs. To begin with, the "adventurer-merchant" who accompanied his wares gradually gave way to the sedentary merchant who directed and organized transport from his business's headquarters. This obviously led to problems with control of the process and trust between the principal and his agents. Even if no single system could eliminate such problems, it is clear that the period of commercial revolution saw the emergence of various methods designed to reduce uncertainties and, consequently, make long-distance exchanges more efficient.

Family and economic growth

Naturally the merchant's family made up the primary environment in which to find resources and support. The evolution of the family structure within Italian firms in the medieval period seems fairly clear, but apparently it was not so uniform for the large mercantile cities. Florence boasts a vast group of scholars who have analyzed the city's economic structures and developments, in search of the origins of modern capitalism. The merchant entrepreneur, the search for profit, and new financial and accounting techniques have all been considered components of a new way of operating in the economic sphere. In this context, the family has also been analyzed as a crucial factor; the family, however, is assumed to shrink during the expansion phase of the Renaissance, which validates the hypothesis linking economic growth to the smaller nuclear family.

There is some support for the argument that at the start of the eleventh century family units began to expand. In the city, the prosperous classes organized themselves along family lines and groups that were more generously defined than in the past (Herlihy 1969). Analogously, commercial companies reflect the central role of the family. Initially we often come across feudal clans with broad interests in the countryside and a place in the urban lineages as well (Greci 1986). Later, however, some households emerged that specialized in business. The larger Tuscan mercantile companies and banks operating between the thirteenth and fourteenth centuries provide good examples. The Castracane family from Lucca devoted itself to the profession of money-changing for generations; by the 1270s there were at least seven associates, of whom only two were not related to the family. But with the expansion of commercial activity the social space of the partners grew (Blomquist 1971). Founded in 1244 by four brothers, the Velluti company lasted at least until 1312 with the inherited rights of the founders. The famous banking and commercial house of the Peruzzi family, which symbolized Florentine economic life in the first half of the fourteenth century, counted about half of its male family members among the partners. It is true that in merely quantitative terms the weight of the Peruzzi in the larger complex of company partners and employees was not predominant, but it bears noting that family members made the important decisions.

The policy of expanding to include new partners, furthermore, seems to have followed a logic that was influenced by familial ties (de La Roncière 1977: 235; Luzzatti 1971: 15–30; Sapori 1955: 653–694). Analogously, in the fourteenth century the Strozzi company was little more than an extension of the powerful clan (Spallanzani 1978). The Alberti company, one of the prominent Florentine commercial enterprises in the fourteenth and fifteenth centuries, was founded by three brothers and over time their sons were also brought into its administration. In 1347 the next generation saw a division between the "new" and the "*antichi*" Alberti. The latter group split further to form two separate companies in 1372. Thus, around 1400, several different Alberti companies operated throughout Europe, all of them descendants of the three founding brothers but now apparently separate (De Roover 1974:

56–58; Sapori 1955: 975–1012). In any event it was inevitable that companies based on family ties should split into different firms over the course of two or three generations.

The Black Death of the mid fourteenth century is considered a watershed for the history of the family, in particular for its economic organization. Before the plague, large family-run firms were dominant, while afterwards significant changes occurred. According to some scholars, the central role of lineage in the organization of companies faded away. In contrast to the thirteenth- and fourteenth-century model, from the end of the fourteenth century on the large companies were structured like holdings, a sort of galaxy of overlapping autonomous partnerships that circled around the main firm. The firms of Marco Datini and those of the Medici represent this new model (Melis 1962: 173–279; Sapori 1967). The merchant enjoyed great freedom of movement and fully embodied the individualism of the Renaissance man (Goldthwaite 1968), while according to other scholars the family continued to exercise a steady influence on the choices made by Florentines (Kent 1977). Beyond the question of the Renaissance ethos, however, what were the dynamics of the social institutions in relation to the economic growth?

If we consider the politics of marriage among Florentine merchants, the clear impression is one of a broad network that includes a large number of families. This was a flexible system that, for example, was reorganized after the political turmoil of the 1378 *ciompi* (woolworkers) revolt to expand the area of political and social consensus. The clans that had been tepid toward the workers' revolt were absorbed by the traditional elite and there developed a partnership system, reinforced by interfamilial and client relationships, particularly in the sectors of finance and international commerce (Padgett and McLean 2006). The result is illustrated in Table 10.2, which shows the high degree of business and family relations that developed in Florence in the early fifteenth century.

The behavior of groups was fairly different: high-status bankers tended to seek new partners among high-status outsiders, while in other industries family ties were more important than status. The result, however, was an extremely solid social class, in which the degree of homogamy among the lineages of the elite was fairly high, even if one cannot speak of a closed caste (Molho 1994: 274–297; Padgett 2010). Cemented by blood, marriage, and neighborhood ties, the Florentine ruling elite survived in the face of adversity and economic and political upheavals for centuries. From the 1530s on, moreover, the warring factions that had characterized Florentine political life disappeared, which reinforced the degree of across-group trust.

Table 10.2 *Early-fifteenth-century Florentine partnerships and social relations*

	Flowing through family	Flowing through *gonfalone*[a]	Flowing within status group	Total partners
Banking sector	158	50	226	296
%	53.4	16.9	76.4	
Wool sector	168	58	172	318
%	52.8	18.5	54.1	
Silk industry	42	20	56	98
%	42.9	20.4	57.1	

Source: McLean and Padgett 2004: 203.
[a] The *gonfalone* was the spatial unit (sixteen districts) into which Florence was divided, thus providing a measure for neighborhood (see also McLean and Padgett 2006).

The role of women is fundamental here. Not only do they represent the bond linking different families, but they are directly involved, along with their dowries, in the fate of the family firms. Florentine practice provided in fact for the imprisonment of wives and the holding of their dowries when the husband went bankrupt. Furthermore, there are various cases which show members of the same family working in different companies, not only to diversify risk but also to maintain a wide network of relationships. All of this leads us to conclude that the degree of competition among Florentine merchants was particularly mild. The same conclusion holds for the businessmen of Asti between the thirteenth and fourteenth centuries. Here we find a complex network of relationships that spread across the Piedmont and Flanders, connecting different companies engaged in issuing loans. This allowed for considerable management flexibility and a solid systemic cohesion (Castellani 1998).

Let us now leave Florence and move to Genoa, the most important western Mediterranean port between the late medieval and early modern period. The Ligurian city enjoyed a lively political culture, characterized by factional conflict, revolts, and general disorder. It is a commonplace to regard the Genoese state as extremely weak in the face of the power of family clans. But this did not impede the Genoese in their construction of a large dominion, first territorial and later financial. From the fourteenth century to the beginning of the sixteenth, Genoa's *alberghi* – that is, multifamily, largely noble clans united by ties of blood, marriage, clientage, and neighborhood – were at the center of the city's social and economic life. While in Florence the structures of lineage and clientage were unrecognized institutionally, in Genoa the *alberghi* performed functions of debt raising, tax distribution, and military mobilization and participated actively in government (Grendi 1987: 49–102; Heers 1961: 564–576). It is interesting to note that some magistrates, when unable to fulfill the obligations of their offices, could be replaced by relatives (Shaw 2005: 51). Toward the end of the fourteenth century there were around one hundred *alberghi*, during the following century the number shrank to around forty, and in 1528 their number was fixed at twenty-three. From the beginning of the sixteenth century on, the activities of these institutions were limited to helping financially needy members, and managing the clan networks.

Regarding the economic aspects of the *alberghi*, the interfamily relationships represented a crucial aspect of Genoese economic growth during the late middle ages. From the middle of the twelfth century, the importance of family ties increased considerably in the sector of long-distance commerce. This led to the formation of specialized networks and consequently to the reinforcement of those family ties. The customs documentation from the port of Genoa in the years 1376 and 1377 indicates that three-quarters of the names had intra-*alberghi* relationships. In 1445 members of the principal clans were positioned along the maritime routes to support trade, and representatives of Genoese families could be found in all of the important European centers. In the fifteenth century the powerful Spinola family dominated trade with the kingdom of Granada thanks to the support of and relations with the Centurione and Lomellini families (García Porras and Fábregas García 2010: 37–38; Petti Balbi 2000; Van Doosselaere 2009: 178–182). The financial dominance of the Genoese within the Spanish empire was based on their capacity to manage the flow of financial resources across a vast area, through a broad kin and extra-familial network. The bankers working in Madrid displayed strong family relationships, which undoubtedly reinforced both business and personal ties (Alvarez Nogal 2005: 77–78, 89).

Venice offers a different picture from that of Florence or Genoa. The lagoon city developed a long tradition of state interests trumping private ones, and thus the family had little to no importance compared to the public good, which defined the state of St. Mark. Careful analyses, nonetheless, have highlighted the crucial role of family relationships in both the political arena and the economic sphere. With regard to the nobility, the great lineages split into branches which over time shared only their original last name. In contrast to Florence, and similarly to Genoa, in Venice the juridical institution of the *fraterna* (brotherhood) had a long life. Upon the death of the head of the family, his sons shared the administration of a large part of the family patrimony and lived under the same roof. Usually only one son was chosen to perpetuate the family line. In a society dedicated primarily to commerce, like that of medieval Venice, the equal division of wealth did not create problems, and permitted each heir to engage in entrepreneurial commerce even with outsiders. The advantages of this family partnership were considerable, and analogous to those of the Genoese *alberghi*. In the first place, the higher degree of uncertainty regarding long-distance commerce encouraged the head of families to choose, not a single heir but rather to involve all of the male heirs in the family business, thus diversifying the risk. By contrast, in a land-based economy, which was less subject to dramatic fluctuations in either the short or the long term, it was less risky to put all of one's chips on a single son (Boone III 1986: 868). Second, the family wealth remained intact and could be managed by the brothers according to their individual specialties. Third, this allowed sons to build political careers that often took them away from Venice, to foreign courts or aboard a warship. Finally, this practice created a sort of an economy of scale, in which shared living quarters allowed for more modest expenses on the home front. The *fraterna* as a family partnership faded away over the sixteenth century, as the shift from commercial to landed investments brought about the limitation of the marriages among the patricians (Hunecke 1995). Accordingly, partnerships developed for several aims of business.

The picture that emerges from this overview of family systems and the structure of commercial firms in the large mercantile cities of late medieval Italy is particularly interesting. We find before us a complex network of family, institutional, and economic ties which were at the base of a gigantic trust composed of thousands of people. Several hundred merchants and firms were scattered across Europe forming the Italian diaspora. This system stretched beyond city walls across a vast area that comprised the Mediterranean, the Black Sea, and the North Sea. The competitive advantages of Italian merchants, that is their capacity to create money of account and transfer it wherever necessary, in addition to their ability to make use of sophisticated credit mechanisms, positioned them within an informal network dominated by family ties and friendships. This undoubtedly facilitated the circulation of both goods and credit, as well as the transmission of economic information. It is worth asking if in this context real market competition could exist. The large commercial and financial markets seem rather to have been characterized by oligopolistic groups that, even when in competition against each other, did not reject cooperation at all, as happened between Genoese bankers in Madrid or between Tuscan and Venetian merchants (Alvarez Nogal, 2005: 75; Goldthwaite 1987: 23–24; Goodman 1981; Luzzatti 1971: 18; Padgett and MacLean 1997; Soldani 2011: 27–39; Vallet 1999: 27–39).

The central role of the family should not be underestimated, if only because it supported at least the first major phase of the commercial revolution. The family environment allowed for the transmission of values and trust, which smoothed cooperation among family members, clients, and neighbors who boasted a tradition of affective and business ties. The family and local networks thus consolidated strong relationships of trust, and made possible the intergenerational transfer of skills and knowledge (de La Roncière 1977: 237; Petralia 1989: 34–36). It could also operate in place of the market in cases of scanty information or the scarce enforcement of the agreed-upon rules. But the great advantage that family ties delivered to the market was the principle of family responsibility. In this case, we can trace an evolving line along which there is a passage in commercial ventures from collective responsibility to that of individual partners in proportion to their participation quotas. Initially the commercial firms reflected the social structure of the urban political landscape, largely influenced by clans and family cliques. As a result, there was no difference between social capital and a family's patrimony (Sapori 1955: 803). The goal behind the principle of collective responsibility was clearly to make the rupture of contracts extremely costly for the whole family. The family network was able to furnish insurance and credit, thus constituting a sort of risk pool. Nor should we underestimate the sense of honor that guided the behavior of mercantile family members. Dishonest behavior would have incurred both collective and family sanctions; the latter was considered a sort of social collateral that supported merchant activity.[1]

A system based on family firms created certain disadvantages. To begin with, it did not protect against internecine battles, and dramatic failures. Second, the central mechanisms governing family and neighborhood relationships were not always capable of furnishing the necessary financial resources to expand the business. Furthermore, in the case of bankruptcy, all of the family members found themselves implicated, even if they had not been directly involved in the problematic economic activity. To avoid these problems, Italians relied on legislative tools like the *ripudio*, which allowed part of the family wealth to be saved from creditors (Kuehn 2008).

---

1 I rely on the model proposed by Besley and Coate (1995), adding the family factor.

A long tradition of scholarship has found that organizations governed by strong barriers and family relationships often experience slow economic growth. Did a structure characterized by vast and robust family ties and solidarity have consequences for the well-being of the society (Fukuyama 1995)? Since the creation of strong, closed groups necessarily impedes cooperation with external members, let us analyze the degree of openness in the system that we are examining here. In the early phase of the commercial revolution Genoa displayed a lively social mobility, reflected in the many small overseas investments from the 1330s on, which were connected to the professionalization of merchants. In Venice, this phenomenon appears only later, but similarly to Genoa the twelfth and thirteenth centuries are a period of extreme mobility (Romano 1987: 18; Van Doosselaere 2009: 123, 146). In Florence, we find a notable social mobility as well, within the mercantile environment. In 1369, out of 106 Florentine commercial companies that used the port of Pisa, 51 belonged to *gente nuova* (Goldthwaite 2009: 104–105). The centuries of Italian commercial expansion appear not to be marked by an impenetrable class system, the central role of traditional networks notwithstanding.

In addition to the informal familial system, there existed legal tools to reduce transaction costs, in particular to attenuate the uncertainties relative to principal–agent relationships. It is important to note that there were (and still are) no methods to resolve this problem definitively. Nonetheless it is clear that during the medieval period several systems were adopted to reduce the uncertainties (Greif 2006). The transformation of the traveling merchant into the sedentary merchant brought the adoption of contracts that involved actors with the same goal. The commenda was a contract that ensured that profits and losses would be divided between the sedentary investment partner and the partner who engaged in trade overseas. Before the adoption of the commenda, the most used contract in the Mediterranean was the sea loan. This provided a fixed payment to the investor, who in turn took on the whole risk of the sea venture. Obviously the investor's high risk implied a high rate of return. Although the origins of the commenda can be found in Roman law with subsequent Byzantine and Arab influences, the development of this type of contract became particularly important in the medieval age.

The contract represented a powerful tool to transform savings into commercial investments, in a context in which information was widely disseminated (Gonzáles de Lara 2008; Pryor 1977). The social base of overseas ventures was composed of several hundred small merchants connected through commenda contracts. While the commenda was used mainly in shipping business, the company was the typical contract of land trading. Unlike the commenda, whose duration ended with the end of each business venture, the company was formed for some years and could be renewed. Profits and losses were proportional to the capital provided by each member. The key feature of the company lay in its capacity to raise funds from outside investors. In order to increase its primary capital (the so-called *corpo*), the company could accept time deposits (the *sovraccorpo*) from the general public providing a fixed return, as is the case with today's bonds. In fifteenth-century Florence, the usual return on deposits was 8 per cent and did not incur the prohibition of usury as the rate of interest took the form of a gift at discretion of the borrower (Goldthwaite 2009: 438).

Another method of financing, which was developed in the late thirteenth century, was the bill of exchange. In order to avoid the difficulties of transferring large amounts of coins merchants resorted to a written order of payment in foreign currency abroad (Goldthwaite 2009; Mueller 1997). The protagonists of this mechanism are four: in one place there are the remitter (or drawee), who wants to transfer the money, and the taker (or drawer, usually a merchant banker) who receives the sum in local currency and makes out the draft on his agent. In the other place there is the beneficiary (or payee), who receives and presents the letter for payment to his counterpart, that is the banker's correspondent (or payer), who pays on the order of the drawer. Obviously this tool involved a network of operators linking the different markets and a deep knowledge of the money market.

The bill of exchange met success because it facilitated international payments and masked the interest rate linked to the credit operation. In fact, the interest rate resulted from two rates of exchange between the currencies involved in the transaction, which was highly uncertain given market swings. Established as a means of payment, by the fourteenth century the bill of exchange became a true credit instrument not linked at all to the movement of goods. The operation of change could be renewed; the bill was retransferred (*rechange*) until the amount, and its interest, was paid back. It is worth noting that, though some earlier evidence can be found among Italian merchants, a further innovation occurred in late sixteenth-century Antwerp, as bills of exchange could be negotiated and easily transferred by endorsement. By the early seventeenth century, the diffused practice of the endorsement and the use of printed forms allowed merchants to issue bills of exchange on their own (Melis 1984: 68–70; Van der Wee 1993: 145–166).

The great complexity of commercial institutions brought about also accounting innovations. The adoption of the double-party system was considered an answer both to the need of the sedentary merchant to control the activities of the overseas agents, and to distinguish family accounts from partnership ones, as well as a tool to legitimize commercial transactions (Carruthers and Espeland 1991). It is interesting to note that this accounting practice, probably borrowed from the mercantile world, was adopted by the Commune of Genoa in 1340 to manage its own budget (Felloni 2005: 65–69). But, as with other practices, accounting techniques were immersed in economic and cultural environments and their diverse needs (Gonzáles de Lara 2008; Lane 1945; Williamson 2010).

The urban commercial world was based, in addition to kinship and local relations, on state organizations that were often considered the institutional emanation of mercantile interests. In effect, the northern and central Italian city-states can be rightly defined as patrimonial systems, in which rulers and corporations "jointly carry out political tasks and share the prerogatives of sovereignty" (Adams 2005: 6). In the following section, we will analyze the three major mercantile centers of medieval Italy, Venice, Genoa, and Florence, in an attempt to determine if and how their governments favored or limited economic success.

Three political systems

Venice was the head of a dominion which had been expanding overseas since the thirteenth century, first in the northern Adriatic Sea and later down to Crete, Cyprus, and several centers of the Aegean Sea. During the fifteenth century, it had conquered a large portion of the Po valley, including important cities such as Padua, Verona, and Brescia. From the mid-fifteenth century, the republic had to contend with the Ottomans, who gradually succeeded in eroding Venice's overseas dominion by conquering territories in Greece, Cyprus, and finally Crete. The Venetian state was made up of a center (Venice), which was physically separated from the rest of its dominion, and the dominion itself, which was in turn divided between the so-called *stato da terra* (the Italian mainland) and the *stato da mar* (the overseas colonies).

Beginning in the fourteenth century, the republic of Venice was run by an oligarchy of patricians. This was composed of families with the right to participate in the Great Council, the large assembly that elected the offices of the government. The Great Council also selected the doge, the highest representative of the state sovereignty, who held the office until his death. But the most important government organ was the senate, comprising about two hundred patricians, whose population changed over time. It was the senate that decided major issues concerning foreign policy, trade, finance, and so on. Below the patricians there were the so-called citizens (*cittadini*), namely individuals who were Venetians either by birth or who had been granted citizenship, who exercised liberal professions, and provided personnel for the bureaucracy. It is important to stress that only the patricians and the citizens had the right to trade overseas; they furthermore enjoyed commercial advantages and privileges in custom duties. By 1385, for example, only citizens (the *cittadini*) by birth were allowed to trade with German merchants in Venice (Bellavitis 2001: 27–28). Immigrants residing for twenty-five years in Venice could obtain the citizenship (*de intus et de extra*) by privilege and enjoy the same advantages reserved to nobles and citizens by birth. The commoners (craftsmen, workers, petty traders, and the like) represented the rest of the population.

By the early fifteenth century the patriciate had become a true caste. Nobody new could aspire to enter the restricted number of patrician families, who transmitted their political rights through familial ties. Only on rare and urgent occasions did the patriciate open their doors to new families. For example, new blood poured in during the war with Crete (1645–1669), when the government offered the chance of obtaining the patrician dignity in return for a huge amount of money. Many families, mostly from Venice and the mainland, took the opportunity to enter halls which until that moment had seemed eternally closed to mere mortals. As for Venetian citizenship, although it was governed by apparently rigid norms, it could become a quite elastic body, which expanded or shrank in response to demographic and social events. Between 1300 and 1500 at least 3,600 persons were granted various kinds of citizenship. After the Black Death, the authorities' benevolence was spurred by the desire to fill the gaps left by the disease. In the period between 1351 and 1400, more than 1,600 people were elevated to the status of Venetian citizen, while in the preceding fifty years only 777 people had been so fortunate. This practice continued into the following centuries, but the incentives to obtain citizenship diminished with the decline of Venice's role in international commerce; in the period between 1551 and 1600, the government collected only 159 requests (Bellavitis 2004; Mueller 2010).

One of the outstanding features of the Venetian mercantile world was the widespread trust that sustained transactions. This phenomenon has recently been analyzed by economic historians, who have emphasized the same element within trading communities. Trust, however, was not an inherent factor: it had to be created and cultivated. Various formal institutions had been emerging across Europe in order to protect merchants: fairs, specific courts, and guilds. Recently, scholars have also stressed the role played by those informal institutions (habits, widespread practices, ideologies) representing endogenous elements of the system as written rules and norms (Greif 2006; Ogilvie 2011).

In Venice, as well as elsewhere, merchants preferred to avoid the courts' halls and to settle disputes within their world through arbiters. State judges were called for only in case the dispute became extreme and extrajudicial solutions were impracticable. It is interesting to note that in Venice, unlike elsewhere, professional judges did not exist. Instead, judges were patricians who were elected for running courts for a specified period, after which they could be selected for the navy, for an ambassadorial or a financial office, or for a governorship in a subject city. This meant that the feuding parties did not address their grievances to law specialists and that – above all – judges enjoyed considerable discretion. Custom, furthermore, generally trumped written norms. Venetian law met the requirements of being fast and easy, typical of and necessary for the merchant world. Nonetheless, Venetian law constituted one of the foundations of republican identity, within a European context dominated by Roman law. It is superfluous to point out that the patrician judge embodied both a legal and a political role. In sum, one might see Venice as a city where rulers exercised political power, administered justice, and were largely engaged in economic activity. This should have brought about severe social and political strains in the city. A caste of rulers exercising political and judicial powers would have been able to dominate the economic sphere without being subject to legal constraints. But this did not occur, at least until the sixteenth century. The reason is that the shared identity between political rulers and economic protagonists lay at the base of the Venetian economic growth. Nevertheless, this autocratic model alone does not suffice to account for Venetian success: one has to set it against a context where the ruling group was able to distribute profits generated from international trade in an effective and widespread way.

Venice is an example of state-led growth. Its government was particularly concerned about the economy and took up an active role in the market. Unlike Florence, for example, where several small and medium-sized banks operated, a few banks existed in Venice and were subject to the strict government's control (Goldthwaite 1987; Mueller 1997). Taking advantage of the Byzantine empire's weakness, the Venetians were able to obtain legal and tax privileges from Constantinople. Another classic example is provided by state convoys of merchant galleys. Beginning in the early fourteenth century, Venice organized a system of protected convoys of great galleys rented out to merchants. The mechanism was quite simple: the government auctioned off the management and use of merchant galleys (more powerful than the light galleys) that, once rigged, manned, and loaded, sailed in convoys (*muda*) under the command of a captain. Thus, centered on the Rialto, a network of connections linked the ports of the Levant and the Black Sea, the coasts of the western Mediterranean and Africa, Flanders and England. The merchant galleys carried high-value and low-volume commodities like spices, silks, and precious metals. This system tended to provide all the merchants with the same opportunities of access to information and profit and Lane has rightly stressed its importance (Lane 1966: 226).

Communal ownership of galleys expressed the solidarity of the Venetian nobility and strengthened that solidarity. The system of annual auctions, combining the advantages of private operation with communal control and ownership, was a vital element in giving to the Venetian government the efficiency and stability which distinguished it from so many other Italian city-states of the fourteenth century.

The advantages of the *muda* system were considerable. First of all, it addressed the needs for defense as well as those of commerce. The convoys were well protected and able to defend themselves against pirates by means of mutual aid. Second, the ships themselves were equipped for any eventuality; state-owned vessels could be used if necessary for military purposes. Third, the convoys facilitated scale economies by lowering operating costs. Merchants could also avoid having to mobilize huge resources in ship-building, investing them instead in commodities to be traded. The state galleys enjoyed a more favorable market access than private ships. The latter were permitted to load luxury goods only if the former had their holds full. It is important to note that all investors enjoyed the same prerogatives and conditions. In addition, the network of Venetian consuls and representatives in overseas ports provided information on market conditions and possible cheating. This state-managed system reduced incentives to behave dishonestly, since a cheater risked losing the benefits of the system itself. The arrivals and departures of merchant galleys set the rhythm of supply and demand in the Venetian market. This permitted the prediction of fluctuations in commodity prices and the cost of money (Mueller 1997; Tucci 1962). Young noblemen who served on board the galleys as crossbowmen were able to gain valuable experience in maritime and commercial activities. Finally, the free oarsmen constituted a trained reserve for the war fleet (Doumerc 1991; Lane 1966; Luzzatto 1954). Thus, the Venetian state furnished both protection and services that acted as incentives for merchants to remain under the wing of the Lion of St. Mark (Gonzáles de Lara 2008). The social and ethical obligations typical of the mercantile communities worked, in the case of Venice, to the advantage of the state institutions.

Between the sixteenth and seventeenth centuries, however, there was a structural transformation in the Venetian economy. During the fifteenth and especially the sixteenth centuries, the city became an important industrial center (Tucci 1991). Venice became a leader in the production of woolen cloth as well as in printing. In the sector of long-distance commerce, however, storm clouds were forming. Venice's hegemony in the eastern Mediterranean was progressively eroded by a number of factors. First, Ottoman pressure forced the Venetians to abandon strategic positions along commercial routes. The commercial relations themselves did not diminish, but undoubtedly the system of protection for commercial galleys was weakened. The costs of commercialization grew due to the growing competition from the "northerners," who showed themselves to be more efficient then the Venetians in naval transport. Third, Venetian textiles were gradually supplanted in Levantine markets by English and French cloth, which was at lower prices thanks to lower transaction and production costs. Thus, structural difficulties with traditional commerce severely weakened the manufacturing sector. The city did not experience a drastic decline, but rather a significant restructuring of its productive apparatus. Some sectors managed to resist (glass-making, the manufacture of silk and other luxury products) and the service industry grew.

At first glance, Genoa presents a very different case from Venice (Epstein 1996; Grendi 1987; Heers 1961). Genoa's history is filled with disorder, revolts, and intervention by foreign powers. Between 1257 and 1528, eighty-one events of revolts and changes in government have been identified (Epstein 1996: 325–327). Some constitutional reforms in the sixteenth century stabilized the political framework and consolidated the hegemony of the nobility. It is surprising, however, that the splendor of the Genoese economy coincided with continuous and grave turmoil in the political life of its citizens. The problem is not to discover the causes of Genoese success, but rather to understand how it came about despite the bitter factional battles.

The political and economic organization of Genoa was significantly different from that of Venice. As we have already mentioned, the institutional and political basis of the Ligurian city was the *albergo*, an extended clan of kin and clients that was even recognized by municipal laws. During the first phase of the commercial expansion, it seems there was a close relationship between households and long-distance trade. From the mid thirteenth century, family clusters became progressively more important. Familial ties in the Genoese case, therefore, represented an effective lever for economic growth (Van Doosselaere 2009: 178–80). It is significant that in 1445, out of ninety-two Genoese merchants located overseas, as many as 80 percent belonged to the most important clans, and their location was strategically situated along the trade routes. In addition, the clans carried out various economic and political functions. Some members were engaged in trade, others in domestic politics, while others were in charge of patrimony management.

The *albergo* therefore represented an element of strength as well as one of weakness. One can think of the clan as a large family firm that was fully engaged in political activity as well. The biggest problem, however, lay with the competition with other clans. If Venice had managed to construct over time an equilibrium among its great families, bound by common interests in overseas commerce, in Genoa the solution was found both in the non-local authority that imposed cooperation among the different groups (Greif 2006), and above all in the search for informal agreements among the classes with shared interests in commercial activity (Van Doosselaere 2009). The high level of political conflict was provoked in particular by the control over the nomination of the doge, the supreme head of the republic (Shaw 2005), but at the moment when it was necessary to mobilize strength and resources for a common goal – whether a war or a commercial enterprise – the Genoese mustered considerable efficiency. Unlike Venice, the Genoese government did not provide a regulated system of state-owned convoys, but ensured protection of private vessels with its warships. It was the government that rented ships from private companies in case of need. Moreover, while in Venice the government directly controlled the arsenal and the construction of ships, in Genoa this activity was not centralized and remained a field controlled by private entrepreneurs. From the sixteenth century on, moreover, the Genoese were able to transfer the costs of protection to the Spanish Crown (Arrighi 2004).

One could even hypothesize that the real difference between Venice and Genoa lay in reliance on formal institutions in the former city, and informal ones in the latter. In effect, what differentiates the two republics was not so much the sense of state on the part of their respective elites as much as the means chosen to establish ties of cooperation, in addition to a different philosophy regarding access to investment opportunities. The Venetian system, which was represented at its highest level by the convoys of merchant galleys, imposed a certain parity among merchants, and limited the formation of enormous wealth on the part of individuals. Naturally, this did not eliminate vast economic disparities, as in any other city, but various indices lead us to conclude that in the 1370s the distribution of wealth in Venice was less unbalanced compared to other cities (Kedar 1976; Romano 1987).

Florence shows structural differences from the two port cities of Venice and Genoa. The political history of the low middle ages here was dominated by lively internal conflicts between magnates and the popular classes, Guelfs and Ghibellines, in an institutional framework that was republican in nature. One part of the citizenry in fact could be elected to commune offices. This principle, despite the government crisis of the corporations and the reinforcement of the oligarchy between the fourteenth and fifteenth centuries, endured even during the Medicean government and during the turbulent years of the Italian wars. From the 1530s on, with the establishment of the principate of the house of Medici, an institutional structure was formed, topped by the duke and his court, and supported by a permanent bureaucracy that was built on local, commune-based institutions. In contrast to Venice and Genoa, the Medicean state relinquished in part its urban traditions, and opened the way to political and administrative participation in the elites throughout its state. It is also worth noting that unlike Venice and Genoa, where merchant corporations did not exist, in medieval Florence the merchant corporations played a critical role, especially those of the moneychangers and wool merchants. The close ties between political leaders and merchants in the port cities made such an institution unnecessary.

While in the middle ages the merchants of Venice and Genoa were inextricably linked to overseas trade, the Florentines looked instead to land trade, textile manufacturing, and finance (Goldthwaite 2009). As long as merchants assured continual provisions of wool and partially finished cloth from northern Europe, the local industry enjoyed advantages due to the high quality of production and the efficient distribution across international markets. When problems with the importation of English wool emerged in the sixteenth century, the Florentines turned to Castile, which offered a lower-quality product, and above all left control over their imports to Castilian and Genoese merchants. In quantitative terms, the levels of production in the second half of the sixteenth century were analogous to those of the great fourteenth-century expansion, even if the internal market had undergone profound changes. From the end of the sixteenth century, however, there were ever-increasing signs of trouble, and the contraction of the market quota caused a drastic reduction in production. The Florentine woolworkers by now were working to satisfy local demand, and at low cost (Malanima 1982).

The other large sector of cloth production was silk. Though largely absent in the fourteenth century, the silk industry grew throughout the following century and developed considerably over the course of the early modern period. Between the second half of the fifteenth century and the first half of the seventeenth, silk cloth production tripled, and grew further in the eighteenth. This success was not limited to Florence but engaged all of northern Italy. Nonetheless, between the success of the sixteenth century and the comeback of the eighteenth, the production structure had changed. Luxury products, like the golden silk cloths which were produced in the city, had lost their primacy of place in the face of French competition, while the medium-low sector had become more vigorous. The diffusion of hydraulic twisting allowed semi-finished products to gain preeminence in the international marketplace; the countryside, moreover, could furnish enormous quantities of raw silk, which became the principal Italian export product in the eighteenth and nineteenth centuries (Battistini 2003; Federico 1994; Poni 2009).

Even if the trajectory of wool production in the principal manufacturing centers followed different patterns, the general picture leaves little doubt that by the early seventeenth century the sector had peaked, while within a century only the vestiges of wool output remained. The production structure, however, changed accordingly, so that luxury textile production was progressively abandoned, and there developed in its place the production of imitations of northern European textiles. Furthermore, production areas moved in large numbers to the countryside. As wool production declined, silk production rose, which in part made up for the losses in the woolen market. The response to these difficulties in the city was high-end niche markets, and the relocation of wool production in the countryside. If on the one hand it is likely that these responses did not succeed in maintaining the high levels of Renaissance wealth, they did mitigate the overall effects of the crisis in the textile sector.

Compared to the imposing presence of the state in Venice, and the pervasive role of clans in Genoa, the Florentine case at first glance seems to fall between the two structures. The great Florentine merchants do not seem to have profited from their positions of power to promote their own interests in the international marketplace (Goldthwaite 2009: 113). For their limited maritime endeavors, between the 1420s and the 1470s, the Florentine government tried to follow the Venetian example by organizing state convoys. The system was designed to support imports of Spanish and English wool, but the difficulties of the Florentine wool industry made the convoy organization obsolete (Mallett 1967). The government's role, however, cannot be denied. The Florentine nobility was among the few Italian ruling classes investing largely in the commercial and industrial sectors well into the seventeenth century. But after the end of the Medici rule in 1737 and the advent of the Lorena their involvement in partnerships dropped, probably because of the uncertainty felt by people who until then had traditionally controlled state courts and financial offices (Litchfield 1969). Likewise, the end of the protection on the silk industry in the 1770s brought about a dramatic decline of the sector, unable to face effectively the competition of French and northern Italian silk industries (Litchfield 1986: 243).

Reducing transaction costs: insurance

Insurance is one of the most effective means to limit risk in long-distance trade. The system originated from a rather close-knit environment composed of personal relations. The real medieval innovation lies in the transfer of the risk to a third party. Early maritime insurance probably dates to the early fourteenth century. Until the late fifteenth century there were two major forms of insurance: the first was a fictitious loan, whose amount was paid in the event of loss of the goods. The other one, according to the usage in Florence, provided for the payment of an up-front premium based on the value of goods insured. The former contract called for a notary, while the latter was a private agreement (Ceccarelli 2009). Beginning in the late fifteenth century, the Florentine system prevailed due to its simplicity. The insurance procedures became more standardized, which was part of a larger development by which market practices became more routine. By the end of the sixteenth century insurance policies were printed in both Florence and Venice.

The most important characteristics of the insurance market were the interchangeability of actors and the high barriers to entry. Many merchants were both underwriters and policyholders (Genoa in the fifteenth century; Florence in the 1520s; Venice in the late sixteenth century). This implies particular relationships among merchants, and low information asymmetry due to the social homogeneity of actors. No surprise, then, that in 1433 the Venetian Andrea Contarini was willing to underwrite a policy in favor of Andrea Zorzi although the former had no information about the trip, the goods, or the premium. In fact, the latter had committed himself to provide coverage to Contarini on a following occasion. The prominence of kinship ties continued to characterize the market at least until the seventeenth century. Within this context, underwriting a policy could be considered more a social duty than an economic act. Despite the tendency to institutionalize the rules, decisions based on trust and informal relations persisted. The insurance companies that were established in Venice in the second half of the sixteenth century, for example, were still centered around kinship and did not represent a true innovation that could enlarge the market. This was to occur throughout the eighteenth century in northern Europe.

The case of the insurance market shows how informal rules could work quite well within a given context: a market composed of a limited group of actors whose roles were interchangeable and relatively linked through parental ties. Of course, this pattern would have been extremely weak *vis-à-vis* exogenous shocks. The bankruptcy of a merchant would have provoked a dramatic sequence of failures. However, the low amount per capita being underwritten reduced this risk and, furthermore, the size of the market sufficed to spread and diminish the risks.

Property rights

Florence 1576: a certain Salvestro dal Borgo was sentenced to the galleys for having shredded a public document. He confessed after being tortured (Lapini 1900: 193). The punishment seems to us disproportionate to the crime, but indicates to what extent the Florentine authorities were anxious to protect the sanctity of public records. In effect, from the high middle ages on, property rights had to be defined with a legal document, and the prominent role of notaries emerged earlier in Italy than elsewhere in Europe. The capacity to understand and ultimately write such documents became a prerequisite for a person's economic life and, more generally, a factor in economic growth (van Bavel 2008).

As early as the ninth century we find a considerable percentage of people able to write and thus able to understand the significance of written law (Wickham 1981: 125). From the thirteenth century on, Italian cities boasted a substantial range of schools, both communal and independent. These increased in number in the fourteenth century, while Church schools had nearly disappeared by the end of that period (Grendler 1989). Analogously, communal schools for the training in abacus appeared in the fourteenth century out of the need to train merchants, scribes, and artisans of the building trade. The communal authorities understood the close tie between technical literacy and their merchants' and artisans' prosperity. The literacy rate in north central Italy in the period between the late middle ages and the Counter-reformation appears to have been quite high. In Villani's Florence (1330s) and according to the Catasto of 1427, probably seven out of ten adult males were able to read and write; in 1587 in Venice, the rate of literacy among boys (six to fifteen years) was about 33 percent. Even in the countryside, it was not unusual to encounter peasants who were able to understand and sign a document (Balestracci 1984: 18; Black 2007: 35, 42; Carlsmith 2010; Grendler 1989: 44–46, 78). Given the strong mercantile environment, it is not surprising to find a high level of literacy, not only among the upper classes but also among the lower social strata as well. But property rights were not recognized only through public contracts.

First of all, custom constituted a fundamental element in personal relationships and was the interface between law and social practice (Thompson 1993: 97). Just as a marriage could be made valid simply through public, social acknowledgment, thus were some rights recognized via their use and tradition. Regarding the control of lords over peasants, northern and central Italy saw an early decline with respect to the rest of Europe. Both peasant and urban communities drastically reduced the power of the lords and their customary rights. This contributed to the separation of land rights from rights over men. Both in Tuscany and the Veneto, feudal institutions were not important and seigniorial rights were quite limited. The presence of fiefs and lordships was significant in Liguria, however. The principal clans of the Genoese aristocracy enjoyed seigniorial rights in the countryside (Heers 1961, 513). Lords, however, did not hold full rights over their vassals and – it seems – were unable to prevent them from selling their goods. Apart from some areas – for example in the Sienese countryside – there were no manorial encumbrances on the land. In much of the Italian countryside, nonetheless, the cities imposed their own legislative systems that tended to favor urban property over that of the countryside. In this context, customary rights that rural communities enjoyed over farmland, grazing land, and forests were progressively eroded, at the expense of both citizen property holders and rural elites.

Although customary rights were largely recognized within the community and were still important elements of the regulatory system, written rules gradually acquired a paramount importance. The growing demand for written regulations was satisfied by a higher number of notaries. In the north central Italy of the late middle ages, the figure of the notary was part of daily life. In the 1280s, cities like Bologna and Milan counted around twenty-five notaries for every thousand inhabitants (Cipolla 1973: 41; Jones 1997: 157); subsequently the percentage diminished considerably, as the range of legal instruments directly available to the public expanded. Fiscal and commercial records, as well as custom, were considered to have a legal value equal to a legal instrument. From the fourteenth century on, for example, Florentine workers no longer sought out notaries for help in disputes with artisan masters, but rather trusted in the justice system of the corporations (Goldthwaite 2009: 352).

The institutions that certified property rights were manifold, because the actors were considered according to their origins and their social status. Men, women, citizens, artisans, nobles, clergy, foreigners, subjects of feudal or ecclesiastical lords, Jews, all had at their disposal specific courts. This legal pluralism consisted of coexisting bodies of law, sometimes conflicting, sometimes complementary. There were state, municipal, and guild courts, feudal and ecclesiastical jurisdictions, customary and merchant laws, each with their own judges. In a framework of deep uncertainty about rights, it was common to turn to the tribunals, to better define the terms of transaction and those same property rights (Ago 1998). Nonetheless, it was in this context that some Genoese merchants, in contrast to their Florentine colleagues (Goldthwaite 2009: 113), preferred to avoid the courts because the judicial system could be inefficient and inadequate to their needs (Court 2004).

Of course we have to consider that this concept of property was far from our modern one. With regard to land ownership, for example, it was not always easy to distinguish between private and public goods, not to mention between rights of property and rights of possession. Also, from the later middle ages on, laws and customs differentiated between the part of the family property that could be alienated and the part that was inalienable. The interests of the household took precedence over those of the individual. City laws ensured that relatives linked through agnatic kinship, for example, had the right to exercise control over the alienation of property. These same cities succeeded in eliminating, between the thirteenth and fourteenth centuries, the entails that limited the sale of land in the lordships of the countryside (Carocci 2004: 208; *Degli statuti* 1622: 148; Grendi 1987: 70; Owen Hughes 1976: 945; *Statuti di Padova* 1551: 65–66). Land under ownership or possession could be acquired or alienated through inheritance or purchase.

Unlike medieval England, much of north central Italy was not bound by feudal limits on the purchase and sale of land. In ninth- and tenth-century Tuscany, peasants bought and sold land freely. This should not be interpreted as a purely economic phenomenon; the peasants acted according to a logic dictated by parish and faction membership, in which the transfer of land played a central role (Wickham 1987). Analogously, land prices seem to have been influenced more by a familial and community context than merely by supply and demand. In seventeenth-century Puglia, relatives enjoyed lower land prices than did outsiders. Land was not a simple commodity, as it made up a large part of daughters' dowries, and generated complex flows within the family and between different lineages. It was not by chance that the majority of land purchases took place around the weddings of daughters, particularly when the middle and lower classes were involved (Delille 1988: 142–146). However, it would be a mistake to assume that the rules restricted the degrees of freedom of all individuals and, consequently, the land market. Legal devices such as *fedecommesso* and primogeniture were intended to protect the assets of the family in the context of lineage, but other practices allowed individuals and families to circumvent such constraints.

Although a myriad of rights, the origin of which are lost in time, created multiple claims on land, they did not prevent the land market from functioning. One has to take into account, however, how heavily constrained noble (land) property was by the *fedecommesso*, a sort of strict settlement. This was a legal device that limited the possibility of alienating the inherited patrimony. Beginning in the fifteenth century in Florence, and later in Venice, it became a means of protecting elites, possibly in order both to combat the hemorrhagic outflow of wealth due to rising expenses, and to sustain lineage identity. The main disadvantage lay in the difficulties of exploiting the patrimony in a profitable and dynamic manner. Recent research, however, has downsized the role of the *fedecommesso* in inhibiting aggressive practices. Around half of noble land was bound by some clauses. The regulations governing the transmission of land among the privileged classes have often been considered insuperable to the point that they shaped the economic and social structure. The analysis of actual cases, however, has shown that juridical rules were often circumvented, and that partible or impartible inheritance does not seem to have influenced the transmission of property between generations. In fifteenth-century Tuscany the diffusion of the patrilineal system was strictly limited by the high mortality of parents and by the availability of land for dowries to compensate for divided inheritances. Similarly, between the seventeenth and eighteenth centuries, women of the Veneto countryside assumed a crucial role in the family economy (Emigh 2003; Povolo 1985).

Property rights, at any rate, were formally guaranteed. Municipal statutes treated everybody as equal, whether a patrician, a citizen, a merchant or a foreigner. One of the most nagging concerns of the Venetian authorities, however, was the safeguard of their merchants' rights, which were regarded as the true pillar of the republic. It is noteworthy that Venetian law forbade tax assessors to use bankers' records to find out the wealth of taxpayers (Mueller 1997: 493). The bankruptcy law was severe, and dishonest bankers, even if they belonged to the ruling group, were rigorously prosecuted. Likewise, the Florentine justice system worked quite well. Property rights were protected and "in the few known cases of disputes about breach of contract between artisans and capitalist the former had no reason to be unhappy with the decision" (Goldthwaite 2009: 352).

The Venetian government is famous for having become the first – to the best of our knowledge – to grant patents. European epicenter of technological innovation during the Renaissance, the lagoon city welcomed artisans and inventors from everywhere. Between 1474 and 1788 the Venetian senate granted 1,904 patents (Berveglieri 1995: 22). The yearly average number of patents (5.6) was slightly over that granted by the Dutch States General from 1590 to 1680, while the number in the southern Netherlands (0.6) in the years 1598–1700 lagged behind; between 1660 and 1699 in England the average was 6.1 (Davids 1995: 347; MacLeod 1988: 150). The late Renaissance turns out to be the period when the Venetian government accepted a record number of applications, but it would be wrong to consider the high number of patents alone a clear sign of growth. The second half of the eighteenth century, for example, which witnessed a huge number of patents, was hardly a period of economic expansion for Venice. It is, however, important to stress that patents were granted particularly for inventions that were already known elsewhere and were now to be exploited within the state borders. Accordingly, this favored those who were able to spread the innovation throughout the republic rather than the innovators themselves. As for Florence, starting from the second half of the sixteenth century the dukes were quite willing to grant patents to inventors and petitioners. Between 1540 and 1739 the government granted 271 privileges (1.3 annually). In some cases these privileges mobilized an initial start-up capital, which would have been difficult to amass with the usual partnerships and contracts. Moreover, this practice became important not only for its practical results but also for the potential connections between innovation and economic rewards (Goldthwaite 2009: 491–492; Malanima 1982: 148–152). It is worth stressing that a market for patents emerged whose protagonists were inventors and financiers as well. Partnerships were established to exploit eventual profits within a legal framework which facilitated the diffusion of technological knowledge (Molà 2007).

The financial sector

So far we have examined some features of Italian economic history concerning mostly international trade; now we will deal with finance, the other great sector which made the fortune of the peninsula. If it is true that central northern Italy was precociously endowed with a (relatively) highly commercialized agriculture, we should expect capital markets to be equally precocious and efficient. Actually, looking at banking techniques and deficit financing methods developed in late medieval Italy the primacy could not be denied. This picture, however, is not wholly bright as the brilliance of high finance and bankers was counterbalanced by a wide area of the countryside where haziness seemed to dominate. This section concerns these two apparently separated financial worlds: on the one hand, that of cities and princes, and on the other, that of countryside and peasants.

We have seen how the commercial expansion of the great Italian cities was linked to growing warfare. Venice and Genoa invested huge amounts of money in fleets, fortifications, and garrisons, which formed the protection system for the commercial routes in the eastern Mediterranean. Florence conquered most of Tuscany in order to supervise its supply routes and to protect them from foreign threats. Likewise, in the early fifteenth century Venice formed a dominion in the Italian mainland to avoid the rise of a strong political rival, to control the land routes to central Europe and, accordingly, to consolidate its interests overseas. The Italian peninsula witnessed a recurring struggle between cities and states over the later middle ages, but the period between the late fourteenth and the early fifteenth centuries was characterized by an extraordinary rise of conflict. As communal armies were composed mostly of citizens hired *ad hoc* and poorly trained, from the fourteenth century governments progressively resorted to the professional soldiers of mercenary companies. The continuous state of war favored those governments better provided with financial resources. The gigantic capital accumulation, the high rate of urbanization, and the weakness of feudal institutions in central northern Italy allowed the large employment of mercenaries. While in the mid fourteenth century the average size of an army was a few thousands of soldiers, by the early fifteenth century the major states could deploy as many as 20,000 men. Consequently, warfare costs grew to unprecedented levels. In the years 1377 and 1378 defense costs and debt servicing absorbed from 60 per cent to 80 per cent of the Genoese budget; between the mid fourteenth and the early fifteenth centuries the military expenditure of the Florentine government increased by two thousand times (Becker 1965; Day 1963: xxiv). The very heated interstate struggle, thus, urged some Italian governments to develop effective methods to mobilize ever-growing financial resources (Parker 1988).

In case of need urban governments had to resort to various expedients to raise money, and permanent indebtedness resulted from repeated episodes of deficit financing. Since the twelfth century, cities such as Venice and Genoa had requested voluntary loans from their wealthy citizens, guaranteeing future tax revenues or public properties as collateral. In 1140 the Genoese government farmed out some tax duties to citizens who had committed themselves to anticipate money to the commune. Optionally, foreign lenders could also be involved (Cammarosano 1996: 48–49). The steady growth of financial need, however, brought the government to call for more and more loans, mainly forced. They were collected on the base of registers that represented the taxable capacity of each citizen. Creditors had the right to receive payments on a regular basis from fiscal revenues until the principal was paid back. Florence and Venice too witnessed an analogous shift from extraordinary voluntary loans to ordinary obligatory loans. The ever-increasing demand on citizens and the parallel difficulties in paying back the principal in due time led to the logical consequence of funding the debt, changing the floating debt into a long-term debt, redeemable at the government's discretion and with a relatively low interest rate guaranteed by specific fiscal revenues. Venice consolidated its debt in 1262, when the government committed itself to pay regularly 5 percent to creditors; in 1274 Genoa gathered various series of its debt into one fund at 8 percent; while as late as 1345 Florence decided to establish a *Monte Comune* at 5 percent. The fund that consolidated loans was called *Monte* in Venice and Florence, and *Compera* in Genoa; each fund was divided into *luoghi* (shares). The governments thus acknowledged their inability to repay creditors but at the same time allowed creditors to negotiate shares freely, which facilitated the emergence of a true secondary market (Ginatempo 2000; Pezzolo 2005).

The methods for managing debt differed among the Italian cities. In Venice and Florence the debt was strictly managed by government agencies, which raised loans and were in charge of interest payment. In Genoa, by contrast, the commune handed the management of revenues earmarked for interest payments over to its creditors (Felloni 1999; Sieveking 1905–6). Underwriters were grouped into consortia named after the tax linked to their payments: the *Compera salis*, for example, put together lenders who were paid by the proceeds of the tax on salt. The *Compera* had a legal status and was run by representatives, periodically elected by creditors, who were expected to safeguard their interests. Even after the consolidation of 1274 the Genoese commune launched new series of debts at different interest rates, so by the end of the fourteenth century there were five main *Compere* with interest rates between 5 and 10 percent. In 1407 the government decided to consolidate the previous debts into the *Officium comperarum Sancti Georgii*, that is the House of St. George, which from then on managed most of the Genoese debt and functioned as a bank as well. A consortium of creditors, run by eight patrons, was also established. The house managed the tax proceeds assigned to interest payments and, above all, had a broad jurisdictional power over some territories of the republic. The government, confronted with more and more difficulties in finding resources to pay St. George's creditors, handed over to the house the control of Famagosta (1447), Caffa and Corsica (1453), as well as some localities of Liguria (Balard 2006; Graziani 2006). These grants, however, eventually did not prove to be profitable to St. George, and in 1562 the commune resumed full jurisdiction in exchange for a consistent financial subsidy.

The House of St. George represents one of the most evident examples of the prevailing institutional practices in Genoa. At first glance it would appear that the state had relinquished some of its own functions to a private institution, which nevertheless performed "public" duties. This judgment goes as far back as Machiavelli's age, who in a famous page of his *Istorie fiorentine* had called the house a state within a state (Machiavelli 1962). Through revolts and changes of governments, St. George always kept a surprising autonomy and an apparent detachment from the harsh factional struggles that affected the city over the fifteenth and sixteenth centuries. The factions and the people who governed the commune, however, also ran the house. This paradox is likely resolved by noting that while the factions struggled for the election of the doge, the highest representative for the republic, in other fields the Genoese showed a remarkable aptitude for cooperation (Shaw 2005: 57–64). It was this very cooperation, based on a broad interfamily network, that supported the Genoese success in the international market.

The house did not always enjoy the full trust of its own shareholders. Looking at the market prices of St. George's securities, it is evident that the stormy political events of the city influenced the market heavily. Starting in the 1560s, however, as the house relinquished the burden represented by Corsica, prices skyrocketed, a further evidence of the confidence of the market in that institution. St. George in fact proved to be quite efficient in providing money to the government and, at the same time, flexible enough in safeguarding creditors, so that it could be said that the Genoese were less concerned than others with taking profit from government debt (Fratianni 2006; Shaw

2005: 82). The house monitored the flows of public resources earmarked to interest payments and, accordingly, also flows of information about the financial health of the government and the international political context. Between the 1620s and the 1630s, state finance faced a severe strain due to war commitments, whereas apparently the house was not wholly involved. The short-term loans the Genoese government had urgently issued in 1625 were gathered into the *Monte di San Bernardo* and two years later another fund, the *Monte di San Giovanni Battista*, was founded. These two funds, disconnected from St. George, paid to investors an interest rate of 5 percent, 3 percent in 1638 and as little as 2 percent in 1666, when both series were put together into the *Compera di Santa Maria*.

Seventeenth-century Genoa was the breeding ground for some interesting financial tools that were to spread throughout Europe, such as the *tontine*. In 1636 in order to complete the construction of the new harbor, the house issued a life annuity at 3 percent, with the clause, however, that the returns would be enjoyed by surviving underwriters until the death of the last nominee (Schiaffino 1624). This was a tool that was widely exploited in the eighteenth century by Britain and mainly by France.

Although the Genoa commune occasionally resorted to forced loans, they lost their obligatory characteristic much earlier than elsewhere in Italy. In Venice and Florence, loans were obligations on citizens until the fifteenth century. As long as the government was able to pay interest regularly, creditors could be satisfied because a return of 5 percent, although not very high, was safe. The high returns possible from trade, on the contrary, were quite uncertain. But governments increasingly accumulated large arrears, which grew along with their demand for forced loans, whose prices accordingly dropped in the secondary market. The citizen lenders thus became true taxpayers; and as such they addressed their complaints to the government or asked help from the tax assessors (McLean 2005). This process highlights the limits of the concept of public debt in medieval Italy. Although public revenues were used as collateral for creditors, the system rested first of all upon citizens above a certain wealth threshold. Moreover, the mandatory character of the loan undermined the investor's free choice.

Since the early 1530s, however, Venice began determinedly to issue securities in the open market, gradually reducing the use of forced loans (Pezzolo 2006). The new series, the so-called *Depositi in Zecca* (deposits in the mint) were tax-free bonds, fully negotiable and not sequestrable. As the deposits offered a higher return than forced loans, it is worth asking the reasons for the shift from low-cost loans to relatively high-cost securities. It is likely this was necessary to revive investors' potential trust and therefore to restructure the base of a debt system that had radically been changed due to the blows of repeated financial crises. The deposits in the mint constituted an effective response within an institutional framework particularly suited to financial markets. In Florence the path toward an open credit market was taken only as late as the sixteenth century, while previously the dukes had collected short-term loans from local and foreign bankers. Probably the stabilization of ordinary fiscal revenues helped the dukes to resort to voluntary loans.

But the real innovation brought about by the debt system in Italian cities was the formation of a solid secondary market of securities. As already mentioned, the possibility of negotiating government credits easily – unlike in France – paved the way to a lively market, one not just dominated by speculators. Fluctuations, sometime dramatic, of prices could advantage those people who had access to information and at the same time held liquidity. The growing demand for new loans could cause difficulties to many lender taxpayers, forcing them to sell old securities in order to raise cash. Accordingly, market prices dropped and favored speculators. Securities, moreover, were used for buying and selling, as collateral for further loans, to fund dowries and ensure a safe income to orphans and widows. The security market favored the formation of submarkets where one negotiated options to buy in future claims on government credits (Goldthwaite 1985: 40). Once again, the Genoese case is exemplary. At first the House of St. George paid interest (*paga*) every three months, but from the mid-fifteenth century the time span widened so as to reach even nine years by the mid sixteenth century; after which in 1575 the extension was set at five years. Thus, due claims were bought and sold and priced according to the date of their (actual or presumed) maturity. One could sell a *paga* (claim) expiring in a year to obtain a sum discounted, therefore below the face value (Heers 1961; Kirshner 1977). Along with the actual and widespread use of discount in a vast and articulated social context, it is interesting to note that in 1631 the house established an office for the monopoly of the *paghe* market, but with little success. Although there were similar markets in Venice and Florence, it is worth stressing that only in Genoa was this particular segment of the market subject to control.

At first, government debts of Italian city-states saw the voluntary involvement of a few lenders; as financial needs grew the tendency to call for forced loans from a larger base of citizens emerged. The successive transformation of an ever-broader class of taxpayers into lenders brought about the formation of

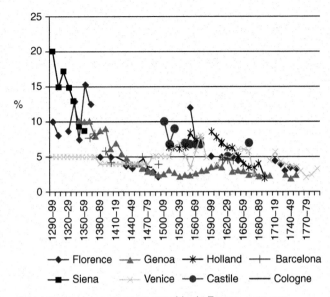

Figure 10.1 Interest rates on government securities in Europe, 1290–1779.
Source: author's database.

a true public debt issued in the open capital market. Unlike the short-term debt system (floating debt), characterized by opaque relations between rulers and powerful lenders, the funded debt showed the typical features of an impersonal market, where transactions were regulated by demand and supply and where investors largely shared information. This process occurred in different phases, overlapping and developing in relation to the institutional and financial framework. It is worth wondering whether the Italian security markets proved more efficient then elsewhere. A measure, albeit rough, to determine the efficiency of financial institutions is the interest rate (North 1990: 69). Figure 10.1 compares the yields of sovereign debt issued by various Italian and other city-states or provinces.

Before putting forward some observations it is necessary to stress that until the fifteenth century it is inappropriate to compare interest rates on obligatory loans (Venice and Florence) and rates on the open market. Considering Genoa and Barcelona in the second half of the fourteenth century, the spread was rather large against the Ligurian city, while a century later the situation was reversed. Genoa actually managed to get cheap credit at rates that were among the lowest in the continent. In the seventeenth century, the Netherlands became the most developed financial market in Europe and reduced its interest rates to the Genoese level. While it is evident that the cost of borrowing in Italy was lower than in major European countries, it must be said that both the Netherlands and England, unlike most Italian states, were engaged in long and costly wars. Only Venice had to face long conflicts against the Ottoman empire, and in fact the negative spread in the years 1650–1669 is due to the war over Crete. In short, financial innovations enabled Italian cities to support military policies at relatively low cost. The formation of Italian territorial states brought about also the strengthening of economic spaces and control tools over trade routes. Taxes on both imports and expanding exports provided the means to service reliably the ever-rising stock of debt. In the long run, therefore, financial investments in war proved profitable if victorious, considering that it was basically impossible to expand without coping with commercial competitors and rival powers.

The private sector in Italy responded positively to the developments of managing public debt. There can be no doubt that medieval Italy was the most fertile ground for some financial innovations. There was a synergy between the opportunities for long-distance trade and the sophistication of credit instruments. As far as high finance is concerned, Italians enjoyed a monopoly in medieval Europe. The so-called "Lombards," Tuscans, and Genoese covered a wide area stretching from the Baltic to the Mediterranean Sea; they provided financial services for both local notables and sovereigns. Italian merchant bankers' supremacy rested on the unquestioned ability to master the techniques of money exchanges and a wide network of correspondents covering the European markets. In the great financial centers a sharp distinction emerged between the domestic sector of exchange and deposit, which was usually managed by local operators, and the foreign sector of international trade financed by bills of exchange, which was controlled by the Italians. The accounting techniques of the Italians allowed the creation of money of account that was largely recognized in the business world and that facilitated transactions in international circuits (Boyer-Xambeau, Deleplace, and Gillard 1986; Petralia 1989: 28–31; Pezzolo and Tattara 2008).

Accordingly, until well into the sixteenth century Italian merchants enjoyed more favorable conditions of borrowing than their European colleagues, who faced severe difficulties in competing with them (Gascon 1971: 84; Spufford 1995: 316–318). The relatively low cost of capital and wide networks allowed Italians abroad in the 1330s to lend among themselves at 10 to 18 percent as opposed to foreigners who were charged as high as 50 to 60 percent (Dini 2001: 93). Unlike in Holland, where kin networks provided needed capital until an efficient financial market emerged in the early seventeenth century

(Gelderblom 2003: 630–631), in Italy cheap commercial credit was largely available as early as the fourteenth century. As we have already seen, between the fourteenth and the fifteenth century Florentine firms paid 8 to 10 percent for loans that had to be paid back at creditor's discretion (Goldthwaite 1985: 12, 32–33). It is necessary, however, to look at what happened in cities and the countryside to determine whether the success of high finance had a positive impact on Italian credit markets too.

The forms of credit in medieval Italy were manifold; the variety at the disposal of lenders went from a free-charge loan to a usurious one, from a loan for a few days to a loan redeemable at the borrower's discretion. Instruments and interest rates generally depended on economic and social environments, on actors' status, and on borrower's guarantee. It is worth noting that in the long run the cost of capital declined, in some case significantly before the Black Death, and the array of interest rates narrowed considerably. While in the late middle ages variance in rates – conditions being equal – was quite large, over the early modern period it tended to reduce, as Table 10.3 shows. This means that financial institutions emerged that made credit markets less personalized than before and made them more efficient.

Table 10.3 *Interest rates on long-term loans in Europe, 1150–1800*

	England	Holland	Germany	France	Central-northern Italy	Castile
1151–1200	20			20		
1201–1250	10.3	10	11	10.8	12.5	
1251–1300	10.2	10	10.8	11.1	12.5	
1301–1350	11.2	10	10.1		12	
1351–1400	4.5	10	9.7	10	10	
1401–1450		6.2	8.5	10	8	
1451–1500	4	6	6.5	9.2	6	
1501–1550	4.6	6	5	8.2	6.5	
1551–1600	5.5	6.2	5	8.3	6.5	7.0
1601–1650	8.7	5.9	5	6.5	6.2	4.8
1651–1700	6	4.4		4.9	5.8	4.1
1701–1750	4.9	4.3		4.8	4.6	3.0
1751–1800	4.4	5.7		4.2	4.3	2.2

Sources: Allen 1988; Alvarez Vázquez 1987; Baum 1985: 33; Benassar 1967: 257ff.; Clark 1988, Clark 1998: 74; Hoffman, Postel-Vinay, and Rosenthal 2000; Homer and Sylla 2005: 119–120; Malanima 2002: 280; Neumann 1865: 266–267, 272; Schnapper 1957; Winter 1895: 172; Zuijderzuijn 2009; author's database.

Comparing the data it is striking to note that in Italy during the commercial revolution the cost of long-term borrowing was higher than elsewhere. It is not easy at all to find an explanation. It is likely that during the period of expansion the money demand was too high with respect to supply, although the area witnessed a considerable degree of monetization. What stands out, however, is that Italian interest rates lined up with European levels during the early modern period, as credit demand in the peninsula dropped as a result of the massive shift of capital from commerce to land (Malanima 2002: 280–281).

Did the birthplace of commercial and financial capitalism, therefore, fail to spread on a large scale the benefits of innovations? Although Italian borrowers did not enjoy more favorable conditions than the other Europeans, it is true that some financial institutions improved the working of markets. Starting from 1462, as the first *monte di pietà* (pawn shop) was established at Perugia, a network of institutions developed aiming to meet both consumer credit demand of poorer segments of population, helpless in the face of usurious credit, and the need of well-to-do people to invest their savings in risk-free funds. The pawn shops collected money from voluntary deposits, bequests, and charity ensuring a moderate yield, while they lent at a slightly higher rate to cover managing costs. It is interesting to note that initially credit was granted upon the oath of the borrower of being a member of the community, be it urban or rural, and using money for his own need. Soon, however, this constraint disappeared and also commercial investment was accepted. In the sixteenth century the *monti di pietà* opened their doors to wealthy borrowers seeking cheap loans (Prodi 2009: 160–161). While the *monti di pietà* addressed, at least in theory, people in difficulties, the international fairs of exchanges had as protagonists the great Genoese and Florentine bankers.

The fairs of exchanges can be rightly regarded as one of the highest examples of financial capitalism. They functioned as a clearing house between various European markets. Between the sixteenth and the seventeenth centuries the Genoese bankers dominated the fairs thanks to their relations with the Spanish Crown, the control over American silver, and the ability to mobilize enormous financial resources in the various war fronts of the Habsburgs. Skill in managing currencies and exchanges as well as a wide financial and information network constituted the pillars of the Genoese system. Their acquired expertise with the payment system of western Europe allowed the Genoese to create a permanent institution, the quarterly fairs, that facilitated not only bankers' investments, but also investments from a wide area of petty investors (Pezzolo and Tattara 2008). These institutional arrangements in the sixteenth century made exchange rates less volatile and, accordingly, lowered interest rates.

By the late seventeenth century Italy had achieved an articulated array of financial institutions ranging from consumer credit to international fairs of exchanges, although the primacy achieved in the Renaissance did not bring about a remarkable comparative economic advantage over other countries. The cost of capital in Italy was in line with the European average, but northern Europe implemented and diffused further financial innovations in a much more dynamic context, thanks to the expansion of the Atlantic economies (Neal 2000).

Innovations in a traditional society

During the late middle ages, central northern Italy witnessed the emergence of a new urban and mercantile society. It was a phenomenon – political for the communes and economic for the merchants – unparalleled in both past history and in Europe today. Despite factional struggles and conflicts between cities, the Italians succeeded in making a social and economic organization that permitted them to dominate the sea routes between the Levant and the North Sea. Organizational and technological innovations supported what has rightly been called a "commercial revolution." The social fabric that strengthened this phenomenon was constituted by a system of kin interrelations, friendship, and neighborhood, which formed an extraordinary stock of social capital. Similar to what was to occur in seventeenth-century England and in Golden Age Holland, where most financiers of the chartered companies had kin relations (Adams 2005, 82; Brenner, 1972, 372; Chaudhuri 1978, 21–22; Hejeebu 2005, 506; Rabb 1967, 97), Renaissance Italy had built the same structure.

Although such family and clientage relations have extensively been analyzed as fundamental elements of social structures and political practices, the attempts nevertheless to link this system to economic performance have been very few. A fabric formed of both formal (family, kin, and godkinship) and informal (friendship, clientage, neighborhood) relations characterized as much the political system as the economic world. The key principle – more or less manifest – was that of reciprocity. When in 1433 the Venetian merchant Andrea Barbarigo wrote to his correspondent in the Levant to take care of "my business on all accounts as you would wish me to do for you and on my part be assured that I will do good for you as if it were mine," he disclosed a tacit rule committing all the actors (*Lettere* 1951: 5). Young people who were introduced into the mercantile world were key elements of the exchange. A further letter shows how a merchant sent his son to a colleague stressing the reciprocity: "act like I would in the future for a son of yours" (*Lettere* 1957: 18). The system based on kinship therefore involved other people, so building a broad network of mutual relationships. This mechanism, allegedly typical of Mediterranean society, formed in its turn the basis of a wide trust exceeding the limits of kinship and neighborhood and thus involving those who held further relational capital as a fundamental asset. During the late middle ages in the main Italian cities a new system, one that combined the advantages of family firms with the formation of scale economies, had been forming.

Between the sixteenth and seventeenth centuries, however, the international market witnessed structural changes; the economic center began to move from the Mediterranean to the North Sea and new countries emerged in the international competition. Italy, though it did not undergo a dramatic decline and reacted positively to changes, showed its weakness and was heavily reduced in the new context. The Venetian network shrank and was replaced by Greek and Jewish operators; Florentines reduced their role in western Europe and maintained significant positions in eastern Europe; the Genoese saw a relevant reduction of their control radius as well. Thus, the network advantages decreased as did, as a consequence, the information flows and degree of trust among merchants. What was the response of the kith and kin system to new conditions? Although it is not easy to find an answer, it is evident that the transformation of the economic base of the elites into immovable (land) and movable (public and private credit) goods brought about the enhancement of constraints on family patrimonies. It is likely that some incentives to transmit skill and knowledge between generations, now become rentiers, weakened. This does not mean that trade disappeared, but its central role in urban and elite environments weakened. Italians' choices depended on economic changes in the international market and the awareness that the most dynamic sectors of long-distance trade were controlled by "Northerners."

In the manufacturing sector the guilds' role changed drastically. While in the middle ages they helped to reduce some transaction costs and to ease the transmission of knowledge, in the early modern period they became the tool to define a marked separation between masters and laborers, as well as to limit access to the higher ranks of professions to the former's offspring. During a prolonged period of difficulties, artisans of the guilds tended to privilege both the transmission of skill and knowledge and social status within the family as a defense of acquired positions (D'Amico 2000: 12). This phenomenon can be found as much in highly specialized sectors, such as glass-making (Trivellato

2000: 35), as in the whole sector, so as it is not surprising that in 1773 a great many Venetian masters were sons of masters (Tucci 1990: 833–836). The circulation of cadets as apprentices among master fellows could solve the problem of the transmission of the workshop among sons and, at the same time, cement alliances and solidarity among the members of the guild. This tendency toward professionalization, that is a criterion of social stratification, reduced both the flow of information, and consequently the degree of trust within the whole social system (Cerutti 1992: 190–205, 257–258), and the openness of the labor market to outsiders.

The central problem of early modern Italy was the low degree of openness of social and institutional structures. The transformation of guilds into organisms heavily controlled by a few families, the growing brakes on vertical mobility within political institutions, the narrowing of the chances to take profits from international trade were all signs of a tendency toward crystallization of Italian society. The lights of commercial and financial capitalism dimmed as a result of structural changes in international markets and because of the inability of Italian ruling groups to give up their advantageous positions at the local level. It would be, however, naïve to believe that the ruling groups could have behaved differently. Only after an exogenous shock, in this case the arrival of the Napoleonic troops, were the power relations and the structure of vested interests forced to modify. But the dramatic political changes created in the aftermath of the French invasions do not appear to have affected the economic field significantly; it would take a long time to for the seeds of economic innovation to take root in ground rendered infertile for centuries. Well into the nineteenth century, the Italian countryside, apart from some exceptions in Lombardy and Piedmont, was encumbered by legal requirements that were extremely unfavorable to peasants. Without their demand for goods and products, most of Italy suffered grave economic stagnation. Consider that in 1860 in Romagna a contract between the landowner and the peasant stated that the latter's family could not purchase textiles in the market without permission from the landowner (Giorgetti 1974: 70). A further evidence that the burden of the *ancien régime* had not yet been eliminated from social relationships and, therefore, from the economic structures of the new united state.

References

Abulafia, D. (1977). *The Two Italies*. Cambridge University Press.
Adams, J. (2005). *The Familial State: Ruling Families and Merchant Capitalism in Early Modern Europe*. Ithaca: Cornell University Press.

Ago, R. (1998). *Economia barocca. Mercato e istituzioni nella Roma del Seicento.* Rome: Donzelli.

Allen, R. (1988). "The Price of Freehold Land and the Interest Rate in Seventeenth and Eighteenth Centuries," *Economic History Review* 41: 33–50.

Alvarez Nogal, C. (2005). "Las compañías bancarias genovesas en Madrid a comienzos del siglo XVII," *Hispania* 65: 67–90.

Alvarez Vázquez, J. A. (1987). *Rentas, precios y crédito en Zamora en el antiguo régimen.* Zamora: Colegio Universitario.

Arrighi, G. (2004). "Spatial and Other 'Fixes' of Historical Capitalism," *Journal of World Systems Research* 10: 527–539.

Balard, M. (1978). *La Romanie génoise (XIIe–début du XVe s.).* Rome: Bibliothèque des Écoles françaises d'Athènes et de Rome.

(2006). "Il Banco di San Giorgio e le colonie d'Oltremare," in G. Felloni (ed.), *La Casa di San Giorgio. Il potere del credito.* Genoa: Società Ligure di Storia Patria, pp. 63–73.

Balestracci, D. (1984). *La zappa e la retorica. Memorie familiari di un contadino toscano del Quattrocento.* Florence: Salimbeni.

Battistini, F. (2003). *L'industria della seta in Italia nell'età moderna.* Bologna: Il Mulino.

Baum, H.-P. (1985). "Annuities in Late Medieval Hanse Towns," *Business History Review* 59: 24–48.

Bavel, J. P. B. van (2008). "The Organization and Rise of Land and Lease Markets in Northwestern Europe and Italy, c. 1000–1800," *Continuity and Change* 23: 13–53.

Becker, M. (1965). "Problemi della finanza pubblica fiorentina nella seconda metà del Trecento e dei primi del Quattrocento," *Archivio storico italiano* 123: 433–466.

Bellavitis, A. (2001). *Identité, mariage, mobilité sociale. Citoyennes et citoyens à Venise au XVIe siècle.* Rome: École Française de Rome.

(2004). "'Ars mechanica' e gerarchie sociali a Venezia tra XVI e XVII secolo," in M. Arnoux and P. Monnet (eds.), *Le technicien dans la cité en Europe occidentale, 1250–1650.* Rome: École Française de Rome, pp. 161–179.

Benassar, B. (1967). *Valladolid au siècle d'or. Une ville de Castille et sa campagne au XVIe siècle.* Paris: Mouton.

Berveglieri, R. (1995). *Inventori stranieri a Venezia, 1474–1788. Importazione di tecnologia e circolazione di tecnici, artigiani, inventori. Repertorio.* Venice: Istituto Veneto di scienze, lettere ed arti.

Besley, T. and S. Coate (1995). "Group Lending, Repayment Incentives and Social Collateral," *Journal of Development Economics* 46: 1–18.

Black, R. (2007). *Education and Society in Florentine Tuscany: Teachers, Pupils, and Schools, c. 1250–1500.* Leiden: Brill.

Blanshei, S. (1979). "Population, Wealth, and Patronage in Medieval and Renaissance Perugia," *Journal of Interdisciplinary History* 9: 597–619.

Blomquist, T. (1971). "Commercial Association in Thirteenth-century Lucca," *Business History Review* 45: 157–178.

Boone III, J. (1986). "Parental Investment and Elite Family Structure in Preindustrial States: A Case Study of Late Medieval Early-Modern Portuguese Genealogies," *American Anthropologist* 88: 859–878.

Boyer-Xambeau, M.-T., G. Deleplace, and L. Gillard (1986). *Monnaie privée et pouvoir des princes. L'économie des relations monétaires à la Renaissance.* Paris: CNRS.

Brenner, R. (1972). "The Social Basis of English Commercial Expansion, 1550–1650," *Journal of Economic History* 32: 361–384

Broadberry, S. N., B. Campbell, A. Klein, M. Overton, and B. van Leeuwen (2011). "British Economic Growth, 1270–1870." London School of Economics, www2.lse.ac.uk/economicHistory/whosWho/profiles/sbroadberry.aspx.

Bruce, T. (2006). "The Politics of Violence and Trade: Denia and Pisa in the Eleventh Century," *Journal of Medieval History* 32: 127–142.

Cammarosano, P. (1996). "Le origini della fiscalità pubblica delle città italiane," *Revista d'història medieval* 7: 39–52.

Carlsmith, C. (2010). *A Renaissance Education: Schooling in Bergamo, 1500–1650.* University of Toronto Press.

Carocci, S. (2004). "Poteri signorili e mercato della terra (Italia ed Europa Occidentale, secc. XI–XIV)," in S. Cavaciocci (ed.), *Il mercato della terra, secc. XIII–XVIII.* Florence: Le Monnier, pp. 193–221.

Carruthers, B. and N. Espeland (1991). "Accounting for Rationality: Double-entry Bookkeeping and the Rhetoric of Economic Rationality," *American Journal of Sociology* 97: 31–69.

Castellani, L. (1998). *Gli uomini d'affari astigiani. Politica e denaro fra il Piemonte e l'Europa (1270–1312).* Turin: Paravia.

Ceccarelli, G. (2009). "Dalla compagnia medievale alle Compagnie assicuratrici: famiglie mercantili e mercati assicurativi in una prospettiva europea (secc. XV–XVIII)," in S. Cavaciocchi (ed.), *La famiglia nell'economia europea, secc. XIII–XVIII / The Economic Role of the Family in the European Economy from the 13th to the 18th Centuries.* Florence University Press, pp. 389–408.

Cerutti, S. (1992). *Mestieri e privilegi. Nascita delle corporazioni a Torino, secoli XVII–XVIII.* Turin: Einaudi.

Chaudhuri, K. N. (1978). *The Trading World of Asia and the English East India Company, 1660–1760.* Cambridge University Press.

Cipolla, C. M. (1973). "The Professions: The Long View," *Journal of European Economic History* 2: 37–52.

Clark, G. (1988). "The Cost of Capital and the Medieval Agricultural Technique," *Explorations in Economic History* 25: 265–294.

(1998). "Land Hunger: Land as a Commodity and as a Status Good, England 1500–1910," *Explorations in Economic History* 35: 59–82.

Coleman, J. S. (1989). "Social Capital in the Creation of Human Capital," *American Journal of Sociology* 94: 95–120.

Court, R. (2004). "'Januensis ergo mercator': Trust and Enforcement in the Business Correspondence of the Brignole Family," *Sixteenth Century Journal* 35: 987–1003.

D'Amico, S. (2000). "Crisis and Transformation: Economic Organization and Social Structures in Milan, 1570–1610," *Social History* 25: 1–21.

Davids, K. (1995). "Shifts of Technological Leadership in Early Modern Europe," in K. Davids and J. Lucassen (eds.), *A Miracle Mirrored: The Dutch Republic in European Perspective.* Cambridge University Press, pp. 338–366.

Day, J. (1963). *Les douanes de Gênes, 1376–77.* Paris: Sevpen.

De Roover, R. (1974). *Business, Banking, and Economic Thought in Late Medieval and Early Modern Europe.* University of Chicago Press.

Degli statuti civili della serenissima republica di Genova (1622). Genoa: Pavoni.

Delille, G. (1988). *Famiglia e proprietà nel Regno di Napoli*. Turin: Einaudi.

Dini, B. (2001). *Manifattura, commercio e banca nella Firenze medievale*. Florence: Nardini.

Dotson, J. E. (1994). "Safety Regulations for Galleys in Mid-fourteenth Century Genoa: Some Thoughts on Medieval Risk Management," *Journal of Medieval History* 20: 52–62.

(2003). "Venice, Genoa and Control of the Sea in the Thirteenth and Fourteenth Centuries," in J. Hatterdorf and R. Unger (eds.), *War at Sea in the Middle Ages and the Renaissance*. Woolbridge: Boydell Press, pp. 119–135.

Doumerc, B. (1991). "Le galere da mercato," in A. Tenenti and U. Tucci (eds.), *Storia di Venezia. Il mare*. Rome: Istituto della Enciclopedia Italiana, pp. 357–93.

Emigh, R. (2003). "Property Devolution in Tuscany," *Journal of Interdisciplinary History* 23: 385–420.

Epstein, S. A. (1996). *Genoa and the Genoese, 958–1528*. Chapel Hill: University of North Carolina Press.

Federico, G. (1994). *Il filo d'oro. L'industria mondiale della seta dalla restaurazione alla grande crisi*. Venice: Marsilio.

Felloni, G. (1999). *Scritti di storia economica*. Genoa: Società Ligure di Storia Patria.

(2005). *Genova e la storia della finanza. Una serie di primati?* Genoa: Banco di San Giorgio.

Fratianni, M. (2006). "Government Debt, Reputation and Creditors' Protection: The Tale of San Giorgio," *Review of Finance* 10: 487–506.

Fukuyama, F. (1995). *Trust: The Social Virtues and the Creation of Prosperity*. New York: Free Press.

García Porras, A. and Fábregas García, A. (2010). "Genoese Trade Networks in the Southern Iberia Peninsula: Trade, Transmission of Technical Knowledge and Economic Interactions," *Mediterranean Historical Review* 25: 37–38.

Gascon, R. (1971). *Grand commerce et vie urbaine au XVIe siècle. Lyon et ses marchands (environs de 1520 – environs de 1580)*. Paris: Sevpen.

Gelderblom, O. (2003). "The Governance of Early Modern Trade: The Case of Hans Thijs, 1556–1611," *Enterprise and Society* 4: 606–639.

Ginatempo, M. (2000). *Prima del debito. Finanziamento della spesa pubblica e gestione del deficit nelle grandi città toscane (1200–1350 ca.)*. Florence: Olschki.

Giorgetti, G. (1974). *Contadini e proprietari nell'Italia moderna. Rapporti di produzione e contratti agarari dal secolo XVI a oggi*. Turin: Einaudi.

Goldthwaite, R. (1968). *Private Wealth in Renaissance Florence: A Study of Four Families*. Princeton University Press.

(1985). "Local Banking in Renaissance Florence," *Journal of European Economic History* 14: 5–55.

(1987). "The Medici Bank and the World of Florentine Capitalism," *Past and Present* 114: 3–31.

(2009). *The Economy of Renaissance Florence*. Baltimore: Johns Hopkins University Press.

Gonzáles de Lara, Y. (2008). "The Secret of the Venetian Success: A Public-order, Reputation-based Institution," *European Review of Economic History* 12: 247–285.

Goodman, J. (1981). "Financing Pre-modern European industry: An Example from Florence 1580–1660," *Journal of European Economic History* 10: 415–435.

Graziani, A.-M. (2006). "Ruptures et continuités dans la politique de Saint-Georges en Corse (1453–1562)," in G. Felloni (ed.), *La Casa di San Giorgio. Il potere del credito*. Genoa: Società Ligure di Storia Patria, pp. 75–90.

Greci, R. (1986). "Una famiglia mercantile nella Bologna del Duecento: i Principi," in G. Rossetti (ed.), *Spazio, società, potere nell'Italia dei Comuni*. Naples: Liguori, pp. 105–141.

Greif, A. (2006). *Institutions and the Path to the Modern Economy: Lessons from Medieval Trade*. Cambridge University Press.

Grendi, E. (1987). *La repubblica aristocratica dei genovesi*. Genoa: Il Mulino.

Grendler, F. P. (1989). *Schooling in Renaissance Italy: Literacy and Learning, 1300–1600*. Baltimore: Johns Hopkins University Press.

Heers, J. (1961). *Gênes au XVe siècle*. Paris: Sevpen.

Hejeebu, S. (2005). "Contract Enforcement in the English East India Company," *Journal of Economic History* 65: 496–523.

Herlihy, D. (1969). "Family Solidarity in Medieval Italian History," in D. Herlihy, R. Lopez, and V. Slessarev (eds.), *Economy, Society and Government in Medieval Italy*. Kent State University Press, pp. 173–184.

Hoffman, P., G. Postel-Vinay, and J.-L. Rosenthal (2000). *Priceless Markets: The Political Economy of Credit in Paris, 1660–1870*. University of Chicago Press.

Homer, S. and R. Sylla (2005). *A History of Interest Rates*. Hoboken, NJ: Wiley.

Hunecke, V. (1995). *Der venetianische Adel am Ende der Republik 1646–1797. Demographie, Familie, Haushalt*. Tübingen: Max Niemeyer Verlag.

Jacoby, D. (2009). "Venetian Commercial Expansion in the Eastern Mediterranean, 8th–11th centuries," in M. Mundell (ed.), *Byzantine Trade, 4th–12th Centuries: The Archaeology of Local, Regional and International Exchange*. Farnham: Ashgate, pp. 371–391.

Jones, P. (1997). *The Italian City-state: From Commune to Signoria*. Oxford: Clarendon Press.

Katele, I. (1988). "Piracy and the Venetian State: The Dilemma of Maritime Defence in the Fourteenth Century," *Speculum* 63: 865–889.

Kedar, B. (1976). *Merchants in Crisis: Genoese and Venetian Merchants of Affair and the Fourteenth-century Depression*. New Haven: Yale University Press.

Kent, W. (1977). *Household and Lineage in Renaissance Florence: The Family of the Capponi, Ginori, and Rucellai*. Princeton University Press.

Kirshner, J. (1977). "The Moral Problem of Discounting Genoese Paghe, 1450–1550," *Archivum Fratrum Praedicatorum* 47: 109–167.

Kuehn, T. (2008). *Heirs, Kin, and Creditors in Renaissance Florence*. Cambridge University Press.

Lane, F. (1945). "Venture Accounting in Medieval Business Management," *Bulletin of the Business Historical Society* 19: 164–173.

(1966). *Venice and History*. Baltimore, MD: Johns Hopkins University Press.

(1969). "The Crossbow in the Nautical Revolution of the Middle Ages," *Explorations in Economic History* 7: 161–171.

Lapini, A. (1900). *Diario fiorentino dal 252 al 1596*, Corazzini Giuseppe Odoardo (ed.). Florence: Sansoni.

La Roncière, C.-M. de (1977). "Une famille florentine au XIVe siècle. Les Velluti," in *Famille et parenté dans l'Occident medieval*. Rome: École française de Rome, pp. 227–48.

Lettere di commercio di Andrea Barbarigo mercante veneziano del '400 (1951), Sassi Salvatore (ed.). Naples: Arti grafiche La Nuovissima.

Lettere di mercanti a Pignol Zucchello (1336–1350) (1957). Morozzo della Rocca Raimondo (ed.). Venice: Comitato per la pubblicazione delle fonti relative alla storia di Venezia.

Leverotti, F. (1999). "Strutture familiari nel tardo medioevo italiano," *Revista de història medieval* 10: 233–264.

Lieber, A. E. (1968). "Eastern Business Practices and Medieval European Commerce," *Economic History Review*, ns 21: 230–243.

Litchfield, R. B. (1969). "Les investissements commerciaux des patriciens florentins au XVIIIe siècle," *Annales ESC* 24: 685–721.

(1986). *Emergence of a Bureaucracy: The Florentine Patricians, 1530–1790*. Princeton University Press.

Lopez, R. (1977). *The Commercial Revolution of the Middle Ages*. Cambridge University Press.

Luzzatti, M. (1971). *Giovanni Villani e la compagnia dei Buonaccorsi*. Rome: Istituto della Enciclopedia Italiana.

Luzzatto, G. (1954). *Studi di storia economica veneziana*. Padua: Cedam.

Machiavelli, N. (1962). *Istorie fiorentine*, ed. Franco Gaeta. Milan: Feltrinelli.

MacLeod, C. (1988). *Inventing the Industrial Revolution: The English Patent System, 1660–1800*. Cambridge University Press.

Malanima, P. (1982). *La decadenza di un'economia cittadina. L'industria di Firenze nei secoli XVI–XVIII*. Bologna: Il Mulino.

(2002). *L'economia italiana. Dalla crescita medievale alla crescita contemporanea*. Bologna: Il Mulino.

(2003). "Measuring the Italian Economy 1300–1861," *Rivista di storia economica* 19: 265–295.

(2011). "The Long Decline of a Leading Economy: GDP in Central and Northern Italy, 1300–1913," *European Review of Economic History* 15: 169–212.

Mallett, M. (1967). *The Florentine Galleys in the Fifteenth Century*. Oxford: Clarendon Press.

McLean, P. (2005). "Patronage, Citizenship, and the Stalled Emergence of the Modern State in Renaissance Florence," *Comparative Studies in Society and History* 47: 638–664.

McLean, P. and J. Padgett (1997). "Was Florence a Perfectly Competitive Market? Transactional Evidence from the Renaissance," *Theory and Society* 26: 209–244.

(2004). "Obligation, Risk, and Opportunity in the Renaissance Economy: Beyond Social Embeddedness to Network Co-constitution," in F. Dobbin (ed.), *The Sociology of Economy*. New York: Russell Sage Foundation, pp. 193–227.

(2006). "Organizational Invention and Elite Transformation: The Birth of Partnership Systems in Renaissance Florence," *American Journal of Sociology* 111: 1463–1568.

Melis, F. (1962). *Aspetti della vita economica medievale (Studi nell'Archivio Datini di Prato)*. Siena: Monte dei Paschi di Siena.

(1984). *L'economia fiorentina nel Rinascimento*. Florence: Le Monnier.

Mineo, I. (1995). "Stati e lignaggi in Italia nel tardo medioevo. Qualche spunto comparativo," *Storica* 1: 55–82.

Molà, L. (2007). "Stato e impresa. Privilegi per l'introduzione di nuove arti e brevetti," in P. Braunstein and L. Molà (eds.), *Il Rinascimento italiano e l'Europa. III: Produzione e tecniche*. Treviso: Colla, pp. 533–572.

Molho, A. (1994). *Marriage Alliance in Late Medieval Florence*. Cambridge, MA: Harvard University Press.

Mueller, R. (1997). *The Venetian Money Market: Banks, Panics, and the Public Debt, 1200–1500*. Baltimore: Johns Hopkins University Pres.

(2010). *Immigrazione e cittadinanza nella Venezia medievale*. Rome: Viella.

Neal, L. (2000). "How it all Began: The Monetary and Financial Architecture of Europe during the First Global Capital Markets, 1648–1815," *Financial History Review* 7: 117–140.

Neumann, M. (1865). *Geschichte des Wuchers in Deutschland bis zur Begründung der heutigen Zinsengesetze (1654)*. Halle: Verlag der Buchhandlung des Waisenhauses.

North, D. (1990). *Institutions, Institutional Change and Economic Performance*. Cambridge University Press.

Ogilvie, S. (2011). *Institutions and European Trade: Merchant Guilds, 1000–1800*. Cambridge University Press.

Owen Hughes, D. (1975). "Urban Growth and Family Structure in Medieval Genoa," *Past and Present* 66: 3–28.

(1976). "Struttura familiare e sistemi di successione ereditaria nei testamenti dell'Europa medievale," *Quaderni storici* 9: 929–952.

Padgett, J. (2010). "Open Elite? Social Mobility, Marriage, and Family in Florence, 1282–1494," *Renaissance Quarterly* 63: 357–411.

Parker, G. (1988). *The Military Revolution: Military Innovation and the Rise of the West, 1500–1800*. Cambridge University Press.

Petralia, G. (1989). *Banchieri e famiglie mercantili nel Mediterraneo aragonese. L'emigrazione dei Pisani in Sicilia nel Quattrocento*. Pisa: Pacini.

Petti Balbi, G. (2000). *Negoziare fuori patria. Nazioni e genovesi in età medievale*. Bologna: Clueb.

Pezzolo, L. (2005). "Bonds and Government Debt in Italian City States, 1250–1650," in W. Goetzmann and G. Rouwenhorst (eds.), *The Origins of Value: Financial Innovations that Created the Modern Capital Market*. Oxford University Press, pp. 145–163.

(2006). *Una finanza d'ancien régime. La repubblica di Venezia fra XV e XVIII secolo*. Naples: Edizioni Scientifiche Italiane.

(2007). "Violenza, costi di protezione e declino commerciale nell'Italia del Seicento," *Rivista di storia economica*, 23: 111–124.

Pezzolo, L. and G. Tattara (2008). "'Una fiera senza luogo'. Was Bisenzone an International Capital Market in Sixteenth-century Italy?" *Journal of Economic History* 68: 1098–1123.

Poni, C. (2009). *La seta in Italia. Una grande industria prima della rivoluzione industriale*. Bologna: Il Mulino.

Povolo, C. (1985). "Vincoli di stirpe, legame degli affetti," in C. Povolo (ed.), *Dueville. Storia e identificazione di una comunità del passato*. Vicenza: Pozza, pp. 733–854.

Prodi, P. (2009). *Settimo non rubare. Furto e mercato nella storia dell'Occidente*. Bologna: Il Mulino.

Pryor, J. (1977). "The Origins of the Commenda Contract," *Speculum*, 52: 5–37.

Rabb, T. K. (1967) *Enterprise and Empire: Merchant and Gentry Investment in the Expansion of England, 1575–1630*. Cambridge, MA: Harvard University Press.

Romano, D. (1987). *Patricians and Popolani: The Social Foundations of the Venetian Renaissance State*. Baltimore: Johns Hopkins University Press.

Sapelli, G. (1997). *Storia economica dell'Italia contemporanea.* Milan: Bruno Mondadori.

Sapori, A. (1955). *Studi di storia economica.* Florence: Sansoni.

(1967). "Dalla 'compagnia' alla 'holding'," in A. Sapori, *Studi di storia economica,* III. Florence: Sansoni, pp. 121–133.

Schiaffino, A. (1624). *Memorie di Genova.* www.quaderni.net/WebCAB/1624.htm.

Schnapper, B. (1957). *Les rentes au XVIe siècle. Histoire d'un instrument de credit.* Paris: Sevpen.

Shaw, C. (2005). "Principles and Practice in the Civic Government of Fifteenth-century Genoa," *Renaissance Quarterly* 58: 51.

Sieveking, H. (1905–6). *Studio sulle finanze genovesi nel medioevo e in particolare sulla Casa di S. Giorgio.* Genoa: Società Ligure di Storia Patria.

Soldani, M. E. (2011). *Uomini d'affari e mercanti toscani a Barcellona nel Quattrocento.* Barcelona: CSIC.

Spallanzani, M. (1978). "Una grande azienda fiorentina del Trecento. Carlo Strozzi e compagni," *Ricerche storiche* 8: 417–436.

Spufford, P. (1995). "Access to Credit and Capital in the Commercial Centres of Europe," in K. Davids and J. Lucassen (eds.), *A Miracle Mirrored: The Dutch Republic in European Perspective.* Cambridge University Press, pp. 303–337.

Statuti di Padova (1551). Padua: Fabriano.

Tangheroni, M. (1996). *Commercio e navigazione nel Medioevo.* Rome-Bari: Laterza.

Thompson, E. (1993). *Customs in Common.* London: Penguin.

Trivellato, F. (2000). *Fondamenta dei vetrai. Lavoro, tecnologia e mercato a Venezia tra Sei e Settecento.* Rome: Donzelli.

Tucci, U. (1962). "Alle origini dello spirito capitalistico a Venezia: la previsione economica," in *Studi in onore di Amintore Fanfani.* Milan: Vita e pensiero. Vol. III, pp. 545–557.

(1990). "Carriere popolane e dinastie di mestiere a Venezia," in A. Guarducci (ed.), *Gerarchie economiche e gerarchie sociali, secoli XII–XVIII.* Florence: Le Monnier, pp. 817–851.

(1991). "Venezia nel Cinquecento: una città industriale?" in V. Branca and C. Ossola (eds.), *Crisi e rinnovamento nell'autunno del rinascimento a Venezia.* Florence: Olschki, pp. 61–83.

Vallet, E. (1999). *Marchands vénitiens en Syrie à la fin du XVe siècle.* Paris: Adhe.

Van der Wee, H. (1993). *The Low Countries in the Early Modern World.* Aldershot: Variorum.

Van Doosselaere, Q. (2009). *Commercial Agreements and Social Dynamics in Medieval Genoa.* Cambridge University Press.

Wickham, C. (1981). *Early Medieval Italy: Central Power and Local Society 400–1000.* London: Macmillan.

(1987). "Vendite di terra e mercato della terra in Toscana nel secolo XI," *Quaderni storici* 12: 355–396.

Williamson, D. (2010). "The Financial Structure of Commercial Revolution: Financing Long-distance Trade in Venice 1190–1220 and Venetian Crete 1278–1400," mimeo.

Winter, G. (1895). "Zur Geschichte des Zinsfusses im Mittelalter," *Zeitschrift für Sozial- und Wirtschaftsgeschichte* 4: 161–175.

Zanden, J. L. van (2009). *The Long Road to Industrial Revolution: The European Economy in a Global Perspective, 1000–1800.* Leiden: Brill.

Zuijderduijn, C. J. (2009). *Medieval Capital Markets: Markets for Renten, State Formation and Private Investment in Holland (1300–1500).* Leiden: Brill.

II

The Low Countries

OSCAR GELDERBLOM AND JOOST JONKER

Introduction

The profound economic breakthrough of the industrial revolution tends to obscure the groundwork of market development on which it was based. Though much slower and more uneven, this transformation encompassed the switch from autarkic or tributary modes of production to voluntary market exchange of goods, labor, land, and capital. Radiating out from northern Italy, the Low Countries, and Britain, the development of product and factor markets also affected urbanized regions of Spain, France, and Germany, but bypassed many rural areas and did not penetrate deeply into eastern Europe until the nineteenth century.[1]

The dynamics of European market development before 1800 are demonstrated to good effect by the Low Countries. Despite the limited size of this area, it offers a unique opportunity to explore long-term changes of market institutions under very different political and economic circumstances. A patchwork of independent countries and duchies in the late middle ages, the Low Countries in the fifteenth and sixteenth centuries displayed an ever-greater legal, political, and economic unity, until a civil war, the Dutch Revolt (1568–1572), set the northern and southern part of the Netherlands on very different paths of economic and political development. In the north, the Dutch Republic became what has been termed the first modern economy,

This work was supported by a grant from The Netherlands Institute for Advanced Study in the Humanities and Social Sciences (NIAS) in Wassenaar. The authors thank Bas van Bavel, Maarten Prak, and participants in the urban history seminar at Antwerp University for their valuable comments and suggestions.

1 For a general treatment of early market development see de Vries 2001. Cf. also Braudel's emphasis on the existence of highly localized pockets of economic growth before 1800 (Braudel 1979). Cf. for Italy: Epstein 2000; for the Low Countries de Vries and Van der Woude 1997; for France: Hoffman 1996; for Spain: Grafe 2012; for Russia: Dennison 2011.

while in the south the virtual stoppage of maritime trade forced a reorganization of the economy that compensated for some of the ground lost, yet could not prevent a prolonged crisis that lasted until 1750.

The dynamics of European market development before 1800 are demonstrated to good effect by the Low Countries, which underwent several distinct phases of evolution and in addition present a highly illuminating contrast between a considerable degree of economic integration among regions and continuing local variations in the organization of markets.[2] There were four growth phases between 1000 and 1800, starting with Flanders's late medieval heyday which, around 1300, culminated in Bruges becoming northwestern Europe's leading entrepôt. The second upswing started during the late fifteenth century with the rise of Antwerp as commercial and financial metropolis. Following the political split between north and south with the Dutch Revolt, the economic center of gravity shifted away from Brabant and Flanders to Holland, initiating a third phase of dynamic growth there, while the southern Low Countries endured an era of comparative stagnation. However, toward the end of the eighteenth century positions reversed. The south entered a new, fourth phase, entrepreneurs in Liège and Ghent pioneering an industrial transformation, whereas the north languished until its belated industrialization during the later nineteenth century.

Now we might have expected the area's geographic diversity and political and legal fragmentation, preconditions it shared with Europe at large, to have handicapped the development of markets. Indeed, constraints on capitalist development did exist, notably in regions where agricultural productivity remained low and the rural elite captured most of the surplus. However, we argue in this chapter that diversity and fragmentation promoted their development, in two distinct ways. First, the abundance of navigable waterways crisscrossing the area, in conjunction with very diverse local resource endowments, stimulated competition and regional specialization based on the market exchange of farm products, raw materials, and manufactures as well as, on a more moderate scale, labor and capital (Blockmans 2010b; van Bavel 2010a). The second way, closely connected to the first, was the nature of the interregional competition itself. Historians have often emphasized the negative effects of urban rivalry on economic performance, but there were

---

2 For a quantitative appraisal of the growth performance of various parts of the Low Countries until the nineteenth century: Aerts 2004; de Vries and van der Woude 1997; Lis and Soly 1997b; Mokyr 1976; van der Wee 1963, 1988; van Zanden and van Riel 2004.

marked benefits to competition within the Low Countries, notably in the realm of contracting institutions. Because most of the area was accessible in more ways than one, urban councils and territorial overlords had to remain on their toes if they wanted to maintain their position in commercial networks, while the towns possessed a keen interest in developing institutions to support market exchange (Davids 1996: 100–112; Dijkman 2011; Gelderblom 2013; Stabel 1997; 161–172). For this purpose contracting institutions were borrowed from nearby regions and adapted to local circumstances.

These factors gave the Low Countries a head start but, if market evolution was more pronounced there than elsewhere in Europe, this was a difference in degree, not kind. That difference was rooted in its specific conditions, notably the large number of towns with considerable legal and political autonomy whose connectivity was much higher than that of towns in, say, the German lands, France, or the interior of Spain. Because of these favorable circumstances the Low Countries did not need a strong central government or major improvements in transportation technology to stimulate economic exchange across regions. Conversely, the area's comparative advantage diminished once the governments of rival states began fostering their own economic interests by excluding Low Countries merchants and manufacturers from domestic markets and by improving their own infrastructure.

Cross-country connections

Geography forms the basis of the Low Countries' diversity.[3] Northern and western parts of the area are flat and lie low, partly below sea level, but as we move east and notably south the land becomes first gently undulating and then mountainous towards the Meuse valley. Most areas have easy access to the sea, either via inlets or by way of the rivers and, increasingly from the early middle ages, man-made canals that crisscross the country. Soil types vary from rich clay and loam to marshy peatlands, poor sand soils, and rock-strewn hillsides. Widely different patterns of settlement and exploitation across the area reflected this diversity of soils. Combined with the ease of transporting surpluses, this variety stimulated specialization and exchange between regions, and in time also the emergence of bigger settlements.

---

3 Cf. van Bavel (2010a: 15–50) for the definitive statement and references to the older literature.

The southern part already possessed towns in Roman times, but following the empire's collapse most of them disappeared with the exception of those in the southern tip of Flanders. There, walled settlements at Cambrai, Tournai, and Arras held on long enough to take part in the urban revival that started to manifest itself from the seventh century onward. In the Meuse valley fortresses remained and served as a basis for a repopulation at places like Huy, Namur, Tongeren, and Maastricht (van Bavel 2010a: 102). Elsewhere, notably in the area north of the River Rhine not conquered by the Romans, the urban revival favored more recent nodes of settlement, such as castles, manors, episcopal seats, or abbeys. Whatever their origin, the early emerging towns shared one salient characteristic. They were all situated to profit from passing trade, i.e. on navigable water. A finely woven network of towns emerged, linked by waterways and serving hinterlands with market facilities and administrative functions. One such cluster centered on Ypres, Lille, Arras, and Cambrai in the southern Flanders–Artois area, another on Bruges and Ghent in northern Flanders, a third one along the Meuse river, and a fourth one emerged a little later on the eastern side of the Zuider Zee.

Over time these towns gained considerable freedom of action in shaping the local institutional framework for the organization of exchange. The growth of towns offered opportunities which overlords, be they clerical or temporal, could not afford to let go, such as a boost to tax revenue, the possibility of raising debt, the provision of key services such as administration and education, and support against rival lords. As a consequence all towns benefitted from the protection and favors of their overlords. In return, overlords bestowed privileges on the towns in their territory (Dijkman 2011: 389–392; van Bavel 2010a: 110–113). These privileges ranged from fairly simple economic benefits such as a trade entrepôt, a weekly local market, or a regional fair, to comprehensive codifications of a town's legal and administrative rules, usually referred to as town charters.

Urban charters resulted from combining the bottom-up shaping of institutions within the towns and by the communities themselves with a top-down contribution from the overlords concerned. However, they also show a third, horizontal factor driving the institutional dynamics of medieval towns, and that is the collaboration and competition between towns. The articles of urban charters were usually lifted from other codifications, resulting in families of related, very similar sets of rules stretching across the Low Countries. There were at least six such families. Some of the more extended networks, like the well-known one fanning out from the Deventer charter first granted in 1123, linked up to fifteen towns together in a common legal framework. This often transcended the boundaries between territories on purpose, with towns importing charters from elsewhere so as to emphasize their independence, distance themselves from powerful neighbors, and position themselves differently on regional markets (van Engen and Rutte 2008: 74–78). Zutphen, for instance, did not in 1190 adopt the charter from nearby Deventer, but the one from Roermond, more than a hundred kilometers to the south as the crow flies.

Towns not only fashioned their relationship with overlords after each other's examples; their initial emulation also led to a more continuous calibration of institutional arrangements between towns. The links between the members of a charter family were more or less regularly maintained by a custom called *hofvaart*, literally court trip, in which officials from affiliated towns visited their parent town to discuss points of law. Thus magistrates from the island of Texel at the northern tip of Holland would consult their immediate forebear Alkmaar. If that failed to settle the matter, Texel and Alkmaar officials travelled together to Haarlem, the next one up, and if necessary with their Haarlem colleagues to Louvain in Brabant, the parent of them all. Though the *hofvaart* mechanism must have helped to achieve a degree of legal homogeneity between the members of one family, the number of charter families suggests that heterogeneity continued to be the norm. But the point really is that urban officials across the Low Countries knew well enough how things worked elsewhere and had a choice if they wanted to stimulate trade by optimizing local conditions.

Thus the urban charter families are a striking manifestation of the information flows that facilitated the exchange of legal concepts and other institutional arrangements among the diverse regions of the Low Countries. These families were possibly the most important conduit, but definitely not the only one. Overland trade routes were another. Town officials along the Dutch section of the cattle route from Denmark to Cologne and Brabant met regularly to smooth trade flows (Benders 1998: 63, 64, 73, 74; Gijsbers 1999: 33–38). The Church was yet another, different one. Financial techniques like the short-term lease, the *rente* or real estate bond, and the property mortgage spread between monasteries in a way that suggests that these organizations exchanged information on how best to manage resources (Rijpma 2012: 160–167: van Bavel 2009: 192–194; Vercauteren 1947: 226–227). The guilds, on the other hand, do not appear to have organized regular information flows by having trainees travel around, as they did in for instance France or Germany, but given the scale of migration and notably the high mobility of artisans they probably saw no need for formal arrangements (Epstein and Prak 2008: 16–17; Lis and Soly 1997; Lucassen 1987; cf. Stabel 2004: 198–204). Consequently, the process of administrative harmonization and centralization introduced by the dukes of Burgundy when they began to organize the various principalities of the Low Countries into a more coherent territorial unit during the fifteenth century really came on top of much older structures that had already forged links between them.

Land markets

Though Low Countries land markets were, as elsewhere, somewhat shielded from competition because land cannot be shifted, they were not immune to competitive pressures. The relative ease of communication and the ready availability across the Low Countries of an array of commercial institutions for marketing agricultural produce meant that the economic and social effects of land reclamation, new institutions governing access to land, new crops or farming techniques, new forms of demand, or the opening of new markets would be felt from one region to the next. Throughout the Low Countries farmers stood to gain from specialization but the extent to which commercial opportunities were grasped varied greatly. Differences in soil quality and in social property relations dampened the commercial impact in one region, tweaked the effects in another, leading to wide differences in land markets across the Low Countries (Hoppenbrouwers and van Zanden 2001; van Bavel 2010a: 86–93).

During the early middle ages no such thing as clearly defined and absolute property rights to land existed. As a rule various parties held different kinds of rights to a particular plot, such as the right to exploit it, to use a part or all of it in a particular season or all year round, to receive a share of its produce, to alienate it, to have a say over its alienation amounting to preemption or even retrospective purchase, to have the right of way, or the right to inherit any or some of these rights (Godding 1987: 150–151). Those rights overlapped with each other and might be bundled with similar or other rights to other plots, and they might depend on oral traditions, not on written documents, so transferring them was difficult (van Bavel 2010a: 51–52). The degree of this fragmentation of property rights to land differed across the Low Countries. In some areas, notably parts of Flanders, Brabant, and the Guelders river delta, well-organized lordly manors occupied most or all of the land and claimed possession of most of the rights, or else at least power over them in the form of binding transfer procedures. Elsewhere, Holland for instance, manors were weaker and the fragmentation consequently greater. Or they might be entirely absent, which was the case in Friesland and the sandy regions of marginal farming in Drenthe, eastern Overijssel, the Veluwe, and the Campine. There rights to land tended to remain undifferentiated, often communal, sometimes until well into the nineteenth century (van Zanden 1991, 1999; cf. however, Bieleman 1990).

From the eleventh century onward the manorial framework declined until by 1400 only a few relics remained, even in areas where manorialism had been strong (van Bavel 2007: 289–290). We do not know all the causes of the manorial decline, but it had at least partly natural origins. Here, soil erosion undermined the manors' economic viability, there flooding wiped their land away, elsewhere subsidence and rising groundwater tables forced farmers to let the land return to wilderness. Contributing factors include the rise of towns, which by offering an escape to hard-pressed peasants siphoned off the manorial labor supply. Aspiring monarchs also strained manors by rolling back feudal prerogatives, for instance setting up public courts to replace the manorial jurisdiction over property disputes. The response of manorial lords to these challenges varied, both in its timing, its precise form, and in its specific consequences, but everywhere it had the same generic effect, that of giving an impetus to properly defining different rights to land, including ownership and tenure, thereby opening up access to land to competitive pressures, that is to say, boosting market-oriented farming by having tenants increase productivity in order to compete for land. We will first analyze why and how lordly responses varied, and then discuss their impact on the emergence of land markets.

The patterns of response, the likely motives behind them, and their effects are best understood by looking at the available options. Large landowners in the middle ages could exploit their holdings in three different ways, analytically alternative modes, though in practice landowners often mixed elements of them (van Bavel 2009: 200–202). First, they could run the land as a manor, recruiting labor by exacting manorial services from the peasants in their territory. Second, they could exploit their land themselves with hired labor. Third, they could lease out their lands to peasants, either in hereditary or in limited tenure. A fourth option crept in through the desire to reclaim land derelict through flooding or rising water tables. In such cases the territorial prince to whom such land had reverted licensed one or more entrepreneurs to reclaim it, granting them full ownership of the soil in return for a token recognition payment. In the Flanders coastal area the reclamation was as often as not undertaken by urban investors who then rented out the plots to peasants on short leases, but the Holland-Utrecht peat lands area was reclaimed and settled by owner occupiers from the eleventh century onwards (Dekker and Baetens 2010; Thoen 1988; van Bavel 2010a; van der Linden 1956).

The transition from feudalism to market orientation meant that landlords moved increasingly from option one to options two, three, and/or four: they needed to find ways other than the manorial exchange of service for safety to attract labor for exploiting the soil. The short-term lease of option three, and option four, was most conducive to widening the access to land. The spread of short-term leasing is the best proxy we have for gauging when and where landlords moved, and in which direction. Where the manorial system was strong, landlords as a rule stuck to the first and second options as long as they could. But their success in doing so depended rather on circumstances, more specifically on what happened in their immediate surroundings. In urbanized counties such as Artois, Flanders, and Brabant, for instance, landlords moved early towards a mixed exploitation. As often as not they succeeded in reinforcing their position, though sometimes they lost it through disastrous timing. Landlords in parts of southern Flanders and Artois let out their land in hereditary leases at fixed rents before a period of high inflation set in from the late twelfth century, so manorialism in these areas declined quickly without producing the rise of short-term leasing associated with its decline elsewhere (Thoen 2001; van Bavel 2009: 200–201). As a consequence of this and other circumstances the balance between various modes of exploitation differed considerably between the regions and even within regions. By 1500 short-term leasing dominated in coastal Flanders, covering an estimated 80–90 percent of the soil as against only 40–50 percent in inland Flanders – a level similar to that of Brabant (30 percent) and Artois (40–50 percent) (Soens and Thoen 2009: 32–39; van Bavel 2009: 191).

An equally strong difference characterized the Guelders river area. Here the exploitation of peasants through manorial services remained strong in the east, but landlords in the western part faced mounting competition for labor from the free ownership offered to settlers in the nearby Holland-Utrecht reclamation area, so they changed tack and started leasing early (van Bavel 2009: 202). Conversely, Holland's early market orientation is linked to the absence of manorialism and tied to the dominance of peasant ownership (van Bavel and van Zanden 2004). However, the short lease spread slowly there, averaging 30–40 percent by 1500, because landowners found it difficult to enforce such terms in an environment used to hereditary leases or full ownership. Only when the government started backing landowners during the sixteenth century did the short lease find wider adoption (van Bavel 2009: 199–200). Short-time leasing spread widely in one area without manors, coastal Friesland, where by 1500 it covered 80–90 percent of the land, so the better definition of property rights necessary for increased productivity there did not depend on being derived from feudal origins. But adjoining Groningen, also without manors and with very similar soil conditions, had a totally different land market dominated by hereditary leases and only 30 percent short-term leasing (van Bavel 2009: 191, 199–200). Neither Friesland nor Groningen were urbanized, at least not nearly to the same degree as for instance Flanders or Brabant, so the presence of towns was at most a contributing factor in some cases, not a decisive one.

Summing up, judging by the spread of short-term leasing, manorialism had been replaced by other, more market-oriented forms of exploitation across the entire area by 1500, opening up access to land. This is not to say that the land market worked smoothly everywhere; we simply do not know. Though short-term leasing must have stimulated a better definition of property rights and other rights to land, the sale and purchase of real estate, and especially farm land, often remained difficult until well into the nineteenth century on account of the variety of parties which a transaction might have to involve (Godding 1987: 150). In areas where manorialism had been strong it was expensive, too, landlords putting a levy of 10–16 percent on land transfers. Land sales rose slowly in the early modern era, but even in the most dynamic regions they rarely affected more than 2 percent per year of all land (van Bavel 2003a: 130–131, 134–135). Indeed, perhaps short-term leasing spread because it avoided the complications of transferring ownership. Attitudes toward the buying and selling of land also needed to change, and the pace of change is likely to have differed considerably from one place to the next. Even in a commercial center like Ghent the idea of treating real estate like any other commodity penetrated rather slowly (Howell 2010: 19–42). Our key point is really that, when manorialism disappeared, the social, economic, legal, and geographic diversity of the Low Countries combined to produce wide differences in land markets, even between neighboring areas. The uneven spread of short leases underlines that necessary legal and economic concepts had spread over the entire country, but local conditions determined whether or not they were applied.

We may thus conclude that, while there were plenty of opportunities for market-oriented production throughout the Low Countries, the creation of well-functioning land markets to capture the gains from agricultural specialization depended on a combination of four factors: first, property rights and contracting institutions such as the relative strength of manorialism and legal concepts such as the short-term lease; second, social property relations, say the power of large landowners or the presence of urban investors on the market; third, conceptions about the nature of land and the proper order of society, for instance the resistance to treating land similarly to movables, or Holland's dominant peasant proprietorship retarding the spread of short leasing; and fourth, local contingencies, like soil quality, environmental constraints, or the unfortunate timing of hereditary leases in parts of southern Flanders and Artois. Different combinations of these four basic determinants produced very different outcomes: in Flanders land reclamation reinforced urban power over the surrounding countryside, while in Holland it bolstered the position of owner occupiers against both feudal lords and neighboring towns. This particular difference in power proved enduring, for Holland's large-scale reclamations during the seventeenth century, though financed by urban merchants, did not really strengthen the position of the cities concerned (van Zwet 2009). However, similar outcomes did not necessarily have similar roots: short-term leasing in Friesland originated in, and led to, social property relations totally different from those in the Guelders river area.

The rise of wage labor

One of the key differences between feudalism and capitalism is the extent to which people work for wages.[4] Feudal manors and similarly self-supporting economic units such as monasteries usually included a number of artisans and workshops for leatherworking or textile production within their domain, but this labor would be bound to the lord and earned no wages beyond the manor's produce consumed. We can thus gauge the advance of capitalism in the Low Countries by considering the switch from feudal services to labor paid in kind or in money.[5]

From the thirteenth century onwards the importance of wage labor rose steadily everywhere in the Low Countries. Its timing and rate of growth, however, differed markedly between regions and even within regions. During the sixteenth century wage labor had risen to an estimated third of all labor performed in the Low Countries, but its incidence still varied greatly, between peaks of more than 50 percent in Holland and the Guelders river area to at most 25 percent in inland Flanders (van Bavel 2003b). This disparity was largely the result of the way in which property rights to land evolved. In

4 For the rise of wage labor as a key element in the transition debate, compare van Bavel 2010b, with references to the older literature.
5 This may be done by looking at the relative importance of coins minted for wage payments in various regions, as Lucassen 2007 shows.

areas where peasants were able to hold on to land, their holdings fragmented to such an extent that households soon possessed far more labor than their farmsteads required, pushing individual members into other employment for part or most of their time.[6] These peasant economies possessed a large and hidden labor reserve, the extent of whose employment depended on the fluctuations of business in the wider economy (Hoppenbrouwers 1992: 264–273). Over time the phenomenon of peasants working part time in other sectors disappeared. It characterized the Holland economy until the late sixteenth century, but continued in inland Flanders for another two centuries, in Twente and the northern part of Brabant until after 1800, and in eastern Brabant, Drenthe, and the Veluwe, with their poor sandy soils, later still (Hoppenbrouwers 1992: 498–499, 678; Stabel 2001: 146–147, based on Thoen 1988; van Bavel 2007: 289–294, with references to the older literature).

Textiles, especially linen weaving, dominated inland Flanders, where it may have provided up to 40 percent of the population with additional income, whereas tapestry weaving in the region may have employed another 5 to 10 percent of the rural workforce part time (van Bavel 2003b: 1120–1122). These peasant families combined subsistence grain growing with some marketing of cash crops and work in the manufacturing sector. Tapestry weaving was mostly wage work, but in linen weaving and in the preparation of wool for urban cloth production peasants worked as independent craftsmen with their own capital and tools, though, for reasons that will become clear soon, their remuneration lay considerably below what waged urban craftsmen earned (van Bavel 2003b: 1145–1150). Elsewhere, textile production, though important, dominated to a lesser extent. Brabant, for instance, had an important brick-making industry near Antwerp, and peasant households in the Holland area between Rotterdam, Leiden, and Utrecht also supplemented their income with seasonal employment in brick works (Hollestelle 1961: 38–44; Limberger 2001: 163–165). For a long time Holland's fishing and shipping sectors also provided a ready source of part-time peasant employment (Boon 1996: 150–162). During the eighteenth century thousands of cottagers in the Liège hinterland produced nails (van Bavel 2003b: 1110).

In other areas the decline of feudalism consolidated the land into large farms and eliminated peasant holdings, structuring rural labor in an entirely

---

6 Underlying this analysis is the distinction between a peasant model and a specialization model, as drawn by de Vries 1974: 4–17. For the various permutations of these two models within the Low Countries: Hoppenbrouwers and van Zanden (2001). In a more detailed study of Brabant in the sixteenth century Limberger (2008) actually finds the coexistence within one region of both models.

different form. The rise of short-term leasing in the Guelders river area, for instance, concentrated leaseholds in the hands of increasingly wealthy tenant farmers and forced the remainder of the rural population off the land and into wage labor (van Bavel 2006). Between the fourteenth and sixteenth centuries wage labor developed similarly in Friesland farming and in the coastal Flanders manufacturing sector. Textiles again drove developments in the south of inland Flanders, employing the rural population of the Nieuwkerke area to produce heavy woolens and at Hondschoote to weave says (thin silk or satin cloths) during the fifteenth and sixteenth centuries (Stabel 2001: 143–146). Some villages even worked their way up to urban settlements on the back of textile production, as happened to Duffel in Antwerp's Brabant hinterland as a result of large-scale serge weaving (Limberger 2001: 161–163). In Holland the switch from an economy based on peasant by-employment to wage labor occurred only during the sixteenth century, when commercialization led to the rise of large-scale and specialized farms employing local landless laborers supplemented by seasonal migrant workers (de Vries 1974; van Bavel 2007: 289–294).

However, property rights to land were not the only factor shaping the labor market structure; the balance of economic and political power between towns and countryside mattered as well (de Vries 1974). Flanders's four major cities, for instance, subjected the labor markets in their hinterlands to their specific interests, which explains the low wages earned by the independent peasant cloth producers. Urban power effectively bridled some of the potential for economic growth and upward mobility in inland Flanders created by its easy access to foreign markets. By contrast, peasants in late medieval Holland also combined subsistence farming with waged work, but they had a much stronger economic position because the regional labor market offered them a range of options in several sectors, from primary production in fishing, dairy farming, and peat digging, via secondary-sector activities in cloth production and brick-making, to the service sector of shipping and even the public sector of digging and dyking. Moreover, the markets for the goods and services produced by peasants were not under urban control. Towns and even small villages competed in creating outlets, a key characteristic of Holland's rural economy that offered peasants a good chance to maintain themselves as independent producers and service providers (Dijkman 2011; van Bavel 2003: 1124, 1143).

The continuing importance of peasant production was one of the reasons why, until well into the early modern era, most people were self employed, whether as farmers, artisans, service providers, skilled or unskilled workers, at least part of their time (Brenner 2001; Du Plessis and Howell 1982; van Zanden 1993). When needed they would supplement that with wage labor or work swapped for one thing or another: payments in kind or in services, such as access to a piece of land, or the use of a cart, a boat. Thus, wage labor formed only a part of the way in which people earned their living, and they would switch in and out of it, depending on the availability of work, the wage offered, other opportunities, and personal circumstances such as family composition or specific needs (Lucassen 1982: 327–329).

From the later sixteenth century economic growth in the northern Low Countries boosted demand for wage labor. The maintenance of dykes and sluices had always absorbed some peasant labor, but now a series of ambitious land reclamation projects recruited large numbers of wage-laborers (van Bavel 2007: 297; van Zwet 2009). Shipping also scaled up. The sector had always been strong in the northern Low Countries, based on the comparative advantages of the rural labor surplus, a widespread willingness to invest private savings in *partenrederijen* or shipping companies, and the need to import grain to make up for the lack of local supplies caused by deteriorating soil conditions. By 1650 Holland boasted the largest merchant fleet of Europe with over three thousand ships connecting ports from Archangel in northern Russia to Constantinople and Aleppo in the Levant. Ocean shipping had become a multimillion guilder business employing thousands of sailors drawn from all over the northern Low Countries, and also drawing migrant workers from Germany and Scandinavia (Van Lottum 2007). Employment in fishing, whaling, and in river transportation also numbered thousands of workers (van Bochove 2009: 213; van Bochove and van Zanden 2006: 564).

Concentrated in the ports of the Meuse estuary around Rotterdam, the ports on the western side of the Zuider Zee, and the coastal towns of Friesland and Zeeland, the maritime labor market also had to meet a strong demand for sailors and soldiers from the navy and from the Dutch East India Company (VOC) (Bruijn and Lucassen 1980; Van Lottum 2007). During the initial stages of the Dutch Revolt the breakaway provinces in the north could still successfully defend their independence with a motley fleet of fishing vessels and merchantmen modified for warfare, but in the seventeenth century the republic built a navy manned by regular sailors and soldiers. Supplemented in wartime with converted merchant ships, employment could peak at some 20,000–24,000 men in the sixty out of a hundred years of armed conflict involving the Dutch during the seventeenth century (Bruijn 1993: 131). The Republic's standing army numbered about 30,000–40,000 men in peacetime, which could rise to 90,000 during war (Israel 1995: 263, 479, 498–499, 507, 602–603, 970; van Nimwegen 2010: 46).

The VOC also exerted a continuous, high demand for manpower. During the seventeenth century the company operated a fleet of eighty to a hundred ships, many of which were stationed in Asian waters (Parthesius 2010). Together with the men sent out to staff the numerous trading posts this required 3,000–4,000 men embarking annually in Dutch ports on company ships (Bruijn, Gaastra, and Schöffer 1987: 156). Between 1602 and 1795 the VOC employed a total of 975,000 men. Though aggregate maritime demand for labor was thus very high, the sector was not labor intensive. The ton-per-man ratio of merchant ships and fishing boats was very high and continued to rise, with only twelve to fourteen hands on herring busses and crews of similar size on merchant ships sailing to the Baltic around 1700 (de Vries and Van der Woude 1997: 250; Lucassen and Unger 2000: 130). Barges on the busy inland transportation network of towboats were typically run by a shipmaster and one helper, with a single urban official keeping tabs on income and expenditure (de Vries 1978: 139).

The industrial sector that rose in tandem with the Republic's commercial expansion also exerted a growing demand for labor, notably in the processing of imported foodstuffs and raw materials (de Vries and Van Der Woude 1997: 522). By the mid sixteenth century timber, beer, herring, and salt were well-established sectors, soon followed by newer branches such as sugar, diamonds, dyewoods, silk, a little later also coffee, tobacco, and import substitution industries such as madder (Priester 1998: 323–374). Processing industries were economically the most dynamic sectors in the northern Low Countries, and at the same time the most vulnerable. From about 1650 their competitive edge in the export markets for low-quality manufactures was blunted by the adoption of mercantilist trade protectionism by Britain and France. Some sectors successfully changed tack by transferring production to the countryside of Twente and Brabant and reorganizing it as putting-out networks to cut cost. Others, such as those grafted on the colonial trade and on specialized farming, continued to thrive in urban environments, entrepreneurs seeking to cut wage bills with new technology. By contrast, textile manufacturing in the southern Low Countries responded entirely differently to the rise of trade protection. Producers consolidated and switched successfully to luxury fabrics for both domestic and foreign markets (van der Wee 1988: 324–327, 330–335, 368–370). During the sixteenth century Oudenaerde tapestry weaving stood out, workshops counting scores of workers coexisting with single-worker units (Stabel 2001: 151), but with consolidation fairly large production units staffed with wage labor became the norm (De Peuter 1999: 244–248; Lis and Soly 1987: 30–40).

The growth of wage labor changed the structure and organization of the labor market. Farm owners found they could reduce the number of regularly employed hands and hire casual workers, usually on a seasonal basis, a contrast with the market for maritime labor which came to offer more steady employment to sailors who could now sign with the same shipmaster year after year and sometimes even for a full year. In the processing industry, the owners of production units typically relied on a workforce of casual laborers headed by trained artisans. At the same time the scale of production units remained small. Until the late eighteenth or, in many areas, even the mid nineteenth century the world of work consisted overwhelmingly of small businesses, typically consisting of a self-employed owner working with two or three employees plus an apprentice or so. Amsterdam bakers seldom had more than two or three extra hands (Kuijpers 2008: 225–248). Firms employing ten or twenty people were rare. Even the largest and most capital-intensive Holland industries such as brewing and sugar refining seldom counted more than ten workers. In some sectors, notably textile production, arms manufacturing, and clock-making, subcontracting could create integrated supply chains with large numbers of workers, but these were formally self employed, if often totally dependent on an entrepreneur (Lis and Soly 2008).

Indeed, self-employment continued at a high level, even as wage labor became more important. Until well into the early modern era most people were, at least part of their time, self-employed, whether as farmers, artisans, service providers, skilled or unskilled workers. The three successive industrial growth phases in the southern Low Countries were all buoyed up by self-employed artisans, be it Flemish cloth manufacturing during the thirteenth and fourteenth centuries, the Brabantine and Flemish industry during the two following centuries, or the luxury weaving of the seventeenth and eighteenth centuries (Lis and Soly 1997b: 219–221; Ryckbosch 2012; van Damme 2007).

Services also offered widespread opportunities for self-employed labor, and not just in highly commercialized provinces such as Holland. During the first half of the seventeenth century, for instance, Amsterdam numbered some 8,600 self-employed merchants, retailers, artisans, and other independent producers of goods and services out of a population of 120,000. If we take each of these entrepreneurs as heading a household of four people, self-employment was a major source of income for at least a quarter of all households in Amsterdam (Gelderblom 2009). This will not have been much lower in the numerous small towns and large villages that characterized the Low Countries. As a rule local amenities included not just a baker, carpenter, and smith, but a much wider group of retailers and artisans (de Vries and Van der Woude 1997: 509–510, 522–523; cf. also van Deursen 1994; for the southern Low Countries: Blondé 1999). Indeed, the comparatively high level of locally available skills combined with a surplus of unskilled workers to give the countryside a comparative advantage in competing with towns for high-quality work (Lis and Soly 1997b: 219–221; Munro 1990 cited in Lis and Soly 1997b: 226). As a result town and countryside developed different employment structures over time, towns concentrating on skilled and continuous work, the countryside on low- or unskilled and discontinuous, that is to say seasonal, work, so in the end the relocation of production facilities to the countryside remained limited to sectors which fit its employment pattern (Lis and Soly 1997b: 224–225).

However, these employment patterns differed in degree, and not in kind. The boundary between waged work and self-employment was a fuzzy one, many people combining the two categories or switching between them on a more or less permanent basis in an economy of makeshift. Many waged jobs, notably in farming, but also in shipping, the army, public works, churches, and in urban defense, did not entail permanent and full-time employment, forcing men and women to combine several jobs or generate income with self-employment (e.g. Kuijpers 2009; Soens 2009; Soly 1977; van Tielhof and van Dam 2006; van Wijngaarden 2000; van Zwet 2009). This included petty farming, landless laborers with a right to use the commons for grazing some animals or collecting firewood. Even urban dwellers hung on to small plots of land outside the town walls to supplement their income (Stabel 2001: 150). Conversely, if and when needed self-employed producers of goods and services would supplement their income with wage labor, Moreover, many jobs were waged at least partly in kind. Seasonal farm workers, domestic servants, sailors, and soldiers all received a considerable part of their wages in the form of board and lodging (Vermeesch 2006).

We might consider constantly shifting work arrangements as beneficial in providing the economy with a large and flexible pool of labor. This certainly was the case for the seasonal migration of farm hands and of sailors to join the merchant navy or the VOC, and also for authorities looking to mobilize large numbers of workers for emergency public works (Lucassen 1987; van Zanden 1993). But the flip side was a precariousness for household income that reduced labor mobility. Wage-dependent workers needed social networks for survival and such networks, once ruptured, could not easily be rebuilt somewhere else. Moving a household required finding work for its individual members all at once if income levels were to be sustained, difficult for people holding the usual combination of jobs (Kuijpers 2009: 254). The social welfare system did nothing to reduce precariousness, indeed, it was geared to prolong it. Rather than paying full benefits to those staying at home, charities tended to supplement the wage incomes of other household members while trying to cut out the very poorest of society, people without a fixed residence, a regular job, and therefore hardly any social network to fall back on (e.g. Van Wijngaarden 2000). In the southern Low Countries poverty relief was tailored to keeping wages down by forcing women and children to accept manufacturing work (Lis and Soly 1997b: 225). Thus, the economy of makeshift within which poor households fought to survive explains why, in an otherwise highly integrated economy, where goods flowed freely between regions, fairly large wage differentials continued to exist, notably for unskilled labor (Aerts 2004: 217; van Zanden 1999). In that sense the Low Countries economy during the early modern age was not really modern or fully capitalist.

Commerce and capitalism

Commodity markets appeared early in different parts of the Low Countries. Norse and Frisian traders pioneered overseas trade during the eighth to tenth centuries and by the turn of the first millennium settlements existed with a regular trade, protected by rulers. This is also best understood from favorable geographic factors. The area's infrastructure favored both farming specialization and local and regional trade while the ubiquity of navigable waterways kept transportation costs low. Food, building materials, and fuel could thus be easily shipped, lowering the threshold for urbanization.[7] The countries' central location also helped to bring about an early integration with other parts of Europe. Regular exchange across the North Sea with northern France, eastern England, northern Germany, and Denmark existed as early as the year 1000. In addition rivers facilitated trading links with the Rhineland and down the Meuse valley, which, from the twelfth century, extended as far as the Champagne fairs, where Flemish fabrics were exchanged for Italian luxury products (Blockmans 2010b: 73–123).

These factors combined to produce a dense scattering of market towns, first of all in Flanders, where scores of small towns developed into specialized cloth production centres tied to regional and interregional trade flows through a fair

---

7 Cf. on the impact of transportation costs on the cost of living in cities: Ballaux and Blondé 2007: 62–63, 76–79.

cycle which competed for business with the Champagne fairs (Stabel 1997). In neighboring Brabant, Antwerp was the first among at least a dozen towns involved in regional and international trade. In the north, towns on the Zuider Zee rim and along the IJssel traded with the German hinterland from the thirteenth century. Holland's trade emerged a century later, fostered by the worsening ecological conditions that forced its inhabitants down the road of marked economic specialization. They switched from growing bread grains to importing them, first from southern Flanders and northern France, then by the second half of the fifteenth century increasingly from the Baltic. Instead of grain, farms started producing dairy goods, flax, and hemp, while surplus farm labor found work in fishing and transportation services (van Bavel and van Zanden 2004).

The most striking aspect of the way in which Low Countries commodity markets developed is the apparent ease with which aspiring market towns succeeded in obtaining a position in regional or international trade. Other European towns and regions profited from the medieval rise of long-distance overland trade, but the high degree of urban autonomy in Low Countries combined with the intensity of interurban competition to produce dynamic institutional development. Here and there feudal lords organized annual fairs, as successive heads of the Wassenaar family did, but the development of commodity markets was primarily driven by town magistrates, who could shape their town's economic destiny in response to perceived threats and opportunities elsewhere. They were more or less free to do so, having obtained substantial legal and fiscal autonomy from their sovereign overlords in return for successive donations of money (Blockmans 2010b; Dijkman 2011).

This enabled town councils to promote trade by every means: by maintaining a legal infrastructure to support private contracting, by offering protection to itinerant and resident merchants, by creating market spaces or dedicated halls, by building port facilities, offering residential accommodation to groups of merchants, granting privileges, setting up institutions such as exchange banks, or even by paying premiums to individuals moving in (Gelderblom 2013). Magistrates monitored the work of local service providers, defined rules for payment, credit and the registration of credit, and set up courts to resolve disputes. The urban charter families offered practical frameworks for devising institutional solutions, as did the Hanseatic League for the towns on the Zuider Zee rim, because the towns united in the League bound themselves to common rules and norms about the organization of commercial transactions. At times these frameworks also served to facilitate a degree of regional coordination and collaboration. Towns coordinated the timing of their local, periodic trade fairs into cycles so as to create quasi-permanent markets, and also joined together in promoting the interests of their merchants abroad (Gelderblom 2004). Flemish cities united in supporting merchants traveling to Britain or to the Champagne fairs as early as the eleventh century, the IJssel towns formed a support network from the twelfth century, Holland towns did the same for their Hanseatic traders from the fifteenth century.

However, competition remained the norm and its intensity was rooted in the Low Countries' geography. Every town strove to maintain or improve its market position in the face of nearby competitors with access to virtually the same production areas and outlets (de Vries and Van der Woude 1997: 172–174). At times towns succeeded in buttressing a favorable location with commercial privileges obtained from overlords to establish a market monopoly. Dordrecht maintained a general staple privilege on the Meuse and Rhine trade for a considerable time during the fourteenth through sixteenth centuries, although, as we shall see, with variable success, and Middelburg had a wine staple for the Zeeland–north Flanders area during the sixteenth century (Dijkman 2011: 159–200; Wijffels 2003). But, as a rule, producers and traders possessed alternatives. They could sell or purchase elsewhere in another town, or avoid one market's commercial privileges by taking an alternative route to another market, knowing that one town's rights were not easily enforced in others. Some markets, such as those for horses and cattle, were highly mobile anyway and thus easily poached by local rulers wanting to stimulate trade (Gijsbers 1999; van der Wee and Aerts 1979).

The pressure of competition drove cities to mobilize every means available, political, legal, fiscal, and if necessary armed force, to secure their position. Bruges repeatedly sent armed men to stop business seeping away to its outport, Sluys, and in 1356 cajoled the count of Flanders to subject Antwerp to its rule (Murray 2005: 35–7, 253). Ghent resorted to arms in order to prevent trade being diverted by the digging of a new canal in 1379, Haarlem did so in 1513 to frustrate the building of a lock obstructing traffic (Blockmans 2010b: 280–281; van Dam 1998: 46–47). In Flanders the three dominant cities Bruges, Ypres, and Ghent managed over time to subject the countryside to their interests and stifle the growth of smaller towns. Groningen in the far north also wielded considerable political and economic power over its surrounding countryside, the Ommelanden (de Vries and Van der Woude 1997: 509). At different points in time, Aalst, Antwerp, and Rotterdam suffered serious trade restrictions imposed by neighboring towns (Dijkman 2011: 147; Gelderblom 2013). When the Holland economy entered its climacteric during the late seventeenth century, hitting the local beer industry, urban magistrates responded with prohibitive tariffs on imports from elsewhere (Yntema 2009). For a time, political centralization limited the impact of urban rent-seeking. Once the duke of Burgundy had gained control over Brabant in 1406, he halted Bruges's check on the development of Antwerp. From the mid fifteenth century towns could challenge urban rivals thwarting their economic ambitions before a central court instituted by the duke. This court ruled in favor of Antwerp when it fought Middelburg's wine staple, and Rotterdam won a similar case against Dordrecht's general staple. Here again the Revolt cut across centralization. In the southern Low Countries the supreme court's power remained undiminished, but it could not break the iron grip of the leading Flemish cities over their province. The Dutch Republic failed to establish a central supreme court, though litigants in Holland and Friesland could appeal against verdicts of their respective provincial courts to a joint *Hoge Raad* or Supreme Court (Verhas 1997).

However, the key point about urban rent-seeking is that its success varied greatly from one region to the next, creating marked structural differences between markets. The three Flemish cities succeeded in controlling the countryside economy, resulting in commodity markets, notably those for grain and textiles, being sharply tilted in their favor, just like the labor markets noted above. By contrast, similar control attempts in Holland largely failed. Dordrecht's comprehensive staple right in the river delta faced continuous and often successful challenges from small, downriver ports vying to poach trade away, until nearby Rotterdam's irresistible rise effectively ended the monopoly (Dijkman 2011). Small towns and villages got away with dodging the market privileges of nearby cities because the count would not risk siding with the cities and incurring the wrath of these smaller communities (Dijkman 2011). When the Amsterdam council, pressed by labor unrest, imposed restrictions on timber processing, the industry simply left town and moved north to the Zaan, drawing ship-building in its wake (de Vries and Van der Woude 1997: 301–302). With cities unable to gain grip, Holland's labor and commodity markets remained much more flexible and responsive than the corresponding ones in Flanders.

It was also the inter-urban competition that from the thirteenth century propelled the Low Countries into dominating international trade.[8] The hub function which Bruges, Antwerp, and Amsterdam successively assumed for European commodity flows could have been exercised equally well by

---

8 This paragraph and the next are based on Gelderblom 2013.

ports in neighboring Britain, France, or Germany. However, those ports all occupied commanding positions in relation to their hinterlands, large areas possessing little or nothing in the way of alternative access to super-regional markets. This situation was conducive to a fiscal exploitation of trade and to institutional sclerosis, at the same time reducing the hinterland's economic scope to low-value activities in the production of basic foodstuffs and manufactures. Leading ports in the Low Countries always attempted to obtain similar power over their hinterlands, and they sometimes succeeded in getting it, but they always needed to reckon with the high urban potential of neighboring regions giving producers and consumers alternative markets. They also had to compete to attract international traders from around Europe, essentially a footloose crowd easily persuaded to move elsewhere if conditions there suited them better. The Bruges market was highly dependent on the German Hanse and on Italian and Spanish merchants, for instance, Antwerp on Rhine merchants, English cloth merchants, and on Portuguese spice traders. If one of those groups moved the others might do so, too, which rendered local councils responsive to demands for better facilities.

The contribution of foreign merchants to the growth of international trade in the Low Countries is usually expressed in terms of their particular product specialization and business expertise. This, however, fails to capture the essence. The real importance of foreign merchants lay in their promoting a continuous adaptation of institutional arrangements to changing economic needs, first as a corporate body, but increasingly, in Antwerp after 1490 and subsequently also in Amsterdam, as individuals. As more and more foreigners used the commercial, legal, and financial infrastructure, town councils strove to optimize conditions, building dedicated market amenities and residential accommodation, promoting good contracting institutions, incorporating foreign customs into law, and adapting legal proceedings to commercial needs. It was this interaction between local markets and foreign merchants that stimulated the spread of commercial institutions such as double-entry bookkeeping and maritime insurance, instruments such as the bill of exchange, public and private bonds, and money market techniques such as bill discounting, securities trading, repos, forwards, futures, and derivatives.

Moreover, the inter-urban competition combined with the ease of communication to ensure that best practices spread quickly from the commercial centers outwards to satellite towns. Foreign merchants could therefore credibly threaten to leave a town, or leave in fact, and they frequently did one or the other. This combination of footloose traders and the determination of urban magistrates to facilitate their commercial transactions also explains the relative ease with which commercial primacy shifted from Bruges to Antwerp in the late fifteenth century, and from Antwerp to Amsterdam following the Dutch Revolt.

The colonial challenge

The keen inter-urban competition also manifested itself in the intercontinental trade, with surprising and innovative results. From the 1560s Flemish merchants seized part of the sugar trade with the Canary Islands and Madeira, but the Crowns of Portugal and Spain kept them out of trading with the Americas, Africa, and Asia. Once the fall of Antwerp in 1585 had removed this obstacle merchants in the northern Low Countries started sending out expeditions to west Africa, to the Caribbean, and, from 1595, to Asia. For the African and the Caribbean trade the traditional forms of business organization sufficed, that is to say, ships run as private companies that coordinated their movements when necessary. But the Asian trade posed a different set of challenges. The initial expeditions during the 1590s were initiated by special-purpose partnerships between merchants running the venture and investors recruited to provide capital, with local and provincial governments providing subsidies in the form of military hardware. Sent out from rival ports, these Dutch expeditions competed with each other and non-Dutch rivals, sending product prices up in Asia and down in Europe, at the same time undermining the fragile Dutch Republic in its fight for independence from the Spanish empire. Without coordination the Dutch stood to lose out against the Portuguese and Spanish traders, already firmly established and backed by the same state power that tried so hard to crush the Dutch Republic. These considerations led the Estates General to push for a merger between competing intercontinental trade interests under its auspices.

Chartered in March 1602 with a capital of 6.4 million guilders, the United Dutch East India Company or VOC obtained a monopoly on the Asian trade and therefore ended private enterprise in that line of business. It marked a step up from the preceding special-purpose partnership in having a clear separation between ownership and management, transferable shares, and limited liability for shareholders. Corporations with such characteristics only became the norm during the nineteenth century, so historians have hailed the VOC as a remarkable achievement of Dutch capitalism. However, we must question whether the company's 1602 design was indeed as modern as is sometimes claimed, because it was tailored to the specific needs of the Asian trade at a particular moment in time, and was not generally adaptable to other types of business.

The VOC was a curious hybrid, indeed an anomaly. For one thing, the Estates General were its principal. It did not have formal representatives on the board of directors, but the 1602 charter did give the Estates the right to overturn decisions of the board, so military considerations, more specifically the demands of carrying the war against Spain overseas by gaining a firm foothold in Asia, came first, business second, shareholders last (Gelderblom, de Jong, and Jonker 2011). For another, to placate competing local interests company operations had to be spread over separate departments or chambers in six cities, and it took the board some twenty years to weed out the most glaring inefficiencies of that decentralization (Schalk, Gelderblom, and Jonker 2012).

Admittedly, the VOC did acquire two other defining characteristics of modern corporations, permanence and limited liability for managers, but this had never been the founders' intention. Rather, it was an inescapable remedy to structural flaws in its corporate finance (Gelderblom, de Jong, and Jonker 2013). The company's first ten-years' account faced statutory liquidation in 1612. It would then be replaced with a second ten-years' account, giving shareholders the option to either take their money back or roll it over to the successor. But the investment required by the overseas presence in the first decade of the company's existence starved shareholders of dividends, so directors realized that the statutory liquidation needed lifting to secure the continuity of the Asian trade. In July 1612 they obtained the necessary waiver from the Estates General, giving the VOC *de facto* though not *de jure*, permanence.

Moreover, the 6.4 million guilder capital had been conceived as a revolving fund to be replenished from sales revenues as ships returned. The six chambers were individually responsible for running their part of the combined operations and they remained suspicious of each other's doings, which restricted the scope for a mutual bridging of periodic shortfalls between income and expenses. Large chambers such as Amsterdam could easily raise debt locally, but the smaller ones faced bankruptcy if their ships failed to return in time. In a process of slow, piecemeal engineering the board built sufficient confidence between the chambers to allow first the circulation of surplus commodities to help out needy chambers, then debts in current accounts, and finally a centralized financial policy tied to managers' limited liability for debt (Gelderblom, de Jong, and Jonker, 2013; Schalk, Gelderblom, and Jonker 2012).

At the end of the day the VOC's permanence and managerial limited liability resulted from a triumph of might over right, and not from the judicious balancing of stakeholders' interests that otherwise characterized

Dutch business. The shareholders were not consulted about the blatant breach of the charter and their rights in 1612, but fobbed off with a dividend in kind at rigged prices. Shareholders who refused the goods had to wait years before the company finally gave them the money. As a result, the 1621 charter lapse turned into an epic fight over shareholder rights, which the shareholders lost because the VOC directors, hand-in-glove with local and provincial authorities, could mobilize the Estates of Holland in support (de Jongh 2011). In 1623 the directors, emboldened by years of getting their way, unilaterally discarded their unlimited liability for debt simply by dropping the clause which referred to it from the preprinted bond forms in 1623 (Gelderblom, de Jong, and Jonker, 2013).

Though the investor protests failed to steer the VOC in the right direction, they did succeed in materially altering the design of its sister intercontinental trading company, the West India Company or WIC, launched in 1621 to take the war against the Luso-Spanish empire to South America and the Caribbean. Its original charter was a copy of the VOC's, so despite vigorous canvassing by the authorities subscriptions remained paltry because by now investors knew that a company combining warfare with trade under political direction made no commercial sense. Bowing to the obvious, the board amended the charter and gave shareholders more power over the company, after which subscriptions closed quickly on a total of 7.1 million guilders (de Jong, Jonker, and Röell, 2013). But then, while the VOC after its rocky start became a distinct commercial success, paying regular, high dividends from the mid-1630s, the WIC faltered following a disastrous attempt to wrest Brazil away from Portugal. By the mid-1640s the heavily indebted company had become an agency licensing its monopoly to private merchants.

Comparison of the VOC and the WIC highlights the fact that corporations working on a large scale possessed no trade advantage unless they succeeded in duping investors into mobilizing the heavy investment needed to build a large territorial presence, as the VOC had done. Both companies remained anomalies in Dutch business by their hybrid corporate form, their scale, and their monopoly. Their size lent their operations some impact on society in the form of a standardization of product specifications, the organization of sales such as auctions, the labor market, and coin production, but they were otherwise dwarfed by other sectors. As a rule the intra-European trade, entirely in the hands of sole proprietors and partnerships of various kinds, amounted to more than 70 percent of total trade (Jonker and Sluyterman 2000: 62, 81). The Dutch economy offered neither the scope nor the need for large-scale ventures, and investors fully realized this. As a result, the attempts in 1720 to inflate a bubble following the examples in Paris and London misfired completely, and investors judiciously picked the one or two projects that offered some commercial prospects from the speculative rest (Gelderblom and Jonker, forthcoming). It was only during the 1740s that larger businesses with a longer lifespan and transferable shares made their appearance as a result of consolidation in processing industries such as brewing and sugar refining (de Jong, Jonker, and Röell, 2013).

The impact of colonial enterprise on the Low Countries' economy remained limited in other respects as well. The VOC was sufficiently well organized to seize a leading role in the European competition over the Asian trade and the very modern-looking labor market formed an integral part of its strength. That provided a marked difference from the organization of labor in agriculture, manufacturing, and services, which did not have a large and mobile labor supply because the self-employment component remained high, businesses were small, highly skilled workers remained strongly tied to their employers, and precariousness of income prevented low-skilled workers in both rural and urban settings from moving. The qualitative economic transformation effected by the colonial trade did not stretch beyond the processing industries concerned and, in some cases, like tobacco, madder, and earthenware, the production of local substitutes for exotic goods. Throughout the Low Countries the main engines of growth were, depending on the region, textile manufacturing, commercial agriculture, and shipping, and, in the cities, retailing and other urban services.

Financial markets

The arrested development of the joint-stock corporation in the Dutch Republic warrants two seemingly opposite conclusions. On the one hand, it is clear that the commercial orientation of local rulers in the Low Countries stimulated the development of important, new contractual forms. On the other hand, the limited use of these new forms shows an essentially Smithian economy, in which growth depended on the efficient circulation of labor, capital, and goods. The concomitant dominance of floating over fixed capital, in turn, determined the structure of financial markets.

Financial markets in the Low Countries reveal a high degree of dynamism and variation from very early on. Financial techniques spread throughout the Low Countries with the same ease as other types of information. As early as the eleventh century, for instance, the property mortgage appeared in the Meuse valley, then economically the most dynamic region (Vercauteren 1947).

From there it travelled first to Flanders and Hainaut, when economic growth began to manifest itself there, and from there to other provinces (van Werveke 1929). By the fourteenth century the mortgage had become the instrument of choice for territorial lords wishing to raise money by mortgaging assets ranging from land to tolls, offices, and fiscal resources (van Bavel 2010a: 182–183, 266–267; Vercauteren 1947).

The settlement pattern of Lombard moneylenders differed from the spread of mortgages. They started their activities not in the Meuse valley, but in the Flanders–Artois–Hainaut region during the first half of the thirteenth century (Bigwood 1921: 319–320). By 1250 they were active in Oudenaerde, Tournai, Courtrai, Furnes, Poperinghe, Mons, Ypres, and Bruges, by the late 1260s also in Brussels, Louvain, and Utrecht, where in 1267 a mob chased three Italian moneylenders into the cathedral and killed them (Tihon 1961: 340, 342, 345; van Bavel 2010a: 185). Some of these Italian bankers formed syndicates to operate licensed pawnshops, the count of Flanders granting licenses for no fewer than fourteen towns during 1280–1282 (Tihon 1961: 348). The duke of Brabant gave blanket permits for his entire territory, where some forty Lombard businesses operated in 1309 (Tihon 1961: 350). By that date Lombards were active in nearly all major towns in the southern Low Countries, and in most major towns in the western part of the northern provinces (Maassen 1994: 41–43).

Though occasionally prosecuting moneylenders for usury, the Church clearly lacked the power to stop them from expanding their businesses across the Low Countries (van Bavel 2010a: 184–185; Wyffels 1991). The increasing use of alternatives that sidestepped the ban on usury rendered clerical objections redundant anyway. In 1228–1229 Tournai issued what are likely to have been the first public life annuities, perpetual annuities following close behind (Tracy 2003). Some twenty years later the practice had reached Ghent, by 1300 it was engrained in both Holland and Brabant. Indeed, towns in the former county had already become so familiar with annuities that they clubbed together to underwrite annuities on behalf of their overlord, thereby laying the foundations for the province's later famously capacious credit (Zuijderduijn 2010: 341, 345ff.). Such paper possessed a fair degree of security for creditors because the law of reprisal allowed them to arrest any burghers of a defaulting town for arrears. As a result annuities were often held at a surprising distance from the issuing town (Zuijderduijn 2009).

We have noted above the spread of wage labor which occurred across the Low Countries during the high and late middle ages, familiarizing increasing numbers of people with the concept of money as a standard of value. However, recurrent deficiencies in the coin supply restricted the extent to which money could be used as a means of payment in the medieval as well as the early modern period. Though no doubt impractical in many instances, coin shortages do not appear to have harmed the economy unduly. People possessed a wealth of alternatives to settle transactions, as often as not through barter or clearing (van der Wee 1979: 101). Intermediaries appeared for squaring multiple transactions. The fragmentary administration of one such intermediary, a cloth merchant active in the eastern Twente region during the first half of the seventeenth century, shows him operating a form of multilateral clearing over considerable distances, compensating, say, goods sold by him with services rendered by one person and debts of a second one to yield a single claim on a third person (Hesselink, Kuiper, and Trompetter 2008). Individual items were always priced in money, but the final tally was usually carried over and not paid with coin. Some debts and claims carried interest, others did not, without apparent connection to other aspects of transactions, for instance the duration of credit or the amount of money involved.

We do not know how common intermediaries such as this merchant were, but given the fact that early modern society revolved around credit they were probably very common indeed. Presumably their scope decreased with the onset of more ordered coinage conditions, in the Dutch Republic during the later seventeenth century and in the southern Low Countries, by then part of the Austrian empire, from 1749. The availability of coin clearly stimulated cash transactions and thus reduced credit; Antwerp estates show a rising proportion of cash to debts plus claims during the eighteenth century (Willems 2009). Even so most people held comparatively little cash long after the arrival of more ordered coinage conditions, so they continued to prefer settling transactions with means other than money.

Members of the aristocracy appear to have been exceptional in keeping surprisingly large amounts of cash in times of coin shortages, that is to say the late fifteenth and early sixteenth century (Spufford 2008). Given the nobility's stereotypical reputation for poor payment of suppliers such sums presumably did not represent the kitty for household expenses and may say more about the need for status-enhancing gestures such as conspicuous largesse. Aristocrats may also have avoided alternative modes of settlement such as clearing, either because counterparties would likely be social inferiors, or because they preferred to let debts hang until ripe for bargaining.

By contrast, a merchant's reputation depended on prompt payments, but preferably not in coin. Merchants employed various means of settlement to minimize both their cash holdings and the need to use coin (Spufford 2008). They cleared claims and debts via current accounts with each other or with cashiers, moneychangers, or bankers, they wrote bills of exchange and IOUs to pay debts, and as often as not they circulated each other's paper. In this they were aided by local councils, which defined terms for accepting business records as legal proof and for endorsing commercial paper. Antwerp provided a key contribution by shaping regulations concerning endorsement to bearer, resulting in a great expansion of commercial credit because paper could now circulate more widely. From at least the mid 1530s bills of exchange were also discounted, that is to say, sold before term to a third party (van der Wee 1978: 102–104). At the end of the 1530s the Emperor Charles V decreed the Antwerp rules about commercial paper-binding for the entire Low Countries (De Smedt 1940–1).

Even so the speed with which commercial payment and credit techniques spread depended less on the adoption of particular legal clauses or new instruments than on the scale and character of business. The Bruges market served as the testing ground for most of them during the thirteenth and fourteenth centuries, and Antwerp's endorsement clauses put in the capstone (Murray 2005; van der Wee 1978).[9] But traders elsewhere adopted these techniques only if and when business warranted it. The basic legal framework governing bills of exchange, for instance, was sufficiently clear for them to spread, but their actual use depended on the availability of highly specific information about trade flows, commodity prices, interest and exchange rates, and about counterparties, all of these at home and abroad. Consequently bills of exchange only spread beyond commercial centers like Bruges or Antwerp if and when foreign trade reached a scale sufficient to repay the gathering and dissemination of such information. Antwerp already reached this position by the late fifteenth century, but more than a century later Amsterdam traders, though already conducting a large and fast-growing international business, showed themselves still wary of being paid with bills (Jonker and Sluyterman 2000; van der Wee 1963).

The bill market's reach was thus determined by the balance between the cost and benefits of collecting the information required, which turned positive only for the top of the commercial and financial hierarchy. However, that reach appears to have widened over time, the fairly small number of international bankers active in Bruges growing first into a large community of brokers, international traders, and bankers at the Antwerp exchange, and

---

9 Amsterdam's late seventeenth-century innovation of turning bills of exchange into acceptances may have been an exception, but at present we simply know too little about the origins and economic importance of this innovation to make a firm statement. (Houwink 1929; Wallert 1996).

then into the specialized and articulated crowd of bill brokers, traders, and merchant bankers that turned Amsterdam into Europe's leading settlement center once the Iberian trade and finance had left Antwerp for its northern rival following the Peace of Westphalia in 1648 (Baetens 1976; Jonker forthcoming).

The arrival of this key business coincided with a period of profound reorientation at Amsterdam's Wisselbank or Exchange Bank (Dehing 2012; Gillard 2004; van Nieuwkerk 2009). Modeled on a famous Venetian example and set up in 1609, seven years after the launch of the VOC and two years before the opening of the city's first commodity exchange, the bank initially served three purposes: first, defending the guilder against the inferior coins flooding in; second, providing merchants with a stable means of payment in the form of banco money; and third, holding a stock of quality coins available for merchants having to pay cash overseas. Existing intermediaries such as cashiers already ran a payments circuit and supplied coins for export. They might well have continued doing so, as their Bruges and Antwerp colleagues had done before, thereby obviating the need for a central clearance institute (Aerts 2011; van der Wee 1978: 104). However, in the Dutch Republic a powerful coalition sought to achieve a higher degree of monetary coordination than Amsterdam's fledgling cashiers could muster. The city council, Holland's Estates, and the Estates General wanted to assert control over the currency, and the VOC needed large amounts of silver for export to Asia. These interests combined to launch the Wisselbank as a strong public body, but the intention of replacing the cashiers failed, their services having become indispensable to merchants. Over time a division of labor emerged, the cashiers becoming the hinge between the Wisselbank and the Amsterdam market, an essential and, one assumes, remunerative function, but one that prevented their further evolution to fully fledged bankers in the way some of their Antwerp colleagues did.

By 1650 the Wisselbank had succeeded in stabilizing the guilder sufficiently to render that part of its function redundant to merchants, so deposits stagnated. Casting around for new ways to attract business, the directors came up with a new type of instrument, the *recepis* or tradable depositary receipt for bullion deposited with the Wisselbank. In essence cheap options on gold and silver, the *recepissen* boosted deposits and transformed operations by handing directors a tool for macroeconomic policies by levering the money supply (Quinn and Roberds 2010). Consequently, though conservative in the sense of not providing credit or issuing notes, the bank was highly modern in pioneering functions that most central banks adopted only during the late nineteenth century. The *recepissen* also reinforced the Amsterdam market's already highly developed facilities to attract gold and silver, lowering the price for obtaining liquidity to levels unobtainable elsewhere and giving the city a competitive edge in the routing of international payments. The further refinement of bills into acceptances, which cut the risk of non-payment and thus the cost of bills on Amsterdam, helped to keep that edge sharp. Consequently the money market enabled Dutch merchants both to hold on to commodity flows, propping up the Republic's foreign trade in the face of mounting competition, and to reinvent themselves as merchant bankers, pioneering a burgeoning foreign loan business on the back of their commodity trade and acceptance dealing (Jonker and Sluyterman 2000).

The character of Amsterdam's financial market must therefore be understood from the huge pool of liquidity at its heart. Foreign merchants rushed in to profit from that liquidity and the low interest rates associated with it, swelling the Wisselbank deposits. By the mid-eighteenth century bills on Amsterdam financed grain traders in Berlin and cotton manufacturers in Brussels (de Jong-Keesing 1939; De Peuter 1999; Schnabel and Shin 2004). The origins of that liquidity can be traced back to the formation of the VOC in 1602. Trading in the company's shares started almost immediately upon the closing of subscriptions, with forwards and options following in its wake (Gelderblom and Jonker 2004, 2005; Petram 2011). By the 1680s one allied transaction, *prolongatie* or repo lending on collateral of securities, had become a standard technique for short-term credit, which it was to remain until 1914 (Jonker 1996). However, this was not the VOC's only contribution to the Dutch market's facilities. In 1608 its directors devised a system of transferable IOUs with which sailors and soldiers could obtain an advance on future pay so as to either buy food and lodging while awaiting embarkation, or to provide for their family during the tour of duty. As often as not debtors sold these bonds, discounted by the going interest rate plus a mortality risk premium, to specialized intermediaries who by grouping them managed to offset the individual mortality risks and thereby keep debtors' costs relatively low.

This system did not remain limited to Amsterdam. All six of the VOC's local chambers operated it and the Dutch navy, equally rooted in local admiralties, adopted something similar (van Bochove and van Velzen 2011). By at least 1670 the kind of intermediation on which the VOC's IOUs depended had also spawned a private IOU system in Amsterdam, which the city council sanctioned that year by defining a standard format and giving legal preference in case of default to claims on officially stamped paper (van Bochove and Kole 2013). We have no idea how widely such paper was used, but surviving specimens suggest that it filled a key gap between the informal credit common at the lower end of the market and the techniques such as bills and repos used by the upper end. By the end of the eighteenth century private, preprinted IOU forms were also sold by Leeuwarden stationers (van Bochove and Kole 2013). The two types of IOU were important innovations because they extended the market's reach further down the social ladder and as such they underline that Amsterdam possessed a highly articulated market meeting a wide variety of needs, ranging from the high volumes of debt raised by the government and the colonial trading companies to small-scale private loans. Consequently, though having a large bank at its center, Amsterdam finance was not bank oriented but fully market oriented (contrary to Carlos and Neal 2011). It was the market, not the Wisselbank, which supplied all credit, and key credit techniques such as *prolongatie* were market based and survived the bank's demise at the end of the eighteenth century for over a hundred years.

The circulation of formalized IOUs highlights another structural aspect typical of northern markets. A fairly wide public of savers willing to buy paper claims appears to have existed from quite early on, long before Holland's upswing. Data from a community north of Amsterdam show people of modest means holding shares in ships and government annuities during the 1530s (De Moor, van Zanden, and Zuijderduijn 2009). Those shares and annuities were clearly available in small denominations, presumably a consequence of the need to mobilize money for investments among a population where wealth was both relatively scarce, compared to Flanders or Brabant, and distributed more evenly (van Dillen 1941). Mobilizing money therefore required mechanisms for getting small contributions from many people rather than large ones from a few. Shipping shares were commonly split into fractions of 1/64th or even smaller. Until the switch to excises as the main source of fiscal revenue at the end of the sixteenth century taxes were raised by allotting each community its share in the total burden, after which community officials spread that share over households using periodic detailed assessments of individual wealth. Holland's public loans were similarly apportioned to communities and households until the 1550s, when officials discovered that investors would buy them willingly (Gelderblom and Jonker 2011). The dispersed placing of loans continued, however, with eighteen local tax receivers doubling as agents for selling debt and paying interest. This had the dual effect of widening the province's access to investors and avoiding the concentration of debt in the hands of a narrow elite.

Consequently Amsterdam differed from Bruges and Antwerp in not being the central market for public debt in the Dutch Republic or even in Holland.

The Antwerp exchange functioned as the hub of Charles V's finances, raising the huge sums needed for bribing German princes into electing him emperor and floating short-term debt, both for his government in the Low Countries and also for the Spanish Crown in the form of *asientos* or short-term bonds (Blanchard 2009; Tracy 2002). The *asientos* cemented the Brabant city firmly at the heart of a European settlement network, which cleared commercial credit, public debt, and bullion flows with each other (Aerts 2004: 222–223). Antwerp possessed a large group of merchants and bankers who could carry out such transactions and absorb debt, while the Brabant aristocracy also tended to invest heavily in it (Tracy 1985). Fiscal centralization under Charles V and Philip II brought about a gradual harmonization of taxation and debt policy across the Low Countries, but following the Dutch Revolt two distinct patterns emerged (Gelderblom and Jonker 2013). The breakaway provinces in the north adopted a fiscal system relying chiefly on indirect taxes levied by provincial governments, supplemented by debt issued on their own credit, and secured on future tax receipts. Combined with a soaring economy this enabled the seven provinces to raise very high amounts of debt to achieve and then defend their independence.

However, in the south the trend toward greater fiscal autonomy for the provinces reversed as the representative assemblies that should have assumed responsibility fell apart into their constituent factions, which continued to assert their fiscal privileges against each other and against the Spanish and, from 1715 on, the Austrian government in Brussels. This had three major consequences. First, taxation and debt remained comparatively low in the southern Low Countries, both at the provincial and at the central level. Second, fiscal policy remained firmly in the hands of local and provincial elites, who kept debt issues largely to themselves. Third, key parts of public financial services such as tax collecting and organizing payments were bestowed as favors on well-connected businessmen. During the eighteenth century prominent banking houses emerged in the southern Low Countries, growing out of payments services, fiscal services, or both (Baetens 1976; Bronne 1969; Degryse 2005; De Peuter 1999; Houtman-De Smedt 1982, 1983). Those fertile substrata were absent in the north, because the Wisselbanken served the commercially most important part of the payments system and frequent public auctions kept profit margins on tax farms at a minimum. Banking houses did emerge, but, rooted as they were in trade finance and the securities market, they concentrated on short-term lending and eschewed longer-term commitments. Conversely, the southern Netherlands market structure appears to have favored financiers accumulating capital for allocation in just such commitments. Thus when, during the early nineteenth century, Belgium's industrialization really took off, its financial market structure could facilitate the concomitant rise in demand for fixed capital.

That said, financial markets in the north and in the south never reached the vast majority of people, whose low income effectively locked them out of all formal financial services except for the occasional pawning of whatever possessions they could offer as collateral. The IOUs might have given the Amsterdam market a somewhat wider reach than those in Antwerp or Bruges, but that was a difference in degree, not kind. From the same point of departure and using highly similar instruments markets in north and south developed very different institutions and forms of intermediation, but this mattered for the few at the top, not for the many at the bottom.

Conclusion

The most striking aspect of capitalism in the Low Countries is its variety, that is to say, the marked differences in the actual organization of transactions between ostensibly similar, free markets driven by supply and demand in which people participated willingly. On the one hand, there clearly did not exist a specific set of preconditions or circumstances, or a particular institutional framework necessary for the development of product and factor markets; on the other, local circumstances continued to shape markets throughout the period under consideration.

The variety had its roots in the area's diversity of soil conditions and natural resources which, transformed into specific social property relations, ultimately determined the distribution of income and wealth, structured the power of local and central authorities, and shaped the contracting institutions organizing agriculture, trade, and industry. However, the relative ease of trade and communication combined with the inter-urban competition to produce a fairly rapid diffusion of information, production techniques, legal concepts, and ways of organizing transactions from one region to the next, the autonomy of local rulers allowing economic actors to choose the institutions that best suited them. The power and wealth of aristocratic magnates, monasteries, and other Church institutions, towns, individual merchants, and artisan guilds might look impressive, but there were always limits, barriers, and countervailing forces preventing any one of them or even coalitions between them from achieving long-term dominance over wide areas and using their vested interests to stifle innovation. Moreover, the keen intercity rivalry prodded elites to embrace innovation when at all possible, since failing to keep up might make business move away to places where perceived restrictions did not apply, to rival cities, or into the countryside.

Now of course capitalism did not develop smoothly everywhere all the time. Opportunities were missed or passed up for one reason or another, innovations were dropped when they failed to live up to expectations, and a few pockets long succeeded in resisting the pressures of change, usually because poor soil conditions cemented the social and political balance. The point is, rather, that as a result of the balance between rulers, economic actors, and local circumstances the structure and shape of factor markets, notably those for labor and for capital, did not become more uniform across the Low Countries, but increasingly different, with a great variety of contracting institutions.

Thus it was not, as is often argued, the early decline of feudalism that stimulated successive phases of economic growth, but the interaction between resource endowments, infrastructure, and political and legal fragmentation. It was this continuous interaction that produced both a dynamic evolution of contracting institutions to govern market exchange, and the creation of political and legal constraints on local and central executives. As such it explains why the Low Countries' political and legal fragmentation did not end in economic stagnation, as it did in northern Italy, why violent disruptions such as social upheaval or political strife remained isolated instances, and why cities or rulers rarely succeeded in harming competitors' trade whether by monopolies, punitive tolls or taxes, or armed force.

In the final balance it was the split between north and south which put the Low Countries at a disadvantage within Europe by drastically reducing both the scope for regional interaction and the size of the internal market. As a result neither half reaped the full benefits of economic growth in the other part, be it the north's seventeenth-century Golden Age, or the south's renewed dynamism feeding into early industrialization during the eighteenth century. The protectionist policies of England and France, countries with much bigger internal markets, made matters worse. However, both halves of the Low Countries retained the long-term legacy of the area's political and legal fragmentation: when international markets opened up in the nineteenth century growth resumed, grafted not just on to the social, human, and financial stock accumulated over time, but also on the accumulated stock of institutions. This really amounted to an oversupply: not only did individual areas possess alternative rules for organizing specific transactions, as for instance the international commodity trade showed, but economic actors in most regions were familiar with a much bigger set of contracting institutions for them to adopt if and when economic opportunities presented themselves. As a result the Low Countries were at the same time resilient enough to absorb exogenous shocks and sufficiently flexible to seize new opportunities. This showed for instance in even the more peripheral areas adopting in the course of the nineteenth century, with apparent ease, modern institutions such as savings and loan banks for middle-class groups, mutual insurance schemes and other forms of risk management, paper money, various forms of investment, and new corporate forms such as the limited liability company.

References

Acemoglu, D., S. Johnson, and J. Robinson (2005). "The Rise of Europe: Atlantic Trade, Institutional Change, and Economic Growth," *American Economic Review* 95(3): 546–79.

(2012). *Why Nations Fail: The Origins of Power, Prosperity, and Poverty*. London: Profile Books.

Aerts, E. (2004). "Économie, monnaie, et société dans les Pays-Bas méridionaux de Charles Quint," in W. Blockmans and N. Mout (eds.), *The World of Emperor Charles V*. Amsterdam: University of Chicago Press, pp. 201–226.

(2011). "The Absence of Public Exchange Banks in Medieval and Early Modern Flanders and Brabant (1400–1800): A Historical Anomaly to be Explained," *Financial History Review* 18: 91–117.

Ballaux, B. and B. Blondé (2007). "Landtransportprijzen en de economische ontwikkeling van Brabant in de lange zestiende eeuw," *Tijdschrift voor Sociale en Economische Geschiedenis* 4(2): 57–85.

Baetens, R. (1976). *De nazomer van Antwerpens welvaart. De diaspora en het handelshuis De Groote tijdens de eerste helft der 17e eeuw*, 2 vols. Brussels: Gemeentekrediet van België.

Bavel, B. J. P. van (2003a). "The Land Market in the North Sea Area in a Comparative Perspective, 13th-18th Centuries," in S. Cavaciocchi (ed.), *Il Mercato della Terra Secc. XIII–XVIII. Atti della "Trentacinquesima Settimana di Studi," 5–9 Maggio 2003*. Prato: Istituto Internazionale di Storia Economica "Fondazione Datini," pp. 119–145.

(2003b). "Early Proto-Industrialization in the Low Countries? The Importance and Nature of Market-Oriented Non-Agricultural Activities in the Countryside in Flanders and Holland, c. 1250–1570," *Revue Belge de Philologie et d'Histoire* 81(4): 1119–1165.

(2006). "Rural Wage Labor in the Sixteenth-century Low Countries: An Assessment of the Importance and Nature of Wage Labor in the Countryside of Holland, Guelders, and Flanders," *Continuity and Change* 21(1), 37–72.

(2007). "The Transition in the Low Countries: Wage Labor as an Indicator of the Rise of Capitalism in the Countryside, 1300–1700," *Past and Present* 195, Suppl. 2: 286–303.

(2009). "The Emergence and Growth of Short-Term Leasing in the Netherlands and Other Parts of Northwestern Europe (11th–16th Centuries): A Tentative Investigation into its Chronology and Causes," in B. J. P. van Bavel and P. Schofield (eds.), *The Development of Leasehold in Northwestern Europe, 1200–1600*. Turnhout: Brepols, pp. 179–213.

(2010a). *Manors and Markets: Economy and Society in the Low Countries, 500–1600.* Oxford University Press.

(2010b). "The Medieval Origins of Capitalism in the Netherlands," *Low Countries Historical Review* 125: 45–79.

Bavel, B. J. P. van and J. L. van Zanden (2004). "The Jump-start of the Holland Economy during the Late-medieval Crisis, c. 1350–c. 1500," *Economic History Review* 57: 503–532.

Beekman, A. A. and P. J. Blok (1915). *Geschiedkundige Atlas van Nederland. De Bourgondische Tijd. De Noordelijke Nederlanden in 1476. Het Bourgondische Rijk in 1476.* The Hague: Nijhoff.

Benders, J. (1998). "Over ossen en keurslagers. De stad Groningse, Overijsselse en Gelderse veehandel tussen 1350 en 1550," in D. E. H. de Boer, R. W. M. van Schaïk, and R. Nip (eds.), *Het Noorden in het midden. Opstellen over de geschiedenis van de Noord-Nederlandse gewesten in Middeleeuwen en Nieuwe Tijd.* Assen: Van Gorcum, pp. 61–86.

Bieleman, J. (1990). "De verscheidenheid van de landbouw op de Nederlandse zandgronden tijdens 'de lange zestiende eeuw'," *Bijdragen en mededelingen betreffende de geschiedenis der Nederlanden* 105: 537–552.

Bigwood, G. (1921). *Le régime juridique et économique du commerce de l'argent dans la Belgique du Moyen Âge.* Brussels: Académie Royale, pp. 319–320.

Blanchard, I. (2009). *The International Economy in the Age of Reason: Antwerp and the English Merchants' World.* Stuttgart: Steiner, pp. 19–78.

Blockmans, W. P. (2010a). "Inclusiveness and Exclusion, Trust Networks at the Origins of European Cities," *Theory and Society* 39: 315–326.

(2010b). *Metropolen aan de Noordzee. De geschiedenis van Nederland, 1100–1560.* Amsterdam: Bert Bakker.

Blondé, B. (1999). *Het Brabantse stedelijke netwerk (ca. 1750 – ca. 1790).* Brussels: Koninklijke Vlaamse Academie van België voor Wetenschappen en Kunsten.

Bochove, C. J. van (2004). "De Hollandse haringvisserij tijdens de vroegmoderne tijd," *Tijdschrift voor sociale en economische geschiedenis* 1(1): 3–27.

(2009). "The 'Golden Mountain': An Economic Analysis of Holland's Early Modern Herring Fisheries," in L. Sicking and D. Abreu-Ferreira (eds.), *Beyond the Catch: Fisheries of the North Atlantic, the North Sea and the Baltic, 900–1850.* Leiden/Boston: Brill, pp. 209–243.

Bochove, C. J. van and H. Kole (2013). "The Private Credit Market of Eighteenth-Century Amsterdam," forthcoming in *Tijdschrift voor Economische- en Sociale Geschiedenis.*

Bochove, C. J. van and T. van Velzen (2011). "Loans for Salaried Employees: The Case of the Dutch East India Company, 1602–1795." Unpublished paper.

Bochove, C. J. van and J. L. van Zanden (2006). "Two Engines of Early Modern Economic Growth? Herring Fisheries and Whaling during the Dutch Golden Age (1600–1800)," in S. Cavaciocchi (ed.), *Ricchezza del mare, ricchezza dal mare. Secoli XIII–XVIII.* Prato: Fondazione Istituto Internazionale di storia Economica/Fondazione Datini, pp. 557–574.

Boon, P. A. (1996). *Bouwers van de zee, zeevarenden van het Westfriese platteland, c. 1680–1720.* Stichting Hollandse Historische Reeks.

Boone, M., K. Davids, and P. Janssens, eds. (2003). *Urban Public Debts: Urban Government and the Market for Annuities in Western Europe (14th–18th centuries).* Turnhout: Brepols.

Brandon, P. (2013). "Masters of War: State, Capital, and Military Enterprise in the Dutch Cycle of Accumulation (1600–1795)." Ph.D. thesis, University of Amsterdam.

Braudel, F. (1949). *La Méditerranée et le monde méditerranéen à l'époque de Philippe II*. Paris: Colin.

(1979). *Civilisation Matérielle, économie et capitalisme, XVe–XVIIIe siècles*, 3 vols. Paris: Colin.

Brenner, R. (2001). "The Low Countries in the Transition to Capitalism," in Hoppenbrouwers and van Zanden (eds.), pp. 275–338.

Bronne, C. (1969). *Financiers et comédiens au XVIIIe siècle. Madame Nettine banquière des Pays Bas suivi d'Hannetaire et ses filles*. Brussels: Goemaere.

Bruijn, J. R. (1993). *The Dutch Navy of the Seventeenth and Eighteenth Centuries: Studies in Maritime History*. Columbia: University of South Carolina Press.

Bruijn, J. R. and J. Lucassen, eds. (1980). *Op de schepen der Oost-Indische Compagnie. Vijf artikelen van J. de Hullu, ingeleid, bewerkt en voorzien van een studie over de werkgelegenheid bij de VOC.* Groningen: Historische Studies Instituut voor Geschiedenis der Rijksuniversiteit Utrecht.

Bruijn, J. R., F. S. Gaastra, and I. Schöffer, eds. (1987). *Dutch-Asiatic Shipping in the 17th and 18th Centuries*. Vol. 1: *Introductory Volume*. The Hague: Martinus Nijhoff.

Brusse, P. (1999). *Overleven door ondernemen, de agrarische geschiedenis van de Over-Betuwe 1650–1850*. Arnhem: Vereniging Gelre.

Carlos, A. and L. Neal (2011). "Amsterdam and London as Financial Centers in the Eighteenth Century," *Financial History Review* 18: 21–46.

Dam, P. J. E. M. van (1998). *Vissen in veenmeren. De sluisvisserij op aal tussen Haarlem en Amsterdam en de ecologische transformatie in Rijnland 1440–1530*. Hilversum: Verloren.

Damme, I. van (2007). *Verleiden en verkopen. Antwerpse kleinhandelaars en hun klanten in tijden van crisis (ca. 1648–ca. 1748)*. Amsterdam: Aksant.

Davids, C. A. (1996). "Neringen, hallen en gilden. Kapitalisten, kleine ondernemers en de stedelijke overheid in de tijd van de Republiek," in C. A. Davids, W. Fritschy, and L. A. van der Valk (eds.), *Kapitaal, ondernemerschap en beleid. Studies over economie en politiek in Nederland, Europa en Azië*. Amsterdam: NEHA, pp. 95–119.

Degryse, K. (2005). *De Antwerpse fortuinen. Kapitaalaccumulatie, -investering en -rendement te Antwerpen in de 18de eeuw*. Antwerp: Genootschap voor Antwerpse Geschiedenis.

Dehing, P. W. N. M. (2012). *Geld in Amsterdam. Wisselbank en wisselkoersen, 1650–1725*. Hilversum: Verloren.

Dekker, C. and R. Baetens (2010). *Geld in het water. Antwerps en Mechels kapitaal in Zuid-Beveland na de stormvloeden in de 16e eeuw*. Hilversum: Verloren.

De Moor, T., J. L. van Zanden, and J. Zuijderduijn (2009). "Micro-Credit in Late Medieval Waterland: Households and the Efficiency of Capital Markets in Edam and De Zeevang, 1462–1563," in S. Cavachiocci (ed.), *La famiglia nell'economia europea secoli XIII–XVIII [The Economic Role of the Family in the European Economy from the 13th to the 18th Centuries]*. Florence University Press, pp. 651–668.

Dennison, T. (2011). *The Institutional Framework of Russian Serfdom*. Cambridge University Press.

De Peuter, R. E. M. A. (1999). *Brussel in de achtiende eeuw. Sociaal-economische structuren en ontwikkelingen in een regionale hoofdstad*. Brussels: VUB Press.

De Smedt, O. (1940–1941). "De keizerlijke verordeningen van 1537 en 1539 op de obligaties en wisselbrieven," *Nederlandsche historiebladen* 3: 15–35.

Deursen, A. Th. van (1994). *Een dorp in de polder. Graft in de zeventiende eeuw*. Amsterdam: Bakker.

Dijkman, J. (2011). *Shaping Medieval Markets: The Organisation of Commodity Markets in Holland, c. 1200–c. 1450*. Leiden: Brill.

Dillen, J. G. van (1941). *Amsterdam in 1585. Het kohier der capitale impositie 1585*. Amsterdam.

DuPlessis, R. S. and M. C. Howell (1982). "Reconsidering the Early Modern Urban Economy: The Cases of Leiden and Lille," *Past and Present* 94: 49–84.

Epstein, S. (2000). *Freedom and Growth: The Rise of States and Markets in Europe, 1300–1750*. London: Routledge.

Epstein, S. R. and M. R. Prak, eds. (2008). *Guilds, Innovation and the European Economy, 1400–1800*. Cambridge University Press.

Engen, H. van and R. Rutte (2008). *Stadswording in de Nederlanden. Op zoek naar overzicht*. Hilversum: Verloren.

Gelderblom, O. (2004). "The Decline of Fairs and Merchant Guilds in the Low Countries, 1250–1650," *Jaarboek voor Middeleeuwse Geschiedenis* 7: 199–238.

(2013). *Cities of Commerce: The Institutional Foundations of International Trade in the Low Countries, 1250–1650*. Princeton University Press.

Gelderblom, O. and J. Jonker (2004). "Completing a Financial Revolution: The Finance of the Dutch East India Trade and the Rise of the Amsterdam Capital Market, 1595–1612," *Journal of Economic History* 64(3): 641–72.

(2005). "Amsterdam as the Cradle of Modern Futures Trading and Options Trading, 1550–1650," in W. G. Goetzmann and K. G. Rouwenhorst (eds.), *The Origins of Value: The Financial Innovations that Created Modern Capital Markets*. Oxford University Press, pp. 189–205.

(2011). "Public Finance and Economic Growth: The Case of Holland in the Seventeenth Century," *Journal of Economic History* 71: 1–39.

(2013). "Low Countries Finance, 1348–1700," in G. Caprio (ed.), *Handbook of Key Global Financial Markets, Institutions, and Infrastructure*, Vol. 1. Oxford: Elsevier, pp. 175–183.

(forthcoming). "Mirroring Different Follies: The Character of the 1720 Bubble in the Dutch Republic," in C. Labio, W. Goetzmann, K. Rouwenhorst, and T. Young (eds.), *The "Great Mirror of Folly": Finance, Culture, and the Crash of 1720*. New Haven: Yale University Press.

Gelderblom, O., A. de Jong, and J. Jonker (2011). "An Admiralty for Asia, Business Organization and the Evolution of Corporate Governance in the Dutch Republic, 1590–1610," in J. Koppell (ed.), *The Origins of Shareholder Advocacy*. New York: Palgrave Macmillan, pp. 29–60.

(2013). "The Formative Years of the Modern Corporation: The Dutch East India Company VOC, 1602–1623," forthcoming in *The Journal of Economic History*.

Gijsbers, W. M. (1999). *Kapitale ossen. De internationale handel in slachtvee in Noordwest-Europa (1300–1750)*. Hilversum: Verloren.

Gillard, L. (2004). *La Banque d'Amsterdam et le florin européen au temps de la République néerlandaise (1610–1820)*. Paris: Éditions de l'EHESS.

Godding, P. (1987). *Le droit privé dans les Pays-Bas méridionaux, du 12e au 18e siècle*. Brussels: Académie Royale de Belgique.

Grafe, R. (2012). *Distant Tyranny: Markets, Power, and Backwardness in Spain, 1650–1800*. Princeton University Press.

Groeneveld, F. P. (1940). *De economische crisis van het jaar 1720*. Groningen: Noordhoff.

Hesselink-Van der Riet, T., W. Kuiper, and C. Trompetter (2008). *Het schuldboek van Arend Kenkhuis*. Amsterdam University Press.

Hoffman, P. T. (1996). *Growth in a Traditional Society: The French Countryside, 1450–1820*. Princeton University Press.

Hollestelle, J. (1961). *De steenbakkerij in de Nederlanden tot omstreeks 1560*. Assen: van Gorcum.

Hoppenbrouwers, P. C. M. (1992). *Een middeleeuwse samenleving. Het land van Heusden (ca. 1360- ca. 1515)*, 2 vols. Wageningen: Afdeling Agrarische Geschiedenis.

Hoppenbrouwers, P., and J. L. van Zanden, eds. (2001). *Peasants into Farmers? The Transformation of Rural Economy and Society in the Low Countries (Middle Ages–19th Century) in light of the Brenner Debate*. Turnhout: Brepols.

Houtman-De Smedt, H. 1982. "Charles Proli als ondernemer," *Economisch en sociaalhistorisch jaarboek* 44: 84–92.

(1983). *Charles Proli. Antwerps zakenman en bankier, 1723–1786, een biografische en bedrijfshistorische studie*. Brussels: Paleis der Academiën.

Houwink, A. (1929). *Acceptcrediet: economische en bankpolitieke beschouwingen over den in het bankaccept belichaamden credietvorm*. Amsterdam.

Howell, M. C. (2010). *Commerce before Capitalism in Europe, 1300–1600*. New York: Cambridge University Press.

Israel, J. I. (1995). *The Dutch Republic: Its Rise, Greatness, and Fall 1477–1806*. Oxford: Clarendon Press.

Janssens, V. (1957). *Het geldwezen der Oostenrijkse Nederlanden*. Brussels: Paleis der Academiën.

Jong, A. de, J. Jonker, and A. Roëll (2013). "Dutch Corporate Finance, 1602–1850," in G. Caprio (ed.), *Handbook of Key Global Financial Markets, Institutions, and Infrastructure*, Vol. 1. Oxford: Elsevier, pp. 73–83.

Jong-Keesing, E. E. de (1939). *De economische crisis van 1763 te Amsterdam*. Amsterdam: Internationale Uitgevers- en Handelmaatschappij.

Jongh, M. de (2011). "Shareholder Activists *avant la lettre*: The 'complaining participants' in the Dutch East India Company, 1622–1625," in J. Koppell (ed.), *The Origins of Shareholder Advocacy*. New York: Palgrave Macmillan, pp. 61–88.

Jonker, Joost P. B. (1996). *Merchants, Bankers, Middlemen: The Amsterdam Money Market during the First Half of the 19th Century*. Amsterdam: NEHA.

(forthcoming). "Wedged between the Market and the World: The Amsterdam Haute Banque, 1650s-1914," in R. Dartevelle (ed.), *La Haute Banque en Europe*.

Jonker, J. P. B. and K. E. Sluyterman (2000). *At Home on the World Markets: Dutch International Trading Companies from the 16th Century until the Present*. The Hague: Sdu Uitgevers.

Kuijpers, E. (2005). *Migrantenstad, immigratie en sociale verhoudingen in 17e-eeuws Amsterdam*. Hilversum: Verloren.

(2009). "Who Digs the Town Moat? The Public Works of Leyden and the Performance of the Markets for Labour and Capital in Late Medieval Holland." Unpublished paper, http://vkc.library.uu.nl/vkc/seh/research/Lists/Working%20Papers/Attachments/24/Who%20digs%20the%20townmoat%20working%20paper.doc.pdf.

Limberger, M. (2001). "Early Forms of Proto-industries in the Backyard of Antwerp? The Rupel Area in the 15th and 16th Centuries," in B. Blondé, E. Vanhaute, and M. Galand (eds.), *Labor and Labor Markets between Town and Countryside (Middle Ages–19th Century)*. Turnhout: Brepols, pp. 158–174.

(2008). *Sixteenth-century Antwerp and its Rural Surroundings: Social and Economic Changes in the Hinterland of a Commercial Metropolis*. Turnhout: Brepols.

Lis, C. and H. Soly (1987). *Een groot bedrijf in een kleine stad. De firma De Heyder en Co. te Lier, 1757–1834*. Lier: Liers Genootschap voor Geschiedenis.

(1997a). *Werelden van verschil, ambachtsgilden in de Lage Landen*. Brussel: VUB Press.

(1997b). "Different Paths of Development: Capitalism in the Northern and Southern Netherlands during the Late Middle Ages and the Early Modern Period," *Review: Fernand Braudel Center for the Study of Economies, Historical Systems, and Civilizations* 20(2): 211–242.

(2008). "Subcontracting in Guild-based Export Trades, Thirteenth–Eighteenth Centuries," in Epstein and Prak (eds.), pp. 81–113.

Lucassen, J. M. W G. (1982). "Beschouwingen over seizoensgebonden trekarbeid naar het westen van Nerderland, ca. 1700-ca. 1800," *Tijdschrift voor sociale geschiedenis* 8: 327–358.

(1987). *Migrant Labor in Europe: The Drift to the North Sea*. London: Croom Helm.

(1995). "Labour and Early Modern Economic Development," in K. Davids and J. Lucassen (eds.), *A Miracle Mirrored: The Dutch Republic in European Perspective*. Cambridge University Press, pp. 367–409.

Lucassen, J. and R. W. Unger (2000). "Labour Productivity in Ocean Shipping, 1450–1875," *International Journal of Maritime History* 12(2): 127–141.

(2007). "Wage Payments and Currency Circulation in the Netherlands from 1200 to 2000," in J. M. W. G. Lucassen (ed.), *Wages and Currency: Global Comparisons from Antiquity to the Twentieth Century*. Berne: Lang.

Maassen, H. A. J. (1994). *Tussen commercieel en sociaal krediet, de ontwikkeling van de bank van lening in Nederland van lombard tot gemeentelijke kredietbank 1260–1940*. Hilversum: Verloren.

Mokyr, J. (1976). *Industrialization in the Low Countries, 1795–1850*. New Haven: Yale University Press.

Murray, J. M. (2005). *Bruges, Cradle of Capitalism 1280–1390*. Cambridge University Press.

Nieuwkerk, M. van (ed.) (2009). *The Bank of Amsterdam: On the Origins of Central Banking*. Arnhem: Sonsbeek.

Nimwegen, O. van (2010). *The Dutch Army and the Military Revolutions, 1588–1688*. Woodbridge: The Boydell Press.

Parthesius, R. (2010). *Dutch Ships in Tropical Waters: The Development of the Dutch East India Company (VOC) Shipping Network in Asia 1595–1660*. Amsterdam University Press.

Petram, L. (2011). "The World's First Stock Exchange. How the Amsterdam Market for Dutch East India Company Shares Became a Modern Securities Market, 1602–1700." Ph.D. thesis, University of Amsterdam.

Prak, M. R. (2005). *The Dutch Republic in the Seventeenth Century: The Golden Age*. Cambridge University Press.

Priester, P. (1998). *Geschiedenis van de Zeeuwse Landbouw circa 1600–1910*. Wageningen: Afdeling Agrarische Geschiedenis Landbouwuniversiteit.

Quinn, S. and W. Roberds (2010). "How Amsterdam got Fiat Money." Unpublished paper. Texas Christian University 2010(17).

Rijpma, A. (2012). "Funding Public Services through Religious and Charitable Foundations in the Late-medieval Low Countries." Ph.D. thesis, Utrecht University.

Ryckbosch, W. (2012). "A Consumer Revolution under Strain: Consumption, Wealth and Status in Eighteenth-century Aalst (Southern Netherlands)." Ph.D. thesis, University of Antwerp.

Schalk, R., O. Gelderblom, and J. Jonker (2012). "Schipperen op de Aziatische vaart. De financiering van de VOC kamer Enkhuizen, 1602–1622," *Low Countries Historical Review* 127(4): 3–27.

Schnabel, I. and H. S. Shin (2004). "Liquidity and Contagion: The Crisis of 1763," *Journal of the European Economic Association* 6: 929–968.

Soens, T. (2009). *De spade in de dijk? Waterbeheer en rurale samenleving in de Vlaamse kustvlakte (1280–1580)*. Ghent: Academia Press.

Soens, T. and E. Thoen (2009). "The Origins of Leasehold in the Former County of Flanders," in B. J. P. van Bavel and P. Schofield (eds.), *The Development of Leasehold in Northwestern Europe, 1200–1600*. Turnhout: Brepols, pp. 31–55.

Soly, H. (1977). *Urbanisme en kapitalisme te Antwerpen in de 16de eeuw. De stedebouwkundige en industriële ondernemingen van Gilbert van Schoonbeke*. Brussels: Gemeentekrediet van België.

Spufford, P. (2008). *How Rarely did Medieval Merchants Use Coin?* Utrecht: Geldmuseum.

Stabel, P. (1997). *Dwarfs among Giants: The Flemish Urban Network in the Late Middle Ages*. Leuven: Garant.

  (2001). "Urban Markets, Rural Industries and the Organisation of Labor in Late Medieval Flanders: The Constraints of Guild Regulations and the Requirements of Export Oriented Production," in B. Blondé, E. Vanhaute, and M. Galand (eds.), *Labor and Labor Markets between Town and Countryside (Middle Ages–19th Century)*. Turnhout: Brepols, pp. 140–157.

  (2004). "Guilds in Late Medieval Flanders: Myths and Realities of Guild Life in an Export-oriented Environment," *Journal of Medieval History* 30: 187–212.

Thoen, E. (1988). *Landbouwekonomie en bevolking in Vlaanderen gedurende de late middeleeuwen en het begin van de moderne tijden. Testregio. De kasselrijen van Oudenaarde en Aalst, eind 13de – eerste helft van de 16de eeuw*, 2 vols. Ghent: Belgisch centruum voor landelijke geschiedenis.

  (2001). "A 'Commercial Survival Economy' in Evolution: The Flemish Countryside and the Transition to Capitalism (Middle Ages–19th century)," in Hoppenbrouwers and van Zanden (eds.), pp. 102–157.

Tielhof, M. van and P. J. E M. van Dam (2006). *Waterstaat in stedenland. Het hoogheemraadschap van Rijnland voor 1857*. Utrecht: Matrijs.

Tielhof, M. van and J. L. van Zanden (2009). "Roots of Growth and Productivity Change in Dutch Shipping Industry, 1500–1800," *Explorations in Economic History* 46: 389–403.

Tihon, C. (1961). "Aperçus sur l'établissement des Lombards dans les Pays Bas aux XIIIe et XIVe siècles," *Revue Belge de Philologie et Histoire* 39: 334–364.

Tracy, J. D. (1985). *A Financial Revolution in the Habsburg Netherlands: Renten and Renteniers in the County of Holland, 1515–1565*. London: University of California Press.

  (2002). *Emperor Charles V, Impresario of War: Campaign Strategy, International Finance, and Domestic Politics*. Cambridge University Press.

  (2003). "On the Dual Origins of Long-term Public Debt in Medieval Europe," in M. Boone, K. Davids, and P. Janssens (eds.), *Urban Public Debts: Urban Government and the Market for Annuities in Western Europe (14th–18th centuries).* Turnhout: Brepols, pp. 13–26.

Van der Linden, H. (1956). *De cope. Bijdrage tot de rechtsgeschiedenis van de openlegging der Hollands-Utrechtse laagvlakte.* Assen: Van Gorcum.

Van Lottum, J. (2007). *Across the North Sea: The Impact of the Dutch Republic on International Labor Migration, c. 1550–1850.* Amsterdam: Uitgeverij Aksant.

Vercauteren, F. (1947). "Note sur l'origine et l'évolution du contrat de mortgage en Lotharingie, du IXe au XIIIe siècle," *Historische bijdragen aangeboden aan Leo van der Essen.* Brussels: Éditions universitaires, pp. 218–227.

Verhas, C. M. O. (1997). *De beginjaren van de Hoge Raad van Holland, Zeeland en West-Friesland: . . . tot onderhoudinge van de Politique ordre ende staet der Landen van Hollandt, Zeelandt, Vrieslant.* The Hague: Algemeen Rijksarchief.

Vermeesch, G. (2006). *Oorlog, steden en staatsvorming. De grenssteden Gorinchem en Doesburg tijdens de geboorte-eeuw van de Republiek (1572–1680).* Amsterdam University Press.

Vries, Jan de (1974). *The Dutch Rural Economy in the Golden Age, 1500–1700.* New Haven: Yale University Press.

(1978). *Barges and Capitalism: Passenger Transportation in the Dutch Economy, 1632–1839.* Wageningen: Landbouwhogeschool.

Vries, J. de and A. Van der Woude (1997). *The First Modern Economy: Success, Failure, and Perseverance of the Dutch Economy, 1500–1815.* Cambridge University Press.

(2001). "Economic Growth before and after the Industrial Revolution: A Modest Proposal," in M. Prak (ed.), *Early Modern Capitalism, Economic and Social Change in Europe, 1400–1800.* London: Routledge, pp. 177–194.

Wallert, J. A. F. (1996). "Ontwikkelingslijnen in praktijk en theorie van de wisselbrief 1300–2000." Ph.D. thesis, Nijmegen University.

Wee, H. van der (1963). *The Growth of the Antwerp Market and the European Economy (14th–16th centuries),* 3 vols. The Hague: Nijhoff.

(1979). "Geld-, krediet- en bankwezen in de Zuidelijke Nederlanden," P. Blok *et al.* (eds.), *Algemene geschiedenis der Nederlanden,* Vol. VI. Haarlem: Fibula-Van Dishoeck, pp. 98–108.

(1988). "Industrial Dynamics and the Process of Urbanization and De-urbanization in the Low Countries from the Late Middle Ages to the Eighteenth Century: A Synthesis," in H. van der Wee (ed.), *The Rise of Urban Industries in Italy and the Low Countries (Late Middle-Ages – Early Modern Times).* Leuwen University Press, pp. 307–381.

Wee, H. van der and E. Aerts (1979). "The Lier Livestock Market and the Livestock Trade in the Low Countries from the 14th to the 18th Century," in E. Westermann (ed.), *Internationaler Ochsenhandel (1350–1750). Akten des 7th International Economic History Congress. Edinburgh 1978.* Bamberg: Klett-Cotta, pp. 235–254.

Werveke, H. van (1929). "Le mortgage et son rôle économique en Flandre et en Lotharingie," *Revue belge de philologie et histoire* 8: 53–91.

Wijffels, A. (2003). "Ius Commune and International Wine Trade: A Revision (Middelburg c. Antwerp 1548–1559," *Tijdschrift voor Rechtsgeschiedenis/The Legal History Review* 71(3–4): 289–317.

Wijngaarden, H. van (2000). *Zorg voor de kost. Armenzorg, arbeid en onderlinge hulop in Zwolle 1650–1700.* Amsterdam: Prometheus/Bert Bakker.

Willems, B. (2009). *Leven op de pof. Krediet bij de. Antwerpse middenstand in de achttiende eeuw.* Amsterdam: Aksant.

Wyffels, C. (1991). "L'usure en Flandre au XIIIe siècle," *Revue Belge de Philologie et Histoire* 69: 853–871.

Yntema, R. (2009). "The Union of Utrecht, Tariff Barriers and the Interprovincial Beer Trade in the Dutch Republic," in O. Gelderblom (ed.), *The Political Economy of the Dutch Republic.* Aldershot: Ashgate, pp. 255–289.

Zanden, J. L. van (1991). "From Peasant Economy to Modern Market-oriented Agriculture: The Transformation of the Rural Economy of the Eastern Netherlands 1800–1914," *Economic and Social History in the Netherlands* 3: 37–59.

(1993). *The Rise and Decline of Holland's Economy: Merchant Capitalism and the Labor Market.* Manchester University Press.

(1999). "The Paradox of the Marks, the Exploitation of Commons in the Eastern Netherlands, 1250–1850," *Agricultural History Review* 47: 125–144.

Zanden, J. L. van and A. van Riel (2004). *The Strictures of Inheritance: The Dutch Economy in the Nineteenth Century.* Princeton University Press.

Zuijderduijn, C. J. (2009). *Medieval Capital Markets: Markets for Renten, State Formation and Private Investment in Holland (1300–1550).* Leiden: Brill.

(2010). "The Emergence of Provincial Public Debt in the County of Holland (Thirteenth–Sixteenth Centuries)," *European Review of Economic History* 14: 335–359.

Zwet, H. van (2009). *Lofwaerdighe dijckagies en miserabele polders. Een financiële analyse van landaanwinningsprojecten in Hollands Noorderkwartier, 1597–1643.* Hilversum: Verloren.

12

The formation of states and transitions to modern economies: England, Europe, and Asia compared

PATRICK KARL O'BRIEN

> The essence of the system lies not in some doctrine of money or of the balance of trade; not in tariff barriers or protective duties, or navigation laws; but in something far greater: namely in the total transformation of society and its organizations as well as of the state and its institutions, in the replacing of a local and territorial economy by that of the national state.
>
> G. Schmoller, *The Mercantile System and its Historical Significance*
> (1897 republished New York, 1967, p. 57).

The formation of states and the construction of capitalist institutions for early modern economies

In recent decades modern economics and economic history have expanded their agendas to include matters that Cunningham recommended to Marshall and they have sustained enlightening programs of classifying, theorizing (and occasionally measuring) how a range of institutional variables promoted or retarded both the flow and the productivity of the inputs of land, labor, capital, technology, and other proximate determinants behind the divergent rates, paths, and patterns that one observes for the economic growth of nations. Re-engaging with traditions of enquiry initiated by the German historical school, we have been reminded that for centuries production and exchange across early modern Eurasia had been more or less embedded in disabling frameworks of law, institutions, and cultures that were shaped and sustained by states (Hodgson 2000). States (or rather states in the process of formation) created and sustained the legal and institutional frameworks within which productive and counterproductive activities occurred (Smelser and Swedberg 2006; Stasavage 2010, 2011). States defined and enforced property rights. States solved or failed to solve the legal, contractual, and infrastructural problems involved in extending, integrating, and coordinating markets. States reordered or neglected to reorder ideologies, religions, and cultures of behavior that reduced shirking, cheating, freeriding, and transaction costs and encouraged thrift, work, and the discovery of new knowledge (Chang 2007; Persson and Tabellini 2003)

As a recent text on "why nations fail" has at least recognized, during pre-modern centuries of intensified international conflict and imperialism states provided or failed to provide national economies bounded by vulnerable frontiers but engaged in foreign trade with some overwhelmingly important public goods, namely internal order, external security, and protection for commerce at sea (Acemoglu and Robinson 2012). Without these state services, private investment, production, innovation, and trade could only have remained below the levels required for discernible growth in real per capita incomes. Our problem is, however, to account for any observed variations in the effectiveness with which the necessary state services were supplied.

Theories that "endogenize" the actions and policies of states and predict that their constitutions and the rules they promulgated for the protection and operation of economic activity altered as and when it became sufficiently profitable for rulers, innovators, or "revolutionaries" to bring about more economically efficient political and institutional change seem unconvincingly reductionist. After all, the traditional preoccupation of political history has always been with evidence, acquired with difficulty, but concerned with the evolution of the states, laws, rules, organizations, religions, ideologies, and cultures conditioning personal and group behavior. History's libraries are dominated by volumes of research into these matters for specific places at particular times. That research does not reveal that the formation of states over the centuries can be simulated to arenas where the actions, inactions, and failures of rulers and their servants can be explained with reference to "rent-seeking" or "revenue-maximizing" behavior. It shows there was too much violence, path dependence, vested interest, custom, inertia, and bargaining recorded for national and local histories of political change in the early modern period. There was no overarching and definable objective that rulers attempted to maximize for general theories from economics or political science to be of real help in dealing with the interrelated problems of state formation, state policies, conditions for their implementation, and connections to rates of material change (Prendergast 1999; White 2009).

Furthermore, and until well into the nineteenth century, the negative view of states associated by liberals with rent-seeking under all *anciens régimes* (and which has been foregrounded by new institutional economics) can be more plausibly represented as unavoidable payments for the centralization of power (Ekelund and Tollison 1997). Before, say 1815, political constraints on the construction of governmental departments and organizations nominally under the control of rulers and their advisors, (with longer-term dynastic interests in delivering governance at lower cost and sustaining institutions that facilitated the extension of taxable private enterprise) continued to be formidable. Historians will continue to insist that the modes and techniques deployed by governmental organizations, the systems in place for the recruitment of personnel, levels of corruption, degrees of rigidity, and rent-seeking simply exemplify the multiple objectives pursued and restraints operating upon *anciens régimes* of all political forms (Teichova and Matis 2003). In those times rulers made political bargains and compromises and incurred the unavoidable costs required to retain sovereignty but their long-term interest was to maintain and increase their dynastic powers and bases for fiscal extraction by supplying external security, protection overseas, victories in war, and internal order in ways and at levels of taxation and expenditure that secured stability and general compliance (Tilly 1975; Timmons 2005).

During the long transition toward modern forms of state sovereignty the scope for functional levels of efficiency from the administrative and organizational capacities available to any and every conceivable kind of political regime (imperial, monarchical, absolutist, republican, and parliamentary alike) remained severely constrained and difficult to develop (Chang 2007). That constraint looks less obvious at the courts and capitals of emperors and kings and the chambers of oligarchies where rulers benefitted from the advice and services of talented men, often recruited from the Church and the law (Reinhard 1996). In China they were selected through an examination system – admired by Voltaire and other enlightened intellectuals of his day (Brook and Blue 1999). These loyal servants of states have been superficially portrayed as corruptible rent-seekers, pursuing interests that were antithetical to economic progress (Ekelund and Tollison 1997). Nevertheless, their albeit sycophantic devotion to sovereigns and opposition to rival centers of power might also be represented as missions to centralize and to rationalize the formulation of rules; to create organizations in order to universalize, monitor, and enforce their execution, to establish procedures for adjudication, and, above all, to mobilize and secure the fiscal and financial resources required for effective governance (Dincecco 2011).

Beyond bureaucracies employed at the courts of kings and by councils of cities serious problems for the execution of policies persisted across the entire range of operations conducted by states for the delivery of public goods – even for defense and aggression supplied by armies and navies commanded by aristocratic officers who often pursued strategies and agendas of their own to the cost and detriment of rulers and national economies (Lachmann 2000). For the implementation of almost all the manifold functions involved in ruling empires, kingdoms, republics, or cities, states everywhere, by necessity, resorted to markets and franchising. Politically appointed hierarchies of advisors and bureaucracies networked in tandem with private firms to deliver public goods (Bowen and Encisco 2006). Debate on the boundaries of private and public sectors, their organizational forms, contractual arrangements, modes of operation, and levels of efficiency goes way back in history and is the dominant theme in a recent wave of books on the political economy of states (Sanchez-Torres 2007). Without adequate and regular inflows of funds states lacked the capacity necessary to supply the requisite levels of protection, to enforce regulations for the efficient operation of capitalist markets for commodities and factors of production, and to support institutions for the promotion of innovation. This is why Schumpeter recognized that historical analyses of how states constructed and sustained fiscal and financial systems and how effectively administrations set up to assess and collect an astonishing variety of direct and indirect taxes operated was a precondition for any understanding of their relative successes and failures as they competed with rivals operating in a mercantilist international economic order (Mann 1986; O'Brien 2002).

The origins and evolution of England's fiscal naval state

Long ago, Schumpeter observed that:

> The fiscal history of a people is above all an essential part of its general history. In some historical periods the immediate formative influence of the fiscal needs and policy of the state on the development of the economy and with it on all forms of life and all aspects of culture explains practically all the major features of events; in most periods it explains a great deal, but there are few periods when it explains nothing. (Schumpeter 1954: 7)

Schumpeter (and latterly his followers in historical sociology) have appreciated that whereas economics might specify, model, and occasionally measure connections between particular institutions and economic growth, only historical narratives can properly explain why some countries formed states that established and sustained the bureaucracies, departments, and complex organizations required to raise taxes and loans and allocated revenues to guarantee external security, preserve internal stability, and deliver the array of public goods that established and sustained the institutions for capitalism and sooner in some polities than others (Hall 1985; Hall and Schroeder 2006). Because Britain continues to be recognized as the first national economy to complete a transition to a modern industrial market economy some understanding of why the state ruling the offshore island became hospitable to and promotional toward material progress might provide not a paradigm case, but a point of reference for the study of connections between the global process of state formation and transitions to industrial market economies (Horn 2010). To comprehend the basic forces behind the formation of the English state the most heuristic place to start is at an endpoint or the "conjuncture" in its long history, when Castlereagh signed the Treaty of Vienna.

In 1815 at the close of twenty-two years of warfare against revolutionary and Napoleonic France, the monarchy, in conjunction with the aristocratic and plutocratic elite in charge of governing the, by then, United Kingdom of England, Wales, Scotland and Ireland, offered its deferential subjects superior standards of external security, internal stability, protection for property rights, support for hierarchy and authority, legal frameworks for contracts and for the extension and integration of markets, encouragement for technical and business innovation, and, above all, more extensive and better-protected entries to imperial and other overseas markets than any other state in the world. As envious mercantilists from the mainland observed, the United Kingdom's propertied elites enjoyed almost complete safety from foreign invasion derived from the hegemony of their navy at sea (Hampson 1988). They possessed ready access to the markets and resources of the largest occidental empire since Rome. Furthermore, they operated within a culture defined by an established religion and basked in the deferential behavior of British citizens toward monarchy, aristocracy, and all persons of wealth and status managing an economy en route to becoming an industrial "workshop for the world" (Mokyr 2009; O'Brien 2011a).

Some historians are disposed to discover "distant origins" for this clear position of primacy in conjoined geopolitical and economic spheres – a position retained by Britain and its empire for roughly a century after 1815. They refer back to the high middle ages when the realm was supposedly ruled by one of the best-funded, centralized, and relatively powerful states in Europe. Yet any scrutiny of data for total taxes collected for kings measured in grams of silver and at constant prices exposes the claim as unfounded (Bonney 1999: Chapter 1). Looking back to an era succeeding the Magna Carta and the first Hundred Years

War from the perspective of more continuous and costly warfare from 1651 to 1815, the endeavors of successive medieval monarchs to create a fiscal base, to maintain sovereignty, to support internal colonization within the Isles and, above all, to extend and defend their dynastic claims to territory across the Channel in France, leaves us with Ormrod's more plausible view that England's "Plantagenet regime presided over the almost complete disintegration of its overseas territories between 1200–1450, losing not only the potential profit from those lands, but also large amounts of England's wealth expended in the ultimately futile campaigns of re-conquest" (Bonney, 1999: Chapter 1; Ormrod, Bonney, and Bonney 1999: 13).

Defeat and withdrawal from colonization on the mainland of Europe placed serious geopolitical, political, and economic constraints on the capacities of the Tudor and Stuart monarchies to fund strategies and policies for the formation of a more powerful government on the Islands (O'Brien 2006). Eventually, about 150 years after the accession of the Tudor dynasty in 1485, political tensions provoked by fiscal constraints on the formation of a centralized state led to a constitutional crisis and a destructive civil war. The extensions and innovations to the scale, scope, and administration of taxation, which emerged as experiments during that interregnum of armed conflict between elites and across the ancient provinces of a composite island realm continued under a restored Stuart monarchy as shown in Figure 12.1, which traces the trajectory of total taxation for central government from 1600 to 1820 (Ormrod et al. 1999). After 1688 they were consolidated into a stable, politically acceptable, and highly productive fiscal and financial regime that continues to be represented by Whig historians as a core component of a Glorious Revolution that flowed from a Dutch *coup d'état* of 1688 (Sowerby 2011; O'Brien 2002 and 2011a includes extended bibliographies).

For historians of capitalism the exaggerated discontinuity of 1688 can be more heuristically contextualized in contradiction to a historical background marked by some two centuries of fiscal stasis, financial mismanagement, internal disorder, and geopolitical weakness. Why not represent that "event" as part of a longer conjuncture in English history that occurred within little more than four decades after the death of Oliver Cromwell, when the fiscal system was extended to fund the reformulation of the country's strategic, foreign, and imperial policies along far more aggressive lines (Brenner 2003; O'Brien 2006)? In retrospect and outcome (as Europe's political and intellectual elites recognized) the island state's rigorous pursuit of mercantilism turned out to be detrimental to its national interests but positive for the long-run development of the British economy (Hampson 1988; O'Brien 2002).

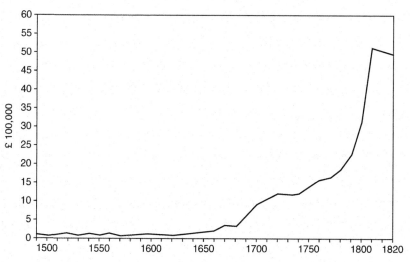

Figure 12.1 Trends in total taxes 1490–1820 (expressed as nine-year moving averages in £100,000 at constant prices of 1451–1475)
Source: Bonney (1999: Chapter 2).

For the construction of a short narrative designed to historicize the recon-struction of the English state over a half century of profound political disconti-nuities marked by civil war, an interregnum of republican rule, the restoration of monarchy, and a Dutch invasion, there seems to be no need for economic historians (concerned basically with the role of states in promoting or restrain-ing economic growth) to engage with unresolvable ideological controversies as to which among this sequence of events can be plausibly represented as a tipping or turning point along the trajectory towards the evolution of a state promotional for the development of capitalism (for the contrary view that reifies 1688 see Acemoglu and Robinson 2012; North and Weingast 1989; Pincus 2009). Historically it is sufficient to note that the whole process began with a highly destructive civil war that for several generations thereafter left the propertied classes from all parties and provinces of a composite island kingdom predisposed to favor some form of strong and more centralized government with the fiscal and financial capacities required to maintain internal order under established and hereditary hierarchies. As Hobbes recognized, what England's propertied elites wanted was a monarchy to maintain stability, to remain committed above all else to defend the realm, and when opportunities arose to engage in potentially profitable aggression against rivals and enemies from the mainland of Europe (Appleby 2010: Parts IV and V; Brenner 2003; Findlay et al. 2006).

Major constitutional "understandings" between restored monarchs and Parliament coupled with revised structural and organizational arrangements for taxation had been more or less settled some years before the Glorious Revolution of 1688. Both sons of England's executed king (Charles I) knew that in order to appropriate taxes or borrow money for purposes of state from their loyal subjects they would have to seek formal consent from assemblies of aristocrats and notables elected by their bribed and/or intimidated adult male inferiors. Before 1832 electorates constituted less than 2 percent of the kingdom's adult population. Furthermore, experiments to cope with desperate circumstances of civil war had demonstrated the feasibility of levying excise and stamp duties upon an extensive range of goods and services produced, sold, and consumed within the kingdom. They had also exposed the strong resistance provoked by coercive Cromwellian attempts to revalue liabilities for the direct taxation of land and other fixed and visible manifestations of family wealth (Coffman 2008).

Meanwhile the gradual structural shift to more regressive forms of indirect taxation, favored by Parliament, was helped on its way by transforming the long-established franchised systems for their assessment and collection into proto-professional public bureaucracies for the administration of customs duties in 1671 and excises in 1683 (Wong and Sayer 2006). Under surveillance from a reorganized Treasury these reforms terminated centuries of tax-farming and jacked up the proportion of the sovereign's revenues from taxes that flowed into the London exchequer. This left the state with the unsolved financial problem of "tax smoothing" or obtaining ready access to liquidity during shorter and longer interludes of time when necessary, unpredicted, and unavoidable levels of expenditure exceeded inflows of revenues (Ormrod et al. 1999). This omnipresent contingency, which invariably became more urgent and serious in wartime, had for centuries been resolved (often with difficulty) by royal borrowing from financiers and tax-farmers who loaned money to the Crown (at more or less extortionate terms) on the security of sovereign revenues as part of the trade-off for leasehold agreements providing for their control and management over royal revenues (Caselli 2008).

The Glorious Revolution of 1688 certainly included an invasion of the Isles by 40,000 Dutch troops and a *coup d'état* against an established monarch – who supposedly harbored realizable and subversive plans for the overthrow of the English constitution and predatory designs on private property (Sowerby 2011). In a seminal article Julian Hoppit has degraded the thesis that in general private property rights become better protected after 1688. He concluded that parliamentary sovereignty operated basically to strengthen centralized power to override vested private interests in order to secure the integration and coordination of markets (Hoppit 2011; and *vide* Epstein 2000; Irigoin and Grafe 2012). Furthermore, whether it was "necessary," let alone "necessary and sufficient," to complete the on-going reconstruction of the fiscal and financial foundations required for a state that may or may not have been willing to pursue an altogether more aggressive and costly commitment to those trans-European mercantilist objectives of power with profit will remain for ever on an agenda for ideologically charged debate.

Meanwhile, two outcomes of the civil war have become reasonably uncontentious for historians versed in the politics and geopolitics of the interregnum (Morrill 1993). First, England's short-lived republican regime had brutally circumscribed traditional threats from Scotland and Ireland to a centralized state ruling over a composite kingdom of the Isles. Secondly, and initially for its survival against royalist inspired invasions from the mainland, the republic's victorious military elite, aware of the advantages of England's location, adopted the strategy for national defense of defending the Isles from offshore. Cromwell and his ministers jacked up public investment in the warships, cannon, and onshore infrastructures for a significantly enlarged and centrally organized navy as the first bastion for external security of the Isles (Knight 2011; Rodger 2004). That strategy involved a sustained commitment to promote a range of symbiotic connections between commerce overseas, merchant shipping (as a nursery for seamen), and domestic ship-building, on the one hand and naval power on the other. England's protestant republicans revived, extended, and aggressively implemented a navigation code for the regulation of seaborne trade in and out of the ports of the Isles and its empire overseas. That strategy advocated by a line of mainstream mercantilist economists from Thomas Mun (through Adam Smith), George Chalmers, and Patrick Colquhoun was persistently revised to secure increased gains from seaborne trades at the expense of England's Dutch protestant and republican rival (Hont 2005; Reinert 2011).

The British merchant marine was established and consolidated by the first Anglo-Dutch war (1652–1654), and then sustained by "jealousy" of Dutch primacy in global trade, shipping, ship-building, and the provision of commercial services (Hont 2005). Republican priorities for the expansion of a mercantile marine networked to enterprises for banking, insurance, and other commercial services remained as national objectives through two further Anglo-Dutch wars pursued under Stuart monarchs (O'Brien 2000; Jones 1999; Ormrod 2003). Indeed, several interconnected policies concerned with defense, mercantilist

diplomacy, and aggression, commerce, and imperial expansion (normally com-
partmentalized by academic experts) can with hindsight be represented as the
English state's enduring and consistent pursuit of geopolitical hegemony at
sea combined with mercantile and imperial expansion overseas in order to
maximize and retain rising shares of the taxable gains from global trade and
commerce. This grand strategy (generating a network technology) has been
recently and aptly labeled as "gentlemanly capitalism" (to signify the essential
features of an alliance between the kingdom's monarchy, aristocracy, and
mercantile oligarchy) and provided its capitalists with the public goods necessary (but hardly sufficient) to invest and to move the economy towards its
precocious transition as an industrial market economy several decades ahead of
its rivals on the mainland (Akita 2002). The origins and basis for that political,
fiscal, and administrative strategy certainly predated the Glorious Revolution
of 1688. That unpredicted and unpredictable event can now be realistically
contextualized as one of a succession of events that formalized an alteration in
the balance of power between the monarchy and Parliament, derived from civil
war. It gave nothing more than an impetus to the kingdom's anti-French and
anti-Catholic orientation in foreign policy and accelerated an on-going reconstruction of the combined fiscal and financial basis for a state that thereafter
matured into Europe's paradigm example of successful mercantilism (Hoppit
2000; Reinert 2011).

Far and away the most significant and immediate outcome of a *coup d'état*
that placed a Dutch protestant monarch in charge of the country's foreign
and strategic policies was nine years of open warfare against Louis XIV and his
allies (referred to at the time as King William's war). That conflict endured,
after a breathing space (1698–1702), into the most protracted, costly, and
dangerous war for the security of the realm since 1453 (Jones 1988). Peace
settlements negotiated at Augsburg in 1698 and Utrecht in 1713 secured the
containment of French ambitions in Europe and confirmed the decline of the
Netherlands as a serious geopolitical rival for gains from empire and commerce overseas. Above all, and despite an interlude of fiscal exhaustion that
promoted peaceful coexistence from 1713 to 1740, the treaties marked the onset
of an era in the realm's geopolitical and economic relations with the mainland
that François Crouzet has aptly titled as the "second hundred years' war"
between Great Britain and France" (Crouzet 1996).

This protracted conflict, which opened with two decades of extraordinarily
costly warfare, intensified fiscal and financial pressures to fund the military
and naval forces mobilized for the security of the realm. King William's and
Queen Anne's wars (1689–1713) involved the commitment of armies to fight on

the mainland of Europe; further engagement for the pacification of Ireland and Scotland; a pronounced upsurge in expenditures on the navy; a marked structural shift away from the direct levies on incomes and wealth toward indirect taxation, particularly excise duties; and what Peter Dickson celebrated as a financial revolution (Dickson 1967; Jones 1988).

Eventually extraordinary demands for funds for three wars stimulated the inauguration and sustained a process of political and administrative reform designed to create an institutional framework (including a central bank) that allowed the English/British state ready and stable access to cheap credit and longer-term loans on the security of future tax revenues to meet its on-going requirements for liquidity as well as those unprecedented upswings in levels of expenditure that invariably occurred during frequent interludes of armed conflicts with rival powers. In all the process took decades of exper- imentation and episodic crises (including the infamous South Sea Bubble) to arrive at an efficient conclusion that provided the state with a framework of institutions, mechanisms, and techniques for the management of a rapidly accumulating national debt. With innovative responses from financial inter- mediaries and cooperation between the Treasury and the Bank of England a wider and deeper capital market developed in London to service the financial needs of agriculture, internal trade, and commerce overseas alongside the provision of credit and loans for the state (Carlos and Neal 2006; Caselli 2008; Neal 2000).

In some reductionist sense the emergence and ultimately successful devel- opment of a set of institutionalized arrangements for the management of England's sovereign debt that rose from a nominal value of around £2 million in the reign of James II to reach £824 million, some 2.5 times the national income (at the conclusion of the second hundred years war in 1815) was predicated on two conditions. First and foremost that the state would remain capable of expanding its fiscal base for the assessment and collection of taxes to the extent necessary to accord top priority to debt-servicing obligations that rose from an insignificant fraction of total taxation before the Glorious Revolution to peak at more than 60 percent of the vastly augmented flows of tax revenues received at the Exchequer at the close of twenty-two years of warfare against revolutionary and Napoleonic France.

Secondly, the unprecedented accumulation of sovereign debt into such a reliable and significant sinew of British power could only have remained operational decade after decade in a polity where creditors anticipated that sovereigns and their ministerial advisors would not renege on debts but repay them in full at the time and on the terms specified in a range of standardized contracts (bills and bonds) issued to secure the credits and loans required to fund expenditures by the state (Murphy 2013; Neal 1990; Wennerlind 2012). After protracted negotiations with a Dutch protestant prince, who lacked legitimacy and whose most urgent priority was to expand England's fiscal and financial resources to mobilize the Stuart realm's already considerable military and naval power to defeat Louis XIV's designs to take over the Netherlands, an assembly of intermarried families of aristocrats and notables managed to negotiate and sustain a constitutional settlement that reaffirmed and redefined the fundamental shift in the balance of power between the monarchy and Parliament that originated as an outcome of civil war. They guarded their grip on sovereignty over taxation by insisting that both Houses of Parliament (Lords and Commons) should meet annually to oversee and discuss revenues and expenditures under a tighter, transparent, and reformulated set of conventions and procedures to replace feudal traditions of sporadic negotiations for the granting extra supplies to fund extraordinary uplifts in expenditures by the monarchy (Hoppit 2000). The ratio of debt servicing to tax revenues rose to permanently higher levels as a result (Figure 12.2).

After 1694 (not 1688), England's constitutional disputes concerned with the locus of sovereignty inextricably linked to taxation, loans, and expenditures never emerged again. A restored balance of power between the monarch and Parliament (along with the reinforcement of trends toward indirect and more

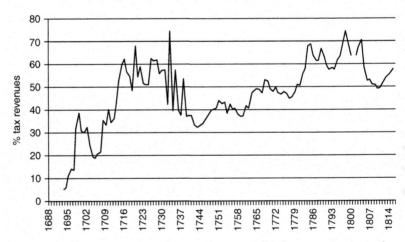

Figure 12.2 Debt servicing ratios 1688–1814 (percentage of total tax revenues received by the state)
Source: from data recorded in Parliamentary Paper, 1868–1869.

regressive forms of taxation) played a major part in securing a high level of compliance from the propertied elites represented in Parliament with the Crown's vastly augmented demands for taxes with loans between 1689 and 1815. With unquestioned sovereignty and with nominal control over annual budgets Parliaments of that period hardly ever resisted demands by governments of the day for extensions to the fiscal base for higher rates of taxation or for loans. Furthermore, and despite the clamor of debate between Tories and Whigs, neither the regularly assembled Lords and Commons nor informed public opinion presumed to interfere with the prerogatives of the Crown to determine the allocation of some 80 percent to 90 percent of the kingdom's revenues to foreign and strategic objectives. Those objectives continued to be formulated by monarchs advised by their selected coteries of aristocratic ministers reporting to manipulated Parliaments of their peers and relatives whose antipathies to higher taxes were assuaged by their command over state patronage, their investments in sovereign debt, and above all by a consensus across the propertied elite that geopolitical power would turn out to be good for the security and stability of the realm and profitable for them.

Backed by a majority of loyal, patriotic, and deferential Britons, Hanoverian kings and their English ministers continued to pursue a Cromwellian strategy that combined naval power for external security and aggression with the range of mercantilist measures commonplace across Europe such as Navigation Acts for shipping; higher tariffs to support import substitution and infant industries; the regulation of the economies of colonial and neocolonial possessions in the Caribbean, North America, and Ireland; legislation to safeguard and promote the development of domestic ship-building and ancillary industries; protection for overseas trade and commerce, etc. These measures extended and deepened the state's fiscal base that funded the supply of ships, seamen, victuals, armaments, and nautical expertise for the Royal Navy's persistent and ultimately successful drive to secure and retain command of the oceans (see Figure 12.3). (The bibliography of secondary sources behind my interpretation of the strategy pursued by Britain's fiscal-naval state is referenced in O'Brien 2002; 2011a; Backhaus 2012; vide Knight 2011.)

The persistence among modern economists pursuing counterfactual speculations about the real costs of pursuing this mercantilist strategy for security and stability from 1689 to 1815 begins to look like anachronistic regrets for the absence of a theoretically convenient liberal international economic order many decades before several geopolitical conditions, including the hegemony of the Royal Navy and fiscal sclerosis across Europe, came into place as foundations for a more peaceable and efficient way of conducting global

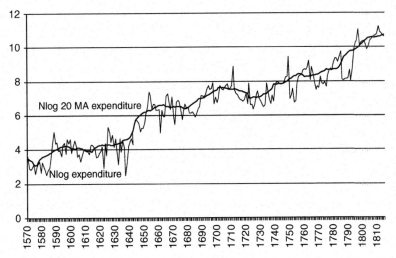

Figure 12.3 Trends in expenditure on the Royal Navy (in constant prices of 1660)
Note: Nlog expenditure: natural logarithm of Royal Navy expenditure in real 1660 pounds;
Nlog 20 MA expenditure: natural logarithm of twenty-year-centered moving average of
Royal Navy expenditure in real 1660 pounds.
Source: Duran and O'Brien 2011.

commerce (Mokyr 2006; Nye 2007). Meanwhile and for the times the strategy
in most of its essentials appears in retrospect to have served and serviced
British capitalism in major ways that assisted swathes of the Islands' economy
to attain the levels of development observed with hostility and envy by
European rivals and competitors. Thus is it not less anachronistic and more
enlightening to relocate Adam Smith and his liberal predecessors and successors to histories of economic theory in retrospect? Arguments of the day over
policy are more realistically linked to the state's really heavy commitment
to naval power combined with Navigation Acts to expand the country's
mercantile marine and associated industries in order to accumulate a workforce of experienced seamen and to secure the gains from international trade
and profits from servicing a global economy maturing toward higher levels
of connection and integration and generating taxable imports. The arguments
were, of course, nuanced and display differences but an "English" tradition
of political economy for this period is marked by a remarkable degree of
consensus about the role of the state and the policies it should pursue for the
security, stability, and prosperity of the economy (Findlay 2006; Hutchinson
1988: Parts v and vi).

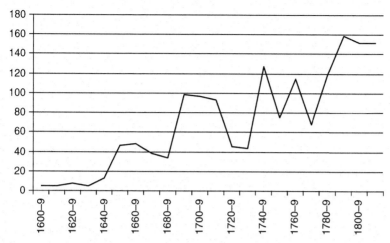

Figure 12.4 Expenditure on the Royal Navy compared to conjectures for private gross domestic fixed capital formation (GDFCF), 1600–1815
Source: Duran and O'Brien 2011.

For example, between 1689 and 1815 public expenditures on the Royal Navy that absorbed around half of total allocations to support the armed forces of the Crown averaged somewhere between 60 percent and 140 percent of aggregated national outlays on private gross domestic capital formation rarely attracted criticism inside or outside Parliament (Figure 12.4).

That came to pass because public consumption or (in perceptions of the time) public investment on that scale provided a range and quality of public goods that were widely perceived to provide tangible benefits as well as less visible spin-offs and externalities for the prosperity of the kingdom. The first, and most obvious, was that the Hanoverian state's consistent commitment to the construction and onshore maintenance of an intimidating fleet of heavily armed, fully manned warships – that in numbers and tonnage exceeded the combined fleets of France, Spain, and the Netherlands by factors of two and eventually of three – could only have assuaged the anxieties of British and foreign capitalists about the security of their stakes in the realm (Figure 12.5).

Although patriotic claims by British naval historians that the productivity of warships, guns, dockyards, and manpower employed by the Royal Navy became, through processes of learning and innovation, significantly higher than the efficiency of rival fleets dominate the historiography, these claims are not proven. Most of the competitive advantages of deploying a strategy based

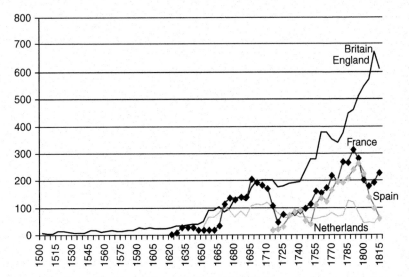

Figure 12.5. Sizes of the Royal Navy and rival navies (displacement tonnage 1,000s)
Source: Duran and O'Brien (2011).

on naval power probably emanated in large part from several other sources (Backhaus 2011; Harding [2004] does not agree). First, it allowed governments of the day to exploit knowledge of the natural endowments (location, coastline, harbors, tides, winds, rivers) of an island realm to maximum effect. Secondly, the Royal Navy combined with the merchant marine reaped increasing returns to scale from their shared use of infrastructural facilities such as harbors, docks, lighthouses, coastal fortifications, warehouses, and shipyards. Both marines benefitted from their joint access to a cumulating volume of nautical, strategic, and commercial knowledge and above all from an increasingly elastic supply of trained and experienced seamen as well as the ancillary skills of workforces employed to construct, repair, outfit, arm, provision, and coordinate the movement of sailing ships for purposes of commerce, defense, and mercantilist aggression.

Multiple loops of symbiotic and tensile interconnections between the two fleets of a large-scale capital and skill-intensive sector of the British economy operated to raise the efficiency of domestic ship-building and shipping, extended, stabilized, and protected markets for British commodities and services overseas and helped make expenditures on the Royal Navy more cost effective and acceptable to taxpayers. With just two lapses in 1692 and 1778 when admirals lost command of approaches to the Isles, the Royal Navy not only protected the realm and its growing interests in markets, territories, and imports overseas but performed in cost-effective ways that left just over half of the state's revenues (taxes plus loans) for allocation to the military forces of the Crown. These revenues "released" from allocations for external security funded a weak second line of defense, maintained internal order within a composite and urbanizing kingdom, and purchased mercenaries (from client states) to fight on the mainland and thereby prevented France and its allies from concentrating more resources on augmenting commitments to naval power (O'Brien 2005 and the bibliography cited there).

Unsurprisingly, the naval and military history of this final period of intensi-fied mercantilist competition and geopolitical warfare between 1689 and 1815 includes a disastrous attempt to suppress colonial rebellion in North America and exposes numerous costly episodes of failures in battle, expeditions, and campaigns that occurred in wartime. Nevertheless, in retrospect the broad thrust of British fiscal and financial policies combined with naval mercantilism can be represented as effective support for the endeavors of private capitalist enterprise carrying the economy through a process of Smithian growth into a transition for the technological breakthroughs for a first industrial revolution. Economic historians who continue to denigrate the role played by a state responding relatively efficiently to the unavoidable risks and challenges of a mercantilist economic order are, I suggest, logically required to outline an ontologically plausible counterfactual strategy for the pursuit of power with profit that might have led to a comparably successful outcome.

Reciprocal comparisons: Britain and its rivals from the mainland

Perhaps a better way to widen and conduct this on-going debate and to deepen historical understanding of economic growth might be to represent Britain as a paradigm case for successful capitalism during Europe's final phase of mercantilism (1659–1815) and to inquire why its leading rivals on the mainland failed to countervail the powers of a small island state vigorously committed to seizing and retaining an inordinate share of the gains from trade in a globalizing economy. The question cannot be dismissed as malposed or chronologically misplaced because recently calibrated European data for the tax and, by extension, financial revenues received and borrowed by the early Stuart regime to fund its ambitions for the pursuit of power with profit were nothing more than on a par with inflows of taxes into the hands of Venetian and Dutch oligarchies. They remained well below the revenues passing circuitously under the control of the territorial monarchies of France and Spain in command of much larger populations and fiscal bases on the mainland (Bonney 1995, 1999).

Quantified in per capita terms or expressed as proxies for tax "burdens" levied upon the unskilled majorities of their subjects, from European perspectives both Tudor and early Stuart monarchies (1485–1642) (so a base of imperfect and recently calibrated data suggests) presided over untapped fiscal potential compared with their Venetian and Dutch as well as Spanish and French rivals (Dincecco, 2009a, 2011; Karaman and Pamuk 2010b). This ostensibly favorable position for English taxpayers, and presumably for the national economy during those reigns, persisted for nearly two centuries after the kingdom's ignominious defeat and virtual withdrawal from sustained and costly imperialistic ventures on the mainland to an island fortress that could be defended relatively cheaply. For a long and fortuitous interlude in its history after 1453 England remained not isolated but relatively insulated from the intensified and costly engagements in state formation, territorial expansion, wars of religion, geopolitical and dynastic conflicts, and competition for resources that preoccupied and afflicted monarchies, aristocracies, and mercantile oligarchies coordinating and centralizing states on the continent (O'Brien 2011a and the bibliography appended there).

Unfortunately, economic historians have not found it feasible to add up, tabulate, compare, and rank plausible estimates for the aggregated amounts of revenue that could serve as proxies for the volume of real resources appropriated by European or Asian states prior to 1648. They probably cannot produce estimates of more revealing figures for the relative amounts allocated by agencies of the state (broadly defined) upon the extension and consolidation of their claims to sovereignty, for territorial expansion and conquest in Europe, on the personnel and means of coercion required to maintain internal order, for the maintenance of external security, the formation of social overhead capital, and as investments designed to establish and monopolize gains from colonization and commerce overseas with Africa, Asia, and the Americas. Unfortunately, historical records for public expenditures are conceptually less tractable and almost as impossible to aggregate as records for revenues received by central governments (Bonney 1995; Dincecco 2011).

Nevertheless, two plausible conjectures can be supported with reference to the vast bibliography in European political, geopolitical, imperial, military, and naval history now in print for the sixteenth and seventeenth centuries. First, that the pressures on Europe's nominally sovereign states to construct and exploit fiscal bases to fund one, more or all of these common objectives became more intense and persistent than anything confronted by rulers of the offshore isles (Blockmans 1997; Bonney 1991; Casalilla and O'Brien 2012).

Secondly, among a group of rival European states, in competition with England for the economic gains derivable from commerce and colonization overseas, the process of constructing and exploiting fiscal bases had begun early in response to an intensified phase of capital-intensive and rising costs of endemic warfare (Downing 1992; Glete 2002; Parker 1996). A semblance of peace had settled in after the treaties at Westphalia (1648) and the Pyrenees (1659) but it coincided with the rise of England emerging to challenge the primacy of the Dutch and the subsidiary positions of Spain, Venice, Scandinavia, and France in seaborne commerce and colonization in the Americas and Asia (Gerace 2004). That challenge came at a time when Europe's fiscal systems (after nearly two centuries of high pressure) had run into diminishing returns.

By the second half of the seventeenth century England's leading rivals had already augmented revenues by designing productive mixes of direct with indirect taxes levied on consumption and production. For many decades they had already attempted, without much political or administrative success, to "universalize" rules for taxation to ensure that they applied across their dominions without regard to ancient territorial boundaries, the legacies of feudal immunities and privileges embedded within composite polities on the mainland (Bonney 1995). They had also tried to improve prospects for compliance with demands for taxes by enclosing evolving regional, structural, and personal changes in the distributions of wealth, incomes, and patterns of consumption within stable and inclusive nets for taxation. Their common ambitions for universal fiscal rules could not avoid confrontation with established regional, ecclesiastical, and urban (even village) interests and hierarchies endowed with traditional powers and responsibilities that persisted after they became political components of composite and confederated kingdoms and republics charged to provide monarchies and oligarchies with the taxes demanded to fund state policies for defense, expansion, and the maintenance of internal order as well as the formulation of rules for the operation and coordination of markets (Epstein 2000; Genet and Le Mené 1987; Zmera 2001).

To secure steady inflows of taxes, credits, and loans, particularly in times of warfare and disorder, even the most "absolutist" of Europe's rulers could do little more than "negotiate" with established authorities and with syndicates of private tax-farmers to whom they had leased or sold responsibilities for the assessment, collection, and despatch of whole ranges of tolls, customs, and excise duties (Dincecco 2009). Both local and regional political authorities and franchised administrations extracted very high prices for their services in providing states with revenues (taxes with loans on the security of future revenues) (Blickle 1997). That cost could, in theory, be measured as gaps between realistically estimated and collectable totals of liabilities for taxation and the amounts actually received for allocations by states. Alas, data to measure and compare levels of efficiency in completing annual assessments and the rates of interest and other charges paid by states to obtain access to credits and loans from subordinate political authorities and tax-farmers are again not quantifiable (Winch and O'Brien, 2002). Nevertheless, the well-documented and voluminous literature from fiscal and financial history records the top priorities accorded by generations of finance ministers and their advisors from all over Europe to programs to universalize the wide range of taxes at their disposal and to reduce the very considerable shares of revenues from taxes, credits, and loans siphoned off as extortionate charges for administration and the servicing of debt (Bonney 1995; 1999).

In circumstances of increasing pressure to raise revenues to fund warfare and maintain internal stability at all costs the unavoidable failures to reform the fiscal and financial systems of European states are explicable. Nevertheless, they weakened compliance with demands from the center, strengthened vested interests in the status quo, and reduced the net inflows of funds available to states for military, naval, and other potentially profitable mercantilistic purposes (Hoffman and Norberg 1994). Between 1492 and 1815 progress in the construction of fiscal and financial infrastructures to support the formation of more powerful and centralized states depended upon balances of power across the territories, societies, cities, and communities of composite realms, confederated republics, and agglomerated empires (Blockmans and Tilly 1994; Hall and Schroeder 2006). Shifts in the structures of taxation toward indirect taxes and privatizing their assessment and collection worked for some states for a time before running into the malign effects of corruption, clientalism, political necessities, and above all the emergencies of unpredictable geopolitical and religious warfare (Dyson 1980). Yes, states made war but war both made and frustrated the formation of economically efficient states (Besley and Persson 2008; Gat 2006; Tilly 1990).

For reasons elaborated in the first section of this chapter, the major afflictions that beset the formation of rival states on the mainland had either been absent for centuries or remained significantly weaker on the offshore Isles. For England defense and a greater commitment to aggression beyond the frontiers of the realm could be more easily and cost-effectively maintained by investing more easily than rival powers with landed frontiers in capital-intensive naval power (Storrs 2009). Except for an increasingly insignificant direct tax on land, the tax revenues of the British state never depended on quotas negotiated with nominally subordinate but powerful representatives of ancient kingdoms, regions, or counties (Ertman 1997). Taxes imposed by monarchs, designed by ministers and almost invariably ratified by subservient Parliaments had long been and remained universal and all inclusive. Liabilities applied at least in law throughout the kingdom.

After a civil war, which in outcome led in time to the formal restoration of parliamentary sovereignty over taxation and expenditure, a productive framework for taxation evolved which was rebalanced to favor indirect taxes, extended to include underutilized levies upon domestic production (denigrated as foreign excises), and placed under the control of comparatively efficient central bureaucracies reporting to ministers of the Crown. When net receipts from an undertaxed fiscal realm exposed an elastic response to ever-increasing demands for a widening range and elevated rates of taxation propertied Englishman (and foreigners) represented by their kin and kind in Parliament became more confident in lending money to the state (Brewer 1989).

To sum up: in a European mirror England's fiscal-cum-financial constitution was reconstituted at a propitious period in the realm's political and geopolitical history. In contrast to its rivals on the mainland the powers of its ancient kingdoms, feudal aristocracies, and ecclesiastical corporations had been reduced by a reformation that created a national religion and by Cromwell's army, which subdued its Celtic peripheries (Ertman 1997). In the Isles fiscal reconstruction could not be frustrated by nominally subordinate but quasi-autonomous and distant local authorities, privileged nobilities, bishops, and venal office-holders with entrenched privatized property rights to collect taxes. England's major Iberian, Dutch, and French rivals emerging in 1648 from long periods of destructive and costly warfare were not fiscally well placed to enter an arms race with the Royal Navy (Gat 2006; Glete 2002). By that time the Iberians and the Dutch had, moreover, already undertaken the basic investments in nautical research, infrastructural facilities, and commercial organizations required to establish regularized commerce and trade with Africa, Asia, and the Americas. Moving on from Tudor piracy, England's well-protected mercantile marine stood poised to appropriate a rising share of gains available from seaborne and oceanic trade both within and well beyond traditional European waters and boundaries. While multiple symptoms of fiscal sclerosis afflicted its rivals on the mainland, a political consensus for a strong centralized state forged in the white heat of civil war promoted the reconstruction of a fiscal constitution that provided a politically constrained *ancien régime* with sinews of power (taxes with loans) to support a sustained uplift in "investments" upon several economically significant public goods: unassailable external security, regime stability for a monarch and aristocracy, operating through sovereign but subservient Parliaments and the military coercion mobilized from time to time to sustain institutions supporting private investment and innovation (O'Brien 2011). Above all, in following a strategy inaugurated by a republican regime the realm built up and maintained a very large and powerful navy that protected and promoted trade, commerce, and colonization that extended way beyond the coastlines of western Europe.

The outline of an analytical narrative for wider reciprocal comparisons: European states and Asian empires in a mercantilist and globalizing economy 1492–1815

As Europeans expanded overseas down the coasts of sub-Saharan Africa and westward to the rediscovered Americas, they found almost no states or societies capable of resisting either their weapons and methods of warfare, their pathogens, and their drives to expropriate natural resources and exploit a potential for unequal exchange (Abernethy 2000). When merchants, corporations, armies, navies, missionaries, and migrants sailed in the direction they had traditionally favored, namely, eastward from western Europe, they encountered developed agrarian empires in west, south, and east Asia ruled by dynastic states claiming absolute powers over extensive territories and large populations. As connections with them solidified it gradually became apparent that these imperial states lacked the powers, fiscal capacities, and institutions either to absorb and adapt potentially useful European knowledge or to regulate the terms and conditions for commerce with outsiders from the west (Modelski and Thompson 1998; Pagden 1995).

Thus, and with benefit from advances embodied in a recent wave of revisionist research into the economic histories of the Ottoman, Mughal, Safavid, and Ming-Qing empires, as well as the island polities of southeast Asia and Japan, historians can now revisit and analyze major economic outcomes that flowed from an intensifying volume and range of economic connections between the Occident and the Orient that followed from Iberian voyages of discovery linking the maritime regions of known and new worlds from the end of the fifteenth century (Pohl 1990; Tracy 1991).

They now recognize that for some two centuries after the encounters with Iberian merchants, Europeans traded with maritime economies and their hinterlands in Asia that, in terms of scientific and technological knowledge, craft skills, and commercial institutions for the organization and coordination of markets, were as "capitalist" as anything operating in port cities of the west (Chaudhuri 1990). Indeed, before Marx no western mercantilist seems to have reported upon any oriental economy as a system approximating to his ineptly disparaged "Asiatic mode of production" (Arrighi 2005). In Asia the onshore activities of Europeans continued to be confined to an exchange of a limited range of manufactures and principally with silver, expropriated from the colonization of the Americas, traded for tropical foodstuffs, organic materials, porcelain, textiles, and exquisite metal wares, which they transported back to Europe and sold to realize supernormal levels of profit (Pohl 1990). Asian merchants and shippers not only showed no desire to compete directly with Europeans for shares of these profitable transcontinental trades but they also cooperated to facilitate their entrée into established and lucrative networks of commerce around the Indian and Pacific oceans, as well as the Mediterranean, China, Arabian, and Red Seas (Mielants 2007; Tracy 1991a, 1991b).

Over time, as the Iberian presence in Asia increased, other Europeans (Dutch, English, and French) challenged their monopoly and entered into mercantilist competition and conflict with each other for the rising gains available from servicing transoceanic trades across the Atlantic and by forging links between the Occident and Orient. In oceanic commerce Europeans also displayed little hesitation in using their superior corporate forms of organization with naval (and eventually military) power to secure territorial and commercial and fiscal concessions from Asia's imperial hegemons but more often from virtually autonomous local rulers. In essence, they carried mercantilism, which had dominated intra-European trade for centuries and characterized their operations in the Americas, into Asian waters and ports where, for reasons to be elaborated, their ambitions to monopolize and maximize the gains from commerce with and within the Orient encountered only limited and ultimately futile resistance from dynastic states ruling over Chinese, Ottoman, Safavid, and Mughal empires as well as the islands and peninsulas of southeast Asia (Findlay and O'Rourke 2007; Lieberman 2009).

Two meta-questions now preoccupy historians of this famous encounter in global history. First, and granted that the representation of Asia's so-called "pre-capitalist" economies as backward, technologically retarded, or underdeveloped compared to western economies is now regarded as eurocentric and probably untenable, why did states redolent in courtly splendor and ostensibly in command of the extensive and productive economies with the fiscal potential of Ottoman, Safavid, Mughal, Ming-Qing empires, and other smaller Asian polities not do more to meet, adapt to, and countervail economic and geopolitical challenges from the west (Mielants 2007)? After all, the nature of those threats first appeared with Da Gama's violent entry into the port of Calicut in 1498, closely followed by visitations from Christian missionaries with aspirations to subvert local religions and moral codes (Doyle 1986). Furthermore and in short compass colonization and traditional mercantilist conflict among European powers and between European and Asian states was transferred to the east (Munkler 2007). Secondly, to what degree did oceanic connections operate to propel private enterprise and capitalism from a western promontory of Eurasia toward an early transition to an industrial revolution? And conversely did this first wave of proto-globalization seriously retard that transition in the east (Frank 1998; Hopkins 2002; Thompson 2000)?

This chapter will refrain from covering connections between the west and the maritime economies of southeast Asia and Japan and concentrate upon Asian empires (Lieberman 2009). Even then only cursory and simplified summaries of responses to such questions could appear in a chapter that offers little more than contexts, guides for critical reading, and lines for future research. In dealing with the first question euro-centered economic historians have taken a critical Ricardian view of the restrictive commercial policies pursued by China and Japan. More significantly they have concluded that states ruling over the geographically vast and ethnically diverse empires with very long frontiers in the west, south, and east of Asia lacked the penetrative powers, fiscal means, and navies to deter intruders from far away. Furthermore, they had no access to the modern technologies and effective organizations required to regulate opportunities for trade with outsiders from the west on terms that could be balanced in their favor (Burbank and Cooper 2010; Colas 2007; Etemad 2005).

At present statistical evidence to quantify the fiscal, financial, monetary, military, and organizational capacities of the dynasties and bureaucracies nominally in command of Ming-Qing, Safavid, Mughal, and Ottoman empires is under construction, remains of contestable reliability, and is open to interpretation (Casalilla and O'Brien, 2012). Nevertheless there are some data and a bibliography of recent histories concerned with the endeavors of Asia's imperial states to centralize the means of coercion, to supply public goods and sustain institutions for the operation of markets for commodities, capital labor, and useful knowledge (for data *vide* Karaman and Pamuk 2009, 2010a). This supports a case for more research into the current euro-centered but plausible hypothesis that states ruling all four empires lacked both the military and fiscal-cum-financial capacities to promote and protect the development of institutions for economic growth and structural change. For example, scattered statistics currently in print suggest that both revenues and military and bureaucratic manpower per unit of territory, per kilometer of frontier, and per head of population, could only have been decidedly lower – compared that is to the officials and forces employed, the taxes appropriated, and money borrowed – for the smaller scale and more spatially compact polities of western Europe (Vries 2002, 2003). Traditional eurocentric views that the supposedly "pre-capitalist" or "proto-command" economies of oriental empires were too underdeveloped to generate taxable surpluses on the scale of those accessible to western states have been convincingly qualified. Nevertheless their fiscal bases were hardly coterminous either with subject populations or with territories, trade, and production over which they asserted claims for taxes. States ruling Asian empires seem to have been constrained less by any lack of potentially taxable wealth, incomes, production, and trade and far more by deficiencies in their political powers and administrative capacities to levy taxes. Agreed the levels and types of taxes contemplated by emperors, sultans, and their advisors may seem to have been conditioned by Islamic and Confucian norms in favor of low taxation (Gerlach 2005; Ghazanfar 2007; Liu 2006).

Nevertheless, in their endeavors to form productive fiscal systems they were seriously constrained by the multiplicities of quasi-autonomous and potentially secessionist polities contained within their conglomerated and polycentric empires, by outbreaks of serious tax revolts and, above all, by the omnipresent threats to stability from predatory horsemen from the steppes, deserts, and hills along stretches of their extended frontiers. The scale and scope of the tasks involved in maintaining governance over such extensive heterogeneous and vulnerable empires certainly look daunting (Burbank and Cooper 2010; North et al. 2009). The problems of containing, never mind taxing, tribal societies, rebellious princes, dissatisfied nobles, disgruntled officials, ambitious military commanders, and predators from beyond the frontiers seem more severe than anything confronted by Europe's dynastic states and cohesive aristocracies in pre-modern times (Barkey 1994; Darwin 2007; Stoler, Mcgranahan, and Perdue 2007). In the absence of adequate and stable levels of revenues prospects for establishing and utilizing financial systems for regularized access to loans and credits was correspondingly restrained (Levi 1998). Furthermore, the interest and commitment of oriental states to maintaining imperial monetary systems for the payment of taxes, the mobilization of loans, and the facilitation of internal and external trade was likewise almost certainly more limited than was the case in the smaller, territorially more consolidated, socially less heterogeneous and altogether better-integrated maritime economies to the west (Neal 2000; Poggi 1990).

With systematic and reciprocal comparisons as guiding principles a reading of modern historical scholarship on the fiscal systems supporting Asia's imperial states leaves an impression (that might never be validated by hard statistical evidence) that the albeit variable capacities to tax and to effectively command and control their sovereign revenues by western states was almost certainly superior (possibly far superior) to the powers exercised by rulers of oriental empires depicted by generations of eurocentric intellectuals as autocratic, despotic, and predatory (Tilly 1975). In relation to the territories, capital assets, populations, and economies nominally under their command, as well as the sums actually appropriated, the amounts flowing as *net* receipts from taxation that became regularly available to rulers of Ming-Qing, Mughal, Safavid, and Ottoman empires almost certainly remained "low" and inadequate compared to revenues actually received from taxes appropriated for states (such as Portugal, Spain, the Netherlands, France, and England) supporting the penetration of their merchant marines and navies into Asian territorial waters (Alam and Subranmanyam 2000; Barkey 1994; Brook 2009; Deng 2011).

Even the benign, realistic, or prudentially modest claims to taxation for centralized governance in Asian empires were everywhere not only more severely compromised in terms of compliance but more seriously reduced by the illegal extortions of unofficial and official collectors. Very high charges were withheld by provincial, urban, and village authorities and officials as well as tax-farmers franchised to assess, despatch, and extend credit on the security of the sovereign's taxes (Darling 1996; Dunstan 1996; Karaman 2000; Quataert 2000; Zelin 1984). Politically negotiated settlements to utilize taxes assessed and collected from specific locations for purposes decided by semi-autonomous local and regional structures of power further reduced the revenues available to fund policies for the security, stability, and economic development of empires as a whole (Richards 1993; Rowe 2009). Unless and until statistics prove otherwise historians may suggest that while *laissez-faire* capitalism generated respectable rates of Smithian growth in the imperial economies of the Orient, smaller more centralized states with access to exploitable fiscal, financial, and monetary systems can surely be represented as a precondition for a next stage of mercantilistic growth led by western Europe (Bernholz and Vaubel 2004; Kuran 2011; Pamuk 1987; Stoler *et al.* 2007)?

But after centuries of denigration by liberal economists and economic historians can anything be positively claimed for the contributions of mercantilist thought and policy to the rise of Western capitalism?

In dealing with the historical significance of mercantilism there will be no need to revisit exhausted debates about its provenance for the history of economic thought. This chapter is not concerned to trace the "progress" of economic theory in retrospect but simply amalgamates and summarizes a sample of the publications from a familiar list of European mercantilist intellectuals whose views reflect their times, locations, epistemological frameworks, and the priorities that they accorded to problems and themes in political economy in order to educate and influence policies formulated by European rulers and statesmen of the period (Rashid 1980; Reinert 1999).

Mercantilism never became a creed with a priesthood purveying injunctions derived from canonical texts or from general axiomatic theories. Nevertheless, now that scholars in the history of economic thought have virtually degraded liberal caricatures of its entelechies, it has recently become possible to summarize its major objectives, assumptions, and recommendations (Magnusson 1993).

For that purpose, and to contest the role that economic ideology may have played in the formation of occidental and oriental states, historians only need surveys that represent the consensual core of mercantilism. This can, moreover, be derived from a more or less coherent body of influential thought in political economy informing and conveyed to the ruling elites of states across western Europe for some three centuries of proto-globalization between the voyages of discovery and the industrial revolution (Magnusson 1994).

At some fundamental moral level statesmen and their mercantilist consultants believed that progress could follow from releasing the passions and appetites for wealth of men from the constraints of medieval Christian theology (Reinert and Jomo 2005). Moving on to address the basic and persistent concerns of monarchies and mercantile oligarchies, with the formation of sovereign states mercantilists designed measures to integrate and coordinate national markets that included the abolition of tolls, the establishment of common and stable monetary systems, national standards for weights and measures, and better legal protection for property rights. They supported the maintenance of the strong coercive forces required to sustain internal order and external security. One way or another all major surveys of mercantilist political economy have noted its antipathies to more moral economies, to local military and/or aristocratic power structures, and to feudal fealty and privileges (Epstein 2000; Reinert 1999, 2004; Schmoller 1967).

While exposing its theoretical errors, conceptual inadequacies, and blatant inconsistencies some economists have latterly recognized the strong intellectual support accorded by mercantilists for mutually reinforcing national economies and centralized states that could create conditions for prosperity by widening and deepening fiscal bases to fund an efficient domestic economic order, external security, and protection for the expansion of commerce within and beyond national frontiers (Cardoso, Chapter 18 in this volume; Findlay 2006; Reinert 2004, 2005; Tribe 2006).

As the "ism" of merchants and before the end of the sixteenth century, securing gains from internal, international, and trans-continental trade matured into the core preoccupation of Europe's mercantilistic political economy and a major policy concern for states seeking to preserve shares in the revenues derived from regulated transactions conducted by diverse and more or less close forms of partnerships with merchants (Reinert 2011; Tracy 1991). Mercantilist assumptions and modes of thought became more influential, particularly in maritime states with smaller domestic economies (Gomes 1987).

Europe's mercantilists certainly never shared the Chinese physiocratic reification of agriculture. They welcomed the widening of home markets emanating from population growth but remained skeptical about prospects for development based upon interregional trade and specialization and market integration within smaller polities. Although by the late seventeenth century many had come round to higher wages as a superior way of increasing levels of consumption by stimulating harder work and promoting endeavors to acquire skills (Perrotta 1997). Citing the examples of Genoa, Venice, Portugal, Spain, and the Netherlands they placed their faith in prospects for their nations' wealth, prosperity, and power in commitments to international and trans-continental trade (Reinert 2011). Mercantilists soon became fully aware that new markets that had developed in the Americas and in Asia for the exchanges of European manufactures and expropriated American silver for a range of novel imports of foodstuffs, raw materials, and manufactures embodied a significant potential to stimulate industriousness among western workforces, to create opportunities for investment and jobs in processing imported raw materials (Cox 1959). They clearly appreciated how Asian commodities that sold well on European domestic markets could foster processes of emulation, transfers of oriental knowledge, and import substitution (Tracy 1991a, 1991b; Wallerstein 1980).

At the same time and until well into the nineteenth century mercantilists and the European states that they served and advised based their regulations for commerce, with each other and the rest of the world, on the infamous assumption that trade was, in modern parlance, a zero-sum game and gains could only be realized and maintained at the expense of rival national economies (Ekelund and Tollison 1997; Mokyr 2006). That assumption, traceable to Aristotle, was included among commonplace perceptions of a national interest that was sustained by omnipresent threats and outbreaks of geopolitical, dynastic, and religious warfare between European states over the centuries before the Treaty of Vienna in 1815 (Appleby 2010; Blitz 1967). It lay behind the design of a more or less effectively executed range of strategic policies predicated upon a conception that national gains from trade could only occur if and when the values of exports exceeded the values of imports – detectable but hardly measurable with reference to inflows and outflows of bullion, the hard or reserve currency of the period. A fundamentalist and irrational fringe of this mode of thought may – as Adam Smith's famous caricature of mercantilism suggests – have confused bullion with wealth (Skinner and Wilson 1976).

Nevertheless, the well-known example of Spain, allegedly afflicted by imports of expropriated American silver rather than its wasteful misallocation to religious warfare together with the reputations that Venice, Antwerp, Amsterdam, and London had acquired as highly prosperous cities while they continued to exchange precious metals for commodities, convinced a majority of mercantilists and the statesmen they advised to formulate wider and altogether more strategic views of gains from trade than that conveyed by an obsession with balances between exports and imports and inflows and outflows of bullion (Perrotta 1991). As merchants they knew that value added from servicing, shipping, financing, insuring, brokering, and facilitating and stabilizing trade exceeded by a large margin the profits derived from merely buying commodities in inelastic demand from natural and lower-cost locations for production overseas and selling them at prices that were higher in the west (Magnusson 1994; Wallerstein 1980).

As intellectuals reflecting upon the political and social benefits from trade and pressurizing European aristocratic elites to support monopoly privileges and protection at sea, mercantilists, as Schmoller observed, expounded upon the full range of externalities and spin-offs that could conceivably flow for a state and its national economy from a fully committed but efficiently formulated set of policies to foster commerce by land and sea (Schmoller 1967). Their arguments were elaborated at length and with a sophistication that falls short of that axiomatic rigor demanded by competitive but countervailing theories from several schools in modern international economics. Nevertheless, as recent scholarship in the history of "European" economic thought exposes, most of the benign outcomes that might conceivably flow from policies promoting exports and encouraging "selected" imports perceived to embody potential for increasing returns and the long-run growth of national economy are included in the writings of mercantilist precursors of English classical political economy (Finkelstein 2000; Reinert 1999, 2004, 2005; Tracy 1991a, 1991b).

Some outstanding and major differences did, however, persist before arguments for *laissez-faire* and free trade became hegemonic. For example, mercantilists, even the minority advocating approximations to freer trade, never formulated a theory of comparative advantage as an intellectually persuasive basis for the invisible hands of unregulated markets, the harmonization of national interests and gains for all nations from a more rapid expansion that could theoretically flow from unregulated global trade and commerce. As far as they and the statesmen they influenced could tell the global economy was not expanding rapidly enough to generate sufficient gains to satisfy all the economies of Europe. They observed that rival states continued to pursue policies designed to maximize their own national interests (Findlay and O'Rourke 2007; Tribe 2006). Thus, and within an international order riven by dynastic and religious competition, diplomatic conflict and vicious warfare – that led over centuries to the absorption of hundreds of nominally autonomous but small polities into larger, more powerful sovereign nation states – the top priorities of rulers and their advisors continued to be with revenues (taxes with loans) – allocated in high proportion (up to 80–90 percent) to armies and navies mobilized and armed to maintain external security, internal order, and as extensions to fiscal bases as sources of power (Contamine 2000; Tilly 1990).

Meanwhile, in the course of the sixteenth century at the margin, the expansion of commerce, overland as well as overseas, emerged as the most promising way of extending fiscal bases for purposes of taxation and loans and for the procurement of hard currency (bullion) as a basis for more stable and elastic monetary systems and financial intermediation. It also functioned as a "war chest" available for outlays upon the projection of power within and beyond the frontiers of particular realms, city-states, and republics (Blitz 1967; Gat 2006). Most statesmen recognized the sense in mercantilist admonitions to unify and integrate domestic markets and to pursue policies that combined incentives to promote exports that increased employment and raised returns for domestic labor and capital. They saw the point of encouraging the import of the kind of commodities that would generate revenues from customs and excise duties; stimulate industrious behavior among households with desires to buy luxuries; foster the processing and finishing of foreign raw materials and increasing bases for import substitution (Perrotta 1997). In short, Europe's national states in formation (and/or danger) promoted and protected the interests of their economies. They regulated international economic relations to secure national objectives and whenever necessary and expedient resorted to predation and colonization (Contamine 2000). Of course, they also took full but diplomatically viable advantage of the opportunities provided by bouts of warfare to seize and retain markets for exports and procure essential imports (Greenfeld 2001). The entelechies of mercantilism became commonplace in discourses about political economy among the statesmen of western Europe. As formulated and executed policies to capture higher shares of the gains from trade display differences of degree (not of kind), that reflect variations across polities in internal balances of power and wealth between landed aristocracies and mercantile oligarchies, their geopolitical locations and, above all, their fiscal and financial capacities to invest in sustained commitments to secure these gains (Appleby, 2010; Cox 1959; Gomes 1987; Tracy, 1991a, 1991b).

Led by Fernand Braudel historians and historical sociologists have constructed a historiography to account for the rise and decline of a sequence of leading Western national economies operating along mercantilist lines evolving after 1492 within a proto-global international economic order (Wallerstein, 1974, 1980, 1989, and 2011). Primacy in securing the highest (alas unmeasurable) share of the gains from inter-European (maturing into Eurasian) trade and translated into a league table of prosperous, secure, and stable western polities has been posited and analyzed for a series of national economies with leading maritime sectors including Genoa, Venice, Portugal, Spain, the Netherlands, France, and England (Arrighi 1994, 2005; Kindleberger 1996; Pezzolo, Chapter 10 in this volume).

Explanations for interludes of primacy and analyses of their subsequent but relative decline have been elaborated in libraries of secondary literature in European economic history and synthesized by Braudel's magisterial three-volume work on *Civilization and Capitalism* (1981–1984). There will be no need to offer another critical survey of the writings of his followers networked into a "school" of world systems historical sociology. Preceded by Schmoller (not Heckscher) their particular emphases and concerns have been to reconfigure the role of power, to contextualize the rationalities of mercantilism and the significance of states for revisions to a modern wave of economic history dealing with the rise of capitalism that had become infused with neoclassical economic theories and neoliberal ideologies of how economies had developed historically and should continue to develop in future. What the record, as elaborated by previous generations of European historians in closer touch with the bibliography of "European" mercantilist political economy and above all with the policies of states in formation, reveals is that the establishment and maintenance of a range of capitalist institutions that appear *ceteris paribus* to have supported and promoted the evolution of competing national economies on trajectories toward transitions to urban industrial market economies depended far less on bourgeois virtue or the unexplained enlightenment of

English (and other?) elites and far more upon the formation, integration, and the fiscal and financial capacities of states geared for purposeful mercantilistic action (Coleman 1969; Findlay *et al.* 2006).

Exhausted by warfare, culminating in the long, destructive, and costly global conflict that flowed from a succession of revolutions against *anciens régimes* in the west that began in 1789 and concluded in 1815 with defeat for the bid by Napoleon for French hegemony over the whole of Europe, the restoration and then reconstruction of western states with fiscal and bureaucratic capacities to sustain institutions for the progress of capitalism on the mainland took several decades to converge in range and efficiency to those established several decades earlier on the offshore isles (Cardoso and Lains 2010; *vide* Chapter 18 by Cardoso in this volume).

Setting aside the ostensibly analogous cases of smaller maritime polities of southeast Asia, the influence of anything resembling the political economy of European mercantilism on the strategic and economic policies pursued by Ottoman, Safavid, Mughal, and Ming-Qing dynasties and elites ruling over territorially extensive densely populated and culturally heterogeneous empires seems hard to detect (Lieberman 2009). Similar ideas and recommendations have been discovered in the writings of isolated intellectuals published for Japan (Oka and Smits 2010). Cases of proto-mercantilism have been exposed for warrior states challenging Mughal hegemony in south Asia for the years immediately before their takeover by the East India Company (Parthasarathi 2011). For entirely explicable reasons – some particular to a polity and its history but most common to all overextended territorial empires during the era of primitive transport and communication, they may be disregarded as minor deviations from the ideologies and priorities of Asian empires (Munkler 2007).

Informed by Confucian, Islamic, Buddhist, and Hindu belief systems the autocratic military elites managing imperial economies and societies of east, south and west Asia remained antagonistic to the adoption of an ideology for the formation and operation of imperial states based upon sustained commitment to the pursuits of power with profit in alliance with merchants (Bayly 1998). Their attitudes reflected support for politically prudent and fiscally soft ideological power exercised within cultures suffused with mandates from heaven, filial pieties, traditional deference to hereditary and caste hierarchies, resignation to Brahminical and other religious authorities, military loyalties, and other norms (Duchesne 2011). As elites managing weak states they sought internal order, compliance, and political stability (along with some detached semblance of centralized rule) across spatially extensive, heterogeneous but otherwise ostensibly ungovernable empires (Adshead 1995; Alam and Subrahmanyam 1998; Brook 2009; Casalilla and O'Brien 2012; Crossley 2006; Kuran 2011; Leonard and Watts 1992; Pamuk 1987; Perlin 1985).

Within these empires minorities of Asian merchants operated and to a degree prospered in conditions approximating to repressive tolerance. They coordinated and integrated markets and fostered commerce across politically extended geographical spaces that allowed them and the economies they serviced to reap greater returns to scale than might theoretically have been the case for their counterparts operating within the geographically constricted, less stable, fiscally onerous frontiers of smaller polities to the west of Eurasia. Nevertheless, Asian merchants played negligible roles in the councils for imperial governance. They lacked the social and political status of their Italian, Dutch, and English counterparts whose liquid wealth probably enjoyed greater security from predatory raids by the emperors and aristocracies of the West.

Although advances between 1492 and 1815 along paths of Smithian growth continued at more impressive rates than generations of eurocentric historians have suggested, is it not plausible to represent the histories of pre-modern capitalism and commercialization that evolved within the Ottoman, Ming-Qing, Safavid, and Mughal empires as progress that occurred despite the strategic objectives and economic policies pursued by their ruling elites (Darwin 2007; Munkler 2007; Thurchin 2009)?

Throughout historically observable stages of expansion and contraction from 1492 to 1815, Asian states persisted with traditional, almost irrestible logics, leading to imperial "overstretch." Eventually, but clearly by 1700, after attaining peaks in scale, reach, and revenues the Mughals and Ottomans ceded territory, taxable assets, and human capital to secessions from within and to rival empires and predatory warrior tribes from outside their vulnerable and contested frontiers (Faroqhi and Quataert 1997; Lieberman 2009; Quataert 2000; Richards 1995). Historical accounts for aggregating the gains from expansion, plunder, tribute, and the formation of an underutilized political potential for large markets followed by the losses incurred from subsequent contractions and internal disorder will remain impossible to reconstruct. But a case has yet to be made that the swings in gains and losses added up to positive effects for the long-term development of the imperial economies and societies of south and west Asia. Yes, the Ottoman empire adapted and survived from its particular history of imperial expansion and overstretch all the way down to the Great War (Quataert 2000). But the Mughal empire collapsed under the strains from a combination of intensifying internal insurrections and a military takeover organized and funded by one large private trading corporation – the

English East India Company (Alam and Subrahmanyam 1998; Bayly 2004; Richards 2012). Meanwhile, the cost of successful conquests by the Qing regime which virtually doubled the size of the Manchu empire almost certainly exceeded cumulative material gains for the Chinese economy and its rapidly growing population over the period immediately preceding a century-long cycle of internal instability and stasis down to 1911 (Deng 2011; Perdue 2005; Rowe 2009; Struve 2004).

The historical record does indeed show that geopolitical declines to the east certainly accompanied and facilitated the economic rise of the West. Nevertheless, now that most pre-modern Eurasian economies have been recently reconfigured as parts of a globalizing economy of "surprising resemblances" undergoing comparable patterns and respectable rates of Smithian growth, the failures of oriental states to provide their businessmen with the public goods and social overhead capital required to reach plateaux of possibilities required for earlier transitions to industrial market economies calls for further analysis and debate (Wong 1997, 2012). Before the imperial states of the Orient were destabilized or taken over by western powers their claims to sovereignty embraced large populations, heterogeneous regional economies, and spaces that prima facie included favorable endowments of exploitable natural resources and political possibilities to foster the integration, coordination, and extension of markets necessary for increasing returns to scale and specialization (Parthasarathi 2011; Richards 1995). Ceteris paribus, they could conceivably have generated larger revenues and allocated more funds to provide for public goods such as external security, greater protection for overseas trade, internal order, social overhead capital, systems for legal adjudication, etc. more cheaply (upon per capita, per square kilometer of territory, or per unit of taxation basis) than the smaller, more homogeneous polities of western Europe (Bayly 2004; Rosenthal and Wong 2011).

General explanations for their ostensible neglect of opportunities to support economic growth from taxation and loans mobilized within the political frameworks of larger-scale polities and markets have emphasized the diseconomies of scale, preoccupations with secessionist tensions and the undefeated armies of nomadic predators within and along frontiers as widespread enduring geopolitical and economically malign features of all pre-modern Eurasian empires (Darwin 2007; Munkler 2007). When the military stage of empire building associated with plunder and tribute ran into the buffers of serious resistance, empires often disintegrated (Colas 2007; Doyle 1986). Alternatively, as the varied and complex early modern histories of the Ottoman, Mughal, Safavid, and Manchu empires reveal, failures ultimately attended their attempts to establish states based upon fiscal and financial systems providing regular inflows of revenues (taxes with credits and loans) on a sufficient scale to define and consistently defend realistic frontiers, deal with nomadic predation, contain secessions, maintain internal order, manage natural disasters, and (once they had comprehended the threat) to build up military and above all naval forces to deter encroachments from western imperialism (Burbank and Cooper 2010; Gat 2006).

Of course, historical records of successes and failures, costs and benefits in providing the public goods and sustaining institutions that have been represented post hoc as promotional for the development of efficient partnerships between states and private enterprise display considerable variance and complexity across Eurasia. It is only with hindsight that economic historians are beginning to claim that pre-modern empires located both to the west (e.g. the Habsburg dominions) but particularly to the east of Eurasia, can be plausibly represented as suboptimal polities and states for the promotion of long-term economic growth (Casalilla and O'Brien 2012). For these centuries of primitive technologies for transportation, communication, and organization the sheer size and heterogeneity of territorial empires rendered them vulnerable to attack and/or prone to mount costly preemptive strikes along their lengthy and indefensible frontiers. Their ruling dynasties settled realistically for a status of remaining politically incapable of constructing centralized fiscal, financial, and monetary systems and even of enforcing standardized weights and measures (Dincecco 2011). After external security their second priority was to retain some negotiable measure of control over the provincial officials, military governors, magnates, notables, tribal warriors, and village authorities that constituted the power structures of heterogeneous and far-flung empires. Secessions from imperial rule could be contained by the sporadic deployments of military force but were usually resolved by reluctant but expedient devolutions of power over fiscal, economic, and even military coercion to a multiplicity of local and virtually autonomous officials and/or to established, traditional, and armed authorities who, under military threat, had agreed to collaborate with projects for empire.

Rulers and even dynasties changed while empires often remained more or less intact throughout the era of European mercantilism, but their provision for public goods, investment in social overhead capital, and the maintenance of institutions required to transform imperial polities into efficiently integrated and coordinated markets with productive levels of regional specialization look inadequate when compared to the smaller maritime economies of Europe. By the end of an imperial meridian (1776–1815), empires of the west (including the British empire) had been truncated. In the east the Mughal empire had been taken over by a western corporation. The Ottoman and Safavid empires had been reduced in scale and fragmented into confederations of loosely connected, local, and more or less autonomous polities (Bayly 2004). Even the Chinese empire can be represented as another loose confederation of local power structures held together by the benign rule of a Manchu regime that abided by traditional Chinese ways and principles (Deng 2011). The Qing regime's "enlightened" emperors and Han Confucian advisors had acquiesced in their lack of penetrative power by allowing the fiscal and military capacities of the imperial state to become degraded to a degree that left their successors unable to cope with a century and more of highly destructive internal disorders and external attacks on the integrity and sovereignty of that great empire (Deng 2011; Rowe 2009).

Meanwhile at sea Britain's Royal Navy won and retained command of the oceans, which created the conditions to bring a long era of mercantilism to a close and to usher in a liberal international economic order for another cycle or novel stage in the history of Eurasian capitalism that became politically, institutionally, and technologically superior for the promotion of material progress.

Negotiable conclusions

Apart from definitions and specifications, prefaces to histories of capitalism will be concerned with chronologies. My narrative has concentrated upon a stage or conjuncture in global economic history when Britain, followed by several economies from mainland western Europe, passed through transitions to emerge as modern industrial market economies some three or more centuries before the imperial economies of west, south, and east Asia.

This analytical narrative is based on a key assumption that was shared by generations of economic historians working within paradigms for research established by the German historical school and which had recently been restored to a position of prominence by new institutional economics and economic history (Chang 2007; Helpman 2004; Hodgson 2000; Menard and Shirley 2005; North 1981, 1990).

That traditional premise is that variations in institutions across space and time could be the most significant chapter for analytical narratives designed and constructed to explain differences in the performance of Eurasian economies over the long run. Nevertheless, the narrative also shares the presumptions of critics of new institutional economics that observed variations in the institutions framing and conditioning economic activity across preindustrial Eurasia could be referred (if not reduced) to: differences in geographies, explicable variations in religious and other hegemonic beliefs or cultures and, above all, explicated as emanating from the actions and inactions of states. Thus, my chapter for a volume on the history of capitalism joins forces with a "school" of historians and latterly a band of economists and sociologists who insist that institutional variables can only be comprehended and become persuasive when contextualized (as Schmoller told us) within histories of states and state formation (Andrade 2010; Arrighi 2005; Bernholz and Vaubel 2004; Chang 2007; Downing 1992; Elias 1982; Epstein 2000; Ferguson 2002; Genet and Le Mené 1987; Hall and Shroeder 2006; Herbst 2000; Landers 2003; Perlin 1985; Reinert 1999; Stasavage 2011; Thompson 2000; Wade 2004; White 2009 et al.).

Long ago Schumpeter suggested that the most heuristic way to achieve some comprehension of connections between states and state formation and the rise of capitalism is through historical investigations into, and comparisons of, their fiscal systems. His approach promises to provide some statistical indicators of the different and evolving capacities of states for effective action in the sphere of political economy. Regardless of their varied constitutional form, the fiscal problem certainly appears in the records as the central preoccupation of elites governing empires, countries, republics, realms, and princedoms across Eurasia in pre-modern and modern times.

Comparisons and contrasts in the formation of fiscal, and by extension financial systems, can be exposed and analyzed by referring to published historical literatures that contain evidence and analysis of relevance to the question of when, how, and why the British state appropriated sufficient resources (taxes and loans) to promote the first transition to an industrial market economy. What delayed the convergence by states in charge of follower countries on the mainland of Europe? Why did the imperial states of west, south, and east Asia after promising interludes of efflorescence in their early histories remain less and less successful as harbingers and promoters of economic progress?

Theory is invariably helpful for the specification of questions. But alas there seems to be no prospect for a general theory that might cover a multiplicity of Eurasian countries and cases. That is because there could be no parsimonious model to encompass and weight the geographical, geopolitical, and political forces and factors behind the formation of fiscal capacities for purposeful, sustained, and centralized actions to provide that necessary and sufficient range of public goods (including effective institutions) to promote and sustain capitalism.

This sadly agnostic observation could only be strengthened by wider reading in political histories which reveals how often the fiscal capacities of states altered fundamentally as outcomes of unpredicted political events such as an English civil war, a Mughal emperor's invasion of the Deccan or outbreaks of White Lotus and Taiping rebellions in Qing China. Since early modern state formation has been so evidently and convincingly represented as a process punctuated by unpredictable events economic historians can only agree that while efficient institutions are clearly necessary for economic growth they have no way of knowing when, how, and why states might establish, sustain, or repress such institutions. Schmoller's view of mercantilism is surely more enlightening than Heckscher's but both lack any theory of when, how, and why transformations of states and their institutions might occur (Findlay 2006; Schmoller 1967).

In retrospect it looks fortuitous but fortunate that the formation of a powerful, well-funded Britain occurred as an outcome of two centuries of detachment from warfare on the mainland, a bloody civil war, and decisive naval victories over its leading economic rivals – first the Netherlands and then France (Baugh 2011; Jones 1999; Neal 1977; O'Brien 2005, 2011b).

British historians will, however, point out that without an upswing in funding provided by English taxpayers the Royal Navy could hardly have obtained and retained command of the oceans all the way down to 1941. Nevertheless, one final and decisive victory at Trafalgar created conditions to bring a long era of "inefficient" mercantilism, navigation acts, piracy, and privateering to a close. The outcome of that famous naval battle kept the industrial revolution on course and ushered in a liberal international economic order for another long cycle in the history of Eurasian capitalism that became and has remained politically, institutionally, and technologically superior for the promotion of capitalism with material progress.

References

A comprehensive bibliography, which includes references to economic theories of fiscal state formation and the fiscal histories of the United Kingdom and other European states, is included in O'Brien (2011a) and Casalilla and O'Brien (2012).

Abernethy, D. (2000). *The Dynamics of Global Dominance: European Overseas Empires 1415–1980.* New Haven: Yale University Press.

Acemoglu, D. and J. Robinson (2012). *Why Nations Fail: The Origins of Power, Prosperity and Poverty.* London: Profile.

Adshead, S. (1995). *China and World History.* Basingstoke: Macmillan.

Akita, S. ed. (2002). *Gentlemanly Capitalism: Imperialism and Global History*. Basingstoke: Palgrave Macmillan.

Alam, M. and S. Subrahmanyam, eds. (2000). *The Mughal State 1526–1750*. New Delhi, Oxford: Oxford University Press.

Andrade, T. (2010). "Beyond Guns, Germs and Steel: European Expansion and Maritime Asia," *Journal of Early Modern History* 14: 165–186.

Appleby, J. (2010). *The Relentless Revolution: A History of Capitalism*. London: W. W. Norton.

Arrighi, G. (1994). *The Long Twentieth Century: Money, Power and the Origins of our Times*. London, New York: Verso.

(2005). "States, Markets and Capitalism, East and West," in M. Miller (ed.), *Worlds of Capitalism: Institutions, Economic Performance and Governance in the Era of Globalism*. London: Routledge, Chapter 6.

Backhaus, J., ed. (2012). *Navies and State Formation*. Berlin: LIT Verlag.

Barkey, K. (1994). *Bandits and Bureaucrats: The Ottoman Route to State Centralization*. Ithaca: Cornell University Press.

Baugh, D. (2011). *The Global Seven Years War, 1754–63*. London: Longman.

Bayly, C. (1998). *Origins of Nationality in South Asia: Patriotism and Ethical Government in the Making of Modern India*. Oxford University Press.

(2004). *The Birth of the Modern World 1780–1914*. Oxford: Blackwell.

Besley, T. and T. Persson (2008). "Wars and State Capacity," *Journal of the European Economic Association* 6: 522–530.

Bernholz, P. and R. Vaubel, eds. (2004). *Political Competition, Innovation and Growth in the History of Asian Civilizations*. Cheltenham: Edward Elgar.

Blickle, P., ed. (1997). *Resistance, Representation and Community*. Oxford: Clarendon Press.

Blitz, R. (1967). "Mercantilist Policies and the Pattern of World Trade 1500–1750," *Journal of Economic History* 27(2): 39–55.

Blockmans, W. P. (1997). *A History of Power in Europe: People, Markets, States*. Antwerp: Fonds Mercator Paribas.

Blockmans, W. P. and C. Tilly (1994). *Cities and the Rise of States in Europe AD 1000 to 1800*. Boulder, CO: Westview Press.

Bonney, R. (1991). *The European Dynastic States: 1494–1660*. Oxford University Press.

Bonney, R., ed. (1995). *Economic Systems and State Finance*. Oxford: Clarendon Press.

(1999). *The Rise of the Fiscal State in Europe*. Oxford University Press.

Bowen, H. and A. G. Encisco, eds. (2006). *Mobilizing Resources for War: Britain and Spain at Work in the Early Modern Period*. Pamplona: Ediciones Universidad de Navarra.

Braudel, F. (1981–84). *Civilization and Capitalism*, 3 vols. London: William Collins.

Brenner, R. (2003). *Merchants and Revolution: Commercial Change and London's Overseas Traders 1550–1653*. London: Verso.

Brewer, J. (1989). *The Sinews of Power: War, Money and the English State, 1688–1783*. London: Unwin Hyman.

Brook, T. (2009). *The Troubled Empire: China in the Yuan and Ming Dynasties*. Cambridge, MA: Harvard University Press.

Brook, T. and G. Blue, eds. (1999). *China and Historical Capitalism: Genealogies of Sinological Knowledge*. Cambridge University Press.

Burbank, J. and F. Cooper (2010). *Empires in World History and the Politics of Difference.* Princeton University Press.

Cardoso, J. and P. Lains, eds. (2010). *Paying for the Liberal State: The Rise of Public Finance in Nineteenth-Century Europe.* Cambridge University Press.

Carlos, A. and L. Neal (2006). "The Micro Foundations of the Early London Capital Market," *Economic History Review* 59: 498–538.

Casalilla, B. Y. and O'Brien, P., eds. (2012). *The Rise of Fiscal States: A Global History, 1500–1914.* Cambridge University Press.

Caselli, F., ed. (2008). *Government Debts and Financial Markets in Europe.* London: Pickering and Chatto.

Chang, H. J., ed. (2007). *Institutional Change and Economic Development: Theory, History and Contemporary Experience.* Tokyo: United Nations University Press.

Chaudhuri, K. (1990). *Asia Before Europe: Economy and Civilization of the Indian Ocean from the Rise of Islam to 1750.* Cambridge University Press.

Coffman, D. M. (2008). "The Fiscal Revolution of the Interregnum: Excise Taxation in the British Isles, 1643–1663." Ph.D. thesis, University of Pennsylvania.

Colas, A. (2007). *Empire.* Cambridge: Polity.

Coleman, D., ed. (1969). *Revisions in Mercantilism.* London: Methuen.

Contamine, P. (2000). *War and Competition between States.* Oxford University Press.

Cox, O. (1959). *Foundations of Capitalism.* New York: Abe Books.

Crossley, P. et al., eds. (2006). *Empire at the Margins: Culture, Ethnicity and Frontier in Early Modern China.* Berkeley: University of California Press.

Crouzet, F. (1996). "The Second Hundred Years' War with France," *French History* 10: 432–450.

Darling, L. (1996). *Revenue Raising and Legitimacy: Tax Collection and Finance Administration in the Ottoman Empire 1560–1660.* Leiden: Brill.

Darwin, J. (2007). *After Tamerlane: The Global History of Empire.* London: Penguin.

Deng, K. (2011). *China's Political Economy in Modern Times: Changes and Economic Consequences, 1800–2000.* London: Routledge.

Dickson, P. G. M. (1967). *Financial Revolution in England: A Study in the Development of Public Credit, 1688–1756.* London: Macmillan.

Dincecco, M. (2009a). "Fiscal Centralization, Limited Government and Public Revenues in Europe 1650–1913," *Journal of Economic History* 69: 48–103.

　(2009b). "Political Regimes and Sovereign Credit Risk in Europe 1750–1913," *European Review of Economic History* 13: 48–103.

　(2011). *Political Transformations and Public Finances: Europe, 1650–1913.* Cambridge University Press.

Downing, B. (1992). *The Military Revolution and Political Change: The Origins of Democracy and Autocracy in Early Modern Europe.* Princeton University Press.

Doyle, M. (1986). *Empires.* Ithaca: Cornell University Press.

Duchesne, R. (2011). *The Uniqueness of Western Civilization.* Leiden: Brill.

Dunstan, H. (1996). *Conflicting Counsels to Confuse the Age: A Documentary Study of Political Economy in Qing China, 1644–1840.* Ann Arbor: University of Michigan Press.

Duran, X. and P. O'Brien (2011). "Total Factor Productivity for the Royal Navy from Victory at Texel (1653) to Triumph at Trafalgar (1805)," in Richard Unger (ed.), *Shipping and Economic Growth.* Leiden: Brill, pp. 279–309.

Dyson, K. (1980). *The State Tradition in Western Europe: A Study of an Idea and an Institution.* Oxford: Martin Robertson.

Ekelund, R. and R. Tollison (1997). *Politicized Economies: Monarchy, Monopoly and Mercantilism.* College Station, TX: Texas A&M University Press.

Elias, N. (1982). *The Civilizing Process.* Vol. II: *State Formation and Civilization.* Oxford: Blackwell.

Epstein, S. (2000). *Freedom and Growth: The Rise of States and Markets in Europe, 1300–1750.* London: Routledge.

Ertman, T. (1997). *Birth of the Leviathan: Building States and Regimes in Medieval and Early Modern Europe.* Cambridge University Press.

Etemad, B. (2005). *De L'utilité des empires. Colonisation et prospérité de l'Europe.* Paris: Armand Colin.

Faroqhi, S. and D. Quataert (1997). *An Economic and Social History of the Ottoman Empire.* Cambridge University Press.

Ferguson, N. (2002).*The Cash Nexus: Money and Power in the Modern World, 1700–2000.* New York: Basic Books

Findlay, R. and K. O'Rourke (2007). *Power and Plenty: Trade, War and the World Economy in the Second Millennium.* Princeton University Press.

Findlay, R., R. G. H. Henriksson, H. Lindgren, and M. Lundahl, eds. (2006). *Eli Heckscher, International Trade and Economic History.* Cambridge, MA, London: The MIT Press.

Finkelstein, A. (2000). *Harmony and Balance: An Intellectual History of Seventeenth Century English Economic Thought.* Ann Arbor: University of Michigan Press.

Frank, A. G. (1998). *ReOrient: Global Economy in the Asian Age.* London: University of California Press.

Gat, A. (2006). *War in Human Civilization.* Oxford University Press.

Genet, J. P. and M. Le Mené (1987). *La Genèse de l'état modern. Culture et société politique en Angleterre.* Paris: Presses universitaires de France.

Gerace, M. (2004). *Military Power, Conflict and Trade.* London: Routledge.

Gerlach, C. (2005). *Wu Wei in Europe: A Study of Eurasian Economic Thought.* London: LSE, Department of Economic History Working Paper 12/05.

Ghazanfar, S. M. (2003). *Medieval Islamic Thought: Filling the "Great Gap" in European Economics.* London: Routledge Curzon.

Glete, J. (2002). *War and the State in Early Modern Europe.* London: Routledge.

Gomes, L. (1987). *Foreign Trade and the National Economy.* Basingstoke: Macmillan.

Greenfeld, L. (2001). *The Spirit of Capitalism.* Cambridge, MA: Harvard University Press.

Hall, J. (1985). *Powers and Liberties: The Causes and Consequences of the Rise of the West.* Oxford: Blackwell.

Hall, J. and R. Schroeder, eds. (2006). *An Anatomy of Power: The Social Theory of Michael Mann.* Cambridge University Press.

Hampson, N. (1988). *The Perfidy of Albion: French Perspectives of England during the French Revolution.* Basingstoke: Macmillan.

Harding, R. (2004). "Sea Power: The Struggle for Dominance, 1650–1815," in G. Mortimer (ed.), *Early Modern Military History, 1450–1815.* New York: Palgrave Macmillan.

Helpman, E. (2004). *The Mystery of Economic Growth.* Cambridge, MA: The MIT Press.

Herbst, J. (2000). *States and Power in Africa.* Princeton University Press.

Hodgson, G. (2000). *How Economics Forgot History: The Problem of Historical Specificity in Social Science.* London: Routledge.

Hoffman, P. and K. Norberg, eds. (1994). *Fiscal Crises, Liberty and Representative Government.* Stanford University Press.

Hont, I. (2005). *Jealousy of Trade: International Competition and the Nation-State in Historical Perspective.* Cambridge, MA: Harvard University Press.

Hopkins, A. G., ed. (2002). *Globalization in World History.* London: Pimlico.

Hoppit, J. (2000). *A Land of Liberty: England 1689–1722.* Oxford University Press.

(2011). "Compulsion, Compensation and Property Rights in Britain 1688–1830," *Past and Present* 210: 93–127.

Horn, J., L. N. Rosenband, and M. Roe Smith, eds. (2010). *Reconceptualizing the Industrial Revolution.* London: MIT Press.

Hutchison, T. (1988). *Before Adam Smith.* Oxford: Basil Blackwell.

Irigoín, A. and R. Grafe (2012). "Bonded Leviathian: Or why North and Weingast are only Right on the Right Half." London: LSE, Department of Economic History Working Paper 164/122.

Jones, D. (1988). *War and Economy: In the Age of William III and Marlborough.* Oxford: Blackwell.

Jones, J. (1999), *The Anglo Dutch Wars of the Seventeenth Century.* London: Longman.

Karaman, K. and S. Pamuk (2010a). "Different Paths to the Modern State: The Interstate Competition." Unpublished paper, Department of Economics, Bogazici University, Istanbul.

(2010b). "Ottoman State Finances in Comparative European Perspective, 1500–1914," *Journal of Economic History* 70: 593–629.

Knight, R. (2011). "Changing the Agenda: The New Naval History of the British Sailing Navy," *Mariner's Mirror* 97: 225–242.

Kindleberger, C. (1996). *World Economic Primacy 1500–1990.* Oxford University Press.

Kuran, T. (2011). *The Long Divergence.* Princeton University Press.

Lachmann, R. (2000). *Capitalists in Spite of Themselves: Elite Conflict and Economic Transitions in Early Modern Europe.* New York: Oxford University Press.

Landers, J. (2003). *The Field and the Forge: Population, Production, and Power in the Pre-Industrial West.* Oxford University Press.

Leonard, J. and J. Watts, eds. (1992). *To Achieve Security and Wealth: The Qing Imperial State and the Economy, 1644–1911.* Ithaca: Cornell University Press.

Levi, M. (1988). *Of Rule and Revenue.* Berkeley: University of California Press.

Lieberman, V. (2009). *Strange Parallels: South East Asia in Global Context c.800–1830,* Vol. II. Cambridge University Press.

Liu, J. (2006). "Cultural Logics for the Regime of Useful Knowledge during the Ming and Early Qing China c. 1400–1700." Unpublished paper of Ninth Global Economic Network Conference, Kaohsiung, Taiwan.

Magnusson, L. (1994). *Mercantilism: The Shaping of an Economic Language.* London: Routledge.

Magnusson, L., ed. (1993). *Mercantilist Economics.* Boston: Kluwer Academic.

Mann, M. (1986). *The Sources of Social Power.* Vol. I: *A History from the Beginning to 1760 AD.* Cambridge University Press.

Menard, C. and M. Shirley, eds. (2008). *Handbook for New Institutional Economics.* Berlin and Heidelberg: Springer.

Mielants, E. (2007). *The Origins of Capitalism and the Rise of the West.* Philadelphia: Temple University Press.

Modelski, G. and W. Thompson (1998). *Seapower in Global Politics, 1494–1993*. London: Macmillan.

Mokyr, J. (2006). "Mercantilism, the Enlightenment and the Industrial Revolution," in Findlay *et al.* (eds.), pp. 269–304.

(2011). *The Enlightened Economy: Britain and the Industrial Revolution 1700–1850*. London: Longman.

Morrill, J. (1993). *The Nature of the English Revolution*. London: Longman.

Munkler, H. (2007). *Empires: The Logic of World Domination from Ancient Rome to the United States*. Basingstoke: Macmillan.

Murphy, A. (2013). "Demanding Credible Commitment: Public Reactions to the Failures on the Early Financial Revolution," *Economic History Review* 6: 178–197.

Neal, L. (1977). "Interpreting Power and Profit in Economic History: A Case Study of the Seven Years War," *Journal of Economic History* 37: 20–35.

(1990). *The Rise of Financial Capitalism: International Capital Markets in the Age of Reason*. Cambridge University Press.

(2000). "How It all Began: The Monetary and Financial Architecture of Europe during the First Global Capital Markets," *Financial History Review* 7: 117–140.

North, D. C. (1981). *Structure and Change in Economic History*. London: W. W. Norton.

(1990). *Institutions, Institutional Change, and Economic Performance*. Cambridge University Press.

North, D. C. and B. R. Weingast (1989). "Constitutions and Commitments: Evolution of Institutions Governing Public Choice in Seventeenth Century England," *Journal of Economic History* 49: 803–822.

North, D. C., J. J. Wallis, and B. R. Weingast (2009). *Violence and Social Orders: A Conceptual Framework for Interpreting Recorded Human History*. Cambridge University Press.

Nye, J. (2007). *War, Wine and Taxes*. Princeton University Press.

O'Brien, P. (2000). "Mercantilism and Imperialism in the Rise and Decline of the Dutch and English Economies," *De Economist* 148: 469–501.

(2002). "Fiscal Exceptionalism: Great Britain and its European Rivals from Civil War to Triumph at Waterloo," in Winch and O'Brien, pp. 245–267.

(2005). "Fiscal and Financial Preconditions for the Rise of British Naval Hegemony 1485–1846." London: LSE Department of Economic History Working Paper 91.

(2006). "Contentions of the Purse between England and its European Rivals from Henry V to George IV: A Conversation with Michael Mann," *Journal of Historical Sociology*, 19(4): 126–141.

(2011a). "The History, Nature and Significance of an Exceptional Fiscal State for the Growth of the British Economy," *Economic History Review*, 64(2): 408–446.

(2011b). "The Contributions of Warfare with Revolutionary and Napoleonic France to the Consolidation and Progress of the British Industrial Revolution." Department of Economic History, LSE Working Paper, 150.

Oka, B. G. and G. Smits, eds. (2010). *Economic Thought in Early Modern Japan*. Leiden: Brill.

Ormrod, D. (2003). *The Rise of Commercial Empires: England and the Netherlands in the Age of Mercantilism, 1650–1770*. Cambridge University Press.

Ormrod, W. M., M. Bonney, and R. Bonney (1999). *Crises, Revolutions and Self Sustained Growth: Essays in European Fiscal History 1130–1830*. Stamford (UK): Shaun Tyas.

Pagden, A. (1995). *Lords of All the World: Ideologies of Empire in Spain, Britain, and France c. 1500–c. 1800*. New Haven: Yale University Press.

Pamuk, S. (1987). *The Ottoman Empire and European Capitalism, 1820–1913*. Cambridge University Press.

Parker, G. (1996). *The Military Revolution: Military Innovation and the Rise of the West, 1500–1800*, 2nd edn. Cambridge University Press.

Parliamentary Papers, Accounts and Papers 1868–69 (xxxv).

Parthasarathi, P. (2011). *Why Europe Grew Rich and Asia Did Not*. Cambridge University Press.

Perdue, P. (2005). *China Marches West: The Qing Conquest of Central Eurasia*. Cambridge, MA: Harvard University Press.

Perlin, P. (1985). "State Formation Reconsidered," *Modern Asian Studies* 19: 415–480.

Perrotta, C. (1991). "Is the Mercantilist Theory of the Favorable Balance of Trade Really Erroneous?" *History of Political Economy* 23: 301–333.

(1997). "The Pre-classical Theory of Development: Increased Consumption Raises Productivity," *History of Political Economy* 29: 295–325.

Persson, T. and G. Tabellini (2003). *The Economic Effects of Constitutions*. Cambridge University Press.

Pincus, S. (2009). *The First Modern Revolution*. New Haven: Yale University Press.

Poggi, G. (1990). *The State: Its Nature, Development and Prospects*. Stanford University Press.

Pohl, H., ed. (1990). *The European Discovery of the World and its Economic Effects on Pre-Industrial Society 1500–1800*. Stuttgart: Franz Steiner.

Prendergast, C. (1999). "The Provision of Incentives in Firms," *Journal of Economic Literature* 37: 7–63.

Quataert, D. (2000). *The Ottoman Empire 1700–1922*. Cambridge University Press.

Rashid, S. (1980). "Economists, Economic Historians and Mercantilism," *Scandinavian Economic History Review* 28: 1–14.

Reinert, E. (1999). "The Role of the State in Economic Growth," *Journal of Economic Studies* 26(415): 268–326.

Reinert, E., ed. (2004). *Globalization, Economic Development and Inequality*. Cheltenham: Edward Elgar.

Reinert, E. and K. S. Jomo, eds. (2005). *The Origin of Development Economics*. London: Zed Publications.

Reinert, S. (2011). *Translating Empire: Emulation and the Origins of Political Economy*. Cambridge, MA: Harvard University Press.

Richards, J. (1993). *Power, Administration and Finance in Mughal India*. Aldershot: Ashgate Variorum.

(1995). *The Mughal Empire*. Cambridge University Press.

(2012). "Fiscal States in Mughal and British India," in Casalilla and O'Brien, pp. 410–441.

Rodger, N. (2004). *The Command of the Oceans: A Naval History of Britain 1649–1815*, Vol. II. London: W. W. Norton.

Rosenthal, J. L. and R. B. Wong (2011). *Before and Beyond Divergence: The Politics of Economic Change in China and Europe*. Cambridge, MA: Harvard University Press.

Rowe, W. (2009). *China's Last Empire: The Great Qing*. Cambridge, MA: Harvard University Press.

Sanchez-Torres, R., ed. (2007). *War, State and Development: Fiscal, Military States in the Eighteenth Century*. Pamplona: Ediciones Universidad de Navarra.

Schmoller, G. (1967), *The Mercantile System and its Historical Significance*. New York: Macmillan.

Schumpeter, J. (1954). "The Crisis of the Tax State?" *International Economic Papers* 4: 1–17.

Skinner, A. and T. Wilson, eds. (1976). *The Market and the State: Essays in Honour of Adam Smith*. Oxford: Clarendon Press.

Smelser, N. and R. Swedberg, eds. (2006), *Handbook of Economic Sociology*. Princeton University Press.

Sowerby, S. (2011). "Pantomime History," *Parliamentary History* 30: 236–258.

Stasavage, D. (2010). "When Distance Mattered: Geographic Scale and the Development of European Representative Assemblies," *American Political Science Review* 104: 625–643.

(2011). *States of Credit: Size, Power and the Development of European Polities*. Princeton University Press.

Stein, B. (1985), "State Formation and Economy Reconsidered," *Modern Asian Studies* 19: 387–413

Stoler, A. L., C. McGranahan, and P. C. Perdue, eds. (2007). *Imperial Formations*. Santa Fe: School of American Research Press.

Storrs, C., ed. (2009). *The Fiscal-Military State in Eighteenth Century Europe*. Aldershot: Ashgate.

Struve, L., ed. (2004). *The Qing Formation in World Historical Time*. London:

Teichova, A. and H. Matis, eds. (2003). *Nation, State and the Economy in History*. Cambridge University Press.

Thompson, W. (2000). *The Emergence of Global Political Economy*. London and New York: Routledge.

Thurchin, P. (2009). "A Theory for the Formation of Large Empires," *Journal of Global History* 4: 191–218.

Tilly, C. (1975). *The Formation of National States in Western Europe*. Princeton University Press.

(1990) *Coercion, Capital and European States 990–1990*. Oxford: Blackwell.

Timmons, J. (2005). "The Fiscal Contract: States, Taxes and Public Services," *World Politics* 57: 530–567.

Tracy, J., ed. (1991a). *The Rise of Merchant Empires: Long Distance Trade in the Early Modern World 1350–1750*. Cambridge University Press.

(1991b). *The Political Economy of Merchant Empires: State Power and World Trade 1350–1750*. Cambridge University Press.

Tribe, K. (1993) "Mercantilism and the Economics of State Formation," in Magnusson (ed.), pp. 175–186.

Vries, P. (2002). "Governing Growth: A Comparative Analysis of the Role of the State in the Rise of the West," *Journal of World History* 13: 67–139.

(2003). *Via Peking and Back to Manchester: Britain, the Industrial Revolution and China*. Leiden: Brill.

Wade, R. (2004). *Governing the Market: Economic Theory and the Role of Government in East Asian Industrialization*. Princeton University Press.

Wallerstein, I. (1974–2011). *The Modern World System*, 4 vols. Berkeley and Los Angeles: University of California Press.

(1980). *Mercantilism and the Consolidation of the European World Economy, 1600–1750*. Berkeley and Los Angeles: University of California Press.

Wennerlind, C. (2012). *Casualties of Credit: The English Financial Revolution 1620–1770*. Cambridge, MA: Harvard University Press.

White, C. (2009). *Understanding Economic Development: A Global Transition from Poverty to Posterity*. Cheltenham: Edward Elgar.

Winch, D. (1996). *Riches and Poverty: An Intellectual History of Political Economy in Britain 1750–1834*. Cambridge University Press.

Winch, D. and P. O'Brien (2002). *The Political Economy of British Historical Experience*. Oxford University Press.

Wolfgang, R., ed. (1996). *Power, Elites and State Building*. Oxford University Press.

Wong, R. B. (1997). *China Transformed and the Limits of European Experience*. Ithaca: Cornell University Press.

(2012). "Taxation and Good Governance in China," in Casalilla and O'Brien (eds.), pp. 353–377.

Wong, Y. S. and D. Sayer (2006). *Twenty Years of the Journal of Historical Sociology*. Vol. I: *Essays on the British State*. Oxford: Blackwell.

Zelin, M. (1984). *The Magistrate's Tael: Rationalizing Fiscal Reform in Eighteenth Century Ch'ing China*. Berkeley and Los Angeles: University of California Press.

Zmera, H. (2001). *Monarchy, Aristocracy and the State in Europe, 1300–1800*. London: Routledge.

13

Capitalism and dependency in Latin America

RICHARD SALVUCCI

Introduction

We begin by briefly considering the historical debate over "capitalism" and economic development in Latin America. There are four salient points: the evolution of institutions in Mesoamerica and the Andes prior to the Conquest; the nature of existing factor endowments; their radical change under the pressure of conquest; and the implications of these changes for the nature of colonialism across agriculture, mining, industry, and trade and commerce.

As a prelude to what follows, we may be permitted some reflection on whether capitalism in Latin America is or could be a homegrown phenomenon, at least to the extent that capitalism depends on free exchange. Of course, the discussion is made infinitely complex by semantics and more. Is it "commercial," "industrial," or "dependent" capitalism of which we speak (or some variation of all), not to mention its relation to the broader international economy, or to colonialism, imperialism, and national liberation? Here I propose to look at a slightly different question. Could we legitimately ask whether capitalism based on a market economy arrived only with the agents of European conquest, or is there evidence of some independent, indigenous evolution of markets that would have ultimately pointed in a similar direction? I consider this question in more detail in the next section, and its implications in the overall conclusions.

Regime change and the great reversal

In 1492, there were probably about 50 million inhabitants in what was to be called America. Some 60 percent resided, roughly, in Mesoamerica and the Andes. However, *any* figure concerning the so-called "contact" population (meaning, the indigenous population at first contact with the Europeans) is conjectural: over the past seventy years, such estimates have ranged from 8 to

100 million. If we accept the conclusion of Massimo Livi Bacci (2006: 281) that the indigenous population of Mexico prior to the arrival of the Europeans will never be known with any certainty, it is probably advisable to leave the "numbers game" behind. In reality, very little depends on it, for we have considerable evidence, both in contemporaneous eyewitness accounts, and indirectly, through physical evidence, of very dense populations in Mexico and the Andes, if not in the Caribbean. The Europeans, not much given to precision in these matters, lumped the *altepetl* (ethnic states) of Tenochtitlan and Tlatelolco into one city whose population, markets, and physical structure they could only compare to what they *had seen* in Rome or Constantinople.

There was no Tenochtitlan in the Andes, but there was an equally impressive accumulation of physical capital, in roads, state storehouses, canals, terracing, raised fields, and irrigation works that were indications of the mobilization of massive amounts of labor from a population that could simultaneously realize agricultural surpluses. Even Livi Bacci's much-reduced estimates for the initial population of the island of Hispaniola stand between 120,000 and 200,000 or the equivalent of an insular Tenochtitlan. The larger point is simply that any reasonable appreciation of all the evidence we possess about indigenous America is that it was densely urbanized, well established, and culturally sophisticated in the Mesoamerican *altiplano* and in the Andean highlands.

There are basically two ways of looking at the growth of population in the Americas prior to the arrival of the Europeans. One tradition, often associated with the "Berkeley School," views the expansion of the indigenous population as a problem. As it grew, the carrying capacity of Mesoamerica was strained to breaking point. Periodic dearth, intense social and political conflict, and the emergence of a nobility with access to private property and slave labor were symptoms of social stress and decline. Over time, as tensions increased, the ensuing conflict would have inevitably caused collapse. The arrival of the European conquerors accelerated the process, but did not cause it (Cook 1949a, 1949b).

Indeed, in the Andes, a civil war over dynastic succession was already under way when the Europeans arrived, a conflict of which they took full advantage (Hemming 2003). In Mesoamerica, various rebellious ethnic groups, such as the Tlaxcalans, turned against the Mexica, the masters of the Aztec empire. They joined the Europeans in overthrowing their erstwhile masters. In this view, the arrival of the Europeans constituted one more episode in a cyclical process of the rise and collapse of native empires that had already gone on for the better part of a millennium. The new masters took advantage of the latest phase of the cycle.

Yet there is an alternative, and in many ways, quite more imaginative view of what had occurred. The expansion of the indigenous population had led to a process of what Ester Boserup (1965) termed agricultural intensification. The Mesoamerican and Andean innovations of raised ridge fields, *chinampas*, terracing, multicropping, irrigation works, and canals were evidence of the process whereby total agricultural product could rise even as the marginal product of individual agricultural workers fell. Sociocultural and property arrangements dictated that producers earned their average product, which was distributed through clan or kinship groups (known as *calpulli* in Mexico or *ayllu* in Peru). Very dense populations were thus possible. The intensification of agriculture provided an incentive toward further agricultural innovation in the hands of what Gene Wilken (1990) calls the sophisticated "good farmers" of Mesoamerica, not exactly improving landlords, but cultivators highly adept at enlarging food supplies for their communities using "traditional" techniques. The resulting surplus sustained a generally well-nourished population (Ortiz de Montellano 1990) that provided the basis for a more advanced economy in which growing exchange based on specialization took place. Large numbers of nonagricultural producers, such as priests, nobles, warriors, and artisans could be sustained as well. As the leading student of colonial land tenure, Carlos Sempat Assadourian (2006: 278) succinctly put it, "there [was] no preemptive Malthusian break." Clearly, these were economies where *markets* existed, for as the conquerors recorded, their presence was well-nigh ubiquitous, at least in Mesoamerica, if not in the Andean highlands. But they were not *market economies* – at least not yet – where supply, demand, and the possession of private property governed the allocation and distribution of resources and rewards.

These were the civilizations that the Europeans found on their arrival. It was precisely their subsequent development that conquest arrested. By warfare and the introduction of unknown diseases, the conquerors decimated the Amerindian populations. Indigenous labor, which had been the abundant factor of production prior to their arrival, now became scarce. Precisely the opposite happened with land. So while the artifacts of intensive agriculture gradually fell into disuse and disrepair, the indigenous population, previously abundant, was placed in a different position. Its labor was potentially very valuable, for as the now-scarce factor of production, it had the upper hand. Money wages – and money wages were mandated for native workers by the New Laws in 1542 – would inevitably rise in real terms, that is, in the amount of goods and services the surviving indigenous population could command. This put the conquerors in a most awkward position. If they were to follow market signals in the allocation of labor, the indigenous people would become rich and the new masters of the land would end up poor. But, clearly, this is not what they had in mind for themselves. As Cortés is said by Bernal Díaz to have remarked, he did not come to till the soil like a peasant. That is what "Indians" were for.

So the conquerors were constrained to devise or modify existing institutions for the distribution and use of previously abundant labor. Their purpose was now to ignore or circumvent labor's increasing and novel scarcity. This, in the final analysis, is what the bewildering roll call of institutions named *encomienda, repartimento,* and *peonaje* were about. One acquired labor in the early decades of the conquest through these means, through status as a conqueror, the use of connections at court, through royal favor, or through illegal payments – by rent-seeking in a modern phrase. This was not "capitalism" as we might understand it: the colonists did not bid for resources on the basis of how productively they could employ them. Economic evolution, not to say thriving economies, were stopped dead in their tracks by the conquest and its demographic aftermath. Scarcity now ran, so to speak, in the wrong direction, and demographic disaster was the reason why.

The magnitude of the decline of the indigenous population under European pressure was nearly inconceivable. Rather than attempt the implausible – to find average population densities for "Mexico" or "Peru" in the sixteenth century and seventeenth centuries – a better course would be to examine some well-documented regions as examples. In Mexico, thanks to the meticulous research of Eleanor Melville (1994), we can calculate the ratio of Indian tributaries to land in the Valle del Mezquital.

In the 1560s, the figure was about $1.7/\text{km}^2$. By the 1570s, it had fallen to $1.2/\text{km}^2$. By the 1580s, the ratio was $0.8/\text{km}^2$. By the 1590s, the population density was $0.5/\text{km}^2$. In other words, to the extent that the estimator is both reliable and representative, the tributary population of Mexico – essentially adult males, or, anachronistically, the "labor force" – fell by over 50 percent in the second half of the sixteenth century. Nor was the Valle de Mezquital unique. Emma Pérez-Rocha (2008: 49) calculates that the tributary count for Coyoacán, one of the most important *encomiendas* in New Spain, fell by 41 percent between 1563 and 1598. Tributary counts for Peru over roughly the same period (1561 and 1591) reveal an analogous, albeit relatively less severe decline of 25.6 percent, while a population count based on 146 *encomiendas* between 1573 and 1602 presents a fall of 30 percent. In other words, the ratio of the indigenous population to land fell by 30 to 50 percent *in the final half of the sixteenth century* in the core areas of European incursion. A comparison of the terminal date with the contact populations, albeit of uncertain size, would yield an even larger decline.

The collapse of the native populations – caused by a well-known combination of European epidemic disease, the violence of the conquest, and the disruptive consequences of the social disorganization that accompanied them – had, at bare minimum, two significant consequences.

First, to the extent that the conquerors had a clearly conceived plan of exploitation rather than simply a series of more or less brilliantly successful improvisations, it depended on what José Miranda (1980) termed the "superposition" of societies, or what others (García Martínez 2012: 1915–1978) term "indirect rule" in the encomienda that the conquerors insisted on implementing. "The Spaniards employed [prehispanic tribute] as they had found it in the beginning, and modified it according to European standards in the socioeconomic regime in New Spain." In essence, and with suitable changes – including monetization, standardization, and adjustments to compensate for population decline – they would step in and collect the taxes that had gone to the ruling Triple Alliance (the confederation of city-states at the apex of the Aztec empire) and other native ethnic states or altepetl as well. Yet for this strategy to work, obviously enough, the productive class had to reproduce itself and it did not. Miranda (1980: 35, 247) offers two striking examples of what occurred to the tribute, the pre-conquest in-kind tax, a reasonable, if not virtually unique proxy for indigenous surplus output. In Metatuyca (Mexico) the tribute before 1537 was fixed at seven to nine "loads" of "cloth"; by the 1550s, it had fallen to two to three loads; and by the 1560s, to one load – or by 50 percent after 1550 and by a much higher percentage from before. This is similar to what Melville (1994: 171–177) found for the tributary population in the Mezquital. In the Mixteca of Tuxtepec, the story, if not the commodity (cacao) was no different. The pattern over a broad area of central Mexico was of falling indigenous population, production, and surplus.

Charles V had been seeking to bring the powerful settler class (the encomenderos) to heel since the 1540s, and the decline of the native population yielded a supportive, if ironic result. The "superposition" model embodied in the encomienda presupposed the continuing existence of a dense tributary population or labor force. The evaporation of this population meant that the material basis for the model had ceased to exist, the continuing attempts of royal authorities to ensure a supply of labor to mining, agriculture, and public works – the so-called repartimiento – notwithstanding. The specifics differ by colony. In Mexico, after an unsuccessful experiment in channeling native labor into public works, the repartimiento was abolished, with what results to the labor supply of the private sector being most difficult to deduce but, perhaps, related to the so-called "depression" of the seventeenth century studied by

Woodrow Borah (1951). In Mexico, Borah argued, the decimation of the native population, upon whom the settler class depended for both labor and taxes, experienced a lengthy period of impoverishment that would not be reversed until the late seventeenth century. For it was not until then that the population of Mexico would begin its uncertain recovery, and even then, with significant demographic alterations underway, including the emergence of a new class of *casta* or mixed blood, rather than indigenous populations.

Miners, markets, and capitalism

The most subtle and revealing examples of the way in which the Europeans confronted changing factor endowments are demonstrated by the long-term shift from intensive agriculture to extensive pastoralism and then to extensive agriculture and ruralization in Mexico and, to some extent, Peru. But mining offers instructive evidence as well. While much has been written about silver mining and free labor in Mexico and its important role at Potosí, the effort of the Europeans to *avoid* dependence on the market and free labor in Peru is, perhaps, most striking. If there were much chance for capitalist markets to develop at all, it was in Mexico, and in silver mining, rather than in Peru.

For example, according to Brooke Larson (1998: 61–62) and other historians of Andean mining, the use of *mita* (hispanicized from *mit'a*) or Indian draft labor in the late sixteenth century augmented the Indian labor force by one-third to one-half. As Larson emphasizes, *mitayos* received one half the wage of free laborers at Potosí, four *reales* daily as opposed to a peso. *Mitayos* had no rights to a portion of the ore mined, as was common among free miners in Mexico and Peru. In addition, there was an ample share of "pocket Indians" (*indios de faltriquera*) perhaps a minimum of 20 percent of the mining labor force, in some cases, who paid their way out of *mita* service. In other words, there were "miners" whose "production" represented nothing more than a tax on indigenous labor. While estimates put the size of the subsidy to the Potosí mines in the 1610s at 3.8 million pesos when their output was in the area of 30 million pesos per year, that figure seems not to include the value of output sacrificed by the *mitayos* in their villages. That implies that a subsidy of *at least* 15 percent was provided by the use of something that was in no sense free, wage labor. The existence of pocket Indians meant an additional distortion. This was not capitalism: it was rent-seeking on an enormous scale by the Crown and its agents, the miners: it is difficult to imagine that an allocation that reflected real labor costs would have looked anything like it. Nor was this simply a transient phenomenon. Enrique Tandeter (2006: 343) flatly concludes "the key to survival and expansion of Potosí was the *mita*."

The situation in silver mining in Mexico is ordinarily described in rather different terms, and perhaps justifiably so. The general tenor of "forced" versus "free" labor that has surfaced in discussion of Peru and Mexico since the eighteenth century is nowhere more evident than in this industry. The distinction – between "free" versus "forced" labor in Mexico and Peru, and by extension, between market- and non-market-based exchange – supports, on the face of things, a sense that the two economies had been evolving in different directions well before the arrival of the Europeans. In Peru, any evolution toward market exchange and "capitalism" had been largely blocked by transportation costs and what John V. Murra (1978) termed "verticality." The only analysis of relative transportation costs (Castillero Calvo 1980: 31) available confirms this. In Peru (on the Huancavelica–Potosí route) transportation costs were 3.5 times as high per ton-kilometer as they were in Mexico (on the Acapulco–Veracruz route) in the colonial period. As a result, exchange between ethnic groups in different ecological niches or micro-climates was carried on largely by reciprocity and redistribution – ceremonial exchange among kinfolk – rather than by market exchange, at least in the central Andes.

The argument that markets and free labor had developed more in Mexico than in Peru is not a new one, although modern historians have tended to neglect it. Yet the vast differences across the empire were certainly evident enough to contemporaries. In the eighteenth century, José Antonio de Areche, a Spanish official sent to Peru to report on the state of the colony, made the comparison explicitly:

> This land is not like Mexico in any way. There, in general, one finds justice; here, daily tyranny. There, the Indians buy what suits them; here, what the *corregidor* (local magistrate) allots them. There, they deal in a free market; here, in forced sale . . . [The presence of Indian labor drafts] and [the nature] of provincial trade keep [Peru] moribund. (Borah 1983: 411)

The effect of presumably freer labor markets in Mexico produced greater competition for labor, and, therefore, higher wages and better working conditions. Moreover, if silver mines in Mexico were compelled to pay higher wages and employ free labor, they could also afford to do so.[1]

---

[1] Very crude calculations comparing per capita income in Peru and Mexico around 1800 are possible. Mexico was, as one might expect, considerably wealthier. My estimate (1997) for Mexico, which follows the generally reliable calculations of José María Quirós (1821), is 34

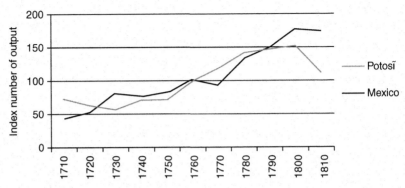

Figure 13.1 Indices of physical silver output, Mexico and Potosi, 1710–1810
Source: data drawn from Enrique Tandeter (2006: 340–341).

While historians have argued that Mexican mines in the eighteenth century were becoming less profitable, this seems doubtful. The argument is based on a confusion between the purchasing power of silver in terms of maize, and the quantum of silver produced. Since the Mexican peso was defined in terms of its weight, the "nominal" value of silver mined was, more or less, its quantum. There is no reason, and, indeed, no sense in "deflating" this to obtain "real" values. Silver's production was what it was; its purchasing power defined over some basket of commodities was something else. Hence my use of Tandeter's index (Tandeter 2006: 340, 341) of "physical silver production" to produce an index of output in Figure 13.1.

By the early years of the eighteenth century, Mexico had replaced Peru as the Spanish empire's leading producer of silver. After 1770, the growth of Mexican output exceeded Peru's until the outbreak of the wars of independence in 1810. It is inconceivable that comparative advantage and growing profitability did not explain the progress of Mexican silver mining over forty years.

Moreover, something distinctly unusual was happening to productivity in Mexican mining. In Figure 13.2, I employ Richard Garner's data on mercury consumption (the vital element used in refining ores by amalgamation) and silver production. Until about the last quarter of the eighteenth century, these series track each other, which is not surprising if the extractive technology was constant. Subsequently, a gap then opened between them. One might interpret the gap as evidence of a rise in the productivity of a major input and

pesos. Nominal per capita income in Peru, based on data collected by Marcel Haitin (1983), was higher, at around 40 pesos, but, adjusted for a substantial difference in colonial price levels (Arroyo Abad *et al.* 2012: 6), a Peruvian estimate at parity would be about 25 pesos.

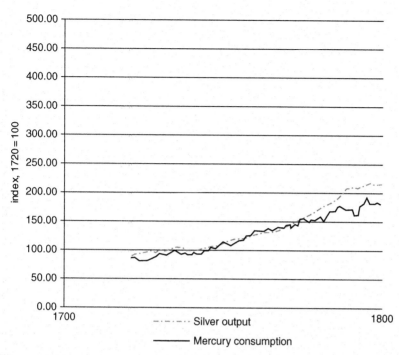

Figure 13.2 Silver output versus mercury consumption, twenty-four-year moving average, 1700–1800.

Source: taken from data sets provided by Richard Garner, www.insidemydesk.com/hdd. html (accessed May 21, 2013).

hence, as indicative of a presumptive reduction in costs. Whether that was or was not the case is unclear. But the Crown's vigorous fleecing of Mexico's miners and merchants coincided with both the apparent change in productivity, and with the clear acceleration of Mexican production. The community of Mexican silver miners was doing very well – or at least well enough to pay the competitive wages that dazzled such observers as Humboldt, even if the Crown and its agents, like José Gálvez, would have liked lower miners' wages so that the court in Madrid could have taxed higher owners' profits (Costeloe 1986; Marichal 2007).

Coase, Hunt and some variations on the themes: industry and agriculture in a colonial setting

While Mexican mines were able to compete for free labor, other sectors of the American economy and their actors were not. Here the dilemma of how to produce commodities that were vital, but which fetched relatively low relative prices, was omnipresent. This was, in essence, a kind of "diamonds and water" paradox brought to the colonial world. It seemed profitable to produce commodities, like silver, that had no value in terms of consumption, but unprofitable to produce those, like maize or cloth, that clearly did. With a rapidly diminishing labor force and what, for all purposes, was essentially "empty" free land, rising real wages would, as Evsey Domar (1970) pointed out, dissipate any available economic surplus. In some places, namely the Caribbean, Brazil, and some coastal lowland regions of Mexico and Peru, African slavery was permitted, adopted, and encouraged. But according to the New Laws of 1542 Indians could not be made chattel slaves, unless they were taken as prisoners of war. The Europeans, however dearly they wished to pay no more than lip service to the restriction, found this particular law difficult to ignore, if only because it offered the Crown a *de jure* instrument with which to contest the *encomenderos'* (and later, large landowners' or *hacendados'*) *de facto* autonomy. The archives are full of cases in which the Crown insisted on the notional freedom of the indigenous people, which the colonists pretended to accept, while taking practical steps to insure that the Crown's legal agents (*alcaldes, corregidores*) would never enforce the laws which they were supposed to uphold. This arrangement – a kind of early modern version of regulatory "capture" – bedeviled the long-standing debate over "capitalism" in Latin America, for the outcome, "free" labor that was too often by no means free in a modern sense, seemed to turn as much on semantics as on substance. It also reflected, as José F. de la Peña (1983: 189–238) illustrated, the tendency of the Habsburg monarchy to reward contending peninsular retainers with colonial lands. In so doing, it purchased stability at home, but at the price of creating a landed oligarchy in the colony all too able to dispute royal prerogative. This was a crucial development, for large colonial landowners and other entrepreneurs contested, used, and sometimes usurped royal prerogatives for their own rent-seeking purposes.

At first glance, it is difficult to think of two institutions that had less in common than haciendas and *obrajes* (textile manufactories) in colonial Spanish America. One was rural, agrarian, and devoted to primary production; the other was principally (if not exclusively) urban, industrial, and focussed mainly on woolens, if not cottons. They were, to an oversimplification, peasant and "proletarian" in composition, but both represented a rational response to the collapse of the indigenous population because both tried to substitute a more abundant factor of production, e.g. land in the hacienda, or even skilled supervision in the *obraje*, for increasingly scarce labor. Yet neither involved free labor in a modern sense, and in the case of agriculture, it was required that labor *not* be divorced, at least not entirely, from the means of production, land. The resulting complex of institutional adaptations made it impossible for historians to call what they found "capitalism," even if profit-maximizing behavior was clearly in evidence. The problem, once again, was to avoid rewarding the scarce factor, labor, which would have undermined the entire colonial enterprise.

One of the more vexing issues was to keep consumers adequately supplied with ordinary wage goods, such as food and cloth, once expansion of the settler population began in earnest, certainly between 1570 and 1620. For the most part, these goods were grown or manufactured in the Americas: any other course would have rendered colonization impossible, for imports were far too costly. The profits of the Sevillian commercial ventures to the Indies were in this period astounding. Antonio-Miguel Bernal (1992: 178, 192), on the basis of exhaustive archival research, calls them "fabulous." Returns on investments in ventures to the Caribbean, Central America, Mexico, and Peru were as high as 100, not to say 200 to 300 percent in commodities like olive oil and wine. In general, the price level in the Americas was estimated to be from 10 to 35 percent higher (depending on location) than what it was in Seville. So the incentive to substitute for olive oil and wine as well as for common cloth was overwhelming.

Cotton (unlike wool – there were no sheep or draught animals) was indigenous to Mexico and Peru. Its use as a tributary item stemmed from the fact that it could not be grown on the *altiplano*, where the bulk of the surviving indigenous population was to be found. Under the Aztecs, cottons were brought up from the coastal lowlands, evidence, perhaps, that they were too costly to transport given ordinary "market" incentives (to the extent these functioned), and was therefore supplied, effectively, by coerced labor instead. Something similar was to occur under the Europeans, as cotton cloth became a staple product of the *repartimiento*, especially in southern Mexico, in Yucatán, and in Guatemala. Here the cotton industry was financed and organized by merchants, or by colonial magistrates, or both, who assumed broad control of its trade. As Robert Patch (2002: 9–10), the principal student of the institution has remarked, although technically illegal, at least in Guatemala, "the *repartimiento* was important because it allowed Spanish *corregidores, alcaldes mayors* and governors to acquire valuable goods much below market price." Patch concludes "in practice [the *repartimiento*] became a coercive kind of putting out system that forced the Maya to work for Spaniards for below-market wages."

The manufactories (*obrajes*) became famous as much for their oppressive working environments as they did as a sort of proto-factory in which the as-yet unmechanized stages of production were largely integrated in one operation and under one roof. The existence of such "manufactories" has always involved a consideration of their ostensibly capitalist nature: clearly profit maximizing but with fixed costs that were not offset by advanced technology, even as late as the eighteenth century. The conclusion to which historians have been logically driven is that the "closed" nature of the *obraje* was related to a largely successful effort to reduce labor costs by impairing, not to say hindering, the mobility of the workforce. The *obraje* was not a factory, but a sort of prison, and its widespread use of convict labor, as well as recourse to what was termed "debt peonage" had one purpose, and one purpose only: to recruit, retain, or detain a labor force that could not otherwise be hired at competitive wages. Records surviving from the industrial center of Querétaro (Mexico) in the 1790s would seem to underscore the success of coercion, where labor costs represented an unexpectedly (and perhaps implausibly low) share of total costs. Salvucci (1987: 44), with even better data from Querétaro in the 1840s where some mechanization existed, suggests that labor costs account for about 50 percent of value added in textile production, rather than a more conventional 75 percent.

Restrictions on labor mobility were widespread enough to raise difficult questions about the existence of "free labor" in their context. Indeed, in Mexico, there was a lengthy period, from the late sixteenth through the middle seventeenth century, when African slave labor was employed, substituting for indigenous labor, whose real wages had risen sharply in the face of population decline, especially in Puebla and Tlaxcala. In the Andes, work in *obrajes* was always associated with the *mita* and the *encomienda*. With the recovery of the native population in the eighteenth century, the sale of African slaves through the British South Sea Company in Mexico dried up, but what replaced slave labor was not "free labor" in an unambiguous sense.

Devices such as advances on wages or loans, once flatly termed "debt peonage," were impediments to labor mobility, but often in unexpected ways. Such access to credit and even subsistence (in the form of a food ration) from *obrajes* were not taken for granted by urban workers whose standard of living was linked to volatile maize prices. Finally, the organization of *obrajes* corresponded to Ronald Coase's theory of the firm, in which internal hierarchies organize production more efficiently than markets, especially when the use of markets is costly. Resource markets in the colonial period were not always good at transmitting market information accurately, much less quickly, because conditions of communication were poor. Labor markets were seemingly made less reliable by a labor–leisure trade-off that occurred at relatively low levels of real wages. The endless complaining of the Europeans about the "natural indolence" of the indigenous people (Schwartz 1978) served as a justification for their coerced labor, and reinforced the Europeans' refusal to turn to labor markets they considered unreliable. This messy reality may not have looked much like "capitalism" to Adam Smith and subsequent observers. It did not serve to distribute income or wealth particularly broadly. But it was rational from the standpoint of the Europeans and the way they did business in a colonial environment.

Historians have looked at this situation in a number of ways, not all of them mutually consistent. There are some who regard indigenous adaptation to markets, especially in Mexico, as relatively straightforward. Some emphasize the resistance of the natives and their desire to manage their own affairs largely independent of, or in subtle opposition to, European rule, or even indigenous opportunism, turning the colonial system to their own ends as much as they could. It is sometimes difficult to know what to make of such tensions, or necessary, perhaps, to embed them in a more nuanced model of how labor markets actually functioned under colonialism. This is precisely what Shane Hunt has done in his account of "haciendas and plantations in Latin America" (2011: 425–485).

Hunt's account of labor and land tenure is explicitly neoclassical in orientation, but does not depend on models of perfect competition for its operation. Rather it considers an implication of the fundamental material reality that colonialism imposed: inequality of power and disparities in access to land and labor between landlord and peasant. The hacienda and the multiple forms of peasant smallholding that emerged in the wake of conquest and its impositions were complementary aspects of a single economy.

The essential outlines of Hunt's argument can be summarized, and much oversimplified, in the following way. The dispossession of native communities and their lands by the Europeans evolved in response to the relative scarcity of labor and abundance of lands. "Employing" peasants in some fully capitalistic framework, as an agricultural proletariat (Hunt's definition of a "plantation," in effect) was impracticable in most places because their productivity on hacienda lands measured by value was simply too low: regional markets were limited in extent and transportation costs to larger commercial markets were high. Hiring scarce labor would have exhausted the hacienda's profits and, in Hunt's judgment, been insufficient to maintain labor at a subsistence level.

The alternative was to compensate peasants in land, which was, in a global sense, abundant to the Europeans, and hence, cheap, and subject to political manipulation. The indigenous people, in any event, found their own access to land limited, and as a result, were forced to wring the most out of it that they could through intensive strategies, such as double-cropping. Andean historians, like Brooke Larson (1998: 171–172) call the surpluses that the indigenous people could produce "shallow and periodic," by which she probably means inadequate *in themselves* to supply the rural population, but adequate *in conjunction with the surplus of the hacienda* to support regular markets, at least in places like Cochabamba. Or as Enrique Florescano put it for Mexico, "The owner employed his most abundant and cheapest resource, land, to attract the scarcest and costliest resources, seasonal labour" (Florescano 1984: 169). Indeed, Hunt's model describes almost exactly the pattern of agrarian labor and income distribution in the state of Morelos a few decades before the outbreak of the Mexican Revolution. "According to [the landlords]," writes Alicia Hernández Chávez, "the solution for a resident of Anenecuilco or any other town there was to put their entire family to work in the cane fields or the sugar mill. They'd earn three times what they did playing the small parcels of land over which they fought so much" (Hernández Chávez 1993: 107).

Landlords seeking to maximize profits and minimize costs never behaved in classically "capitalist" fashion. Yet even if the arrangement were efficient in the sense that disturbing it would make either the *hacendado* or the peasants worse off, there was little chance that it would lead to the dynamic growth that characterized export agriculture ("plantations") in the nineteenth century. So agricultural output probably grew at more or less the same rate that population did, except in areas of extraordinary fertility, like the Mexican Bajío, or what were to become the coffee regions of southeastern Brazil (Vidal Luna and Klein 2003).

The general applicability of Hunt's model is not limited to agriculture and the hacienda alone. The wages paid to weavers in Mexico's *obrajes* were also consistent with their relatively low marginal productivity, a little more than 50 pesos per worker per year in Mexico City at the end of the sixteenth century (Salvucci 2000: 27). But in major weaving centers, like Coyoacán and San Miguel el Grande, home-spinning of yarn went hand in glove with the *obrajes*, the industrial equivalent of the relationship between peasant producers and *hacendados*, which reflects the transaction costs that any complex or coordinated economic activity faced, where, for instance, market information moved very slowly, as little as 100 miles in a week, so that the response of suppliers and supply of inputs could be delayed in the event of unanticipated demand for cloth (Salvucci 1987: 51, 95).

Hence the enormous impact that railroads had throughout Latin America in the nineteenth century: by raising productivity and enlarging and linking previously small and isolated markets, they made specialization, commercialization, and, ultimately, proletarianization a reality. It is no exaggeration to suggest that, in Latin America, capitalism rode the rails (Summerhill 2006).

Trade and commerce

The Spanish empire was known as a "seaborne empire," and the far-flung commercial links between the Iberian Peninsula, Europe, Asia, and the Americas have long been seen as the epitome of commercial capitalism. After an initial period of uncontrolled trade (1494–1503), commerce was in theory tightly regulated by Spain. Regular fleets assembled and sailed under military convoy, first from Seville, and then from Cadiz. Arriving in Portobelo (Isthmus of Panama) and Veracruz, there were great trade fairs in which American silver produced under state control was offered in payment for European and Asian goods, particularly textiles and luxury items. Behind the impressive façade, however, lay a more complex reality. Virtually every western European power connived at eroding the "Spanish" monopoly on the merchandise trade by fair means or foul (Carrasco González 1997). France, in particular, struggled to maintain its international power and financial balance through access to American silver, and by the eighteenth century, had successfully installed a branch of the Bourbon monarchy on the Spanish imperial throne in response to the demise of the Habsburgs, whose progressive debility presented both extraordinary opportunities – and problems – to rival European monarchies. In the eighteenth century, under Charles III, Spain undertook a concerted effort to revive its sagging commercial fortunes and imperial sovereignty with the so-called Bourbon reforms, a series of administrative measures reconfiguring trade, the bureaucracy and colonial governance, that proved only partially successful because of the determined resistance of the "reformed" (Stein and Stein 2000, 2003, 2009).

Yet even partial success meant that America was far more important as a source of imperial revenues in the eighteenth century than it had been at any previous time. David Ringrose (1996: 93, 96) estimates that "an estimated 45 percent of peacetime income [of the Crown] was directly or indirectly derived from the colonies." Financing the trade to the Indies had always been a very profitable activity for the merchants of lower Andalusia, not to say to other communities, such as the Basques. The amount of long-term credit required to lubricate the cumbersome and far-flung imperial trade was simply vast (González Carrasco 1997: 66–67). It was an activity in which foreigners played a typically smaller, if still not insignificant role. In a more general way, the broader economic significance of the American trade to the Spanish monarchy was less its ability or inability to transform the productive structure of the peninsular economy through aggregate demand than its function as the glue that held the diverse pieces of the Spanish political nation together. A wide section of the elites ultimately depended on the profits on empire – not so much as capitalists, perhaps, but as rentiers. Politicians, career bureaucrats, diplomats, military officers, large merchants, and high clergy in the peninsula shared no common body of interests other than those provided and under-written by a successful, unified, and, ultimately, intact empire. In this sense, the economic function of the Spanish seaborne empire was more like the second British empire than historians have until now realized, with the rents of empire doing as much to unify the political classes and to sustain their larger economies as to multiply income (Costeloe 1986; Davis and Huttenback 1986). Nevertheless, very recent work (Lamikiz 2010) has once more turned our attention to the very significant, if underappreciated, changes in the commercial regime in the eighteenth century that the early Bourbons brought. With the end of the Portobelo trade fair in 1739 and the temporary (1739–1757) demise of the fleet-convoy system, individual ships sailing from the peninsula played a far greater role in the merchandise trade. In the case of Peru, an upswing in imports carried on these so-called "register ships" appears to have had subtle, but wide-ranging effects on the colonial market, rendering it both more competitive and thus responsive to changes in demand than it had been under the Habsburgs. By the evidence of Peru, in contrast to Mexico, some "renationalization" of the colonial trade may have occurred, along with a corresponding revitalization of Iberian commercial houses with wide-ranging personal connections in the Atlantic world.

A related, but more difficult question, is whether trade and imperial monopoly were ultimately the mechanisms whereby "Spain underdeveloped America," to use the terms that *dependentistas* employed when the debate was current forty years ago. But answering the relevant counterfactual – how America would have developed in the absence of European interference – is nearly hopeless. No deep insight is required to see that the introduction of exotic flora and fauna, pathogens, and in the case of the transatlantic slave trade, the African peoples changed the hemisphere in unalterable ways whose efficiency or lack of it is unknowable. There was, simply, no going back to a world lost, better or not, or more efficient or not, with independence from Spain or Portugal. Yet historians have queried and measured the relative burdens of actual empires, and the answers to which they have come are nothing if not provocative.

The classic, not to say canonical statement of the "burden of empire" position was clearly defined and enunciated by John Coatsworth (1978) who influenced an entire generation of scholars with two conclusions. The first was that, if anything, the burden of Spanish imperialism (relative to the first British empire's) was large, positive, and significant. The second was that the adjustment to the rupture in this relationship, at least in the Mexican colony, was so large as to have literally been responsible for Mexican underdevelopment in a statistical sense. Never again would the per capita output of the periphery be so large relative to that of the core states of the north Atlantic as it was in 1800, an outcome that has been echoed for other parts of Latin America.

The economic position of Latin America at independence was a bad equilibrium: costly in which to remain, but equally, if not more costly to disturb. The source of this observation is Leandro Prados de la Escosura (2009), whose recent survey of the national literature supports a rather different picture. First, Prados de la Escosura points out that the empire enjoyed economies of scale in administration, economies whose loss led almost directly to the first debt crisis of 1825 in London, as the revenue-hungry republics defaulted on their bond issues one after another (Salvucci: 2009). Second, the performance of the Latin American economies was in line with that of Asia and Africa at least in the period up to 1840, which may, perhaps, be a more relevant comparison. And third – while not Prados de la Escosura's observation directly – comparative advantage is comparative advantage. It is a truism that the commodity composition of exports from Latin America changed very little, barring some outstanding exceptions, such as the demise of Cuban coffee, through 1840. If colonialism had substantial costs, its impact on international trade is very hard to discern. Studies of the net barter terms of trade are not definitive: some improved after political independence, some declined, and the changes were mostly exogenous anyway (Bates *et al.* 2007: 933). Nevertheless, as Alejandra Irigoín (2003: 4) has accurately observed, "Independence in Spanish America also meant the disintegration of the largest fiscal and monetary union known to that date." Irigoín has, not unreasonably, emphasized the costs of the break-up of this union, but there were positive consequences as well, consequences that were integral to the development of "capitalism" in Latin America. The argument is best seen by comparing monetary perspectives in Mexico and the La Plata region.

In Mexico, for all of the variations in fineness that regional mints imposed after independence, the basic unit of currency was the Spanish dollar or peso. In a general way, the peso had retained its nominal value since a spate of monetary reforms in the early eighteenth century. By independence, some observers had begun to argue that the fixed exchange rate that the peso effectively imposed was a source of trade-offs that we today recognize as the "trilemma" of a small open economy with capital mobility and virtually no control over its money supply. The trilemma refers to the macroeconomic policy inconsistency between fixed exchange rates, free capital flows, and domestic autonomy in shaping monetary policy: at any given moment, two conditions are possible, but not three. Perhaps as early as the 1780s, as a consequence of the relentlessly deflationary fiscal policies of the later Bourbons that Carlos Marichal (2007) has described, a slowing of growth occurred that was aggravated, but certainly not caused, by the economic consequences of the insurgency that broke out in 1810. The remedy for stagnation, so one observer wrote in the 1830s, was monetary reform, and specifically a fiduciary issue linked to silver, but one that could nevertheless depreciate (Salvucci: 2005). There was, in other words, support for a flexible exchange rate.

Argentina, and in particular, Buenos Aires, presented a different picture. There the expansion of pastoral products such as hides, wool, and tallow was proceeding at a rapid pace – perhaps as much as 5 percent per year – in the later eighteenth century both as a result of the Bourbon reforms and the expansion of international demand. Since pastoral products still accounted for no more than 20 percent of exports (Lynch 1985: 615) by value at independence – the remainder was silver – it is difficult to see how their share in exports could have been much more than 1 or 2 percent when the viceroyalty of La Plata was established in 1776. Unlike Mexico, then, Buenos Aires and its hinterlands were growing rapidly before the Spanish empire dissolved.

But the interruption of supplies of specie from Potosí caused by the break-up of the empire led the authorities in Buenos Aires to experiment with fiduciary issue, which, as Irigoín (2000) notes, became one of the pillars of Buenos Aires economic and political leadership over neighboring regions. As Irigoín demonstrates, the result was a sustained fall in the inconvertible paper peso against gold after 1826, with especially sharp bouts of depreciation in the 1840s. However "disorderly" the Argentine monetary experience had been, it had no negative effects on export performance at the time.

To the contrary, Argentine sales of hides, wool, and tallow in Great Britain, not to mention elsewhere in Europe, prospered. From the 1790s through the 1820s, hide prices in Great Britain fluctuated broadly, if trendlessly (Amaral 2002: 233). After 1820, their prices fell pretty steadily into the 1840s, roughly paralleling the depreciation of the inconvertible paper peso. As a sort of natural experiment in what monetary union and its dissolution brought to the very different parts of the Spanish empire, the record was predictably mixed. A uniform currency standard did not, and could not, encourage capital accumulation and entrepreneurship, let alone prosperity, across the sprawling empire in which factor mobility was, to say the least, highly restricted. It may well be that the Mexicans sought to emulate the Argentine example, but were simply unable to do so. On the other hand, as Jeffrey Williamson (2011: 132–133) argues, the boom in the net barter terms of trade that Mexico experienced after 1828, if not before, was relatively weaker than it was elsewhere in Latin America precisely *because* the price of Mexico's principal export, silver, was broadly stable. These are complex issues that will require further exploration, but Williamson has raised the level of debate surrounding the role of international trade and its impact on Latin America well beyond the often simplistic terms in which the dependency writers of the 1960s cast it.

Brazil and the Caribbean: some further considerations

Actions in Brazil (with an estimated indigenous population of about 2.4 million [IBGE 2000: 222]), and by extension, much of the Caribbean were a direct outcome of the disappearance of the population. There was no alternative, in the world as it then existed, to a massive recourse to the transatlantic slave trade. The result suggests a radically different outcome in terms of economic efficiency. For example, David Eltis (1995) estimated per capita income on the sugar island of Barbados in the mid seventeenth century as one-third to two-thirds higher than that of England and Wales. He then observes: "Barbados was able to overtake Bahia in terms of both total and per capita output." The in-depth study of Bahian sugar by Stuart Schwartz (1986: 233) by no means suggests an opulent standard of living there in the mid seventeenth century – quite the contrary, Schwartz frequently speaks of "hard times" on the plantations – but wide swings between profitability and loss making seem more the rule. If per capita income in Bahia was, at best, half that of Barbados, per capita income would have been 70 to 80 percent of levels found in England and Wales. That seems rather remarkable for what could only be regarded as a backwater, albeit the political capital of one.

Stuart Schwartz has very little difficulty in describing plantation society in Bahia through the nineteenth century as, in essence, patriarchal but profit maximizing, slavery or no. This seems accurate because the commodity cycles of Brazilian history through the nineteenth century were the clear outcome of the evolution of comparative advantage, and, ultimately, in adjustments in the international market for African slave labor. The process was similar in Cuba, but there the long-run result was the highest level of exports per capita in Latin America by around 1850. The puzzle, perhaps, is why Brazil, at only half the Cuban level of exports, lagged so far behind. The answer may well lie in a far more extensive development of the internal market in Brazil, which supplied the sugar plantations with a substantial amount of foodstuffs from Rio Grande de Sul, São Paulo, and Santa Catarina. Cuba, more completely specialized, imported foodstuffs from the United States, and paid for them with larger exports of sugar abroad (Eltis 1987; Fragoso 1992: 83–93).

Plainly, the cause was not a shortage of labor. If anything, Brazil was the land of cheap labor, or, at least, of cheap slave labor (Fragoso and Florentino 1993: 50). Slavery was ubiquitous, and not simply confined to the plantation economy or the export sector. Rather, slaves were employed in domestic agriculture and mining: uniquely in Latin America, the slave population of Minas Gerais, the region of the eighteenth-century gold boom, was able to reproduce itself. Studies of patterns of wealth holding in Rio de Janeiro portray slave ownership that was broadly dispersed throughout all socio-economic levels of urban society, a pattern strikingly different in most ways from other slave-holding societies, such as the antebellum United States South (Bergad 1999: 218–219; Florentino 2000: 82; Vidal Luna and Klein 2003: 130–181; Wright 2006: 71).

The answer, or at least, one that has the merit of yielding testable hypotheses, has been best posed by William Summerhill (2007). Summerhill, too, dismisses external dependency as "simplistic." Rather, he attributes Brazil's performance to "geography that hobbled exchange over distance and institutions that obstructed exchange and investment by either restricting them to the point of exclusion, or making the activities risky to the point of being wholly uncertain." While the stock response might be that one could, with equal justice, say this about Mexico or Peru – and that for Mexico, Coatsworth (1978) has – there is a larger point at stake. The dependency narrative found something intrinsic to the process of market exchange, for which "capitalism" stood as a metaphor. The argument for Brazil, albeit cast in terms of *transaction costs*, implied an inability to employ markets because of the costs of using them. It may well be that the inability or unwillingness to use markets as a device for allocating resources may or may not come down to the same thing, but the consequences of ignoring, thwarting, or simply failing to recognize relative scarcity are, in the end, the most powerful obstacle to economic development.

In passing, at least, the overwhelming role of slavery in the Brazilian economy cannot be ignored. The African slave trade to Rio de Janeiro did not come to an end until 1850, and the number of captives brought to Brazil through the slave trade between 1501 and 1867 was simply staggering, nearly 4.9 million individuals (Eltis and Richardson 2008: 18). Moreover, the capital accumulated in the trade to Brazil stayed in Brazil, apparently financing the further acquisition of slaves and creating enormous fortunes for the families of merchants and traders involved (Fragoso 1992: 153–178). In this context, it may be appropriate to reconsider the "crowding out" hypothesis (that is, that the ownership of slaves displaced investment in physical capital, such as machines) raised by Roger Ransom and Richard Sutch (1998) for the United States South, if only because it is not easy to see how the allocation of capital accumulated in the trade to finance further purchases of slaves could have had *no* effect on savings and investment in physical capital in Brazil. Here, indeed, one inevitably wonders if there were "capitalists without capital" rather than "capital without capitalists" as in much of the rest of Latin America.

Conclusions

At least from the perspective of Ester Boserup, Mesoamerica and the Andes had evolved in line with their factor endowments. Labor was the abundant factor of production. It was, indeed, so abundant as to induce the widespread appearance of intensified agricultural practices. In part of Mesoamerica, at least, intensive agriculture supported an early or emergent form of market exchange, or an exchange-based response to relative scarcities. There was no labor market properly speaking, but labor markets are late-bloomers in the history of economic development (Boldizzoni 2011: 99–104). In the Andean highlands, natural factors, "vertical" geography and transportation costs, above all, impeded similar development. Whatever the case, a response to relative scarcity was at least present, if not to the degree in Mesoamerica.

Where these developments were leading is a question as important as it is unanswerable. At the great risk of teleological simplification, "Mexico" if not "Peru" was, perhaps, evolving as a market economy, and an impressive one as well. The accumulations of physical capital and sumptuary wealth that stimulated both the awe and open greed of the conquerors remain as testimony to the productive potential of these economies. No scholar, to my knowledge, has ventured so much as a guess as to the relative productivity of the Indies at the time of contact. But we can read what the Pizarro brothers or Bernal Díaz thought. If output per person were below the levels to which they were accustomed in Europe, they certainly never said so. Indeed, they said quite the opposite.

Nevertheless, these civilizations were turned upside down, if not quite destroyed, by conquest. Their development was profoundly altered, and permanently so, in a process that has not yet abated. Vital continuities of language, culture, religious practice, and political authority, to name only a few, certainly remained far more rooted than historians once believed. Nor does anyone doubt that indigenous survivals were more enduring as well. Yet it is equally pointless to deny the radical changes in factor endowments that occurred because of the introduction of alien pathogens, or the gross modifications of the natural environment because of the introduction of alien flora and fauna into the Americas (Crosby 1986). Labor, previously abundant, became scarce. Land, previously scarce, became abundant. In a market economy, the logic of scarcity is everything. Scarce labor should command a larger share of output than abundant land. Yet this was hardly the distribution that the conquerors desired nor could it possibly be.

For the enterprise of conquest to prosper, it was necessary, as Victor Bulmer-Thomas (2003:127) puts it succinctly, for the Europeans to refuse to recognize relative scarcity. And refuse to recognize it they did by employing the nearly endless variety of devices and means outlined here. The oppression of the indigenous people stood scarcity on its head. A competitive market economy, capitalism if you will, rewards factors of production according to their relative productivity, which, in turn, depends on scarcity. Yet this was not what empire in the Indies valued. It rewarded instead the bonds of kinship, influence, and power, or, at best, the contrived scarcity that these provided with its *flotas*, *haciendas*, and *repartimentos*. These were rent-seeking institutions par excellence. One has only to recall the open disgust with which Adam Smith categorized the Spanish empire in *The Wealth of Nations*. If Smith was the prophet of modern capitalism, he failed to recognize what had become its Latin American variant.

Ironically, the places where the Spanish and Portuguese had no choice but to recognize scarcity was where their presence had left no indigenous peoples to oppress: in Brazil, and most famously, throughout the Caribbean. The business of slavery, it is well known, was carried on in an unimpeachably capitalist fashion, according to most historians. The distribution and employment of African slaves was, by all accounts, determined by relative prices and comparative advantage. Here, given the institutional arrangements of the time, the slave owners had no choice but to "recognize" the scarcity of labor because they possessed a property right in it. As economic historians have often reminded us – although admittedly not without dissent – property rights in human beings bring with them the benefit of economic efficiency dubious though it might seem in this case. In Latin America, capitalism and slavery uniquely sustained each other because the labor was, literally, human capital.

But does this matter in anything other than an ideological sense?

There are perhaps few places in which a history of the development of capitalism is *less* a purely academic question than in Latin America. A unique combination of circumstances, political (the end of colonialism in Asia and Africa) and economic (successful import substitution industrialization and its expression in mass populist regimes) rendered the dominant historical discourse there in the 1960s and 1970s about little else than the history of capitalist development. The conclusions that historians drew were deeply ideological, but the literature was nuanced, sophisticated, and vast (Packenham 1992; Stern 1988). While there may well have been better-known expositions of the immediate relevance of what was known in the region as the "capitalist since the Conquest" school of historical thought, one of its clearest exponents, and deeply influential, was the Chilean (Argentine by birth) Marxist and intellectual, Luis Vitale (1968: 36, 41–42). As Vitale put it, "Spanish capitalism in the fifteenth century was not modern industrial capitalism but an incipient capitalism, primitive, essentially commercial and with remnants of feudalism..." Thus, "[b]ackwardness was caused, not by feudalism, but by Latin America's role as a producer of raw materials and its dependence on the world market." And "[i]t is a mistake to claim as the reformers do, the phase of capitalist development can be attained through the 'progressive bourgeoisie.'"

Vitale's (and many others') reading of Latin American history indicated that its laggard economic performance vis-à-vis the developed countries could *not* be remedied by liberal reformism and the liquidation of feudal social and economic relations. The larger goal was social, anti-capitalist revolution and the progressive "delinking" from the international market by building socialism. The academic question was, above all, political: it was as if the Cuban Revolution of 1959 had invested the study of economic history with a significance completely out of proportion to its more modest vocation in the developed countries.

Of course, the concerns of historians change with the times. If the immediacy of this debate has, today, a faintly dated air, it is because the questions raised were, literally, an aspect of the moment itself, roughly encompassing the period between the Cuban Revolution and the collapse of the Eastern Bloc socialist economies after the fall of the Berlin Wall in 1989.

As the curves in Figure 13.3 illustrate, patterns of citation to two key terms in Spanish, *dependencia* and *capitalismo*, usually linked in discussions of

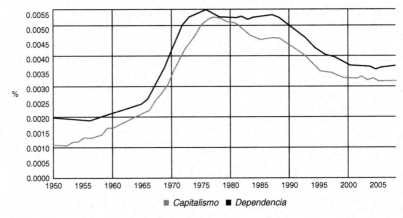

Figure 13.3 *Capitalismo, Dependencia*
Source: Google N-Gram frequency search.

"dependent capitalism" in Latin America provide some insight into the phenomenon. While interest is Latin America had been rising since the mid-1950s, the "take-off," to use the Rostovian term of the day, came in the mid-1960s. Interest in "dependency" may have peaked slightly before interest in "capitalism" *per* se, but by 1980 or so, something seemed to have changed. Today, patterns of publication have, at least in terms of relative frequency, returned to where they were, more or less, in 1970. However, whether persistence or decline is emphasized, a nuanced account would insist that historical discourse underwent a permanent alteration in the 1970s and 1980s, with such socio-economic questions receding somewhat in importance, at least in Latin America, but by no means totally disappearing.

Postmodernism, increasingly influential in the 1980s, may have had very little effect on economic history in a larger sense, but in the United States, its impact on historians of Latin America was substantial. Marxism, the *Annales* school, the highly congenial work of Witold Kula on the feudal economy (1976), all of which had informed the research programs of many younger US scholars working on early Latin America, was largely elbowed aside (Iggers 1997: 51–140). The value of subaltern studies, or of work undertaken under the rubrics of the cultural or linguistic "turns" is not at issue. Yet there is little question that the empirical research agenda stimulated by "the dependency movement," whatever its political agenda, was hindered in a fundamental way. Important questions that bore on the nature of economic change, especially after 1700, were not so much answered as dropped. In the process, substantial damage was done to the program of understanding the historical trajectory of capitalism and economic change in Latin America from virtually *any* perspective, not simply from the left. It is more than high time to return to the study of historical political economy, not for the purpose of rehashing old debates, but for the purposes of attempting to resolve old questions, and indeed, of opening an entire range of new ones that developments in economic history have brought since the 1980s.

References

Amaral, S. P. (2002). *The Rise of Capitalism on the Pampas: The Estancias of Buenos Aires, 1785–1870.* New York: Cambridge University Press.

Arroyo, A. *et al.* (2012). "Between Conquest and Independence: Real Wages and Demographic Change in Spanish America, 1530–1820," *Explorations in Economic History* 49: 149–166.

Bates, R. *et al.* (2007). "Lost Decades: Postindependence Performance in Latin America and Africa," *The Journal of Economic History* 67: 917–943.

Bergad, L. (1999). *Slavery and the Economic and Demographic History of Minas Gerais, Brazil, 1720–1888.* New York: Cambridge University Press.

Bernal, A. M. (1992). *La Financiación de la Carrera de Indias (1492–1824). Dinero y Crédito en el Comercio Colonial con América:* Seville: Fundación El Monte.

Boldizzoni, F. (2011). *The Poverty of Clio: Resurrecting Economic History.* Princeton University Press.

Borah, W. (1951). *New Spain's Century of Depression.* Berkeley, CA: University of California Press.

(1983). *Justice by Insurance: The General Indian Court of Colonial México and the Legal Aides of the Half-Real.* Berkeley, CA: University of California Press

Boserup, E. (1965). *The Conditions of Agricultural Growth: The Economics of Agrarian Change under Population Pressure.* Chicago, IL: Aldine Publishing Company.

Bulmer-Thomas, V. (2003). *The Economic History of Latin America since Independence,* 2nd edn. New York: Cambridge University Press.

Carrasco, G. and M. Guadalupe (1997). *Comerciantes y casa de negocio en Cádiz.* Cadiz: Universidad de Cádiz.

Castillero Calvo, A. (1980). *Economía terciaria y sociedad. Panamá siglos XVI y XVII.* Panama: Instituto Nacional de Cultura de Panamá.

Coatsworth, J. H. (1978). "Obstacles to Economic Growth in Nineteenth-Century Mexico," *The American Historical Review* 83: 80–100.

Cook, S. (1949a). *The Historical Demography and Ecology of the Teotlalpan.* Berkeley, CA: University of California Press.

(1949b). *Soil Erosion and Population in Central Mexico.* Berkeley, CA: University of California Press.

Costeloe, M. P. (1986). *Response to Revolution: Imperial Spain and the Spanish American Revolutions, 1810–1840.* New York: Cambridge University Press.

Crosby, A. W. (1986). *Ecological Imperialism: The Biological Expansion of Europe, 900–1900.* New York: Cambridge University Press.

Davis, L. E. and R. Huttenback (1986). *Mammon and the Pursuit of Empire: The Political Economy of British Imperialism, 1860–1912*. New York: Cambridge University Press.

De la Peña, J. F. (1983). *Oligarquía y propiedad en Nueva España, 1550–1624*. Mexico, DF: Fondo de Cultura Económica.

Domar, E. (1970). "The Causes of Slavery or Serfdom: A Hypothesis," *Economic History Review* 30: 18–32.

Eltis, D. (1987). *Economic Growth and the Ending of the Transatlantic Slave Trade*. New York: Oxford University Press.

(1995). "The Total Product of Barbados, 1664–1701," *The Journal of Economic History* 55: 321–338.

Eltis, D. and D. Richardson (2010). *Atlas of the Transatlantic Slave Trade*. New Haven, CT: Yale University Press.

Florentino, M. G. (1995). *Em Costas Negras. Uma história do tráfico atlântico dos escravos entre a África e o Rio de Janeiro (Sèculos XVIII e XIX)* Rio de Janeiro: Arquivo Nacional.

Florescano, E. (1984). "The Formation and Economic Structure of the Hacienda in New Spain," in Leslie Bethell (ed.), *The Cambridge History of Latin America*, Vol. II. New York: Cambridge University Press.

Fragoso, J. L. R. (1992). *Homens de grossa aventura. Acumulação e hierarquia na praça mercantil do Rio de Janeiro, 1790–1830*. Rio de Janeiro: Arquivo Nacional.

Fragoso, J. L. R. and M. Florentino (1993). *O Arcaísmo Como Projeto. Mercado Atlântico, Sociedade Agrária e Elite Mercantil no Rio de Janeiro, c.1790–c.1840*. Rio de Janeiro: Diadorim.

García Martínez, B. (2011) "Encomenderos españoles y British Residents: el sistema de dominio indirecto desde la perspectiva novohispana," *Historia Mexicana* 60: 1915–1978.

Haitin, M. (1983). "Late Colonial Lima: Economy and Society in an Era of Reform and Revolution." Ph.D. thesis, University of California, Berkeley.

Hemming, J. (2003). *The Conquest of the Incas*. New York: Mariner Books.

Hernández Chávez, A. (1993). *Anenecuilco. Memoria y vida de un pueblo*. México, DF: Fondo de Cultura Económica.

Hunt, S. J. (2011). "La economía de las haciendas y plantaciones en América Latina," in Shane J. Hunt, *La formación de la economía peruana. Distribución y crecimiento en la historia del Perú y América Latina*. Lima: Instituto de Estudios Peruanos.

IBGE (2000). *Brasil. 500 anos de povoamento*. Rio de Janeiro: IBGE.

Iggers, G. G. (1997). *Historiography in the Twentieth Century: From Scientific Objectivity to the Postmodern Challenge*. Middletown, CT: Wesleyan University Press.

Irigoín, M. A. (2000). "Inconvertible Paper Money, Inflation and Economic Performance in Early Nineteenth Century Argentina," *Journal of Latin American Studies* 32: 333–359.

(2003). "Macroeconomic Aspects of Spanish American Independence: The Effects of Fiscal and Currency Fragmentation, 1800s–1860s," Working Paper 03–45. Madrid: Universidad Carlos III.

Kula, W. (1976). *An Economic Theory of the Feudal System: Towards a Model of the Polish Economy, 1500–1800*. London: NLB.

Lamikiz, X. (2010). *Trade and Trust in the Eighteenth-Century Atlantic World: Spanish Merchants and Their Overseas Networks*. Woodbridge, Suffolk: Royal Historical Society.

Larson, B. (1998). *Cochabamba 1550–1900: Colonialism and Agrarian Transformation in Bolivia*. Durham, NC: Duke University Press.

Livi Bacci, M. (2006). *Los Estragos de la Conquista. Quebranto y Declive de los Indios de América.* Barcelona: Crítica.

Lynch, J. (1985). "'The Origins of Spanish American Independence," in L. Bethell (ed.), *The Cambridge History of Latin America,* Vol. III. New York: Cambridge University Press.

Marichal, C. (2007). *Bankruptcy of Empire: Mexican Silver and the Wars Between Spain, Britain and France, 1760–1810.* New York: Cambridge University Press.

Melville, E. G. K. (1994). *A Plague of Sheep: Environmental Consequences of the Conquest of Mexico.* Berkeley, CA: University of California Press.

Miranda, J. (1980). *El Tributo Indígena en la Nueva España Durante el Siglo XVI.* Mexico, DF: El Colegio de México.

Murra, J. V. (1978). *La Organización Económica del Estado Inca.* Mexico, DF: Siglo XXI Editores

Ortiz de Montellano, B. R. (1990). *Aztec Medicine, Health and Nutrition.* New Brunswick, NJ: Rutgers University Press.

Packenham, R. (1992). *The Dependency Movement: Scholarship and Politics in Development Studies.* Cambridge, MA: Harvard University Press.

Patch, R. (2002). *Maya Revolt and Revolution in the Eighteenth Century.* New York: M. E. Sharpe.

Pérez-Rocha, E. (2008). *El tributo en Coyoacán en el Siglo XVI.* Mexico, DF: Instituto Nacional de Antropología e Historia.

Prados de la Escosura, L. (2009). "Lost Decades: Economic Performance in Post Independence Latin America," *Journal of Latin American Studies* 41: 279–307.

Quirós, J. M. (1821). *Memoria de estatuto; idea de la riqueza que daban a la masa circulante de Nueva España sus naturales producciones en los años de tranquilidad, y su abatimiento en las presentes conmociones . . . leida en la primera junta de gobierno celebrada en 24 de enero de 1817.* Veracruz.

Ransom, R. L and R. Sutch (1988). "Capitalists Without Capital: The Burden of Slavery and the Impact of Emancipation," www.escholarship.org/uc/item/56m1k703.pdf; origin=repeccitec.

Ringrose, D. (1996). *Spain, Europe and the "Spanish Miracle", 1700–1900.* New York: Cambridge University Press.

Salvucci, R. (1987). *Textiles and Capitalism in Mexico: An Economic History of the Obrajes, 1539–1840.* Princeton University Press.

  (1997). "Mexican National Income in the Era of Independence, 1810–1840," in Stephen Haber (ed.), *How Latin America Fell Behind: Essays on the Economic Histories of Brazil and Mexico, 1800–1914.* Stanford University Press, pp. 216–242.

  (2000). "Las manufacturas en Hispanoamérica," in *Historia general de América Latina,* 9 vols. Paris: Ediciones UNESCO, Vol. III: 1, pp. 247–268.

  (2005). "Algunas Consideraciones Económicas" (1836). Análisis Mexicano de la Depresión A Principios del Siglo XIX," *Historia Mexicana* 55: 67–97.

  (2009). *Politics, Markets, and Mexico's "London Debt," 1823–1887.* New York: Cambridge University Press.

Schwartz, S. B. (1978). "Indian Labor and New World Plantations: European Demands and Indian Responses in Northeastern Brazil," *The American Historical Review* 83: 43–79.

  (1985). *Sugar Plantations in the Formation of Brazilian Society: Bahia, 1550–1835.* New York: Cambridge University Press.

Sempat Assadourian, C. (2006), "Agriculture and Land Tenure," in Victor Bulmer-Thomas et al. (eds.), *The Cambridge Economic History of Latin America*, Vol. I. New York: Cambridge University Press, pp. 275–314

Stein, B H. and S. J. Stein (2009). *Edge of Crisis: War and Trade in the Spanish Atlantic*. Baltimore, MD: Johns Hopkins University Press.

Stein, S. J. and B. H. Stein (2000). *Silver, Trade and War: Spain and America in the Making of Early Modern Europe*. Baltimore, MD: Johns Hopkins University Press.

(2003). *Apogee of Empire: Spain and New Spain in the Age of Charles III, 1759–1788*. Baltimore, MD: Johns Hopkins University Press.

Stern, S. J. (1988). "Feudalism, Capitalism, and the World System in the Perspective of Latin America and the Caribbean," *The American Historical Review* 93: pp. 829–872.

Summerhill, W. (2006). "The Development of Infrastructure," in V. Bulmer-Thomas et al. (eds.), *The Cambridge Economic History of Latin America*, Vol. II. New York: Cambridge University Press, pp. 293–326.

(2007). "The Origins of Economic Backwardness in Brazil: Colonialism, Slavery, and Dependency Reconsidered." Unpublished paper.

Tandeter, E. (2006). "The Mining Industry," in V. Bulmer-Thomas et al. (eds.), *The Cambridge Economic History of Latin America*, Vol. I. New York: Cambridge University Press, pp. 315–356.

Vidal Luna, F. and H. S. Klein (2003). *Slavery and the Economy of São Paulo, 1750–1850*. Stanford University Press.

Vitale, L. (1968). "Latin America: Feudal or Capitalist," in J. Petras and M. Zeitlin (eds.), *Latin America: Reform or Revolution?* Greenwich, CT: Fawcett Publications, pp. 32–43.

Wilken, G. C. (1990). *Good Farmers: Traditional Agricultural Resource Management in Mexico and Central America*. Berkeley, CA: University of California Press.

Williamson, J. G. (2011). *Trade and Poverty: When the Third World Fell Behind*. Cambridge, MA: MIT Press.

Wright, G. (2006). *Slavery and American Economic Development*. Baton Rouge, LA: Louisiana State University Press.

14

The emergence of African capitalism

MORTEN JERVEN

To what extent did capitalism come into being in Africa before 1850? If by capitalism we mean the production of goods for exchange by capitalists who combine their own capital and land with labor bought from free workers without land, then the accumulative historical evidence tells us that only to a limited extent had capitalism emerged before 1850, and it was most certainly not the dominant system of production in Africa (Iliffe 1983). This does not mean that there was no production for the market. Nor does it imply that there was no wage labor, or that exchanges of capital did not take place. Finally it does not mean that there was no economic growth in sub-Saharan Africa before 1850. As will be analyzed here, markets did exist, there was some wage labor, and there were means of exchange that facilitated some economic growth, though growth mostly occurred on the extensive margin.[1]

This chapter examines the long "precolonial" African economic history up to 1850 (Reid 2011). This encompasses the time both before and after the rise and fall of the Atlantic slave trade (and the trans-Saharan and Indian Ocean slave trades). The term "legitimate commerce" denotes the exchange of goods other than slaves, and is usually used to denote the period of commerce following the abolition of the slave trade in 1807 (Law 1995). The slave trade is of course crucial to understanding the relationship between external trade and the emergence of capitalism in this period. Moreover, the question of labor coercion is crucial to the question of the emergence of capitalism, as it pertains to labor markets. However, goods were traded for external and domestic markets both before and alongside the slave trades – so although the issue of

---

1 Following Jones (1983), Austin (2008b), and Jerven (2010a), among others, extensive growth is based on expansion of the quantity of inputs in order to increase the quantity of outputs, in contrast to intensive growth. Extensive growth is thus likely to be subject to diminishing returns and is therefore often viewed as having no effect on per capita income in the long run.

slavery remains central to the historiography of this period, this chapter goes well beyond a discussion of the slave trades.

Before setting the stage with some considerations of long-term economic growth and the expansion of markets in precolonial Africa, it is worth saying a few words about the periodization and regional focus in this chapter. Reflecting the state of the literature on capitalism in Africa this chapter is biased in its coverage in at least two ways. First, more is written about precolonial markets, production, and exchange in western Africa, than in the central, eastern or southern Africa. The focus here is on sub-Saharan Africa, but on balance, more material from West Africa is discussed than from other regions, quite simply because the development of commerce between Europeans and Africans is better documented for this region. The second bias is again shared with some of the literature in that there is a focus on external economic relations. Such a focus is justified because a discussion of capitalism is intimately linked to a discussion of international trade, and here we will fundamentally focus on how the growth of interaction with external markets affected the expansion and function of local markets.

That means that I will only briefly touch upon very early, long-term, and slow expansion of African societies, the emergence of food-producing communities and the impact of metals, or other central developments in African history before roughly 1500. These topics have been well discussed and synthesized elsewhere (Austen 1987; Iliffe 1995). I will discuss the basic constraints and possibilities that "initial conditions" such as geographical and demographic factors had on technological and institutional change in the fourth section of this chapter.

The title chosen here, "Emergence of African capitalism," is the same title as that chosen for the publication of John Iliffe's four essays on capitalism in Africa (1983). In his four essays, Iliffe focussed mainly on the period of colonial rule and the question of rural capitalism, then on the choices of development model and ideology in independent Africa in the twentieth century. In his brief first essay, he did analyze the state of "indigenous" capitalism in Africa in the mid-nineteenth century, but the relationship between capitalism and economic history before 1850 was not discussed in any great detail. Thus, this chapter makes two central contributions. First, it focusses on the period before the mid nineteenth century. Second, it re-emphasizes the importance of international markets in interaction with local markets.

This chapter is organized in the following way. First it discusses the extent to which economic growth existed in Africa before 1850. According to most aggregate accounts Africa was stagnant, but recent scholarship shows that there was significant economic expansion in the pre-modern era. While growth occurred particularly on the extensive margin, driven by population increases, Africa also had recurring periods of intensive economic growth with increases in per capita income (Jerven 2011; Jones 1988). In the second section of the chapter the relationship between external trade, exports, and economic growth is analyzed. The discussion then moves to the importance of the market as an institution in precolonial Africa. Karl Polanyi and others have argued that precolonial prices were set not by market forces but by custom or command (1966), but despite North's fear that the claims of substantivism were unfalsifiable (1977), Robin Law and others have documented that markets did exist according to formal definitions (Austin 2005; Hopkins 1973; Latham 1971, 1973; Law 1992). The third section discusses the literature on domestic markets in precolonial Africa.

To demonstrate the existence and functions of markets in precolonial Africa is not the same as the question of factor markets. Markets for the factors of production of land, labor, and capital were constrained in precolonial Africa. Such markets form as a response to scarcity (Austin 2009b). With some exceptions, precolonial Africa was typically characterized by a relative abundance of land and scarcity of labor. Therefore, markets for land were limited, and labor was recruited with coercion – thus the importance of the institution of slavery in precolonial Africa. Meanwhile, means of exchange that facilitated long-distance trade and enabled savings did exist (Austin 2009b: 38), but a relative absence of intermediation meant that effective markets for credit and capital for third parties did not form. Consequently, we discuss to what extent there were institutional constraints on economic development in precolonial Africa.

Low population densities, high transport costs, and scattered areas where cultivation of economic surpluses was possible were among the factors that constrained state formation and state centralization in precolonial Africa (Austin 2008; Herbst 2000; Iliffe 1995). The study of the emergence of capitalism in Africa is then linked closely to what extent institutions that governed exchange and production did emerge, and to what extent these were enforcing the "rules of the game" (North 2005). It is beyond doubt that low population densities and geographical factors hampered the growth of markets in precolonial Africa. As pointed out already, the corollary is that states and centralized institutions were similarly constrained. A central question then is to what extent institutional shortcomings, such as a lack of a coordinating power to secure property rights either in land for cultivation or in goods for exchange, affected the effectiveness of markets and therefore economic growth. The question of institutional constraints will be addressed in the fifth section of this chapter, but first the record of economic growth in premodern Africa needs to be established.

Economic growth in precolonial Africa

The study of African economic growth is not only constrained by low data quality, but also by low availability of data (Jerven 2013). The study of economic growth is often supported and aided by the availability of a reliable data set of GDP per capita estimates. Such estimates have only been published regularly by national statistical offices since World War II. For most other regions of the world, economic historians have provided historical national accounts, but for the majority of African economies such estimates are not available before 1950 (Jerven 2012). The Angus Maddison data set only provides a few single-year estimates of GDP per capita for Africa before 1870 (Maddison 2003). According to these numbers, which include north Africa and south Africa, the continent's average growth in the precolonial period growth was negligible, or indeed negative. Table 14.1 shows a decline from 472 dollars per capita in year 1, to 420 dollars per capita in 1820, and finally a marginal increase to 500 dollars in 1870.

These data paint a picture of steady stagnation, but aggregating Africa in this manner does not make much sense. The data hide large regional diversity and skip across large periods of time. The slow growth rates may seem incompatible with what is otherwise known about the economic and political changes taking place during this period. There were large flows both of factors of production and commodities, both internally and externally, during the Atlantic slave trade and the cash-crop revolution. Kingdoms rose and fell;

Table 14.1. *African and world GDP per capita, 1 (CE)–1950*

	I	1000	1500	1600	1700	1820	1870	1900	1913	1940	1950
Total Africa	472	425	414	422	421	420	500	601	637	813	889
World	467	453	566	596	615	667	871	1,262	1,525	1,958	2,109

Source: Maddison (2007). All values in constant 1990 International Geary-Khamis dollars. Note that the only African countries for which Maddison has individual income estimates in this period are Algeria, Egypt, Libya, Tunisia, and Morocco. Presumably the decline from year 1 parallels the decline of the Roman empire in northern Africa, whereas the marginal increase in the late nineteenth century is driven by recorded export growth in western Africa.

colonial empires were established, railways and mines developed and yet the GDP per capita measure barely blinks (Jerven 2010a).

Part of the reason is that these growth "data" are only to a limited extent based on historical evidence. These estimates rely first and foremost on assumptions and projections. Gareth Austin recommends caution when approaching these observations and reminds us that the literal interpretation of the word data is "things that are given" and that therefore many of the historical income or population estimates used in the literature for African economies should not be considered as data in the strictest sense (Austin 2008a: 1002), because "all aggregate figures for the population of pre-colonial sub-Saharan Africa, or its major sub-regions, are 'guestimates' based on backward projection from colonial census reports" (Austin 2008b: 590).

The lack of reliable population estimates for large parts of historical Africa, and sub-Saharan Africa in particular, thus continues to hamper long-term analyses of African economic development. Wrigley neatly summed it up: "One thing, perhaps only one thing, is certain about African historical demography. It takes a bold and determined scholar to embark on the study of numbers, and of changes in numbers, in countries where until very recently nobody was even counting, let alone recording the results" (Wrigley 1981). For the precolonial period the direct empirical evidence is very thin indeed. Thus, while it is possible to use a demographic lens to discuss general patterns of transformation, expansion, and movements of societies and systems of production based on linguistic and demographic evidence (Iliffe 1995), it is very difficult indeed to be specific about rates of economic change in precolonial Africa.

A unique quantitative study work based on baptismal records from missionaries in the kingdom of Kongo exists (Thornton 1977). His finding was that the population in Kongo for the period 1650–1700 was much lower than commonly assumed (*c.* 500,000 compared to 2 million), thus suggesting that the civil wars and slave trades of the seventeenth and eighteenth centuries had a much less disastrous impact on populations than previously thought. The colonial censuses are in turn widely discredited (Kuczynski 1937, 1948, 1949), and therefore not used as authoritative benchmarks (Fetter 1987) and, while the populations in postcolonial states of Africa are better recorded, census taking has been very uneven, irregular, and incomplete (Jerven 2013; Tabutin and Schoumaker 2004). So, while it is the only viable option, backward projections based in both the colonial and postcolonial period remain hazardous.

Recently, Patrick Manning, one of the key participants in the scholarly exchange on the population impact of the slave trade, has boldly rekindled the debate on the African population database, with a re-estimate of the total colonial and precolonial population for Africa (Manning 2010). Manning suggests that precolonial populations around 1850 may have been 50 percent higher than previously estimated. Even with such bands of error, it seems inescapable that for comparative historical purposes most areas of pre-modern Africa were sparsely populated (Austin 2008b), and furthermore that factor ratios would imply that the region in most areas was characterized by an abundance of cultivable land in relation to labor (Austin 2009b). But the large margins of error mean that it is not possible to use population growth as a direct proxy for estimating the impacts of slave trades and colonial rule, simply because although the direction or rate of change in population has been vigorously debated, it has been difficult to settle these debates with hard facts (Jerven 2013).

Consequently, the study of growth in Africa, particularly during the precolonial era, but also during the colonial and to some extent during the postcolonial period, must make use of circumstantial evidence and interpret visible trends in trade, population, and taxation to make conjectures on rates and direction of economic change. The average GDP data presented here may well be within the reasonable range of guesses one could make for such a long time period, but it is perhaps of greater interest to see what happened to particular polities, states, and regions, and also to go beyond quantitative evidence and consider qualitative evidence on economic growth in precolonial Africa.

To begin a discussion of economic growth in Africa before 1850, it is useful to distinguish between intensive and extensive economic growth (Jones 1988). Extensive growth is a simple expansion of production by adding more factors of production, which is essentially observed by historians as more people using more land. It is this focus that is applied in John Iliffe's demographic interpretation of Africa's long-term history (1995). The study of modern economic growth in general focusses on intensive growth. It refers to the process of getting more for the same, and thus is the type of economic growth that is associated with technological change. Such changes therefore also increase living standards, and if properly recorded and measured, could be summarized as sustained increases in GDP per capita (Kuznets 1966).

Agriculture has been and remains the main economic activity, and until the advanced stages of the cash-crop revolution starting in the late nineteenth and running into the twentieth century, food production was the mainstay of this sector. The archaeological evidence on origins and diffusion of food production is contested, but the origins of the food production in west Africa did not lag far behind centers of origin in the Near East (Hopkins 1973: 29; Iliffe 1995: 12–17) though with different patterns of spread in the savannah and forest regions. The spread of food production from the west African forest is associated with the adoption or invention (another contested point) of iron-working peoples, specifically Bantu-speaking groups (Austen 1987: 13). Food production with iron tools is thought to have spread with the Bantu migrations from west Africa (about 1000 BCE) as far south as contemporary Namibia, as far inland as to borders of contemporary southern Sudan and eastwards towards the Great Lakes region and beyond toward the Indian Ocean (Iliffe 1995: 17).

As noted, growth occurred mostly on the extensive margin. Relative abundance of land to labor meant that economic growth was occurring by putting more land into production. There were exceptions to this rule (thus affirming a rational choice interpretation). Intensive agriculture (defined as adding capital to land, chiefly by capitalization of labor), did occur in some places in precolonial Africa. With a few geographical exceptions precolonial Africa was severely underpopulated. The commonly noted exceptions are found in the areas today covered by Ethiopia, Rwanda, and Burundi, where also intensive techniques and technologies, such as the plow, were adopted, in addition to locations with particularly good transport access (Austin 2009b). Furthermore, although land was not physically scarce, it could be so in periods for some populations. Disruptions arising from the slave trade meant that at times some groups in west and central Africa had to turn to intensive production methods (Hawthorne 2001). Similarly, it has been documented that ecological pressures and stress deriving from warfare led to "islands of intensification" at different places and times in African history (Widgren and Sutton 2004).

The most important sources of intensive growth in the premodern period were the introduction of new cultigens. Food crops such as cassava, banana, and maize made large impacts on productivity when introduced (Austin 2008b: 588). Similarly, crops primarily grown for exports, such as cocoa and tobacco, could be interpreted as growth arising from introduction of new technologies and investment. As emphasized by Jared Diamond (2005), culti-gens travel more easily across parallel latitudes, and thus the major innova-tions here arrived in Africa via external contact over the oceans. The first gains were introduced through the Indian Ocean trade with the imports of Asian rice, Asian yams, and what grew to be a very import food crop – the banana– plantain family. This occurred before the Atlantic trade. Crops like maize, cassava, and groundnuts were introduced from the Americas over the last five hundred years, and became the most important food crops in contemporary Africa (Austin 2008b: 607).

Another important stimulant of economic growth is market integration. When markets integrate, specialization takes place, opportunities for expansion arise, and growth occurs as economies of scale make production more efficient. Moreover, an expanded market may allow the use of underutilized factors of production, such as land and labor, to generate new production for the market. Growth arising from production for local and regional markets and even long-distance trade goes back many centuries. Herein lies the primary challenge to Diamond's contention of Africa's geographical disadvantage (2005). Vertical diversification proved very beneficial for early economies, which found opportunities for continued trade between different ecological zones. According to Hopkins, the most important trade routes went along the south and north axis, where for instance the people of the savannah traded livestock, salt, dried fish with people of the forest zones in exchange for kola nuts, slaves, ivory, and iron ware (Hopkins 1973: 59–60). However, these opportunities were sometimes constrained by the availability of transportation routes.

It is worth restressing that it is not as if all agricultural production in the premodern era went toward own production; local markets existed for agricultural goods. In addition markets for handicrafts, textiles, metals, and currencies were all widespread and important in the precolonial era (Austen 1987). Moreover, the interaction with markets precedes the slave trade and goes beyond the Atlantic trade. Internal markets in northern and sub-Saharan Africa were linked by the trans-Saharan trade (Austen 2010). On the Horn, eastern and southern Africa caravans linked with the vibrant Indian Ocean trade (Reid 2002; Sheriff 1987). Nevertheless, the main source of economic growth during this period was arguably external trade.

Exports and economic growth in precolonial Africa

Harms, writing on the Zaire basin in central Africa, stressed the vigor of local markets, while emphasizing the importance of external trade (1981). Equatorial African society and economy was not static. European traders were only able to come to the coast, and the extent of the trade that has been observed is testament to the existence of the basic institutions necessary for trade and capitalistic behavior (Harms 1981: 234; Latham 1971, 1973). However, it is still argued that expansion in trade and further investment in production would not have been possible without the existence of an external market. Thus, the emphasis on external factors in this economic transformation is in Harms's view still justified.

However, as has been frequently pointed out, until the nineteenth century only a small part of the territorial gross product entered external trade (Curtin 1975). In a monograph marshaling an impressive amount of quantitative evidence to analyze the precolonial economic history of Senegambia, *Economic Change in Pre-colonial Africa*, Philip Curtin does not discuss external trade until the final chapter, and only devotes less than 10 percent of the pages to this topic. This was a deliberate choice: "External trade usually comes first in writing about African economic history, mainly because the historiography tradition was laid down by Europeans who first saw Africa through the commerce that linked the two societies. This time it has been left till last" (Curtin 1975: 309).

Curtin left the discussion of external trade for last presumably to maintain a perspective in which Senegambian agency is central in the account of historical change, but also because he argues that this is the appropriate order of importance and analysis. According to Curtin, only a small part of territorial gross product entered external trade, and it only makes sense to analyze these trade flows and their relative importance once the domestic conditions for production of export commodities and slave trade have first been discussed in detail. The relative importance of internal markets and external markets in terms of contribution to GDP is hard to pinpoint with much accuracy.

It has been guessed that the export economy only accounted for 15 percent of the total Nigerian economy in 1900 (Helleiner 1966). Similarly, it was suggested that as much as 90 percent of all production remained outside the cash-based coastal economies in west Africa in the middle of the nineteenth century (Flint and McDougall 1987). With these parameters in mind, it is easier to make some judgments about how expansion in external markets made an impact on exchange and growth in domestic economies. While the growth rates derived from observing external market growth should not be interpreted literally, they do testify to a rapid export growth that may have facilitated further growth in the domestic economy. However, less is known regarding the exact effect and the relative importance for growth of the local economy (Cooper 1993: 91–92).

The basic heuristic device that has been used to analyze this process is the dual economy models from classical economics. The vent-for-surplus model assumes that there was a surplus of factors of production, particularly labor and land, and that the world market provided a vent for these factors (Myint 1958). Thus when we see increased export volumes, the opportunity cost of this growth is zero. The assumption of modern sector growth being an absolute gain to the aggregate economy is also made in the classical dual economy model proposed by Arthur Lewis (1954). The main distinction is that in the Lewis model, land was assumed to be scarce and marginal productivity of labor in the rural sector was zero. In the vent-for-surplus model, both land and labor are abundant. In effect, both models assume the opportunity cost of modern sector growth and increased export volumes is zero. Scholarship has in different ways contested these assumptions and by extension the validity of the model applied to Africa, particularly for the colonial period (Austin 2008b).

It has been pointed out that labor was only seasonally abundant and was very scarce in certain periods – particularly in areas outside the west African forest belt (Tosh 1980). Furthermore, the production of exports involved both innovation and capital; that is, investment in new technologies, and expansion in production was made possible through labor migration (Berry 1993; Hill 1963). Most importantly, the opportunity costs of engaging in production for exports were not necessarily zero, as they could have an impact on food quality and security, the division of labor, and on local manufacturing (Smith 1976). Though sometimes and in some places the assumptions of the vent-for-surplus model largely holds (Martin 1988), these, and other empirical contributions, remind us that when we see aggregate modern sector growth it is not necessarily equivalent to observing aggregate economic growth.

To illustrate the importance of external markets, let us turn to the experience of precolonial Dahomey. The kingdom could be considered typical for west and central African coastal states, many of which were deeply integrated in the Atlantic economy at this time. According to Manning, 2 million slaves were exported from the west African region through the kingdom of Dahomey between 1640 and 1865 (Manning 1982). Like Asante and Oyo, Dahomey grew from a small state to a major kingdom in this period (Austin 2008a: 1005). This pattern was not replicated throughout west Africa, however. Some states chose to disengage from the slave trade, like Benin and Kongo, and in other areas low political concentration prevailed (Klein 2001). The slave trade had millions of African victims, but it is generally agreed upon that African agents, be they states or networks of merchants, engaged in this trade because they were able to realize sizeable economic gains from these economic transactions (Behrendt, Latham, and Northrup 2012; Northrup 2002: 56). European traders generally did not have the means to coerce African leaders to sell slaves (Thornton 1992). This topic has been extensively debated and studied, and many scholars have argued that the slave trade had lasting negative economic effects. The direct effect of lost manpower and the persistence of low labor concentrations in sub-Saharan Africa figure prominently. Inikori argues that "the transformation of the Gold Coast into a major exporter of captives to the Americas retarded the developing inter-regional specialization and the growing commercialization of agriculture"

(Inikori 2007: 84). It has further been suggested that the persistence of poverty in Africa was caused by the slave trade either through negative effects on state formation, or social capital such as trust (Nunn 2008). The latter work tends to understate the economic motivations for states engaging in the slave trade, and has not explicitly dealt with the implications of short-term gain versus long-term effects (Austin 2008b).

The data presented by Patrick Manning span from the end of the slave trade and into the period of "legitimate commerce." A central thesis, suggested by A. G. Hopkins, is that the closing of the Atlantic slave trade market meant stagnation and loss of power for centralized states as fiscal capacity disappeared; this is referred to as the "crisis of adaptation" (1973). It did not always mean the end of slavery as a mode of production, as documented by Paul Lovejoy and Jan Hogendorn: "At the time of the colonial conquest (1897–1903), the Sokoto Caliphate had a huge slave population, certainly in excess of 1 million and perhaps more than 2.5 million people" (1993:1). Furthermore, in some areas such as Dahomey, the banning of the slave trade actually led to an intensification of trade in slaves in the middle of the nineteenth century (Flint and McDougall 1987).

Manning's estimates reproduced in Table 14.2 provide a suggestive quantitative study of effects of the slave trade in Dahomey. It is estimated that during the height of the slave trade the per capita export revenue in Dahomey was comparable to that of Great Britain (Manning 1982: 3). This probably led

Table 14.2. *Income and growth, Dahomey 1800–1950*

	Real national income growth (avg. annual %)	Per capita domestic product (1913, British pounds)
1800s–1840s	1.1	1.5
1840s–1860s	3.4	1.9
1860s–1890s	2.7	3.4
1890s–1910s	1.7	5.8
1910s–1930s	2.8	6.7
1930s–1950s	0.1	9.5

Source: Manning (1982). The data for national income growth are proxied by import purchasing power, and the per capita income is estimated by assuming that the per capita export revenue multiplied by seven equals per capita domestic product. We should not accept these data as "facts," but they are an indication of the rate of change, and of the economic resources at the state's disposal.

to a rapid increase of GDP per capita, while total GDP might have declined because of the loss of manpower. In the longer run this kind of economic growth was not sustainable (Manning 1982: 4). The economic specialization in slave trading suggests that, from the point of view of the states, the return on slave exports was superior to the return on labor that could be captured in other domestic production (Manning 1982: 12). The profitable slave business thus facilitated the growth of stronger states. Imports of money and other commodities further spurred exchange and growth in the domestic economy for some actors. When the slave trade ended in the nineteenth century, this undermined the fiscal basis of Dahomey as well as other west African states (Austin 2008b: 1005).

The end of the slave trade opened up new economic opportunities. It paved the way for what has been called the period of "legitimate commerce," referring to the expansion of trade between 1807 and colonization (Law 1995). Hopkins (1973) suggested that a "crisis of adaptation" occurred as trade shifted from slave to legitimate trade. To what extent this important change in external trade constituted a "crisis of adaptation" for African rulers has been a central historiographical question. The thesis was that the shift undermined rulers' control over the income from trade and thus that the ending of the slave trade resulted in economic and political upheaval and dislocation that ultimately resulted in European intervention and colonization. Hopkins's view has not been universally accepted. It is recognized that changes did occur as a result of the shift from slave to legitimate commerce, but that institutions adapted (Law 1995), and that therefore the transition to legitimate trade constituted more of an evolutionary than a revolutionary process.

The term "cash-crop revolution" refers to the colonial period. This was largely a peasant response, though some crops were produced at plantations. Some of these were worked by slaves like those involved in palm production in the Sokoto caliphate, as referred to above. The cocoa boom at the end of the nineteenth century was a different matter and involved African peasants. Polly Hill argues that they should rather be called "capitalists" (Hill 1963). Her insight was that land, and particularly trees, in cocoa farming should be considered capital assets. The growth in Dahomey recorded in Table 14.2 was underpinned by palm oil and palm kernel exports. If we take Manning's data seriously this would mean a tripling in GDP per capita during a half century of export-based growth (Manning 1982: 17).

The example of growth from precolonial and colonial Dahomey, with export booms first in slaves and second in palm oil and kernels, shows that the external market can function as a "vent for surplus." However, as has been pointed out, it was not simply a reallocation of previously idle resources, labor and land, but the evidence reviewed here points further to the existence of a functioning and expanding domestic market in interaction with the world market. The slaves that were exported were often procured in internal markets (which could be considered factor markets), and slave prices changed in response to supply and demand (Lovejoy and Richardson 1995). Moreover, the organization of the slave trade meant that an elaborate system of credit was developed (Austin 2005; Latham 1973; Lovejoy and Richardson 1999). The extent and impact of this spurt of growth observed in response to external forces in Dahomey must of course be moderated by an appreciation of the drain on labor supply – thus the growth had negative externalities for other activities and more importantly for other surrounding areas that supplied the slaves.

The presence of markets in precolonial Africa

As Austin reminds us, six decades ago it was generally assumed that no markets besides that for slaves for export across the Atlantic and Sahara existed in precolonial Africa (2009b: 23). However, research to date has established that while they emerged, "the forms of property, and some of the other institutions with or within factor markets operated were different from those which spring to mind in European history, such as regular wage labor, land titling and financial intermediation" (2009b: 24). So while markets and the institutions that governed them were distinct, it has been amply demonstrated, from the pioneering work of Dike (1956), Latham (1971), and Hopkins (1973) that the operation of these markets can be explained and analyzed in terms of market economics.

This broke with perspectives from orthodox Marxists who generally posited that economic rational behavior was specific to capitalist societies. The classic statement of the substantivist position was provided by Karl Polanyi, who also made an empirical contribution with a study of the aforementioned kingdom of Dahomey (1966). In *Markets in Africa*, Bohannan and Dalton used three categories to classify societies. First there were marketless societies, then there were societies in which markets did exist, but remained peripheral, and finally there were market economies. Bohannan and Dalton applied the two first categories to African societies. Substantivism inspired and provoked historical research on markets in Africa for years after (Good 1973). The question was not only an empirical one, as in this chapter where it concerns whether a market economy had emerged or not in precolonial Africa; it also had great methodological significance. If markets were peripheral, and not fundamental, then production decisions, choice of techniques, and institutional design could not have been explained with reference to rational choice or more generally market behavior.

Already a decade later, Hopkins (1973: 52) could state that "[Bohannan and Dalton's] claim that peripheral markets do not influence market is at variance with the evidence. The extent to which market activity failed to mobilise the factors of production fully is better explained in terms of economics (technological limitations and constraints on demand) than in terms of social controls based on anti-capitalist values." Hopkins argued that although some markets were periodical rather than continuous, this was explained by the seasonal volume of traded goods and local purchasing power. Seasonality did not mean that these markets functioned with different motivations (Hopkins 1973: 53–55). Contrary to claims put forward by Hodder (1965), local markets had not arisen simply because of long-distance trade. Local markets served local exchange needs, and were further stimulated by long-distance trade, not only in west Africa. Gray and Birmingham (1970) established that the same pattern was observable in central and eastern Africa. Thus, Hopkins could draw the conclusion that the "indigenous distributive system was not made redundant by the 'impact of modern capitalism'. On the contrary, the skill, efficiency and adaptability of local trades assisted the rapid expansion of internal trade during the colonial era."

The most explicit tests of substantivist propositions were conducted later (Law 1992; Lovejoy 1982), and focussed on the claims of "ports of trade" and "price-fixing." Lovejoy investigated the validity of the concept of "ports of trade" for nineteenth-century Kano and Salaga, two important commercial centers in the Sokoto caliphate and the Asante kingdom respectively. Whereas Polanyi's model of administered trade held that prices would be fixed and not regulated by supply and demand (which he specifically argued also applied to caravan trading), Lovejoy found that while there was a separation between local markets and long-distance exchange so that the markets were not fully integrated, the price structure was not fixed in the way that Polanyi thought (Lovejoy 1982: 277).

Polanyi had specifically argued that Dahomey was not a market economy, and rather that the state administered trade in order to maintain traditional structures, and not for profit (1966). Again, the key testable proposition was price stability, or that prices were not responding to supply and demand. Law's careful study of prices and currency markets in Dahomey from the seventeenth century until the nineteenth century clearly demonstrated that prices changed, in both local and European markets. His study showed that the local currency of cowry shells experienced great price inflation, caused by excessive European imports of cowries in the nineteenth century. Even more striking, Law's study revealed that while prices for foodstuffs were increasing during this period, wages collected by local porters were kept stable and thus real wages were falling. State intervention thus did not keep the market from operating, and nor did the state intervene to change wages with respect to a notion of equity as Polanyi would have us expect (1966). In sum, markets did exist. The term "subsistence economy" has been proven to be a misnomer; even food crops were exchanged on local markets, higher-end consumer goods were exchanged in regional trade, and these markets linked with, and benefitted from external market growth.

Factor markets in precolonial Africa

While there were markets with responsive prices in precolonial Africa, a full-fledged capitalist market system implies factor markets for labor, land, and capital as well as markets for final consumption goods and services. As Iliffe reviews, in the mid nineteenth century there existed a capitalistic sector of exchange. This is particularly well documented in the savannah region of west Africa, which was well linked with in trade with northern Africa (Iliffe 1983: 5). The merchants of the savannah used imported currencies of silver and cowrie shells (Johnson 1970), and systems of credit and commercial papers were also in use to facilitate long-distance trade across the Sahara (Iliffe 1983: 5).

However, this capitalistic sector of exchange existed alongside a production sector that still in the nineteenth century could be characterized as predominantly pre-capitalist. A true proletariat, according to the orthodox definition, exists only when the labor is alienated from the means of production. Marxist scholarship in the 1970s searched for the African "mode of production," and sought to explain whether African states predominantly relied on feudal, tributary, slave, or other modes of production (Freund 1985). Tracing the emergence of capitalism in precolonial Africa has tended to focus on the prevalence of wage labor and whether this was a characteristic component of production.

The relative abundance of land to labor explains the prevalence of slavery in precolonial Africa. Consistent with Nieboer's (1900) hypothesis as formalized by Domar (1970), where land is abundant and labor and capital are scarce, long-term hiring of free labor is absent because the wage rate would be too high for employers to accept, and coercion, specifically slavery, emerges as the dominant form of labor (Austin 2009b). Only where urban centers formed, wage labor appeared, especially when craft production was associated with it. The most prominent example of this is the textile production and cloth dyeing in Kano, Nigeria (Shea 1975). In east and central Africa, however, wage labor in craft production was not common (Iliffe 1983). There were some examples of wage labor in craft production, and where capitalism had most clearly emerged in precolonial Africa, it was in relation to trade. Some of this trade was linked to external trade, but equally important was long- and shorter-distance trade within the continent.

Agricultural production would normally rely on family labor. Larger estates in west and east Africa existed, but these made use of slave labor. Use of slaves was widespread, particularly in the vicinity of trading centers (Iliffe 1983: 6). Much of the hired labor in this period was related to long-distance trade. In order to move the goods for trade, porters were hired. This was prominent in the trans-Saharan trade – in the trade caravans connecting west and central Africa with the Atlantic coast, as well as in the Swahili-organized trade caravans in east Africa (Rockel 2006). Caravans also employed full-time porters. Slaves formed an integral part of this activity because the trade in other goods coincided with the slave trade. Slaves could carry commodities and be sold on arrival. Bundy documents an anomaly on the African continent in nineteenth-century South Africa, where African capitalist farmers emerged in response to the market demand created by the European settlements at the Cape (1979). As in the case of the previously discussed commercial cocoa production and palm oil in west Africa, these are movements toward rural capitalism that belong to the latter half of the nineteenth century.

Rural capitalism emerged in west Africa with the shift from the slave trade to legitimate trade on the Atlantic coast (Austin 2009a). This shift preceded colonial rule. Before and under colonial rule there was an expansion in production of primary products for exports. This could be considered rural capitalism, not because of its reliance on wage labor – although that also featured – but rather because it entailed the investment of borrowed or saved capital for expansion in production for a market (Hill 1963). New land was bought and cleared, and investments were made in perennial crops. This expansion was characteristic in west Africa in the production of cocoa, but it also occurred simultaneously in other crops (for example, coffee, cotton, tobacco, palm products, kola nuts, and groundnuts) and in other areas (south, central, and east Africa). In the latter half of the nineteenth century, as factor ratios changed, and land became scarcer, property rights did develop (Austin 2007).

However, before the cash-crop revolution that occurred in the late nineteenth century and continued into the twentieth, cultivable land was relatively abundant in precolonial Africa, and consequently it is hard to find any evidence of a market in cultivation rights (Austin 2009b: 33–34). It has been documented that land was available for rent, though not for purchase, for immigrant farmers (Austin 2005). Generally, rents for land was the exception, and natural rents could be captured from controlling specific natural resources, such as gold, or access to grazing lands in arid regions (Austin 2009b: 34; Johnson 1976).

As already touched upon, lack of financial intermediaries meant that credit was not widely available, and when it was, interest rates were high (Austin 2009b: 35–36). The lack of a market in land also meant that it could not be mortgaged, but credit or security could be taken in the form of pawns or hostages. Lovejoy and Richardson have documented how this system of keeping hostages facilitated the slave trade at Calabar and Bonny (Lovejoy and Richardson 1999, 2004). This meant that European traders could extend credit to slave merchants at the coast. Hostages were kept as security, and slavers could venture inland to purchase and procure slaves.

Constraints: factor endowments, technology, and institutions

It was tempting, on the basis of the data presented in the first section on economic growth, to dismiss Africa's economic past as a chronic growth failure. Indeed, this may also seemingly make sense judging by Africa's relative poverty today. The link between economic growth and income made in the economic growth literature is fairly straightforward: low income today must be a result of a lack of income growth in the past. If one accepts a linear understanding of economic growth, the next logical step from this stylized fact of a chronic growth failure is, and has been, to concentrate research on explaining the persistence of low incomes in African economies. By making almost exclusive use of statistics that show average growth over time, the literature has not explained periods of growth and stagnation, and by extension, since most poor economies have displayed slow growth on average, explaining slow growth has been conflated with explaining low income (Jerven 2010b).

This "compression of history" (Austin 2008a) has biassed the evaluation of the underlying growth constraints in Africa. Specifically, such analysis has tended to overstate the extent to which African economies were trapped by growth hindering institutions (Acemoglu and Robinson 2010, 2012; Acemoglu, Johnson, and Robinson 2001, 2002). While growth in precolonial Africa was not triumphant, there were growth episodes. These were mainly rooted in trade and the world economy, but this growth was only possible due to a reorganization of factors of production, a combination of investment and technological growth that in turn also led to institutional change. The growth episodes raise questions about the extent to which precolonial institutions were growth inhibiting, and furthermore raise the issue of to what extent initial conditions, such as geographical factors and factor endowments, were indeed shackling economic growth in precolonial Africa.

It is of course important to note that geography should not be solely considered as an "initial condition." Resource conditions change partly because of human responses to them. So that for instance, as Austin (2008b) has argued, the fact that Africa exported slaves should not be considered exogenous institutional change; it was a response to the resources and techniques available, as well as to overseas demand.

If one accepts a rational choice interpretation of history then also the choice of technology, defined as innovation rather than invention, was typically conditioned by the environment. An illustrative example is the wheel, for only in places where there were draught animals and a landscape that allowed the building of wide roads did it emerge as an important new technology. The wheel was well known, but not adopted in west Africa (Law 1980). The implication is that the rationality of choices regarding technology, institutions, or production techniques is dependent on the conditions under which these choices were made. In his economic history of precolonial West Africa, Anthony Hopkins noted that:

> comparing the natural resources and climates of different parts of the world in order to draw conclusions about whether they stimulated or retarded the economic progress of particular societies is a tempting but unprofitable exercise – rather like trying to decide if life is more difficult for penguins in the Antarctic or camels in the Sahara. (Hopkins 1973: 13–14).

Issues such as the choice of production techniques and the level of investment in physical and human capital need to be evaluated within specific environments and local conditions, a discussion that will be extended in the fourth section of the chapter. To begin with the question of interest here is not whether capitalism failed or succeeded, but rather to trace its incomplete emergence before 1850; thus a different approach to economic growth, markets, and institutions is required.

Jack Goody made the point that the crucial difference between Africa and Eurasia does not lie in the absence or presence of markets, and furthermore, a recurring theme here, the concept of nonmonetary economics, is not applicable to precolonial Africa. In his evaluation of the mercantile system, parts of Africa were not dissimilar to western Europe in the same period (Goody 1971

22–24). In his comparative study of feudalism, Goody argues that the crucial difference was that of the plow. Without the plow and livestock no system of tribute similar to that of feudal systems in Europe developed. In turn this explains the lack of centralized states in precolonial Africa. These states were not able to withstand colonization in the late nineteenth century. Again, Ethiopia is the exception that confirms the rule, as the Ethiopian army was able to defeat the Italian forces at Adwa in 1896.

Daron Acemoglu and James Robinson ask why farmers in the precolonial kingdom of Kongo in sub-Saharan Africa did not adopt the plow. Their answer is because of the institutions or that "they lacked any incentives to do so" (Acemoglu and Robinson 2012: 61). More specifically, Acemoglu and Robinson argue that it was the fear of expropriation of crops, output, and manpower by an absolutist king that took away incentives for productive investment. The slave trade, colonial rule, and the postcolonial regime of Mobuto all contrived to keep this region poor, and therefore, "The interaction of economic and political institutions five hundred years ago is still relevant for understanding why the modern state of Congo is still miserably poor today" (90).

This rather general statement does undoubtedly have some truth in it, but it is generally conceded that the political institutions were not the primary factor explaining the slow or lack of adoption of the plow in sub-Saharan Africa. In the tropical forest zone, including the Congo basin, the prevalence of trypanosomiasis made it impossible to keep cattle, and thus, a plow was not efficient (Hopkins 1973). Furthermore, in many places land was relatively abundant, and therefore investment in land was discouraged, not by excessive state intervention but by the abundance of land (Austin 2008a). Finally, as many colonial administrators would later find out, the plow is not universally desirable. In tropical soils fertility is shallow and therefore the plow increases the risk of soil erosion.

In sum, factor endowments did have an impact on institutional development in precolonial Africa, and the evidence supports the view that when factor ratios changed, and there were returns for states or other agents to provide property rights in land or labor or to provide capital for exchange and production, institutional changes did occur. The institution of slavery and the slave trade were definitely a response to factor ratios. While some states were able to internalize positive returns from the slave trade, the overall impact on African economic development was probably to slow down population growth, though we do not have the evidence to measure this effect accurately. What we do now is that the trade in legitimate goods that preceded, coexisted with, and followed the slave trade was only made possible by functioning domestic markets, which were founded on well-established trade routes and networks. Institutional innovations facilitated this trade.

Conclusion

If by capitalism we mean the production of goods for exchange by capitalists who combine their own capital and land with labor bought from free workers without land, then capitalism had not emerged before 1850. While it was not the dominant system of production in Africa as per the orthodox definition, as has been documented here, this does not mean that there were no markets or economic growth according to formal definitions. Goods markets did exist, whereas factor markets were limited. As seen in other places in world economic history, slavery was not incompatible with economic growth. Slaves were used in domestic production, facilitated long-distance trade across the continent, and were central in the trades with other regions of the world. Africa was integrated with the rest of the world economy through the Indian Ocean, the Mediterranean, the Atlantic trade, and the trans-Saharan trade – a flow of ideas, goods, and people for centuries. The expansion of external contacts from sporadic contacts that led to established trading posts eventually led to formal colonization of the majority of the continent by European powers in the late nineteenth century.

References

Acemoglu, D. and J. A. Robinson (2010). "Why is Africa Poor?" *Economic History of Developing Regions* 25(1): 21–50.

(2012). *Why Nations Fail: The Origins of Power, Prosperity, and Poverty*. New York: Crown Publishers.

Acemoglu, D., S. Johnson, and J. A. Robinson (2001). "The Colonial Origins of Comparative Development: An Empirical Investigation," *The American Economic Review* 91(5): 1369–1401.

(2002) "Reversal of Fortune: Geography and Institutions in the Making of the Modern World Income Distribution," *The Quarterly Journal of Economics* 117(4): 1231–1294.

Austen, R. A. (1987). *African Economic History: Internal Development and External Dependency*. London: James Currey, Portsmouth, NH: Heinemann.

(2010). *Trans-Saharan Africa in World History*. New York: Oxford University Press.

Austin, G. (2005). *Labor, Land, and Capital in Ghana: From Slavery to Free Labor in Asante, 1807–1956*. University of Rochester Press.

(2007). "Labor and Land in Ghana, 1874–1939: A Shifting Ratio and an Institutional Revolution," *Australian Economic History Review* 47(1): 95–120.

(2008a). "The 'Reversal of Fortune' Thesis and the Compression of History: Perspectives from African and Comparative Economic History," *Journal of International Development* 20(8): 996–1027.

(2008b). "Resources, Techniques, and Strategies South of the Sahara: Revising the Factor Endowments Perspective on African Economic Development, 1500–2000," *The Economic History Review* 61(3): 587–624.

(2009a). "Cash Crops and Freedom: Export Agriculture and the Decline of Slavery in Colonial West Africa," *International Review of Social History* 54(1): 1–37.

(2009b). "Factor Markets in Nieboer Conditions: Pre-colonial West Africa, c.1500-c.1900," *Continuity and Change* 24(1): 23–53.

Behrendt, S. D., A. J. H. Latham, and D. Northrup, (2012). *The Diary of Antera Duke, an Eighteenth-Century African Slave Trader.* New York: Oxford University Press.

Berry, S. (1993). *No Condition is Permanent: The Social Dynamics of Agrarian Change in sub-Saharan Africa.* Madison, WI: University of Wisconsin Press.

Bohannan, P. and G. Dalton, eds. (1902). *Markets in Africa.* Evanston, IL: Northwestern University Press.

Bundy, C. (1979). *The Rise and Fall of the South African Peasantry.* Berkeley, CA: University of California Press.

Cooper, F. (1993). "Africa and the World Economy," in F. E. Mallon, S. J. Stern, A. F. Isaacman, and W. Roseberry (eds.), *Confronting Historical Paradigms: Peasants, Labor and the Capitalist World System in Africa and Latin America.* Madison, WI: University of Wisconsin Press, pp. 84–204.

Curtin, P. D. (1969). *The Atlantic Slave Trade: A Census.* Madison, WI: University of Wisconsin Press.

(1975). *Economic Change in Pre-colonial Africa: Senegambia in the Era of the Slave Trade.* Madison, WI: University of Wisconsin Press.

Diamond, J. M. (2005). *Guns, Germs, and Steel: The Fates of Human Societies.* New York: W. W. Norton.

Dike, O. K. (2011). *Trade and Politics in the Niger Delta, 1830–1885: An Introduction to the Economic and Political History of Nigeria.* Oxford: Clarendon Press.

Domar, E. (1970). "The Causes of Slavery or Serfdom: A Hypothesis," *Journal of Economic History* 30(1): 18–32.

Fetter, B. (1987). "Decoding and Interpreting African Census Data: Vital Evidence from an Unsavory Witness," *Cahiers d'Études Africaines* 27: 83–105.

Flint, J. E. and McDoughall, E. A. (1987). "Economic Change in West Africa in the Nineteenth Century," in J. F. Ajayi and M. Crowder (eds.), *History of West Africa*, Vol. II. New York: Columbia University Press.

Freund, B. (1984). "Labor and Labor History in Africa: A Review of the Literature," *African Studies Review* 27(2): 1–58.

Good, C. M. (1973). "Markets in Africa: A Review of Research Themes and the Question of Market Origins," *Cahiers d'Études Africaines* 13(52): 769–780.

Goody, J. (1971). *Technology, Tradition, and the State in Africa.* London: Oxford University Press.

Gray, R. and D. Birmingham (1970). *Pre-Colonial African Trade: Essays on Trade in Central and Eastern Africa before 1900.* London: Oxford University Press.

Harms, R. W. (1981). *River of Wealth, River of Sorrow: The Central Zaire Basin in the Era of the Slave and Ivory Trade, 1500–1891.* New Haven: Yale University Press.

Hawthorne, W. (2001). "Nourishing a Stateless Society during the Slave Trade: The Rise of Balanta Paddy-rice Production in Guinea-Bissau," *The Journal of African History* 42(1): 1–24.

Helleiner, G. K. (1966). *Peasant, Agriculture, Government, and Economic Growth in Nigeria.* Homewood, IL: R. D. Irwin.

Herbst, J. I. (2000). *States and Power in Africa: Comparative Lessons in Authority and Control.* Princeton University Press.

Hill, P. (1963). *The Migrant Cocoa-farmers of Southern Ghana: A Study in Rural Capitalism.* Cambridge University Press.

Hodder, B. W. (1965). "Some Comments on the Origins of Traditional Markets in Africa South of the Sahara," *Transactions of the Institute of British Geographers* 36: 97–105.

Hopkins, A. G. (1973). *An Economic History of West Africa.* New York: Columbia University Press.

Iliffe, J. (1983). *The Emergence of African Capitalism: The Anstey Memorial Lectures in the University of Kent at Canterbury 10–13 May 1982.* London: Macmillan.

(1995). *Africans: The History of a Continent.* Cambridge University Press.

Inikori, J. E. (2007). "Africa and the Globalization Process: Western Africa, 1450–1850," *Journal of Global History* 2(1): 63–86.

Jerven, M. (2010a). "African Growth Recurring: An Economic History Perspective on African Growth Episodes, 1690–2010," *Economic History of Developing Regions* 25(2): 127–154.

(2010b). "The Relativity of Poverty and Income: How Reliable are African Economic Statistics?" *African Affairs* 109(434): 77–96.

(2012). "An Unlevel Playing Field: National Income Estimates and Reciprocal Comparison in Global Economic History," *Journal of Global History* 7(1): 107–128.

(2013). *Poor Numbers: How We Are Misled by African Development Statistics and What to Do about It.* Ithaca, NY: Cornell University Press.

Johnson, M. (1970). "The Cowrie Currencies of West Africa Part I," *The Journal of African History* 11(1): 17–49.

(1976). "The Economic Foundations of an Islamic Theocracy: The Case of Masina," *Journal of African History* 17(4): 486.

Klein, M. A. (2001). "The Slave Trade and Decentralized Societies," *The Journal of African History* 42(1): 49–65.

Kuczynski, R. R. (1937). *Colonial Population.* London: Oxford University Press.

(1948). *Demographic Survey of the British Colonial Empire.* Vol. I: *West Africa.* London: Oxford University Press.

(1949). *Demographic Survey of the British Colonial Empire.* Vol. II: *East Africa.* London: Oxford University Press.

Kuznets, S. S. (1966). *Modern Economic Growth: Rate, Structure, and Spread.* New Haven: Yale University Press.

Latham, A. J. H. (1971). "Currency, Credit and Capitalism on the Cross River in the Pre-Colonial Era," *Journal of African History* 12(4): 599–605.

(1978). *Old Calabar 1600–1891: The Impact of the International Economy upon a Traditional Society.* Oxford: Clarendon Press.

Law, R. (1980). "Wheeled Transportation in Pre-Colonial West Africa," *Africa* 50: 249–262.

(1992). "Posthumous Questions for Karl Polanyi: Price Inflation in Pre-Colonial Dahomey," *The Journal of African History* 33(3): 387–420.

Law, R. ed. (1995). *From Slave Trade to "Legitimate" Commerce: The Commercial Transition in Nineteenth-century West Africa*. Cambridge and New York: Cambridge University Press.

Lewis, A. W. (1954). "Economic Development with Unlimited Supplies of Labor," *Manchester School* 20: 139–191.

Lovejoy, P. E. (1982). "Polanyi's 'Ports of Trade': Salaga and Kano in the Nineteenth Century," *Canadian Journal of African Studies* 16(2): 245–277.

(2000). *Transformations in Slavery: A History of Slavery in Africa*. Cambridge and New York: Cambridge University Press.

Lovejoy, P. E. and J. S. Hogendorn (1993). *Slow Death for Slavery: The Course of Abolition in Northern Nigeria, 1897–1936*. Cambridge and New York: Cambridge University Press.

Lovejoy, Paul E. and David Richardson (1995). "British Abolition and its Impact on Slave Prices along the Atlantic Coast of Africa, 1783–1850," *Journal of Economic History* 55(1): 98–119.

(1999). "Trust, Pawnship, and Atlantic History: The Institutional Foundations of the Old Calabar Slave Trade," *American Historical Review* 104(2): 33–55.

(2004). "'This horrid hole': Royal Authority, Commerce and Credit at Bonny 1690–1840," *Journal of African History* 44(3): 363–392.

Maddison, A. (2007). *Contours of the World Economy, 1–2030 AD: Essays in Macro-economic History*. Oxford and New York: Oxford University Press.

Manning, P. (1982). *Slavery, Colonialism and Economic Growth in Dahomey, 1640–1960*. Cambridge University Press.

(2010). "African Population. Projections 1850–1960," in K. Ittman, D. Cordell, and G. Maddox (eds.), *The Demographics of Empire: The Colonial Order and the Creation of Knowledge*. Athens, OH: Ohio University Press, pp. 245–275.

Martin, S. M. (1988). *Palm Oil and Protest: An Economic History of the Ngwa Region, South-eastern Nigeria, 1800–1980*. Cambridge and New York: Cambridge University Press.

Miller, J. C. (1988). *Way of Death: Merchant Capitalism and the Angolan Slave Trade, 1730–1830*. Madison, WI: University of Wisconsin Press.

Myint, H. (1958). "The 'Classical' Theory of International Trade and the Underdeveloped Countries," *Economic Journal* 68: 317–337.

Nieboer, H. J. (1900). *Slavery as an Industrial System: Ethnological Researches*. The Hague: M. Nijhoff.

North, D. C. (1977). "Markets and other Allocation Systems in History: The Challenge of Karl Polanyi," *Journal of European Economic History* 6: 703–716.

(2005). *Understanding the Process of Economic Change*. Princeton University Press.

Northrup, D. (1978). *Trade Without Rulers: Pre-colonial Economic Development in South-eastern Nigeria*. Oxford: Clarendon Press.

(2002). *Africa's Discovery of Europe: 1450 to 1850*. New York: Oxford University Press.

Nunn, N. (2007). "Historical Legacies: A Model Linking Africa's Past to its Current Underdevelopment," *Journal of Development Economics* 83(1): 157–175.

(2008). "The Long-term Effects of Africa's Slave Trades," *The Quarterly Journal of Economics* 123(1): 139–176.

Polanyi, K. (1966). *Dahomey and the Slave Trade: An Analysis of an Archaic Economy*. Seattle: University of Washington Press.

Reid, R. (2002). *Political Power in Pre-colonial Buganda: Economy, Society and Warfare in the Nineteenth Century*. Oxford: James Currey, Kampala: Fountain Publisher, and Athens, OH: Ohio University Press.

(2011). "Past and Presentism: The Pre-colonial and the Foreshortening of African History," *The Journal of African History* 52(2): 135–155.

Rockel, S. J. (2006). *Carriers of Culture: Labor on the Road in Nineteenth-century East Africa*. Portsmouth, NH: Heinemann.

Shea, P. J. (1975). "Economies of Scale and the Indigo Dyeing Industry of Pre-colonial Kano," *Kano Studies* 1(2): 55–61.

Sheriff, A. (1987). *Slaves, Spices and Ivory in Zanzibar: Integration of an East African Commercial Empire into the World Economy, 1770–1873*. London: James Currey.

Smith, S. (1976). "An Extension of the Vent-for-Surplus Model in Relation to Long-Run Structural Change in Nigeria," *Oxford Economic Papers* 28(3): 426–446.

Tabutin, D. and B. Schoumaker (2004). "The Demography of Sub-Saharan Africa from the 1950s to the 2000s," *Population (English Edition)*, 59(3–4): 447–556.

Thornton, J. (1977). "Demography and History in the Kingdom of Kongo, 1550–1750," *Journal of African History* 18(4): 507–530.

(1992). *Africa and Africans in the making of the Atlantic World, 1400–1680*. Cambridge, New York: Cambridge University Press.

Tosh, John (1980). "The Cash-Crop Revolution in Tropical Africa: An Agricultural Reappraisal," *African Affairs* 79(314): 79–94.

Widgren, M. (2004) "Towards a Historical Geography of Intensive Farming in Eastern Africa," in M. Widgren and J. E. G. Sutton (eds.), *Islands of Intensive Agriculture in Eastern Africa: Past and Present*. London: British Institute in Eastern Africa.

Wrigley, C. C. (1981). "Population and History: Some Innumerate Reflexions," in *African Demography*. Vol. II: *Proceedings of a Seminar Held in the Centre of African Studies, University of Edinburgh, 24th and 25th April 1981*. Edinburgh: Centre of African Studies, University of Edinburgh, pp. 17–31.

15

Native Americans and exchange: strategies and interactions before 1800

ANN M. CARLOS AND FRANK D. LEWIS

Introduction

North American aboriginals are not often included among those who had capitalist economies.[1] Most were hunter-gatherers, moving across the landscape in keeping with the seasonal availability of game, wild grains, and other food sources. The groups tended to be small, and reliant on similar resources, which left little scope for market exchange, while their nomadic lifestyle made significant capital accumulation virtually impossible. Also inhibiting complex market activity was the fact that, until the nineteenth century, native peoples had no written language. Nevertheless, anthropologists and archaeologists are discovering that, throughout North America, natives were engaging in trade, including long-distance trade; and in areas with high population densities, trade was an important component of their economies.

In this chapter we consider the record of economic exchange among aboriginals, a record that predates European contact. We also discuss the later and much more extensive trade that took place between natives and Europeans. Although natives have not been viewed as market oriented, evidence has been accumulating that some groups engaged in sophisticated exchange. Their mechanisms included reciprocity and redistribution, which played a much greater role than in Western societies. Indeed, universal among the aboriginals of North America was an ethic of generosity. Since the 1920s

Frank Lewis conducted research on this chapter while a visitor at the University of Colorado, and a research associate at the National Bureau of Economic Research, Cambridge, MA. In addition to the editor and those at the volume conference in Madrid, the authors thank Stanley Engerman, Michael Huberman, Sally Cole, and participants at the 2012 Canadian Network for Economic History Conference, Banff, Alberta. Support was provided by the Social Sciences and Humanities Research Council of Canada.
1 Our discussion will be limited to those groups who lived north of Mexico. For a discussion of the areas further south see Chapter 13 by Richard Salvucci in this volume.

publication of Marcel Mauss's seminal, *The Gift: The Form and Reason for Exchange in Archaic Societies*, the place of gifts in aboriginal societies has received increasing attention. Mauss defines gift-giving as equal exchange between symmetrically placed individuals or groups (Gamble 2008: 234). Gifts received one year were expected to be returned in another, and thus were a form of saving for the giver and borrowing for the receiver. We explore some of the factors that contributed to gift-giving among North American aboriginals.

Trade was not introduced to Native Americans with the arrival of Europeans, but it was greatly expanded, both in terms of the number of goods and the complexity of the trading arrangements. Both sides faced enormous challenges. The Europeans had to establish operations on both sides of the Atlantic, and both parties had to develop mechanisms for dealing with peoples unfamiliar with their goods, their means of trading, and their language. Our focus is on the fur trade and on the main European player in the north central part of the continent, the Hudson's Bay Company. How the English company was able to establish a successful trade of European goods for furs in the interior of North America is one of the great stories of business history.[2] Equally remarkable was the engagement of the natives. They traveled hundreds of miles by canoe to Hudson's Bay Company posts on a schedule that was limited by the navigable season and their need for game. They acquired trade goods that helped them trap beaver, which was the cornerstone of the trade, and firearms that improved their ability to hunt. In the northern fur trading regions guns were used mainly for waterfowl and small game, not as instruments of warfare. Natives also received blankets and kettles, and a wide range of luxury items including cloth, jewelry, tobacco, and alcohol. As the price of beaver pelts in Europe rose, due to greater demand for felt hats, and as French competition in the region increased, the native traders, who were astute bargainers, extracted higher prices for their furs. They used the additional income to raise their living standards by purchasing more luxury goods. So, even though market exchange had played a limited role in aboriginal society, the natives quickly exploited the mechanisms and responded to the incentives of European trade.

The aboriginals of North America did not have capitalist economies in the sense of accumulating significant levels of capital; nevertheless, their societies

---

2 The extensive literature on the Hudson's Bay Company of which E. E. Rich's two-volume *Hudson's Bay Company: 1670–1870* (1958), is the classic, is due not just to the achievements of the company, but also to the unparalleled historical records it has left.

had market features including barter trade and, for a few groups, trade that was facilitated by money. More importantly, they institutionalized gift-giving, which provided a capital market, in that it allowed for borrowing and lending. Gift-giving also served an insurance function, a role that was essential to native communities, who produced close to subsistence and whose food supply was variable. In some societies, notably those in the Pacific northwest, gift-giving was also a means of reducing conflict and preserving resources. As emphasized in the introduction to this volume, an important feature of capitalist economies is secure property rights, typically enforced through formal legal or other institutional structures. In the case of North American aboriginal societies, property rights did exist, but the mechanisms were based on societal norms that were sufficient to allow for a capital market, an insurance market, and a means of protecting resources.

Such mechanisms were by no means unique to North America. In *The Art of Not Being Governed*, James Scott, political scientist and anthropologist, emphasizes the preference for non-state institutions in the isolated upland communities in "Zomia," a roughly 2.5 million square kilometer region of southeast Asia. Mirroring, at least in some respects, the characteristics of Native American society, the region, as described by Scott, had "widespread craft specialization and complexity, but in a context that appears politically decentralized and relatively egalitarian" (Scott 2009: 325–326). And anthropologist David Graeber (2011: 89–126) draws examples from a wide range of regions and cultures to illustrate both the imperatives associated with making a gift, and the understanding that receiving a gift entailed a debt to be repaid. In fact, the use of gifts as a mechanism for facilitating trade has a history that goes back at least to the Phoenicians, as archaeologist Maria Eugenia Aubet (2001: 127–138) describes in her important book, although in this case gift exchange was mainly among the social elites.

Native American mechanisms for gift-giving and the norms associated with generosity predate the coming of Europeans to North America, but once the aboriginals had access to European goods they quickly took advantage of the opportunities by adapting their practices and past trading experience to the now more complex arrangements. The record of native-European exchange, best preserved in the remarkable archives of the Hudson's Bay Company, reveals Native Americans as energetic traders, who traveled hundreds of miles to company posts; astute consumers, who demanded a quality and range of goods suitable to their environment; tough bargainers, who played off the English and French where they competed; and industrious workers, who raised their effort in the trade in response to higher fur prices. Importantly, the Native American experience has implications that go beyond the fur-trading regions. Theirs was a society with no written language, a relatively small array of goods, and limited experience with complex trade; nevertheless they were able to adapt to an economic system drawn from the most advanced economies of the already industrializing world.

Exchange among Native Americans in the early and pre-contact periods

Trade was an element of aboriginal societies, but from the time preceding European contact until well into the nineteenth century, Native Americans were primarily subsistence producers. In the northern part of the continent they were hunters, with a diet based on big game, although in some regions freshwater fish were a key supplement to the diet, and in others waterfowl were important, especially after firearms were introduced. As well, the flesh of small game, such as rabbit and beaver, provided energy, especially during periods of scarcity. In a typical year, however, large ungulates, whether deer, moose, or woodland caribou in the boreal forest, or bison on the plains, made up the bulk of the native diet. Along parts of the Pacific coast, fish and marine mammals were the main food sources, while along the Mississippi river and in other regions, natives grew corn, beans, and other foods. As was true of pre-nineteenth-century Europe, Native Americans had an economy based on the land. Not only food, but even clothing and often shelter were derived from hunting, being produced mainly with animal skins. In such an environment the opportunity and motivation for trade was limited. Nevertheless, in some parts of North America, especially in California and the Pacific Northwest, natives engaged in significant levels of market exchange prior to European contact, and trade was also taking place in the interior of the continent.

As archaeologists have shown, native activities included the long-distance movements of goods over routes that in some cases had been used for thousands of years. In large parts of the northern half of North America evidence has been found of trade in silver, silica, copper, and obsidian (Carlson 1987). Like the other materials, obsidian, a dark glass-like volcanic rock, valued for cutting, has been discovered at widely dispersed sites. These scarce, high-value goods speak of interconnected exchange that took place over great distances. Although their trade was more confined geographically, the Chumash of southern California and neighboring tribes specialized in a variety of activities including the "minting" of money from the shells of sea snails.[3] In other parts of the continent, wampum, a form of money made with beads, was used after European trade was introduced.

There is also evidence of trade in food. Natives hunted bison on the Great Plains almost from their arrival in the Americas. Most hunting was on a limited scale, the killing of small numbers of animals at separate locations to meet the food requirements of the individual groups.[4] But starting about two thousand years ago, there is evidence of production of meat for trade. At Head-Squashed-In, an area in southern Alberta, there was intensive hunting and processing of bison. The area contains "over a million projectile points, hundreds of thousands of potsherds, and millions of kilograms of rocks" that were carried several kilometers and "used in stone boiling to render bone grease" (Bamforth 2011: 8). The bone grease was used to produce pemmican, a nutritious mixture of powdered meat mixed with melted fat that was easy to trade. The output at Head-Squashed-In far exceeded what was required to meet local demand. This industrial level of production coincided with the expansion of exchange networks on the Plains. There is also evidence of trade in pottery that extended from Illinois and Ohio to the Rocky Mountains (Bamforth 2011: 10).

The Chumash of southern California

The Chumash of southern California, who lived in what is now Santa Barbara county, had perhaps the most elaborate trading relationship in all of North America.[5] Some tribes occupied several of the Channel Islands located about 50 kilometers from the mainland, some resided near the coast, and others lived inland. As a result of this diversity, the various groups making up the Chumash had access to very different resources. In the late eighteenth century, the time of first Spanish settlement, it is estimated that the Chumash numbered between 15,000 and 25,000, and lived in an area no more than 20,000 km² (Gamble 2008: 9). In fact nearly all the population occupied less than 7,500 km² on the mainland, while the three Channel Islands occupied by the Chumash, Santa Cruz, Santa Rosa, and San Miguel, totaled just 500 km². With the possible exception of some native groups along the

---

3 King has written extensively on the Chumash. One of his early works, which effectively lays out the nature of their economy, deals with inter-village economic exchange (King 1971). Gamble (2008) is a wide-ranging study of Chumash society.
4 Bamforth (2011) provides a detailed description of the various techniques used for hunting bison on the Great Plains. Contrary to a popular perception, natives rarely used the method of driving bison over steep arroyos.
5 Our discussion of Chumash trade is drawn mainly from King (1971) and Gamble (2008).

coast of the Pacific Northwest, the Chumash had the highest population density north of central Mexico.[6] The wide variation in their environment and the close proximity of the groups encouraged trade. And because of its complexity, this trade was underpinned with currency that took the form of beads strung on threads of different lengths. These bead strings not only acted as a medium of exchange, they were also a luxury good, and a symbol and store of wealth.

The variety of resources was much greater on the mainland than on the Channel Islands, where the natives relied mainly on fish, although sea otters were hunted for their skins, both for trade and personal use. The currency was supplied by the island Chumash, who fashioned the bead strings from shells. Many of the beads were based on *olivella biplicata*, a sea snail with a very hard shell composed of enamel. The value of the string was determined by its length and the degree of fineness of the beads, which reflected the labor involved in shaving and polishing. In addition to beads, the islanders traded other goods, including stone rings (also called digging stick weights), stone tools, and probably fish. In exchange they received, among other items, acorns, seeds, skins, and bows and arrows. Importantly, the island Indians were net importers of goods, and they made up the difference by, in effect, purchasing the goods with the money that they produced. The inland and coastal Chumash also traded with each other, and facilitating that trade were the bead strings.

Although the island Chumash traded mammal skins, primarily sea otters and seals, and fish, they mainly sold the manufactured beads. The chert on Santa Cruz Island was ideal for fashioning tools, and shells were needed to make the beads, but, despite the need for a raw material, the beads were essentially labor produced (King 1971: 38). Figure 15.1 illustrates the trade between the island and mainland economies. Resource-based goods, f (food), are produced with labor and resources, while manufactured goods, b (beads), are produced with labor alone. The production possibilities curves of the two economies are represented by PP^I and PP^M, where I refers to the islands and M to the mainland; and consistent with the historical discussion only the island Chumash produce beads. Even if island and mainland natives had equal ability, the comparative lack of resources meant that the island Chumash could not produce as much food as mainlanders. Trade equalizes the relative price of food and manufactured goods at the slope of the line segments, $P^I C^I$ and $P^M C^M$. The island Chumash produce at P^I and consume at

6 A density of more than one person per km² in the region occupied by the Chumash compares, for example, with less than one person per 100 km² in Canada's boreal forest.

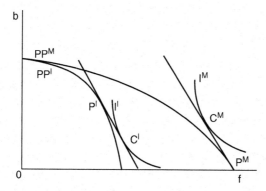

Figure 15.1 A model of trade between the island and mainland Chumash
Note: line segments P^IC^I and P^MC^M have the same slope and are of equal length.

C^I, while the mainland Chumash produce at P^M and consume at C^M. Thus, as Figure 15.1 illustrates, the island Chumash trade manufactured items to the mainland Chumash for food. The exchange allows both groups to consume beyond the limits of their own productive potential, and provides them higher living standards, represented by indifference curves, I^I and I^M.

Island natives traded manufactured goods, not because of a greater innate ability at fashioning beads and stone tools, but rather because of their comparative lack of resources, which, as Figure 15.1 shows, implies a lower living standard than the mainland Chumash (I^I versus I^M). The accounts of the Spanish do in fact describe the island Chumash as the poorest of the three groups, even though they too benefitted from trade. Another feature of the trade may also have been determined in part by the distribution of resources. Nearly all trade took place on the mainland. Thus, it was mainly the islanders who provided the transportation. Just as in the case of beads and other manufactured goods, the smaller resource base gave the island Chumash a comparative advantage in this labor-intensive activity.

Beads, the main trade item of the island Chumash, acted as currency, facilitating exchange not only between those on the island and the mainland, but also among the various mainland groups. Anthropologists have suggested that, as the quantity of beads increased, the price of beads relative to food and other trade goods would fall, ultimately undermining beads as a medium of exchange and limiting its other money-related functions (King 1971: 36; Gamble 2008: 247–248). This did not happen. The likely reason is that the multiple uses of the beads magnified the effect of the physical depreciation rate on the stock of beads, and as long as that rate matched the rate of production, the stock remained stable. To illustrate: if b is annual production and δ is the annual (physical) depreciation rate, then over time the stock of beads will approach b/δ. The greater the depreciation rate, δ, the smaller will be the stock and the higher the price of the beads relative to goods. The nature of the beads, their use beyond the Chumash community, and aspects of Chumash culture, apparently led to a high enough depreciation rate to maintain their value.

While beads circulated as currency, they also served other functions. Bead strings, often worn around the head or as belts, were ornamental and a symbol of wealth or status. These additional uses magnified the effect of depreciation on the "money supply"; that is, they kept the money supply at a lower level.[7] There were other forms of leakage. It was usual practice at mortuary-related events to bury the deceased with their possessions, including their beads. In addition, beads became part of a secondary trade with non-Chumash peoples. The wide variety of uses of the beads, along with native custom, seemed to provide for a stable system.

The overall composition of trade among the Chumash, captured in Figure 15.1, highlights the fact that island natives traded mainly manufactured (non-resource based) goods and received in return mainly food (resource-based goods), but natives also demanded variety within these broad categories. Santa Rosa Island was rich in otter. The skins were brought to the mainland and exchanged for acorns and other resource-based goods. Meanwhile, the islanders purchased fox and other types of skins and furs from the mainland Chumash. The islanders made baskets that they sold to mainland villages, but they also purchased larger baskets from the mainland. Stone tools, a manufactured good, were exported from the islands, while bows and arrows, another manufactured good, were imported. Food was the chief import to the islands, but there is evidence that they exported fish, likely to the inland natives. The Chumash's desire for variety and how they met it through exchange is an early illustration of what has become an important feature of international trade.[8]

---

7 Suppose B^M is the stock of beads used as money, and B^W the stock used as jewelry and for displays of wealth. If δ is the physical depreciation rate of beads, then assuming a constant level of non-money uses, the rate of depreciation of the money supply is: $\delta\,(1+ B^W/B^M)$. For example, if half the beads are used as jewelry, the depreciation rate of the money supply is doubled. This simplified characterization treats beads as a single good. In fact there were many types of beads, some of which were used almost exclusively as jewelry (the finer beads) (King 1978).

8 Krugman's (1979) seminal "Increasing Returns, Monopolistic Competition, and International Trade," focusses on variety as a central feature of the gains from trade.

Trading on the northern plains

Little information exists on the overall dimension of the trade among aboriginal peoples, but archaeologists have found evidence of exchange over long distances and in a wide variety of goods. Prior to European contact, there was trading throughout the continent as Baugh and Ericson document in *Prehistoric Exchange Systems in North America* (1994). In the maritime peninsula, comprising the Canadian maritime provinces and parts of Quebec, New York, and New England, a wide range of exotics (non-local items) has been found in burial mounds. Stone and mineral tools have been unearthed as well as ceramics and other artifacts (Bourque 1994: 29–35). Along the St. Lawrence river basin and in the Great Lakes region, evidence from archaeological sites has been used to describe the major trade routes for varieties of silica, silver, copper, and marine shells (Wright 1994). Michael Stewart (1994) infers from the sites in the middle Atlantic region that there were two systems of exchange. Broad-based exchange involved goods indigenous to the area and took place among or within local groups or bands. Such items are generally found at sites close to their source. Focussed exchange, on the other hand, involved goods produced for trade often over long distances. It appears that both broad-based trade and focussed trade declined after 800/900 CE, a shift that coincided with the emergence of sedentary agriculture (Stewart 1994: 92). Although Stewart finds the decline puzzling, it may be that the range of goods provided by subsistence agriculture, which would have included some hunting, and the comparative stability of output, mitigated the need for trade.

The northern plains were lightly populated, yet as in other regions, aboriginal peoples developed elaborate, long-distance, trading arrangements. In a prehistoric site in South Dakota, archaeologists have found artifacts from Florida, the Gulf coast, and both the Atlantic and Pacific coasts (Wood 1980: 99). But more revealing of the nature and extent of trading on the northern plains are the journals of Lewis and Clark, and later explorers. They describe a trade in nondurable goods which cannot be revealed by burial sites. Trading in the northern plains appears to have come about mainly because of the coexistence of sedentary horticulturalists, including the Arikara, Mandan, and Hidasta, who lived in the Dakotas, and nomadic hunters, among them the Cheyennes, Arapahoes, and Comanches. The horticulturalists traded corn,

Broda and Weinstein (2006) estimate that greater import variety increased the real income of US consumers, over the period 1972 and 2001, by the equivalent of 2.6 percent of GDP. It seems safe to conclude that, if the alternative was no trade in similar goods, the Chumash gained much more. For an explanation of the gains from trade due to scale economies and imperfect competition, see Markusen (1981).

beans, and other garden produce, and in return received dried meat and such animal products as bison robes, sheep bows, and leather goods. Much of the trading activity took place in village centers, which for the Arikara, Mandan, and Hidatsa, were located along the Missouri river (see Map 15.1).

In the Pacific Northwest the trading structure was similar. The main center, the Dalles Rendezvous, was located at major rapids on the Columbia river, and attracted native groups from the coastal region. But it was also part of an overall trading system that included the plains. The coastal natives exchanged mainly dried fish in return for the products of the hunting economy. Other trade items included fish oil, feathers, shells, and root and seed foods (Wood 1980: 102). The long-distance exchange was facilitated by an intermediate trading center, the Shoshone Rendezvous in southwestern Wyoming, which like the Dalles Rendezvous was located on an important water route, the Bear river. The Crows brought goods there from the northern plains and the Utes came from the southwest. The Shoshone, Nez Percés, and Flatheads were among the groups that completed the trading network to the west coast. Despite the high transport costs implied by the long and elaborate trade routes, the sharing of technology and the increased variety in consumer items was sufficient compensation. Most natives did not engage in long-distance trade directly, rather the involvement of middlemen allowed them to participate in the benefits.

Gift-giving and sharing among Native Americans

Native groups traded; nevertheless, far more important than the exchange of one item for another, was an institutional arrangement that allowed for the transfer of goods, usually food, with no explicit compensation. Whether called the good Samaritan rule or an ethic of generosity, gift-giving appears to have been universal among North American aboriginals. There is a large literature on gift-giving, generosity, cooperation, and related behavior, where the emphasis is on individual motivation.[9] While not ignoring this aspect, anthropologist Bruce Winterhalder (1997) explores the potential gains to the economy from societal norms based on generosity. He characterizes two explanations for gift-giving in pre-modern societies as "tolerated theft" or "scrounging," and risk minimization. Indeed, Karl Polanyi (1957) points to uncertainty about the environment as a key factor in giving.

In aboriginal society, tolerated theft, which was regarded as giving rather than theft, has been viewed by anthropologists as a mechanism that raised welfare by equalizing the distribution of income. The notion is that, with

---

9 As we noted, Marcel Mauss's classic, *The Gift* (2002), is the cornerstone of this literature.

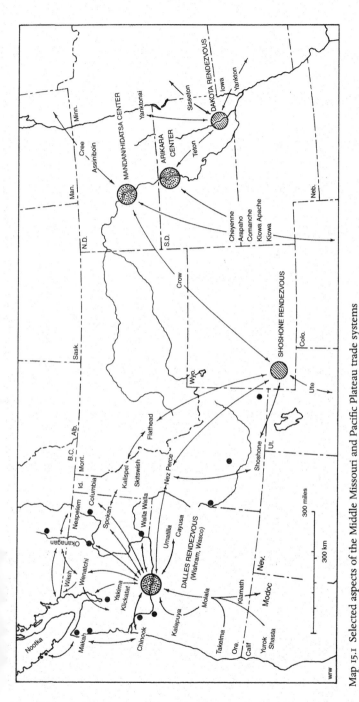

Map 15.1 Selected aspects of the Middle Missouri and Pacific Plateau trade systems

Note: large stippled circles indicate major trade centers; large hatched circles indicate secondary trade centers; small black circles represent minor trading points.

Source: Wood (1980: 101). The authors thank Raymond Wood for permission to reproduce the map.

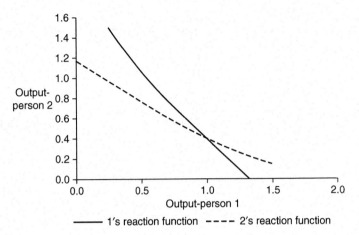

Figure 15.2 Reaction functions with full sharing
Notes: the equations underlying the reaction functions are: $U = \frac{c^{1-\delta}}{1-\delta} - l^{\alpha}$ and $q = kl$, where
U is utility, c is consumption, l is labor (effort), q is output, k is labor productivity,
δ is relative risk aversion, and $\alpha-1$ is the elasticity of the marginal disutility of labor.
Output is normalized such that person 1 produces one unit of output with one unit of labor
($k_1 = 1$). Person 2 is assumed to produce 0.75 units of output with one unit of labor ($k_2 = 0.75$).
The parameter values are: $\alpha = 1.5$ and $\delta = 3$.

diminishing marginal utility of consumption, the loss in utility of the (higher-income) giver was less than the gain in utility of the receiver. This essentially utilitarian view takes utility across individuals as additive. As Winterhalder points out, there is the question of what motivates the giver; but, even if that is resolved, a more general issue is how giving affects work effort, with its implications for output and consumption. The problem is that sharing acts as a tax on both the giver and receiver since each keeps only a portion of any additional output that they produce. Figure 15.2 depicts the reaction functions of two persons who share equally. Each function shows the optimal (utility-maximizing) output of each person for a given level of output of the other. In the illustrated case, person 2 is assumed to be 25 percent less productive than person 1, yet in equilibrium his output is 60 percent less (0.4 as compared to 1). The gap is larger because person 1's effort is greater. Since their consumption is the same, however, it follows that, ignoring prestige or other utility effects of sharing, the lower-productivity person is better off.

The literature on generosity does not claim that gift-giving led to full income equality, and the implication, that those with lower productivity will be better off, highlights why such an outcome is implausible. But might partial sharing have been a way of raising total utility? Figure 15.3 describes the

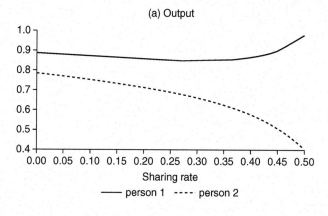

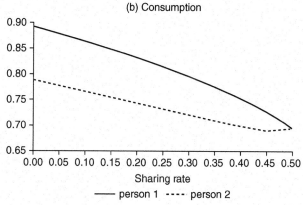

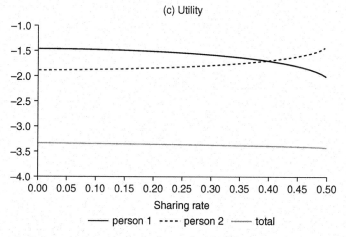

Figure 15.3 Output, consumption, and utility with partial sharing

Note: see Figure 15.2. Because of the form of the utility function, utility is negative. Utility is increasing in consumption and decreasing in labor.

range of outcomes, from no sharing to full sharing, for output, consumption, and utility. As the sharing rate increases, the high- and low-productivity persons both produce less because of the disincentive effects (see Figure 15.3(a)). It is only when there is almost full sharing that person 1's output goes up.[10] Throughout all sharing ranges, total output falls and the consumption even of the person receiving the transfer declines (see 15.3(b)). The utility of person 2 does go up because their effort is less, but this is at the expense of the giver (see 15.3(c)). Total utility does not increase, with the exception of a range where sharing rates are very low. Thus, even if we take a utilitarian approach, gift-giving is hard to justify on the sole basis of equalizing income.[11] It should be emphasized, however, that this conclusion applies only to transfers that are always in the same direction. As outlined below, where gift-giving is reciprocal the benefits can be very great.

Another form of sharing was the good Samaritan principle. This required that even if a native group had nominal hunting rights to a territory, outsiders were permitted to kill any potential food-source animal for personal use. In *Commerce by a Frozen Sea* (2010) we argued that this rule benefitted a native economy based on large game (such as moose or caribou), because it increased the Indians' incentive to cooperate over a resource that was depletable.[12] Since game migrated, and various native groups had access to the herds, it was in their common interest to behave as a single monopoly exploiter of the resource, rather than to compete. Where two groups compete for a depletable resource, each maximizing their own long-run harvest given the harvest of the other, their harvest is smaller and their level of hunting effort much greater than if they cooperate. The good Samaritan rule was, therefore, a mechanism that encouraged conservation and more efficient hunting.

In the eastern part of the continent, property rights to game were stricter than those in the interior. Native groups even to the level of the family had exclusive rights to specific areas. Chrétien Le Clercq, a Franciscan missionary, gives the following seventeenth-century description of property rights among a group of Algonquians:

10 Over this range the income effect of the implicit tax on person 1, which leads to increased effort, dominates the substitution effect.

11 Figures 15.2 and 15.3 are based on specific parameter values, but the main conclusions would apply if other plausible values were assumed.

12 The "good Samaritan" rule extended to beaver and other animals that had value in the fur trade, but if a beaver was killed, the hunter was not allowed to sell the pelt. See Carlos and Lewis (2010: Chapter 6 and appendix C).

It is the right of the head of the nation . . . to distribute the places of hunting to each individual. It is not permitted to any Indian to overstep the bounds and limits of the region which shall have been assigned to him in the assemblies of the elders. These are held in autumn and in spring expressly to make this assignment.

And fur trader Joseph Chadwick described in 1764 how Maine Indians divided their land into heritable family hunting territories: "Their hunting ground and streams were parceled out to certain families, time out of mind [into the distant past]" (Carlos and Lewis 2010: 156).

Even where native groups had exclusive hunting grounds, sharing/gift-giving may have played a role in conservation. Suppose each person's productivity depends positively on the resource stock. In the absence of gift-giving, a decline in the animal stock will lead to increased hunting effort as natives try to maintain their consumption. If the increase in effort is large enough the animal population will decline further. The advantage of a sharing rule is that it moderates the overall rate of exploitation. In effect, the sharing rule shifts hunting to the region where the resource stock has remained high and reduces the overall labor input.

Another explanation for sharing is what Winterhalder calls "risk minimization." In regions where output is highly variable, sharing has been shown to result in improved nutritional outcomes. The key is that health is determined less by average consumption over time than by the periods when consumption falls below a threshhold. In the subarctic winter, adult males needed between 4,500 and 5,000 calories per day. The extraordinary energy demands made starvation a particular threat, especially given the uncertainty about weather and the movements of game.[13] Gift-giving greatly reduced the risk by allowing natives to diversify over territories that varied over time in productivity. In fact, because of the precarious nature of their environment, the insurance role, implicit in reciprocal gift-giving sharing, did not just raise the utility of natives, it was an essential survival mechanism.

The natives of the Pacific Northwest had perhaps the highest incomes in North America, but they too faced periods of scarcity. Gift-giving through the potlatch was an important feature of their society. As Stuart Piddocke (1965: 244) describes it, "the potlatch had a very real pro-survival or subsistence function, serving to counter the effects of varying resource productivity by

---

13 The calorie estimates by anthropologists Edward Rogers and James Smith are for the Canadian shield west of Hudson Bay. Energy demands were less further south, but a daily requirement of three pounds of meat from large game per day was likely the minimum in the northern part of the continent. See Carlos and Lewis (2010: 163).

promoting exchanges of food from those groups enjoying a temporary surplus to those groups suffering a temporary deficit." And Asen Balikci (1970: 17) points to the vital role of sharing among the Netsilik Eskimos (Inuit) of Nunavut (eastern Northwest Territories): "Whenever game was abundant, sharing among non-relatives was avoided, since every family was supposedly capable of obtaining the necessary catch. In situations of scarcity, however, caribou meat was more evenly distributed throughout the camp."

The southern Kwakiutl Indians of British Columbia have received particular attention because of their elaborate potlatches, which greatly expanded after European contact. Potlatches not only lowered risk and helped preserve resources, they also reduced conflict, a role highlighted by Bruce Johnsen (1986) – see also Allen (1956). The Kwakiutl occupied the salmon-rich inland waterways of Queen Charlotte Sound. Each kinship unit, or *numaym*, had exclusive ancestral rights to specific streams, an arrangement that helped preserve the salmon stocks, since it encouraged each group to fish at a sustainable rate.[14] However, salmon runs varied, and in years when the run was low there could be privation and an incentive to overharvest, with serious implications for future salmon populations. But the problem emphasized by Johnsen was the close proximity of the groups, which made it tempting for those having a bad fishing year to encroach on their neighbors' streams. If this happened, conflict was likely, and Johnsen points to evidence that, in earlier times, warfare was common. Variability in salmon runs aside, the differential productivity of streams in typical years was also a potential source of conflict. The transfer of wealth through the potlatch acted as a safety valve, mitigating the threat.

In the hunter-gatherer world of North America, gift-giving and other forms of generosity raised long-run welfare, perhaps even ensured native survival. Yet to be sustained as a societal norm, gift-giving had to be in the interest of individuals. In the language of game theory, it had to be incentive compatible. Drawing on Marcel Mauss, the father of gift-giving theory, anthropologist Chris Gregory (1982: 19) explains the difference between commodity and gift exchange this way: "commodity exchange establishes a relationship between the objects exchanged, whereas gift exchange establishes a relationship between the subjects." In contrast to commodity exchange, where no further interaction between the parties is implied, a gift creates a debt to be repaid. Rank and prestige are other features of gift-giving. Gifts are seen as a way of

---

14 Although natives had no formal knowledge of fish dynamics, they were aware of the effect of overfishing on future stocks.

maintaining or gaining rank and enhancing prestige, features absent from commodity exchange. Prestige and status are recurring themes in the anthropological literature.

The most studied groups in regard to gift-giving lived in the Pacific Northwest. Their mechanism for gift-giving was, as we noted, the potlatch, which varied in form depending on the tribe, although some features were common.[15] The chief of a clan or kinship group, or someone of lower rank, would invite the guests and assume the role of host. There would be a feast, but the main purpose was to distribute goods. In the case of large potlatches called by a chief, other members of the clan would also provide the gifts. But whatever the exact makeup of the donor group: "participation [was] direct and the return in prestige [was] immediate" (Barnett 1938: 350).

With European contact, the volume and types of gifts expanded. Gilbert Sprout, a colonial magistrate on Vancouver Island in the mid nineteenth century, described gift-giving by the Aht, who lived on the west coast of the island:

> the principal use made by the Aht of an accumulation of personal chattels is to distribute them periodically among invited guests ... the giver does not now consider that he has parted with his property ... he regards it as well invested, for the present recipients of his largess will strive to return to him at their own feasts more than he has bestowed. (Bracken 1997: 33–34)

Israel Powell, the first Indian superintendent of British Columbia, saw potlatches in much the same way: "The gifts are dealt out with profusion, but it is attended with a strange feature; for an equivalent in return at a future gathering is expected to be presented" (Bracken 1997: 36).[16] Another motivating factor was the prestige and status associated with the ceremonies. Sprout did not see this as unusual: "The habit of the 'Patlach' is based on the common human desire for distinction which appears to be as strong among uncivilised as among civilised people" (Bracken 1997: 44). Thus, even though there was no legal commitment to reciprocate, societal norms provided enough of an incentive. Over time the potlatches became more elaborate and prestige

---

15 Anthropologists have written extensively on the Kwakiutl and other groups including the Tlingit, who occupied parts of southern Alaska and northern British Columbia, the Haida, who lived in the area of the Queen Charlotte Islands, and the coast Salish, who lived near Puget Sound. In fact, a 1938 article by anthropologist H. G. Barnett (1938: 349) begins: "So much has been written about the potlatch of the Northwest Coast that almost everyone has some ideas about it."

16 Some discussions of gift-giving suggest that reciprocity included the expectation of a greater return in the future. The larger amount could have reflected an implicit positive discount rate made higher by the possibility that the "loan" would not be repaid.

became associated with the volume of gifts, but this was a post-contact phenomenon. In earlier years the amounts distributed remained roughly the same.

Exchange between Native Americans and Europeans

With the arrival of Europeans, trading by Native Americans increased by orders of magnitude both in volume and variety, and was a major change relative to the more limited exchange that had been part of traditional native society. The Dutch had some involvement in the fur trade in the early years, but the North American fur trade, indeed all trade with the Indians, was dominated by the English and French, with the French playing the much larger role. In setting up a mechanism that would work, Europeans faced challenges of distance, time, language, and culture. The trade in furs took place thousands of miles from the markets where the furs were ultimately sold. Transport included not only ocean shipping from Europe to North America, but also the movement of furs and goods within the continent.

The French operated through various monopoly companies until the loss of New France in 1763, while the main English player in the interior of the continent was the Hudson's Bay Company. Both Europeans and Native Americans met the challenges of the new commercial relationship. As we have described, not only did trading take place among aboriginals, but the Chumash and some other groups even used specie. The Europeans, however, introduced a complex trading regime and a vast array of goods. Beaver pelts, which had been a minor part of the native economy, became the cornerstone of the trade. As fur trader Andrew Graham put it, Indians had seen the beaver as an: "animal whose pelt made poor clothing and was too small to be used for tipi covers or other practical purposes" (Williams 1969: 97). But once Native Americans recognized that beaver pelts were a means of acquiring European goods, they dramatically increased their trapping, even transforming the way they hunted beaver, now using ice chisels, nets, and knives purchased from the Europeans.

The accommodation that developed over time among Europeans and Native Americans is explored by Richard White, who in *The Middle Ground* describes French-native, especially Algonquian, interactions. As White (1991 x) puts it: "people try to persuade others who are different from themselves by appealing to what they perceive to be the values and practices of others."

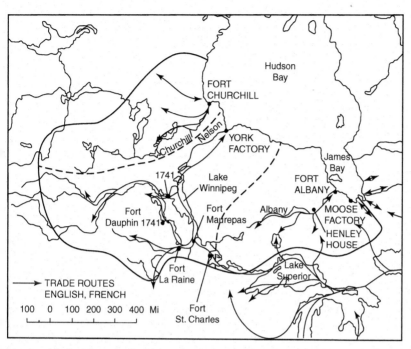

Map 15.2 Trading hinterland of the Hudson's Bay Company
Source: Ray (1987, plate 60)

There are often misunderstandings, but "from these misunderstandings arise new meanings and through them new practices – the shared meanings and practices of the middle ground."

In *Commerce by a Frozen Sea* our focus was on the region south and west of Hudson Bay, and on the trade between the Indians and the Hudson's Bay Company (see Map 15.2). This English company, chartered in 1670, operated solely from the coast of Hudson Bay until the later part of the eighteenth century, when inland posts were also established. There is a large literature on the company of which E. E. Rich's, *Hudson's Bay Company 1670–1870*, published in 1958, remains the classic work. From 1718 to 1763, the Hudson's Bay Company faced competition from French traders operating out of Montreal and Quebec City under the umbrella of the Compagnie des Indes. After the conquest of New France by the British, the trade from Montreal was taken over by Scottish merchants, who in 1779 formed the North West Company; but the trading relationships within the Hudson Bay region remained much the same. The Hudson's Bay Company's long-term survival and its extraordinary records have allowed us to develop a comprehensive picture of how both parties, Europeans and natives, adapted.

The Structure of the trade

The Hudson's Bay Company's approach was one of centralized control. It established trading posts along the coast of Hudson Bay at the mouths of major rivers, and sent men to operate the posts and conduct the trading operations. Map 15.2 shows the company's main trading posts and the approximate trading hinterlands that they served. Natives arrived during the summer to trade furs for the European goods that had been delivered to the posts the previous year by the annual ship from London. The furs were transported to England on the next ship, which came to the post toward the end of the summer. In England, the company auctioned the pelts to furriers and hatters. The company's head office in London made the key decisions concerning the number of men to send to the posts and the quality and types of goods to trade. Reports on native preferences were central to these decisions. The head office also gave guidance to the post traders about the rates of exchange between trade goods and furs. All correspondence between the post governors and the company officials in London was carried by the annual ship, which meant that the company was effectively operating in an extended futures market. The furs sold in London were exchanged in North America for trade goods that the company had purchased at least eighteen months earlier.[17]

The correspondence between each post and the head office in London included a daily journal kept by the chief factor. James Isham's journal for the 1740/41 trading year at York Factory provides a picture of life at the post and describes how the trade was conducted. York Factory and the other trading posts were set up to be self-sufficient. There was a doctor, armorer, tailor, carpenter, blacksmith, cooper, bricklayer, and other men, mainly laborers. The full complement was between thirty-six and fifty, although in 1740/41 there were fewer than thirty men. On August 1, 1740 the annual ship left York Factory for London with its cargo of furs and timber.[18] Few canoes arrived in August and September, none to trade furs. Those natives who did come to the

---

17 For example, furs auctioned in November 1741 were purchased with goods that were sent from England no later than May 1740. Moreover the correspondence on which decisions about trade goods were based would have been on the ship that arrived in England in late 1739.

18 Typically the main ship was accompanied by a smaller vessel.

post were the "home guard" Indians, who spent the year in the general vicinity of the post, supplying the men with meat and fish. Their presence helped make the trade viable, but their direct contribution in terms of furs was limited. On September 29, Isham reported the river "full of ice," and other than the occasional native who came on foot, there was no further contact with the natives until April.

Twenty-six families, numbering 130 individuals, came in April for the goose hunt. It was the end of May, however, that marked the start of the fur-trading season, which was very short. It occupied less than a month; in fact, nearly all the trade was conducted during the week beginning June 12. On Monday eighty-five canoes arrived, representing at least four different native groups. The natives stayed just a few days, often one or two. The journey to the trading post was long, the rivers were navigable for a short period, and the natives needed to return to hunting. With trading effectively over by the end of June, company men spent the summer preparing for the arrival of the ship from England. The furs were sorted, counted, packed into bundles, and placed in casks. In late July, buoys were readied, and on August 2, the *Churchill* arrived along with a sloop. By August 6, the vessels were unloaded, and over the next three days the homeward cargo of furs and lumber were boarded. On August 12, having spent just ten days at the post, the vessels weighed anchor, and the next day set sail for London.

The annual cycle of trade at York Factory, which was developed over many years, required coordination between the head office in London and the post governor, who together made the key decisions on goods and prices. This was achieved entirely through the extensive and detailed correspondence that accompanied the ship. But even though communication was infrequent, the company was able to conduct a profitable business. Natives in the region also adapted, even specializing in activities related to the trade. As noted, some groups, the "home guard" Indians remained in the general vicinity of the posts, including those who came for the goose hunt. They supplied food, mainly meat and fish, rather than furs. Other natives acted as middlemen. They traveled to the posts from far in the interior, bringing furs obtained by other hunters.

Trading mechanisms and the nature of the trade goods

The Hudson's Bay Company and the natives developed mechanisms to deal with this complex barter trade. More than sixty types of European goods and as many as fifteen to twenty types of fur and skins were exchanged. An important element in the success of the trade was how the company adapted to native practice. The trade began with a gift-giving ceremony that mirrored the reciprocal exchange that was such an important element of native society. In one ceremony, the governor presented the native trading captain with a suit of clothes and other items, while all the natives in the group were given bread, prunes, tobacco, and brandy. The Indians also received other gifts that included the wide range of goods they obtained through trade. As part of the ceremony, the chief would present the governor some furs, but in contrast to gift-giving among natives, the transfers were nearly all from the company to the natives. The trade was conducted in the language of the natives, Cree in much of the region. The company gave language instruction to its personnel, providing them with phrase books and dictionaries.

The trading stage highlights the Hudson's Bay Company's creativity. All furs and trade goods were denominated in a new unit account, the made beaver. The company also established an official standard, which set rates of exchange for all furs and goods in terms of the made beaver. Table 15.1, drawn from the accounts of the company's largest post, York Factory, lists some of the more than sixty trade items that were purchased by the Indians in the 1740 trading year, along with their prices.[19] The items have been grouped into a few broad categories: producer goods, household goods, alcohol and tobacco, and other luxuries.

The producer goods were those used mainly for hunting food game, including waterfowl, but some items, such as twine and ice chisels, were used to trap beaver. The household goods, kettles, and blankets were also functional. In the early years, natives purchased mainly producer and household goods, which were the sorts of goods that helped them reach subsistence. But over time, as fur prices rose, they increasingly traded for luxuries. These included various types of beads and high-quality, brightly colored cloth, which they used to decorate clothing. They also purchased jewelry, vermilion, and a

---

19 The made beaver accounting mechanism developed by the Hudson's Bay Company was similar to the forms of money used in the African slave trade. In Senegambia a monetary unit based on cloth, the guinée, was first used to establish relative prices in the slave trade, but in the mid seventeenth century the iron bar came to be the standard against which goods and slaves were priced. And just as was true of the Hudson's Bay Company's official standard, bar prices in the slave trade were nominally fixed. Actual prices in the fur trade deviated from the official standard in that company traders typically exchanged goods for furs at different rates depending on market conditions. In the slave trade the adjustment was made through the mix of goods offered for slaves. An important distinction between the bar iron measure and the made beaver is that, whereas the bar iron unit was also a physical currency, the made beaver was only a unit of account. See Curtin (1975: 233–253) and Carlos and Lewis (2010: 51–62).

Table 15.1 *Quantities and prices of European trade goods at York factory, 1740*

	Quantity	Price (mb/unit)		Quantity	Price (mb/unit)
Producer goods			Other Luxuries		
Files	308	1	Bayonets	150	1
Flints	2313	1/12	Beads (lb)	159	2
Guns	250	14	Buttons	40	1/4
Gun worms	340	1/4	Cloth (yd)	987	3.5
Hatchets	762	1	Combs	346	1
Ice chisels	472	1	Egg boxes	142	1/3
Knives	3,312	1/4	Flannel (yd)	19	1.5
Net lines	218	1	Gartering (yd)	364	2/3
Powder horns	181	1	Handkerchiefs	12	1.5
Powder (lb)	3,360	1	Hats	35	4
Scrapers	216	1/2	Lace (yd)	184	2/3
Shot (lb)	7,388	1/4	Needles	410	1/12
Twine (skein)	114	1	Pistols	26	7
Household goods			Rings	471	1/8–1/3
Awls	840	1/8	Sashes	48	1.5
Blankets	189	7	Scissors	56	1/2
Fire steels	376	1/4	Shirts	90	2.5
Kettles	679	1.5	Spoons	24	1/2
Tobacco and alcohol			Stockings	26	2.5
Alcohol (gallon)	412	4	Trunks	37	4
Rundlets	350	1	Vermillion (lb)	19	16
Tobacco (lb)	2,272	2			
Tobacco boxes	162	1	Total value (mb)		27,457

Note: the made beaver (mb) was the unit of account used by the Hudson's Bay Company at its trading post. The official price of a prime beaver pelt was one made beaver.

Source: Carlos and Lewis 2010: 60–61.

variety of other luxury items. The other important luxury goods were alcohol and tobacco.

The prices in Table 15.1 are given in the Hudson's Bay Company's unit of account, the made beaver (mb), where a prime beaver pelt had a price of 1 mb. In 1740, for example, the natives traded for 250 guns, which at a price of 14 mb, were worth 3,500 mb. This means that, at the official rate, natives would have exchanged 3,500 prime beaver pelts, or the equivalent, for the guns. The actual rate varied according to market conditions, but still, the official price list guided the company's traders in their dealings with the Indians. The price list was not posted, nor could the Indians have interpreted it, but they knew from past experience the approximate rates of exchange between furs and European goods.

The accounts allow us to determine how the natives were allocating their income from the fur trade across the different goods. In 1740 the natives traded for a total of 27,500 mb in trade goods of which 12,000 mb or just over 40 percent were producer goods. These composed mainly firearms and related goods. The 3-ft guns that they purchased were particularly effective for geese and small game, not warfare. Blankets and kettles made up 10 percent of the trade goods, while the remaining 50 percent of income was spent on luxuries, divided about equally between tobacco and alcohol, and other luxuries, mostly cloth.

Given the emphasis that has been placed on it in the literature, surprisingly little was spent on alcohol. The roughly 400 gallons accounted for less than 6 percent of total expenditure. Much more was spent on each of tobacco and cloth, and more was spent on blankets and kettles. The mix of goods and the way the natives allocated their income presents a picture of producers, who used the goods they received to better hunt and trap, and consumers, who acquired new luxury goods that improved their quality of life.

The French fur trade – a comparison

The French had begun participating in the fur trade in the sixteenth century, and during the first half of the eighteenth century they were the Hudson's Bay Company's main rivals, and also the main rivals of the English merchants operating out of Albany. In 1700 control of the French trade passed from the Northern Company, a joint French-Canadian venture, to the Colony Company, whose board of directors was exclusively Canadian. Perhaps through mismanagement, disruptions in the fur market, or lack of capital, the company was unsuccessful; and it was only in 1718 with the formation of the Compagnie des Indes that trade increased.[20] Like the Hudson's Bay Company, the Compagnie des Indes was given a monopoly.

The literature on the English fur trade is much more extensive, due in part to the superb historical records of the Hudson's Bay Company; but, in fact, the trade of the Compagnie des Indes far surpassed not only that of the Hudson's

20 For a review that includes the French trade during the first half of the eighteenth century, see Miquelon (1987).

Bay Company, but the trade of all the English. Over the period 1720 to 1760, while London was receiving on average 70,000 beaver pelts per year of which 51,000 were brought in by the Hudson's Bay Company, beaver pelts received by the Compagnie des Indes in Paris averaged 166,000 (Wien 1990: 309).[21] The greater trade of the Compagnie des Indes, twice that of the English and three times that of the Hudson's Bay Company, reflected its much larger trading area. The French operated not just in the northeast and Great Lakes regions, but also in areas that extended down the Mississippi river basin. French traders even competed with the Hudson's Bay Company in its own trading hinterland, especially after 1730.

The Compagnie des Indes imported far more furs than the Hudson's Bay Company, but it was a much smaller presence in North America, employing just two or three receivers, a few clerks, and an agent in Quebec City.[22] The company was really little more than a wholesaler. It brought in European goods on hired merchant ships; sold the goods to independent French fur traders, called *voyageurs*; purchased the furs that the *voyageurs* obtained through trade with the Indians; and transported the furs to France, where it sold them at auction. The prices the company paid to *voyageurs* were based on a fixed scale that was periodically adjusted according to market conditions. Thus, the *voyageurs* knew in advance what they would be receiving for their furs and could determine the appropriate rates of exchange to offer the Indians. In contrast to the Hudson's Bay Company, which conducted all its trading along the bay coast, at least until late in the eighteenth century, the *voyageurs* went to the Indians, locating their trading posts in the interior. The French, therefore, reduced the distance the Indians needed to travel, and this was reflected in the market. In hinterlands where the *voyageurs* and the Hudson's Bay Company competed, the English company offered the Indians much more favorable rates of exchange.

The mix of trade goods sold by the companies also differed, mainly because of transport costs. The Hudson's Bay Company had a great advantage in that it brought supplies and trade items to the trading posts directly by ship. This allowed the company to trade European goods with a much lower

---

21 The English trade also included a small number of furs received in New York.
22 In addition to paying the salaries of the workers, the company hired guards to curtail smuggling and was required to pay a tax on its beaver receipts of about 4 percent (Wien 1990: 299). Each Hudson's Bay Company post, by contrast, had a complement of roughly thirty to fifty men. With four major posts in the first half of the eighteenth century, Hudson's Bay Company employed more than a hundred on the Canadian side of its operation (Carlos and Lewis 2010: 47).

value-to-weight ratio than the furs they were receiving in exchange, such as kettles. The ships also brought supplies for the men at the post. As a result, each ship arrived fully loaded, and left with furs whose weight was far less than the ship's tonnage. The difference was normally made up with lumber, which provided the company a small additional source of revenue. By contrast, the *voyageurs* canoed thousands of miles to the interior of the continent. It was therefore more profitable for the French to trade goods with a value-to-weight ratio that more closely matched the furs they were transporting back.

We have limited information on precisely what the French were exchanging, but an invoice of trade goods sent in 1742 to St. Joseph, a post on the southeast coast of Lake Michigan, reveals sharp contrasts with the accounts of York Factory. Producer goods, which include axes, ice chisels, and firearms, tended to be the most difficult to transport. At York Factory in 1740, the value of these goods was 44 percent of the total, whereas at St. Joseph they were just 10 percent (Carlos and Lewis 2010: 81–85; Miquelon 1987: 152–153). The various types of cloth, including blankets, were much more important at the French post, accounting for more than 75 percent of the value of trade goods. At York Factory, the same types of goods made up less than 20 percent of the total. The share of brandy, however, was similar at the two posts, about 6 percent, even though it was a low value-to-weight item.[23]

The structure of the Compagnie des Indes gave much more independence to the individual French traders. Nevertheless, the interactions of the *voyageurs* and the English with the Indians were fundamentally the same. Gift-giving was a key part of the initial phase of fur trading for the French as it was for the English, and the bargaining that was so important at Hudson's Bay Company posts was also an element of the *voyageurs'* exchanges. Where the English competed with the French, native traders were able to extract better prices for their furs. And, as was true at Hudson's Bay Company posts, trade was conducted in the language of the natives.

Following the British conquest in the Seven Years War of 1756–1763, control of the St. Lawrence fur trade passed from the French to mainly Scottish merchants operating out of Montreal. The structure of the interior trade, however, remained much the same, as the *voyageurs* continued to be the ones who dealt directly with the native fur traders. In 1779 the Montreal companies formed an association, the North West Company, built new posts, and greatly extended their trading network, even reaching the Rocky Mountains. In

---

23 It might be noted that five years later, brandy's share was considerably higher at York Factory, but still only 10 percent (Carlos and Lewis 2010: 81–85).

Table 15.2 *The value of gifts received at York factory (selected items), 1740*

	Made beaver		Made beaver
Producer goods		Other luxuries	
Flints	51	Baize	12
Guns	70	Beads	24
Hatchets	11	Cloth	123
Knives	28	Gartering	20
Powder	439	Hats	28
Shot	379	Lace	100
Household goods	11	Rings	8
Alcohol	328	Sashes	12
Tobacco	198	Shirts	8
		Trunks	16
		Vermilion	32
		Total (all items)	2,024

Source: Carlos and Lewis 2010: 85–86.

response the Hudson's Bay Company, which previously had done all its trading along the bay coast, set up posts in the interior. In 1821, after forty years of competition, the Hudson's Bay Company and the North West Company merged.[24] With Jay's Treaty and the delineation of the border between the United States and Canada, the North West Company's Mississippi operation was sold to John Jacob Astor's American Fur Company, which became a major competitor.

Gift-giving in the fur trade

Before the trading began, native and company traders, as we noted, participated in a gift-giving ceremony. These ceremonies had been adopted by the Europeans much earlier, when the fur trade was introduced to eastern North America. The Hudson's Bay Company's early ceremonies were modest, but as the price of furs rose in Europe, and French competition in the region increased, gift-giving expanded. Table 15.2 shows the value in made beaver of the gifts distributed at York Factory in 1740. They amounted to 7 percent of value of goods received in trade, and, while the range of goods was similar, there were differences in the composition. Alcohol made up a much larger share, 16 percent rather than 6 percent, and more was received as gunpowder and shot (but not as guns).

24 See Carlos (1986) and Carlos and Hoffman (1986).

Gift-giving between natives and Europeans was similar in form to the exchanges among natives. In substance, though, it was entirely different. Gift-giving in the aboriginal world was reciprocal, involving status and prestige. It was understood that generosity would be compensated in the future. There was no such understanding in the fur trade. Each year it was the Hudson's Bay Company providing the gifts, receiving little in return. Moreover, the value of the gifts increased over time. Meanwhile the natives made clear that their acceptance of the gifts entailed no commitment to return to the posts the following year. They based their decision entirely on what they expected to receive from the company and, where there was French competition, on the gifts and rates of exchange offered by the French. In other words it was the promise of future gifts, along with the expected rates of exchange between goods and furs, that mattered.

Gift-giving also had little impact on the particular goods the Indians ultimately consumed. All goods received as gifts were also purchased in the trading phase. This meant that the relative prices of the goods in the trading phase determined consumption. Figure 15.4 illustrates the choice for alcohol. Where some alcohol is received as gifts, the budget line, B, is truncated, but the optimal consumption point of alcohol, A, is not affected. At York Factory,

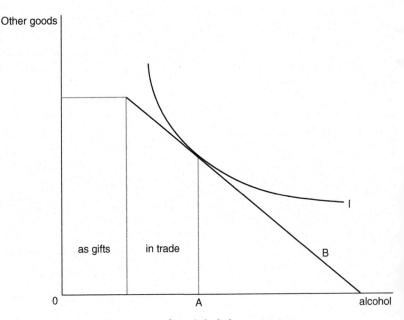

Figure 15.4 Gifts and alcohol consumption

gifts of alcohol varied over time, but, in years where gifts of alcohol increased, the natives correspondingly reduced what they purchased in the trading phase. The gift-giving ceremonies were a necessary adaptation to native culture, but did not materially affect what was purchased in the fur trade.

Native labor and consumption responses

The response of Native Americans to economic incentives has been an important theme in the history and anthropology literature. As archaeologist Robert McGhee (2010: 8) puts it: "Much of aboriginal history . . . tends to treat indigenous societies as so distinctive that comparison with western society is either impossible or at least unproductive." The works of E. E. Rich (1958), preeminent historian of the Hudson's Bay Company, and geographer Arthur Ray (1974), have led to more nuanced interpretations of native behavior (see also Ray and Freeman 1978). Natives faced a different physical environment from Europeans, but their bargaining ability and their choices of trade goods reveal them as remarkably similar in terms of fundamental motivations.

On the question of labor supply to the fur trade, however, views about native behavior have just started to change. In an influential 1960 publication, Rich (1960: 47) laid out what would become the accepted view: "English economic rules did not apply to the Indian trade. On the contrary, all who had any knowledge of the trade were convinced that a rise in prices would lead to the Indians bringing down fewer furs." The origin of Rich's statement was a 1749 Parliamentary Commission report that investigated whether the Hudson's Bay Company should lose its exclusive charter. The felters and hatters of England supported increased competition as a way of raising fur prices to the Indians and increasing the supply of furs. Hudson's Bay Company officials argued instead that raising prices would have the opposite effect. According to these officials the Indians wanted only a given quantity of trade goods, and so higher prices would bring fewer furs. Whether the Parliamentary Commission accepted the argument or made their decision for other reasons, the company was allowed to keep its charter.

A review of the full commission report shows that those witnesses who were currently associated with the Hudson's Bay Company claimed that higher prices would lead to fewer furs, but former employees, who had spent time at Hudson Bay, gave the opposite picture. They said that natives would bring more furs if prices at the posts were higher. During the eighteenth century the company was increasing fur prices at its trading posts, and the pattern of purchases by the natives in terms of the types and quantities of goods is revealing of their response. Figure 15.5 compares the price of furs

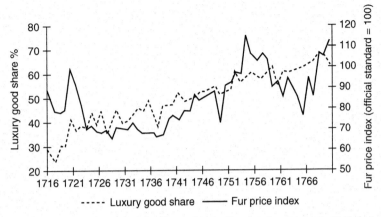

Figure 15.5 The price of furs and the share of expenditure on luxury goods: York factory, 1716–1770

Source: Carlos and Lewis 2010: 146.

at York Factory and the share of native income that was allocated to luxury goods. Over the period 1737/41 to 1766/79, the 40 percent increase in fur prices corresponded to a roughly 50 percent increase in the share of income spent on luxuries, implying a positive, elastic, labor response on the part of natives. The "lazy Indian" view is contradicted by this evidence, and has also been rejected by John Lutz (2008) for the aboriginals of the West Coast.

Much has been written about the influence of alcohol on native society. Peter Mancall's *Deadly Medicine* has documented its destructive effects on natives in the more southerly trade, while Daniel Usner (1987: 178) has addressed its use specifically among the Choctaw, who lived in the southeast. The trade accounts from York Factory, while involving different native groups, offer another perspective on the place of alcohol. In 1740, as shown in Tables 15.1 and 15.2, natives received 412 gallons of alcohol in trade and another 82 gallons in the gift-giving ceremonies. The total, 494 gallons, for the approximately 8,600 natives in the York Factory hinterland, translates to 0.06 gallons per person or four two-ounce drinks per year. Limiting the comparison to adult males, and even more restrictively to those who were directly involved with the fur trade, still gives a picture of natives who drank far less than the British and, even more so, the American colonists. In the 1740s English per capita consumption was 1.4 gallons, and in 1770 North American colonists were consuming 4.2 gallons (Carlos and Lewis 2010: 93). Thus, by the standards of their contemporaries the natives of the Hudson Bay region were abstemious. Alcohol may be a serious problem in many Native American communities today, but in the Hudson Bay region during the early days of the fur trade, alcohol had little impact on native society. The evidence on alcohol is of a piece with the overall composition of the trade and the response of natives to prices. The fur trade was a mechanism for improving their condition.

European trade and native living standards[25]

Richard Steckel and Joseph Prince (2001) argue that the traditional native economy made possible a biological standard of living higher than in Europe. The Indians of the Great Plains, including the Assiniboin, who lived much of the year in the boreal forest south of Hudson Bay, were among the "tallest in the world," a clear indication that they were better nourished. Health-based measures are one approach to living standards, but a comprehensive method requires that we take account of all consumption. In the case of the natives of the Hudson Bay region this includes the variety of goods they obtained through trade.

The great advantage of Native Americans over Europeans in nutrition is illustrated in Table 15.3, which compares the diets of low-wage English workers in the mid eighteenth century with the diets of the natives of the boreal forest. Daily calorific intake was much greater, 3,500 kcal versus 2,500 kcal for adult males, but this gap is a reflection of different energy demands. More revealing is the composition of the diets. Because of the greater meat component, natives consumed much more protein, close to 500 grams per day versus 100 grams per day by the English. English workers derived just 5 percent of their calories from meat, 14 percent if dairy products are included. Their diet was mainly grain based. In contrast, Native Americans obtained nearly all their calories from meat and fish, and most of that came from the flesh of large ungulates, the highest-priced type of food in Europe. This means that a measure of living standards based on food gives natives a decided advantage.

Native clothing, which was made from animal skins that were often decorated, was superior to the low-quality cloth worn by English workers. Budget studies reveal that the cost of English workers' clothing was far less than the value of the deer, caribou, beaver, and other skins that were used in native clothing. On the other hand, natives, because of their nomadic lifestyle, had inferior housing, living in tipis or wigwams in the winter and communal log houses in the summer. And despite the volume of luxury goods they

---

25 Much of this section is based on Carlos and Lewis (2010: Chapter 7).

Table 15.3 *Calorie and protein content of the eighteenth-century diet of English workers and Native Americans (adult males)*

English workers	Budget share percent	Price per calorie meat =1	Calories	Protein (grams)	Native Americans	Calories	Protein (grams)
Bread	22.2	0.34	555	22	Big game	2,500	375
Wheat flour	30.0	0.33	775	32	Other meat and fish	750	100
Oatmeal	14.4	0.22	572	19	Vegetal products	250	
Potatoes	5.6	0.19	249	5			
Beef	3.3	1	29	4			
Mutton	3.3	1	29	4			
Pork	7.8	1	67	5			
Milk	5.6	0.43	110	6			
Butter	4.4	0.59	65	0			
Cheese	3.3	0.59	49	6			
Total	100	0.34	2,500	103		3,500	475

Source: Carlos and Lewis 2010: 172.

received from the fur trade, native purchases of luxuries, especially alcohol, were much less than in England. Arriving at an overall comparison of living standards requires weighting the categories of consumption goods. Weights can be derived from the choices of these eighteenth-century consumers. Where weights corresponding to English budgets are used, natives in the Hudson Bay region are derived to have real incomes between 10 and 25 percent less than English workers. But if native weights are used, the positions are reversed. The real income of natives is 10 to 20 percent higher. The implication is that in the mid eighteenth century Native Americans and low-wage English workers had similar living standards. Richard Salvucci, in Chapter 13 of this volume, argues similarly that at contact the productivity of aboriginals in Mexico was at least the level of the Europeans', and later their per capita incomes were higher.

Our comparison for natives in the Hudson Bay region may, in fact, be understating their relative incomes. Native Americans certainly had inferior housing as measured on a cost basis, but natives, being nomadic, did not require the more substantial dwellings of the Europeans. Moreover, the fact that they spent more time outdoors, and that their population densities were very much less, likely led to a healthier environment. The European diseases, such as smallpox, did not arrive until the late eighteenth century and may not have been as serious as generally reported (Carlos and Lewis 2012). It might also be noted that the greater consumption of luxuries by Europeans, an important element in the comparison, was largely due to their greater use of alcohol. Furthermore, the Hudson Bay region did not include the natives with the highest living standards. Although taller than Europeans, the Assiniboin were shorter on average than Indians of the Great Plains (Steckel and Prince 2001: 289). The natives of the Pacific Northwest had perhaps the highest standards of living as judged by their plentiful supply of fish and their elaborate clothing and artifacts.

Beginning in the late eighteenth century, however, the position of nearly all natives relative to Europeans declined. In the Hudson Bay region dwindling fur and game resources contributed to an absolute decline. But more importantly, a commercial trade based on furs rather than agriculture or manufacturing could not promote long-run economic growth, especially the modern economic growth of Europe and colonial North America. The number of fur-bearing animals was limited by the capacity of their habitat, and so the fur trade could offer no more than the constraints dictated by that habitat.

Conclusion

Modern economies are underpinned by markets, but trade and exchange were central to preindustrial Europe, and also played an important role in the aboriginal societies of North America. Prior to contact or to significant involvement with Europeans, Native Americans had developed exchange mechanisms that allowed them to better deal with their environment. In most of North America the options and advantages of trade were limited. Natives were mainly hunter-gatherers, possibly supplementing their food sources with small-scale farming. They produced similar goods in similar ways, and as a result there was little scope for the comparative advantage that is fundamental to trade. Nevertheless, in regions where hunters and horticulturalists coexisted, trade took place, and exchange over time implied by gift-giving was a feature of nearly all native societies, perhaps allowing their survival. It was a system of lending and borrowing made possible by the understanding, underpinned by custom, that giving was reciprocal. In a world with fluctuating supplies of food and resources, gifts helped natives to equalize consumption, preserve game, and other food resources, and avoid conflict. The potlatch and other forms of gift-giving ceremonies formalized the arrangement.

There was little trade in most of North America, less for cultural reasons than because the gains from trade were limited. The archaeological evidence reveals, however, that there was long-distance trading among aboriginals in some goods, especially those used for hunting. But it was in the areas of high population density that trade was most fully developed. The Chumash of southern California lived in close proximity but included groups with access to very different resources. The result was a trade complex enough to require the use of money. The Chumash, who lived on the Channel Islands, responded by producing bead strings which served that function. The Chumash exchanged a wide range of goods, and their trading extended to natives who lived far in the interior. Moreover, just as preference for variety is a feature of modern trade, so it was among the Chumash, who traded among themselves similar but not identical goods.

The arrival of Europeans led to conflict in some regions, but in many areas where beaver were present, trade offered the natives access to new hunting technologies and more consumption options. Meanwhile the Europeans, both English and French, had open to them a new source of furs. They responded with arrangements for transporting the trade goods and furs, and they established effective trading mechanisms that adapted to native practice. These included the introduction of gift-giving and the learning of native languages. The aboriginals also adapted, becoming effective bargainers and traders.

Trade among aboriginal peoples and trade between aboriginals and Europeans was a response to the potential for mutual gain. The goods they consumed were different, their technologies were different, and their institutional arrangements were different; but the nature of the exchanges and the ways the groups responded to their opportunities were, fundamentally, very much the same.

References

Allen, R. A. (1956). "The Potlatch and Social Equilibrium," *Davidson Journal of Anthropology* 2: 43–54.

Aubet, M. E. (2001). *The Phoenicians and the West: Politics, Colonies, and Trade*, 2nd edn. New York: Cambridge University Press.

Balikci, A. (1989). *The Netsilik Eskimo*. Prospect Heights, IL: Waveland Press.

Bamforth, D. B. (2011). "Origin Stories, Archaeological Evidence, and Post-Clovis Paleoindian Bison Hunting on the Great Plains," *American Antiquity* 76: 24–40.

Barnett, H. G. (1938). *The Nature and the Function of the Potlatch*. Eugene: University of Oregon Press.

Baugh, T. G. and J. E. Ericson, eds. (1994). *Prehistoric Exchange Systems in North America.* New York: Plenum Press.

Bourque, B. J. (1994). "Evidence for Prehistoric Exchange on the Maritime Peninsula," in T. G. Baugh and J. E. Ericson (eds.), *Prehistoric Exchange Systems in North America.* New York: Plenum Press, pp. 23–46.

Bracken, C. (1997). *The Potlatch Papers: A Colonial Case History.* University of Chicago Press.

Broda, C. and D. Weinstein (2006). "Globalization and the Gains from Variety," *Quarterly Journal of Economics* 121: 541–585.

Carlos, A. M. (1986). *The North American Fur Trade, 1804–1821: A Study in the Life Cycle of a Duopoly.* American Business History Series, ed. Stuart Bruchey. New York: Garland Publishing.

Carlos, A. M. and E. Hoffman (1986). "The Making of a Joint Profit-Maximizing Contract by a Duopoly: A Case Study from the North American Fur Trade, 1804–1821," *Journal of Economic History* 46: 967–986.

Carlos, A. M. and F. D. Lewis (2010). *Commerce by a Frozen Sea: Native Americans and the European Fur Trade.* Philadelphia: University of Pennsylvania Press.

(2012). "Smallpox and Native American Mortality: The 1780s Epidemic in the Hudson Bay Region," *Explorations in Economic History* 49: 277–290.

Carlson, R. L. (1987). "Prehistoric Trade," in R. Cole Harris (ed.), *Historical Atlas of Canada,* Vol. I. University of Toronto Press, plate 14.

Curtin, P. D. (1975). *Economic Change in Precolonial Africa: Senegambia in the Era of the Slave Trade.* Madison, WI: University of Wisconsin Press.

Gamble, L. H. (2008). *The Chumash World at European Contact: Power, Trade, and Feasting among Complex Hunter-Gatherers.* Berkeley: University of California Press.

Graeber, D. (2011). *Debt: The First 5,000 Years.* New York: Melville House Publishing.

Gregory, C. (1982). *Gifts and Commodities.* London: Academic Press.

Johnsen, D. B. (1986). "The Formation and Protection of Property Rights among the Southern Kwakiutl Indians," *Journal of Legal Studies* 15: 41–68.

King, C. D. (1971). "Chumash Inter-Village Economic Exchange," *The Indian Historian* 4: 31–43. Reprinted in L. Bean and T. Blackburn (eds.), *Native Californians: A Theoretical Retrospective.* Ramona, CA: Ballena Press, pp. 289–318.

(1978). "Protohistoric and Historic Archaeology," in *Handbook of North American Indians.* Vol. VIII: *California,* ed. Robert Heizer. Washington, DC: Smithsonian Institution, pp. 58–68.

Krugman, P. (1979). "Increasing Returns, Monopolistic Competition, and International Trade," *Journal of International Economics* 9: 469–479.

Lutz, J. S. (2008). *Makúk: A New History of Aboriginal-White Relations.* Vancouver: UBC Press.

Mauss, M. (2002). *The Gift: Forms and Functions of Exchange in Archaic Societies.* New York: Routledge.

Mancall, P. C. (1995). *Deadly Medicine: Indians and Alcohol in Early America.* Ithaca: Cornell University Press.

Markusen, J. R. (1981). "Trade and the Gains from Trade with Imperfect Competition," *Journal of International Economics* 11: 531–551.

McGhee, R. (2010). "Demythologizing the Fur Trade: A Review of Commerce by a Frozen Sea," *Literary Review of Canada* 18: 7–8.

Miquelon, D. (1987). *New France, 1701–1744: "A Supplement to Europe,"* The Canadian Centenary Series. Toronto: McClelland and Stewart.

Piddocke, S. (1965). "The Potlatch System of the Southern Kwakiutl: A New Persepctive," *Southwestern Journal of Anthropology* 21: 244–264.

Polanyi, K. (1957). "The Economy as Instituted Process." in K. Polanyi, C. Arensberg, and H. Pearson (eds.), *Trade and Market in the Early Empires: Economies in History and Theory*, Glencoe, IL: The Free Press, pp. 243–269.

Ray, A. J. (1974). *Indians in the Fur Trade: Their Role as Hunters, Trappers and Middlemen in the Lands Southwest of Hudson Bay, 1660–1870.* University of Toronto Press.

(1987). "Bayside Trade, 1720–1780," in R. Cole Harris (ed.), *Historical Atlas of Canada*, Vol. 1. University of Toronto Press, plate 60.

Ray, A. J. and D. Freeman (1978). *"Give Us Good Measure": An Economic Analysis of Relations Between the Indians and the Hudson's Bay Company Before 1763.* University of Toronto Press.

Rich, E. E. (1958). *Hudson's Bay Company 1670–1870*, 2 vols. London: Hudson's Bay Record Society.

(1960). "Trade Habits and Economic Motivation among the Indians of North America," *Canadian Journal of Economics and Political Science* 26: 35–53.

Scott, J. (2009). *The Art of Not Bring Governed: An Anarchist History of Upland Southeast Asia.* New Haven: Yale University Press.

Steckel, R. H. and J. M. Prince (2001). "Tallest in the World: Native Americans of the Great Plains in the Nineteenth Century," *American Economic Review* 91: 287–294.

Stewart, M. R. (1994). "Late Archaic through Late Woodland Exchange in the Middle Atlantic Region," in T. G. Baugh and J. E. Ericson (eds.), *Prehistoric Exchange Systems in North America.* New York: Plenum Press, pp. 73–98.

Usner, D. H. Jr. (1987). "The Frontier Exchange Economy of the Lower Mississippi Valley in the Eighteenth Century," *William and Mary Quarterly*, 3rd Series, 44: 165–192.

White, R. (1991). *The Middle Ground: Indians, Empires, and Republics in the Great Lakes Region, 1650–1815.* New York: Cambridge University Press.

Wien, T. (1990). "Selling Beaver Skins in North America and Europe, 1720–1760: The Uses of Fur Trade Imperialism," *Journal of the Canadian Historical Association* 1: 293–317.

Williams, G., ed. (1969). *Andrew Graham's Observations on Hudson's Bay, 1767–1791.* London: Hudson's Bay Record Society.

Winterhalder, B. (1997). "Gifts Given, Gifts Taken: The Behavioral Ecology of Nonmarket, Intragroup Exchange," *Journal of Archaeological Research* 5: 121–167.

Wood, W. R. (1980), "Plains Trade in Prehistoric and Protohistoric Intertribal Relations," in W. Raymond Wood and Margot Liberty (eds.), *Anthropology on the Great Plains.* Lincoln: University of Nebraska Press, pp. 98–109.

Wright, J. V. (1994). "The Prehistoric Transportation of Goods in the St. Lawrence River Basin," in T. G. Baugh and J. E. Ericson (eds.), *Prehistoric Exchange Systems in North America.* New York: Plenum Press, pp. 47–71.

16

British and European industrialization

C. KNICK HARLEY

Modern economic growth – the simultaneous doubling of income and population in fifty or seventy years – has been capitalism's greatest triumph. It first became apparent in Britain in the mid-nineteenth century and spread to America and continental Europe. Modern growth did not, however, spread elsewhere and a great divergence developed between income per capita in the few leaders and the rest (Figure 16.1).

It is common to attribute modern growth to the factory-based industrialization that emerged from British inventions in textile production and steam power in the later eighteenth century – the industrial revolution, represented dramatically by the patents of both Richard Arkwright's water frame for the mechanical spinning of cotton thread and James Watt's improved steam engine in 1769. These inventions created an explosion of urban factory-based industry, particularly in textiles, that made Britain the "workshop of the world" by the 1850s. By that time British factories provided some two-thirds of the world's output of "new technology industries" (Bairoch 1982: 288). Growth seemed to be the product of novel urban factory-manufacturing and the social changes that it brought about. Marx and Engels, starting with the *Communist Manifesto* in 1848, put forward a forceful theory of economic growth in which "the class of modern capitalists, owners of the means of social production and employers of wage labor," occupy center stage as the agents of disruptive but productive change (Marx and Engels 1848: Chapter 1). The spread of modern economic growth is usually seen as the spread of the British factory system to continental Europe and America. Marx remarked "the country that is more developed industrially only shows, to the less developed, the image of its own future" (Marx 1867: ix). Economic historians, however, now question the closeness of the connection between urban factory industrialization and the emergence of modern economic growth. Estimates of overall income show a modest connection with the famous industrial breakthroughs. Britain was already relatively rich when the industrial revolution

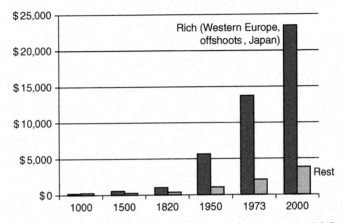

Figure 16.1 Great Divergence 1000–2000 (per capita GDP, 1990 international dollars)
Source: Maddison 2007.

occurred and the innovations that created urban factory industrialization were the product of an already advanced economy. Similarly, incomes in continental Europe in the nineteenth century are not well explained by adoption or non-adoption of the technology that Britain pioneered.

The emergence of Britain's modern economic growth depended more on a long history of capitalism than on the industrial revolution. That capitalism occurred in large measure in enterprises of modest scale and created institutions – particularly markets – that supported efficient allocation, and reallocation, of resources and provided incentives consistent with wealth accumulation and innovation. As Chapter 1 pointed out, the displacement of custom and command with durable and long-lasting markets was potentially of key importance. Goods and factor markets were well established in late medieval Britain and Holland and persisted through the following centuries. These societies developed an economic lead that was apparent by the sixteenth century and rested on agricultural productivity and efficient service industries as much as on industrialization. The emergence of growth in continental Europe in the nineteenth century depended less on the spread of British-style industrialization and more on the spread of British-type capitalism and the institutions that supported it. Rising productivity across the economy created growth; excessive concentration on the spread of factory manufacturing overlooks much of a broader process.

The British industrial revolution

Estimates of aggregate economic activity underlie understanding of the beginnings of modern economic growth. Early quantitative analysis of the growth of British national income appeared to support the traditional view of late eighteenth-century inventions creating an industrial revolution (Deane and Cole 1967; Hoffmann 1955). Deane and Cole's systematic use of the early censuses to estimate national income showed that per capita income accelerated during the industrial revolution. Revision of the aggregate estimates since, however, has questioned sudden aggregate change arising from great factories of industrial capitalists. Some historians, most notably Sir John Clapham, who also drew on census data on occupations, had earlier questioned the representativeness of the new factory industries and the impact they had on the fundamental issue of raising standards of living (Clapham 1926). Using the Deane and Cole income estimates, D. N. McCloskey published a revealing calculation that suggested that technological advances in the "new technology industries" were insufficient to explain the acceleration of national income and concluded that technological change had become pervasive in early nineteenth-century Britain, although it was still slow by twentieth-century standards (McCloskey 1981: 114).

Views of a broader process of change and a revision of the timing of change were strongly supported when scholars revisited the pioneering estimates in the mid 1980s and concluded that Hoffmann and Deane and Cole unconsciously exaggerated the discontinuity in the final decades on the eighteenth century. Harley pointed out that Hoffmann's estimate of industrial production dealt with the incomplete coverage of manufacturing industries with an implicit assumption that other industries, in aggregate approximately the size of cotton textiles, shared cotton's exceptional growth following Arkwright's inventions (Harley 1982). Crafts re-examined Deane and Cole extrapolation of nineteenth-century census data into the eighteenth century and their conversion of estimates of income in current prices into real income and concluded that aggregate growth was substantially slower between 1770 and 1840 (Crafts 1976, 1985). The difference between the Deane and Cole estimate of real per capita income and the Crafts–Harley revisions is illustrated in Figure 16.2. Slower growth in the late eighteenth and early nineteenth centuries implied that eighteenth-century Britain must have already been richer than we had previously thought and that nineteenth-century income levels depended less on the famous technological breakthroughs (the shaded years are the conventional dating of the Industrial Revolution).

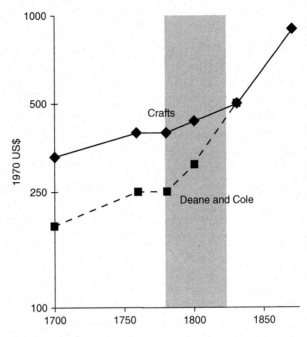

Figure 16.2 British national income, 1700–1870
Source: Crafts (1976); Deane and Cole (1967).

Research (initially spearheaded by historians of the Asian economies (Parthasarathi 1998; Pomerantz 2001) has also placed British and European economic growth in a broader framework. Multinational comparisons of economic performance are tricky even when data are extensive and much harder in data-scarce historical circumstances. However, labor income makes up the majority of national income. It can also be reasonably argued that the well-being of ordinary people is the best indicator of societal well-being and their income is almost entirely labor income. It is also the case that labor income is the most readily available component of historical income because corporate, public, and private bodies whose archives make up most of the historical record regularly hired wage labor. Scholars have collected this material for the earlier developers and increasingly for later-developing societies. The records are, of course, not perfect indicators of societal well-being particularly as in many societies only a small part of labor income passed through organized labor markets. Nonetheless, wage data deflated by indicators of the cost of living provide us with significant insights into historical economic performance.

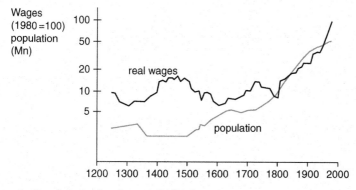

Figure 16.3 Population and real wages: England, 1250–1980
Sources: Clark 2005; McEvedy *et al.* 1978; Wrigley and Schofield 1989.

Prior to the nineteenth century, the balance between population and resources was the prime determinant of real wages. Figure 16.3 shows this clearly in the case of England. The fourteenth-century Black Death which killed off over one-third of the population resulted in a dramatic increase in real wages. Real wages declined to near pre-plague levels when the population eventually recovered, beginning at the end of the fourteenth century. Slower population growth after 1650 led to a rise of wages that ended in the mid eighteenth century when population growth resumed. Only after the first quarter of the nineteenth century did increases in real wages accompany continued population growth – a transformation to modern economic growth which reinforces traditional narratives of transformation at the end of the eighteenth century.

Placing England's experience in the context of other European regions, however, reveals a different picture (Allen 2001). The Malthusian fall in real wages of the fifteenth century occurred throughout Europe but by the sixteenth century another dynamic appeared. In the North Sea economies – the Low Countries and England – real wages declined significantly less than elsewhere and in the early seventeenth century wages began to grow. This phenomenon, which Allen called the great divergence in European wages and Jan Luiten van Zanden the "little divergence" (to distinguish it from the great divergence between developed economies and the rest) directs attention to a period well before the classical industrial revolution.

Wage data are not as extensively available outside Europe and its offshoots but research is beginning to fill the gaps (Allen 2001; Allen *et al.* 2011). Preliminary results show that in the eighteenth century real wages in major Asian cities were comparable to those in most of Europe, with the important exception of the

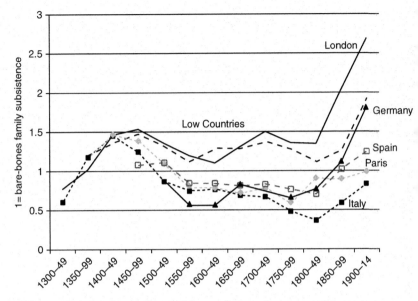

Figure 16.4 Urban real wage Europe, laborers, fourteenth to twentieth centuries
Source: Allen 2001.

North Sea economies. European wages generally started to trend upwards in the nineteenth century but Asian wages declined until mid century and fell behind those in all but the poorest areas in Europe. The wage data challenge most economic historians' supposition that European incomes generally were superior to those in Asia in the early modern period and those who have postulated general features of European society as causes of modern economic growth. Perhaps we should not be surprised, however. Allen found that in most of Europe an unskilled laborer's real earnings fell in early modern times to below levels needed to support a modest family on the cheapest diet available (the unit on the vertical axis of Figure 16.4 is the cost of supporting a family of a man, a wife and two small children on a bare subsistence diet primarily of oatmeal gruel or its equivalent).

Although long-run comparative data have made it clear that we need to take a longer and broader view of the process of industrialization, the industrial revolution between 1770 and 1840 remains important. The famous new technologies did not, in and of themselves, transform the economy, but they were early manifestations of the acceleration of the rate of technological change that characterizes modern growth. Most inventive activity undoubtedly arises from conscious search, and successful technological improvement seldom emerges fully formed but rather requires expensive continuing research and development. Market conditions in late eighteenth-century Britain greatly increased the likelihood that new technologies that saved labor with machinery, mechanical power sources, and mineral fuels would occur there rather than elsewhere.

First, as we have seen, British workers earned higher wages than workers elsewhere (the Low Countries excepted). Second, only in Britain had coal been extensively mined and technologies for its use as residential and industrial fuel evolved (Allen 2009b; Hatcher 1993; Nef 1932). Consequently, British manufacturers chose cost-minimizing techniques that used capital and energy to save labor, and British research and development had a machinery-using, fuel-intensive starting point. Elsewhere there was much less incentive to explore possibilities of this sort because firms were not currently employing coal-using and labor-saving techniques. In addition, outside of Britain small improvements that used capital and fuel to save labor would not lower costs of production. It is hardly surprising, then, that the breakthroughs in machine-based cotton spinning, steam engines, and coke-iron production were British (Allen 2009b, 2010).

Of course, the innovations in machine-based cotton spinning, steam engines, and coke iron production were not small improvements but massive breakthroughs. Arkwright's water frame – the most spectacular – reduced the price of coarse cotton yarn to about a third of its mid-eighteenth-century price by the early nineteenth century and the price of finer yarn by much more (Harley 1998); Watt's steam engine revolutionized power supply; Cort's puddling-furnace and rolling-mill made coke production of wrought iron on a large scale profitable. Nonetheless, these changes modified existing practices adapted to high wages and cheap energy. While there seems to be no a priori reason to think that capital-intensive and energy-using techniques were more likely to generate technological breakthroughs than other techniques, it appears that for the past two centuries technological change has mostly clustered around improvements of techniques used in rich economies that employed capital, energy, and raw materials intensively (Allen 2011). It is unclear whether this reflects the nature of possible technical improvement or identifies technologically advanced societies with advanced engineering skills and advanced capacity for innovation, and consequently high income levels.

The argument that machine technology emerged from a conscious search process undertaken by entrepreneurs experienced in using capital-intensive methods because they operated with expensive labor and cheap energy seems compelling. As an explanation as to how and why economies entered into the era of modern economic growth, however, it is unsatisfactory. Crudely, Allen argues that Britain became richer in the nineteenth century because it was already rich in the eighteenth. This is likely true, but it begs the basic question: why was eighteenth-century Britain rich? Just as national income estimates and comparative real wages drive us to consider earlier developments, so does the search for the sources of the technology of the British industrial revolution.

British prosperity: productive agriculture

Nineteenth-century international comparisons provide insights into the sources of Britain's development leadership. The common perception is that economic advancement arose from superior productivity in modern manufacturing but when data allow comparison in the nineteenth century, Britain, although it pioneered the industrial revolution and developed a much larger manufacturing sector than its rivals, does not have much higher output per worker in manufacturing than France or Germany. Patrick O'Brien and C. Keyder (1978) in their reinterpretation of French economic growth, estimated that labor productivity in French industry exceeded that in Britain during the first half of the nineteenth century by between 10 and 40 percent. These estimates may overstate the French achievement but Britain had little or no lead in industrial labor productivity (Crafts 1984a). Nonetheless, Maddison estimates French per capita income for 1830 at barely over two-thirds the British level and Allen reports real wages in Paris as between half and three-quarters of those in London. Similarly, comparison with Germany for later in the century yields similar results. Stephen Broadberry estimated that labor productivity in German manufacturing in 1871 was 93 percent of British manufacturing productivity even though GDP per worker was only 60 percent (Broadberry 1997).

A main determinant of Britain's higher per capita income was much higher productivity in agriculture. Low agricultural productivity characterized Europe outside the Low Countries. In Britain around 1840 (at a per capita income level of about $550, 1970 US dollars) the share of the labor force (25 percent) and the share of income (24.9 percent) in agriculture and extraction were very nearly equal. The average European experience at that income was an agricultural labor force share of 54 percent and an income share of 37 percent. This implies that while output per worker in British agriculture was about the same as in the rest of the economy, the European norm of labor productivity in agriculture was only half of that elsewhere (Crafts 1984b, 1985). Broadberry finds that German agricultural productivity was 56 percent of British in 1870. The gap between agricultural productivity in Britain and the continent (outside the

Low Countries) appeared between the early seventeenth century and the mid eighteenth century, well before the industrial revolution (Allen 2000).

The distinctive, highly capitalistic nature of British agriculture appears to have generated high productivity. In most of western Europe the typical farm was a peasant operation with customary tenancy and family control of farm operations and labor input. In contrast the typical British farmer was an entrepreneur who rented land from a landowner, provided the farm's working capital, and employed hired labor (Shaw-Taylor 2005, 2012; Caird 1852). In older views improving landlords and enclosure of the open fields drove British agricultural change but research has firmly established that in the seventeenth and eighteenth centuries yeoman farmers on modest size farms initiated and adopted productivity enhancing changes in open-field villages as well as on enclosed farms (Allen 1992, 1999, 2009b, Chapter 3). Underlying driving forces cannot be firmly established but British agriculture's high level of market orientation, both in selling its produce and in organizing its inputs, played a key role. This market orientation was long-standing, going back to medieval times and reinforced in the aftermath of the Black Death.

Robert Brenner's theory on the origin and nature of British agricultural precocity based in theories of capitalism provides a useful framework (Aston and Philpin 1987; Brenner 1976; Pamuk 2007). He saw capitalist farming evolve from late medieval class struggles. In Britain, the feudal elite became landlords with large land holdings and secure property rights. At the same time, all vestiges of medieval servile labor – where serfs were required to work on the lord's demesne – disappeared. Markets replaced customary and power relationships. Landlords had to compete for tenants to farm their land and tenants depended on the market for access to land. A regular agricultural wage labor market developed, particularly for young adults. Farmers who increased productivity were able to offer higher rents, hire labor, and increase the size of their operations while less successful farmers gradually became wage laborers without the option of remaining family workers on customary tenancies.

In contrast, in most of Western Europe, particularly in France and western Germany, late medieval change abolished un-free feudal labor, but failed to provide elites with clear property rights. Instead, direct agricultural producers gained control of the land on customary tenures from which they could be removed only with difficulty. The elites integrated into state structures and extracted resources through taxation. Incentives to increased productivity were much weaker than in England. Landowners had little opportunity to select successful tenants to increase rental incomes. Less successful farmers did not depend on a rental market for access to land. Consequently, it was much more difficult for successful farmers to acquire larger holdings and less productive peasants were much less likely to be forced into wage labor. Customary relationships remained strong and family workers tended to remain on agricultural holdings when marginal product fell below wages elsewhere in the economy because they had access to a share of the returns of the family agricultural holding.

The dating of the dominance of capitalist agriculture in Britain and its relationship to productivity advance is a matter of some dispute. The best-documented evidence of the evolution of efficiency and agricultural structure comes from R. C. Allen's study of the south Midlands (Allen 1992, 1999). He shows that the most impressive gains in agricultural productivity occurred between 1600 and 1750. Although he argues that these were the product of the family farm, his evidence shows the importance of capitalist agriculture. He defines three farm categories: peasant farms of less than 60 acres relying on family labor; capitalist farms over 100 acres, where hired labor dominated the workforce; a transitional category completed the taxonomy. In the south Midlands in the early seventeenth century, enclosures occupied about 17.5 percent of all land and 90 percent of this was in farms over a hundred acres (although most of this was in very large holdings that may have been sublet). In open-field villages land was approximately evenly divided among the three classes of farm size. Overall, farms over a hundred acres occupied a little over 40 percent of all land and the other classes under 30 percent each. By the early eighteenth century the proportion of enclosed land had nearly doubled to about a third of the total. The dominance of large farms on enclosed land had declined somewhat but they still occupied nearly three-quarters of the land. Large farms gained ground in open-field villages where they now occupied over half the land. Overall, large farms occupied nearly 60 percent of the land in the south Midlands around 1700. Medium sized farms that employed labor on a continuous basis occupied another 20 percent of the land. Peasant families on the French model where the decision margin regarding the use of labor was the peasant patrimony and not the labor market formed only the remaining 20 percent of the land (Allen 1992: 31, 73).

Recently, Leigh Shaw-Taylor has examined Allen's conclusion. He confirms that the data from the south Midlands appear representative of the English heartland, although it cannot hold for all of England. He also finds that capitalist farming reached smaller farms than Allen supposed. The majority of farms between 20 and 30 acres in Buckinghamshire reported to the 1851 census that they employed at least one male worker on 31 March, a slack date in the agricultural calendar (Shaw-Taylor 2005). He finds that "in 1700 small-scale capitalism predominated in the south-east with three-quarters of the adult male agricultural workforce being proletarian" (Shaw-Taylor 2012: 57).

It is perhaps strange that capitalist farming arose so strongly in England since in the early middle ages (eleventh and twelfth centuries) feudal manorialism, where elites held nonmarket rights to labor of the agricultural population, was particularly strongly entrenched. In contrast, in the Low Countries, where capitalist agriculture and high productivity also emerged, manorialism was never strong. Productive agriculture in both parts of the North Sea economy emerged in conjunction with well-organized markets for factors of production (land, labor, and capital). Product markets in peasant economies are common and developed in most parts of medieval Europe. Markets for occasional labor are also common but very unusually a labor market emerged in the North Sea economies that played a primary role in labor allocation.

The underlying determinants of labor market development are hard to trace but it seem associated with another unusual feature of northwestern Europe – the early emergence of the European marriage pattern where newly married couples established a new household independent of the previous generation. The marriage union was consensual and brides were much older than typical in other societies. In late sixteenth-century England brides were typically about twenty five and grooms two or three years older. Elsewhere, marriages were usually arranged by parents, new couples integrated into families of the preceding generation and teenage brides typically married substantially older men. In late medieval England and the Low Countries young men and women left their parental home in their early teens to work for wages, usually in agriculture. They accumulated resources for about a decade and established independent households on marriage. Wage labor markets became well established, with young men and women forming the majority of participants. There is uncertainty as to the exact timing and extent of this market. Christopher Dyer has estimated that in fourteenth-, fifteenth-, and sixteenth-century England just under half the population was active in the labor market (and probably more in the most commercialized areas of the southeast) (Dyer 2005: 218–220). In the most advanced parts of the Low Countries estimates have up to 60 percent of the population dependent on wage labor (De Moor and van Zanden 2010; van Zanden 2009).

Markets for the sale and leasing of land also developed in late medieval Europe, first in Italy and then in the North Sea economies (although England's strong manorial tradition delayed its emergence somewhat). Modern short-term competitive leasing systems developed in parts of the Low Countries in the fourteenth and fifteenth centuries and perhaps a century later in England (van Bavel 2008).

The precocious allocation of labor to manufacturing

A substantial portion of the English labor force was employed in manufacturing well before the industrial revolution. Deane and Cole's path-breaking quantitative assessment relied heavily on the social tables that Gregory King constructed about 1690 as a starting point. They tentatively concluded that agriculture employed somewhere between 60 and 80 percent of the labor force (Deane and Cole 1967: 137). Indispensable as he was as a starting point, King painted a misleading picture: "a nation consisting of just London and a vast, poor agricultural hinterland ... England and Wales were almost surely more industrial and commercial than he has led us to believe" (Lindert 1980: 707). Peter Lindert and Jeffrey Williamson modified this view (Lindert 1980; Lindert and Williamson 1982, 1983) suggesting that in King's time 56 percent of the labor force was in the primary sector (agriculture), 18 percent in the secondary (manufacturing) and 26 percent in the tertiary sector (services). In this picture Britain was still a highly agricultural economy (Crafts 1985).

The Cambridge University Group for the History of Population and Social Structure (Shaw-Taylor et al. 2010) are currently re-estimating eighteenth-century occupational structure on the basis of information in a large number of baptismal records. Their preliminary results indicate that considerably fewer English men worked in agriculture, and considerably more worked in manufacturing than even Lindert and Williamson's work suggested. The new estimates for about 1710 show that agriculture and mining employed about 43 percent of the occupied male population and manufacturing employed 39 percent. Over the next century, the share of the labor force in agriculture declined only modestly to about 39 percent while the secondary sector's share increased to only 42 percent. These results strongly reinforce the conclusion that Britain was already well on the way to becoming a modern economy at the beginning of the eighteenth century.

Although the great late eighteenth-century innovations in textiles and in iron contributed to rising real incomes by lowering the costs of these products they do not seem to have greatly increased the proportion of the labor force in manufacturing. However, manufacturing concentrated geographically. In the early eighteenth century secondary-sector employment was widely distributed. The proportion of males in the sector in the northern counties (47 percent) was higher than in the agriculturally advantaged southern counties, but the southern proportion was still 39 percent. By the early nineteenth century, industrial employment had concentrated on a crescent of counties running from the West Riding of Yorkshire through Lancashire then south and west to Glamorgan in South Wales. In southern counties, the proportion of manufacturing workers had declined by more than a quarter to 28 percent while in the north, principally in Lancashire and the West Riding, they had increased by close to 62 percent. The bulk of southern deindustrialization occurred in textiles. Male employment in clothing manufacture also declined significantly, presumably due to the rise of ready-made clothing manufacture in the east Midlands and a feminization of the trade (Shaw-Taylor *et al.* 2010). A second factor was replacement of charcoal-based iron production by coal-based technology that drew the industry to the coalfields.

Britain was already substantially an industrialized economy by the early eighteenth century. Manufacturing was widely dispersed and production units were still small. They nonetheless clearly produced for the market and were subject to competitive pressure. Textiles, clothing, leather processing, food and drink processing, and construction were by far the largest sectors, accounting for over three-quarters of manufacturing in the mid eighteenth century (Harley 1982). Metal workers produced a wide variety of hardware and trinkets for consumer markets as well as tools for agriculture, construction, and manufacturing. The high level of manufacturing production was a consequence of the relatively high income levels. Efficient agriculture released labor and there was consumer demand – even building laborers' incomes provided a margin above subsistence and artisans could afford modest luxuries including imported groceries, particularly sugar, tea, and tobacco, and modest amounts of manufactured goods. The well-to-do, including a rising middle class, probably still constituted the major consumer market for manufactured goods.

Exports contributed importantly to Britain's industrialization. Crafts calculated that exports made up about 45 percent of manufactured output in 1801 (Crafts 1985: 127). Exports of woolen cloth to European markets completely dominated British exports until the early eighteenth century. Manufactured goods continued to dominate exports during the eighteenth century but important diversification occurred. By the third quarter of the eighteenth century exports to the Americas nearly equaled exports to Europe and were widely diversified with woolen cloth only a little over a quarter while metal products made up nearly 20 percent and miscellaneous manufactured goods were nearly as important as woolens (Davis 1962, 1979).

Competitive imperial expansion and mercantilism characterized the eighteenth-century Atlantic economy. Britain and France, and to a lesser extent the Netherlands, challenged Spain's imperial claims and established colonies in the Caribbean and the English developed colonies on the North

American mainland. The colonial economies revolved around export staples (principally sugar but also tobacco in the English Chesapeake Bay) produced by African slaves. Mercantilist regulation reserved the trade of each imperial power to its own subjects. In the mercantile contest the English did better than their rivals in developing markets for manufactured exports. Success did not arise from superior colonies in the Caribbean – the British islands were high-cost sugar producers, unable to compete with the rapidly growing output of French Saint Dominique without protection, and their prosperity depended on English consumers paying higher sugar prices to support them. Nor were the English colonies particularly large compared to their rivals. What differentiated the British empire was the large population in the settler colonies of the mainland who had been drawn, at least outside the Chesapeake, not by an export staple but by the prospect of establishing an independent existence in a new land.

The settlers succeeded and population grew rapidly. By the third quarter of the seventeenth century, some 60 percent of English manufactured exports to the Americas went to the mainland colonies (Davis 1979). These colonials financed their imports by selling temperate agricultural and forest products to the sugar islands and providing mercantile and shipping services. In this way the English paid for their sugar imports with manufactured goods exports. To what extent, then, did the growth of English manufactured exports depend on West Indian slavery? Certainly slave products ultimately financed exports to America. However, the answer to the more interesting question of whether those exports would have existed if slavery had not is less clear. The mainland colonies flourished largely independently of slavery. Englishmen probably would have settled and population grown rapidly even if the West Indian slave colonies had not existed. They would still have demanded European industrial goods. Without opportunities in the West Indies, they would have had to find other ways of financing imports that were inferior to those they used and imports would have been smaller, but it is likely that they would have remained substantial and helped to sustain Britain's precocious industrialization.

Conclusions on Britain's industrialization

Britain's industrialization had deep roots; produced in an already well-developed capitalist economy that had long been mediated by markets. Product markets developed well before the Black Death. They may have retreated somewhat with population decline but remained substantial and expanded when the population recovered in the sixteenth century. More importantly and more unusually, late medieval markets for factors of production were also well established. In early modern England most land was held in market contracts. In addition, most English men and women experienced a labor market in the countryside or in towns. Agriculture was unusually productive, probably because of its capitalist organization. The land rental market allowed successful farmers to expand while their less successful rivals lost land. In the early seventeenth century family labor remained important on most English farms but most of the acreage farmed employed hired labor. Under these circumstances, labor decisions were made with reference to a labor market. Feudal relationships had long since disappeared. There was no significant class of peasant cultivators – at least in the sense of small farms that had customary or ownership rights to their land, which were only tangentially involved in the product market, and organized their labor independently of labor markets.

The penetration of markets resulted in what economic historians have come to refer to as "Smithian growth" following Adam Smith's observation that specialization and productivity advance was limited by the extent of the market. Smith recognized three growth-inducing processes: specialization and exchange that exploits comparative advantage; capital accumulation; and technological improvement. These can all be seen in Britain by the eighteenth century. Agricultural improvement was stimulated by market opportunities, presented most conspicuously by the growth of London as a trading, administration, production, and consumption center. Modern industrialization is often seen as a process that substitutes mineral sources of power for pre-modern sources based on human and animal muscle and wood, all of which are limited by agricultural resources. Britain developed coal as a source of power and fuel long before the late eighteenth-century industrialization. Englishmen had been learning how to use coal from at least the seventeenth century (Allen 2009a, 2009b; Hatcher 1993; Nef 1932). Builders experimented in the use of coal for domestic heating and by the eighteenth century Newcastle coal heated London houses. Coal also provided heat for many industrial processes from brewing beer to refining copper. Iron masters experimented in using coal but chemical problems remained unsolved until the end of the eighteenth century. Within textile production, the largest pre-modern manufacturing industry, large numbers of merchant manufacturers, many immigrants from warfare in the Low Countries and religious intolerance in France and others inspired by continental examples developed new techniques and fabrics (the so-called New Draperies).

In this view of British development, which rests on statistical analysis, long-run international comparisons of standards of living, and a long view of institutions and innovation, it appears inappropriate to overemphasize the famous decades of the 1760s and 1770s and the achievements of Arkwright, Watt, and Cort. There are two perspectives that are worth reviewing. First, how much did the inventions contribute to economic growth? Here statistical analysis shows that the impact was limited. More importantly, did these developments mark the start of an era of faster and more sustained technological change? By current standards technological change and growth of living standards before the nineteenth century were so slow as to be barely noticeable. Growth, mainly driven by technological change, accelerated in the middle of the nineteenth century to eventually reach twentieth-century levels of about 1 percent per year (Crafts 2004a; Crafts and Harley 1992; Crafts and Mills 2009). Although the technological change in textiles in the late eighteenth and early nineteenth centuries was rapid and had the highly visible impact of enlarging an already large textile sector and concentrating it in urban factories, its impact on overall growth was modest. The innovations of the late eighteenth century can be seen as the result of a sustained research and development program that extended existing ideas in a high-wage environment; the inventions fit within a longer continuum of Smithian growth.

Arkwright transformed and concentrated Britain's largest manufacturing sector in a manner that caught the attention of contemporaries and historians but did not greatly increase aggregate growth. Nonetheless, the successful application of mechanical manipulation ("clock work") on a large scale and the development of the factory as a primary locus of production marked important steps in the evolution of technology. Cotton factories stimulated the development of specialist machine producers who became a locus of improved technology (Rosenberg 1994). That said, however, it is hard to see fundamental changes emerging from the textile innovations. For example, we might ask: did the cotton innovations make the railway more likely? Probably not. In many ways the breakthrough in cotton was not all that different from, say, the expansion of large-scale pottery production in the West Midlands by Wedgwood and others. Watt's improvements in the steam engine and Cort's development of improved methods of using coal to produce wrought iron had similar characteristics. They were the result of conscious application of resources to already defined research and development programs. They both marked stages on the evolution of technological change. Both involved, at least at a modest level, the introduction of science into industrial research and development.

During the nineteenth century the success of the industries of the industrial revolution within the international economy continued to influence Britain. The textile industries, highly concentrated in Lancashire and the West Riding of Yorkshire, and the large coal-based ironworks on the coalfields captured the most attention. Foreign trade contributed the growth of both. Even before the French Revolution, the Lancashire cotton industry enthusiastically supported freer trade and the Eden Treaty with France (1786). Competition drove down the price of yarn dramatically and low yarn prices in England attracted foreign buyers even in the face of severe wartime disruption. By the time peace was restored in 1815 the British cotton mills were selling to foreign customers as much as to their countrymen. Although the technology quickly became available overseas as a result of foreigners copying the English practice, hiring British mechanics and, after the 1843 repeal of the British prohibition of the export of machinery, buying machinery exported by English makers (Jeremy 1981), the British remained the low-cost producer of all but the simplest fabrics and two-thirds of output was exported until the outbreak of World War I. Woolen manufacturers did not capture world markets to the same extent but exported a large portion of their output. Consequently, the textile industries were much larger than they would have been if they had depended on domestic markets (Findlay and O'Rourke 2007).

Puddling and rolling for wrought iron production also grew in response to Britain's changed position in the international market. Before Cort's inventions nearly 60 percent of the wrought iron used in Britain was imported, principally from timber- and ore-abundant Sweden and Russia (Fremdling 2000; Harley 1982; Hyde 1977). The industry initially grew largely by displacing imports. By the early decades of the nineteenth century, however, Britain was exporting pig iron and wrought iron. The railways, first in Britain and then elsewhere, greatly increased the demand for iron and Britain was the principal international provider. Rainer Fremdling calculated that in the late 1840s railway iron consumed a little over a quarter of British iron production and about 40 percent of that was exported for use in the United States and western Europe. Although the importance of railway iron declined in the subsequent decade to a bit over a sixth of output as the pace of British railway construction eased and output increased by about 70 percent as other uses of iron expanded, exports continued to increase primarily to meet the demands of the expanding railway networks in the United States and Europe (Fremdling 1977). Technological leadership also supported the growth of British engineering. In the 1840s the industry succeeded in having prohibitions on the exports of machinery repealed and exports expanded rapidly. British machine-makers dominated world textile markets and were strong in other industries. British engineers and machinery were central to early railway construction on the continent. For example, between 1838 and 1841 the Prussian railways purchased forty-eight of its first fifty-one locomotives from British manufacturers – the dominance of British manufacturers then declined and locomotives were almost entirely of German manufacture (Fremdling 1977).

British technological leadership was enhanced by the isolation engendered by the revolutionary and Napoleonic wars – for twenty years British firms gained experience in the new technologies while potential rivals on the continent had little access to British practice. Lower prices from technological leadership led to extensive exports. We should, however, be careful not to attribute too much gain to the British from these exports. British competitive capitalism eliminated excess profits rapidly. Prices fell as firms entered industries to take advantage of lower costs. The benefits from technological improvement took the form of cheaper goods enjoyed by consumers and not higher profits for firms. Exports grew because prices fell; the foreign consumers of the goods shared the benefits of improved productivity with British consumers (Harley 2004).

In the long run, the steam engine was probably the most important technological development of the classical industrial revolution. Several points need to be made, however. First, Watt clearly drew on earlier developments, particularly Newcomen's pumping engine which had been in use since early in the eighteenth century. Second, the impact of the steam engine depended as much on its further development as on Watt's innovations. Third, the impact of steam engines, even in cotton manufacturing which dominated its earliest use outside of pumping applications, was minor until the 1830s (von Tunzelmann 1978). The great contribution of steam to increased efficiency came from its later application to transportation – railways and steamships. These innovations impressively lowered costs and induced investment that increased the amount of capital per worker (Crafts 2004a, 2004b). Crafts calculated that from 1830 to World War I, steam power and the investments it induced in transportation networks generated about a third of a percent per year growth in labor productivity, but before 1830 its contribution was barely noticeable at one- or two-tenths of a percent per year. The contributions of the other famous industries were much less. The cotton industry's spectacular technological transformation may have increased the growth of the economy by an eighth of 1 percent a year between 1780 and 1860. Improvements in agriculture (a much larger sector with slower technical change) contributed a little more. The other modernized industries together contributed rather less than cotton (Harley 1999).

The sustained growth in per capita income after 1830 (a little over 1 percent per year, three-quarters of which arose from total factor productivity growth) resulted from improvements broadly across the economy and cannot be explained mainly by changes in the famous industries. No historian has yet carried out an accounting exercise to quantify this process but we know changes were widespread. Agricultural productivity continued to rise. New, improved and cheaper chemicals and glass appeared. Food processing improved with such innovations as better flour mills, refrigeration, and packaged food. The sewing machine increased productivity in clothing manufacture and shoe making. Improvements in machine-making and steel contributed to productivity advance but generally it must be concluded that changes were broadly spread through the economy. This was the dynamics of capitalism at work on a broad scale (Bruland and Mowery 2005).

During the industrial revolution (1770–1830) the average real wage of British male workers changed little (Allen 2007; Clark 2005; Feinstein 1998). Wage experiences varied – rural workers in the south of England suffered as population growth and deindustrialization hit their labor market; handloom weavers initially benefitted from cheap yarn but then their swollen numbers were victims of mechanization. Wages increased in urban factories but workers faced an unhealthy environment, loss of freedom, and an absence of amenities (Williamson 1985). During and after the French Revolution, the state responded to war and fear of unrest by suppressing working-class rights and political expression. Child labor intensified and the economic conditions of working-class women probably deteriorated with the enclosure of common lands and the decline of manufacturing in the countryside – certainly the widespread employment in spinning disappeared (Humphries 2011). Optimists, however, point out that factors other than industrialization keep wages down: population grew at 1.5 percent a year – a rate that historically would have been accompanied by falling wages; the revolutionary and Napoleonic wars were extremely expensive and protracted. From the 1830s the real wages of working men clearly trended upwards and were about 50 percent higher by 1880. Many working-class families in Britain at the end of the nineteenth century remained desperately poor but almost all were less poor than their great-grandparents had been at the end of the eighteenth century and few experienced the levels of poverty that were common in Italy or eastern Europe – the poorer parts of Europe.

Industrialization in continental Europe

Narratives of the spread of industrialization in Europe have tended, following Marx's comment that "the country that is more developed industrially only shows, to the less developed, the image of its own future," to revolve around the spread of the leading industries of Britain's industrial revolution – factory-based textiles; iron; mechanical engineering – with tables of cotton consumption, pig iron output, coal production, and railway mileage (Landes 1969; Pollard 1981). This provides insights into the particular industries and the process of technology transfer but is inadequate for three reasons. First, these industries are insufficient to explain Britain's success. Second, local conditions – particularly expensive labor and cheap energy from coal – strongly influenced these industries' success in Britain and affected continental development. Third, Britain's industries grew because falling prices and Britain's continuing first-mover advantage supported massive export markets. Followers could hardly have replicated this experience.

Britain's technological achievement, particularly in textiles and iron, significantly affected continental industries but there were important national differences in responses. Imports from Britain challenged established producers who obtained tariff protection. British technology was copied, particularly in modern textile production, through industrial espionage and more importantly through the employment of skilled British workers and after the 1843 by the purchase of British machinery (Bruland 2003). Textiles emulated British methods but experiences differed from place to place. France adopted heavy tariff protection in the face of cheap British imports after the Napoleonic wars. Consequently, machine-spinning became established with the aid of British skilled workers but with higher costs than in England (Landes 1969: 158–163; Milward and Saul 1973: 270–277, 316–322). In Prussia, however, protection was moderate and consequently, imports of British yarn expanded as did handloom weaving. In the late 1830s about two-thirds of the cotton yarn used in the German states was imported (Pollard 1981: 181).

The spread of coal-based iron production was more complicated because success depended on coal and ore and because the older charcoal-based technology produced superior iron that commanded a higher price. Again tariff policy was important. France adopted complete protection while the German *Zollverein* enacted lower tariffs with a structure that encouraged the import of pig iron for domestic refining. Continental iron masters adopted new iron technologies at different rates and in different combinations depending on resources and markets. Charcoal-smelted pig iron persisted but coal was increasingly used for refining wrought iron. Even in the highly protected French market, coal-smelted pig iron initially had trouble competing. The coming of the railways in the 1840s created a mass demand for lower-quality iron- and coal-based pig iron production finally became established on coalfields in France, Belgium, and Silesia, and, after deep mines were sunk in the 1840s, in the German Ruhr (Evans and Rydén 2005; Fremdling 1997, 2000). Elsewhere the absence of coal precluded the industry's development.

The most important transfer of British technology was undoubtedly the railways. They stimulated investment and finance and transformed the fortunes of the iron industry. More fundamentally they integrated national markets allowing greater specialization in both industry and agriculture.

In narratives that revolve around textiles and iron, Belgium and Germany emerged as the principal successes while France disappointed. Belgium maintained its position as a highly industrialized region with about 30 percent of its national income in the industrial sector in 1870 (only Britain with 34 percent had more) (Broadberry, Fremdling, and Solar 2010: 170). In the mid nineteenth century, factory textile firms took over from traditional textile producers (present from medieval times) but not without creating hardship for traditional handloom weavers. More importantly, engineering firms developed impressive capacity in machine-building (although they were slow to turn to new industries in the final years of the century). The Belgian iron industry continued to grow with the successful switch to steel production and the development of larger firms and plant. It, however, lost its initial continental leadership to German rivals (Milward and Saul 1977: 154–165).

After the 1848 revolutions, Germany was the great success in this narrative. Building railroads and political change began the transformation and the iron and steel industry took pride of place. In the final quarter of the century, German iron and steel firms increased the size, capital intensity, and modernity of their plants, and firms like Krupp became technological leaders. Germans produced a quantity of steel second only to the United States and exported steel, particularly to markets in continental Europe (Landes 1969: 249–269). Along with iron and steel, engineering flourished in the aftermath of the railway. German capitalists supplied not only the domestic market but also much of the machinery, outside of textile machines, demand in Europe.

The conventional narrative delineates the development of some important industries but one must question how much insight it provides into the process of modern economic growth. Although the title of this chapter is "British and European industrialization" the process by which sustained growth of income per head developed is clearly the important issue. In our discussion of Britain we have already seen that the "British model" of textiles and iron can explain only a small proportion of Britain's growth. Similar conclusions are appropriate for continental Europe. Narratives that assume that modern economic growth emerged by emulating the leading sectors of mid-nineteenth-century Britain exaggerate the role and contribution of a few new industries.

First, the industries that are most studied and taken to indicate the emergence of economic growth made up only a modest a share of manufacturing and a much smaller portion of national income. In Germany, the metal industries – including iron, steel, and engineering – contributed about 15 percent of the value of manufacturing around 1870. Since manufacturing, including mining, construction, and utilities, amounted to a little over a quarter of national income these industries amounted to less than 4 percent of national output (Broadberry et al. 2010: 168–174).

The Germany metal industry in 1913 was about ten times as large as it had been in 1870. This is impressive growth but some simple calculations put it into perspective. First we can exaggerate the sector's effect by assuming for simplicity that the growth occurred without increasing the share of resources used in the industry (thus not reducing the output of other sectors of the economy). In fact, although productivity gains in metal production were impressive at 2.4 percent per year (Milward and Saul 1977: 26), this plus an increase in the labor force equal to population growth would have only increased metal output by a little less than fourfold. If all the tenfold growth had been productivity gain it would have increased national income by about 35 percent. This appears to be a large increase but is a growth rate of somewhat under 1 percent annually. German population was growing at 1.16 percent per year so productivity growth of the metal industries alone would have resulted in a decline in per capita income. More realistically, if we assume that the rest of the economy grew at the same rate as population growth, the growth of metal production would have increased per capita income about 20 percent or under half a percent per year. Since German per capita income more than doubled between 1870 and 1913, the contribution of the metal and engineering industries was modest. Many will object to placing much weight on the preceding calculations. After all, the key story of the genesis of dynamic change is absent from the calculation. However, quantitative historians are fond of quoting Samuel Johnson on the effect of simple calculations: "That, Sir, is the good of counting. It brings everything to a certainty, which before floated in the mind indefinitely" (quoted in McCloskey 1981: 105).

Cotton textiles, which led the introduction of the factory system in Britain, is the other industry on which traditional narratives concentrate. Again, unless the goal is to trace emulation of Britain, the focus is strange. Factory-based machine-spinning became established throughout Europe and the textile industries grew but if we were to carry out an exercise like that above we would find a similar result. On average the textile and clothing industries were a little over twice the size of the metal industries but grew more slowly. More troubling, however, is the fact that textile industries in continental Europe depended on protection from the more efficient British industry. This had, of course, also been true of the metal industries until the last quarter of the century when Germany's industry became competitive. No such growing-up of mass-production textile industries occurred and consequently European consumers' real incomes were reduced by the growth of their domestic textile industry. There were, of course, some exceptions. Silk production grew in France and Italy; both thrived in export markets and were never threatened by British firms. French firms successfully held on to high-fashion textiles and clothing. The protected cotton industries introduced urban factories to the continent, and may have stimulated mechanical engineering and generally enhanced the technological capability but most of the industry's machinery was imported from Britain. It is hard to sustain a claim that cotton textiles were the engine of growth.

Railways are the third great indicator of industrialization and here the story is somewhat different. Transportation services are, of course, location specific and not tradable. Railway technology was quickly adopted across Europe, with some modest delays relating to government policy and finance. Technology and finance were readily available internationally although modest commercial prospects in more backward regions led to government involvement in finance either directly with state debt or by guaranteeing interest on railway debt. In either case most of the capital came from foreign investors. The direct impact of railways on transportation varied depending on the pre-existing transportation network and the level of commercial development. In particular the impact was less in regions with well-developed water transportation. Various calculations of the transportation cost saving generated by the railways, while somewhat problematic, are in the neighborhood of 5 percent of national income (Broadberry, Federico, and Klein 2010: 81). Unlike iron and steel or textiles, transportation improvements brought by the railway almost certainly had spillover that affected growth widely.

In particular, cheaper, faster, and more reliable transportation and communications (aided by the telegraph that accompanied railways) integrated national economies allowing greater specialization in both industry and agriculture. Efficient producers expanded at the expense of small local and relatively inefficient firms and household production. For example, Berlin – situated in a backward agricultural area east of the Elbe distant from the main markets in western Germany – become a major producer of engineering and consumer products for all of Germany. Agriculture was profoundly affected. Agricultural historians note that market access was an important determinant of investment and technological improvement (Allen 2003; Grantham 1989; Hoffman 1996). Railways brought remote areas all across Europe into closer contact with urban markets and stimulated productivity advance. Nonetheless, the impact of railways was large only when they successfully interacted with wider forces of economic change.

Per capita income and inadequacy of the 'British model'

Historians have constructed estimates of national income for the past. These figures should be viewed as work in progress and used with care. The data that modern statisticians use are not available before the mid twentieth century and officials who collected earlier statistical material did not think in terms of a concept of national income. Nonetheless it is almost impossible to think about economic growth without an estimate of aggregate activity. Without them, we rely on impressions that overemphasize the novel, the spectacular, and the new. Table 16.1 provides estimates for European countries from the eighteenth century to World War I. They show (as do the long-run real wage figures above) there was a gradient of incomes in Europe prior to the

Table 16.1 *GDP per capita in principal European countries, 1750–1913 (1990 "international" Geary-Khamis dollars)*

	1750	1820	1870	1913
UK	1,485	1,707	3,191	4,921
Denmark		1,274	2,003	3,912
Netherlands	1,861	1,821	2,758	4,049
Belgium	1,297	1,319	2,692	3,923
France		1,230	1,876	3,485
Germany		1,077	1,839	3,646
Switzerland		1,280	2,202	4,266
Italy	1,297	1,117	1,499	2,564
Spain	990	1,063	1,376	2,255
Sweden	1,144	1,198	1,664	3,096
Russia			683	939

Source: Broadberry and O'Rourke 2010: 2; Maddison 2007.

Table 16.2 *Industrial structure (% of manufacturing) United Kingdom, France, and Germany, 1870*

	UK	France	Germany
Food, drink and tobacco	14	17	19
Textiles, clothing	26	34	30
Metals	18	3	15
Other manufacturing	8	20	20
Construction	7	22	9
Mining	25	3	6
Utilities	2	1	1

Source: Broadberry, Fremdling, and Solar 2010: 170–171.

nineteenth-century industrialization. The highest incomes were in the Netherlands and Britain while lower incomes prevailed in the southern and eastern periphery. The national income figures also correspond with the narrative history's conclusion that Germany was a particular success but that success was primarily in overcoming initial backwardness. Even in 1913 Germany does not stand out as having achieved high income per capita. National income statistics also highlight the fragility of narratives of economic growth based on industrialization driven by textiles and iron. They show the success of Germany and Belgium but the companion story of failure of France and the Netherlands must be abandoned.

When we look at the structure of industry in France we are struck almost immediately by the small size of the metal and mining sectors which loom large in conventional narratives (see Table 16.2). The French economy grew quite slowly in aggregate when compared to Britain and Germany (1.6 percent per year in contrast to 1.9 and 2.8 percent for Britain and Germany), but during the same period British population increased by two-thirds and German population nearly doubled while France's increased by only 14 percent. Consequently, as we can see from Table 16.1, German growth per capita only slightly exceeds that of France and France grew considerably faster than Britain. France grew with a very different economic structure than Germany or Britain. Metal and mining were unimportant primarily because France had poor coal resources. Industrialization followed a different path and agriculture declined relatively more slowly without substantially hurting overall growth. In 1870, France and Germany both had half their working population in agriculture; by 1913, the share in Germany had fallen to 35 percent but in France it remained at 41 percent. French slower population growth put less pressure on its rural population.

Research on the French economy now effectively challenges the failure narrative. O'Brien and Keyder demonstrated that productivity in French industry was high during the eighteenth and nineteenth centuries. They summarize the difference between French and British industry as follows:

> Value added per worker remained high in France because industry specialised in higher-value products. For such products, differentiated in quality and style, the workshop unit of production, often organized on a family basis, could train skilled labor and cater effectively for local and other specific demands.
>
> (O'Brien and Keyder 1978: 178–179)

Mechanization, large factories and the extensive use of mineral fuels were among the changes in industrializing Europe but they were not necessary to generate economic growth. In many sectors small-scale capitalist enterprises remained efficient and profitable. By the last years of the nineteenth century new industries were developing and France performed well, achieving leadership in automobile, aviation and electrical engineering, for example. Recent detailed examination of comparative income statistics confirms the high levels of productivity in French industry in the early twentieth century (Woltjer, Smits, and Frankema 2010).

The national income statistics reveal two other successful economies that did not follow the British-German model – the Netherlands and Denmark. The Netherlands is covered in detail in another chapter. Here it is only necessary to note that although a story of relative failure of growth in the Dutch economy in the eighteenth and nineteenth centuries has large elements of truth, per capita income remained high despite the failure to adopt the so-called key industries. Efficient services, specialized agriculture and associated food production, and other light industries provided incomes that rivaled those in Britain through most of the nineteenth century. The Danish story is even more impressive. The economic structure was even more heavily biased towards specialized food production and processing than the Dutch but the Danes attained growth rates of per capita income between 1820 and 1913 that were close to those achieved by Germany by specializing completely differently.

Gerschenkron, relative backwardness, and convergence

Exploring the development of the industries that were at the forefront of Britain's industrial revolution provides information about the spread of technology but fails to provide an adequate basis for understanding the mechanisms involved in the emergence of modern economic growth. In what is probably the most influential essay in European economic history in the past two generations, Alexander Gerschenkron suggested a typology of the history of European industrialization that gave prominence to initial conditions of backwardness at the start of industrialization and focussed on systematic substitutions for the "prerequisites" of growth that had been present in Britain's industrialization (Gerschenkron 1962).

Contemporaries and historians alike were aware that the most advanced economies lay in Britain and the Netherlands in the northwest. Moving east across the north European plain gradation of backwardness seemed obvious. France's relative backwardness *vis-à-vis* the "North Sea economies" was perhaps open to debate. The western states of Germany, however, were clearly more backward than France or the Low Countries. As one crossed the Elbe, the level of backwardness increased and Russia was clearly well behind. Moving from north to south a similar gradient appeared although generalization was more tenuous because legacies of earlier urban commercial success remained and significant differences in climate affected agriculture. The south of France was behind the north; Italy, despite its illustrious past, lagged badly. The Balkans, influenced by their troubled history on the periphery of the Ottoman empire, as well as their fragmented geography, lagged even further behind.

Gerschenkron accepted that backwardness was multidimensional but various indicators yielded the same ranking. The most obvious indicator was per capita income, or general standard of living, but the profile of backwardness was also visible in a range of institutional features. Three, all characteristics of developed capitalism, stand out: the organization of agriculture; the extent of commercialization and urbanization and the general penetration of commodity markets; the development of factor markets for both labor and capital. Capitalist agriculture with well-developed markets in labor and land predominated in Britain and, in a different form in the Low Countries; peasant farmers dominated French agriculture and western Germany; beyond the Elbe aristocratic landlords farmed under feudal relations using forced labor and draft animals or serfs. At the most extreme was Russian serfdom. The extent of markets diminished from west to east. Britain and the Netherlands had well-developed financial markets; France, although it lagged somewhat behind, also had well-developed, if somewhat different, institutions (Hoffman, Postel-Vinay, and Rosenthal 2001). There was some financial development in western Germany but little further east. In Britain and in the Netherlands, labor markets dominated the allocation of labor and most of the population had labor market experience. In France and western Germany some two-thirds of the labor force in the eighteenth century was in agriculture mainly organized on the basis of the custom of the peasant family rather than the labor market. The serfdom east of the Elbe was based on un-free labor under obligation of providing labor to landlords.

Gerschenkron put forward a number of hypotheses regarding the influence of relative backwardness, some of which have survived critical examination better than others. His predictions include the hypothesis that industrialization in a more backward economy started with a more rapid spurt than had characterized more advanced economies. This rapid growth arose out of several related ideas. First, there was a gap between the technological possibilities demonstrated by the advanced economies and the current economy. If the institutional forces preventing development could be overcome, there was a potential for rapid catch-up growth. Second, in backward economies, the majority of the population in low-productivity agriculture and organized on the basis of either family or servile labor (or some combination of both) demanded few goods on the market and so could not provide the basis for development of consumer goods industries. For growth to occur it was necessary to achieve a "development bloc" of producer goods industries that could provide each other markets. Consequently, growth began with a "big spurt."

In conditions of backwardness, markets for finished goods and factors of production were poorly developed and consequently, entrepreneurs could not rely on widespread competition among buyers and sellers to insure that products could be readily sold at competitive prices or that inputs and intermediate goods could be readily purchased in required quantities. In industrial revolution Britain broad markets existed that permitted firms to develop on a small scale and concentrate on a production niche confident that inputs could be readily purchased and output, even intermediate goods in a longer production chain, could be sold. In backward economies, firms found that it was necessary to adopt hierarchical organization within the firm to overcome market limitations. As a result, larger firms emerged that often integrated the entire process from raw material supply to final product sale under managerial control (Harley 1991).

Finance also was less market oriented in more backward economies. In Britain, small firms had been able to finance development by a variety of means because financial transactions were well developed. Firms generally grew from funds accumulated in pre-existing mercantile manufacturing, personal contacts, the existing network of trade credit, and the short-term financing that British commercial banks were willing to offer. Behind these arrangements, well-developed financial markets in bills of exchange, and a stock exchange supported the development of diversified portfolios for investors. For more capital-intensive infrastructure like turnpikes and canals, trusts and companies were organized to tap more extensive sources of funds (Harris 2000: section 2). When railways demanded exceptionally large amounts of capital in a short period of time, they were able to borrow directly on the stock exchange. In conditions of moderate backwardness, in Gerschenkron's narrative primarily Germany but also France and Italy, commercial sources and financial markets did not have the capacity to provide the same financing and substitutes developed in the form of the large universal banks beginning with the Crédit Mobilier in France and then dominating finance in Germany. These institutions accepted deposits and made commercial loans but were also willing to take longer-term positions in the financing of large firms and to act as intermediaries in the issuing and distribution of stock to investors. In conditions of extreme backwardness, exemplified by Russia, conditions were too backward even to support this sort of bank and the state played an important role in industrial finance with public debt proving an instrument that investors, particularly in the richer West, were willing to hold.

Backwardness also influenced the choice of techniques by firms in newly established industries. Backwardness provided a tension for entrepreneurs between employing the latest technology that had been developed in more advanced economies to suit their high-wage conditions and the cheap labor of the backward economy. In fact, however, the dilemma was to a large extent false. To be sure, raw brute labor was cheap but skilled labor and even disciplined labor suitable for factory production was scarcer than in advanced economies. Consequently, and apparently paradoxically, industries like steel in the backward economy installed the most advanced labor-saving technology in key parts of production while using cheap unskilled, or brute, labor as much as possible in auxiliary operations.

Backward agriculture played a major role in Gerschenkron's thinking and was the subject of two of his major works (Gerschenkron 1943, 1966). He concluded that the contribution of agriculture to the growth process declined with backwardness because the poverty of agriculture and the tenuous connection of agricultural workers to the market limited the sector's contribution to demand. Because of its institutional nature the agricultural sector did not release labor and create a market-oriented workforce, as happened in Britain.

Gerschenkron's schema provides substantial insight into the variation within European industrialization, particularly when combined with an awareness of the importance of coal for the development of industry on the British model. It is particularly useful in illuminating differences in institutional structure that emerged in different countries. It is hardly surprising that the general-izations have proven too sweeping to be a totally reliable guide to the complex economic history of modern Europe. Gerschenkron – despite his avowed aim to replace Marx's great generalization that more backward countries follow the path of industrialization carved out by the first example – still thought in terms of emulating the British experience of large urban factories and a vibrant iron industry. The substitutions of prerequisites that he identified – large hierarchical firms, a key role for banks and the state in finance, and the adoption of the most advanced technology to overcome the shortcomings of labor in backward economies – were largely relevant for the "big industries" and, like other discussions with similar focus, are less helpful in understanding the less spectacular development of other sectors.

Gerschenkron's "big spurt" at the start of industrialization has proven hard to find in aggregate statistics (Crafts, Leybourne, and Mills 1991). However, there is connection with the idea of convergence of income levels among economies in particular "growth clubs" in which economies that have initially lower incomes tend to grow more rapidly and converge toward income levels of initially the richest economies. Convergence certainly occurred in western Europe by the late twentieth century, although on the European periphery it was little in evidence until the mid twentieth century. Convergence is, of course, by no means guaranteed. On a global scale the history of the nineteenth and twentieth centuries has been one of "divergence, big time" with a small "club" of successful economies in western Europe and its offshoots growing much faster than poorer economies elsewhere, increasing global inequality.

Agriculture

When we shift our focus from the "great" industries to a more holistic view of economies and the levels of income that they generated, backwardness and its implications for growth across Europe return our attention to agriculture. High agricultural productivity was a leading determinant of Britain's relatively high incomes at an early date. Allen's recent estimates of comparative output per worker in agriculture for some key European countries are presented in Table 16.3 along with estimates for the years just before World War I.

The high productivity of the Netherlands (shared with Belgium) in the late eighteenth century is apparent, but low productivity elsewhere is more striking. Contemporaries did not see these data but the relative backwardness of continental agriculture was apparent and associated with agricultural insti-tutions. In England capitalist agriculture had proceeded to its limit. In France

Table 16.3 *Output per worker in agriculture, England* = 100

	Late 18th-century England = 100	1910 England = 100	1910 (England 1750=100)
England	100	100	150
Netherlands	98	50	75
France	55	74	111
Germany	41	52	78
Italy	43	32	48

Source: col. 2 (Allen 2000: 20); col. 3 (Broadberry, Federico, and Klein 2010: 66); col. 4 (Allen 2006: 43).

and to a somewhat lesser extent in western Germany, peasant proprietors with secure title to land farmed with family labor. In France, peasant security of title was enhanced by the Revolution and as Patrick O'Brien notes, "[b]y abolishing seigniorial dues and suppressing tithes, the Revolutionaries also transferred agricultural income back to those who farmed the land. At a stroke, the tax and judicial reforms of the 1790s lightened burdens on the peasantry and enhanced their capacity to prosper on small plots of land" (O'Brien 1996: 228).

In Germany east of the Elbe a more backward feudal system of estate agriculture – *Gutsherrschaft* – predominated. Aristocrats farmed their estates to the largest possible degree using enforced serf labor of which there were two classes. More substantial peasants with property rights were required to provide draught animals and stipulated labor services. Lesser peasants without legal property provide only labor. The extent of labor required from a peasant farmstead was considerable:

As a rule of thumb, one can say that enforced serf labor did not exceed 2–3 days a week for peasants with property in their land. As for peasants without property, it depended entirely on the requirements of the estates. There were quite often 4, 5 or even 6 days of enforced labor per peasant-farmstead. As the great majority of the peasants . . . had no property rights in their land we can quite confidently say that enforced labor for more than 3 days a week was very widespread in these areas.   (Harnisch 1986: 45)

The system provided cheap labor, draught animal capital and serf-built structures that underpinned a profitable system for the landowning aristocracy. Harnisch quotes a prominent Pomeranian official who wrote that 'managing an estate with enforced labor might not lead to the highest possible yields and would certainly cause a lot of irritation and annoyance . . . but it was 'convenient and cheap'" (Harnisch 1986: 45). In Russia serfdom was even more strongly entrenched with heavier peasant obligations and even less freedom.

The institutions and productivity in agriculture across northern Europe invites further consideration of Robert Brenner's triptych of class structures differing in terms of conditions and priorities for those engaged in agriculture – the means of social reproduction – that emerged in the centuries following the Black Death. Brenner saw the institutions that emerged in the late medieval and early modern era determining the development possibilities into the eighteenth and nineteenth centuries. He emphasized the technological improvements that occurred with the British structure that allowed labor to leave agriculture and expanded the market for nonagricultural goods. From another perspective, landlessness and wage labor in the countryside removed the possibility for the agricultural labor force remaining in subsistence peasant agriculture.

In France, peasant communities gained substantial *de jure* and *de facto* property rights in land that were dramatically reinforced by the Revolution (Brenner 1976: 68–72; O'Brien 1996). Brenner describes the dynamics of the peasant farm as follows:

> On the one hand, the peasant had every positive incentive to hold onto his holding, for it formed the basis for his existence, and that of his family and heirs. On the other hand, purely economic forces seem to have worked to undermine the peasants' property only in the very long term. Thus the point is that the peasant proprietor was under relatively little pressure to operate his plot as profitably or efficiently as his potential competitors in order to survive, for there was no direct means for such competitors to "defeat" him. In other words, the peasant did not have to be competitive, because he did not really have to be able to "hold his place" in the world of the market, either the market for tenants or the market for goods. Unlike a tenant, the peasant proprietor did not have to provide a level of rent equal to what the landlord might get from any other tenant – or else be evicted at the expiration of his lease. Unlike the independent artisan, he did not have to be able to produce cheaply enough to sell his goods profitably at the market price – or else go out of business. All that was necessary for survival for the peasant proprietor (assuming of course that he was a food producer) was sufficient output to provide for his family's subsistence and to pay his taxes. (Brenner 1976: 72–73)

In serf agriculture farther east the dynamics were different again. Here economic relationships were subsumed within power relationships in an aristocratic polity. Brenner's classic essay again provided a stark assessment:

> [The] structure of class relations in the East had as its outcome the "development of underdevelopment", the preclusion of increased productivity in general, and

of industrialization in particular. First of all, the availability of forced laborers whose services could be incessantly intensified by the lord discouraged the introduction of agricultural improvements. Secondly, the lord's increasing surplus extraction from the peasantry continually limited the emergence of a home market for industrial goods. Thirdly, the fact of direct and powerful controls over peasant mobility meant the constriction of the industrial labor force, eventuating in the suffocation of industry and the decline of the towns. Finally, the landlords, as a ruling class which dominated their states, pursued a policy of what has been called "anti-mercantilism"; they attempted to usurp the merchants' function as middlemen and encouraged industrial imports from the West, in this way undermining much of what was left of urban and industrial organization.   (Brenner 1976: 60)

Brenner's assessments are stark and exaggerate backwardness but are good starting points. The French peasants were certainly not so unresponsive to economic opportunities as the quotation above suggests. They reacted to market opportunities as adjustment to the railway and the expansion of quality viticulture demonstrated. Nonetheless, the peasant family's attachment to the farm and the small size of the typical farm characterized French agriculture into the twentieth century. The French farm was small and, by English standards, poorly capitalized. It had only 60 percent of the draught animals per worker of British agriculture; only 24 percent of the value of output consisted of meat and milk (the British figure was 67 per cent) and thus less natural fertilizer (O'Brien and Keyder 1978: 113–119).

The greatest adjustment that French peasants made to support their independence was to reduce fertility dramatically. By the end of the Napoleonic wars, the French birth rate had fallen, achieved by drastically reducing births within marriage well before that occurred elsewhere, so that population grew at 10 percent per generation compared to a rate of about 40 percent elsewhere. Between 1820 and 1913 western Europe's population approximately doubled – German population increasing more than 2.5 times – but French population increased by less than a third. Undoubtedly maintaining the peasant family holding and connection to the land was a key objective. Sons remained even if the farm's income per worker fell to below the wage in non-rural occupations. Peasant ownership and slow population growth made this strategy possible. In contrast in British capitalist agriculture, farmers hired only until marginal product of labor equaled the wage rate so labor input was significantly lower with a higher average product than on a peasant farm (Crafts and Harley 2004; Cohen and Weitzman 1975). O'Brien and Keyder concluded in their sympathetic study of the French economy "that French farmers probably did as well as can be expected given the ... constraints on investment exercised by smaller units of ownership and production" (O'Brien and Keyder 1978: 139). The small units were a product of institutional history and acted as a drag on the economy as a whole. The French peasantry, however, quite clearly preferred the family farm, and ownership of the land allowed them to exercise that preference even at the cost of dissipating potential agricultural rents. Nonetheless, French agriculture performed creditably during the nineteenth century. Output per worker closed some of the gap with Britain; between 1880 and 1910 agricultural productivity grew at 1.5 percent per year, which is slightly faster than per capita national income (Broadberry, Federico, and Klein 2010: 66).

German agricultural change was more complex. The west was broadly similar to France. In the east change revolved around the abolition of servile agriculture. Eighteenth-century East Elbian German agriculture was by no means isolated from markets; noble estates supplied a vibrant grain market fueled by demand in the Netherlands and also increasingly in Britain. More prosperous peasant farmers were also market oriented, often hiring workers to provide the labor services they owed to the aristocratic estates (Harnisch 1986: 50–59). The elimination of serfdom in Prussia and elsewhere in central and eastern Europe was a conscious modernizing policy. Peasant unrest was apparent before the French Revolution and military defeats in 1806 triggered the Stein-Hardenberg reforms in Prussia that started a half-century process of replacing feudal with capitalist agriculture. Reforms emancipated the peasantry from feudal tenures and redefined property right in land. Aristocratic landowners, unlike in France, had the political power to ensure compensation for the loss of feudal benefits and increased the land under their direct control. The aristocratic estates adopted capitalist agriculture using wage labor. Many large and mid-sized peasant farmers also benefitted from secure land tenure and the elimination of feudal services. In the first half of the century for Prussia as a whole output per worker increased by between 40 percent and two-thirds and east of the Elbe, where reforms had most effect, labor productivity in 1860 was more than 2.5 times its 1800 level. From 1850 to 1913 output continued to grow at 2.1 percent per year and output per worker increased at 1.8 percent to more than triple – a faster rate of growth than German per capita income (Pierenkemper and Tilly 2004: 23–29, 76–80).

Poor rural residents without legal land rights became impoverished wage laborers, their numbers swollen by rapid population growth. Unlike France, where the elimination of the remains of feudal tenure strengthened the property rights of the peasants, led to a near cessation of population growth and inhibited the growth of a mobile wage labor force, reform on the East

Elbian estates contributed to the creation of a proletariat for the country's industrialization. Poor rural inhabitants found themselves transformed into wage laborers and at the same time population growth was accelerating to over 1 percent per year (largely due to falling death rates while birth rates declined only in the twentieth century) (Pierenkemper and Tilly 2004: 87–94). East of the Elbe population growth and agricultural change led to dramatic out-migration after 1860. At first many went abroad, mainly to the United States, but as urbanization and industrialization developed in the Rhineland, Westphalia, and around Berlin migrants from the east became urban factory workers. In the twenty-five years to 1907 more than two million people migrated (equal to about two-thirds of the surplus of births over deaths) from the eastern provinces of Prussia. At the same time the Berlin region and the western industrial provinces received about the same number of migrants. Between 1880 and 1910 the agricultural share of the German labor force fell from just under half to 36 percent (Milward and Saul 1977: 45; Pierenkemper and Tilly 2004: 87–104).

The contrast between institutional development in agriculture in France, on one hand, and Germany and England, on the other, highlights a complication in assessing European industrialization. In both England and Germany the conversion of agricultural workers into free wage labor (proletarianization) contributed to industrialization by easing labor recruitment and swelling the numbers of urban consumers (who purchased a disproportionate share of mass-produced consumer goods). In France, rural labor – the peasantry – was free to move but chose to remain on the land, often substantially self-sufficient and at lower material reward than urban alternatives offered. They were able to make that choice because they owned the land. By staying on the land the peasant family chose a lifestyle that misallocated labor if we accept the criterion that marginal product should be the same in alternative uses – the retention of labor on family farms reduced the marginal product of labor in agriculture below that in the rest of the economy. In effect, peasant families chose to expend potential land rent on maintaining rural peasant status. It is hard not to accept that at least for the generations making the choice this was an informed and rational decision. English and German rural workers would almost certainly have made the same choice had they been able to. This poses a dilemma for analysis of industrialization. Mobility of labor enhanced industrialization and allocated labor more efficiently. This increased measured national income in Germany and England relative to France. The measured increase overstates the welfare gain, however, since the increased welfare from peasant existence – whose reality French peasants' choices demonstrated –is not included in national income accounts.

Conclusions: capitalism and European industrialization

European industrialization was a triumph of capitalism. However, large firms employing masses of proletarian workers – a usual conception of capitalism – played a modest role. Modern economic growth was achieved by societies in which markets became pervasive. In the initial leaders, the Netherlands and England, market capitalism was firmly established long before the industrial revolution. In many places elsewhere in Europe, capitalist roots were deep and growth spread quite rapidly during the nineteenth century. In general, per capita incomes tended to converge as more backward economies benefitted from advanced technology, institutional change, and capital inflow from the leaders. The contours of European industrialization varied, influenced particularly by relative backwardness and by the availability of coal. Large capitalist firms, of course, played their role, particularly in highly visible large urban factories and in heavy industry. Nowhere, however, were they extensive enough to drive growth of the entire economy and in some economies that attained the highest levels of income per capita these industries hardly existed.

The capitalism that drove growth pervaded small and medium-sized firms, usually family controlled, that produced most industrial and service output even in Britain and Germany. Also, importantly, capitalism came to prevail generally in agriculture. Agriculture has featured rather more prominently than might be expected in a narrative of European industrialization. However, Europe's transformation would not have happened without vigorous agricultural growth. In 1750 (outside of England and the Low Countries) the proportion of the labor force in agricultural was approximately 60 percent plus a rural nonagricultural population of an additional 20 to 30 percent (Allen 2000: 11). Substantial economic growth was virtually impossible without productivity improvement in the countryside. In many cases, particularly in the east, agricultural change involved institutional change. In the event, productivity advances in agriculture rivaled advances elsewhere in the economies.

Sustained growth in per capita income rests on technological change. Unfortunately, the origin of technological change and the process by which it spreads is elusive. The relevant technological change was not limited to famous inventions. Britain was already rich by the standards of the time when the industrial revolution occurred. A high-wage economy rested on earlier advances in agriculture and a wide range of manufacturing and services that had developed in a capitalist market economy. Even though most firms (and farms were small, the economy was well integrated and product and factor markets were broad. Firms' need to compete insured that costs were controlled and products improved. The possibility of profiting from innovation motivated inventors like Richard Arkwright to undertake research and development.

Continental Europe, except the Netherlands, generally lagged behind Britain in income and industrial technology. The technological gap, although it certainly exhibited a gradient of backwardness as one moved east, should not be overstated. France experienced impressive eighteenth-century growth and its textile industries were not dissimilar to Britain's. The French certainly led in silk and other luxury products. The technological breakthroughs of the industrial revolution occurred in Britain, probably because high wages and cheap coal provided incentives to explore the relevant technology. When relevant to local costs, new techniques moved rapidly to continental Europe as local capitalists sought to emulate British successes, often employing skilled British workmen or purchasing machinery from British engineering firms. Certainly when we focus on factory textiles, iron, coal, and steam the story was one of British leadership and continental emulation. But these industries should not be overemphasized. Their traction in France was limited and they had little impact in the Netherlands or Denmark but income grew in these countries because technology advanced in other industries, sometimes possibly stimulated by the example of British textiles and engineering but also often along original lines. By the second half of the nineteenth century it was clear that technological capacity had developed in all the leading economies and new technology diffused rapidly from place to place. Nonetheless, resources, past experience, and labor force characteristics caused paths taken to differ and an attempt to force the economic history into too rigid a mold only leads to misunderstanding.

Finally, Europe needs to be briefly placed in a broader global perspective. The European story was one of widespread technological change, rapid diffusion, and convergence to similar levels of technological competence and incomes, tempered by institutions of backwardness particularly in agriculture. To be sure convergence was far from complete when Europe tore itself apart with wars and depression in the first half of the twentieth century and was only completed in the second half of the century. Then all of western Europe converged on the United States, now the technological leader. At this time in many continental economies the rapid reallocation of large workforces from low-productivity agriculture and traditional services speeded growth. When, however, we look at global history, we realize that convergence, which apparently seems so natural, is, in fact, exceptional. Most of the world was unable fully to utilize the improved technologies that emerged during and after the industrial revolution and global income inequality increased dramatically. Consequently, when growth economists think about the transfer of technology and income convergence, they emphasize convergence clubs and social capacity to use technology. The history of European industrialization clearly demonstrates that most of Europe belonged to a "convergence club" since at least the beginning of the nineteenth century and it is intriguing to speculate on the nature of the "social capacity" that made this the case.

It is far beyond even the immodest aims of this chapter to answer this question. Certainly, long-developed traditions of markets dating from at least medieval times – capitalism if you like – are central to the answer. So too is the historic unity of Europe in its disunity of competing states which led to competition among polities. Long-distance trade connected the continent. Shared religion and culture played a role – the Renaissance and the Enlightenment contributed. The development of unified and competent states and the emergence of constitutional government also played their role. The underlying determinants of economic success seem likely to rest in the realm of culture, society, and politics rather than in the simply technological.

References

Allen, R. C. (1992). *Enclosure and the Yeoman: The Agricultural Development of the South Midlands 1450–1850*. Oxford: Clarendon Press.

(1999). "Tracking the Agricultural Revolution in England," *The Economic History Review* 52(2): 209–235.

(2000). "Economic Structure and Agricultural Productivity in Europe, 1300–1800," *European Review of Economic History* 4(1): pp. 1–26.

(2001). "The Great Divergence in European Wages and Prices from the Middle Ages to the First World War," *Explorations in Economic History* 38(4): 411–447.

(2003). "Progress and Poverty in Early Modern Europe," *The Economic History Review* 56(3): 403–443.

(2006). "English and Welsh Agriculture, 1300–1850: Outputs, Inputs, and Income." Working paper, Nuffield College, Oxford.

(2007). "Pessimism Preserved: Real Wages in the British Industrial Revolution." Working paper, Nuffield College, Oxford.

(2009a). "Agricultural Productivity and Rural Incomes in England and the Yangtze Delta, c. 1620–c. 1820," *The Economic History Review* 62(3): 525–550.

(2009b). *The British Industrial Revolution in Global Perspective*. Cambridge University Press.

(2010). "The Industrial Revolution in Miniature: The Spinning Jenny in Britain, France, and India," *Journal of Economic History* 69(4): 901.

(2012). "Technology and the Great Divergence: Global Economic Development since 1820," *Explorations in Economic History* 49(1): 1–16.

Allen, R. C. *et al.* (2011). "Wages, Prices, and Living Standards in China, 1738–1925: In Comparison with Europe, Japan, and India," *The Economic History Review* 64: 8–38.

Aston, T. H. and C. H. E. Philpin (1987). *The Brenner Debate: Agrarian Class Structure and Economic Development in Pre-industrial Europe.* Cambridge University Press.

Bairoch, P. (1982). "International Industrialization Levels from 1750 to 1980," *Journal of European Economic History* 11: 269–333.

Bavel, B. J. P. van (2008). "The Organization and Rise of Land and Lease Markets in Northwestern Europe and Italy, c. 1000–1800," *Continuity and Change* 23(1): 13.

(2010). *Manors and Markets: Economy and Society in the Low Countries 500–1600.* Oxford University Press.

Brenner, R. (1976). "Agrarian Class Structure and Economic Development in Pre-industrial Europe," *Past & Present* 70(1): 30–75.

Broadberry, S. N. (1997). *The Productivity Race: British Manufacturing in International Perspective, 1850–1990.* Cambridge University Press.

Broadberry, S. N. and K. H. O'Rourke (2010). *The Cambridge Economic History of Modern Europe.* Vol. II: *1870 to the Present.* Cambridge University Press.

Broadberry, S. N., G. Federico, and A. Klein (2010). "Sectoral Developments, 1870–1914," in S. N. Broadberry and K. H. O'Rourke (eds.), *Cambridge Economic History of Modern Europe.* Vol. II: *1870 to the Present.* Cambridge University Press, pp. 59–83.

Broadberry, S. N., Fremdling, R., and P. M. Solar (2010). "Industry, 1700–1870," in S. N. Broadberry and K. H. O'Rourke (eds.), *The Cambridge Economic History of Modern Europe.* Vol. I: *1700 to 1870.* Cambridge University Press, pp. 164–186.

Bruland, K. (2003). *British Technology and European Industrialization: The Norwegian Textile Industry in the Mid-nineteenth Century.* Cambridge University Press.

Bruland, K. and D. Mowery (2005). "Innovation through Time," in R. Nelson, D. Mowery, and J. Fagerberg (eds.), *The Oxford Handbbok of Innovation.* Oxford University Press.

Caird, S. J. (1852). *English Agriculture in 1850–51.* London: Longman, Brown, Green.

Clapham, J. (1926). *An Economic History of Britain: The Early Railway Age.* Cambridge University Press.

Clark, G. (2005). "The Condition of the Working Class in England, 1209–2004," *Journal of Political Economy* 113(6): 1307–1340.

Cohen, J. S. and M. L. Weitzman (1975). "A Marxian Model of Enclosures," *Journal of Development Economics* 1(4): 287–336.

Crafts, N. F. R. (1976). "English Economic Growth in the Eighteenth Century: A Re-Examination of Deane and Cole's Estimates," *The Economic History Review* 29(2): 226–235.

(1984a). "Economic Growth in France and Britain, 1830–1910: A Review of the Evidence," *Journal of Economic History* 44(1): 49–67.

(1984b). "Patterns of Development in Nineteenth Century Europe," *Oxford Economic Papers* 36(3): 438–458.

(1985). *British Economic Growth during the Industrial Revolution.* Oxford: Clarendon Press.

(2004a). "Productivity Growth in the Industrial Revolution: A New Growth Accounting Perspective," *The Journal of Economic History* 64(2): 521–535.

(2004b). "Steam as a General Purpose Technology: A Growth Accounting Perspective," *The Economic Journal* 114(495): 338–351.

Crafts, N. F. R. and C. K. Harley (1992). "Output Growth and the British Industrial Revolution: A Restatement of the Crafts–Harley View," *The Economic History Review* 45(4): 703–730.

(2004). "Precocious British Industrialization: A General Equilibrium Perspective," in L. Prados de la Escosura (ed.), *Exceptionalism and Industrialisation: Britain and its European Rivals 1688–1815*. Cambridge University Press.

Crafts, N. F. R. and T. C. Mills (2009). "From Malthus to Solow: How did the Malthusian Economy Really Evolve?" *Journal of Macroeconomics* 31(1): 68–93.

Crafts, N. F. R., S. Leybourne, and T. Mills (1991). "Britain," in R. Sylla and G. Toniolo (eds.), *Patterns of European Industrialization*. London: Routledge, pp. 109–152.

Davis, R. (1962). "English Foreign Trade, 1700–1774," *The Economic History Review* 15(2): 285–303.

(1979). *The Industrial Revolution and British Overseas Trade*. Leicester University Press.

De Moor, T. and Zanden, J. L. van (2010). "Girl Power: The European Marriage Pattern and Labour Markets in the North Sea Region in the Late Medieval and Early Modern Period," *The Economic History Review* 63(1): 1–33.

Deane, P. and W. A. Cole (1967). *British Economic Growth, 1688–1959: Trends and Structure*. Cambridge University Press.

Dyer, C. (2005). *An Age of Transition? Economy and Society in England in the Later Middle Ages*. Oxford University Press.

Evans, C. and G. Rydén (2005). *The Industrial Revolution in Iron: The Impact of British Coal Technology in Nineteenth-century Europe*. Aldershot: Ashgate.

Feinstein, C. H. (1998). "Pessimism Perpetuated: Real Wages and the Standard of Living in Britain during and after the Industrial Revolution," *Journal of Economic History* 58(3): 625–658.

Findlay, R. and K. H. O'Rourke (2007). *Power and Plenty: Trade, War, and the World Economy in the Second Millennium*. Cambridge University Press.

Fremdling, R. (1977). "Railroads and German Economic Growth: A Leading Sector Analysis with a Comparison to the United States and Great Britain," *The Journal of Economic History* 37(3): 583–604.

(2000). "Transfer Patterns of British Technology to the Continent: The Case of the Iron Industry," *European Review of Economic History* 4(2): 195–222.

Gerschenkron, A. (1943). *Bread and Democracy in Germany*. H. Fertig.

(1962). *Economic Backwardness in Historical Perspective*. Cambridge, MA: Belknap Harvard University Press.

(1966). "Agrarian Policies and Industrialization: Russia 1861–1917," in *The Cambridge Economic History*. Vol. VI, Part II. Cambridge University Press.

Grantham, G. (1989). "Agricultural Supply during the Industrial Revolution: French Evidence and European Implications," *The Journal of Economic History* 49(1): 43–72.

Harley, C. K. (1982). "British Industrialization before 1841: Evidence of Slower Growth during the Industrial Revolution," *The Journal of Economic History* 42(2): 267–289.

(1991). "Substitution for Prerequisites: Endogenous Institutions and Comparative Economic History," in R. Sylla and G. Toniolo (eds.), *Patterns of European Industrialization: The Nineteenth Century*. London: Routledge, pp. 28–44.

(1998). "Cotton Textile Prices and the Industrial Revolution," *The Economic History Review* 51(1): 49–83.

(1999). "Reassessing the Industrial Revolution: A Macro View," in J. Mokyr (ed.), *The British Industrial Revolution: An Economic Perspective*. Boulder, CO: Westview Press, pp. 160–205.

(2004). "Trade: Discovery, Mercantilism and Technology," in R. Floudand and P. Johnson (eds.), *The Cambridge Economic History of Modern Britain*. Vol. I: *1700–1860*. Cambridge University Press.

Harnisch, H. (1986). "Peasants and Markets: The Background to the Agrarian Reforms in Feudal Prussia East of the Elbe, 1760–1807," in R. J. Evans and W. R. Lee (eds.), *The German Peasantry: Conflict and Community in Rural Society from the Eighteenth to the Twentieth Centuries*. London, Beckenham, Kent: Croom Helm, pp. 37–70.

Harris, R. (2000). *Industrializing English Law: Entrepreneurship and Business Organization, 1720–1844*. Cambridge University Press.

Hatcher, J. (1993). *The History of the British Coal Industry*. Vol. I: *Before 1700*. Oxford: Clarendon Press.

Hoffman, P. T. (1996). *Growth in a Traditional Society: The French Countryside, 1450–1815*. Princeton University Press.

Hoffman, P. T., G. Postel-Vinay, and J. L. Rosenthal (2001). *Priceless Markets: The Political Economy of Credit in Paris, 1660–1870*. University of Chicago Press.

Hoffmann, W. G. (1955). *British Industry, 1700–1950*. Cambridge, MA: Harvard University Press.

Humphries, J. (2011). *Childhood and Child Labour in the British Industrial Revolution*. Cambridge University Press.

Hyde, C. K. (1977). *Technological Change and the British Iron Industry 1700–1870*. Princeton University Press.

Jeremy, D. J. (1981). *Transatlantic Industrial Revolution: The Diffusion of Textile Technologies between Britain and America, 1790–1830s*. Cambridge, MA: MIT Press.

Landes, D. S. (1969). *The Unbound Prometheus: Technological Change and Industrial Development in Western Europe from 1750 to the Present*. Cambridge and London: Cambridge University Press.

Lindert, P. H. (1980). "English Occupations, 1670–1811," *The Journal of Economic History* 40(4): 685–712.

Lindert, P. H. and J. G. Williamson (1982). "Revising England's Social Tables 1688–1812," *Explorations in Economic History* 19(4): 385–408.

(1983). "Reinterpreting Britain's Social Tables, 1688–1913," *Explorations in Economic History* 20(1): 94–109.

Maddison, A. (2007). *The World Economy*. Vol. I: *A Millennial Perspective*; Vol. II: *Historical Statistics*. Academic Foundation.

Marx, K. (1867). *Das Kapital*. Hamburg: Verlag von Otto Meissner, vol. I.

Marx, K. and F. Engels (2002[1848]). *The Communist Manifesto*. Penguin Classics.

McCloskey, D. N. (1981). "The Industrial Revolution 1780–1860: A Survey," in R. Floud and D. N. McCloskey (eds.), *The Economic History of Britain since 1700*. Cambridge University Press, pp. 103–27.

McEvedy, C. and R. Jones et al. (1978). *Atlas of World Population History*. Harmondsworth: Penguin Books.

Milward, A. S. and S. B. Saul (1973). *The Economic Development of Continental Europe, 1780–1870*. London. Allen & Unwin.

(1977). *The Development of the Economies of Continental Europe, 1850–1914*. Cambridge, MA: Harvard University Press.

Nef, J. U. (1932). *The Rise of the British Coal Industry*. London: Routledge.

O'Brien, P. K. (1996). "Path Dependency, or why Britain Became an Industrialized and Urbanized Economy Long before France," *The Economic History Review* 49(2): 213–249.

O'Brien, P. K. and C. Keyder (1978). *Economic Growth in Britain and France, 1780–1914: Two Paths to the Twentieth Century*. London, Boston: G. Allen & Unwin.

Pamuk, S. (2007). "The Black Death and the Origins of the 'Great Divergence' across Europe, 1300–1600," *European Review of Economic History* 11(3): 289–317.

Parthasarathi, P. (1998). "Rethinking Wages and Competitiveness in the Eighteenth Century: Britain and South India," *Past & Present* 158: 79–109.

(2011). *Why Europe Grew Rich and Asia Did Not: Global Economic Divergence, 1600–1850*. Cambridge University Press.

Pierenkemper, T. and R. H. Tilly (2004). *The German Economy during the Nineteenth Century*. Berghahn Books.

Pollard, S. (1981). *Peaceful Conquest: The Industrialization of Europe, 1760–1970*. Oxford University Press.

Rosenberg, N. (1994). *Exploring the Black Box: Technology, Economy and History*. Cambridge University Press.

Pomeranz, K. (2001). *The Great Divergence: China, Europe, and the Making of the Modern World Economy*. Princeton University Press.

Shaw-Taylor, L. (2005). "Family Farms and Capitalist Farms in Mid Nineteenth-century England," *The Agricultural History Review*: 158–191.

(2012). "The Rise of Agrarian Capitalism and the Decline of Family Farming in England," *The Economic History Review* 65(1): 26–60.

Shaw-Taylor, L. and E. Wrigley (2008). *The Occupational Structure of England c. 1750–1871: A Preliminary Report*. Cambridge, UK: Cambridge Group for the History of Population and Social Structure.

Shaw-Taylor, L. *et al.* (2010). *The Occupational Structure of England c. 1710 to c. 1871: Work in Progress*. Cambridge, UK: Cambridge Group for the History of Population and Social Structure.

Tunzelmann, G. N. von (1978). *Steam Power and British Industrialization to 1860*. Oxford University Press.

Williamson, J. G. (1985). *Did British Capitalism Breed Inequality?* Boston: Allen & Unwin.

Woltjer, P., Smits, J. P., and E. Frankema (2010). "Comparing Productivity in the Netherlands, France, UK and US, ca. 1910: A New PPP Benchmark and its Implications for Changing Economic Leadership." *GGDC Research Memorandum*.

Wrigley, E. A. and R. S. Schofield (1989). *The Population History of England 1541–1871*. Cambridge University Press.

Zanden, J. L. van (2009). *The Long Road to the Industrial Revolution: The European Economy in a Global Perspective, 1000–1800*. Leiden: Brill.

17

America: capitalism's promised land

JEREMY ATACK

Introduction

In one of his few memorable (but often misquoted) sayings, "Silent" Cal(vin) Coolidge, the thirtieth president of the United States, famously pronounced, "the chief business of the American people is business." Elaborating upon this theme, he continued that the people "are profoundly concerned with producing, buying, selling, investing and prospering in the world" (Coolidge 1925). Others had also noticed and remarked upon these same traits in America. Werner Sombart (1976), for example, in answering his rhetorical question regarding the absence of American socialism, declared "America is the Canaan of capitalism, its promised land."[1] Earlier still, the English novelist Anthony Trollope, touring the United States as the Civil War began, was struck that while "men in trade in America are not more covetous than tradesmen in England, nor probably are they more generous or philanthropical ... that which they do, they are more anxious to do thoroughly and quickly" and that everywhere there was "that sharp desire for profit, that anxiety to do a stroke of trade at every turn" (Trollope 1863, writing of Lowell, Massachusetts in 1861).

The evidence, both inferential and concrete, suggests that this habit of doing business at every turn goes back to the very origins of the United States and applied to almost every activity – agriculture, manufacturing, and commerce. Moreover, it was set in motion by the very institutions that initiated English settlement in America. It was implicit in the decisions of tens of thousands of the poor who agreed to relinquish their freedoms temporarily

---

[1] This biblical allusion to the land "flowing with milk and honey" is from Exodus 3:8. The translation of Sombart is by Meyer Weinberg "A Short History of American Capitalism" (www.allshookdown.com/newhistory/CH01.htm, visited May 4, 2011) who asserts that Hocking and Husbands (Sombart 1976) mistranslate Sombart. Indeed, although I am not a speaker of German, "Canaan" is clearly in Sombart's original text.

for a period of indentured servitude to pay for their passage to America and the millions who risked their resources and their lives to emigrate to what they hoped would be a better life for them and for their families. It was embodied in the actions of slave owners who overcame any moral qualms they might have had regarding the exploitation of those whom they viewed as weak and inferior. It was certainly manifest in the actions of millions of individual farmers who routinely and deliberately produced more than they could consume and thus actively marketed their surplus so as to secure the best possible price and net the greatest profit. It was the driving force behind farmers who continually pushed westward into new lands. It also propelled those who moved from the countryside to a city in search of better opportunities, each in search of his or her own best advantage. In the actions of these individuals and socially interconnected groups, it might be argued that their quest for gain was tempered by other motivations such as altruism. However, over time, economic activity was increasingly concentrated in the hands of a new breed of "individuals" who, as the Lord Chancellor, Baron Thurlow, is said to have remarked, "have neither bodies to be punished, nor souls to be condemned" (Poynder 1844: I, 268) – corporations, entities which US Supreme Court Chief Justice John Marshall would subsequently describe as "artificial beings existing only in contemplation of the law" (US Supreme Court and Marshall 1819).[2]

Incorporation conveyed several critical rights and privileges. Among these (and implicit within the term "corporation" which derives from the Latin root "corpus" or body) was the ability of a group of individuals to act as a single entity under common seal, independent of the mix of the group, with the right to hold or exchange property, the right to enter into contracts, and the right to sue and to be sued. One especially important implication of the ability to act a single entity regardless of the mix of owners was that the mortality of the institution was no longer tied to the mortality of any individual or group of individuals. This was, I believe, key. In essence, the corporation achieved immortality unless otherwise constrained by its charter. As we will see, some early charters of incorporation did in fact impose such a constraint, often twenty years.[3] But even this seemingly brief "life" compared favorably with

---

2 Also "in corporations . . . there is no personal consciousness, consequently no shame or remorse," attributed to William Wilberforce. See Poynder (1844: I, 267).

3 New York's general incorporation law of 1811, for example, limited corporate charters to twenty years. This, however, represented an extension of life over that often granted in special charters granted earlier by the state which lasted fourteen or fifteen years. See Seavoy (1972).

that of any mortal individual at the time and it was almost certainly longer than the collective mortality experience of any group of humans.

The history of corporations in America begins with the history of permanent English settlement in North America. On April 10, 1606, King James I of England granted a charter creating two companies "to make Habitation, Plantation, and to deduce a colony of sundry of our People into that part of America commonly called VIRGINIA, and other parts and Territories in America" (Thorpe 1909; see also http://avalon.law.yale.edu/17th_century/va01.asp). That action would not only change the world by authorizing what became the first permanent English settlement in North America but also represented a subtle change in the nature and role of corporations. Previously, the most common use of the corporation had been to create public entities such as municipalities (e.g. the City of London), educational institutions, religious bodies, and charities.[4] However, the London and Plymouth companies created by King James's charter represented a quite different model in which there was a significant private element, albeit one with a specific public purpose (that is, claiming territory for the English Crown). Furthermore, unlike their immediate predecessors – the Muscovy Company (1555), the Levant Company (1581), and the East India Company (1600) – which had quite narrowly circumscribed objectives, these new companies enjoyed much greater freedoms.[5]

The earlier trading companies like the East India Company had proved to be quick sources of profit for their investors and promoters, including the state. At the same time, they had freed a fiscally constrained monarchy from underwriting the highly uncertain but almost certainly expensive costs of these ventures and from bearing the risk of failure to their credibility.[6] They might be thought of as the SPVs (special purpose vehicles) of that age. Moreover, those companies created before the London and Plymouth companies also clearly belonged to the mercantilist tradition of the time,

---

4 According to a history of the City of London, in 1067, William the Conqueror confirmed the city's rights which had existed since the time of Edward the Confessor. See www.cityoflondon.gov.uk/Corporation/LGNL_Services/Leisure_and_culture/Local_history_and_heritage/Buildings_within_the_City/Mansion_house/History+of+the+Government+of+the+City+of+London.htm.

5 For histories of these early chartered companies, see Willan (1956) on the Muscovy Company and Epstein (1908) on the Levant Company. There are many histories of the East India Company. See, for example, Robins (2006).

6 Similar ideas are to be found in Grafe and Irigoín (2012) who refer to the British empire as a "shareholder" empire although their focus is the Spanish "stakeholder empire." See also Elliott (2006) and Rei (2009).

with their focus on trade and imbued with extensive and exclusive monopoly rights.[7] Trade, however, was scarcely mentioned in the Virginia charter beyond a prohibition against the transport of any "Wares, Merchandises, or Commodities" outside of the British empire without royal consent. Instead, the goal for these new companies was long-term settlement and nation-building and many rights and privileges were left unspecified. Among these were the right to coin money and the ability to charter corporations – powers that were then reserved to the sovereign and ones which would subsequently be stripped away by the English Parliament (Scott 1910).

While the prospect of private profit lured investors into the London and Plymouth companies, these early corporations also served a clear public purpose which was then central to the grant of the privilege of incorporation. Over time, however, the balance between public and private interest shifted increasingly in favor of the private. In the world of small firms such as that envisaged by Adam Smith (1776), this shift would have been of little or no consequence. But, with dramatic growth in the size and scope of corporations resulting from scale and agglomeration efficiencies and unanticipated consequences from the passage of the thirteenth and fourteenth amendments to the US Constitution in 1865 and 1868, the growth of corporations transformed the world. These amendments were adopted to protect the rights of newly freed slaves. However, in an unsigned Supreme Court decision, the provisions of the fourteenth amendment were extended to corporations in the case of *Santa Clara County* v. *Southern Pacific Railroad* (1886) and corporations thereby achieved most of the rights of *natural* persons under American law as well as potential immortality, something which previously had been the exclusive domain of gods and governments.[8]

These changes have, in turn, increasingly led corporations to become rival forms of human organization to that of the nation-state which had created them. In 2011, for example, WalMart stores had over 2 million employees and annual revenues that exceed $420 billion.[9] This exceeds the population of Latvia and was more than the GNP of Austria, the twenty-seventh biggest country in the world in 2011 in terms of GNP, which has a conscript army and a

---

7 Indeed, the change in British policy to protect the interests of the East India Company through the Tea Act of 1773 was a seminal event for the American Revolution.

8 For the most recent affirmation of "natural" rights for corporations, see *Citizens United* v. *Federal Election Commission*: 558 U.S. 50, 2010.

9 Data from Fortune Global 500 listing for 2011 at http://money.cnn.com/magazines/fortune/global500/2011/full_list/index.html.

seat in the United Nations.[10] So large and powerful have some corporations become that now not only are they "too big to fail" but they have been known to dictate national policy.[11] They have become the distinguishing feature of American capitalism and have been so successful that, like sovereign nations, this innovation has spread around the world. While it is tempting to view this as a recent phenomenon, at least one prescient observer (Charles Adams) forecast the trend over one hundred and forty years ago:

> Our great corporations are fast emancipating themselves from the state, or rather subjecting the State to their own control, while individual capitalists who long ago abandoned the attempt to compete with them, will next seek to control them.   (Adams and Adams 1871: 12)

The corporation in America, however, only began to gain traction after the revolution and it would not become dominant until the late nineteenth century. Even so, corporations would remain rare. Rather, the sole proprietorship was and still is (in terms of sheer number) the dominant organizational form (see, for example, Carter, Gartner et al. 2006b: Part C, Chapter XX). Capitalism, though, was ever present in America from the establishment of colonies onward, as evidenced by reliance upon markets for personal, private gain.

The centrality and dominance of markets in America from an early date

Agricultural markets

Early on, virtually everyone in America was engaged in agriculture (Carter, Gartner et al. 2006a: Table Ba, 814–830). However, farms differed in scale, organization, and crop mix regionally. Some were clearly more capitalist – that is to say market-focussed and market-driven – than others. This was especially true in the South where plantations devoted much of their efforts to the production of non-food staple crops, particularly tobacco during the colonial period and cotton thereafter – crops which had to be sold on markets to satisfy distant needs, often overseas. Since such operations were highly specialized, these plantations had to purchase food and feed for the plantation family, its workforce, and its livestock.

---

10 Population and GNP data are from the *CIA Factbook* for 2011 at www.cia.gov/library/publications/the-world-factbook/geos/xx.html.

11 Avoiding modern debates such as the role of US oil companies in the Middle East in Yergin (1991), see, for example, Mitchener and Weidenmier (2005). Cuba is another case in point.

Nothing about farming – certainly not the type of farming practiced in the northeast and Midwest – required the corporate form. Capital requirements were modest (but larger than for the average manufacturing plant [Atack 1986b]), diversified farm activities potentially made gainful use of all members of the family farm (Craig 1993), and the prospect of an inheritance could be used to induce scarce family labor to stick around (Atack and Bateman 1987). Capital requirements for slave plantations were higher than those for free farms because of the cost of the slaves and some (limited) evidence of scale economies (Fogel and Engerman 1974, 1977). Nevertheless, the corporate form was not adopted by the plantation although plantations were much more obviously run as businesses (for example, professional management, use of business accounts, their concentration upon producing a non-food staple crop that had to be sold out of the area, etc.) than free northern farms.

Homogeneous endowments and low population densities made for limited local trading opportunities. The problem was neatly summarized by one observer as follows: "the land could produce nothing but corn, but as there was no market for the corn, they made it into whiskey; and, as they could not sell the whiskey, they drank it" (Ohio Experiment Station 1920: 50). Nevertheless, markets did emerge and farmers appear to have routinely and systematically produced not only enough for their family needs but also more than they could consume. As a result, most farmers engaged in market trade and ultimately became beholden to the market, despite being in the one activity that had the potential to eschew market involvement and, instead, be self-sufficient. Not all historians agree that farmers throughout the country quickly adopted a market *mentalité* (Henretta 1978), but the empirical evidence suggests that farmers produced more than they needed to produce to live (Atack and Bateman 1987) and, having done so, sought out those markets which offered the best prices (Atack and Bateman 1987; Rothenberg 1981, 1992). Moreover, farmers adapted their land use and crops to markets and prices (Thünen and Hall 1966). Thus, for example, when cheap grains from the Midwest flooded the east coast, farmers on the most marginally productive lands in New England responded quickly to the market signal. Many abandoned their farms and left agriculture for wage work in towns and cities becoming the first industrial workers (Field 1978). Not all left, though, and those who chose to stay on the land switched to other crops and products which could not be imported more economically from elsewhere, notably dairy products – initially butter and cheese and then as transportation improved, fluid milk. These new products required an intensification o labor effort (for example, year-round work in the fields, milking sheds and barns rather than a routine governed by a short growing season) in return for the higher value of output in the manner suggested by Boserup (1965, 1981).

In the South, the cotton monoculture quickly exhausted the soil and labor was the relatively scarce factor of production. As a result, it generally proved cheaper for the slave-owning "labor lords" to migrate westwards to the extensive frontier where cheap virgin cotton land was available rather than try to restore the soil's fertility (Majewski and Tchakerian 2007; Wright 1978). One consequence of this was to reduce the incentives to invest in "place" through urbanization and extensive investment in infrastructure. Such investment as did take place in the region was concentrated in port cities and in a transportation system designed to export cotton to distant markets whether in England or New England. Only after emancipation did these incentives reverse, converting labor lords to landlords (Wright 1986).

One measure of the importance of markets and trade is the extent, availability, and dissemination of knowledge relevant to market decision-making – that is to say, information about supply and demand, in particular information about prices and quantities. Such information enabled both producers and consumers to make informed decisions and helped create well-functioning, deeper, and broader markets.

Beginning in 1719, for example, Philadelphia's *American Weekly Mercury* began to carry lists of prices of a wide range of local, domestic, and imported products trading in that market. These prices were taken from broadsheets which previously had been posted in coffee houses that were frequented by merchants. The transfer of this specific knowledge out of the hands of specialists and its presentation to a broader audience – at a minimum, anyone able to afford the price of a newspaper – is symbolic of the growing depth and breadth of interest in the market (Bezanson, Gray et al. 1935: 3). There are similar but scattered data for New York beginning in 1720 and regularly for New York after 1748 (Warren, Pearson et al. 1932) and for Charleston from 1732 (Taylor 1932; Cole and International Scientific Committee on Price History 1938a, 1938b).

Over time, the quality and quantity of price data increased everywhere. For example, local prices appeared irregularly in Kentucky and Ohio papers as early as 1809 and regularly from about 1816 and even on a daily basis (albeit briefly) in 1825, by which time there was regular steamboat traffic on the rivers. These local prices were also often printed alongside New Orleans prices or those in even more distant markets (Berry 1943: especially 14–18) and those reproduced in Figure 17.1. Similar data, particularly for local farm

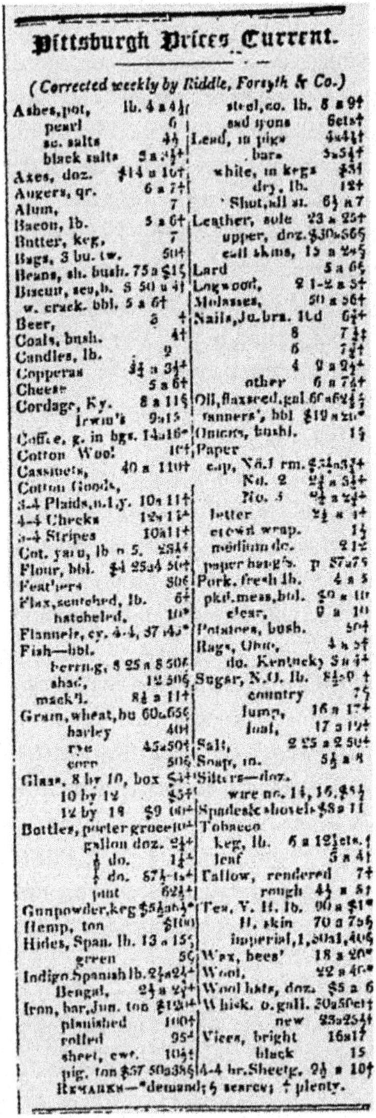

Pittsburgh Prices Current.

(Corrected weekly by Riddle, Forsyth & Co.)

Ashes, pot, lb. 4 a 4½
pearl 6
sc. salts 4½
black salts 3 a 3½†
Axes, doz. $14 a 16†
Augers, qr. 6 a 7½
Alum, 7
Bacon, lb. 5 a 6†
Butter, keg, 7
Bags, 3 bu. tw. 50†
Beans, sh. bush. 75 a $1§
Biscuit, sea, lb. 3 50 a 4†
w. crack. bbl. 5 a 6†
Beer, 5 †
Coals, bush. 4†
Candles, lb. 9
Copperas 3½ a 3½*
Cheese 5 a 6†
Cordage, Ky. 8 a 11§
Irwin's 9a15
Coffee, g. in bgs. 14a16*
Cotton Wool 10†
Cassinets, 40 a 110†
Cotton Goods,
3-4 Plaids, n.l.y. 10a11†
4-4 Checks 12a15*
3-4 Stripes 10a11†
Cot. yarn, lb n 5. 25½*
Flour, bbl. $4 25a4 50†
Feathers 30§
Flax, scutched, lb. 6†
hatcheled, 10*
Flannels, cy. 4-4, 37 a 45*
Fish—bbl.
herring, 3 25 a 3 50§
shad, 12 50§
mack'l. 8½ a 11†
Grain, wheat, bu 60a65§
barley 40†
rye 45a50†
corn 50§
Glass, 8 by 10, box $4½†
10 by 12 $5†
12 by 18 $9 10*
Bottles, porter groce 10*
gallon doz. 2½*
½ do. 1¼*
¼ do. 87½-1a*
pint 62½*
Gunpowder, keg $5½a6½*
Hemp, ton $100
Hides, Span. lb. 13 a 15§
green 5§
Indigo Spanish lb. 2½a2½*
Bengal, 2½ a 2½†
Iron, bar, Jun. ton $120*
planished 100†
rolled 95*
sheet, cwt. 10½†
pig, ton $37 50a38§
steel, co. lb. 8 a 9†
and irons 6cts†
Lead, in pigs 4a4½†
bars 5a5½†
white, in kegs $3½
dry, lb. 12†
Shot, all si. 6½ a 7
Leather, sole 23 a 25†
upper, doz. $30a36§
calf skins, 15 a 24§
Lard 5 a 6§
Logwood, 2 1-2 a 3†
Molasses, 50 a 56†
Nails, Ju. brs. 10d 6½†
8 7½†
6 7½†
4 9 a 9½*
other 6 a 7½†
Oil, flaxseed, gal 60a62½§
tanners', bbl $19 a 20*
Onions, bushl. 1§
Paper
cap, No. 1 rm. $3½a3½†
No. 2 2½ a 3½†
No. 3 2½ a 2½†
letter 2½ a 1†
crown wrap. 1§
medium do. 2 1†
paper hang's. p 37a75
Pork, fresh lb. 4 a 5
pkd. mess, bbl. $9 a 10
clear, 9 a 10
Potatoes, bush. 50†
Rags, Ohio, 4 a 5†
do. Kentucky 3 a 4*
Sugar, N.O. lb. 8½a9 †
country 7§
lump, 16 a 17*
loaf, 17 a 19†
Salt, 2 25 a 2 50†
Soap, in. 5½ a 8
Sifters—doz.
wire no. 14, 16, $5½
Spades & shovels $8 a 11
Tobacco
keg, lb. 6 a 12½cts.
leaf 3 a 4†
Tallow, rendered 7†
rough 4½ a 5†
Tea, Y. H. lb. 90 a $1*
H. skin 70 a 75§
imperial, 1,30a1,40§
Wax, bees' 18 a 20*
Wool, 22 a 40*
Wool hats, doz. $5 a 6
Whisk. o. gall. 30a50cts†
new 23a25½†
Vices, bright 16a17
black 15
4-4 br. Sheetg. 9½ a 10†
Remarks—*demand; § scarce; † plenty.

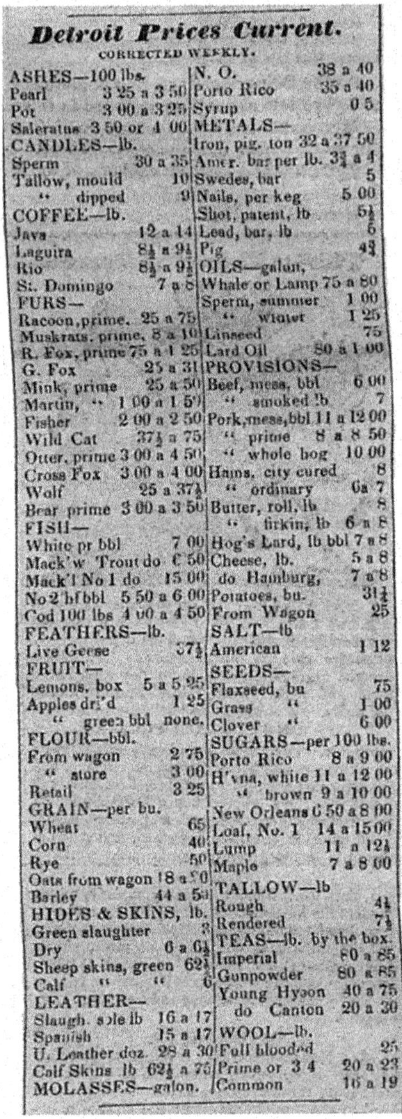

Detroit Prices Current.

CORRECTED WEEKLY.

ASHES—100 lbs.
Pearl 3 25 a 3 50
Pot 3 00 a 3 25
Saleratus 3 50 or 4 00
CANDLES—lb.
Sperm 30 a 35
Tallow, mould 10
" dipped 9
COFFEE—lb.
Java 12 a 14
Laguira 8½ a 9½
Rio 8½ a 9½
St. Domingo 7 a 8
FURS—
Racoon, prime. 25 a 75
Muskrats, prime, 8 a 10
R. Fox, prime 75 a 1 25
G. Fox 25 a 31
Mink, prime 25 a 50
Martin, " 1 00 a 1 50
Fisher 2 00 a 2 50
Wild Cat 37½ a 75
Otter, prime 3 00 a 4 50
Cross Fox 3 00 a 4 00
Wolf 25 a 37½
Bear prime 3 00 a 3 50
FISH—
White pr bbl 7 00
Mack'w Trout do 6 50
Mack'l No 1 do 15 00
No 2 hf bbl 5 50 a 6 00
Cod 100 lbs 4 00 a 4 50
FEATHERS—lb.
Live Geese 37½
FRUIT—
Lemons, box 5 a 5 25
Apples dri'd 1 25
" green bbl none.
FLOUR—bbl.
From wagon 2 75
" store 3 00
Retail 3 25
GRAIN—per bu.
Wheat 65
Corn 40
Rye 50
Oats from wagon 18 a 20
Barley 44 a 50
HIDES & SKINS, lb.
Green slaughter 3
Dry 6 a 6½
Sheep skins, green 62½
Calf " " 6
LEATHER—
Slaugh. sole lb 16 a 17
Spanish 15 a 17
U. Leather doz. 28 a 30
Calf Skins lb 62½ a 75
MOLASSES—galon.
N. O. 38 a 40
Porto Rico 35 a 40
Syrup 0 5
METALS—
Iron, pig. ton 32 a 37 50
Amer. bar per lb. 3¾ a 4
Swedes, bar 5
Nails, per keg 5 00
Shot, patent, lb 5½
Lead, bar, lb 6
Pig 4¾
OILS—galon,
Whale or Lamp 75 a 80
Sperm, summer 1 00
" winter 1 25
Linseed 75
Lard Oil 80 a 1 00
PROVISIONS—
Beef, mess, bbl 6 00
" smoked lb 7
Pork, mess, bbl 11 a 12 00
" prime 8 a 8 50
" whole hog 10 00
Hams, city cured 8
" ordinary 6a 7
Butter, roll, lb 8
" firkin, lb 6 a 8
Hog's Lard, lb bbl 7 a 8
Cheese, lb. 5 a 8
do Hamburg, 7 a 8
Potatoes, bu. 31¼
From Wagon 25
SALT—lb
American 1 12
SEEDS—
Flaxseed, bu 75
Grass " 1 00
Clover " 6 00
SUGARS—per 100 lbs.
Porto Rico 8 a 9 00
H'vna, white 11 a 12 00
" brown 9 a 10 00
New Orleans 6 50 a 8 00
Loaf, No. 1 14 a 15 00
Lump 11 a 12½
Maple 7 a 8 00
TALLOW—lb
Rough 4½
Rendered 7½
TEAS—lb. by the box.
Imperial 80 a 85
Gunpowder 80 a 85
Young Hyson 40 a 75
do Canton 20 a 30
WOOL—lb.
Full blooded 25
Prime or 3 4 20 a 23
Common 16 a 19

Figure 17.1 Two examples of nineteenth-century Midwestern US "Prices Current"

Source: *The Pittsburgh Gazette*, 45(14) (November 6, 1829), p. 2 and *The Signal of Liberty* 6 (10), (June 27, 1846), p. 3 (numbered 39) http://signalofliberty.aadl.org/signalofliberty/SL_18460627-p3-07.

produce, however, were published in small town newspapers throughout the Midwest and elsewhere from relatively early dates in their settlement process (e.g. 1841 in Indiana and Wisconsin, 1851 in Iowa, and 1858 in Minnesota) (Farris and Euler 1957; Marquardt 1959; Mortenson and Erdman 1933; Norton and Wilson 1930; Strand 1942).

Price data such as these also reveal an important nugget of information that stands as a measure of the existence and functioning of markets: the arbitrage of price differences between markets. Economic theory tells us that for tradable goods and in the absence any other institutional barriers, prices should not differ between any pair of markets by more than the cost of moving the good from the market where the price is lower to the market where the price is higher.

The available evidence suggests that price differences bore an increasingly close relationship to the costs of transportation. Moreover, as transport costs declined over the course of the nineteenth century with the transportation revolution, prices in different markets converge as predicted in both the long and the short run for commodity after commodity (Berry 1943; North 1961; Slaughter 1995). For example, Figure 17.2 shows the convergence in wheat prices

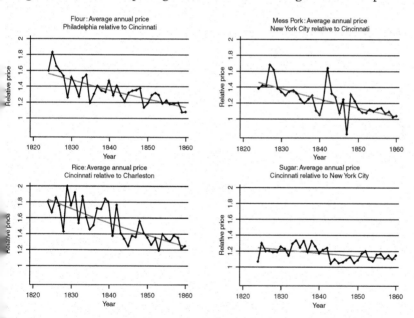

Figure 17.2 Price convergence in spatially separated US markets, 1824–1860
Sources: data from Cole (1938b) available at www.vanderbilt.edu/econ/cipr/cole-historical-data.html.

between Chicago and New York from the 1840s onward. Similar price convergence is also found for manufactures and for wage labor (Slaughter 1995).

Another metric of the existence and importance of markets is the emergence of specialized institutions that support them. None is of greater significance than the establishment of the Chicago Board of Trade (CBoT) in March of 1848 in anticipation of the opening of the Illinois and Michigan canal the following month. The first telegraph message had reached the city just two months earlier. In May, work would begin on the first plank road in the state and in November, 1848 the first wheat shipment was received in Chicago by rail (Taylor 1917: I, 134).

Almost from the start, some transactions on the CBoT involved what today we would call a forward contract involving grain "to arrive" in the city at some near future date (see, for example, Taylor [1917: 157] for delivery in August of 1849). The growing importance of Chicago and the CBoT as a trade center was also evidenced by the posting of market reports from Oswego, Buffalo, Montreal, and New York on the bulletin board by noon each day beginning in 1858. Moreover, the directors of the CBoT revised and strengthened their inspection rules adopted two years earlier, establishing moisture and foreign matter standards for grain deliveries (Taylor 1917). Such rules creating a standardized product of known quality were a *sine qua non* for futures trading. Standardized contract terms would soon follow and by the mid 1860s the market had become regularized, although a futures market as we know it today in which a clearing-house acts as the counterparty to every transaction did not appear until the early 1870s (Hoffman 1932).

Such activities posed a challenge to long-established ways of trading insofar as they involved the sale of a product which one did not own to someone who did not want it (see Rothstein in Gilchrist, Lewis *et al.* 1965) – that is to say, many futures contracts were settled by offsetting transactions with cash settlements through the clearing-house rather than by delivery of the commodity in question.

An active market in land may even have predated the emergence of an active commodities market in America as a result of terms laid down in the colonial charters which dictated that the lands were given and granted "in free and common Soccage only, and not in Capite." This effectively put the American colonies beyond the feudal system and gave the colonists the right to alienate land, a right that was largely denied to their English brethren for two more generations (Charles II 1660).[12] Such tenure provides incentives

---

12 Indeed, notice the especially important qualifier "in free and common Soccage *only*. . ." These provisions regarding land tenure were also generally stipulated in subsequent

for the landowner to exploit the land in an economically productive manner so as to maximize the difference between the fixed annual payments to the allodial owner of the land (the sovereign or state) and the landowner's gain from exploiting the land. The system thus encouraged the transfer of land to those who would use it productively (North and Thomas 1973).

This market for land would only grow ever more active as settlement pushed westward. Moreover, the cession of western land claims to the federal government by the original colonies provided a uniform system for the disposal of these public lands beginning with the Land Act of 1785 and continued by its successor legislation (Johnson 1976). This provided for the systematic survey of lands and their sale at public auction to the highest bidder, subject only to a statutorily set minimum price, until the federal government began giving land away to private individuals under the Homesteading Act of 1862 (Gates 1936; Hibbard 1924; Oberly 1990).[13] Even so, there remained an active secondary resale market in land in which speculators played a central role (Fogel and Rutner 1972; Swierenga 1968).

Labor markets

As a land of *European* settlement, America has always been a land of immigrants. It was also a land of labor scarcity. These characteristics imparted a uniquely American character to the market for labor. Wages were high and the transatlantic voyage was arduous, risky, and expensive. Consequently, the trek was not undertaken lightly but was the result of serious deliberation regarding the likely returns, whether in the form of treasure or a better life for oneself and/or one's descendants (including such considerations as personal freedom or the vote) (Engerman and Sokoloff 2005; Fogel and Rutner 1972; Hatton and Williamson 1993; Thomas 1973; Williamson 1974).

The high cost of travel early on, however, meant that few people could afford to meet the out-of-pocket expenditure themselves while the risks of the voyage (including physical distance) and the perceived difficulty of collecting a debt from someone in a distant and still largely undeveloped land discouraged participation by the developing capital markets in this trade. As a result, a majority of colonial immigrants came to America on some form of long-term labor contract which financed their travel. These contracts were either

charters such as that to Lord Baltimore for the settlement of Maryland (http://avalon.law.yale.edu/17th_century/ma01.asp) and to William Penn for the settlement of Pennsylvania (http://avalon.law.yale.edu/17th_century/pa01.asp).

13 By providing a secure title to a specific piece of land, these surveys also created value and encouraged investment in and improvement of the land. See, for example, Libecap and Lueck (2011).

negotiated in England prior to departure for indentured servants or, in the case of redemptioners, negotiated with would-be employers upon safe arrival in America (Galenson 1981; Grubb 1986, 1988). In each case, however, the term of service was set so that the expected value of the servant's output net of the cost of their maintenance, board, and any other compensation paid (such as a performance bonus at the conclusion of the contract) discounted to the present would cover the cost of passage to the colonies plus a risk premium. In the case of indentured servants, this market quickly became regularized and routine as evidenced by the printing of "fill-in-the blank" standardized contract forms (Galenson 1981).

In America, too, morality and ethics also had a price.[14] Insufficient labor was willing to migrate here for the price that employers were willing to offer for less agreeable tasks such as planting rice, picking cotton, or harvesting sugar. For millions of persons of African descent, this price was the difference between their high productivity in these unpopular tasks and the cost to others of providing them with the minimum subsistence consistent with maintaining their health and capacity for work. The result was the enslavement and exploitation of the weak by the powerful (Ransom and Sutch 1977; Vedder 1975) and these gains to the few (slave owners) at the expense of the many (slaves) undoubtedly played a role in southern intransigence and the outbreak of the Civil War (Gunderson 1974).

While slavery in the northern colonies and states had died out more or less naturally in the late eighteenth and early nineteenth centuries, in the South high and rising demand for cotton – a crop which could not be grown in more northerly climes – and the invention of the cotton gin reinvigorated the system. The opening up of even more productive cotton lands in Alabama, Mississippi, and Texas only reinforced and strengthened the system by raising current returns on the investment (Conrad and Meyer 1958; Fogel 1989; Fogel and Engerman 1974). As a result, slave owners voluntarily moved westward to take advantage of this economic opportunity, dragging their chattel slaves along with them without regard to the costs to those chattels. Moreover, to the extent that the white population in these newly settled areas were a shrinking minority, poor whites in the area found themselves tied ever more closely to the slave-owning elite for mutual protection.

14 For example, the Southern Baptist Convention, which would become the world's largest Baptist denomination in the world and the largest Protestant sect in the United States by the late twentieth century, split from the rest of the Baptist Church in 1845 over the issue of slavery

The market for slaves was deep, long-lived, and is well documented (see, for example, Hall 2000). As with other markets, the evidence suggests that slave prices were set in a manner consistent with the intrinsic value of the asset, that is to say, the slave's productivity (Fogel 1989; Fogel and Engerman 1974). For slaves, their ability to invest in their human capital was severely constrained. Consequently, even following emancipation, making up for these deprivations took time despite the passage of constitutional amendments for their benefit. Instead, most former slaves remained trapped in economically disadvantageous sharecropping contracts and dependent upon the paternalism of the new landlords, their former masters, for access to justice and protection for a generation or more (Alston and Ferrie 1993, 1999; Alston and Higgs 1982; Alston and Kauffman 1998; Higgs 1977; Ransom and Sutch 1977; Wright 1986).

Transportation as a key innovation for incorporation

As the American population pushed westwards to take up new land, there was an increasing mismatch between the locus of production and places of consumption. As a result, the development of improved means of transportation and communication between the two became an ever more pressing concern. That need was clearly articulated by Thomas Jefferson's Treasury Secretary, Albert Gallatin, who, in his report to Congress, argued "Good roads and canals, will shorten distances, facilitate commercial and personal intercourse, and unite by a still more intimate community of interests, the most remote quarters of the United States" (Senate and Treasury 1808). Yet these amenities were lacking. The problem, according to Gallatin, was the high cost of capital and low settlement density which rendered such improvements less profitable than expected or desired, and the challenge posed by large positive externalties associated with such improvements although, as he observed, "The General Government can alone remove these obstacles" (Senate and Treasury 1808). Most roads, for example, were local and did not constitute a network, let alone represent anything necessary to satisfy the continental aspirations and security needs of the country.

Early efforts concentrated on improving the nation's roads, the best of which were privately financed, limited access, fee-for-use turnpikes. Even though most of these were relatively short, their capital cost was still generally beyond the means of an individual or a small group. Consequently, most were built by corporations created especially for that purpose and granted special charters by the state. Insofar as these transportation improvements served the public good, such state grants of incorporation were consistent with existing legal tradition. Incorporation, however, quickly proved to have another important benefit: raising capital through the sale of stock also enabled corporations to mediate the free rider problem whereby landowners lying along or close to the right of way could benefit from enhanced land values regardless of whether or not they used the road. However, by selling stock to such landowners, not only were the locals actively engaged in the construction and routing of the road but they also became vested in its eventual financial success.

Such sales were made easier because turnpike stock, unlike that of banks and industrial corporations also being chartered around the same time, typically carried a low par value. As a consequence, with regard to turnpikes

> Stockholders' lists reveal a web of neighbors, kin, and locally prominent figures voluntarily contributing to what they saw as an important community improvement. Appeals made in newspapers, local speeches, town meetings, door-to-door solicitations, correspondence, and negotiations in assembling the route stressed the importance of community improvement.
>
> (Klein and Majewski 2008; see also Cleveland and Powell, 1909; Coffman and Gregson 1998).

In the final analysis, though, profits (and dividends) from most turnpike ventures were disappointing although such public goods generated valuable and significant positive externalities (Klein 1990; Klein and Majewski 1992, 2008; Taylor 1951). Such low returns to investors in these and other transportation improvements are a key element in the protracted debate regarding the extent to which specific infrastructure investments were "premature" (see, for example, Fishlow 1965; Fogel 1960; Mercer 1969, 1970).

Government – federal, state and local – also intervened to promote transportation improvements. Sometimes these agencies were simply permissive; at other times they were much more proactive. Among the former actions were the approval of risk and capital pooling arrangements through grants of incorporation and access to the court system for eminent domain cases to secure rights of way. The federal government also supplied the services of the Army Corps of Engineers who conducted detailed surveys and feasibility studies for transportation routes (Haney 1908). However, government was often more deeply involved in transportation improvements. The state of New York, for example, famously guaranteed bond payments to would-be investors in the Erie Canal, although *ex post* it never had to make good on that promise. Similarly, Pennsylvania, Ohio, and Indiana were major investors and promoters of canals within their borders (see, for example, Goodrich 1960, 1967; Metzger and Bobel 2009; Sheriff 1996; Taylor 1951; Woods 2008). As a consequence, Ohio and Pennsylvania initially tried to discourage railroads by imposing taxes on those lines which competed directly against canals (quoted in Taylor 1951: 75), while in Indiana, the bursting of the canal bubble forced the state into bankruptcy and led to the drafting of a new state constitution in 1842 limiting the state's ability to borrow.

The federal government was (intermittently) even more deeply involved in internal improvements than state governments. It constructed the National Road (Raitz, Thompson et al. 1996: especially Chapters 3–6) and underwrote a network of post roads (Lord 1907) that eventually evolved into the US highway system. They also built harbors and lighthouses, and removed snags and sandbars from navigable waterways (Hunter 1949). Later on, the federal government would also grant public lands to encourage railroad construction. This provided these businesses with an asset that they could mortgage or sell and it also gave them a vested interest in some of the potential externalities that would accrue through the appreciation of land values contingent upon construction (Gates 1934).

The high cost of transportation improvements made incorporation a virtual necessity. In the northeast, for example, turnpike companies accounted for more than a quarter of all business incorporations by general or special charters between 1800 and 1830 (compiled by Klein and Majewski 2008) and in Ohio, railroads accounted for 45 percent of incorporations in 1836 (Evans 1948: Appendix 4).[15] However, where the financing for roads had been local, it became increasingly national and even international. Money to begin construction of the Baltimore and Ohio railroad had been raised from a few prominent Baltimore merchants and bankers by public subscriptions through the Mechanics Bank in Baltimore, the Farmers' Branch Bank in Frederick and the Hagerstown Bank in Hagerstown. The initial public offering was heavily oversubscribed with the public signing up for 36,788 shares although only 15,000 were available (Stover 1987). Similarly, the Mohawk and Hudson railroad was financed by wealthy New Yorkers (Taylor 1951: 99). However, as the railroad network expanded and railroad mania caught hold in the 1840s, "State Street in Boston and Wall Street in New York began to play a more important role, especially in connection with the construction of western lines" (that is to

---

15 In Pennsylvania, turnpike companies accounted for an even higher share of business incorportations: 46 percent.

say, lines in which they had no immediate local interest either as a supplier of transportation services or a source of local externalities).

> Similarly, the Illinois Central was managed by eastern promoters and was financed in part by funds raised in the eastern states and abroad ... British investments in American railroad securities, especially bonds, increased rapidly, so that by 1853, of the total American railroad bonds outstanding, 26 percent were foreign owned [but] railroad stocks, valued at something less than twice the figure for bonds, were only 3 per cent foreign-owned.
>
> (Taylor 1951: 100)

Moreover, when the Illinois Central railroad found it more difficult to raise money in London during the Crimean War, their stocks and bonds were offered in Amsterdam and found a ready market (see also Veenendaal 1992; Wilkins 1989). As a result, other American railroads also raised money in continental Europe and by 1860 railroads had absorbed more than a billion dollars – a sum equal to the aggregate investment in manufacturing at the time – to build and operate trains on some 30,000 miles of track in the United States (Chandler 1965).

While corporations were essential organizations for the *construction* of these new transportation media, they were essential as *suppliers of transportation services* only on the nation's railroads where coordination of traffic was an absolute necessity. Absent a central planner, faster trains could not pass slower trains on the same track and departures and arrivals had to be strictly timed to avoid head-on collisions on a single-track system. There were, however, few if any barriers to entry for canal barge operators, teamsters, or coach drivers. Even steamboats were, for the most part, affordable by wealthy individuals or a small group (Taylor 1951) and, since they did not survive the rigors of river navigation for very long, the partnerships had a natural turnover quite independent of the mortality of the individual partners. While corporations (for example, the Cincinnati and Louisville Mail Line and other packet lines) were not unknown on the western rivers (Hunter 1949: 320–342), they were common on the rivers of the east coast (for example, Commodore Vanderbilt's operations) and the Great Lakes (Taylor 1951: 69).

These transportation improvements facilitated the development of the Midwest's prodigious agricultural potential, allowed the plantations of the South to concentrate their energies on producing raw cotton for the New England and British textile mills. Meanwhile the northeastern population was freed from the necessity of eking out a marginal subsistence from the land and could, instead, move into the cities to engage in more remunerative manufacturing and trading occupations (North 1961b). Such manufacturing became increasingly concentrated in businesses organized as corporations as capital requirements grew and firms took advantage of economies of scale and efficiency gains.

The emergence and growth of the manufacturing corporation in America

Although early colonial governments had made relatively little use of their presumed ability to create corporations and thus the colonies were largely unaffected by the "pernicious art of stock-jobbing" that accompanied the South Sea Bubble, Parliament extended the Bubble Act of 1720 to the American colonies in 1741 (Scott 1910: 1, 436–437).[16] What few corporations had been chartered in America, like Harvard College and Yale, hewed to the tradition of municipal, educational, charitable and religious organizations (Davis 1917) serving primarily public purposes and without consideration of private profit (Nettels 1962: 290). Indeed, Davis dismisses those colonial corporations which were created with the statement "Business corporations which were colonial both in origin and in activity were few, and on the whole of no great importance" (1917: 87).

Following the Revolution, however, the former colonies began to assert their independence. One of the ways in which they did so was to charter corporations since this power had been so closely associated with that of the sovereign. Indeed, some state incorporations at this time made explicit reference to this fact (Davis 1917: 11, 9). Despite this incentive on the supply side, relatively few corporations were chartered until after the 1789 Constitution was adopted (Davis 1917: 11, 28–29, Figure 1), most of them in transportation and none in manufacturing.[17]

The development of domestic American manufactures had been actively stifled during the colonial period by British mercantilist policy. This generally prohibited the widespread distribution of domestically produced goods that might compete with British manufactures including (but not limited to)

16 Harris (1994) argues that the Bubble Act was of minor importance in Britain.
17 Indeed, one of the more important corporations chartered at this time, the Bank of North America, received its charter from Congress rather than a state. However, questions about congressional authority to charter institutions led it to hedge its bet by also securing a charter from the state of Pennsylvania (Wilson 1942). Similar doubts would also arise under the 1789 Constitution and clouded the creation and operation of the First and Second Bank of the United States.

woolens, iron products (including guns), and glass. In reality, however, the small size of the American market, the low density of settlement and the limited number of skilled artisans were at least as serious impediments to the development of colonial manufactures as any imperial restrictions (Clark 1929).[18] Some crude manufactures such as pig iron were encouraged as input for the British iron industry. So too was the manufacture of wood products, given the scarcity of lumber in Great Britain. One of these products, ships, was especially important as their export to Great Britain was a critical entry in the colonial balance of payments under invisibles (Shepherd and Walton 1972; Walton and Shepherd 1979) with pig iron often serving as ballast.

In the newly minted United States, the development of domestic industry would become a matter of national debate, at least for a while, between competing visions of America. On the one hand, Thomas Jefferson opined "for the general operations of manufacture, let our work-shops remain Europe" (Jefferson and Peterson 1984: 291: Query xix from Notes on the State of Virginia) while, on the other, Alexander Hamilton concluded his report to Congress on the subject of manufactures with the following declaration: "in a community situated like that of the United States, the public purse must supply the deficiency of private resource. In what can it be so useful, as in prompting and improving the efforts of industry?" (House and Treasury 1791: 144). Reflecting this spirit, Hamilton several months earlier had pushed the state of New Jersey to charter what we would today call a state-sponsored enterprise: the Society for Establishing Useful Manufactures with a capitalization of $600,000. The key asset of the new company (aside from its links to the Executive Branch) was the Great Falls of the Passaic around which would grow one of the nation's first industrial centers, the town of Paterson, New Jersey. Perhaps somewhat predictably, the enterprise was a failure and Paterson also fell short of its promise (Davis 1917). Thereafter, with a few notable exceptions such as the willingness of the federal government to pay a very high price for firearms with interchangeable parts (Hounshell 1984), government had little *direct* participation in manufacturing activity until the twentieth century.

After receiving Hamilton's report on manufactures, the House simply tabled the plan without any debate or vote (Irwin 2004). Congressional lack of interest in manufactures reflected the boom in the carrying trade ther

---

18 Both Adam Smith (Smith 2001) and Alexander Hamilton (United States Congress, House, American State Papers [1791]) make these same points to explain the lack of manufacturing development in the American colonies. For new work on colonial manufactures inferred from British trade data see Smith (1998).

on-going. America's merchants and ship-owners were earning large profits on trade not only with Europe but also with the rest of the world, including Asia (Dalzell 1987; Fichter 2010). Moreover, Americans could buy from Europe whatever manufactures they might desire at a lower price and of higher quality than domestic manufacturers could possibly supply. Industrialization was simply irrelevant to American prosperity and living standards at the time despite the success of individual ventures such as the gunpowder works of E. I. DuPont along the Brandywine in Wilmington, Delaware or the Slater Mill in Pawtucket, Rhode Island. This mill, underwritten by Providence merchants Almy and Brown, was the first successful effort to innovate the new British textile technology in the United States, a technology that the British had sought to protect by, for example, prohibiting the emigration of persons such as Samuel Slater who had knowledge of these new machines. This was but the first of several industrial espionage episodes that were crucial to the growth and development of the American cotton textile industry.

The American export and re-export boom that began with the French Revolution in 1789 would, however, collapse when President Jefferson embargoed trade with Europe in 1807 and it lasted through the war of 1812–1815.[19] Suddenly, cheap high-quality foreign manufactures were unavailable at almost any price and America was forced to supply its own wants. The result was involuntary import substitution industrialization, which shows up in a sharp uptick in factory incorporations, particularly in those industries whose products had previously been imported: chemicals, glass, metals, and textiles (Senate and State 1824).[20]

The sudden importance of manufactures also shows up in Congress's belated and haphazard efforts to collect information on manufacturing activity as part of the 1810 Census. These events also transformed former President Jefferson's views: "we must now place the manufacturer by the side of the agriculturalist . . . experience has taught me that manufactures are now as necessary to our independence as to our comfort" (Jefferson and Peterson 1984: 1371: Letter to Benjamin Austin, January 9, 1816).

19 It was in this war that the "bombs bursting in air" over Fort McHenry protecting Baltimore's harbor in 1814 inspired Francis Scott Key to write the words we now know as "The Star-Spangled Banner."
20 The underlying data appear to be from the returns of the 1820 Census. These therefore seriously understate the true number of businesses that were incorporated between 1800 and 1820 since the business had to survive from its incorporation to 1820 in order to be enumerated. Even so the data show a sharp rise in incorporations between 1809 and 1816. See Lebergott (1984).

Slater's mill produced cotton yarn. The weaving of that yarn into cloth would remain a bottleneck in the industry so long as weaving remained a handicraft operation. As with the spinning of thread, this problem had been solved by the British, although its solution would remain hidden from the Americans until Francis Lowell paid a visit to Lancashire in 1810 and, upon his return, was able to work with machinist Paul Moody to produce the first American power looms based upon this pirated technology.[21] These were operational by 1815 in the Boston Manufacturing Company that Lowell had established along the Charles river in Waltham (Dalzell 1987; Shlakman 1935; Weil 1998). The capital and the organizing genius for this new venture came from socially embedded Boston merchants whose trade opportunities and profits had fallen sharply in the wake of Jefferson's embargo and the war that followed. The speed with which these individuals and families switched from one activity to another suggests little in the way of sentimental attachment to traditional employment and little or no stigma attaching to their new activities; only a superior expected rate of return on their abundant, fungible, and mobile capital.

Besides the new power looms, the other key innovation in this factory was the integration of spinning and weaving under one roof, whereas in Rhode Island and back in Britain these two tasks in the production of textiles were kept separate. Both innovations proved to be resounding successes. The location of the mill, however, was less satisfactory because of the limited waterpower potential of the Charles river. This shortcoming was remedied in the following decade by the establishment of a new mill town along the Merrimack river at its confluence with the Concord river. There, the Merrimack river falls 32 feet, providing what was thought to be ample waterpower potential and space for the industry to grow (Hunter, Eleutherian Mills-Hagley Foundation et al. 1979: 1). They named the new town, Lowell, to memorialize Francis Lowell whose power loom and integration of spinning and weaving had revolutionized the industry. Over the course of the next thirty years or so, the Boston Associates would establish dozens of cotton textiles mills in Lowell, a planned industrial community (Dalzell 1987; Shlakman 1935; Weit 1998). More mills would spring up in other cities along the Merrimack river such as Lawrence, Nashua, and Manchester. These promoters expanded the scope and scale of the industry. They also avoided engaging in "ruinous competition" through a web of interlocking directorates among the individual companies and by the careful strategic positioning of a

---

21 The first power loom is credited to Edmund Cartwright in 1785.

new mill's products as complementary to, rather than competing with, those of existing mills.

The return on investment in the Boston Manufacturing Company as well as that in the hundreds of other ventures induced by Jefferson's embargo and the wartime cut-off in foreign trade was threatened by the outbreak of peace following the Treaty of Ghent, which brought with it competition from a flood of cheap, high-quality manufactured imports from Great Britain beginning in 1815. Hamilton had foreseen this circumstance in his report on manufactures twenty-five years earlier:

> The superiority antecedently enjoyed by nations, who have preoccupied and perfected a branch of industry, constitutes a more formidable obstacle, than either of those, which have been mentioned, to the introduction of the same branch into a country, in which it did not before exist. To maintain between the recent establishments of one country and the long matured establishments of another country, a competition upon equal terms, both as to quality and price, is in most cases impracticable. The disparity in the one, or in the other, or in both, must necessarily be so considerable as to forbid a successful rivalship.   (United States Congress. House. American State Papers [1791])

The solution, he suggested, was "the extraordinary aid and protection of government" (United States Congress. House. American State Papers (1791) by means of a temporary protective tariff for these infant industries – again, an alliance between the public and private sector to resolve issues associated with externalities and thus the failure of a pure (private) market economy. This would allow workers and capitalists to gain experience through learning by doing, enabling them to compete on quality terms (Bils 1984; David 1970; Williamson 1972). The breathing room and profits from tariff protection would also allow domestic industry to achieve the scale necessary to compete on price with larger, more mature foreign rivals. The result, according to Taussig (1967), was a shift in tariff policy away from simply serving as a revenue source for the federal government to providing protection for specific domestic industries (Bils 1984; David 1970; Irwin 2008; Pincus 1977).

While cotton textiles were significant beneficiaries of tariff policy (Bils 1984; David 1970; Harley 1992; Irwin and Temin 2001) many other industries also gained protection (Hawke 1975; Irwin 2008). This policy also skewed national income between different groups (favoring capitalists and industrial workers over agriculturalists and landowners, for example) and regions (James 1981) and led to secessionist talk in the South culminating in the nullification crisis of 1832 over the 1828 Tariff Act. While this crisis was temporarily resolved by the lowering of tariffs, the regional disparity in the costs and benefits of tariffs never disappeared and would again become a force in the crisis leading up to the Civil War (Irwin 2008; Ochenkowski 1982; Taussig 1888). Moreover, tariffs would remain high for the rest of the nineteenth century, reflecting, in part, the North's political and economic ascendancy following its Civil War success (Beard and Beard 1927; Hacker 1940).

By the time the 1820 census was taken, there was a fairly extensive industrial sector in the northeast. Census coverage of manufacturing for the South and Midwest was much less complete but even making allowance for this it is clear that there was what historian Charles Ramsdell (1936) would describe as a "deplorable scarcity" of manufacturing in the South (Bateman and Weiss 1981). This would prove to be a factor in the Confederacy's loss in the Civil War: the South simply lacked the means to fight a modern war based around iron and machinery so long as the North's blockade kept out imports.

While average per capita income in the South compared favorably with that in the Midwest, the distribution of income was far more unequal in the South. Slaves had no dollars and thus no market power. There were also disproportionately more poor southern whites than poor midwesterners. As a result, the mass southern market demand was weak and failed to support a local domestic industry. This shows up in a smaller range of consumer products and smaller producers serving the southern market (Bateman and Weiss 1981). Many southern politicians of the time, most notably John C. Calhoun of South Carolina, pushed for more industry – especially cotton textiles – in the South through speeches, editorials, and commercial conventions (Calhoun, Meriwether et al. 1959, especially November 13, 1845) and there was a commercial press, particularly DeBow's Commercial Review published out of New Orleans that also championed the cause. Little, however, came of this public debate so long as the South enjoyed a comparative advantage in raw cotton production and operated within the common market of the United States until cheap southern labor began attracting northern and midwestern industry to relocate there after the Civil War (Wright 1986).

The theft of ideas seems to have been common in early America as the piracy of British inventions by Slater and Lowell show. Similar "appropriations" occurred domestically and several notable American inventors – Oliver Evans and Eli Whitney, for example – complained bitterly that existing patent protection promised by the US Constitution and supposedly secured by the passage of a federal patent law in 1791 failed to secure their rights (and rewards) for the promised limited period of time (Bathe and Bathe 1935; Evans and Stevens 1805; Mirsky and Nevins 1952; Olmsted and Sillimar

1846). Despite this weak protection, however, Americans would prove to be amazingly creative and inventive. American inventors came from all walks of life so that invention, like so much of American life, was relatively democratic and open. Many of these early inventors were workers in occupations and industries directly affected by their invention – they saw the need and found the means (Khan 2005; Lamoreaux and Sokoloff 1996; 2001; Sokoloff 1988; Sokoloff and Khan 1990;). Over time, however, patenting came to be increasingly identified with businesses rather than individuals and there was a sharp uptick in the rate of invention, measured by patents per million residents following the Civil War (Lamoreaux 2005; Lamoreaux and Sokoloff 1996, 2001).

The adoption of these inventions would have a profound effect upon the ways in which goods and services were produced. Many, particularly those adopted in manufacturing, substituted the skill and creativity of the machine-builder for the skill of the worker thus reducing the average skill level in the typical workplace (Atack, Bateman et al. 2004; Cain and Paterson 1986; Goldin 1982; Goldin and Katz 1998; Goldin and Sokoloff 1984). They also had a profound effect upon the nature and operation of the firm. The introduction of ever-more complex machinery required the use of an inanimate source of power and reduced firms' mobility by tying them to a particular place (Atack, Bateman et al. 1980; Hunter, Eleutherian Mills-Hagley Foundation et al. 1979). The complexity of machinery also inevitably increased the specificity of capital and tended to raise the capital/labor ratio (Cain and Paterson 1986; Chandler 1977; Hounshell 1984). Given greater sunk costs, firms operated longer each day and for more days per year at significantly greater output levels and rates of throughput to spread these added costs over more units of production (Atack 1986b; Atack, Bateman, et al. 2002; Chandler 1977).

Firm size increased, primarily as a result of sharp increases the relative size of the very largest firms, which were those best suited to take advantage of the new technologies embodied in inanimately powered machines (Atack 1985, 1986a; Atack, Bateman et al. 2004). The machine technology had a profound effect upon firm size and output. Consider for example, the production of cheap boots for men. Hand production involved 83 operations by two men and required over 1,400 man-hours to produce 100 pairs. Machine production broke down the production process into 122 operations performed by 113 workmen who took just over 154 man-hours to produce the same 100 pairs of boots (United States Congress, House and Labor [1899]). Adopting machine production therefore vastly expanded the scale of the business and required access to bigger markets.

Each of these changes also had the effect of increasing the incentives for firms to avoid the destructive forces of competition whether by seeking government protection through tariffs and the like, by merging, or by finding other ways to cooperate rather than compete (Chandler 1977; Hawke 1975; Lamoreaux 1985; Schumpeter 1947). In short, the very market mechanisms that symbolize and stimulate capitalism also contain the seeds to destroy the system:

> That process, impressive in its relentless necessity, was not merely a matter of removing institutional deadwood, but of removing partners of the capitalist stratum, symbiosis with whom was an essential element of the capitalist schema ... [T]he capitalist process in much the same way in which it destroyed the institutional framework of feudal society also undermines its own.   (Schumpeter 1947: 139)

The rise in the capital costs of manufacturing associated with the use of power, the increasing scale of the business, the cost, complexity, and specificity of the new machinery conspired to push firms to adopt more robust, longer-lived forms of business organization that also spread that risk. These attributes were to be found in the very organizational form that had first promoted English settlement in North America: the corporation.

According to Chief Justice John Marshall, this entity was:

> the mere creature of law, it possesses only those properties which the charter of its creation confer upon it either expressly or as incidental to its very existence ... Among the most important are immortality, and ... individuality – properties by which a perpetual succession of many persons are considered as the same, and may act as a single individual. They enable a corporation to manage its own affairs and to hold property.
>   (US Supreme Court and Marshall 1819)

Subsequent court decisions, however, made one seemingly small change to Chief Justice John Marshall's decision with consequences that continue to reverberate to the present. Marshall had declared the corporation "an *artificial being*" (emphasis added), but in the *Santa Clara* decision (US Supreme Court 1886), the Supreme Court, in a unanimous decision, extended the fourteenth amendment's "equal protection" rights to corporations as if they were natural persons. Importantly in the context of the current debate over the role of the corporation in American (political) life, Justice Marshall continued that "this being does not share in the civil government of the country, unless that be the purpose for which it was created." This shift has, in turn, led directly to *Citizens United* v. *Federal Election Commission* (2010) and is what allowed Republican presidential candidate Mitt Romney to famously retort to a heckler at the Iowa State Fair in August 2011: "corporations are people too, my friend" (Mark 1987; Oliphant 2011).

The rise of the corporation to dominance (in terms of size and output share but not numbers) began slowly. As one legal scholar (Friedman 1985: 511) noted "in 1800, corporation law was a torpid backwater of law, mostly concerned with municipalities, charities and churches. Only a bridge or two, a handful of manufacturing enterprises, a few banks or insurance companies, disturbed its quiet."[22] This would not long remain so. "By 1870 corporations had a commanding position in the economy. They never lost it. In the decade of the 1880s, pulpit and platform resounded with battle cries about trust and antitrusts" (Friedman 1985: 511).

Early on, incorporations were by special charter with each company created by a private (and thus often personalized) act of the legislature (Sylla and Wright 2012). This process was expensive, cumbersome, and potentially corrupt. Consequently, an increasing number of states adopted general incorporation laws by which the privilege of incorporation was open to all who agreed to abide by a specific set of rules. The first state to adopt such legislation was North Carolina in 1795 (initially just for canal companies but subsequently extended to other activities), followed by Massachusetts in 1799, and New York in 1811 (Seavoy 1972). These latter two states were, of course, particularly important as they were major industrial and commercial states from the beginning. Moreover, while many have made light of the 1811 New York law in part because corporations chartered under its provisions were limited to twenty years of life (a similar restriction was contained in most special acts too) and restricted with regard to industry and capitalization, Kessler (1940) shows that more manufacturing firms were incorporated under its provisions before the Act was superseded in 1848 than under special acts which remained available. Perhaps more importantly, the 1811 Act stipulated that "the persons then composing such company shall be individually responsible to the extent of their respective shares of stock in said company and no further" (Angell and Ames 1931: 363) – in other words, stockholders enjoyed limited liability as we understand it today.

22 Banking seems to have been the one area where an operating permit from the state – a charter of incorporation – was almost always required.

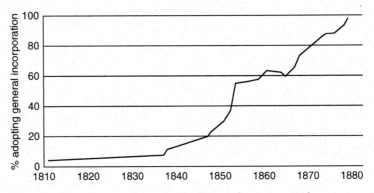

Figure 17.3 Fraction of states and territories with general incorporation laws
Source: Hamill (1999).

There were, however, sufficient caveats and exclusions in the early Massachusetts, New York, and North Carolina incorporation laws, for most legal scholars to cite Connecticut as adopting the first truly broad-based general incorporation law in June 1837 (Connecticut 1837). This authorized the creation of a corporation to "engag[e] in and [carry] on any kind of manufacturing or mechanical or mining or quarrying or any other lawful business" without securing a special charter.[23] Other states would follow. Still, by the end of the 1830s, only three states had adopted general incorporation laws. Six more passed laws in the 1840s, fifteen in the 1850s and fourteen during the 1860s (Figure 17.3). Though, by 1875, forty-four of forty-eight states and territories had general incorporation laws on their books (Hamill 1999). Moreover, in several of these (for example, Alabama and Louisiana [Friedman 1985]), the general incorporation law was the only way in which to secure a corporate charter as special acts to do so were prohibited.

Despite the legislative record created by special and general incorporation laws, however, there is no comprehensive accounting for business incorporations nationwide prior to the twentieth century and certainly no comprehensive view regarding the state of business organization until manufacturing establishments enumerated in the twelfth census in 1900 were required to provide information regarding their manner of organization, or what was

23 Perhaps not surprisingly, it was also in 1837 that banking moved away from special charters to general incorporation, or so-called free banking, beginning with Michigan (Michigan 1837a, 1837b, 1838). Interestingly, however, there is not a one-to-one mapping between general incorporation states and free banking states.

called "character" (US Bureau of the Census and North 1902). The problem is that while entry was tracked, there was no accounting for exit. However, for a variety of reasons we believe that exit rates were lower and survival rates were higher for corporations than for other forms of business organization. At the census of 1900, 512,254 establishments were enumerated, of which just 40,743 were incorporated (8 percent). Nevertheless, these incorporated establishments accounted for 59 percent of all manufacturing output (United States Bureau of the Census and North 1902: lxvi).

By making some heroic (but, I would argue, reasonable) assumptions, it is, however, possible to get a rough estimate of the "character" of firms at an earlier date based upon the names recorded for these establishments in the manuscripts of earlier censuses of manufactures. I have used the coding sheets underlying the Bateman–Weiss national samples from the censuses of manufacturing for 1850–1870 to do just that.[24] Manufacturing establishments doing business as "John Smith," for example, have been classified as sole proprietorships, those doing business as "Smith and Jones" as partnerships; those listed as "John Smith and Sons" as family business, and so on. Those establishments with a business name that is not the name of a specific individual or a group of individuals, such as "Boott Mills" and "The Ohio Iron Co." have been classified as incorporated businesses.[25]

Based upon this analysis, sole proprietorships (individuals doing business on their own account) were the median business in every state and in almost every activity (Table 17.1). These were easy to create, typically requiring no formal action and enjoying no real privileges that the individual did not already possess. Similarly, partnerships in their many different configurations greatly outnumbered corporations. Two-name partnerships were almost twice as numerous – and much more than twice as numerous in 1850 – as corporations.

Weighting firms by some measure of size radically changes the data in Table 17.1, tilting shares in favor of corporations regardless of what measure of

---

24 Unfortunately, the Atack–Bateman sample from the 1880 censuses of manufacturing was entered directly from microfilm into a PC database without the names of the individual firms being recorded (although the page number and line number of each observation were recorded so that it would be possible to track each observation by going back through the microfilm records). This has not been done.

25 The organizational form of each firm is generally easy to interpret with the sole exception of businesses styled as "Smith and Company" or similar. I do not believe that these businesses were incorporated under state law but rather operated essentially as partnerships where some of the partners were unnamed. Such organizations were common in Great Britain prior to the passage of that country's general incorporation law.

Table 17.1 *Percentage of manufacturing firms by form of business organization,*
1850–1870

	1850	1860	1870
Sole proprietorship	82.7	77.4	78.3
Family firm	3.6	4.3	4.3
Two-person partnership	7.7	8.7	8.4
Three or more person partnership	0.2	0.1	0.3
". . . & Co."	4.3	6.8	5.8
Incorporated	1.7	2.8	2.9

Source: computed from data underlying the Bateman–Weiss national samples from the manufacturing census using the procedure described in the text.

Table 17.2 *Percentage of manufacturing firms by form of business organization*
weighted by output, 1850–1870 and 1900

	1850	1860	1870	1900
Sole proprietorship	56.6	42.3	35.5	20.6
Family firm	4.2	6.7	5.7	19.8
Two-person partnership	10.7	12.3	10.4	
Three or more person partnership	0.3	0.5	1.0	
". . . & Co."	13.0	22.6	18.2	
Incorporated	15.2	15.7	29.3	59.6

Source: 1850–70: computed from data underlying the Bateman–Weiss national samples from the manufacturing census using the procedure described in the text. 1900: United States Bureau of the Census and North (1902: lxvi).

size used. Table 17.2 reports the shares using output as the weight because this same measure is also possible using data published in the 1900 census.

Indeed, it is particularly instructive to look at the average capital invested in each firm by organizational type on the grounds that raising capital from a large number of investors was one of the goals of incorporation (Table 17.3). Unfortunately, the 1900 census does not provide data for comparison. Variances are large but the hypothesis that there is no difference in average invested capital by organizational type is overwhelmingly rejected. Those firms which our procedure identifies as sole proprietorships had on average

Table 17.3 *Average capital ($) invested in manufacturing firms by type of firm organization, 1850–1870*

	1850	1860	1870
Sole proprietorship	2,752	3,478	3,768
Family firm	6,303	10,165	14,898
Two-person partnership	5,136	9,362	10,768
Three or more person partnership	11,086	67,600	45,910
"… & Co."	13,905	22,324	34,190
Incorporated	78,347	69,749	178,031

Source: Computed from data underlying the Bateman–Weiss national samples from the manufacturing census using the procedure described in the text.

only about one-third as much capital as was invested in the average family firm. Such family firms were also of a similar size to the average two-person partnership. By comparison, partnerships with three or more named partners, were at least twice as large in terms of capital investment as a two-person partnership but broadly similar in terms of size to private companies (identified as "& Co."). Incorporated firms, on the other hand, were on average much larger than other business organizations, regardless of the metric: output, invested capital, or average employment. Indeed, in 1850, the average incorporated firm had about thirty times the capital investment in the average sole proprietorship. By 1870, this had increased to almost fifty-fold.

Shares of public corporations are transferable (though not necessarily publicly traded) and markets quickly arose to facilitate those exchanges and provide better information to both buyers and sellers regarding price. The ability to resell increased the willingness of buyers to invest in the first place and made it easier for companies to raise the capital they required. They also made investing more impersonal and more likely to be driven by the financials such as dividend returns and risk.[26] The first organized securities markets appeared in the 1790s in America although debt obligations had obviously been exchanged long before then (see, for instance, the contents of probate

---

26 Nowadays, capital gains – appreciation in the value of the shares – are an important component of the total return to equity owners but this is in part driven by tax policy which favors capital gains over dividend income. This was not the case in the nineteenth century when companies tended to pay out most of their profits as dividends so as to maintain share price at close to par.

inventories in Jones 1980 or Rothenberg 1992). The New York Stock Exchange, for example, was created when brokers meeting at coffee houses in the Wall Street area signed the so-called Buttonwood agreement in 1792. The formal exchange dates from 1817 (see, for example, Buck 1992; Sobel 1975). Similarly, there was an informal market in Boston from at least 1798 although the formal exchange only dates from 1834 (Barron and Martin 1975). The key role played by a market is to bring buyers and sellers together to determine the best possible price that reflects all relevant information. Since these early markets were small (in terms of the number of buyers and sellers) and thin (as measured by the number of securities being traded at any moment of time), they were organized as call markets on which each security was traded sequentially so that the full attention and liquidity of the market was focussed on that one asset, albeit only briefly, rather than trading any security whenever someone desired to buy or sell. Even so, there would be some days (at least on the Boston market) when not a single stock was traded although there were others, especially during the Civil War, when the trade was described as "enormous" (Martin 1871).

New York City (and the New York Stock Exchange) quickly established itself as the premier securities market in America but it was originally dominated by debt obligations issued by governments, railroads, and the like rather than equities. It did not become the leading equities market, particularly for industrials, that it is today, until the twentieth century. For example, as late as 1898 only twenty industrials were officially listed on the New York exchange although there was a large and rapidly growing trade in unlisted industrials after about 1885 (Snowden 1987, 1990). In contrast, forty-eight industrials were officially listed on the Boston exchange by 1869 (Martin 1871: 68). One reason, perhaps, for the prominence of industrials on the Boston market is that Massachusetts was a leading industrial state and a pioneer in progressive legislation with respect to corporate charters (Dodd 1954). Less than 5 percent of Massachusetts manufacturing firms before the Civil War were organized as corporations and thus issued securities.[27] Fewer still were publicly traded.

One major problem with early equity issues was the high par value of most stocks. This necessarily limited their appeal to all but the wealthiest of customers. For example, many stocks had a par value of $1,000 (that is, several orders of magnitude greater than average per capita income in the mid nineteenth century) compared with a nominal value of a small fraction of a penny today

---

27 Unpublished estimates based upon a review of names of industrial establishments enumerated in the 1850 and 1860 Censuses of Manufactures by Atack and Bateman.

(but a market price of whatever level supply and demand determined).[28] Of the sixteen stocks traded on the Boston market in 1835, for example, thirteen had par values of $1,000; one had a par of $750 and two had par values of $500 (Martin 1871: 64). The rationale behind this is unclear but it may reflect the relatively high cost of maintaining transfer books and of dealing with large numbers of stockholders. It certainly had the effect of limiting ownership to a relatively small group. Indeed, Martin , the historian of the Boston stock market, describes the market for industrials as "an 'exclusive' one; for it is almost exclusively in the hands of certain capitalists, who have no desire to sell when it is up, and can afford to hold when it is down" (Martin 1871: 64).

Over time, and particularly as the market for equities expanded in the twentieth century as par values changed, ownership became more widely dispersed. Capitalism became more democratic. As a result, however, new generations of economists began to worry about agency problems arising from the separation of ownership from control in the capitalist system (Berle, Means *et al.* 1932). These issues still resonate today although there seems little doubt that the vast majority have benefitted (albeit, perhaps, unequally) from the spread of capitalism throughout every region and every activity in America – a process that began with European settlement and which was facilitated and accelerated under the Constitution.

Concluding remarks

Adam Smith emphasized the importance of self-interest and responsiveness to unadulterated market signals as the source of the wealth of nations. This would certainly prove true in the early development of the United States. Although early English settlement took place in a world that was the very antithesis of Smith's doctrine – indeed, was the focus of his attack – the instruments of that settlement, corporations, were accorded unusually broad mandates and the American colonial population enjoyed far greater freedoms and liberties than residents back home. With these freedoms (even if not enjoyed by everyone) and in a world dominated by agriculture, development and growth in a land-abundant economy "took off." That development was almost certainly helped by distance from the mother country which contributed to that sense of freedom and the ability to march to a different beat.

From the very first, markets were important, whether the market for tobacco in England, the market for land and labor in the colonies, or the

---

28 No-par shares first appeared in New York in 1915 (Hamilton 2000).

market for food and other supplies in cities, towns, and communities. Information about those markets was initially quite narrowly held by special-ist merchants and factors but eventually spread by word of mouth and then through newspapers and pamphlets to a population that was more literate than most and had more freedom of action than most in that day and age. Perhaps it was these conditions that allowed Americans to take advantage of "that sharp desire for profit, that anxiety to do a stroke of trade at every turn" which had so impressed Trollope in his visit to America.

The benefits of that activity also seem to have done more than "trickle down" to the common person. Visitors to America in the middle of the nineteenth century were little short of amazed at the dress and manner of the working person. Charles Dickens, for example, on a day trip to the cotton textile mills of Lowell wrote of the mill girls whom he observed:

> [they] were all well dressed: and that phrase necessarily includes extreme cleanliness . . . they were healthy in appearance, many of them remarkably so, and had the manners and deportment of young women: not of degraded brutes of burden . . . I cannot recall or separate one young face that gave me a painful impression; not one young girl whom, assuming it to be a matter of necessity that she should gain her daily bread by the labour of her hands, I would have removed from those works if I had had the power [despite the fact that] they *do* work. They labour in these mills, upon an average, twelve hours a day, which is unquestionably work, and pretty tight work too.
>
> (Dickens 1842)

Dickens went on to describe the culture and literary opportunities (as well as the strict supervision) provided for the Lowell mill girls during their time off work, all of which surprised him but none of which alarmed him. In short, New England factory girls enjoyed a manner of life and work that Dickens found inconceivable based upon his observation of life in the industrial centers of England at that time. American capitalism must indeed have seemed to him as something like the promised land, if not a mirage.

References

Adams, C. F. and H. Adams (1871). *Chapters of Erie and Other Essays*. Boston: James R. Osgood.

Alston, L. J. and J. P. Ferrie (1993). "Paternalism in Agricultural Labor Contracts in the U.S. South: Implications for the Growth of the Welfare State," *The American Economic Review* 83(4): 852–876.

(1999). *Southern Paternalism and the American Welfare State: Economics, Politics, and Institution in the South, 1865–1965*. Cambridge and New York: Cambridge University Press.

Alston, L. J. and R. Higgs (1982). "Contractual Mix in Southern Agriculture since the Civil War: Facts, Hypotheses, and Tests," *The Journal of Economic History* 42(2): 327–353.

Alston, L. J. and K. D. Kauffman (1998). "Up, Down, and Off the Agricultural Ladder: New Evidence and Implications of Agricultural Mobility for Blacks in the Postbellum South," *Agricultural History* 72(2): 263–279.

Angell, J. K. and S. Ames (1831). *On the Law of Private Corporations Aggregate*. Boston: Hilliard, Gray, Little & Wilkins.

Anonymous (1811). Act of March 22. N.Y. Laws III. ch. LXVII.

Anonymous (1886). *Santa Clara County v. Southern Pacific Railroad Company*. 118 U.S. 394, US Supreme Court.

Anonymous (2010). *Citizens United v. Federal Election Commission* 558 U.S. 50, 2010, US Supreme Court.

Atack, J. (1985). "Industrial Structure and the Emergence of the Modern Industrial Corporation," *Explorations in Economic History* 22(1): 29–52.

(1986a). "Firm Size and Industrial Structure in the United States During the Nineteenth Century," *The Journal of Economic History* 46(2): 463–475.

(1986b). "Firm Size and Industrial Structure in the United States During the Nineteenth Century," *Journal of Economic History* 46(2): 463–475.

Atack, J. and F. Bateman (1987). *To Their Own Soil: Agriculture in the Antebellum North*. Ames, IA: Iowa State University Press.

Atack, J. and F. Bateman (1980). "The Regional Diffusion and Adoption of the Steam Engine in American Manufacturing," *Journal of Economic History* 40(2): 281–308.

(2002). "Part Year Operation in Nineteenth Century American Manufacturing: Evidence from the 1870 and 1880 Censuses," *Journal of Economic History* 62(3): 792–809.

(2004). "Skill Intensity and Rising Wage Dispersion in Nineteenth-Century American Manufacturing," *Journal of Economic History* 64(1): 172–192.

Barron, C. W. and J. G. Martin (1975). *The Boston Stock Exchange*. New York, Arno Press.

Bateman, F. and T. J. Weiss (1981). *A Deplorable Scarcity: The Failure of Industrialization in the Slave Economy*. Chapel Hill: University of North Carolina Press.

Bathe, G. and D. Bathe (1935). *Oliver Evans: A Chronicle of Early American Engineering*. Philadelphia, The Historical Society of Pennsylvania.

Beard, C. A. and M. R. Beard (1927). *The Rise of American Civilization*. New York: The Macmillan Company.

Berle, A. A., Gardiner C. Means et al. (1932). *The Modern Corporation and Private Property*. New York and Chicago: Commerce clearing house Inc., Loose leaf service division of the Corporation trust company.

Berry, T. S. (1943). *Western Prices before 1861: A Study of the Cincinnati Market*. Cambridge, MA: Harvard University Press.

Bezanson, A., R. D. Gray et al. (1935). *Prices in Colonial Pennsylvania*. Philadelphia: University of Pennsylvania Press.

Bils, M. (1984). "Tariff Protection and Production in the Early US Cotton Textile Industry," *The Journal of Economic History* 44(4): 1033–1045.

Boserup, E. (1965). *The Conditions of Agricultural Growth: The Economics of Agrarian Change under Population Pressure*. London: G. Allen & Unwin.

(1981). *Population and Technological Change: A Study of Long-Term Trends*. University of Chicago Press.

Buck, J. E. (1992). *The New York Stock Exchange: The First 200 Years*. Essex, CT: Greenwich Publishing Group.

Cain, L. P. and D. G. Paterson (1986). "Biased Technical Change, Scale, and Factor Substitution in American Industry, 1850–1919," *Journal of Economic History* 46(1): 153–164.

Calhoun, J. C., R. L. Meriwether *et al.* (1959). *The Papers of John C. Calhoun*. Columbia, University of South Carolina Press for the South Caroliniana Society.

Carter, S. B., S. S. Gartner *et al.* (2006a). *Historical Statistics of the United States Millennial Edition Online*. New York: Cambridge University Press.

 (2006b). *Historical Statistics of the United States Millennial Edition Online*. New York: Cambridge University Press.

Chandler, A. D. (1965). *The Railroads, the Nation's First Big Business: Sources and Readings*. New York: Harcourt.

 (1977). *The Visible Hand: The Managerial Revolution in American Business*. Cambridge, MA: Belknap Press.

Charles II (1660). An Act Takeing Away the Court of Wards and Liveries and Tenures in Capite and by Knights Service and Purveyance, and for Setling a Revenue Upon His Majesty in Lieu Thereof. S. o. t. R. v.-. (1819), 259–266.

Clark, V. S. (1929). *History of Manufactures in the United States*. New York: For the Carnegie Institution of Washington by the McGraw-Hill Book Company Inc.

Cleveland, F. A. and F. W. Powell (1909). *Railroad Promotion and Capitalization in the United States*. New York: Longmans, Green & Co.

Coffman, C. and M. E. Gregson (1998). "Railroad Development and Land Value," *Journal of Real Estate Finance and Economics* 16(2): 191–204.

Cole, A. H. and International Scientific Committee on Price History (1938a). *Wholesale Commodity Prices in the United States, 1700–1861*. Cambridge, MA: Harvard University Press.

 (1938b). *Wholesale Commodity Prices in the United States, 1700–1861: Statistical Supplement: Actual Wholesale Prices of Various Commodities*. Cambridge, MA: Harvard University Press.

Connecticut (1837). Act of June 10, 1837, Tit. Xiv, Ch. Lxii, § 1. CONN. GEN. STAT. § 1.

Conrad, A. H. and J. R. Meyer (1958). "The Economics of Slavery in the Ante Bellum South," *Journal of Political Economy* 66(2): 95–130.

Coolidge, C. (1925). "The Press under a Free Government." Washington, DC: Address before the American Society of Newspaper Editors.

Craig, L. A. (1993). *To Sow One Acre More: Childbearing and Farm Productivity in the Antebellum North*. Baltimore, MD: Johns Hopkins University Press.

Dalzell, R. F. (1987). *Enterprising Elite: The Boston Associates and the World They Made*. Cambridge, MA: Harvard University Press.

David, P. A. (1970). "Learning by Doing and Tariff Protection: A Reconsideration of the Case of the Ante-Bellum United States Cotton Textile Industry," *The Journal of Economic History* 30(3): 521–601.

Davis, J. S. (1917). *Essays in the Earlier History of American Corporations*, 2 vols. Cambridge, MA: Harvard University Press.

DeBow, J. D. B. (n.d.). *DeBow's Review. Agricultural, Commercial, Industrial Progress & Resources*. American Periodicals Series II.

Dickens, C. (1842). "American Notes for General Circulation." *Collection of Ancient and Modern British authors*, vol. 383. Paris: Baudry's European Library.

Dodd, E. M. (1954). *American Business Corporations until 1860, with Special Reference to Massachusetts*. Cambridge, MA: Harvard University Press.

Elliott, J. H. (2006). *Empires of the Atlantic World: Britain and Spain in America, 1492–1830*. New Haven: Yale University Press.

Engerman, S. L. and K. L. Sokoloff (2005). "The Evolution of Suffrage Institutions in the New World," *The Journal of Economic History* 65(4): 891–921.

Epstein, M. (1908). *The Early History of the Levant Company*. London: G. Routledge & Sons.

Evans, G. H. (1948). *Business Incorporations in the United States, 1800–1943*. New York: National Bureau of Economic Research.

Evans, O. and J. Stevens (1805). "The Abortion of the Young Steam Engineer's Guide Containing an Investigation of the Principles, Construction and Powers of Steam Engines : A Description of a Steam Engine on New Principles . . .: A Description of a Machine, and Its Principles, for Making Ice and Cooling Water in Large Quantities. . . By the Power of Steam. . . : A Description of Four Other Patented Inventions." Philadelphia: Printed for the author by Fry and Kammerer.

Farris, P. L. and R. S. Euler (1957). "Prices of Indiana Farm Products, 1841–1955," *Purdue Agricultural Experiment Station Bulletin* 644: 62..

Fichter, J. R. (2010). *So Great a Proffit: How the East Indies Trade Transformed Anglo-American Capitalism*. Cambridge, MA: Harvard University Press.

Field, A. J. (1978). "Sectoral Shifts in Antebellum Massachusetts: A Reconsideration," *Explorations in Economic History* 15: 146–171.

Fishlow, A. (1965). *American Railroads and the Transformation of the Antebellum Economy*. Cambridge, MA: Harvard University Press.

Fogel, R. W. (1960). *The Union Pacific Railroad: A Case in Premature Enterprise*. Baltimore, MD: Johns Hopkins University Press.

(1989). *Without Consent or Contract: The Rise and Fall of American Slavery*. New York: Norton.

Fogel, R. W. and S. L. Engerman (1974). *Time on the Cross: The Economics of American Negro Slavery*. Boston, Little.

(1977). "Explaining the Relative Efficiency of Slave Agriculture in the Antebellum South," *The American Economic Review* 67(3): 275–296.

Fogel, R. W. and J. Rutner (1972). "The Efficiency Effects of Federal Land Policy, 1850–1900: A Report of Some Provisional Findings," in W. A. Aydelotte (ed.), *The Dimension of Quantitative Research in History*. Princeton University Press, pp. 390–418.

Friedman, L. M. (1985). *A History of American Law*. New York: Simon & Schuster.

Galenson, D. W. (1981). *White Servitude in Colonial America: An Economic Analysis*. New Rochelle, NY: Cambridge University Press.

Gates, P. W. (1934). *The Illinois Central Railroad and Its Colonization Work*. Cambridge, MA: Harvard University Press.

(1936). "The Homestead Law in an Incongruous Land System," *The American Historical Review* 41(4): 652–681.

Gilchrist, D. T. and W. D. Lewis (1965). *Economic Change in the Civil War Era: Proceedings*. Greenville, DL: Eleutherian Mills-Hagley Foundation.

Goldin, C. and L. F. Katz (1998). "The Origins of Technology Skill Complementarity," *Quarterly Journal of Economics* 113(3): 693–732.

Goldin, C. and K. Sokoloff (1982). "Women, Children, and Industrialization in the Early Republic: Evidence from the Manufacturing Censuses," *The Journal of Economic History* 42(4): 741–774.

(1984). "The Relative Productivity Hypothesis of Industrialization: The American Case, 1820 to 1850," *Quarterly Journal of Economics* 99(3): 461–487.

Goodrich, C. (1960). *Government Promotion of American Canals and Railroads, 1800–1890.* Columbia University Press.

(1967). *The Government and the Economy, 1783–1861.* Indianapolis: Bobbs-Merrill.

Grafe, R. and A. Irigoín (2012). "A Stakeholder Empire: The Political Economy of Spanish Imperial Rule in America1," *The Economic History Review* 65(2): 609–651.

Grubb, F. (1986). "Redemptioner Immigration to Pennsylvania: Evidence on Contract Choice and Profitability," *The Journal of Economic History* 46(2): 407–418.

(1988). "The Auction of Redemptioner Servants, Philadelphia, 1771–1804: An Ecnomic Analysis," *The Journal of Economic History* 48(3): 583–603.

Gunderson, G. (1974). "The Origin of the American Civil War," *The Journal of Economic History* 34(4): 915–950.

Hacker, L. M. (1940). *The Triumph of American Capitalism: The Development of Forces in American History to the End of the Nineteenth Century.* New York: Simon and Schuster.

Hall, G. M. (2000). "Afro-Louisiana History and Genealogy, 1699–1860." Baton Rouge, LA: Louisiana State University Press (electronic database on DVD).

Hamill, S. P. (1999). "From Special Privilege to General Utility: A Continuation of Willard Hurst's Study of Corporations," *American University Law Review* 49(1): 81–180.

Hamilton, R. W. (2000). *The Law of Corporations in a Nutshell.* St. Paul, MN: West Group.

Haney, L. H. (1908) *A Congressional History of Railways in the United States.* Madison, WI: Democrat Printing Co.

Harley, C. K. (1992). "International Competitiveness of the Antebellum American Cotton Textile Industry," *The Journal of Economic History* 52(3): 559–584.

Harris, R. (1994). "The Bubble Act: Its Passage and Its Effects on Business Organization," *The Journal of Economic History* 54(3): 610–627.

Hatton, T. J. and J. G. Williamson (1993). "After the Famine: Emigration from Ireland, 1850–1913," *The Journal of Economic History* 53(3): 575–600.

Hawke, G. R. (1975). "The United States Tariff and Industrial Protection in the Late Nineteenth Century," *The Economic History Review* 28(1): 84–99.

Henretta, J. (1978). "Families and Farms: Mentalité in Pre-Industrial America," *William and Mary Quarterly*, 3rd Series 35: 3–32.

Hibbard, B. H. (1924). *A History of the Public Land Policies.* New York: Macmillan.

Higgs, R. (1977). *Competition and Coercion: Blacks in the American Economy, 1865–1914.* Cambridge and New York: Cambridge University Press.

Hoffman, G. W. (1932). *Future Trading Upon Organized Commodity Markets in the United States.* Philadelphia: University of Pennsylvania Press, and London: Oxford University Press.

Hounshell, D. A. (1984). *From the American System to Mass Production, 1800–1932: The Development of Manufacturing Technology in the United States.* Baltimore, MD: John Hopkins University Press.

Hunter, L. C. (1949). *Steamboats on the Western Rivers: An Economic and Technological History.* Cambridge, MA: Harvard University Press.

Hunter, L. C., Eleutherian Mills-Hagley Foundation *et al.* (1979). *A History of Industrial Power in the United States, 1780–1930.* Charlottesville: Published for the Eleutherian Mills-Hagley Foundation by the University Press of Virginia.

Irwin, D. A. (2004). "The Aftermath of Hamilton's 'Report on Manufactures'," *The Journal of Economic History* 64(3): 800–821.

   (2008). "Antebellum Tariff Politics: Regional Coalitions and Shifting Economic Interests," *Journal of Law and Economics* 51(4): 715–741.

Irwin, D. A. and P. Temin (2001). "The Antebellum Tariff on Cotton Textiles Revisited," *The Journal of Economic History* 61(3): 777–798.

James, J. A. (1981). "The Optimal Tariff in the Antebellum United States," *The American Economic Review* 71(4): 726–734.

Jefferson, T. and M. D. Peterson (1984). *Writings.* New York: Viking Press.

Johnson, H. B. (1976). *Order upon the Land: The US Rectangular Land Survey and the Upper Mississippi Country.* New York: Oxford University Press.

Jones, A. H. (1980). *Wealth of a Nation to Be: The American Colonies on the Eve of the Revolution.* New York: Columbia University Press.

Kessler, W. C. (1940). "A Statistical Study of the New York General Incorporation Act of 1811," *Journal of Political Economy* 48(6): 877–882.

Khan, B. Z. (2005). *The Democratization of Invention: Patents and Copyrights in American Economic Development, 1790–1920.* Cambridge and New York: Cambridge University Press.

Klein, D. B. (1990). "The Voluntary Provision of Public Goods? The Turnpike Companies of Early America," *Economic Inquiry* 28(4): 788.

Klein, D. B. and J. Majewski (1992). "Economy, Community, and Law: The Turnpike Movement in New York, 1797–1845," *Law and Society Review* 26(3): 469–512.

   (2008). "Turnpikes and Toll Roads in Nineteenth-Century America," *EH Net Encyclopedia*, from http://eh.net/encyclopedia/article/Klein.Majewski.Turnpikes.

Lamoreaux, N. R. (1985). *The Great Merger Movement in American Business, 1895–1904.* Cambridge and New York: Cambridge University Press.

Lamoreaux, N. R. and K. L. Sokoloff (1996). "Long-Term Change in the Organization of Inventive Activity," *Proceedings of the National Academy of Sciences of the United States of America* 93(23): 12686–12692.

   (2001). "Market Trade in Patents and the Rise of a Class of Specialized Inventors in the 19th-Century United States," *The American Economic Review* 91(2): 39–44.

   (2005). "Decline of the Independent Inventor: A Schumpeterian Story." NBER Working Paper. Cambridge: NBER.

   (2007). *Financing Innovation in the United States, 1870 to the Present.* Cambridge, MA: The MIT Press.

Lebergott, S. (1984). *The Americans: An Economic Record.* New York, W.W. Norton.

Libecap, G. D. and D. Lueck (2011). "The Demarcation of Land and the Role of Coordinating Property Institutions," *Journal of Political Economy* 119(3): 426–467.

Lord, J. W. (1907). "The Post-Roads Power of Congress: An Historical View," *The North American Review* 185(619): 635–644.

Majewski, J. and V. Tchakerian (2007). "The Environmental Origins of Shifting Cultivation: Climate, Soils, and Disease in the Nineteenth-Century US South," *Agricultural History* 81(4): 522–549.

Mark, G. A. (1987). "The Personification of the Business Corporation in American Law," *The University of Chicago Law Review* 54(4): 1441–1483.

Marquardt, R. E. (1959). "Minnesota Agriculture, 1858–1959–Prices," *St. Paul Minnesota-Federal Crop and Livestock Reporting Service.*

Martin, J. G. (1871). *Seventy-Three Years' History of the Boston Stock Market, from January 1, 1798, to January 1, 1871; with the Semi-Annual Dividends Paid from Commencement of the Boston Banks, Insurance, Railroad, Manufacturing, and Miscellaneous Companies.* Boston: The author.

Mercer, L. J. (1969). "Land Grants to American Railroads: Social Cost or Social Benefit?" *The Business History Review* 43(2): 134–151.

 (1970). "Rates of Return for Land-Grant Railroads: The Central Pacific System," *The Journal of Economic History* 30(3): 602–626.

Metzger, L. and P. Bobel (2009). *Canal Fever: The Ohio & Erie Canal, from Waterway to Canalway.* Kent State University Press.

Michigan (1837a). An Act Suspending, for a Limited Time Certain Provisions of Law, and for Other Purposes. Acts of the Legislature of the State of Michigan Passed at the Special Session of 1837. Detroit, MI.

 (1837b). An Act to Organize and Regulate Banking Associations. Acts of the Legislature of the State of Michigan Passed at the Annual Session of 1837. Detroit, MI.

 (1838). An Act to Amend an Act Entitled "an Act to Organize and Regulate Banking Associations" and for Other Purposes. Acts of the Legislature of the State of Michigan Passed at the Adjourned Session of 1837 and the Regular Session of 1838. Detroit, MI.

Mirsky, J. and A. Nevins (1952). *The World of Eli Whitney.* New York: Macmillan.

Mitchener, K. J. and M. Weidenmier (2005). "Empire, Public Goods, and the Roosevelt Corollary," *The Journal of Economic History* 65(3): 658–692.

Mortenson, W. P., H. H. Erdman, and J. H. Draxler (1933). "Wisconsin Farm Prices–1841 to 1933," *Agricultural Experiment Station of the University of Wisconsin, Research Bulletin* 119.

Nettels, C. P. (1962). *The Emergence of a National Economy, 1775–1815.* New York: Holt, Rinehart & Winstin.

North, D. C. (1961). *The Economic Growth of the United States, 1790–1860.* Englewood Cliffs, NJ: Prentice Hall.

North, D. C. and R. P. Thomas (1973). *The Rise of the Western World: A New Economic History.* Cambridge University Press.

Norton, L. J. and B. B. Wilson (1930). "Prices of Illinois Farm Products from 1866 to 1929," *Illinois Agricultural Experiment Station Bulletin* 351: 487–566.

Oberly, J. W. (1990). *Sixty Million Acres: American Veterans and the Public Lands before the Civil War.* Kent State University Press.

Ochenkowski, J. P. (1982). "The Origins of Nullification in South Carolina," *The South Carolina Historical Magazine* 83(2): 121–153.

Ohio Experiment Station (1920). "The Agriculture of Ohio." Wooster, OH: Ohio Agricultutal Experiment Station 326.

Oliphant, J. (2011). "Romney in Iowa," *Los Angeles Times.*

Olmsted, D. and B. Silliman (1846). *Memoir of Eli Whitney, Esq.* New Haven: Durrie & Peck

Pincus, J. J. (1977). *Pressure Groups and Politics in Antebellum Tariffs.* New York: Columbia University Press.

Poynder, J. (1844). *Literary Extracts from English and Other Works*, 2 vols. London: John Hatchard.

Raitz, K. B., ed. (1996). *The National Road: Road and American Culture*. Baltimore, MD: Johns Hopkins University Press.

Ramsdell, C. W. (1936). "Some Problems Involved in Writing the History of the Confederacy," *The Journal of Southern History* 2(2): 133–147.

Ransom, R. L. and R. Sutch (1977). *One Kind of Freedom: The Economic Consequences of Emancipation*. Cambridge, New York: Cambridge University Press.

Rei, C. (2009). "The Organization of Merchant Empires," Ph.D. thesis, Boston University.

Robins, N. (2006). *The Corporation That Changed the World: How the East India Company Shaped the Modern Multinational*. London and Ann Arbor, MI: Pluto Press.

Rothenberg, W. B. (1981). "The Market and Massachusetts Farmers, 1750–1855," *The Journal of Economic History* 41(2): 283–314.

(1992). *From Market-Places to a Market Economy: The Transformation of Rural Massachusetts, 1750–1850*. University of Chicago Press.

Schumpeter, J. A. (1947). *Capitalism, Socialism, and Democracy*. New York and London: Harper & Brothers.

Scott, W. R. (1910). "The Constitution and Finance of English, Scottish and Irish Joint-Stock Companies to 1720," in *Making of Modern Law*. Cambridge University Press.

Seavoy, R. E. (1972). "Laws to Encourage Manufacturing: New York Policy and the 1811 General Incorporation Statute," *The Business History Review* 46(1): 85–95.

Shepherd, J. F. and G. M. Walton (1972). *Shipping, Maritime Trade, and the Economic Development of Colonial North America*. Cambridge University Press.

Sheriff, C. (1996). *The Artificial River: The Erie Canal and the Paradox of Progress, 1817–1862*. New York: Hill and Wang.

Shlakman, V. (1935). *Economic History of a Factory Town: A Study of Chicopee, Massachusetts*. Northhampton, MA: The Department of History of Smith College.

Slaughter, M. J. (1995). "The Antebellum Transportation Revolution and Factor-Price Convergence." NBER Working Paper No. W5303. Cambridge, MA.

Smith, A. (1776). *An Inquiry into the Nature and Causes of the Wealth of Nations*. London: W. Stranhan and T. Cadell.

Smith, S. D. (1998). "The Market for Manufactures in the Thirteen Continental Colonies, 1698–1776," *The Economic History Review* 51(4): 676–708.

Snowden, K. A. (1987). "American Stock Market Development and Performance, 1871–1929," *Explorations in Economic History* 24: 327–353.

(1990). "Historical Returns and Security Market Development, 1872–1925," *Explorations in Economic History* 27: 381–420.

Sobel, R. (1975). *N. Y. S. E.: A History of the New York Stock Exchange, 1935–1975*. New York: Weybright and Talley.

Sokoloff, K. L. (1988). "Inventive Activity in Early Industrial America: Evidence from Patent Records, 1790–1846," *The Journal of Economic History* 48(4): 813–850.

Sokoloff, K. L. and B. Zorina Khan (1990). "The Democratization of Invention During Early Industrialization: Evidence from the United States, 1790–1846," *The Journal of Economic History* 50(2): 363–378.

Sombart, W. (1976). *Why Is There No Socialism in the United States?* White Plains, NY: International Arts and Sciences Press.

Stover, J. F. (1987). *History of the Baltimore and Ohio Railroad*. West Lafayette, IN: Purdue University Press.

Strand, N. V. (1942). "Prices of Farm Products in Iowa, 1851–1940," *Iowa Agricultural Experiment Station Research Bulletin* 303: 907–998.

Swierenga, R. P. (1968). *Pioneers and Profits: Land Speculation on the Iowa Frontier*. Ames, IA: Iowa State University Press.

Sylla, R. E. and R. E. Wright (2012). "U.S. Corporate Development, 1801–1860." NSF.

Taussig, F. W. (1888). "The Tariff, 1830–1860," *The Quarterly Journal of Economics* 2(3): 314–346.

(1967). *The Tariff History of the United States: Including a Consideration of the Tariff of 1930*. New York: A. M. Kelley.

Taylor, C. H. (1917). *History of the Board of Trade of the City of Chicago*. Chicago: R.O. Law Co.

Taylor, G. R. (1932). "Wholesale Prices at Charleston, S.C., 1732–91," *Journal of Economic and Business History* 4: 356–377.

(1951). *The Transportation Revolution 1815–1860*. New York: Holt, Rinehart & Winston.

Thomas, B. (1973). *Migration and Economic Growth: A Study of Great Britain and the Atlantic Economy*. Cambridge University Press.

Thorpe, F. N., ed. (1909). *The Federal and State Constitutions Colonial Charters, and Other Organic Laws of the States, Territories, and Colonies Now or Heretofore Forming the United States of America Compiled and Edited under the Act of Congress of June 30, 1906*. Washington, DC: Government Printing Office.

Thünen, J. H. von and P. Hall (1966). *Isolated State: An English Edition of Der Isolierte Staat*. Oxford and New York: Pergamon Press.

Trollope, A. (1863). *North America*. Philadelphia: Lippincott.

United States Bureau of the Census and S. N. D. North (1902). *Twelfth Census of the United States: Manufactures*. Washington, DC: Government Printing Office.

US Congress. House. American State Papers (1791). *Manufactures*.

US Congress, House. and US Department of the treasury (1791). *Manufactures*. Communicated to the House of Representatives, December 5, 1791.

US Congress, House and United States Department of Labor (1899). *Thirteenth Annual Report of the Commissioner of Labor, 1898*.

US Congress, Senate and US Department of State (1824). Report of the Secretary of State, of Such Articles Manufactured in the United States as Would Be Liable to Duties If Imported from Foreign Countries; as, Also, the Amount of Capital Invested in Each County, Respectively, with a Schedule of Factories Incorporated by State Laws, from 1800 to 1820, Inclusive. Prepared in Obedience to a Resolution of the Senate of the 1st March, 1823. January 27, 1824. Printed by Order of the Senate of the United States.

US Congress, Senate and US Department of Treasury (1808). Roads and Canals. Communicated to the Senate, April 6, 1808.

US Supreme Court and John Marshall (1819). *Trustees of Dartmouth Coll. v. Woodward*, 17 U.S. 4 Wheat. 518. US Supreme Court.

Vedder, R. (1975). "The Slave Exploitation (Expropriation) Rate," *Explorations in Economic History* 12(4): 453–457.

Veenendaal, A. J. (1992). "An Example of 'Other People's Money': Dutch Capital in American Railroads," *Business and Economic History* 21: 147–158.

Walton, G. M. and James F. Shepherd (1979). *The Economic Rise of Early America*. Cambridge and New York: Cambridge University Press.

Warren, G. F., F. A. Pearson *et al.* (1932). *Wholesale Prices for 213 Years, 1720 to 1932.* Ithaca, NY: Published by the University.

Weil, F. (1998). "Capitalism and Industrialization in New England, 1815–1845," *The Journal of American History* 84(4): 1334–1354.

Wilkins, M. (1989). *The History of Foreign Investment in the United States to 1914.* Cambridge, MA: Harvard University Press.

Willan, T. S. (1956). *The Early History of the Russia Company, 1553–1603.* Manchester University Press.

Williamson, J. G. (1972). "Embodiment, Disembodiment, Learning by Doing, and Returns to Scale in Nineteenth-Century Cotton Textiles," *The Journal of Economic History* 32(3): 691–705.

(1974). "Migration to the New World: Long Term Influences and Impact," *Explorations in Economic History* 11: 357–389.

Wilson, J. (1942). "The Bank of North America and Pennsylvania Politics: 1781–1787," *The Pennsylvania Magazine of History and Biography* 66(1): 3–28.

Woods, T. K. (2008). *Ohio's Grand Canal: A Brief History of the Ohio & Erie Canal.* Kent State University Press.

Wright, G. (1978). *The Political Economy of the Cotton South: Households, Markets, and Wealth in the Nineteenth Century.* New York: Norton.

(1986). *Old South, New South: Revolutions in the Southern Economy since the Civil War.* New York: Basic Books.

Yergin, D. (1991). *The Prize: The Epic Quest for Oil, Money, and Power.* New York: Simon & Schuster.

18

The political economy of rising capitalism

JOSÉ LUÍS CARDOSO

The emergence of capitalism as an economic system was a process that spread over a lengthy historical period with a wide-ranging and diversified geographical scope, as documented and discussed in the various chapters of this volume. The full extent of this range and variety of historical experiences cannot be covered in the present chapter. My aim here is simply to identify the main developments in the sphere of economic ideas and doctrines that took place in western Europe in the two centuries prior to the chronological limit established for this volume. Particular attention will be given to the period from 1776 to 1848.

The year of 1776 is generally considered to be the year that brought the good news of the birth of political economy as an autonomous scientific field. The publication of Adam Smith's *Wealth of Nations* represented a point of departure, a crucial moment in the establishment of a set of concepts and instruments of analysis that are still used today in order to express and understand economic reality. The name of Adam Smith is widely venerated, and he is seen as a figure of authority by most schools and currents of economic thought. His contributions were, however, particularly important for the development of the so-called classical political economy throughout the first half of the nineteenth century.

Adam Smith was not alone in the founding of this new science. His work did not appear from nowhere and must also be seen as a point of arrival, a factor of convergence, a point at which the various analytical and doctrinal contributions of the authors who preceded him all came together. It is therefore worth paying some attention to the development of economic discourse in the century and a half prior to the publication of the *Wealth of Nations*.

The year of 1848 was highly symbolic in European political history, and it is not by mere chance that it has been chosen as the point of separation between the two volumes of this *Cambridge History of Capitalism*. As if this key status were not enough, 1848 was also a year that was particularly significant for the history of economic ideas and for the more general history of social and political thought. Indeed, that year witnessed the almost simultaneous publication of John Stuart Mill's *Principles of Political Economy* and Karl Marx and Friedrich Engels's *Communist Manifesto*. The year 1848 therefore stands out as an undeniable chronological milestone marking the publication of both the last great work written in the classical tradition of political economy (Mill's book) and the most famous of the manifestos prematurely heralding the end of the economic system that, according to its promoters, was legitimized and sustained by the discourse of political economy.

The path that will be followed in this synthetic journey through the evolution of economic thought until the mid nineteenth century gives special emphasis to the written texts and the contexts described by the authors who, in their various accounts and reflections, sought to bear witness to the new practices and experiences associated with the rise of capitalism. The primary and secondary sources dealt with in this chapter relate to ideas, interpretations, visions, proposals put forward by protagonists and players in an enduring changing world. I do not mean to suggest that economic discourse is a mere mirror or reflection, or that it only serves as a veil that can be used to either conceal or reveal an ever-changing reality. I believe that it is fundamental to bear in mind that ideas themselves, expressed in their time as a means of inducing political change and social intervention, can acquire an unexpected capacity to transform reality. This is also why it is fundamental to remain in close touch with the sources that provide documentary evidence of the formation of the capitalist system and the scientific bases for its understanding.[1]

Trade and power

The overseas territorial and commercial expansion set in motion by both the Portuguese and the Spanish in the late fifteenth century and throughout the sixteenth century, and in which they were later followed by the Dutch and the English, created an unprecedented trading dynamic at the world level. Whether or not this phenomenon is considered to be a sign of proto-globalization, there is no denying that the opening up of new trade routes and the growing interaction between people, with commodities, goods, and services being produced and traded in different parts of the globe, brought

---

1 Space constraints do not allow for lengthy quotations and references to primary sources. References are provided to fundamental original texts and to narratives serving to substantiate the main arguments.

about a substantial change in the behavior and thinking of an economic world in a state of permanent agitation (Findlay and O'Rourke 2007).

Bills of exchange, insurance contracts, banking houses, paper money, trading companies, Navigation Acts, colonial trading monopolies, stock market operations – these were just some of the instruments and institutions that needed to be afforded a legal status, technical recognition, and political and moral support. The vast mercantilist literature produced in different parts of Europe throughout the sixteenth and seventeenth centuries and the first half of the eighteenth century was heavily influenced by the need to establish a framework for new facts and new economic and financial experiences. The aim was to make transactions easier and to ensure the successful performance of the institutions that were either being newly created or caught in the process of change (Finkelstein 2000).

The descriptions, complaints, suggestions, and recommendations made by traders, businessmen, political advisors, illustrious scholars, and doctors of the Church demonstrate the determination to express their views of the individuals and organized groups that were the driving forces behind the gradual formation of a genuine capitalist spirit. But two types of strategic options serving to reinforce national political unity and the power of the state were regularly to be found: first of all, the staunch defense of the equilibrium and stability of the balance of trade, with its consequent implications for monetary and fiscal policy, and of the protectionist measures that were indispensable to prevent both the importation of manufactured products and the exportation of raw materials (Magnusson 1994); secondly, the establishment of prudent alliances between the state and those economic agents who were well placed in the world of trading and manufacturing. Such alliances were established through systems of exclusive contracts, monopoly practices, the granting of privileges, and any other instruments that could generate the simultaneous and sustained extraction of rents for the state and returns for private individuals (Ekelund and Tollison 1997).

The short pamphlets and long treatises written about trade in the mercantilist era did not limit themselves to discussing the themes listed above. But there was one crucial and emblematic characteristic to be found in them, namely the strengthening of the power of the state, which was essential for sustaining wars, but also fundamental for guaranteeing support, vigilance and direct intervention in economic life.

Along the same lines, the development of initiatives that would assure the maintenance and increase of accumulated wealth, expressed in the stock of bullion, was an essential condition for strengthening the power of the state.

and hence a central motivation of the economic literature produced in most European countries during the second half of the seventeenth century and throughout the eighteenth century. Despite the convergence in general viewpoints, important differences in focus appear in the analysis presented by English (Malynes, Misselden, Mun, Child, and North), French (Bodin, Laffemas, Montchrétien, and Colbert), Italian (Serra and Botero) and Spanish (Ortiz, Cellorigo, Moncada, and the *arbitristas*) authors. There was room for disagreement between the most interventionist positions and those simply motivated by the necessity of regulating international trade. In many cases, the priority given to the accumulation of bullion is the main axis that intersects several authors' arguments. But for others, the essential was the development of instruments which permitted a favorable balance of trade, both for the particular merchants involved and for the national aggregated level, and this was to be achieved through policies which would set incentives to allow bullion to flow in.[2]

The focus on obtaining gold and silver was taken most seriously by those countries without mines, and it was for this reason that the wealth accumulated by the balance of trade represented increased capacity of allocating productive resources as well as placing manufactured goods in outside markets. The attention to detail placed on commercial statistics that appear in the pamphlets and other mercantilist writings shows the importance that the development of trade had in satisfying a growing and well-diversified demand for goods and services in the major European trading areas.

The mercantilist authors wrote about a broad set of matters, and these show well the number of problems that sparked continuous economic inquiry. Princes and merchants requested and commissioned reports and advice on issues such as the status of the trading companies, the regulation of insurance markets, the justification of the legitimacy of banking and financial operations, the enforcement of poor relief laws, the ceilings of interest rates in lending markets, the restrictions and prohibitions in the import of manufactured goods as well as the export of raw materials, the establishment of heavy duties for goods of sumptuary consumption, the infant industry protection, the concession of manufacturing and trading privileges, as well as the specific restrictions applied to the

---

2 If one is restricted to choosing only one of the many tracts and pamphlets produced by the various authors of the mercantilist era, and this choice being informed by its representativeness, the right choice would be Thomas Mun, *England's treasure by forraign trade* (first published in 1664 but written in the 1620s). For a comprehensive vision of the mercantilist literature, especially in its English interpretations, it is still indispensable to read E. Hecksher (1935) and J. Viner (1937: Chapters 1 and 2).

colonial products and their re-exports. The legacy of the authors that contributed the most to this large body of economic literature, certainly motivated by private interests but framed as intended to discuss the right policies underlying the development of an increasingly capitalized commercial society, shows the importance of such writings in designing economic policies almost always intending to solve practical problems under particular circumstances.

Money and stock

The well-known obsession of mercantilist writers in emphasizing the accumulation of precious metals, understood as the definite symbol of a state's strength and power, led later critics to caricaturize the fragility of a purely metal-based conception of wealth. Yet, even if many mercantilist writers were indeed seduced by such symbolic representation, what is important to underline is the way in which they discuss the role of precious metals as a medium of circulation and exchange, unit of account, and store of value. The full understanding of the role and function of money had John Locke as one of its main interpreters (1989). But before him many other authors discussed or described the properties of precious metals as an emergency reserve for state treasure, or as stock for capital investment.

With regard to the pioneer analysis of monetary themes, special emphasis goes to the authors of the Salamanca School from the second half of the sixteenth century. Azpicuelta, Soto, Mercado, Molina, as well as other doctors of the Church, contributed to launch a school of thought with their disciples in the universities of Salamanca (Spain) and Coimbra (Portugal). Their objective was to explain the observed price increases which were happening during this period in the Iberian peninsula, as well as in other areas of Europe. The conventional wisdom argument, frequently heard at the time, was that explanation rested on the new needs induced by the commercial and maritime expansion – this argument was to be laid out in writings by Jean Bodin in the 1570s. The innovation introduced by the Salamanca doctrinaires consisted in recognizing that the price increase was due to a diminishing value of coin, in turn justified by the substantial increase in its production and circulation following the discovery of the almost endless silver mines in Spanish America. In other words, for the writers of the Salamanca school, the explosion of prices was primarily due to the increase in supply of precious metals, the fundamental input in the production of money. Consequently, the formulation of one of the oldest analytical devices in economics was beginning to take form: an embryonic version of a quantity theory of money by means of an intuition of the equation of exchange MV = PT, an accounting identity relating the money supply (M) with the price level (P), under the restriction of considering invariable both the velocity of circulation (V) and the amount of transactions (T).

The acceptance that there exists a stable relation between the quantity of money and the price level has implications which raise doubts about some basic assumptions of the mercantilist literature, namely with regard to the possibility of permanent supremacy and hegemony of a nation over others. In fact, the existence of international trade (even if under protectionist conditions) forces us to consider the following logical line of thought: if in a given country the quantity of money in circulation is small or suffers a sudden decline, the price level will be low, and consequently, outside demand will increase, which will increase exports and result in a flow of money coming into the country. This incoming flux will now generate internal price increases, which will eventually check export growth until an equilibrium is established between the country and its commercial partners. This is the essence of the famous price specie flow mechanism, which describes international trade equilibria and prevents the mercantilist objective of a permanently favorable balance of trade (Cantillon 1755; Hume 1985). In David Hume's summary:

> There seems to be a happy concurrence of causes in human affairs, which checks the growth of trade and riches, and hinders them from being confined entirely to one people; as might naturally at first be dreaded from the advantages of an established commerce. (Hume 1985: 283)

Another important consequence of this mechanism is the demonstration of the non-neutrality of money in the short run, since the flow of gold and silver entrances could be used by the most industrious nations, in this way generating a productive investment which would result in the growth of wealth that anticipates the price increase effects. In this and many other instances, Cantillon and Hume showed an analytic capacity to understand the role of money in a market economy which was more sophisticated than Adam Smith and the classical economists would later show.

In analyzing the problem of velocity (or ease) in circulation of money, the worries which Smith would show later in relation to the emission of paper money had been amply discussed by authors such as Pierre de Boisguilbert and Isaac de Pinto. The latter, indeed, develops a coherent argument in favor of the role of circulation in a given economy, which in his work refers not only to the stimulus given to mass consumption, but also to the acceleration given to monetary circuits and the easy access afforded to means of payment (de Pinto

1771). In other words, the stock of circulating capital depended heavily on the availability of monetary aggregates and therefore the expansion of the economic and financial sectors required a steady increase of the monetary base.

Pinto was also an interested follower of the work of Bishop George Berkeley, both of them stressing the role of the system of national debt and public credit that prevailed in England in the mid eighteenth century.[3] Thanks to the modernity of its financial institutions and instruments, after the creation of the Bank of England in 1690, England had managed to achieve a level of prosperity and development that brooked no comparison with that attained by other more populous countries enjoying greater resources. Now, according to Berkeley followed by Pinto, such success was due to the system of indebtedness adopted by the British Crown toward private individuals and the additional financing that it thus guaranteed. Although Pinto could not express it in these terms, it should be noted in his arguments that the small and large investors who lent money to the state in return for securities, which could be bought and sold and which earned interest, entered into a kind of implicit contract in which economic and financial dividends were added to the advantages of political stability that were of benefit to both parties.

This maturity in thinking about financial issues is of exceptional nature. Despite this discussion, the second half of the seventeenth century and the first half of the eighteenth were fertile in events and instability in the financial markets (Tulipmania, South Sea Bubble, Mississipi System, etc.). John Law inspired innovative financial and banking experiments, though his "splendid but visionary ideas," as Adam Smith qualified them, did not succeed. Yet Law's astute vision on how the international monetary system could work out and flourish without the use of metallic money was indeed an ingenious anticipation of the modern role of money and monetary policy in response to the needs of an extended and global economy (Murphy 1997). Law's system was subject to severe criticism and refutation, almost always in moral terms. This attitude was also representative of one of the identifying characteristics of the rising capitalism. A contemporary author, reflecting on the moral issues associated with investment and having the knowledge of someone who knew the Amsterdam stock market well, confessed his perplexity in face of the actions which made the stage of financial transactions a true *confusion de confusiones* (de la Vega 1688). This expression says much regarding the perception that people then had on the substantial changes that were happening

---

3 Berkeley's ideas on national debt were mainly conveyed through the articles published in *The Querist* in 1735–1737. Cf. Rashid 1990.

to markets at the global scale and which were reflected in the stock market microcosmos (Neal 1990).

Natural order, circular flow, and *laissez-faire*

Economic change channeled through transformations in international trade and monetary systems also gave rise to different forms of perception of a reality that was now being understood through numbers, calculations, measurements, statistical information, and political arithmetic. The development of double-entry bookkeeping suggested the acceptance of the principles of methodological exactitude, precision, credibility, and accuracy, all of which structured the innovative modes of reasoning used by the emergent sciences of wealth and society (Perrot 1992; Poovey 1998). Practical knowledge and the instruments and processes used for capturing the empirical world consequently represented the accumulated capital of a cognitive experience that was essential for the improvement of political economy.

The tradition of political arithmetic, as expressed in the work of William Petty (1690), was indispensable for the formation of a scientific discourse that sought to explain the logic whereby the market operated as a natural order of things. In this context, it is worth stressing the relevance of the framework also provided by the philosophy of natural law for interpreting the foundations of social and economic organization. The existence of universally accepted natural laws that are inherent in human nature, the belief in a natural spontaneous, harmonious, and self-regulating order, were all crucial elements for explaining the economic order of the market and were consequently indissociable from the discourse of the science that sought to elucidate the mechanisms to which this same order was subject (Cardoso 2004; Clark 1992).

The philosophical principles of natural law were also useful for improving individual capacities and motivations (private vices), and for the consequent subordination of collective interests (public virtues). The emergence of an autonomous discourse of political economy, which considered the economic dimension of human action as a proper category of analysis, was related, up to a certain point, to the belief in a spontaneous economic and social order. This belief, in turn, implied the lessening of state intervention in the economic sphere. However, the harmony of civil society might not prove to be an immediately attainable objective, which was why it would be advisable to accept the intervention of a correcting force in the natural order. In other words, the state – though not an integral part of the spontaneous natural order – was entrusted with the supreme task of preserving its coordination and stability.

It is this view that we find in authors such as Boisguilbert, Cantillon, and Quesnay, who, besides being in favor of the adoption of *laissez-faire* policies applied to the domestic and external markets, developed innovative methods and instruments of analysis for studying a theme that was to prove one of the most solid foundations of the burgeoning economic science: the equilibrium resulting from the circular flow of wealth (Hutchison 1988).

In the case of Quesnay and the French physiocratic school, the relations between the different classes were presented in the form of a circuit wherein landowners, producers, and consumers cross each other's paths, a circuit which also serves to quantify output produced in a given period of time, and which ensures the reproduction of economic activity in the following period. The idea that immediately arises from Quesnay's *Tableau Économique* is one of equilibrium and harmony in the economic and social universe as a whole (Larrère 1992; Steiner 1998). As it is economic, such equilibrium is described through the economic relations binding the autonomous interests of different groups and actors to a common project.

The priority given by the physiocrats to the development of agriculture is completely understandable in a country in which the sector employed 85 percent of the population and generated 60 percent of GDP. A similar situation was observed in other European countries, and the physiocratic message echoed in various institutions – enlightened salons, scientific academies, and regional economic societies – that amplified the political sense which the physiocratic message undoubtedly contained: the belief in a natural order of things and the capacity of reproduction of the annually obtained equilibrium, meant to bet on a model of economic organization which made the individual agents less dependent on the state's advice and control.

Indeed, in several European economies we verify that during the second half of the eighteenth century there is a decline in intervention of national states in regulating internal and external markets, and increasing criticism of recipes and policies of a mercantilist nature. There is a deepening of the doctrinal debate on the advantages and disadvantages of government intervention, as shown by the many arguments presented publicly for and against the liberalization of production and distribution of grain. Verri, Galiani, and Genovesi in Italy, Graslin, Forbonnais, Quesnay, and the physiocrats, Condorcet and Turgot in France, Campomanes, Jovellanos, and Ward in Spain, joined public debates on the scarcity of food and on the actions required to avoid it, both through more freedom to produce and circulate these goods and through new protection and regulation measures from the state. The choices and political decisions over such an important matter were naturally dependent on the short-term economic situation, as on the capacity to allocate human resources and capital advances in agriculture. There was almost always some analysis of the role of market forces and agents in establishing an equilibrium price which better corresponded to the necessities of both producers and consumers. These authors also frequently emphasized the mutual interdependency between different markets, both internally and externally.

The call to open markets was not always accepted when it was about applying the principle of *laissez-faire* to international trade, and in particular when the maintenance of colonial commerce was at stake. The validity of the Navigation Acts and the aggressiveness of the measures to protect the empires prevented the complete acceptance of the principles of free trade and contributed to justify the necessity of a state with broad functions for defense and control of the seas – without which the expansion of international trade would not be possible.[4] In this way, the commercial prosperity of the European motherlands depended on a system in which the colonies guaranteed the supply of raw materials and consumer goods both for direct use in the European continent and for later re-export.

They similarly functioned as a protected market for selling the products manufactured in the metropolises, while further insuring that the balance of trade remained favorable and guaranteeing the continued accumulation of the precious metals. They also served as destinations for voluntary or enforced emigration and sources for the collection of tax revenue. The systems of exclusive contracts and monopolies, as well as the financial and fiscal privileges inherent therein, provided firm warranty of success for the different economic agents involved in colonial trading operations, beginning with the state itself. Consequently, the survival of this system of "colonial pact" was guaranteed through a series of security mechanisms and through military protection, as well as through regulatory measures that guarded against the occurrence of any conflicts of interest.

Despite the tacit acceptance of the advantages arising from the "colonial pact" system briefly described above, the enlightened economic literature of the second half of the eighteenth century offers interesting examples of a different attitude towards the role of colonies. In England, Josiah Tucker (1774) was the author who most clearly expressed this radically different attitude toward the colonial question in his works published after 1760. He openly

---

4 For a global contextualization of this topic, cf. Chapter 12 by Patrick O'Brien in this volume.

advocated the possibility of American emancipation, because of the heavy costs of administering and maintaining the most important British colony. His view was that the superiority of the British capital could make itself felt in any part of the globe where British manufactures might reach, so that the hegemony that they exercised would lead the Americans to return to the fold of the old metropolis under the guise of what Tucker rather precociously imagined to be a form of privileged commercial partnership. In his own words:

> While this superiority [of the British capitals] shall last, it is morally impossible that the trade of the British Nation can suffer any very great or alarming diminution. Let the Americans go where they please, and try all the nations of the globe. When they have done, they will suppliantly return to Great Britain, and entreat to be admitted into the number of our customers, not for ours, but for their own sakes. (In Semmel 1970: 23)

Tucker also considered that the restrictive processes inherent in the colonial system were prejudicial to the development of trade as a whole, given that they hindered the free enterprise of a multiplicity of agents and interests. In this sense, he openly declared himself to be in favor of a system that guaranteed greater freedom of trade: "When all parties shall be left at full liberty to do as they please, our North American trade will rather be increased, than diminished, because it is freedom and not confinement, or monopoly, which increases trade" (in Semmel 1970: 23–24).

In France, Mercier de la Rivière and Turgot also defended an identical position in relation to the controlled autonomy of the colonies. The excessive cost of maintaining the colonies, the counterproductive nature of the heavy burden of taxation, and the atmosphere of financial and economic subjugation imposed by the metropolis, were more than sufficient reasons for reviewing the mercantilist administration of the colonies.

Similar concerns to these were being voiced in the Iberian countries, namely through the work of two of the most highly regarded representatives of enlightened economic thought: Pedro de Campomanes in Spain and Rodrigo de Souza Coutinho in Portugal. The relevance of the colonial empire for both countries was absolutely crucial. In their writings and political decisions – since they were both committed to governmental action in Spain and Portugal – Campomanes and Coutinho openly criticized the strategy which based the process of colonization on the mining of precious metals, while leaving all the other sectors of activity to fend for themselves. They also highlighted the fact that colonial trade was founded on exclusive monopolistic systems as representing a major obstacle to making full use of the potentialities that such trade offered. Finally, they both denounced the heavy burden of the tax system imposed on colonial territories (Cardoso 2009; Paquette 2008).

The different positions on the willingness to reform colonial policy as well as the broader understanding of the advantages of a system of international commerce based on the *laissez-faire* doctrine present a complete picture on the dimension of the life changes lived by the commercial society at a global scale. These were changes that demanded a renewed effort from the science called upon to understand them.

The science of the legislator

The idea of equilibrium, which is to be found in the work of the physiocrats, was expressed at that time in other ways, largely being given a more literary flavor. Whether we refer to it as *doux commerce* (Montesquieu), "secret concatenation" (Samuel Johnson), hidden chains of events, or the natural order of things, it is that prodigious harmony between the parts and the whole, between the individual and society, that we are talking about when we refer to the notion of the invisible hand in the work of Adam Smith. (A notion that Smith so rarely used, but which his readers and interpreters make such abundant use of) (Skinner 1979; Winch 1996).

This literary device is nothing more than the reaffirmation of one of the central ideas of the *Wealth of Nations*: by acting in the market, seeking to satisfy their own interests, economic agents spontaneously create situations of equilibrium that correspond to the full satisfaction of the interests of the community. In this way, a new language is developed about harmony and equilibrium: without ever forgetting that economic agents are equipped with a series of moral sentiments of respect, benevolence, and sympathy, which prevent the market from being seen as a place of jealousy, confrontation, and conflict, this same market is endowed with the natural capacity to fix price and to regulate the quantities that are supplied and demanded. Political economy was finally able to acquire maturity with a distinct conceptual corpus (Hont 2005; Hont and Ignatieff 1983; Teichgraeber 1986).

By explaining how the extension of the market affects the scope of the division of labor and hence acts in order to either limit or stimulate the accumulation of capital and long-term economic growth, Smith does not forget the role of the legislator in equipping a nation with the laws and institutions needed to attain this aim of continued and sustained growth.

Smith brings together earlier arguments and creates new arguments to reinforce the credibility of an economic system that is based on individual initiative, but which does not dispense with the coordination and regulatory action of the state. The new science of the market and of the modern institutions that serve the dynamics of the emerging industrial capitalism is also a science that is placed at the service of the legislator, with added responsibility in the design and implementation of the state's new functions. Smith's long digression on "The revenue of the sovereign or commonwealth" in book v of the *Wealth of Nations* is the most eloquent testimony of the full reach and boundaries of this science available to the legislator.

Smith lived in a time of profound economic, social, and political change and intense revolutions (the American Revolution, the French Revolution, the industrial revolution), whose consequences could not be fully grasped or comprehended. The winds of change were blowing at a giddying speed. And the famous pin manufacture was not the most appropriate example for illustrating the innovation introduced by contemporary steam technology. However, the basic ingredients or mental raw material that Smith provided his readers with made it possible for him to explain that the world was different and would continue to be so. His vision of the evolution of the systems of economic and social organization enabled him to intuitively deduce the distinct nature of the new stage that was being formed. In this sense, the science of the legislator is also the science of modernity, a set of principles and laws that help us to understand how wealth is produced and distributed, and to identify the obstacles to its growth over time. Or, in other words, it is the science that allows us to understand the changes and transformations of rising capitalism.

Smith worked out consistently on a line of argument that came from far back, at least since Mandeville, which was intended to explain how private interests contribute to common good. Smith did not invent the wheel. He simply gave new life to an everlasting notion which reveals that the acts of buying and selling benefit those that participate in these acts.

Starting from the assumption that individuals know well how to satisfy their own interests, both as producers and consumers, and assuming that such satisfaction corresponds to a defining feature of human nature, their participation in the market leads to obtaining optimal results for the community as a whole. Private interests are not seen as vicious, but as virtuous ingredients of natural order. In this way self-interest is no longer an end in itself, but rather an intelligent mechanism which generates actions and institutions which converge toward creating common good.

Yet the private area of personal relations and individual interests does not show just as a factor for further sociability. In a certain way, its existence is only conceivable in a public context which is related to the world of commercial relations, contract systems, universal rules of administration and justice, and above all, the very existence of moral sentiments which move individual action toward human improvement, which Smith explains through the concepts of sympathy and the impartial spectator.

The world in which Smith lived showed signals of an economy under great transformation, the fruit of an industrial revolution whose long-term effects could not yet be felt but which presented undeniable evidence of technological innovation as well as wage and standard of living improvements. Furthermore, Smith was representative of the typical conviction of an enlightened political economist, as Joel Mokyr (2009: 452) well summed up: "The Enlightenment view of the economy was that it could be improved and that material life would get better if radical changes were made in the way institutions were set up and useful knowledge was utilized."

The defense of the virtues of both private wealth and the opulence of nations is the result of a will to institute new rules of behavior and new habits of life in society which allow the blossoming of economic life and the attainability of increased prosperity levels, that is, the defense of the moral advantages of the commercial society, of an ethics responsible for the triumph of the future of capitalism as a model of organization of collective life (Hirschman 1977).

Such principles incorporate the defense of private property, free work, the rule of law and an ethical consensus around the legitimacy and the necessity of the development of entrepreneurship and the encouragement of innovations. These are the principles that embody the bourgeois virtues which, in the succinct words of McCloskey "have been the causes and consequences of modern economic growth and modern political freedom" (2006: 22).

The increase in levels of consumption and generalized access to goods that previously had a superfluous connotation illustrate the construction of a decent society where social status is set through a new standard of public prosperity. Luxury is no longer judged by moral conceptions, now it incorporates the virtuous attributes of an instrument of creation and circulation of wealth. The flourishing of commerce generates additional trust of individuals in the capacity of governments to promote freedom, equality, and justice. And there exists a universal disposition of human mind to understand and accept the reforms that will speed up the ways toward progress, as Emma Rothschild (2001) pointed out when discussing the essence of the spirit of the Enlightenment.

The connection between private interests and the common good is well summarized in the following passage from the Wealth of Nations:

587

Political economy, considered as a branch of the science of a statesman or legislator, proposes two distinct objects; first, to provide a plentiful revenue or subsistence for the people, or more properly to enable them to provide such a revenue or subsistence for themselves; and secondly, to supply the state or commonwealth with a revenue sufficient for the public services. It proposes to enrich both the people and the sovereign. (Smith 1776: 428)

Hence the search for self-interest follows a number of norms established by the ruler which individuals freely accept because they know that is the way which permits them to better satisfy their objectives. This leads one to the conception of the functions of the state, which include the explicit recognition of its role in regulating the commercial society.

Smith's concern with prerequisites such as the education of citizens and the legislator's motivation which guarantees the proper functioning of the state shows up in a vast European political literature from the second half of the eighteenth century. The professionalization of the organization and administration of the state are questions specifically addressed by the cameralist literature.[5]

These are matters which were also considered by the different academic societies which invested in the promotion and diffusion of knowledge as a way to improve the human spirit and life in society. The idea of useful knowledge with direct application in the processes of allocation of naturally productive resources is one of the most important heritages of the Enlightenment. The new institutions of production of knowledge also collaborated in the design and institutional reform at both the local and national levels, playing an active part in dismantling the *ancien régime* institutions.

Smith had a large influence in the European intellectual playing field, not only at the theoretical level but especially as regards the development of rhetoric and political arguments. He was a figure of immense authority as a source for economic policy prescriptions adapted to the circumstances of each particular country where his system of thought was imported and used.

Population, returns, and growth

The undeniable fact that Smith can be considered the father of the modern discourse of political economy – once one has safeguarded all the legacies and lineages that demonstrate the ancestral nature of this path – does not mean

5 On German cameralism see Keith Tribe, *Governing Economy: The Reformation of German Economic Discourse, 1750–1840*. Cambridge and New York: Cambridge University Press, 1988.

that there is a perfect continuity guaranteed by his closest followers. It is undeniable that the bases for the development of the theories of value, rent, wages, profits, money, international trade, public finance, and economic growth were all pointed out in the *Wealth of Nations*. The economists of the classical school, especially those working within the British tradition, accepted and recognized that this book was the starting point for their own contributions (O'Brien 2004; Redman 1997). But there is no doubt that the developments that were made in political economy with the works of Malthus and Ricardo (to mention just two of the most important names) notably veered away from the original direction of the Smithian legacy.

The grounds for this divergence are to be found in a different view of the problem of satisfying individual interests through participation in the market. According to the new leading figures emerging in the classical school of political economy, such a problem has to be seen in the light of the effects of a process of long-term economic growth that has different effects on the trends of relative shares of total output (wages, profits and rents). And the answer to the problem lies in the limits to rising real incomes and distributive shares resulting from the simultaneous occurrence of population increase and diminishing returns in agriculture.

Malthus's doctrine of population and Ricardo's theory of diminishing returns are integral parts of an analytical scheme that explains the relentless process of economic growth leading to a stationary state. Contrary to Smith's whimsical view of the goodness of unlimited growth, classical economists share a perspective that accentuates the dark side of a dismal science. However, zero growth in returns (profits that are canceled out, wages that do not rise above subsistence level, rents that reach their maximum level) does not imply that the stationary state is a point of no return. In Ricardo's more elaborate view, the stationary state was a kind of warning about a situation of risk that it was important to avoid or postpone. To this end, it was enough to encourage the development of two factors that could counter this universal trend: innovations and technical progress in agriculture (in order to avoid the formation of diminishing returns) and the increasing openness of the economy to the external world (Eltis 1984).

Ricardo's line of argument in relation to the second factor was to afford him the title of the inventor of one of the most famous principles of economic science, and one of the few concepts created at the beginning of the nineteenth century that is still taught today in economics textbooks: the principle of comparative advantage in international trade. According to this principle, the deepening of commercial exchanges between countries represents the response to the inevitable processes of specialization to which each country devotes itself in those sector(s) of activity in which, given its potential partners and competitors, it manages to produce the same quantity of a good at a lower price. Or, in other words, the commercial advantages that a country can obtain – as a result of its geographical situation, or of its endowment in terms of resources and capital – will be greater the more it specializes in what it best produces. In this way, each country will be able to avoid diminishing returns and a fall in its rate of economic growth.

Ricardo's explanation was based on a political diagnosis of the harmful effects caused by the corn laws, which impeded England from obtaining cheaper grain from the European continent and, in this way, guaranteeing low-wage goods that would make it possible to increase profits in the industrial sector. This is why his argument in favor of expanding international trade also ended up serving the programmatic aims of the industrial capitalism that was beginning to expand in Great Britain in the first half of the nineteenth century.

One of the essential characteristics of the political economy system developed by Thomas Malthus, David Ricardo, Jean-Baptiste Say, Nassau Senior, John R. McCulloch, John Stuart Mill, and so many other authors, mainly of British origin, is about establishing positive and universal laws which help the understanding of economic mechanisms. Population growth, diminishing returns, subsistence wages, capital accumulation, differential rent, markets; these are some of the titles of laws and tendencies which were first rigorously laid out by the political economists who dominated the reasoning on economic issues during the first half of the nineteenth century.

There was abundant production of political economy manuals and textbooks, and this allowed convergence of a number of systematic principles which expressed the fundamental points of this new science. Among the multiple examples which one could choose, let us mention Nassau Senior, whose main political economy message can be summarized in the following postulates:

1 that every man desires to obtain additional wealth with as little sacrifice as possible;
2 that the population of the world, or in other words, the number of persons inhabiting it, is limited only by fear of a deficiency of those articles of wealth which the habits of the individuals of each class of its inhabitants lead them to require;
3 that the powers of labor, and of the other instruments which produce wealth, may be indefinitely increased by using their products as the means of further production;

4   that, agricultural skill remaining the same, additional labor employed on the land within a given district produces in general a less proportionate return, or, in other words, that though, with every increase of labor bestowed, the aggregate return is increased, the increase of the return is not in proportion to the increase of the labour.   (Senior 1836: 26)

In the first postulate Senior presents succinctly the central message of Bentham's utilitarian philosophy, the maximization of self-interest. The second postulate offers a slight variation of Malthus's population doctrine, while the third postulate affirms the basic principle of capital accumulation through the utilization of final products which constitute the production goods for the next period. Finally, the fourth postulate describes the law of diminishing marginal returns in agriculture which dictate the long-run dynamics of an economy threatened by the coming of a stationary state. This is in a nutshell the essence of the laws which describe the economic world according to the construction of the school of classical political economy.

Many of the principles and tenets set up by the economists of this period, throughout the first half of the nineteenth century, reflect the economic transformations which occurred as a consequence of the industrial revolution. Demographic growth, the change in the structure of the economy with growing weight of industry in the growth of GDP, the monetary innovations such as the substantial increase in the usage of paper money, the greater opening to international trade, the development of public debt and, in general, the deep alterations to the system of public finance, are changes documented in other chapters of this book which can here be considered as given. The political economists participated in the public debates around these matters, not just through the vast literature they left us, but also in the journals and magazines in which they wrote (*Edinburgh Review*, *Westminster Review*, *Quarterly Review*), in the clubs they frequented, and in parliamentary debates.

The creation of an educated public sphere ready to discuss economic issues was one result of the labor of economists from this period, which, in this way, gave decisive contributions to the consolidation of the disciplinary status of political economy. Questions such as the repeal of the Corn Laws, the misery of working classes, and the institutional framing of the Poor Laws, the Factory Acts and the problem of technological unemployment, the issuing of money and public debt bonds, the reform of the education system and the organization of trade unions, are some of the areas of intervention and change which occur not only in Great Britain but also in most of the European countries and which had the decisive contribution of the political economy writers. In many cases, we may not observe the mental stature of worldly philosophers, but the policy prescription testimonies reveal a critical motivation with solving practical problems which test the validity of the universal laws in which they believed.

Political economy could not be conceived without its counterpart of policy decision. A science that aimed to explain the functioning of economic realities by means of widespread theoretical principles could not subsist or prove its usefulness without the implementation of measures that were needed to adapt and transform those realities to the vision and purpose of policy-makers.

A science of proportions

Agreement between classical economists on matters of economic analysis and policy was far from being complete (Robbins 1978). One of the most interesting controversies and divergences at the time was the debate that opposed Malthus to Ricardo and Jean-Baptiste Say, regarding the possibility of overproduction and general gluts. Directly at stake was the acceptance of the prevalence of an equilibrium between aggregate supply and demand, under the terms that Say made famous through his *loi des débouchés* ("products are paid for with products," later simplified through the use of the expression "supply creates its own demand"). It is worth looking more carefully at this theoretical debate.

When J.-B. Say gave a first coherent presentation of his ideas (1803) there was a favorable background for the discussion commonly centered upon the limits to output growth and the impossibility of aggregate production being cleared through the market. Say's basic argument, which was also conveyed by James Mill, was conceived in opposition to the views doubting the virtues of the self-regulating capacity of the market and can be summarized as follows. Production of a given output spontaneously and necessarily generates a purchasing power of equal value and consequently leads to an equal demand for other products; economic agents are only interested in selling their goods and services because they wish to buy other goods and services, so that the aggregate quantity supplied is equal to the aggregate quantity demanded; producers bring their output to the market for they realize that this is the precondition for an equal consumption of other products.

According to this argument, the total demand for products is determined by the total amount of products supplied and sold, provided that the entrepreneurial function is efficiently carried out. Therefore aggregate supply and aggregate demand are balanced, which implies that there cannot occur *general* gluts or trade depressions due to overproduction. The occurrence of commercial crises originated by partial overproduction was something that could only happen on a temporary basis, or only affect a particular economic sector, with the market forces always being successful in directing the global economy to a new equilibrium. In keeping with this train of thought, it is worth noting that Say was not interested in putting forward a monetary interpretation of, or solution for, trade depressions, since he explicitly denied any possibility that the excess supply of products might be the consequence of an excess demand for money.

Say has hence created an optimistic outlook concerning the possibilities of economic growth which was strongly opposed by several of the leading economists of the time. Authors like Lauderdale, Sismondi, and Malthus maintained that the symptoms of overproduction, clearly experienced by those economies that had recently undergone profound changes in their industrial structure, could neither be ignored nor simply considered as temporary, passing signs of market imperfections or coordination failures.

The capacity of the economy to keep up the balance between aggregate supply and demand was the main issue arising from the controversy opposing Say to the underconsumption theorists. In the case of Malthus, his well-known critique asserted that a general glut could actually occur due to an insufficient level of effective demand, i.e. the demand for products that is necessary to absorb total output as well as to encourage its sustained growth (Malthus 1951). According to Malthus, the revenue created through production was not all spent in the purchase of new goods; therefore, it was necessary to stimulate unproductive consumption in order to bridge the gap between effective demand and aggregate output. It would be the responsibility of those social classes with high revenues, not only to foster superfluous spending so as to increase the level of effective demand, but also to restrain the economic forces that determine long-term economic and demographic growth, since unproductive consumption would mean a reduction in the amount of productive investment.

Malthus's critique of the law of markets and of the idea that there was no possibility of general gluts being caused by overproduction was newly refuted by Jean-Baptiste Say soon after the publication of Malthus's *Principles* (Say 1996). In his letters addressed to Malthus, Say strengthened the arguments in favor of the possibility of long-run economic growth, which would be the necessary outcome of the fulfillment of the following conditions: a more efficient allocation of available and potential resources, an increase in productivity and technological progress, and an intensification of open trade relations between nations.

Notwithstanding the theoretical issues concerning the ocurrence of gluts, the debate also led Malthus and Sismondi, among others, to opt for broader considerations about the validity of supposedly universal laws and principles. In their opinion, overgeneralizations could be contradicted by empirical evidence that demonstrated the bankruptcy of some principles of political economy. Above all, they questioned the adoption of economic policy guidelines that could accentuate the differences in the levels of development of national economies. In this sense, they considered that political economy should be seen as a "science of proportions," cautiously applied in accordance with the observation of distinct realities and without claiming to reach absolute truths.

This vision was largely present in the American protectionist literature of the early nineteenth century (namely in the works and political actions of Franklin, Hamilton, and Carey), and was later quite influential in the shaping of Friedrich List's national system of political economy, which inspired the fostering of economic growth in the German states from the 1840s onwards. According to this approach, the mission of political economy was to inspire economic policies – namely through tariffs and infant industry protection – that would contribute to the development of a national economy (Tribe 1995).

Besides national imbalances, other areas of tension were created as a result of the negative consequences and perverse effects caused by the rise of capitalism, which, in the eyes of its critics, generated ever-greater social inequalities. The growth of the more advanced capitalist economies did not benefit the different social groups in an equal way, with there continuing to be extremely clear differences in the access that they enjoyed to property and in the distribution of the wealth created. Material and economic progress had no equivalence in terms of social and moral progress. Besides its vibrant descriptions of the humiliating living conditions of the working classes, the European literary and political environment was also shocked by revelations of the irrationality of the system and by calls for the implementation of utopian projects in which alternative models of economic and social organization were tried out. Even before it became consolidated as a system, capitalism was already creating political derivations that threatened its integrity (Winch 2009).

Recantation and reform

The wonders of industrial growth could not conceal the low living standards of the urban working-class population. These were further compounded by a labor market where women and child labor were frequently taken advantage of. Unemployment provoked by the usage of machinery was an open challenge to the bourgeois conventions on human dignity. The pacific mobilization of the proletariat, often motivated by their having nothing to lose, was one of the ingredients present in this era of revolutions.

Among the political economists we can distinguish sharply different views. Ricardo's model has plenty of analytical potential, but Malthus's social prejudices shifted the attention to other fields of debate. Both believed in the virtues of the existing economic and social organization and both were adverse to those who looked to alternative recipes for life in society. But the renewal of tensions and revolts showed that there was a moral dimension in the social and economic organization which forced others into thinking in different social models.

Generally speaking, most of the authors who, during the second quarter of the nineteenth century, began to view the capitalist economic system from the other side of the barricade, had been trained in the spirit and letter of the individualistic and liberal political economy of Smith, Bentham, and Ricardo. The most emblematic change of allegiance was perpetrated by Sismondi (1971).

Another author trained in the classical tradition was John Stuart Mill, who, despite remaining faithful to the principles and laws of political economy as applied to the production and distribution of wealth, vehemently rejected the philosophical principles of utilitarianism and seriously questioned the traditional Ricardian view of the consequences of the stationary state seen from the perspective of the progress of humanity. Mill believed in a system where the aim to reach individual betterment was a major driving force. The foundations of the system could be jeopardized, but Mill believed in reform solutions which would continuously promote social justice and that would cushion situations of unreasonable inequality.

His famous recantation of the wage fund theory shows his opposition to the classical vision in which the determination of the subsistence wage was absolutely dependent on the fixed amount of wage fund that the capitalists would have been willing to employ. But his rejection of such forced equilibrium in the labor market, through wage determination, did not nudge him toward more radical positions taken by authors, who, like Marx, thought these signs of class domination were a symptom of the global fragility of a system that would be fatally taken down by the mobilization of the most vulnerable classes.

Mill's reformist tendencies are well visible in this conception of the stationary state as the anticipation of the ideal moment for the organization of life in society. Being inevitable the process which leads to a situation where sustained economic growth is impossible – in accordance with the laws of production and distribution which are the positive legacy of political economy – Mill sustains that such a fate needs to be seen as an opportunity to build a better world.

The alleged existence of universal laws of political economy permits us to understand the general movement of evolution in society, but does not fix in an unchangeable way the conditions which determine the goals to be achieved. Hence, if the stationary state is inevitable, its occurrence can represent a way to improve the current situation: the next step for mankind would be no longer how to produce more but how to distribute wealth and property better.

In this way, the stationary state was not a risk or a threat to be averted, but rather a moment for the realization of human happiness, a step forward in the construction of moral and social progress:

> I cannot, therefore, regard the stationary state of capital and wealth with the unaffected aversion so generally manifested towards it by political economists of the old school. I am inclined to believe that it would be, on the whole, a very considerable improvement on our present condition. I confess I am not charmed with the ideal of life held out by those who think that the normal state of human beings is that of struggling to get on; that the trampling, crushing, elbowing, and treading on each other's heels, which form the existing type of social life, are the most desirable lot of human kind, or anything but the disagreeable symptoms of one of the phases of industrial progress. (Mill 1848: 113)

Therefore, the essential problem for Mill is to know how the virtues of the stationary state can be anticipated through a series of actions of economic regulation developed by the government, with the main objective of humanizing the capitalist system. Book v of Mill's *Principles of Political Economy* takes on some of the themes also considered in book v of Smith's *Wealth of Nations*, discussing which structure of public finances would be better adapted to contribute to the fairness of the capitalist economy. The attention given by Mill to the inheritance tax is representative of his concern to guarantee the equality of initial opportunities which should not be disturbed by privileges transmitted without any effort from those on the receiving side.

John Stuart Mill's book was published in 1848, the same year that saw the publication of Marx and Engels's *Communist Manifesto*. Marx had also been trained in the classical school of political economy and maintained his elective affinities with it. His reasoning in economic terms – regardless of certain alterations in terminology and the adoption of a different political stance – was always mainly congruent with Ricardian economic thought, particularly with regard to the circumstances that lead an economy to the stationary state.

Despite his still being some way from producing his most famous economic works, in 1848 Marx was already proclaiming the end of a system that, by reaching the stationary state, created the platform for its transformation, thus opening the door to the brilliant dream of a classless society.[6]

Mill's reformist bent contrasts naturally with Marx's catastrophic and revolutionary vision. To Marx the stationary or steady state results from the simultaneous occurrence of the law of the falling rate of profit and other laws of capitalist development such as the increasing misery and poverty of the working class, the growing industrial reserve army, the increasing concentration and centralization of industry, the frequent occurrence of cyclical crisis and commercial depressions. Hence for Marx the stationary state represented the turn-around moment which announced a new model of social organization that would substitute the capitalist mode of production based on the alienation and exploitation of the workforce. The foundations of the market economy could never be accepted by those who saw in them a source of continued greed and plunder. To Marx, the moral bases of commercial society which Adam Smith and other classical economists had idealized were definitely broken. Competition and self-interest were not factors for wealth and progress, but for misery and speculation. The division of labor was not the secret for accumulation but the cause for alienation of the workers with no access to the factors of production. According to Marx, the new capitalist economy ensuing from the industrial revolution and their technological breakthroughs could not be denied. Yet they represented the counterpart to the enormous pain inflicted to those who did not own capital.

Mill's reformist blueprint and Marx's revolutionary spirit offer us clear signs of opposition to an economic system that, despite everything, revealed a prodigious capacity for survival and reproduction. Thus, ironically, 1848 now no longer appears to us as the final year of the rise of capitalism, but rather as the first year of the spread of capitalism.

References

Cantillon, R. (1997 [1755]). *Essai sur la Nature du Commerce en Géneral*. Paris: INED.
Cardoso, J. L. (2004). "Natural Law, Natural History and the Foundations of Political Economy," in J. B. Davis, A. Marciano, and J. Runde (eds.), *The Elgar Companion to Economics and Philosophy*. Cheltenham: Edward Elgar, pp. 3–23.

---

6 Indeed, Marx's magnum opus in the field of political economy, *Das Kapital*, would only be published in 1867.

(2009). "Free Trade, Political Economy and the Birth of a New Economic Nation: Brazil 1808–1810," *Revista de Historia Económica, Journal of Iberian and Latin American Economic History* 27(2): 183–204.

Clark, C. M. A. (1992). *Economic Theory and Natural Philosophy: The Search for the Natural Laws of the Economy.* Cheltenham: Edward Elgar.

de la Vega, J. (1688). *Confusion de confusiones* . . . Amsterdam.

de Pinto, I. (1771). *Traité de la circulation et du crédit* . . . Amsterdam: Marc Michel Rey.

Ekelund, R. B. Jr. and R. D. Tollison (1997). *Politicized Economies: Monarchy, Monopoly and Mercantilism.* College Station: Texas A&M University Press.

Eltis, W. (1984). *The Classical Theory of Economic Growth.* London: Macmillan.

Findlay, R. and K. O'Rourke (2007). *Power and Plenty: Trade, War, and the World Economy in the Second Millennium.* Princeton University Press.

Finkelstein, A. (2000). *Harmony and the Balance: An Intellectual History of Seventeenth-Century English Economic Thought.* Ann Arbor: The University of Michigan Press.

Haakonssen, K. (1981). *The Science of a Legislator: The Natural Jurisprudence of David Hume and Adam Smith.* Cambridge and New York: Cambridge University Press.

Hecksher, E. (1935). *Mercantilism,* 2 vols. London: Allen & Unwin.

Hirschman, A. O. (1977). *The Passions and the Interests: Political Arguments for Capitalism Before its Triumph.* Princeton University Press.

Hont, I. (2005). *Jealousy of Trade: International Competition and the Nation-State in Historical Perspective.* Cambridge, MA and London: Harvard University Press.

Hont, I. and M. Ignatieff, eds. (1983). *Wealth and Virtue: The Shaping of Political Economy in the Scottish Enlightenment.* Cambridge and New York: Cambridge University Press.

Hume, D. (1985 [1752]). "Of Money." In *Essays, Moral, Political and Literary,* Part II. Indianapolis: Liberty Classics, pp. 281–294.

Hutchison, T. W. (1988). *Before Adam Smith: The Emergence of Political Economy, 1662–1776.* Oxford: Basil Blackwell.

Larrère, C. (1992). *Du Droit naturel à la physiocratie. L'invention de l'économie au XVIIIe siècle.* Paris: PUF.

Locke, J. (1989 [1696]). *Several Papers relating to Money, Interest and Trade.* Reprints of Economic Classics, Fairfield, NJ: Augustus M. Kelley.

Magnusson, L. (1994). *Mercantilism: The Shaping of an Economic Language.* London and New York: Routledge.

Malthus, T. R. (1951 [1820]). *Principles of Political Economy.* Reprint, New York: Augustus M. Kelley.

McCloskey, D. (2006). *The Bourgeois Virtues: Ethics for an Age of Commerce.* Chicago and London: University of Chicago Press.

Mill, J. S. (1970 [1848]). *Principles of Political Economy With Some of Their Applications to Social Philosophy.* Harmondsworth: Penguin Books.

Mokyr, J. (2009). *The Enlightened Economy: An Economic History of Britain, 1700–1850.* New Haven: Yale University Press.

Mun, T. (1664). *England's treasure by forraign trade.*

Murphy, A. E. (1997). *John Law.* Oxford University Press.

Neal, L. (1990). *The Rise of Financial Capitalism: International Capital Markets in the Age of Reason.* Cambridge University Press.

O'Brien, D. P. (2004). *The Classical Economists Revisited.* Princeton and Oxford: Princeton University Press.

Paquette, G. (2008). *Enlightenment, Governance and Reform in Spain and its Empire, 1759–1808*. Basingstoke and New York: Palgrave MacMillan.

Perrot, J.-C. (1992). *Une histoire intellectuelle de l'économie politique (XVIIᵉ–XVIIIᵉ Siècle)*. Paris: Éditions de l'EHESS.

Petty, W. (1986 [1690]). *Political Arithmetick*. Reprints of Economic Classics, Fairfield, NJ: Augustus M. Kelley.

Poovey, M. (1998). *A History of the Modern Fact: Problems of Knowledge in the Sciences of Wealth and Society*. Chicago and London: The University of Chicago Press.

Rashid, S. (1990). "Berkeley's *Querist* and its Influence," *Journal of the History of Economic Thought* 12(1): 38–60.

Redman, D. A. (1997). *The Rise of Political Economy as a Science: Methodology and the Classical Economists*. Cambridge, MA and London: The MIT Press.

Robbins, L. (1978). *The Theory of Economic Policy in English Classical Political Economy*, 2nd edn. London: Macmillan.

Rothschild, E. (2001). *Economic Sentiments: Adam Smith, Condorcet and the Enlightenment*. Cambridge, MA and London: Harvard University Press.

Say, J.-B. (1803). *Traité d'économie politique*. Paris: Deterville.

(1996 [1820]). *Lettres à M. Malthus sur différents sujets d'économie politique*. Paris: GF-Flammarion.

Semmel, B. (1970). *The Rise of Free Trade Imperialism: Classical Political Economy, the Empire of Free Trade and Imperialism, 1750–1850*. Cambridge and New York: Cambridge University Press.

Senior, N. (1836). *An Outline of the Science of Political Economy*. London: W. Clowes and Sons.

Sismondi, S. de (1971 [1819]). *Nouveaux Principes d'Économie Politique*. Paris: Calmann-Levy.

Skinner, A. (1979). *A System of Social Science: Papers Related to Adam Smith*. Oxford: Clarendon Press.

Smith, A. (1976 [1776]). *An Inquiry into the Nature and Causes of the Wealth of Nations*, Glasgow edn. Book IV, Introduction.

Steiner, P. (1998). *La "Science Nouvelle" de l'Économie Politique*. Paris: PUF.

Teichgraeber, R. (1986). *"Free Trade" and Moral Philosophy: Rethinking the Sources of Adam Smith's Wealth of Nations*. Durham, NC: Duke University Press.

Tribe, K. (1988). *Governing Economy: The Reformation of German Economic Discourse, 1750–1840*. Cambridge and New York: Cambridge University Press.

(1995). *Strategies of Economic Order, German Economic Discourse, 1750–1950*. Cambridge University Press.

Tucker, J. (1974 [1774]). *Four Tracts on Political and Commercial Subjects*. Reprints of Economic Classics, Fairfield, NJ: Augustus M. Kelley.

Viner, J. (1937). *Studies in the Theory of International Trade*. New York: Harper & Brothers, Chapters 1 and 2.

Wilson, T. and A. Skinner, eds. (1976). *The Market and the State: Essays in Honour of Adam Smith*. Oxford: Clarendon Press.

Winch, D. (1996). *Riches and Poverty: An Intellectual History of Political Economy in Britain, 1750–1834*. Cambridge and New York: Cambridge University Press.

(2009). *Wealth and Life: Essays on the History of Political Economy in Britain, 1848–1914*. Cambridge and New York: Cambridge University Press.

Index